Ecuador & the Galápagos Islands

Danny Palmerlee
Michael Grosberg, Carolyn McCarthy

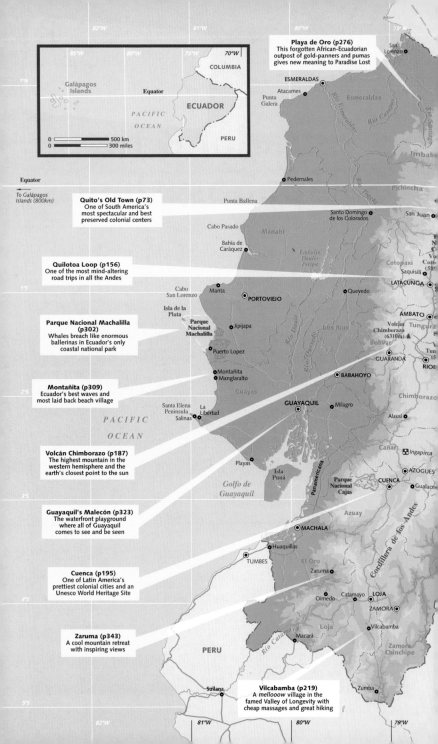

Playa de Oro (p276)
This forgotten African-Ecuadorian outpost of gold-panners and pumas gives new meaning to Paradise Lost

Quito's Old Town (p73)
One of South America's most spectacular and best preserved colonial centers

Quilotoa Loop (p156)
One of the most mind-altering road trips in all the Andes

Parque Nacional Machalilla (p302)
Whales breach like enormous ballerinas in Ecuador's only coastal national park

Montañita (p309)
Ecuador's best waves and most laid back beach village

Volcán Chimborazo (p187)
The highest mountain in the western hemisphere and the earth's closest point to the sun

Guayaquil's Malecón (p323)
The waterfront playground where all of Guayaquil comes to see and be seen

Cuenca (p195)
One of Latin America's prettiest colonial cities and an Unesco World Heritage Site

Zaruma (p343)
A cool mountain retreat with inspiring views

Vilcabamba (p219)
A *mellooow* village in the famed Valley of Longevity with cheap massages and great hiking

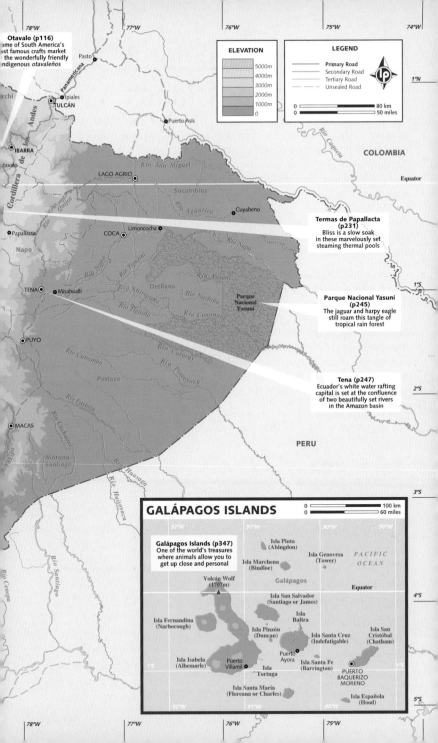

Otavalo (p116)
Home of South America's
most famous crafts market
and the wonderfully friendly
indigenous *otavaleños*

ELEVATION

5000m
4000m
3000m
2000m
1000m
0

LEGEND

Primary Road
Secondary Road
Tertiary Road
Unsealed Road

0 ————— 80 km
0 ————— 50 miles

Pasto

Ipiales
TULCÁN

Puerto Asís

COLOMBIA

IBARRA

tavalo

Río Caquetá

Equator

1°N

LAGO AGRIO

Río San Miguel

Sucumbíos

Río Aguárico

Cuyabeno

Papallacta

Río Quijos

Napo

Limoncocha

COCA

Río Napo

**Termas de Papallacta
(p231)**
Bliss is a slow soak
in these marvelously set
steaming thermal pools

Río Napo

Río Tiputini

Orellana

Río Yasuní

Río Nashiño

**Parque
Nacional
Yasuní**

1°S

TENA   Misahualli

Río Negro

Río Shiripuno

Río Tiputini

Río Curaray

Río Nashiño

Río Cononaco

**Parque Nacional Yasuní
(p245)**
The jaguar and harpy eagle
still roam this tangle of
tropical rain forest

PUYO

Río Cunambo

Río Curaray

Río Pindoyacu

Pastaza

2°S

Río Pastaza

Tena (p247)
Ecuador's white water rafting
capital is set at the confluence
of two beautifully set rivers
in the Amazon basin

MACAS

Morona-
Santiago

Río Chiahuila

PERU

Río Huasaga

3°S

Río Santiago

Río Cenepa

Río Hualyaga

GALÁPAGOS ISLANDS

0 ————— 100 km
0 ————— 60 miles

Galápagos Islands (p347)
One of the world's treasures
where animals allow you to
get up close and personal

92°W   91°W   90°W   90°W

Isla Pinta
(Abingdon)

Isla Genovesa
(Tower)

Isla Marchena
(Bindloe)

*PACIFIC
OCEAN*

Volcán Wolf
(1707m)

Galápagos

Equator

Isla San Salvador
(Santiago or James)

Isla Fernandina
(Narborough)

Isla
Baltra

Isla Pinzón
(Duncan)

Isla Santa Cruz
(Indefatigable)

Isla San
Cristóbal
(Chatham)

Isla Isabela
(Albemarle)

Puerto
Villamil

Puerto
Ayora

Isla Santa Fe
(Barrington)

Isla
Tortuga

**PUERTO
BAQUERIZO
MORENO**

1°S

1°S

Isla Santa María
(Floreana or Charles)

Isla Española
(Hood)

4°S

5°S

92°W   91°W   90°W

78°W   77°W   76°W   75°W

Destination Ecuador & the Galápagos Islands

Nowhere else on earth will you find so much natural diversity – and all the fun that accompanies it – in so tiny a place. Ecuador is the second-smallest country in South America, but its range of offerings is no less than astounding. In one day's drive you can journey from the Amazon Basin – that's *the* Amazon Basin – across glaciated Andean volcanoes, down through tropical cloud forest and sputter into the sunset for a dinner of ceviche on the Pacific coast, where – yes indeed – the water is warm. One day you'll pick through hand-woven wool sweaters at a chilly indigenous market in the Andes, and the next day you'll sweat all over your binoculars while spying on howler monkeys from a canopy tower in the Amazon rain forest.

For nature lovers Ecuador is a dream, with exotic orchids and birds, bizarre jungle plants, strange insects, windswept *páramo* (Andean grasslands), dripping tropical forests and the fearless animals that hop, wobble and swim around the Galápagos Islands. For the adrenaline junky, the choices are outrageous: mountaineering, trekking and white-water rafting are world class. Toss in some horseback riding and surfing and you'll go home with a happily aching body. And for the culture vulture, Ecuador is a labyrinth of indigenous heritage of traditional costumes and highland markets, where a constant rhythm of sound and movement envelops you. As for colonial architecture, few cities top the beauty of Cuenca and Quito, both of which are Unesco World Heritage Sites.

So, no matter if you can't decide *exactly* where to go – just go! The beauty of Ecuador is that you can change your surroundings as quickly as you change your mind.

Natural Wonders

Climb towards the earth's closest point to
the sun, Volcán Cotopaxi (p149)

Flowers in full bloom, Puerto Ayora (p362), Isla
Santa Cruz

Stroll one of the Galápagos' finest beaches, Gardner Bay (p379), Isla Española

Traditional Culture

A young indigenous girl keeps warm at the animal market in Saquisilí (p160)

OTHER HIGHLIGHTS

- Visit Museo del Banco Central (p82) in Quito, and trace the nation's rich history through Ecuador's largest collection of art work
- Celebrate the May Chonta festival (p260) in Macas, with the indigenous Shuar

A multi-talented musician plays *folklórica* (traditional Andean music; p37)

The Otavalo crafts market (p118) is a great place to buy souvenirs for the folks back home

Local women celebrate Carnaval in Baños (p167)

Get into the festive spirit in Quito (p68)

There's no shortage of demand for Panama hats in Cuenca (p205), the capital of the straw hat

8

Colonial Gems

Two blue domes dominate the Catedral de la
Inmaculada Concepción (p196), Cuenca

ALICE GRULICH-JONES

Wander through Palacio Arzobispal (p75)
in Quito's world heritage 'old town'

PAUL KENNEDY

ALFREDO MAIQUEZ

Admire the abundance of intricate work-
manship in Quito's 'old town' (p73)

Contents

The Authors 12

Getting Started 14

Itineraries 18

Snapshot 23

History 24

The Culture 33

Environment 40

Galápagos Wildlife Guide 49

Food & Drink 61

Quito 68
History 69
Orientation 69
Information 70
Dangers & Annoyances 72
Sights 73
Activities 86
Walking Tour 87
Courses 88
Quito for Children 88
Tours 89
Festivals & Events 90
Sleeping 90
Eating 96
Entertainment 102
Shopping 104
Getting There & Away 105
Getting Around 107
AROUND QUITO 107
La Mitad del Mundo 108
Rumicucho 109
Reserva Geobotánica Pululahua 109
Calderón 110

Guayllabamba & Around 110
Sangolquí 111
Refugio de Vida Silvestre Pasochoa 111
Volcán Pichincha 111

Northern Highlands 113
Cochasquí Archaeological Site 114
Cayambe to Oyacachi 115
Otavalo 116
Around Otavalo 122
Reserva Ecológica Cotacachi-Cayapas 127
Intag Valley 127
Reserva Biológica los Cedros 129
San Antonio de Ibarra 129
Ibarra 129
North of Ibarra 134
La Esperanza 134
Río Blanco Area 135
El Ángel 135
Reserva Biológica Guandera 135
Tulcán 136
WESTERN ANDEAN SLOPES 139
Cloud Forest Lodges 139
Santa Lucía 140
Reserva Biológica Maquipucuna 140
Reserva Bellavista 140
Mindo 141
West of Mindo 143

Central Highlands 145
Machachi & Aloasí 147
The Ilinizas 147
Parque Nacional Cotopaxi 149
Latacunga 152
The Quilotoa Loop 156
San Miguel de Salcedo 161
Ambato 162
Around Ambato 165
Baños 167
From Baños to Puyo 175
Parque Nacional Sangay 176
Guaranda 178
Salinas 180

Riobamba 180
Guano & Santa Teresita 186
South of Riobamba 187
Volcán Chimborazo 187
Guamote 189
Alausí 189

Southern Highlands 191

Ingapirca 194
Cañar 195
Biblián 195
Azogues 195
Cuenca 195
Around Cuenca 208
Jima 210
From Cuenca to Machala 210
Saraguro 211
Loja 212
Parque Nacional Podocarpus 216
Zamora 218
Vilcabamba 219
Zumba & the Peruvian Border 223
Catamayo & Around 223
Catacocha 224
Macará 225

The Oriente 226

THE NORTHERN ORIENTE 229
From Quito to Lago Agrio 229
Lago Agrio 232
Along Río Aguarico 236
Reserva Producción Faunística Cuyabeno 236
South from Lago Agrio 237
Coca 238
Vía Auca 241
Lower Río Napo 241
Parque Nacional Yasuní 245
Parque Nacional Sumaco-Galeras 246
Archidona 246
Tena 247
Misahuallí 251
Upper Río Napo 253
Puyo 256
THE SOUTHERN ORIENTE 259
Macas 259
Parque Nacional Sangay 262
Kapawai Ecolodge & Reserve 262
The Jungle from Macas 263

Sucúa 264
From Méndez to Limón 264
Gualaquiza 264
From Gualaquiza to Zamora 265

North Coast & Lowlands 266

WESTERN LOWLANDS 268
Quito to Santo Domingo de los Colorados 268
Santo Domingo de los Colorados 269
North of Santo Domingo de los Colorados 271
South of Santo Domingo de los Colorados 272
Quevedo 272
Quevedo to Guayaquil 272
Babahoyo 272
THE NORTH COAST 273
San Lorenzo 273
Reserva Ecológica de Manglares Cayapas Mataje 274
Limones 274
La Tola 274
Olmedo 275
Borbón 275
Along Río Cayapas 275
Playa de Oro 276
Reserva Ecológica Cotacachi-Cayapas 277
The Road to Esmeraldas 277
Esmeraldas 278
Atacames 280
Súa 283
Same & Tonchigüe 283
Muisne & Around 284
Mompiche 286
Cojimíes 286
Pedernales 286
Canoa 287
Around Canoa 287
San Vicente 288
Bahía de Caráquez 288
Portoviejo 291
Inland from Portoviejo 293
Crucita Area 293
Manta 293
Montecristi 298
Jipijapa 299

The South Coast 300

RUTA DEL SOL 302
Puerto Cayo 302

Parque Nacional Machalilla 302
Puerto López 305
Salango 308
Puerto Rico 308
Las Tunas 308
Ayampe 309
Montañita 309
Dos Mangas 311
Manglaralto 312
Valdivia to Ballenita 312
Santa Elena Peninsula 312
SANTA ELENA PENINSULA TO GUAYAQUIL 315
Chanduy 315
Playas 315
Around Playas 317
Puerto Hondo 318
Bosque Protector Cerro Blanco 318
GUAYAQUIL 318
History 319
Orientation 319
Information 319
Dangers & Annoyances 323
Sights & Activities 323
Tours 326
Festivals & Events 326
Sleeping 326
Eating 329
Entertainment 331
Shopping 332
Getting There & Away 337
Getting Around 338
SOUTH OF GUAYAQUIL 339
Reserva Ecológica Manglares Churute 339
Machala 339
Puerto Bolívar & Jambelí 342
Zaruma 343
Piñas 343
El Bosque Petrificado Puyango 343
To/from The Peruvian Border 344

The Galápagos Islands 347

Isla Santa Cruz (Indefatigable) 359
Around Isla Santa Cruz 368
Isla San Cristóbal (Chatham) 369
Isla San Salvador (Santiago or James) 374
Around Isla San Salvador 375

Isla Isabela (Albemarle) 376
Isla Fernandina
(Narborough) 378
Southern Islands 378
Northern Islands 380

Directory 381

Accommodations 381
Activities 383
Business Hours 386
Children 386
Climate Charts 386
Courses 387
Customs 387
Dangers & Annoyances 387
Disabled Travelers 388
Discount Cards 389
Embassies & Consulates 389
Festivals & Events 390
Food 390
Gay & Lesbian Travelers 390
Holidays 391
Insurance 391
Internet Access 391
Legal Matters 391
Maps 392
Money 392
Photography 393
Post 394
Shopping 394
Solo Travelers 396
Telephone 396
Time 397
Toilets 397
Tourist Information 397
Visas 397
Women Travelers 398
Work 398

Transportation 400

GETTING THERE & AWAY 400
Entering the Country 400
Air 400
Land 403
River 404
Sea 404
GETTING AROUND 404
Air 404
Bicycle 405
Boat 406
Bus 406
Car & Motorcycle 407
Hitchhiking 409
Local Transportation 409

Tours 410
Train 411
Trucks 411

Health 412

BEFORE YOU GO 412
Insurance 412
Recommended
Vaccinations 413
Medical Checklist 413
Internet Resources 413
IN TRANSIT 413
Deep Vein Thrombosis 413
Jet Lag & Motion Sickness 413
IN ECUADOR 414
Availability & Cost of
Health Care 414
Infectious Diseases 414
Traveler's Diarrhea 416

Environmental Hazards 416
Traveling with Children 417
Women's Health 417

Language 418

Glossary 425

Behind the Scenes 426

Index 430

World Time Zones 438

Map Legend 440

Regional Map Contents

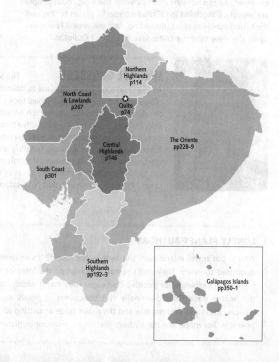

Northern
Highlands
p114

North Coast
& Lowlands
p267

Quito
p74

Central
Highlands
p146

The Oriente
pp228–9

South Coast
p301

Southern
Highlands
pp192–3

Galápagos Islands
pp350–1

The Authors

DANNY PALMERLEE Coordinating Author; Quito, Central Highlands, Southern Highlands

Danny has spent nearly every waking moment of the past seven years studying, traveling in and writing about Latin America, a region he's been no less than infatuated with since he first backpacked through in 1991. He works as a freelance travel writer based in Buenos Aires and travels regularly to Ecuador. His travel articles have appeared in the *Los Angeles Times*, *Miami Herald*, *Dallas Morning News*, *San Francisco Chronicle*, *Houston Chronicle* and other publications throughout the world. Along with other Lonely Planet titles, Danny is also the coordinating author of *South America on a Shoestring*, *Argentina* and *Best of Buenos Aires*.

The Coordinating Author's Favorite Trip

It's the obvious option, but my best trip during this visit was the **Quilotoa loop** (p156). The endless views and steep mountainsides cropped into a patchwork of fields are simply astounding. With the brain a little tweaked on altitude – by the time you reach **Laguna Quilotoa** (p157) you're at 3854m – everything takes on a sort of dreamy appearance. On one trip around the loop, you'll ride in buses, pickups and in a milk truck. The market at **Zumbahua** (p157) is fascinating, the indigenous art at **Tigua** (p157) is excellent, the bus rides are mind blowing, the indigenous people are friendly, **Chugchilán** (p159) has wonderful places to stay and the hiking everywhere is outstanding. And the views? Few stand up to the view over the crater lake of Laguna Quilotoa.

Quilotoa Loop

MICHAEL GROSBERG The South Coast, the Galápagos Islands

After a childhood spent stateside in Washington, DC area and with a valuable philosophy degree in hand, Michael took a job helping to develop a resort on an island in the Pacific, after which he left for a long overland trip through Asia. He later found his way to South Africa where he did journalism and NGO (nongovernment organization) work. He returned to New York City for graduate school in comparative literature focusing on Latin America and spent a summer teaching in Quito and traveling through much of Ecuador. More recently he has taught literature and writing in several NYC colleges in addition to other Lonely Planet assignments that have taken him around the world.

LONELY PLANET AUTHORS

Why is our travel information the best in the world? It's simple: our authors are independent, dedicated travelers. They don't research using just the Internet or phone, and they don't take freebies in exchange for positive coverage. They travel widely, to all the popular spots and off the beaten track. They personally visit thousands of hotels, restaurants, cafés, bars, galleries, palaces, museums and more – and they take pride in getting all the details right, and telling it how it is. For more, see the authors section on www.lonelyplanet.com.

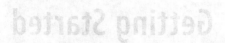

CAROLYN McCARTHY   Northern Highlands, the Oriente,
                                            North Coast & Lowlands

Carolyn McCarthy's first foray to Ecuador was in 2002, when she visited the Galápagos, Shuar territory and various Andean peaks. Her return for this book, her first for Lonely Planet, took her further afield, where her misadventures included a bus fire, uninvited intestinal guests and tripping into a pit of crude oil. Despite the often-precarious state of Ecuador, its gorgeous landscapes, resilient people and natural treasures will keep her going back, rubber boots in tow. A freelancer and Fulbright fellow, she has published in *South American Explorer*, the *Boston Globe* and Spanish-language titles. She lives in southern Chile where she guides treks and is working on a book about rural Patagonia.

CONTRIBUTING AUTHORS

David Andrew took to wildlife-watching the way some people take to sport or religion. Since the age of five he has wanted to explore the Galápagos Islands but first he needed to arm himself with some credentials. He instigated Lonely Planet's Watching Wildlife series and has since coauthored *Watching Wildlife Australia*, *Watching Wildlife East Africa*, *Watching Wildlife Southern Africa* and *Watching Wildlife Central America*. Nature writing has taken David to some of the world's great wild places, including Papua New Guinea, Borneo and Uganda; and as a scientist he has monitored seabirds and whales in Antarctica, and studied the endangered giant panda in southwest China. Working on *Watching Wildlife Galápagos Islands* left him in no doubt that Charles Darwin was oh so right…. David wrote the Galápagos Wildlife chapter (p49).

David Goldberg MD wrote the Health Chapter (p412). Dr Goldberg completed his training in internal medicine and infectious diseases at Columbia-Presbyterian Medical Center in New York City, where he has also served as voluntary faculty. At present, he is an infectious diseases specialist in Scarsdale New York and the editor-in-chief of the website MDTravelHealth.com.

Getting Started

Ecuador is a marvelous country offering a myriad of experiences. Its challenges – dizzying bus rides, travel delays, road blocks, hard-to-reach jungle destinations, long canoe rides, weird market food and street protests – are what make it exciting. They make it *Ecuador*. Some solid pretrip planning will help you get the very most from your trip no matter what happens. This chapter will help you ask – and answer – the right questions *before* you go.

WHEN TO GO

See Climate Charts (p386) for more information.

Ecuador is a year-round destination. Each region of Ecuador – the Andes, the Pacific coast, the Oriente and the Galápagos – has its optimal visiting season. Details are given in respective chapters. In terms of weather, there are only two real seasons – the rainy season and the dry season – but there are significant variations among the geographical regions, and temperature is often a factor of altitude. Even during the rainy season, most days are sunny until the afternoon.

The highland dry season is June through until the end of September. In the Oriente, it rains during most months, but August and December through March are usually the driest. Both seasons have their advantages and disadvantages (see p227).

In the Galápagos, the wildlife is there year-round. If you're at all prone to sea sickness, avoid the rough-sea months of July through October. The dry season (June to December) is also cool and often misty. Also, see p348.

On the coast, the wet season (roughly January to May) sees sunny days with daily afternoon downpours, but it's the best beach weather. The dry season (roughly June to December) is cooler and usually overcast.

Tourist high seasons throughout Ecuador coincide with European, North American and Ecuadorian vacation periods, roughly mid-December through January and June through August. During this time, accommodation rates are highest, and reservations at more popular lodging options are advised.

Accommodations can be hard to find during local festivals, so reserve in advance if you plan to arrive during a town celebration. Dates for these are provided in respective destination sections.

COSTS & MONEY

HOW MUCH?

Bus travel per hour about $1

American breakfast $3-6

Set lunch $1.50-3

Short cab ride in Quito $2

One-way mainland flight $50-70

Also see the Lonely Planet Index inside this book's front cover

Costs in Ecuador have risen since the official currency was changed to the US dollar (see p31), but it's still affordable. Budget travelers can get by on $15 per day, staying in the cheapest hotels, eating *almuerzos* (set lunches) and cheap dinners, and taking buses rather than taxis. Bump it up to $30 per day, and you can stay in modest but comfortable hotels, take cab rides when you're feeling lazy, eat in better restaurants, visit museums, go out at night and cover the occasional $10 national park fee. Spending $50 to $70 per day will allow you to sleep and eat in style and do all the aforementioned fun stuff.

Things get expensive when you start adding tours (climbing, mountain-biking, bird-watching and other tours cost $35 to $80 per day), staying at jungle lodges or haciendas and – priciest of all – when you visit the Galápagos Islands.

TOP TENS
Festivals & Events
Ecuador's festivals, especially the indigenous festivals of the highlands, can be so colorful and exciting they're worth planning a trip around. If you can, hit one of the following. For more on Festivals & Events see p390 and the regional Festivals & Events sections throughout this book.

- Fruit & Flower Festival, Ambato; end February, beginning March (p163)
- Carnaval in Guaranda; end of February, beginning of March (p178)
- Good Friday processions in Quito; Friday before Easter, March/April (p90)
- Corpus Cristi, Pujilí (p157) or Salasaca (p166); usually mid-June (ninth Thursday after Easter)
- Inti Raymi (summer equinox), Otavlao area; June 21 to 29 (p119)
- Founding of Guayaquil, Guayaquil; July 25, although usually begins a few days before (p326)
- Fiesta del Yamor, Otavalo; first two weeks of September (p119)
- Fiesta de la Mamá Negra, Latacunga; September 23 and 24 (p154)
- Founding of Quito, Quito; December 6 (p90)
- Pase del Niño Christmas Eve procession, Cuenca; December 24 (p201)

Traditional Markets
Ecuador's traditional markets are surely one of the country's highlights, and offer the chance to experience Ecuador's unique indigenous culture up close. Plus, you never know what you might find.

- Ambato on Monday (p162)
- Latacunga on Tuesday and Saturday (p153)
- Guamote on Thursday (p189)
- Saquisilí on Thursday (p160)
- Otavalo on Saturday (p118)
- Riobamba on Saturday (p181)
- Zumbahua on Saturday (p157)
- Gualaceo & Chordeleg on Sunday (p209)
- Saraguro on Sunday (p211)

Parks & Reserves
For nature lovers, Ecuador is a paradise. Each and every one of the country's protected areas offers something different, but the following are the pick of the lot.

- Galápagos Islands (p347)
- Parque Nacional Yasuní (p245)
- Reserva Producción Faunística Cuyabeno (p236)
- Parque Nacional Podocarpus (p216)
- Parque Nacional Cotopaxi (p149)
- Parque Nacional Machalilla (p302)
- Parque Nacional Cajas (p208)
- Reserva Ecológica de Manglares Cayapas Mataje (p274)
- Reserva Ecológica Cotacachi-Cayapas (p274)
- Volcán Chimborazo (p187)

DON'T LEAVE HOME WITHOUT...

- A windproof jacket – the highlands get cold.
- Ear plugs – often essential for sleeping.
- A universal sink plug – a must for hand-washing clothes.
- The proper vaccinations (see p412).
- Travel insurance (see p391).
- Dental floss – sews your clothes, laces your shoes and more!
- Duct tape – make your own miniroll around a pencil stub or lighter.
- A hat, sunglasses and sunscreen.
- A pocket flashlight (torch).
- A travel alarm clock.
- A Swiss Army–style pocket knife.
- Ziploc bags.
- A few meters of cord (makes great clothesline).
- Insect repellent (containing 30% DEET).

TRAVEL LITERATURE

If there's one book that nails Ecuadorian culture on the head, it's the eloquent and humorous *Living Poor,* written by Moritz Thomsen, a 48-year-old Peace Corps volunteer on the Ecuadorian coast during the 1960s.

Joe Kane's *Savages* is a more recently written account of life on the *other* side of the Andes, an eye-opening (and sometimes hilarious) look at how the oil industry effects the indigenous Huaoranis and the rain forest.

As for the Galápagos, no list of books is complete without Kurt Vonnegut's whimsical novel *Galápagos,* in which vacationers are stranded on the islands and become the progenitors for a strange new twist in human evolution.

The Panama Hat Trail, by Tom Miller, is a fascinating book about the author's search for that most quintessential and misnamed of Ecuadorian products, the panama hat.

For a more poetic (and surrealist) impression of the country, read *Ecuador: A Travel Journal,* by Henri Michaux, a Belgian-born poet, writer and painter who crafted this strange mix of poetry and travel journal after spending a year here in the 1920s.

Anthony Smith's *The Lost Lady of the Amazon* is a fascinating and gripping reconstruction of Isabela Godin's horrific 18th-century journey from the Andes to the Amazon. Godin was the wife of a scientist on La Condamine's equatorial mission.

In *Floreana,* Margaret Wittmer tells her bizarre (and true) story of living off the land in the Galápagos with her eccentric husband. Murder, struggle and vegetarianism all come into play.

Finally, British climber Edward Whymper's *Travels Amongst the Great Andes of the Equator* is a climbing classic. Although published in 1892, it reads as beautifully today as any in the genre.

INTERNET RESOURCES

For websites about specific topics (such as surfing, volunteer work or Ecuadorian newspapers), see the appropriate section in the Directory (p381). Websites for specific towns and regional attractions are given throughout this book.

Ecuaworld (www.ecuaworld.com) General information site jam-packed with everything from volcano elevations to hacienda reviews.

Ecuador Explorer (www.ecuadorexplorer.com) General travel and tour information and good classifieds.

Latin American Network Information Center (http://lanic.utexas.edu/la/ecuador/) Scores of useful links about everything Ecuadorian.

LonelyPlanet.com (www.lonelyplanet.com) Find succinct summaries on traveling to most places on earth; postcards from other travelers; and the Thorn Tree bulletin board, where you can ask questions before you go or dispense advice when you get back.

Ministry of Tourism (www.vivecuador.com) Suss out everything from health and budget issues to country highlights.

The Best of Ecuador (www.thebestofecuador.com) Packed with information on just about everything you can think of.

Itineraries

CLASSIC ROUTES

BEST OF ECUADOR   Two to Three Weeks/Andes, Galápagos & Amazon

Ecuador is small, and flights are cheap, so you can cover a lot quickly; however if you're planning any high-mountain hiking, allow a few days to acclimatize. Spend three days exploring the splendid colonial streets of **Quito's old town** (p73). Fly to the **Galápagos** (p347) for a cruise around the islands. Back in Quito, swap planes and head to the **Oriente** (p226) for your Amazon visit. Return to Quito and head north to **Otavalo** (p116) for the Saturday market, one of South America's biggest. With an extra week, return to Quito and take the bus south to **Latacunga** (p152) to spend a few days roaming the spectacular **Quilotoa Loop** (p156). Sleep in **Tigua** (p157) or **Chugchilán** (p159) and visit the colorful Saturday market in **Zumbahua** (p157) or the Thursday market in **Saquisilí** (p160). Book yourself into one of the haciendas around **Parque Nacional Cotopaxi** (p149), which are great bases for summit attempts of the volcano, horseback riding or hiking in the park. If colonial cities are more your style, fly round-trip to **Cuenca** (p195) instead, where you can wander the streets of Ecuador's most picturesque city. If you have the time, allow daytrips to **Parque Nacional Cajas** (p208) and **Ingapirca** (p194).

This itinerary will take you from the historic streets of Ecuador's capital, to the animal 'fun park' of the Galápagos, then from the rain forest and back into the Andean highlands all in about three weeks.

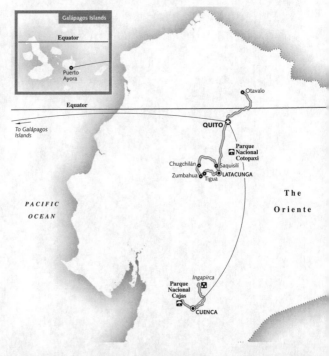

ANDEAN MOUNTAIN HIGH   Two to Three Weeks/Otavalo to Vilcabamba

Begin with a few days in **Quito** (p68), where you can acclimatize to the altitude while exploring one of South America's most beautiful colonial centers. Head south for a night or two in a historic hacienda on the flanks of **Volcán Cotopaxi** (p149), where you can horseback ride, hike and climb to your heart's content. Travel south to **Latacunga** (p152) and beat it up into the magical mountains of the **Quilotoa Loop** (p156) for two to four days. Once you're back in civilization (ie Latacunga), make your way south to the deliciously subtropical town of **Baños** (p167) where you can soak in the thermal baths and take a fabulous downhill bike ride to **Puyo** (p256) in the Oriente. After Baños, move on to **Riobamba** (p180) and do some high-adrenaline mountain biking or hiking around **Volcán Chimborazo** (p187). After a few high-altitude hikes, you might even attempt to summit Chimborazo with a guide. Continue south to the marvelous colonial city of **Cuenca** (p195) either via the famous **Nariz del Diablo** (p186) train ride or the **Inca trail to Ingapirca** (p194). After exploring Cuenca for a couple of days, wind your way south to **Loja** (p212) and the laid-back village of **Vilcabamba** (p219), where you could (easily) kill three days hiking and relaxing. Be sure to take at least a one-day hike in **Parque Nacional Podocarpus** (p216) before flying from Loja back to Quito. Then treat yourself to a few relaxing days hiking and bird-watching in the cloud forests of the **western Andean slopes** (p139). Because you were thinking smart, you saved the **Otavalo market** (p118) for last, so the only place you have to lug all those beautiful ponchos and weavings is to Quito and onto the airplane.

Traverse some 800km of hair-raising, roller-coaster roads as you journey from Quito through the central highlands and make your way toward the laid-back retreat of Vilcabamba, just north of the Peruvian border. You'll see Ecuador's highest peaks, most scenic roads and fascinating indigenous markets.

ROADS LESS TRAVELED

MARIMBAS & MANGROVES   Two to Three Weeks/The Northern Coast

Ecuador's northernmost coastal region is a land of giant mangroves, Afro-Ecuadorian culture, incredible biodiversity, extreme poverty and serious off-the-beaten-track travel. The rewards are great for those adventurous enough to undertake the journey. From **Quito** (p68), travel north to **Ibarra** (p129), and then northwest along the windy road to **San Lorenzo** (p273). From there, explore the rarely visited mangroves and forested islands of **Reserva Ecológica de Manglares Cayapas Mataje** (p274) for a couple of days. Zip through the mangroves by motorboat to the village of **Limones** (stay only if you *really* like the boondocks; p274) and on to **La Tola** (p274). From La Tola walk 15 minutes to **Olmedo** (p275) where you can spend the night and hike the following day to the **Manglares de Majagual** (p275), the tallest mangroves in the world. Back in the boat, motor up to **Borbón** (p275). If you have a thing for nowhere towns spend a night in Borbón, then continue up Río Santiago. This journey will really get you into the wild, especially once you hit **Playa de Oro** (p276) – a must-see jungle cat reserve – and the western reaches of **Reserva Ecológica Cotacachi-Cayapas** (p277), both worth a couple of days exploration. After finding your way back to the ocean, head southwest along the coast (by road) and spend a few days in the sun in **Same** (p283) or **Tonchigüe** (p283). Return to **Esmeraldas** (p278) and jump on the next bus to Quito. Break the ride at **Mindo** (p141), where you can spend several days hiking in the cloud forests before heading back to the capital.

Ecuador's north coast has a magic all of its own. As you travel by boat, bus and beat-up-old pickup truck, this largely Afro-Ecuadorian region will open your eyes to a world most tourists never see – a world of giant mangroves, coastal fishing villages and nature reserves .

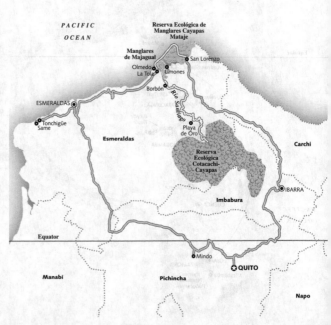

SOUTHERN ECUADOR

Two to Three Weeks/Andes & Amazon

After a day in **Riobamba** (p180), leave the gringo trail and visit the fascinating Thursday market at **Guamote** (p189) before veering east into **Parque Nacional Sangay** (p176) via the new Guamote–Macas road. Stop in Atillo for a couple of days of spectacular hiking around the crystalline **Lagunas de Atillo** (p177). From Atillo continue downhill to **Macas** (p259), a friendly town bathed in the siesta-inducing tropical humidity of the southern Oriente. In Macas hire a guide for a cultural tour to an indigenous Shuar community, or walk (without a guide) to the village of **Sevilla** (p263). You can also hire a guide in Macas to take you down the Río Santiago to the **Cueva de los Tayos** (p264), the cave-home of Ecuador's mysterious oil birds. After a few days in Macas, travel south through **Sucúa** (p264), and the wee town of **Limón** (p264) and stop in whatever jungle village piques your interest. After a day in **Gualaquiza** (p264) either venture uphill to **Cuenca** (likely the prettiest darn town in the southern Oriente; p195) via the scenic dirt road through **Sígsig** (p210) or continue south through the rain forest to **Zamora** (p218), where you can explore **Parque Nacional Podocarpus** (p216). After a day or two in Zamora, climb back into the Andes to **Loja** (p212) where you'll rejoin the tourist trail. Take a breather (and treat yourself to a massage) in laid-back **Vilcabamba** (p219), and then work your way down the western side of the Andes to **Catacocha** (p224). After a day in Catacocha, make your way to **Puyango** (p343) to visit one of South America's largest petrified forests, before winding your way back to Cuenca.

This will take you through the southern sector of Parque Nacional Sangay and into the little visited reaches of the southern Oriente. You'll pass through tiny jungle towns and see indigenous Shuar before climbing back into and over the Andes for a tumble down the western side.

TAILORED TRIPS

SURF & SUN   The Ecuadorian Coast

Ecuador's coast is underrated. Admittedly, it's no Caribbean, but it has some undeniably stunning beaches. The best on the north coast are **Mompiche** (p286), where surfers will find a heavenly wave, and **Canoa** (p287), whose sands seem endless. Visit Tarqui beach in **Manta** (p293) to see the fascinating fish market (it takes place right on the sand) and the nearby wooden-boat yard, the last of its kind in the country.

Next up, visit the **Ruta del Sol** (Route of the Sun; p302), the stretch of beautiful Ecuadorian coastline stretching from Parque Nacional Machalilla in the north, to Ballenita in the south. Spectacular **Los Frailes Beach**

(p304), protected inside **Parque Nacional Machalilla** (p302), is a paradise. The bayside village of **Puerto López** (p305) is the perfect base for exploring the park. Divers should stop at **Salango** (p308) for some underwater fun. South of here, it's beach after beach, with the best lodging at **Ayampe** (p309). At last you arrive **Montañita** (p309) whose surf and laid-back vibe (bring your fire sticks) have made it famous. For the classic upper-class Ecuadorian experience, visit **Salinas** (p180), the country's most famous resort. And to fuel up after all that fun, stop in **Playas** (the poor person's Salinas; p315) for a massive plate of the town's famous crab – have at it with a wooden hammer!

PEAK EXPERIENCE   The 10 Highest Mountains

Ten peaks in Ecuador top 5000m, and whether you climb them, trek around them, or marvel at them from the window of a bus, they're some of Ecuador's most glorious sights. The views from the top of each are outrageous. **Volcán Chimborazo** (p187) is Ecuador's highest mountain and, thanks to the equatorial bulge, the closest point to the sun. Beginners with a guide can climb **Volcán Cotopaxi** (p149), the country's second-highest peak and one of the world's highest active volcanoes. It's tough to find a finer sight than that of **Volcán Cayambe** (p116) towering majestically in the distance behind Otavalo's Saturday morning animal market. The view of Antisana from the thermal

baths at **Papallacta** (p229), however, is definitely more luxurious. Only the headstrong attempt to climb **Volcán Sangay** (p177), the world's most constantly active volcano. **Volcán El Altar** (p177) is also rarely climbed but, for many mountaineers, its nine challenging peaks ringing a gorgeous crater lake make it the most beautiful of the big 10. **Iliniza Norte** (p148) and **Iliniza Sur** (p147) are majestic backdrops for hiking and climbing near the capital. Standing adjacent to Chimborazo, **Volcán Carihuairazo** (p187) is the country's ninth-highest peak and technically more challenging than its domineering neighbor. Near Baños, the sight of **Volcán Tungurahua** (p176) spewing smoke and steam is unforgettable.

Snapshot

From the 2004 Miss Universe pageant – televised *live!* from Quito – to the ousting of President Gutiérrez in 2005, the past few years in Ecuador have been exciting, to say the least. In fact, slow news days have become as rare as the country's honest politicians.

The Gutiérrez debacle came to a head amid massive nationwide protests, when congress voted to sack the president on charges of corruption (see p32). He officially became the third Ecuadorian president ousted in eight years. Initially, Gutiérrez refused to step down, calling his ousting unconstitutional. But once the military withdrew its support, Gutiérrez had no choice but to abandon ship. And that he did, with the military and hoards of angry protesters hot on his heels. It certainly must have been an intense moment as the president choppered in his escape helicopter over to Quito's airport, only to find that the military (and more protesters) had shut it down. The president was forced to take refuge in the Brazilian embassy. Four days later – and against the wishes of interim president Alfredo Palacio – Brazil granted Gutiérrez asylum. The ex-prez then reportedly fled the embassy and evaded police by disguising himself beneath a balaclava.

Ecuador's new president, a 66-year-old political newcomer who refers to himself as a 'simple doctor' rather than a politician, soon announced he would turn his attention to the social problems his predecessor had abandoned. In order to fund health and education programs and kick-start the economy, Palacio announced he would redirect oil profits earmarked for paying the foreign debt. In August 2005, when this proponent of social spending turned to the World Bank for a loan to help pay its foreign debt, the bank – notorious for pushing economic austerity measures alongside its loans – refused.

Within weeks of the World Bank's rejection, Palacio found himself faced with other urgent issues. Protesters in the Amazon region (p226), demanding that private oil companies invest more in the communities where they operate, seized oil installations, attacked pipelines, vandalized oil equipment and effectively brought Ecuador's oil industry to a standstill. Not until the stoppage cost the country some $400 million did oil companies agree to a 'good neighbor pact,' in which they promised to invest in health, education and infrastructure such as roads. According to protestors, the companies later backtracked on their promises.

That same month, the country was grief-stricken after 94 Ecuadorians – mostly immigrants from the southern highlands province of Azuay – died in a shipwreck off the southern coast of Colombia. The passengers were crammed into a wooden boat made for 15 people and were bound for Guatemala, where they would have continued their clandestine journey north to the United States. Most had paid *coyotes* (human smugglers) for the promise of passage to the USA. For more on immigration issues, see p33.

It's not all bad news in Ecuador. In October 2005, the country qualified for its second World Cup, which was celebrated with two days of music, fireworks and merrymaking. And if you're wondering who won the Miss Universe contest staged in this Andean nation, why… none other than a tall, blonde and blue-eyed Miss Australia.

FAST FACTS

Population: 13.3 million

GDP per capita: $3700

Foreign debt (2006): $10.3 billion

Minimum wage: $148 per month

Inflation rate (2006): 2.3%

Unemployment rate: 11%

Adult literacy rate: 92.5%

Annual banana exports: 4.5 million tons

Number of presidents since 1997: nine

Origin of the panama hat: Ecuador

History

Ecuador's history is written in its street signs. One only need stroll around Quito for a day, from Avenida de Los Shyris (named after the pre-Inca tribe of the northern highlands) to the Mariscal Sucre neighborhood (named after Ecuador's greatest independence hero) to get a good lesson in Ecuadorian history. Thanks to the country's undying adoration for one of Latin America's greatest independence heroes, it seems every town in Ecuador has a Plaza Simón Bolívar. Independence heroes aside, what's really fascinating about Ecuador's history is its indigenous past, which is present and palpable throughout the country today. The great majority of the country's indigenous peoples live in the highlands and the Oriente. But to dig deeply into Ecuador's human history – before the Spanish and before the Inca – it's necessary to begin with the coast.

The majority of Ecuador's earliest cultures developed along the southern coast, not in the Andes.

EARLY CULTURES

Any romp down Ecuador's coastline will unveil a long list of names – La Tolita, Bahía, Manta, Valdivia, Machalilla – that together tell the story of Ecuador's pre-Inca past. Along with several important groups from the highlands, these pre-Inca cultures are paramount to Ecuadorian identity, their importance in many ways even eclipsing the Inca, who didn't arrive in present-day Ecuador until shortly before the Spanish.

Although it's now generally accepted that Ecuador was populated by people migrating west from Brazil, the most important early societies developed along the coast, which was a more habitable landscape than the highlands. Ecuador's fist permanent sedentary culture was the Valdivia, which developed along the Santa Elena Peninsula (p312) from nearly 6000 years ago. The Valdivia are famous for their earthenware figurines – likely used in fertility rituals – depicting women with exaggerated breasts and genitalia and in various stages of pregnancy and childbirth. Quito's Museo del Banco Central (p82) and the Museo Guayasamín (p83) both have outstanding examples of these.

While the Valdivia were the first of Ecuador's settled cultures, the Chorrera were the most widespread and influential of the groups that appeared during this so called Formative Period (4000–300 BC). Both the Chorrera and the Machalilla culture (which inhabited southern Manabí and the Santa Elena Peninsula from 1500 BC to 800 BC) are known for the practice of skull deformation. As a form of status, they used stones to slowly elongate and flatten their craniums, and they often removed two front teeth to further enhance their appearance.

Beginning sometime around 600 BC, societies became more stratified; they were ruled by an elite caste of shamans and elite merchants who conducted highly valued long-distance trade. These included the Bahía, Jama-Coaque, Guangala and La Tolita cultures on the coast and the Panzaleo in the highlands. It is likely the Panzaleo were the first culture to practice the technique of shrinking heads – or *tzantza* – for which the Shuar of the southern Oriente are much more famous (they practiced it until the mid-20th century). Cuenca's Museo del Banco Central

TIMELINE	4000 BC	600 BC
	Ecuador's first sedentary culture, the Valdivia, develops around Santa Elena Peninsula	Indigenous societies become more stratified and long-distance trade increases

'Pumapungo' (p200) houses five of what are likely the most impressively displayed *tzantza* in the country – just in case you're interested.

Slowly, beginning probably around AD 800, cultures became integrated into larger, more hierarchical societies. These included the Manteños, Huancavilcas, and Caras on the coast; the Quitus (from which the city of Quito takes its name) of the northern highlands; the Puruhá of the central highlands; and the Cañari of the area around present-day Cuenca. Around the end of the 1st century AD, the expansionist Caras of the coast conquered the peaceful Quitus of the highlands and the combined cultures became collectively known as the Quitu-Caras, or the Shyris. They were the dominant force in the Ecuadorian highlands until about the 1300s, when the Puruhá of the central highlands became increasingly powerful. The third important culture was the Cañari, further south. These were the cultures the Inca encountered when it began its expansion into the north.

The Caras, a powerful, sun-worshiping culture from the coast, was ruled by the Shyri family.

THE INCA EMPIRE

Until the early 15th century, the Inca Empire was concentrated around Cuzco in Peru. That changed dramatically during the rule of Inca Pachacuti, whose expansionist policies set into motion the creation of the vast Inca Empire, Tahuantinsuyo, meaning 'Land of the Four Quarters' in Quechua. By the time the Inca reached Ecuador they were under the rule of Tupac Yupanqui, Pachacuti's successor, and were met with fierce resistance.

Many associate the Andes with the Inca; in Ecuador, the Inca were present for less than a century.

The Cañari defended themselves bitterly against the Inca invaders, and it was some years before Tupac Yupanqui was able to subdue them and turn his attention to the north, where he was met with even fiercer resistance. In one battle the Inca massacred thousands of Caras and dumped them into a lake near Otavalo, which supposedly turned the waters red and gave the lake its name, Laguna Yaguarcocha (Lake of Blood; p131).

The subjugation of the north took many years, during which the Inca Tupac fathered a son with a Cañari princess. The son, Huayna Capac grew up in Ecuador and succeeded his father to the Inca throne. He spent years traveling throughout his empire, from Bolivia to Ecuador, constantly suppressing uprisings from all sides. Wherever possible, he strengthened his position by marriage and in the process produced two sons: Atahualpa who grew up in Quito and Huáscar who was raised in Cuzco.

Inca ruler Huayna Capac had a third son, Manco Capac. He was the last Inca ruler and staged one of the greatest revolts against the Spanish. He was killed by a Spaniard whose life he had saved.

When Huayna Capac died in 1526 he left his empire not to one son, as was traditional, but to two. Thus the Inca Empire was divided for the first time – an event that fatefully coincided with the strange arrival of a group of bearded men on horseback in present-day Esmeraldas province. They were the first Spaniards in Ecuador, led south by the pilot Bartolomé Ruiz de Andrade on an exploratory mission for Francisco Pizarro, who remained, for the time being, further north.

Meanwhile, the rivalry between Huayna Capac's two sons worsened, and the Inca nation broke into civil war. After several years of fighting, Atahualpa finally defeated Huáscar near Ambato and was thus the sole ruler of the weakened and still-divided Inca Empire when Pizarro arrived in 1532 with plans to conquer the Incas.

600–700 BC	1500s
Long-distance, maritime trade begins to develop and reaches as far north as Central America	Inca Empire begins expansion north into Ecuador

THE SPANISH CONQUEST

Pizarro's advance was rapid and dramatic. His horseback-riding, armor-wearing, cannon-firing conquistadors were believed to be godlike, and although they were few in number, they spread terror among the natives. In late 1532, a summit meeting was arranged between Pizarro and Atahualpa. Although Atahualpa was prepared to negotiate with the Spaniards, Pizarro had other ideas. When the Inca arrived at the prearranged meeting place (Cajamarca, in Peru) on November 16, the conquistadors captured him and massacred most of his poorly armed guards.

Atahualpa was held for ransom, and incalculable quantities of gold, silver and other valuables poured into Cajamarca. Instead of being released when the ransom was paid, however, the Inca was put through a sham trial and sentenced to death. Atahualpa was charged with incest (marrying one's sister was traditional in the Inca culture), polygamy, worship of false gods and crimes against the king, and he was executed on August 29, 1533. His death effectively brought the Inca Empire to an end.

When Atahualpa was executed, his war-general Rumiñahui was supposedly on his way to Cajamarca with large quantities of gold and treasure as ransom for the Inca. Legend has it that, upon hearing of Atahualpa's death, Rumiñahui stashed the treasure in the impenetrable mountains of present-day Parque Nacional Llanganates (p165); it has never been found.

The general then continued to fight valiantly against the Spaniards for two more years. The general was so fierce that he supposedly dealt with a Spanish corroborator (and possible heir to Atahualpa's throne) by murdering him, breaking all the bones in his body to bits, extracting them through a hole, and stretching the body – with heads and appendages intact – into a drum. By the time Pizarro's lieutenant, Sebastián de Benalcázar, had finally battled his way to Quito in late 1534, he found the city razed to the ground by Rumiñahui, who preferred to destroy the city rather than leave it in the hands of the conquistadors. Quito was refounded on December 6, 1534, and Rumiñahui was finally captured, tortured and executed in January 1535.

Despite the Inca's short presence in Ecuador (just over 100 years), they left a indelible mark on the country. Quecha (now Quichua in Ecuador) was imposed on the population and is still spoken today by a quarter of all Ecuadorians. The Inca built a vast system of roads that connected Cuzco in the south with Quito in the north, and part of the 'royal highway' – the Inca trail to Ingapirca – can still be hiked today (see p194). Ingapirca itself is Ecuador's most important Inca archaeological site and has splendid examples of the Inca's mortarless stonework.

THE COLONIAL ERA

From 1535 onward, the colonial era proceeded with the usual intrigues among the Spanish conquistadors, but with no major uprisings by indigenous Ecuadorians. Francisco Pizarro made his brother Gonzalo the governor of Quito in 1540. Hoping to conquer the Amazon and find more gold, Gonzalo sent his lieutenant Francisco de Orellana away from Quito to prospect in 1541. The lieutenant and his force ended up floating all the way to the Atlantic, becoming the first party known to descend the Amazon and thus cross the continent. This feat took almost a year and is still commemorated in Ecuador today.

When Pizarro set out to conquer the Inca Empire, he did so with only 150 men.

John Hemming's outstanding The Conquest of the Incas is by far one of the best descriptions of Francisco Pizarro's conquest of the Inca Empire; although mostly about Peru, there are several sections on Ecuador.

1526	1532
Inca ruler Huayna Capac dies and leaves the Inca Empire to his two sons, Atahualpa and Huáscar	Spanish conquistador Francisco Pizarro arrives in present-day Ecuador

During the first centuries of colonial rule, Lima, Peru was the seat of Ecuador's political administration. Ecuador was originally known as a *gobernación* (province), but in 1563, it became known as the Audiencia de Quito, a more important political division. In 1739, the Audiencia de Quito was transferred from the viceroyalty of Peru, of which it was a part, to the viceroyalty of Colombia (then known as Nueva Grenada).

Ecuador remained a peaceful colony during these centuries, and agriculture and the arts flourished. Various new agricultural products were introduced from Europe, including cattle and bananas, which still remain important in Ecuador today. Churches and monasteries were constructed atop every sacred indigenous site and were decorated with unique carvings and paintings, the result of a blend of Spanish and Indian artistic

Written in the 16th century, Bartolomé de las Casas' *A Short Account of the Destruction of the Indies* is a searing and readable account of the Spaniards abuse of the native population at the time of colonization.

ADMINISTRATIVE DIVISIONS

influences. This so-called Escuela Quiteña (Quito School of Art), still admired by visitors today, has left an indelible stamp on the colonial buildings of the time and Ecuador's unique art history.

Life was comfortable for the ruling colonialists, but the indigenous people (and later, the mestizos, or people of mixed Spanish and indigenous descent) were treated abysmally under their rule. A system of forced labor was not only tolerated but encouraged, and it is no surprise that by the 18th century there were several indigenous uprisings against the Spanish ruling classes. Social unrest, as well as the introduction of cocoa and sugar plantations in the northwest, prompted landowners to import African slave laborers. Much of the rich Afro-Ecuadorian culture found in Esmeraldas province today is a legacy of this period.

INDEPENDENCE

The first serious attempt to liberate Ecuador from Spanish rule was by a partisan group led by Juan Pío Montúfar on August 10, 1809. The group managed to take Quito and install a government, which lasted only 24 days before royalist troops (loyal to Spain) were able to regain control.

Independence was finally achieved by Simón Bolívar, the Venezuelan liberator who marched southward from Caracas, freed Colombia in 1819 and supported the people of Guayaquil when they claimed independence on October 9, 1820. It took almost two years before Ecuador was entirely liberated from Spanish rule. The decisive battle was fought on May 24, 1822, when one of Bolívar's finest officers, Mariscal (Field Marshal) Antonio José de Sucre, defeated the royalists at the Battle of Pichincha and took Quito. The battle is commemorated at a stunningly situated monument (p79) on the flanks of Volcán Pichincha, overlooking the capital.

'Bolívar's idealistic dream was to form a united South America'

Bolívar's idealistic dream was to form a united South America, and he began by amalgamating Venezuela, Colombia and Ecuador into the independent nation of Gran Colombia. This lasted only eight years, with Ecuador becoming fully independent in 1830. In the same year, a treaty was signed with Peru, drawing up a boundary between the two nations. This boundary was shown on all Ecuadorian maps prior to 1999. (In 1942, after a war between Ecuador and Peru, the border was redrawn but was not officially acknowledged by Ecuadorian authorities until a peace treaty was signed with Peru in late 1998.) Also see the boxed text, opposite.

POLITICAL DEVELOPMENT

Following independence from Spain, Ecuador's history unfolded with the typically Latin American political warfare between liberals and conservatives. The turmoil between these political groups frequently escalated to extreme violence. In 1875, the church-backed, conservative dictator President García Moreno (who attempted to make Catholicism a requisite for citizenship), was hacked to death with a machete outside Quito's presidential palace (p73). In 1912 liberal President Eloy Alfaro, who attempted to undo much of García Moreno's legacy, was murdered and burned by a conservative mob in Quito. Rivals between these factions continue to this day, albeit on a somewhat more civilized level. Quito remains the main center for the church-backed conservatives, while Guayaquil stands, as

THE BORDER DISPUTE WITH PERU

A glance at any Ecuadorian map published before 1999 will show Ecuador's claim to a large section of jungle extending beyond Iquitos in Peru. The basis of this claim has a long history. After independence in 1822, the new republic of Ecuador claimed lands as far south as Río Marañon (in northern Peru) and as far east as the present border with Brazil. This remote and difficult-to-control area was slowly settled by increasing numbers of Peruvians (as well as Colombians and Brazilians), and Ecuador gradually lost lands to these countries. In 1941, matters came to a head and war broke out with Peru. Each country accused the other of beginning the aggression. The following year, a treaty signed at Río de Janeiro ended the war and allotted to Peru a huge section of the jungle that had formerly belonged to Ecuador.

The Ecuadorians never officially accepted the full terms of this treaty, claiming that the treaty was bulldozed through when most of the world was occupied with WWII; that Peru invaded the country; that the limits of the treaty were geographically invalid; and that the land was theirs in the first place. However, the border as drawn up by the 1942 treaty was internationally accepted.

This dispute resulted in armed skirmishes every few years. The last major battles were in early 1981, when several soldiers were killed and aircraft shot down; and, most recently, in early 1995, when several dozen soldiers were killed on both sides. Some political observers suggest that the wars served politicians by increasing their national popularity during periods of internal crisis or during election years.

Finally, leaders of both countries agreed to a compromise, whereby Ecuador gained a square kilometer of land that was previously Peru's. President Mahuad of Ecuador and President Fujimori of Peru signed a binding peace treaty in 1998, and the countries have not only improved their diplomatic relationship, they have also improved their economic relationship with more trade.

An unfortunate by-product of the war, however, is landmines. An estimated 11,000 remain hidden along the stretch of the border region between Ecuador and Peru and have killed more than 114 people since the end of the war. There is an ongoing effort to clear the landmines, and the base for this operation is the town of Teniente Ortiz, near the town of Santiago in the southern Oriente.

On the positive side – for travelers, especially – the peace treaty means there are more functioning border crossings between the two countries in remote regions, which were previously strictly controlled.

it has for centuries, on the side of more liberal and sometimes socialist beliefs. The rivalry has even seeped into everyday life (see p33).

Throughout much of the 20th century, Ecuador's political sphere was totally volatile, though the country never experienced the bloodshed or brutal military dictatorships suffered by other Latin American countries. That's not to say the military never nabbed the reins of power, with the 20th century having almost as many military as civilian periods of rule. One president, José María Velasco Ibarra, was elected five times between 1934 and 1972 and was ousted by the military before he could complete any one of his terms. Ibarra wasn't alone: in the 10 years between 1930 and 1940, 17 different presidents took a shot at leading Ecuador, not one of whom completed his term.

In 2006, five former Ecuadorian presidents or vice-presidents were either living in exile or in jail, including former presidents Gutiérrez, Mahuad and Bucaram.

YELLOW GOLD TO BLACK GOLD

Until the 1970s, Ecuador was the archetypal 'banana republic,' and the fruit was the country's single most important export. In fact, Ecuador exported more bananas than any country in the world. Although bananas are a staple of the country's economy today, they ceased being Ecuador's sole export after the discovery of oil in the Oriente at the close of the 1960s. By 1973, oil exports had risen to first place, and by the early 1980s, they accounted for well over half of the total export earnings. Distribution of that wealth, however, has been patchy from the get go, and much of the rural population continues to live at the same standard – or worse – that it did in the 1970s.

After oil was discovered, Ecuador began borrowing money with the belief that profits from oil exports would enable the country to repay its foreign debts. But this proved impossible in the mid-1980s due to the sharp decline in Ecuador's oil exports; world oil prices slumped in 1986, and in 1987, a disastrous earthquake wiped out about 40km of oil pipeline, severely damaging both the environment and the economy. The discovery of oil also opened up vast tracts of Ecuador's Amazon Basin and had a dramatic effect on both the rain forest and the indigenous people who lived there, some of whom had never before encountered outsiders.

Ecuador continues to rely on oil as its economic mainstay, but reserves are not as large as had been anticipated. Although oil revenues failed to improve the living standards of most Ecuadorians (most of the profits went into the pockets of oil companies and corrupt Ecuadorian politicians), it did bring with it a period of *relative* political stability.

RETURN TO DEMOCRACY

Ecuador's most recent period of democracy began in 1979, when President Jaime Roldos Aguilera was elected. But he died in a mysterious airplane crash (conspiracy theories point fingers at US constituents with interests in Ecuadorian oil) in 1981, and his term of office was completed by his vice president, Osvaldo Hurtado Larrea.

In 1984, the conservative León Febres Cordero was elected, followed in 1988 by Rodrigo Borja, a social democrat, whose government then leaned to the left. The 1992 elections resulted in the victory of another conservative – Sixto Durán Ballén, a quiteño (person from Quito) of the Republican Unity Party. President Durán's right-wing government attempted to tackle the deficit and reduce inflation, but ran into opposition from trade unions, who opposed privatization proposals, and from indigenous and environmental groups, who opposed the destruction of their homelands and the Amazon rain forest by oil exploration. Widespread protests created major problems for the administration, which was also plagued by corruption scandals, one of which involved Vice President Alberto Dahik, who resigned and left Ecuador after being accused of depositing state funds into private bank accounts.

FROM THE MADMAN TO MAHUAD

The contenders in the 1996 election were two firebrand politicians from Guayaquil, both known for their brash, macho attitudes. The right-wing Jaime Nebot was defeated by the populist Abdala Bucaram, who received about 54% of the vote and was nicknamed 'El Loco' (The Madman) for his fiery, curse-laden style of oration and his penchant for performing at rock concerts as part of his campaign. Bucaram promised cheap public

Approximately 40% of Ecuador's national income goes to the richest 5% of the population.

Mike Tidwell's *Amazon Stranger: Rainforest Chief Battles Big Oil*, is a great read, although the Cofan village chief on whom the book is based, Randy Borman, says to take it with a pinch of salt.

1967	1979
Texaco discovers oil in the Oriente, Ecuador's share of the Amazon Basin	A new constitution under President Jaime Roldos Aguilera, marking Ecuador's return to democracy after decades of military coups

housing, lower prices for food staples and free medicine; but instead he promptly devalued Ecuador's currency, the sucre, and increased living costs while carousing in nightclubs.

Within a few months, massive strikes led by trade unions and Conaie (Confederation of Indigenous Nationalities of Ecuador) paralyzed the country. Congress declared Bucaram 'mentally unfit,' terminated his presidency, and Bucaram fled to Panama.

After Bucaram was ousted, his vice president, Rosalía Arteaga, became Ecuador's first female president, albeit for fewer than two days. Congress voted overwhelmingly to replace her with Fabián Alarcón, the head of congress. He led the government until elections were held again in 1998, when quiteño Jamil Mahuad of the Popular Democracy party defeated businessman Alvaro Noboa by less than 5% of the popular vote.

Mahuad had his political savvy put to the test. The effects of a nasty El Niño and the sagging oil market of 1997–98 sent the economy into a tailspin in 1999, the same year shrimp exports dropped by 80% following devastating shrimp diseases. The sucre depreciated from about 6000 per US dollar at the start of 1999 to about 25,000 by January 2000. When inflation topped 60% – making Ecuador's the worst in Latin America – the embattled president took drastic measures: he pinned Ecuador's economic survival on dollarization, a process whereby Ecuador's unstable national currency would be replaced by the US dollar.

DOLLARIZATION

Dollarization has been used successfully in a few other economically hard-hit countries, including nearby Panama (where the US dollar is called a Balboa), but when President Mahuad declared his plan to dump the national currency, the country erupted in strikes, protests and road closures. On January 21, 2000, marches shut down the capital, and protesters took over the Ecuadorian Congress building, forcing Mahuad to resign.

The protesters were lead by Antonio Vargas, Colonel Lucio Gutiérrez and former supreme court president Carlos Solorzano, who then formed a brief ruling triumvirate. Two days later – and largely due to the international pressure that followed Latin America's first military coup in two decades – the triumvirate turned the presidency over to vice president Gustavo Noboa.

Noboa went ahead with dollarization, and in September 2000, the US dollar became the official currency. Although only one year earlier 6000 sucres bought one dollar, people were forced to exchange their sucres at the dramatically inflated rate of 25,000 to $1. Their losses were severe.

Another immediate effect of dollarization was rounding up. Items that only a month earlier cost 21,000 sucres (or $0.84) were sold for $1 because it was easier to deal with than $0.84. The ubiquitous phrase, 'un dolarcito,' a diminutive and endearing reference to the dollar, became heard throughout the country and the cost of living climbed immediately. Even today you'll be hard pressed to find a cab driver (that great urban social barometer) who won't complain for the entire ride about the ill-effects of dollarization: everything is just *too* expensive now.

Former president Abdala Bucaram (aka The Madman) recorded a CD titled *A Madman in Love.*

For an insider's take on how the USA may have bullied Ecuador into accepting foreign aid which in turn funded lucrative contracts to US development companies, pick up a copy of John Perkin's *Confessions of an Economic Hitman.*

1997	2002
Congress declares President Bucaram – aka 'The Madman' – mentally unfit and terminates his presidency	Leftist colonel and former coup-leader Lucio Gutiérrez is elected president

THE 21ST CENTURY

Along with dollarizing the economy, Noboa also implemented austerity measures to obtain US$2 billion in aid from the IMF (International Monetary Fund) and other international lenders. At the end of 2000, gas and cooking-fuel prices sky-rocketed (largely because of dollarization) and the new year saw frequent strikes and protests by unions and indigenous groups. The economy finally stabilized (relative to the roller-coastering of the late 1990s), and Noboa left office on somewhat favorable terms.

Within a couple of years, dollarization had knocked inflation to under 20% – technically. With the new currency, and the horrendous exchange rate people received when cashing in their sucres, prices seemed higher than ever.

President Noboa was succeeded in 2002 by former coup-leader Lucio Gutiérrez, whose populist agenda and promises to end government corruption won him the crucial electoral support of Ecuador's indigenous population. But shortly after taking office, Gutiérrez began backing down on his promises of radical reform and began implementing IMF austerity measures to finance the country's massive debt instead. If that wasn't enough to turn the population against him, Gutiérrez tossed out almost the entire supreme court, both to rid it of his rivals and to allow himself to change the constitution in order to drop corruption charges on his former ally, ex-president Bucaram. Not surprisingly, protests erupted in the capital, and congress finally voted to throw Gutiérrez out, replacing him with vice president Alfredo Palacio. Palacio held the reins at the close of this edition. For details on what went down after Palacio took the presidential chair, see p23.

April – President Gutiérrez ousted amid nationwide protests; Vice President Aflredo Palacio takes presidency

Gutiérrez campaigns for another presidency only weeks after his release from prison, on charges of endangering national security

The Culture

THE NATIONAL PSYCHE

Most Ecuadorians have three things in common: pride in the natural wealth of their country (both in its beauty and its resources); disdain for the corrupt politicians who promise to redistribute, yet continue to pocket, that wealth; and the presence of a relative in another country (over 10% of the population – some 1.3 million people – have left Ecuador in search of work elsewhere).

From there, the communal psyche blurs, and attitude becomes a matter of altitude. *Serranos* (people from the mountains) and *costeños* (people from the coast) can spend hours telling you what makes themselves different (ie better) than the other. Largely rooted in the historic rivalry between conservative quiteños (people from Quito) and more liberal *guayaquileños* (people from Guayaquil), *serranos* call people from the coast *monos* (monkeys) and say they're lazy and would rather party than keep their cities clean. *Costeños,* on the other hand, say *serranos* are uptight and elitist and that they pepper their interactions with shallow formalities. They jokingly refer to highlanders as *'serranos que comen papas con guzanos'* (hill people that eat potatoes with worms). Of course, *costeños* still speak longingly of the cool evenings of the highlands, and *serranos* pour down to the coast in droves for vacations, and everyone mixes everything up on the beach in peace.

LIFESTYLE

How an Ecuadorian lives is a matter of geography, ethnicity and class. A poor indigenous family that cultivates the thin soil of a steep highland plot lives very differently than a coastal fishing family living in the mangroves of Esmeraldas province, or a family living in the slums of Guayaquil. An indigenous Saraguro family that tends communally owned cattle in the southern highlands leads a dramatically different life than that of an upper-class quiteño family with two maids, a new computer and a Mercedes in the garage. As a visitor you might find yourself surrounded by middle-class folks in a city such as Ambato or Cuenca, or you may find yourself spending a night in a veritable shack with an indigenous family near Laguna Quilotoa.

But one hard fact is certain: an estimated 60% to 70% of Ecuadorians live below the poverty line, a dramatically higher percentage than in the 1970s, despite the country's oil profits. Dollarization has had a dramatic effect on the majority of Ecuadorian's lives, placing everything but the very basics out of economic reach. For many Ecuadorians, paying for cooking fuel and putting food on the table is a constant concern. An increase in poverty, combined with the constant presence of tourists, has led to an increase in begging, both on the streets of major cities and along popular rural trails such as the Inca trail to Ingapirca (p194). But, as most first-time visitors are always astounded to experience, even the poorest Ecuadorians exude an openness, generosity and happiness all too rare in developed countries. Fiestas are celebrated with fervor by everyone, and you'll sometimes roll around in bed, kept awake until dawn by the noise of a nearby birthday bash or soccer celebration.

One lifestyle that's easy not to notice in Ecuador is that of the immigrant who left. The high rates of immigration have had dramatic effects on indigenous communities throughout the highlands, as people

Fabian Basabe, the 25-year-old son of one of Ecuador's wealthiest businessman was on the American TV reality show *Filthy Rich Cattle Drive.*

abandon traditional lives and customs to migrate either to the city or to another country. *Turismo comunitario* (community tourism) projects, such as those in and around Cuenca (p200), Salinas (p180) and Tena (p249), have sprung up in recent years and offer the visitor an excellent way to help contribute to an economic alternative to immigration.

A poor Ecuadorian must save or borrow up to $10,000 to pay a *coyote* (professional smuggler of humans) for illegal passage to the USA. Many never make it.

SOCIAL GRACES

Greetings are important to Ecuadorians, especially in the highland areas. Strangers conducting business will, at the very least, exchange a cordial '*Buenos días, cómo está?* (Good morning, how are you?)' before launching into whatever they are doing. Male friends and casual acquaintances meeting one another in the street shake hands at both the beginning and end of even a short meeting. Women will kiss one another on the cheek in greeting and in farewell. Men often kiss women decorously on the cheek as well, except in a business setting, where a handshake is deemed more appropriate. Close male friends hug one another in the traditional *abrazo* (hug). Indigenous people, on the other hand, rarely kiss, and their handshakes, when they're offered, are a light touch rather than a firm grip. In all situations, politeness is a valued habit.

Personal space is a fully different concept for Ecuadorians than it is for North Americans and Europeans. Conversations tend to take place face to face; streets and market places can get as packed as a fruit crate; standing in line becomes a game of bump-and-nudge; and homes have little individual space. Noise is a part of life: giant speakers blast *cumbia* (dance music originally from Colombia, similar to salsa) from massive storefront speakers, and guests staying in cheaper hotel rooms crank up their TVs so loud that the barber across the street can follow the soccer match.

ECUADOR'S PUNCTUALITY CAMPAIGN

As for most Latin Americans, punctuality is not a strong suit for Ecuadorians. In fact, arriving late is so prevalent in Ecuador that, in 2003, the community group Participación Ciudadana embarked upon a national campaign to stop tardiness. The group called on Ecuadorians to come together at noon on October 1 and do the unthinkable: synchronize their watches.

Campaigning for punctuality is no minor undertaking in a country where an estimated 57% of public events start late. But Participación Ciudadana was determined. And who better to enlist to kick off the campaign than race-walker Jefferson Pérez, the country's only Olympic gold medalist? Certainly no one wanted to rely on then-president Lucio Gutiérrez – who was notorious for arriving to meetings three to four hours late. But the prez did participate and arrived only a few minutes' late! Throughout Ecuador, public authorities, business people, teachers and others vowed to make punctuality a priority. Why all the fuss? Because, according to Participación Ciudadana, tardiness costs Ecuador some $724 million a year – no small change in a country with a GDP of $49.5 billion.

Has the campaign had an effect? It's hard to say. At the government level, where every hour the president is late costs government coffers $45, it seems to have helped; meetings get moving an hour or so after their scheduled start. On a societal level? Not really. It's still entirely normal to arrive late to a social engagement or even a business meeting. If you're wondering whether you should arrive at your Spanish class on time, the answer is yes. Spanish teachers have apparently figured out how to keep their foreign students from getting too jittery and seem invariably punctual (give or take 10 minutes). As for everything else (except soccer matches and church services), don't be offended if you're left waiting a bit – consider it a lesson in lightening up, a campaign that might do some good in the rest of the world.

Spitting, and even urinating, in public is commonplace, particularly in the lower socioeconomic classes; however, burping in public is considered the absolute height of bad manners by everyone.

POPULATION

Ecuador has the highest population density of any South American nation – about 49 people per square kilometer, for those who can wrap their minds around such abstractions. Despite Ecuador's relatively high population-density, the country still feels incredibly wild, mainly because nearly 30% of the population is crammed into the cities of Quito and Guayaquil. Another 30% is mixed into Ecuador's other urban areas, and that leaves a lot of open space for the nature-hungry eye. The rural population is mainly indigenous.

About 25% of the population is indigenous, and the majority of those are Quichua (called Quechua in Peru) and speak Quichua as their first language. Another 65% of the population is mestizo (people of mixed indigenous and European decent). Except in towns such as Otavalo, mestizos own and work in the vast majority of businesses; they are the folks with whom travelers have most of their day-to-day contact. About 4% of the population is Afro-Ecuadorian, the majority whom live in the province of Esmeraldas (in northwestern Ecuador) and the Valle de Chota in the northern highlands. About 6% of the population is of pure European descent, and a small but growing number of people are of Asian descent. The western lowlands town of Quevedo has a substantial Asian-Ecuadorian population (and is likely the best place to pick up an authentic plate of Chinese food!).

The majority of Ecuador's *indígenas* (indigenous people) live in the highlands, and they have distinctive differences in dress depending on their region. Someone familiar with highland dress can tell exactly where an indigenous person is from by the color of their poncho or by the shape of their hat. Some of the best-known highland groups include the Otavaleños, Salasacas, Cañaris and Saraguros.

Several other small groups live in the Amazonian lowlands, including about 60,000 Quichua, 40,000 Shuar (formerly called Jívaro), 2000 Huaorani (formerly called Aucas), 800 Cofán and some 1000 Siona-Secoya peoples. There are also about 4000 indigenous Chachi (formerly called Cayapas) in the rain forests of northern Esmeraldas province, and about 2000 Tsáchilas (also called Colorado) near Santo Domingo de los Colorados. All these groups have their own languages, which are often completely unrelated to one another.

SPORTS
Soccer

The national sport is *fútbol* (soccer), which is played in every city, town, village and outpost in the country. Major-league games are played in Quito and Guayaquil on Saturday afternoons and Sunday mornings, and if you have a chance, they're a spectacle well-worth your participation. People in Ecuador, as throughout Latin America, can be extremely passionate about soccer, and going to a game is usually an exciting experience to say the least. Just as the nation celebrated when Ecuador qualified for the World Cup in 2002 for the first-time ever, it celebrated once again in 2005 when it made it again. The partying began before the game even ended and continued until the next morning. Even in small towns, giant speakers were dragged out onto the street or set up in central plazas, and people danced, drank and sang into the wee hours.

Abya Yala Net/Native Web (www.abyayala .nativeweb.org) provides a good introduction and general overview of Ecuador's indigenous cultures.

The Amazon's indigenous Cofán are one of the most traditional cultures in all of Ecuador. Ironically, it's one of the few indigenous groups with its very own website! See www.cofan.org.

The results of the 2001 census (Ecuador's most recent) can be found at INEC (www.ince.gov.ec), the official website for the National Institute of Statistics and Census.

Bullfighting & Cockfighting

As throughout most of Latin America, bullfighting and cockfighting are popular. The main bullfighting season is during the first week in December in Quito, when bullfighters of international stature may arrive from Mexico and Spain. Perhaps even more exciting than the professional bullfight is the *pueblo* (small town) bullfight. During a *pueblo* bullfight, although the bull is tormented beyond belief, it is never killed. To the great delight of the crowd, the bull may even get the best of the bullfighters by pitching them into the air, trampling them and otherwise scaring the bullfighting urge right out of them. Small town bullfights often end with a game of 'bull soccer' in which (usually drunk) volunteers leave the relative safety of the stands, enter the ring in two teams of five and do their best to tease the bull into chasing them through the opponents' goal posts! Do your best to see one.

Cockfighting is popular nationwide, and most towns of any size will have a *coliseo de gallos* (cockfighting arena). Most foreigners – even those who can stomach a bullfight – find the idea of a cockfight cruel at best. The sport has a long and important history throughout Latin America, and the country's most famous gamecock trainers have even been prominently featured in *El Comercio*, the nation's most important newspaper. Gambling is a key component of the cockfight.

Olympic race-walker Jefferson Pérez took gold in the 1996 Olympic Games, becoming Ecuador's first and only Olympic gold medalist.

Other Sports

The only locally played sport even remotely approaching soccer's popularity is volleyball, known colloquially as 'Ecua-volley,' but even it is played with a soccer ball (most likely because no one would dream of spending money on a volley ball with so many soccer balls lying around). A much rarer ballgame is a sort of paddleball called *pelota de guante*, where players hit a rubber ball with large, spiked paddles. Occasionally in the highlands, you'll spot people playing a game similar to the French game of *boules* or *petanque*, which involves tossing steel balls the size of baseballs along an impromptu dirt court.

RELIGION

As with most Latin American countries, Ecuador's predominant religion is Roman Catholicism. About 95% of the population is Catholic, and the church shows no signs of loosing its importance in the lives of most Ecuadorians. For many, however, attending Sunday services is a low priority – for them it's the classic case of getting religious on holidays and letting it float beneath the surface of the family psyche for the rest of the year.

For indigenous Ecuadorians, Catholicism is often only a veneer laid over millennia-old indigenous beliefs and practices. Ecuador's many religious festivals are perfect examples of this. Around Otavalo, the summer equinox of Inti Raymi is celebrated alongside the nominally Catholic celebration of Saint John, and throughout the highlands, Corpus Cristi celebrations coincide with indigenous harvest festivals. The Catholic church in Saraguro is another obvious illustration: corn stalks and woven corn-husks decorate the entrance, and the Inca commandments '*Ama killa, ama Llulla, ama shua* (Do not be lazy, do not lie, do not steal),' hang over the altar inside.

WOMEN IN ECUADOR

On paper, women in Ecuador have almost identical rights to those enjoyed by women in the USA, France or Canada. Constitutionally, women are equal to men in all spheres of public and private life. In reality, however, things are different.

Women occupy a large part of the workforce, and as a traveler to Ecuador you'll encounter just as many women in the workplace as you will men. Yet a huge of number of working women suffer discrimination in the form of sexual harassment (which ranges from mild but ever-present, to severe), lower wages and difficulty in advancing to positions of real power. Indigenous and Afro-Ecuadorian women experience a harsh form of double discrimination, living both as women and as indigenous or black people in a society dominated by mestizos and men (see the boxed text, p211).

In 1929, Ecuador became the first Latin American nation to grant equal voting rights to women. Today, approximately 10% of Ecuador's government positions are held by women, though only a handful of these are high decision-making positions. On the flipside, women – and especially indigenous and poor women – have played a huge role in politics at the grassroots level. Women have stood on the frontline of countless protests and political movements.

In December, 2005, Guinness Book of World Records crowned 116-year-old Maria Esther de Campovilla from Guayaquil the oldest living person on earth.

ARTS
Music
Most people are familiar with traditional Andean *folklórica* (folk music) without even knowing it: Simon and Garfunkel's version of 'El Cóndor Pasa (If I Could)' was a classic Andean tune long before the popular duo got their hands on it. Despite the fact that hearing it for the umpteenth time in Ecuador may induce insanity, its distinctive and even haunting sound is characteristic of Andean folk music. *Folklórica's* definitive instrument is the *rondador*, or bamboo panpipe. Other traditional instruments include the *quena* and *pingullo* (large and small bamboo flutes) and the *charango*, a mandolin-like instrument with five double strings with a sounding box that was originally made with an armadillo shell.

Inspire your photography by picking Judy Blankenship's *Cañar: A Year in the Highlands of Ecuador*, a beautiful work by a photojournalist who spent a year photographing indigenous families in the highlands of southern Ecuador.

Despite the fact that most people associate Ecuador with *folklórica*, the country's true national music is the *pasillo*, which is rooted in the waltz. Its most famous voice was Julio Jaramillo (known affectionately as 'JJ'; 1935–76), a handsome singer from Guayaquil whose buttery voice popularized the genre throughout Latin America.

Northwest Ecuador, particularly Esmeraldas province, is famous for its marimba music, which is historically the music of Ecuador's Afro-Ecuadorian population. Today it's becoming increasingly difficult to hear it live because many Afro-Ecuadorians have swapped it for salsa and other musical forms.

If there's one music you won't escape without hearing, it's *cumbia*, whose rhythm resembles that of a trotting three-legged horse. Originally from Colombia, Ecuadorian *cumbia* has a more raw (almost amateur), melancholic sound and is dominated by the electronic keyboard. Bus drivers love the stuff, perhaps because it so strangely complements those back-road journeys through the Andes.

As for the kids, Caribbean-born *reggaetón* (a blend of Puerto Rican *bomba*, dancehall and hip-hop) is about the only thing anyone anywhere listens to. The only youth that seem to despise the stuff are the country's *rockeros* (rockers), who prefer foreign heavy metal or the poppy rock 'n' roll sounds of Ecuadorian bands such as Kruks en Carnak, Hijos de Quién and Sal y Mileto.

Architecture
When it comes to colonial architecture, two cities stand high above the rest: Quito and Cuenca. Both have historical centers that are so stunning, each was declared an Unesco World Heritage Site (Quito in 1978 and Cuenca in

1999). Quito's churches are some of the richest, most spectacular colonial buildings in all of South America. Bearing testament to the fact that Spain was under the rule of the Moors for centuries, many of Quito's churches have striking Moorish (Arabic) influences known as *mudéjar*. Many of Quito's churches were built atop sacred indigenous sights, adding yet another layer to the cultural mix. The overall appearance of the city's colonial churches is overpoweringly ornamental and almost cloyingly rich.

In contrast to the opulence of the churches, the houses of the middle and upper classes during the colonial period were elegant and simple, often consisting of rooms with verandas around a central courtyard. The walls were whitewashed and the roofs were of red tile. Many houses had two stories, and the upper floors had ornate wooden balconies with intricately carved balustrades. Cuenca is the true exemplar of these.

The indigenous painting technique known as *tigua* receives colorful treatment in Jean G Colvin's beautiful bilingual coffee-table book *Arte de Tigua*. It's available in Quito or online at www .tigua.org.

Painting & Sculpture

Ecuador's most significant impact on the art world came in the form of the Quito School of Art (see boxed text, below), which reached its creative height between 1600 and 1765. The Quito School died out with the coming of independence (largely because the styles became associated with the Spanish regime), and was followed by the 19th-century Republican period. Favorite subjects during this time were heroes of the revolution, important members of high society in the new republic and florid landscapes.

For an in-depth look at the Otavalo weaving industry and the region's 'indigenous middle class,' read Rudi Colloredo-Mansfield's *The Native Leisure Class: Consumption and Cultural Creativity in the Andes*.

The 20th century saw the rise of the *indigenista* (indigenous lead) movement, whose unifying theme was the oppression and burdens of Ecuador's indigenous inhabitants. The pioneer of the *indigenista* move-

---

THE QUITO SCHOOL OF ART

As the Spanish colonized present-day Ecuador, religious conversion became the key to subduing the native population and remaking the New World in a likeness of the Old. The most successful tool for conversion was art, whose story-telling power and visual representations had long served the Catholic church in matters of gaining believers. At first, the Spanish imported sculptures and paintings from Spain, but beginning in the mid-16th century, the church set up guilds and workshops to train a local base of indigenous artisans. From these workshops blossomed one of the most important artistic genres in Latin America: the Escuela Quiteña, or Quito School of Art.

The beauty of the Quito School is its fascinating blend of indigenous concepts and styles and European art forms. The artisans were mostly indigenous, and their beliefs and artistic heritages crept into their work. If you look closely at paintings in Quito's many religious museums and churches, you'll see many non-European themes: Christ eating a plate of *cuy* (roast guinea pig), or the 12 apostles dining on *humitas* (a type of corn dumpling). Religious figures are often depicted with darker skin or stouter builds that reflect the body types of indigenous Ecuadorians. Inside churches, sun motifs and planetary symbols crop up in ceilings that are decorated in what appear to be simply Moorish patterns.

What the Quito school really became known for was its mastery of the realistic. By the 18th century, artisans were using glass eyes and real hair and eyelashes in their sculptures. They added moving joints, inserted tiny mirrors into the mouth to mimic saliva, and became known for their mastery of polychrome painting (the use of multiple colors). Some sculptures, particularly those of the 18th-century carver Manuel Chili (nicknamed 'Caspicara'), are so real they almost seem to be alive.

After Quito gained independence from Spain in 1822, the religious art of the Quito School lost both its potency and necessity. Today, Caspicara's work can be seen in the Quito's Monastery of San Francisco (p77) and the Museo del Banco Central (p82). Notable painters of the Quito School include Miguel de Santiago, whose huge canvases grace the walls of Quito's Monastry of San Agustín; Manuel Samaniego; Nicolás Goríbar; and Bernardo Rodríguez.

ment was Camilo Egas (1899–1962), who, along with painter Eduardo Kingman (1913–98) placed Ecuadorian modern art on the international map. The country's most famous *indigenista* painter – despite the fact that Kingman's and Egas' works are equally impressive – is Oswaldo Guayasamín (1919–99).

The best places to set your eyes upon the work of Ecuador's contemporary artists are at Quito's Museo del Banco Central (p82) and art galleries (p105). Finally, no discussion of Ecuadorian painting is complete without mentioning *tigua*, an intricate, colorful painting style generally depicting Andean indigenous groups. The art form's major progenitor is the internationally known Alfredo Toaquiza. Also see p157.

Crafts

In Ecuador, indeed in much of Latin America, there is a bridge between 'fine arts' and crafts known as *artesanía*. Literally this means 'artisanship' and refers to textile crafts ranging from finely woven ponchos to hammocks, panama hats, basketwork, leatherwork, jewelry, woodcarving and ceramics. These items are discussed in more detail on p394.

Literature

Ecuador has several notable literary figures, although none have become household names outside the country. Juan Montalvo (1832–89) was a prolific essayist from Ambato who frequently attacked the dictatorial political figures of the time. His best-known work is the book *Siete Tratados* (Seven Treatises; 1882), which includes a comparison between Simón Bolívar and George Washington. Juan León Mera (1832–94), also from Ambato, is famous for his novel *Cumandá* (1891), which describes indigenous life in the 19th century.

Perhaps the most notable Ecuadorian writer of the 20th century was Jorge Icaza (1906–79) from Quito. Profoundly influenced by the *indigenista* movement, his most famous novel is *Huasipungo* (1934), translated as *The Villagers* (1973). This is a brutal story about indigenous Ecuadorians, the seizure of their land and the savage massacre of those who protested.

There are many contemporary Ecuadorian writers. A good introduction to Ecuadorian literature is *Diez Cuentistas Ecuatorianos* (1990), a book of short stories by 10 Ecuadorian writers born in the 1940s. The stories are in Spanish with English translations.

Cinema

One of Ecuador's first internationally applauded directors was Sebastián Cordero, whose *Ratas, ratones, rateros* (1998; English title is the same) tells the story of a quiteño kid whose ex-convict cousin drags him into a nasty life of street crime. The film offers a glimpse into the capital's dark side – one that you likely won't see otherwise. Cordero's more recent *Crónicas* (2004; Chronicles), which takes place in the city of Babahoyo (p272), revolves around a warped deal between a serial killer and a Miami reporter.

Another influential Ecuadorian filmmaker is Camilo Luzuriaga, whose *Cara o cruz* (2004; Heads or Tails) tells the story of two sisters who reunite in Quito after being separated for 25 years. Luzuriaga made his name internationally with his film *Entre Marx y una mujer desnuda* (1996; Between Marx and a Naked Woman), which portrays a group of young communist intellectuals in Quito who get slapped in the face by the realities of Ecuadorian corruption and bureaucracy.

There is simply no better book on highland indigenous dress than Ann P Rowe's *Costume and Identity in Highland Ecuador;* available at bookshops in Quito if you can't find it online.

Pablo Mogrovejo's documentary film *Ecuador vs el resto del mundo* (Ecuador vs the Rest of the World) takes a look at the country's participation in the 2002 World Cup and its significance to ordinary Ecuadorians.

Gustavo Guayasamin's documentary *Hieleros del Chimborazo* (1980; Icemen of Chimborazo), is a fascinating portrayal of the men who hacked ice from the glaciers of Chimborazo to sell in highland markets. Available online.

Environment

THE LAND

Ecuador straddles the equator on the Pacific coast of South America and is bordered by Colombia to the north and Peru to the south and east. Despite its small size, Ecuador is one of the world's most varied countries, making it possible to experience astonishingly different landscapes in a single day.

At 283,560 sq km, Ecuador is about the size of New Zealand or the US state of Nevada, and it's somewhat larger than the UK. The country is divided into three regions. The dramatic Andean mountain range runs roughly north to south and splits the country into the western coastal lowlands and the eastern jungles of the upper Amazon Basin, known as the Oriente. The Andes themselves are virtual skyscrapers, with Volcán Chimborazo – Ecuador's highest peak – topping out at 6310m. The Andes are deservingly known as the highlands.

The central highlands contain two somewhat parallel volcanic mountain ranges, each about 400km long, with a valley nestled between them, appropriately dubbed 'the Avenue of the Volcanoes' by the German explorer Alexander von Humboldt, who visited the country in 1802. Quito lies within this valley and, at 2850m is the world's second-highest national capital, second only to La Paz, Bolivia. The central highlands are also home to countless towns and tiny villages that are often of great interest for their indigenous markets and fiestas. This region has the highest population density in the country.

The western coastal lowlands used to be heavily forested, but most of the natural vegetation has been destroyed for agriculture, and the mangroves have been hacked out in order to create shrimp ponds. The beaches are blessed with warm water year-round and provide decent surfing, but are not as pretty as the beaches of the Caribbean.

The eastern lowlands of the Oriente still retain much of their virgin rain forest, but oil exploitation and colonization are seriously threatening this habitat. The population of the Oriente has more than tripled since the late 1970s.

In addition, Ecuador owns the Galápagos Islands, which are on the equator about 1000km west of the mainland.

WILDLIFE

Ecologists have labeled Ecuador one of the world's 'megadiversity hotspots.' The tiny nation is one of the most species-rich countries on the planet. Part of the reason for this is that it's a tropical country, and the tropics harbor a much greater diversity than do temperate countries. But Ecuador's astounding biodiversity is also due to the simple fact that there are a great number of different habitats within its borders. Obviously, the cold, high Andes support very different species than do the low tropical rain forests. When all the intermediate areas are included, and the coastal region added, the result is a wealth of habitats, ecosystems and wildlife. The transition zones between the lowlands and the highlands, where much species overlapping occurs, are some of the most biodiverse (and least understood) regions on earth. For nature lovers, this place is a dream come true.

Animals

For more detailed information about the wildlife of the Galápagos Islands, see p49.

Thanks to the earth's equatorial bulge, the summit of Volcán Cotopaxi (p149) is the furthest point from the center of the earth and the closest to the sun.

Stay abreast of current volcanic conditions in Ecuador by checking the weekly updates at the Instituto Geográfico Militar's volcanic and seismic information page (www.igepn.edu.ec in Spanish).

Keep your eyes peeled in Ecuador for wildlife photographers Pete Oxford and Reneé Bish's two outstanding photography books, *Amazon Images* and *Ecuador*.

BIRDS

Bird-watchers from all over the world flock to Ecuador for one simple reason: the country is home to more than 1500 species, twice the number found in any one of the continents of North America, Europe or Australia! It's impossible to give a precise number because new species (most of which are already known in other South American countries) are often reported. Very occasionally, a new species is discovered – an incredibly rare event in the world of birds – and it is likely that bird species exist in Ecuador that have never been described by scientists. Bird-watching is outstanding year-round and every part of the country is unique. For more information, see p383.

Ecuador's most emblematic bird is most likely the Andean condor, whose 3m wingspan makes it one of the largest flying birds in the world. In 1880, the British mountaineer Edward Whymper noted that he commonly saw a dozen on the wing at the same time. Today, there are only a few hundred pairs left in the Ecuadorian highlands, so sighting one is a unique experience. Another majestic highland bird is the caruncualted caracara, a large member of the falcon family with bright-orange facial skin, a yellowish bill, and white-on-black wings and body. The bird is often seen in the *páramo* (high Andean grasslands) of Parque Nacional Cotopaxi (p149).

For many visitors, the diminutive hummingbirds found throughout Ecuador are the most delightful birds to observe. About 120 species have been recorded in Ecuador, and their exquisite beauty is matched by extravagant names, such as green-tailed goldenthroat, spangled coquette, fawn-breasted brilliant and amethyst-throated sunangel.

In the Galápagos, about half of the 58 resident species are endemic (meaning they're found nowhere else in the world) to the islands. For more on the islands' bird life, see p49.

> Hummingbirds beat their wings up to 80 times per second in a figure-eight pattern that allows them to hover in place or even to fly backward.

> In two outstanding volumes, Robert Ridgely's *The Birds of Ecuador* is the only bird-watching guide covering the entire country. The first has more details for the serious bird-watcher, while the second has great pictures and descriptions.

MAMMALS

Some 300 species of mammals have been recorded in Ecuador. These vary from monkeys in the Amazonian lowlands to the rare Andean spectacled bear in the highlands. The most diverse mammals are the bats, of which there are easily more than 100 species in Ecuador alone.

For many, the most delightful mammals to spy upon are monkeys. Ecuador's monkey species include the howler, spider, woolly, titi, capuchin, squirrel monkeys, tamarins and marmosets. The best places to see them in their natural habitat include Reserva Producción Faunística Cuyabeno (p236) and Parque Nacional Yasuní (p245) in the Amazonian lowlands, and the rarely visited lowlands sector of Reserva Ecológica Cotacachi-Cayapas (p127) near the coast. A group of marvelously mischievous capuchin monkeys have taken over the central plaza in the Oriente town of Misahuallí (p251), where you're guaranteed an up-close (and sometimes too personal) experience. In the Oriente, you may hear howler monkeys well before you see them; the males' eerie roars carry great distances and can sound like anything from a baby crying to wind moaning spookily through the trees.

Other tropical specialties include two species of sloth: the diurnal three-toed sloth and the nocturnal two-toed sloth. It's very possible you'll spot one of the former while hiking in the Amazon. They are usually found hanging motionless from tree limbs or progressing at a painfully slow speed along a branch toward a particularly succulent bunch of leaves, which are their primary food source. Leaf digestion takes several days, and sloths defecate about once a week. Sloths are most fastidious with their toilet habits, always climbing down from their tree to deposit their weekly movement on the ground. Why they go to all this trouble is one of the mysteries of mammalian life in the tropics.

> Of the world's three species of vampire bats, all are found in Ecuador. The vampire bat is the only mammal that feeds on the blood of other living mammals...including the occasional human!

There are far fewer species of mammals in the highlands than in the lowlands, but commonly seen critters include deer and rabbits and less commonly sighted mammals include Andean foxes. The mammals most commonly associated with the Andes are llamas, which are domesticated and used primarily as pack animals. Their wild relative, the lovely vicuña, has been reintroduced to the Chimborazo area (p187), where you're almost guaranteed to see them as you drive, bus or walk through the park.

Other possible mammal sightings include anteaters, armadillos, agoutis (large rodents), capybaras (even larger rodents, some weighing up to 65kg), peccaries (wild pigs) and otters. River dolphins are occasionally sighted in Amazonian tributaries. Other exotic mammals, such as ocelots, jaguars, tapirs, pumas and the Andean spectacled bear, are very rarely seen.

INSECTS

Many thousands of insect species have been recorded in Ecuador; undoubtedly, tens of thousands more remain undiscovered.

Butterflies, of which there are some 4500 species in Ecuador, are among the first insects that the visitor to the tropics notices. Perhaps the most dazzling are the morphos. With their 15cm wingspan and electric-blue upper wings, they lazily flap and glide along tropical rivers in a shimmering display.

Caterpillars are often masters of disguise themselves. Some species mimic twigs; another is capable of constricting certain muscles to make itself look like the head of a viper, and yet another species looks so much like bird droppings that it rarely gets attacked by predators. Mindo (p141) has a wonderful butterfly farm, as does Misahuallí (p252), and these farms are well worth a visit to see these creatures in their marvelous stages as they morph from caterpillar to cocoon to butterfly.

Ants are also a delightful diversion in the forest. Nearly any walk through a tropical forest will allow the observer to study many different types. Particularly interesting are the leaf-cutter ants, which can be seen marching in columns along the forest floor carrying pieces of leaves like little sails above their heads. The leaf segments are taken into the ants' underground colony where they rot into a mulch, which produces a fungus that feeds the ants.

AMPHIBIANS & REPTILES

The majority of Ecuador's approximately 460 species of amphibians are frogs. There are tree frogs that spend their entire lives in trees and lay their eggs in water trapped inside bromeliads (a type of epiphytic plant). The ominously named poison-dart frog is among the most brightly colored species of frog anywhere. The colors of poison-dart frogs run the spectrum from bright red-orange with jet-black spots to neon green with black wavey lines. Some poison-dart frogs have skin glands exuding toxins that can cause paralysis and death in animals, including (and you probably don't want to hear this) humans.

Of Ecuador's reptiles, four really make an impression on visitors: three of them – land tortoises, land iguanas and marine iguanas – live in the Galápagos and are easy to see. The fourth are the caimans, which inhabit lagoons in the Oriente. With a little patience and a good canoe guide, you'll spot these spooky creatures as well. But that's only four of Ecuador's 410 species, which is over 150 more than are found in all of North America!

Snakes, which are much talked about but seldom seen, make up a large portion of reptiles in Ecuador. They usually slither away into the undergrowth when people are coming, so only a few fortunate visitors get to see them. Perhaps Ecuador's most feared snake is the fer-de-lance, which is extremely poisonous. Visitors are rarely bitten.

FISH

Most visitors' encounters with fish are in the Galápagos. But there is also a vast number of fish in the Amazon. Recent inventories counted some 2500 species in the whole Amazon Basin and roughly 1000 of these are found in Ecuador. Some of them are fearsome. The electric eel can produce shocks of 600V; a school of piranhas can devour a large animal in minutes; stingrays can deliver a crippling zap; and the tiny candirú catfish can swim up the human urethra and become lodged there by erecting its sharp spines. Despite these horror stories, most Amazonian rivers are safe to swim in. Just follow the locals: shuffle your feet as you enter the water to scare off the bottom-dwelling stingrays; wear a bathing suit to avoid having a candirú swim up your urethra; and don't swim with open, bleeding cuts or in areas where fish are being cleaned, because piranhas are attracted to blood and guts.

Plants

Some 25,000 species of vascular plants reside in Ecuador, and new species are being discovered every year. Compare this number to the 17,000 species found on the North American continent! Plants in Ecuador are generally unique to their habitat, and the following are Ecuador's primary habitats.

PÁRAMO

Above the cloud forests lie the Andes' high-altitude grasslands and scrublands, known as the *páramo*. The *páramo* is characterized by a harsh climate, high levels of ultraviolet light and wet, peaty soils. It is an extremely specialized habitat unique to the neotropics (tropical America) and is found only in the area starting from the highlands of Costa Rica to northern Peru.

The *páramo* is dominated by cushion plants, hard grasses and small herbaceous plants that have adapted well to the harsh highland environment, and often look strange and interesting. Most plants up here are small and compact and grow close to the ground. An exception is the giant *Espeletia*, one of the *páramo*'s strangest sights. These Dr Zeussian plants stand as high as a person, and have earned the local nickname *frailejones*, meaning 'gray friars.' They are an unmistakable feature of the northern Ecuadorian *páramo*, particularly in the El Ángel region, near Tulcán (p135).

The *páramo* is also characterized by dense thickets of small trees, often of the *Polylepis* species, which along with Himalayan pines, are the highest-growing trees in the world. They were once extensive, but fire and grazing have pushed them back into small pockets.

TROPICAL CLOUD FORESTS

These forests are found at higher elevations and earn their name because they trap (and help create) clouds, which drench the forest in a fine mist. This continual moisture allows particularly delicate forms of plant life to survive. They have a characteristically low, gnarled growth of dense, small-leaved canopies and moss-covered branches, and support a host of plants, including orchids, ferns and bromeliads. The dense vegetation at all levels of this forest gives it a mysterious and delicate fairy-tale appearance. Some people find them even more beautiful than the rain forests since many of the plants grow closer to the forest floor. This creates a far more luxuriant environment where orchids, bromeliads and other plants are easier to see.

With decent color photos and good illustrations, John Kricher's *A Neotropical Companion* is a comprehensive guide to America's tropical ecosystems.

RAIN FORESTS

Ecuador's slice of the Amazon is known as the Oriente. Of all the habitats in the country, it attracts the most attention – and it's no surprise. The Amazon is the greatest rain-forest habitat in the world, supporting a bewildering variety of plants and animals. Unlike in temperate forests, which have relatively few plant species, if you stand in one spot in the rain forest and look around, you'll see scores of different species.

Lianas (thick dangling vines) hang from high in the canopy beckoning you to swing from them, and the massive roots of strangler figs engulf other trees, slowly choking them of light and life. One of the most impressive characteristics of rain-forest trees are buttressed roots, which are sometimes so massive you can just about disappear inside their weblike supports. Equally impressive are the forest's giant leaves, which are thick and waxy and have pointed tips, called 'drip tips,' that help facilitate water runoff during downpours.

Much of the rain forest's plant and animal life is up in the canopy, rather than on the forest floor, which can appear surprisingly empty to the first-time visitor. If you're staying in a jungle lodge, find out if it has a canopy tower; climbing into it is unforgettable.

Regardless of your science background (or lack of it), the entertaining and highly readable classic, Tropical Nature, by Adrian Forsyth and Kenneth Miyata, is an excellent read before or during any trip to the rain forest.

MANGROVE SWAMPS

Mangroves are trees that have evolved with the remarkable ability to grow in salt water. The red mangrove is the most common in Ecuador and, like other mangroves, it has a broadly spreading system of intertwining stilt roots to support the tree in the unstable soils of the shoreline. These roots trap sediments and build up rich organic soil, which creates a protected habitat for many plants and fish, as well as mollusks, crustaceans and other invertebrates. The branches provide nesting areas for seabirds, such as pelicans and frigatebirds. The shrimp industry has extensively destroyed the mangroves on most of Ecuador's coastline, and most are now found in the far northern and southern coastal regions. For more information, see the boxed text, p285. The tallest mangroves in the world are inside the Reserva Ecológica de Manglares Cayapas Mataje (p274).

Defending Our Rainforest: A Guide to Community-Based Ecotourism in the Ecuadorian Amazon, by Rolf Wesche, is a recommended read covering just what its title says it does.

TROPICAL DRY FORESTS

This fascinating habitat is fast disappearing and is found primarily in the hot coastal areas near Parque Nacional Machalilla (p302) and in southwest Loja Province en route to Macará (p225). Its definitive plant species is the majestic bottle-trunk ceiba (or kapok), a glorious specimen of a tree with a massively bulging trunk and seasonal white-flowers that dangle like light bulbs from the bare tree branches.

THE GALÁPAGOS ISLANDS

The Galápagos Islands support surprisingly diverse plant species within distinctive vegetation zones that begin at the shoreline and end in the highlands. The shorelines of the main islands support low mangroves with bright-green leaves, while slightly higher arid zones are characterized by the islands' eerie cacti, including forests of the giant prickly pear cactus. Trees such as the ghostly looking *palo santo*, the *palo verde* and spiny acacias are also found here. As you move higher, a transition zone supports perennial herbs, smaller shrubs and lichens, and the vegetation becomes increasingly varied and thick. This zone gives way to a cloud-forest type of vegetation, and Scalesia forests with bromeliads, ferns, mosses and orchids. The highest elevations are home to the unique Galápagos tree fern, which grows up to 3m high.

NATIONAL PARKS & RESERVES

Ecuador's first *parque nacional* (national park) was the Galápagos, formed in 1959. Today Ecuador has more than 30 government-protected parks and reserves (of which nine carry the title of 'national park') as well as numerous privately administered nature reserves. A total of 18% of the country lies within protected areas.

Most of the national parks have little tourist infrastructure. Despite being national parks or protected areas many continue to be susceptible to oil drilling, logging, mining, ranching and colonization, threats that are entirely incompatible with true protection.

Many parks are inhabited by indigenous groups, who were living in the area long before it achieved park or reserve status. In the case of the Oriente parks, indigenous hunting practices (which have a greater impact as outside interests diminish their original territories and resources), have met with concern from those seeking to protect the park. The issue of how to protect these areas both from interests such as oil, timber and mining, while recognizing the rights of indigenous people, continues to be extremely tricky.

National park entrance fees vary. On the mainland, most highland parks charge $10, and most lowland parks charge $20 per visitor, but these fees are valid for a week. On the Galápagos Islands, the park fee is $100. Despite the fact that most of these funds end up in a bureaucratic wasteland, the national parks do preserve large tracts of pristine habitat.

The following is a list of the country's national parks. Other important reserves are shown on the map. All of Ecuador's parks can be visited year-round and the 'best' time to visit depends on your interests (climbers may

The Amazon rain forest and its indigenous inhabitants face serious threats from the oil industry, and Amazon Watch (www.amazonwatch.org) spells out the issues on its eye-opening website.

NATIONAL PARKS

Name of Park	Features	Activities	Best Time to Visit
Cajas (p208)	páramo, lakes, small *Polylepis* forests	hiking, fishing, bird-watching	year-round
Cotopaxi (p149)	páramo, Volcán Cotopaxi: Andean condor, deer, rabbits	hiking, climbing	year-round
Galápagos (p347)	volcanically formed islands: seabirds, iguanas, turtles, rich underwater life	wildlife watching, snorkeling, diving	Nov-Jun
Llanganates (p165)	páramo, cloud forest, lowland forest: deer, tapir, jaguars, spectacled bears	hiking	year-round (access difficult)
Machalilla (p302)	coastal dry forest, beaches, islands: whales, seabirds, monkeys, reptiles	hiking, wildlife watching	year-round
Podocarpus (p216)	páramo, cloud forest, tropical humid forest: spectacled bear, tapir, deer, birds	hiking, bird-watching	year-round
Sumaco-Galeras (p227)	Volcán Sumaco, subtropical and cloud forest	off-trail hiking	year-round (access difficult)
Sangay (p176 and p262)	volcanoes, páramo, cloud forest, lowland forest: spectacled bears, tapirs, pumas, ocelots	hiking, climbing	year-round
Yasuní (p245)	rain forest, rivers, lagoons: monkeys, birds, sloths, jaguars, pumas, tapirs	hiking, wildlife watching	year-round

NATIONAL PARKS

chose different seasons than hikers). Here, the 'best time to visit' generally means the most comfortable time to visit.

ENVIRONMENTAL ISSUES

In 1978, Unesco created its first list of World Heritage Sites. Of the 12 sites around the world that made that list, one was the Galápagos Islands.

Deforestation is Ecuador's most severe environmental problem. In the highlands, almost all of the natural forest cover has disappeared, and only a few pockets remain, mainly in private nature reserves. Along the coast, once-plentiful mangrove forests have all but vanished, too. These forests harbor a great diversity of marine and shore life, but they have been removed to make artificial ponds in which shrimp are grown for export.

About 95% of the forests of the western slopes and lowlands have become agricultural land, mostly banana plantations. These forests were host to more species than almost anywhere on the planet, and many of them are (or were) endemic. Countless species have likely become extinct even before they have been identified. An effort is now being made to conserve what little there is left.

Although much of the rain forest in the Ecuadorian Amazon remains standing, it is being seriously threatened by fragmentation. Since the discovery of oil, roads have been built, colonists have followed and the destruction of the forest has increased exponentially. The main drives behind the destruction are logging, cattle ranching and oil extraction.

Clearly, these problems are linked tightly with Ecuador's economy. Oil, bananas and shrimp are the nation's top three exports. However, the serious environmental damage caused by the production of these and other products requires that their value be carefully examined.

The rain forest's indigenous inhabitants – who depend on the rivers for drinking water and food – are also dramatically affected. Oil residues, oil treatment chemicals, erosion and fertilizers all contaminate the rivers, killing fish and rendering formerly potable water undrinkable. Unfortunately, government policies allow oil exploration and encourage the colonization and clearing of land with little regard for forests, rivers, wildlife or residents.

Environmental Groups

The environment has never had a reliable watchdog within the Ecuadorian government, and the country lacks the financial resources to commit itself to strong government-funded conservation programs. Various international conservation agencies have provided much-needed expertise and economic support, and ecotourism projects have largely had a positive effect on habitat protection.

Ecuador's biggest environmental NGO (nongovernmental organization) is Fundación Natura (see p111), which has created and manages several nature reserves throughout the country. At a more grassroots level, local conservation groups have blossomed since the late 1980s. Groups on the coast are particularly concerned with defending the mangrove forests, while those in the Amazon region focus not only on the environment, but also on the protection of the rights of indigenous inhabitants. In the past decade, the organizations that are protecting the fast-diminishing and unique forests on the western Andean slopes, particularly in the Mindo area (p141), have become increasingly important.

The role of indigenous organizations should also be recognized as an effective voice in environmental protection. The struggle in which they have been engaged to secure land rights, particularly in the Amazon regions, has gone a long way toward securing the future of the tropical forests in that area.

Judith Kimmerling's *Amazon Crude* is widely regarded as the most comprehensive examination of the destruction wrought on the Ecuadorian Amazon by the oil industry.

For a thorough explanation of why 30,000 Ecuadorians are locked in a class-action lawsuit against oil giant Chevron Texaco, check out Chevron Toxico www.chevrontoxico.com.

THE BAD BUSINESS OF TRAFFICKING

The illegal trafficking of animals, which are sold on national and international black markets, is a serious problem in Ecuador. To give you an idea of the kind of money being swapped, a rhinoceros beetle from the Amazon can fetch up to US$240 in the USA or Japan. Big bucks are involved, but only as the animals are taken further away from the forests. Those who actually catch or find and sell them might be lucky to pay for a few meals with what they earn. In other words, neither the forest nor its human inhabitants benefit. Despite this, police catch only a fraction of the animals and animal products trafficked in Ecuador.

The most illegally trafficked animals are parrots and monkeys, but there is also a huge *legal* traffic in insects, which is also disastrous for the forest. And imagine visiting the Amazon without seeing one of the magnificent blue-winged morphos butterflies fluttering alongside your canoe as you float down the river. As more and more of these are caught, killed, mounted and sold, this becomes a reality.

That you don't purchase a monkey or a cat skin is a simple no-brainer, and you'll likely never see these for sale in the open anyway. But mounted butterflies, beetles and spiders are a common sight. Sadly, insects are still legally sold both nationally an internationally. Don't buy them. If you buy one in Ecuador, you likely won't be allowed to bring it into your own country (despite the fact that they're sold there). More importantly, the business of bugs is quickly killing off the forest's most beautiful insects which play an important role in the forest's survival. What's more, seeing them in their natural environment, in all their alien and frightening and beautiful forms, is a marvel of the forest – which is exactly where the bugs belong.

UNESCO WORLD HERITAGE SITES

Four sites in Ecuador have been designated World Cultural Heritage Sites by Unesco. Of course, all are worth a visit.

- Quito (p68) – designated in 1978
- Galápagos Islands (p347) – designated in 1978
- Parque Nacional Sangay (p176) – designated in 1983
- Cuenca's historical center (p195) – designated in 1999

In the Galápagos Islands, the **Charles Darwin Foundation** (www.darwinfoundation.org) is a long-established and tireless protector of the archipelago. Conservation, scientific research and the education of both locals and international visitors are among its main goals.

Responsible Tourism

Ron Mader's Planeta (www.planeta.com /ecuador.html) is an outstanding source for travelers with an interest in ecotourism.

Ecuador's tourism industry has grown in recent years and is a significant part of the economy. On the surface, international tourists spending money are a positive force. But tourists and travelers need to look deeper than just spending their money. Hundreds of thousands of foreign visitors can create a negative impact on the society and environment of Ecuador. The Galápagos are a case in point: the islands receive so many thousands of visitors each year that resident populations have skyrocketed and are having a negative impact on the fragile island ecology.

Problems exist with the dichotomy between rich tourists (and even the most budget-oriented backpacker is rich by local standards) and the locals who work for substandard wages to provide services for tourists. For example, demands by groups of non-Spanish-speaking tourists can range from reasonable to rude and obnoxious. Some things that may not seem immediately wrong (taking a person's photograph, demanding toilet paper in a cheap restaurant, expecting the same amenities as you have at home etc) may be unreasonable by local standards.

So what can be done to promote responsible tourism? Start by learning at least enough Spanish to be able to say 'hello,' 'thank you,' 'Ecuador is a beautiful country' and a few more phrases. And don't be afraid to use them! Interact with the local people – don't just take photos and run. Support local artisans by buying locally made handicrafts and artwork, but don't buy illegal artifacts such as pre-Columbian pieces; mounted insects; items made from endangered animals; or jewelry made from sea turtle or black coral. On outdoor expeditions, don't allow your guides to hunt, cut trees for bonfires, harass wildlife or litter. Try to set a good example, but be sensitive to local customs and beliefs.

Galápagos Wildlife Guide

Thanks to countless documentaries and feature articles, the name Galápagos conjures up images of absurdly tame wildlife, and it's true that you can look a sea lion in the eye and be investigated by inquisitive mockingbirds. Early naturalists struggled to understand how the remote, barren Galápagos archipelago could support such a diversity of unique and unusual wildlife. Due to the careful deliberations of a remarkable man named Charles Darwin and countless scientists since, we now know that animals and plants colonized this chain of barren volcanic islands by air, sea and floating vegetation over the course of 10 million years or so. Finding no competition, the few species that survived the sea crossing came to dominate the island ecosystem in a way that they could not on mainland South America, and in the process evolved to fill every available ecological niche.

Thus, in the absence of large herbivores such as deer, vegetarian tortoises have evolved to great size; the first wind-blown daisy seeds grew as large as trees; and an insignificant finch took over the role of woodpeckers in the forest. See for yourself the unique sea-going lizard and tool-using finch, and witness first-hand the other amazing animals that led Charles Darwin to have what has been described as the 'best idea that anyone ever had.'

BIRDS

Even the most casual observer will be intrigued by the spectacular and apparently fearless birds seen on a typical visit. During a week of touring careful bird-watchers should see 40 or so species, including several of the famous Galápagos finches; abundant seabirds, including comical boobies; and some specialties, such as the Galápagos penguin.

SEABIRDS

The term 'seabird' covers a range of bird families that exploit different ecological niches, including some that spend most of their lives at sea, only returning to land to breed; others that fish in more coastal waters; and generalist feeders such as seagulls that may be seen around towns as well as at sea. Many are a joy to watch in flight or when they congregate in great feeding flocks, plunging headlong into shoals of panicked fish herded together by dolphins and other predators.

Boobies

Despite their name, boobies are graceful seabirds whose comical courting behavior and confiding nature make them popular with visitors. Three of the world's five booby species breed in the islands, and on land, at least, they are easily told apart by the color of their feet. Punta Pitt (on Isla San Cristóbal) and Isla Genovesa are the only visitor sites where all three species can be seen together. All boobies feed on fish by plunge-diving from a great height.

The blue-footed booby is often the first booby seen by visitors and is common on many islands. During courtship it picks up its bright-blue feet in a slow, dignified fashion and continues with bowing, wing-spreading and sky-pointing in an enchanting, if rather clownish, display – a highlight of any visit.

The best general guide to the history, geology, and plant and animal life on the Galápagos Islands is the thorough and highly recommended *Galápagos: A Natural History*, by Michael H Jackson.

The Nazca booby is the largest Galápagos booby and this striking black-and-white bird often nests near cliff tops. A blackish area of bare skin surrounding its yellowish bill gives it a 'masked' appearance, and until recently was considered to be a subspecies of the widespread masked booby.

The red-footed booby is the smallest Galápagos booby species and has two color phases – golden-brown and black-and-white – but can be readily identified by its red feet and pale-blue bill. Although it's actually the most numerous of the Galápagos boobies, it is found only on outer islands such as Isla Genovesa.

Frigatebirds

The two species of frigatebird – greater and magnificent – are the largest seabirds commonly seen in the archipelago, although both are mainly glossy black in coloration and difficult to tell apart. They are readily seen riding high on thermals above coastal cliffs and, with a wingspan reaching 2.3m, are dazzling fliers. Both species make their aerobatic living by fishing, but earned their other name – man o' war bird – through piracy: frigatebirds sometimes harass smaller seabirds into dropping or regurgitating their catch and then swoop to catch the booty in midair. Courting males inflate a balloon-sized flap of scarlet skin under their bill and cock their wings to attract females.

Flightless Cormorant

Apart from penguins, the flightless cormorant is the only flightless seabird in the world and is endemic to the Galápagos. When an ancestral population colonized this predator-free archipelago the birds eventually lost the need for flight, but Galápagos cormorants still show characteristics of their flying relatives – to decrease buoyancy when feeding underwater all cormorants lack waterproofing oils in their feathers, and spread their wings to 'dry' on land; flightless cormorants do the same, although their wings are no bigger than a penguin's flippers. In recent centuries the flightless cormorant has become vulnerable to introduced predators, such as feral dogs, and today there are only about 700 to 800 pairs left. To see flightless cormorants you'll need to visit Isla Fernandina or the west coast of Isla Isabela.

Galápagos Penguin

Sometime in the distant past a population of penguins followed the cool Humboldt Current up the west coast of South America from Antarctica and became established in the Galápagos Islands. Today the Galápagos penguin is the most northerly penguin in the world and the only species that lives at the equator. Galápagos penguins normally breed in the western parts of Isabela and on Isla Fernandina, although they occur sporadically around other islands, particularly at Isla Bartolomé. The clumsiness of penguins on land belies their skill and speed underwater and the best way to appreciate this, of course, is to jump in and snorkel with them.

South American penguins reached the Galápagos Islands an estimated four million years ago.

Waved Albatross

The waved albatross is the only albatross species that breeds at the equator and, despite some awkwardness on land, these huge birds are graceful fliers. With an average weight of 5kg and a wingspan of up to 2.4m, this is the largest bird in the archipelago, and its presence here is owed to a precise combination of environmental factors. Only one island, Española, offers these huge birds both a flat surface for nesting and nearby sea cliffs from which to become airborne – they waddle up to the edge and simply drop into the void with wings outstretched. Albatrosses are masters of the wind but helpless in calm weather, and rely utterly on the southeast trade winds to transport them between their feeding areas and Isla Española. Española's 12,000 pairs vanish from the island between December and April, when the trade winds cease to blow. During courtship, pairs perform a mesmerizing display of bowing, bill clicking, bill circling, swaying and freezing, honking and whistling.

Other Seabirds

The brown pelican is often one of the first birds recognized by visitors, and stands out for its huge pouched bill and large size. Brown pelicans can be seen feeding around Puerto Ayora harbor or nesting in just about any good stand of mangroves; young birds sometimes perch on ships' railings and dive for fish attracted to the lights at night.

The unmistakable red-billed tropicbird is about the size of a small gull and is pure white with black flecks and a crimson bill. But its most noticeable feature is a pair of slender feathers (streamers) projecting beyond its tail, often as long as its body. Tropicbirds nest in cliff crevices on most islands and pairs indulge in noisy but graceful courtship flights; Puerto Ayora and Isla Española are good places to see them.

There are two species of endemic seagull – the swallow-tailed and lava gulls. Both are subtly decked out in shades of gray and black, but the swallow-tailed gull also has a white belly and scarlet legs, feet and eyering. The swallow-tailed gull is highly nocturnal, and sometimes follows boats at night emitting weird clicking calls that are thought to be a form of echolocation. This species is easily seen on many islands during the day. The lava gull is the world's rarest gull and its total population numbers only about 400 pairs. Its coloration helps it blend perfectly with lava boulders, but it is widely distributed around the islands.

SHORE & WETLAND BIRDS

There are few permanent freshwater bodies in the primarily arid Galápagos Islands, but the saltwater lagoons and mangrove-lined inlets around the coast support a diversity of waterbirds. Largest of these birds is the great blue heron, which stands at about 1m tall and has a 2m wingspan. Like all herons it has long legs and neck, a daggerlike bill and when at rest it typically sits 'hunched.' Great blue herons are common around Puerto Ayora – even perching on harborside buildings – and are usually found along the rocky coasts of most islands. The heron 'blueprint' has several variations on the islands, including the cattle egret, a whitish bird that feeds among cattle and giant tortoises on Santa Cruz; and the endemic lava heron, a small gray species that blends in perfectly with the lava boulders among which it hunts for crabs and other small animals.

The greater flamingo, that grand pink bird with long legs, is best seen poking around salty lagoons, where it feeds on tiny crustaceans by upending its strangely bent bill. Islas Rabida and Santa Maria (Floreana), and Isabela near Puerto Villamil are good places to look, but nesting flamingos should not be approached as they may desert their nests and leave the young to starve.

Migratory wading birds, such as sandpipers and plovers, visit the islands during the northern winter. Two other waders, the American oystercatcher and the black-necked stilt, are easily recognizable, black-and-white residents. Oystercatchers inhabit rocky coasts, where they eat mollusks such as mussels; stilts are long-legged denizens of salty lagoons that they typically share with other small shorebirds.

The only species of duck resident in the islands is the Galápagos or white-cheeked pintail, which is equally at home in saltwater or freshwater lagoons, such as El Junco on Isla San Cristóbal.

LAND BIRDS

What Galápagos' land birds lack in glamour or size they make up for with scientific interest and sometimes incredible tameness.

Darwin's Finches

'The islands' finches helped change the course of science'

Although they are nothing special to look at, the islands' finches helped change the course of science. All are thought to have descended from a common ancestor, which on arrival in the archipelago found a host of vacant ecological niches and evolved into the 13 species known today. Their different distribution, beak size and shape, and feeding habits helped Charles Darwin formulate his evolutionary theories and today they are commonly known as Darwin's finches.

At least one species is found on each island, and several are easy to see around settlements. Like their namesakes, warbler finches glean insects from foliage; the three species of ground-finch are separated by bill size and typically – but not always – feed on seeds on the ground; and cactus finches are most often seen around stands of opuntia cactuses. The remarkable woodpecker finch grasps twigs in its bill to help extract grubs from holes and cracks under tree bark – a remarkable example of tool use that is very rare among birds. And, an example of evolution in action, the so-called vampire finch of remote Islas Wolf and Darwin is a type of ground-finch that has learned to supplement its moisture requirements by pecking wounds in live seabirds and drinking blood.

Mockingbirds

Fearless parties of mockingbirds are often the first birds to investigate visitors at beach landings, and are famous for poking around in bags and perching on hats. These nondescript, thrush-sized birds are easily recognizable by their down-curved bill and cocky manner, and are actually fine songsters. The four very similar species are endemic to the Galápagos and feed on seeds, insects and small animals such as lizards.

Birds of Prey

The endemic Galápagos hawk is a large raptor with no natural enemies and often allows curious visitors to approach within a meter. Unfortunately, its fearlessness and penchant for preying on domestic chickens led to its persecution by early settlers and it is now extinct on several islands. Just over a hundred pairs remain scattered among the islands; Islas Santiago, Bartolomé, Española, Santa Fé, Fernandina and Isabela are the best on which to see them.

Of the two resident owl species the most commonly seen is the shorteared owl, which commonly hunts by day on islands where there is no competition from Galápagos hawks, such as Genovesa. The barn owl is the same species found the world over, although it is rather more nocturnal on Galápagos and rarely glimpsed by most visitors.

Other Land Birds

The gentle doves are represented by the endemic Galápagos dove, a small, ground-dwelling species that is common on uninhabited islands such as Española, although it is now uncommon around settlements where cats and dogs have taken a toll. A variety of other small land birds are also present year-round, their numbers increased by migratory species during the northern winter.

Widespread in the highlands, the adult male vermilion flycatcher is unmistakable with its bright-red crown and chest. Females are brown above and yellowish beneath, and easily confused with the endemic large-billed (Galápagos) flycatcher, although the latter is also found at sea-level and is much more abundant. The tiny yellow warbler is found in all habitats on just about every island. The dark-billed cuckoo is common, but rather secretive and difficult to see, but another cuckoo species, the smooth-billed ani, is common among secondary growth. This large, all-black bird is thought to have introduced itself from South America and is something of a pest because it preys on native nestlings.

REPTILES

The Galápagos Islands are possibly unique among the world's great wildlife destinations in ranking reptiles among their main draws. Giant, prehistoric-looking tortoises and colorful iguanas are easily observed and photographed on land; you can snorkel with sea-going iguanas at a couple of sites; and sea-turtles are a common sight, especially in the nesting season.

TORTOISES & SEA TURTLES

Nowhere else on earth do tortoises, among the most ancient of land animals, reach the size they do in Galápagos, and snorkelers have an excellent chance of seeing graceful sea turtles in their native element.

Giant Tortoise

The most famous reptile in the archipelago is the giant tortoise, or Galápagos ('saddle' in Spanish), after which the islands are named. Ancestral tortoises, washed out to sea on floods, probably drifted to the islands on their back from South America – tortoises have been recorded living for months in this manner. Finding an abundance of food and no competitors or predators, they evolved into enormous size. Although there is only a single species, its shell varies in shape and size between the islands and, like the finches, demonstrates the soundness of Darwin's theories. On moist, verdant islands, such as Santa Cruz, where there is an abundance of vegetation to browse at ground level, tortoises have a high, domed carapace (upper shell). On arid islands, such as Española, where resources are at a premium, plants tend to sprout higher up and tortoises have a saddle-shaped carapace that allows them to reach overhanging vegetation.

Giant tortoises, which can live for several hundred years, usually mate toward the end of the rainy season, when the males posture and shove other males in contests of dominance before winning a mate. Unsuccessful males have been known to attempt to mate with other males, or even with appropriately shaped boulders, and the grunts of a male in copulation can be heard up to 100m away!

Seafarers killed tortoises for fresh meat in the 18th and 19th centuries, and from an estimated population of 200,000 only some 15,000 now remain. To see these majestic creatures in the wild, visit the tortoise reserve (p361) on Isla Santa Cruz or the Los Galápagos visitor site (p370) on Isla San Cristóbal, or climb Volcán Alcedo (p376) on Isabela. The easiest way to see both tiny yearlings and full-grown adults is at the breeding

Thanks to their ability to metabolize stored fat, Galápagos tortoises can go for more than a year without food or water.

project at the Charles Darwin Research Station (p360) in Puerto Ayora, Isla Santa Cruz.

Sea Turtles

Leatherback and hawksbill turtles have occasionally been recorded in Galápagos waters, but only the Pacific green sea turtle breeds here and it is abundant near many islands. Adult green sea turtles are huge and can reach 150kg in weight and 1m in length. They can be seen readily surfacing for air at many anchorages in calm water and are often encountered underwater when snorkeling.

Green sea turtles mate in the water near the shore – a sight that can sometimes be witnessed in quiet lagoons such as Black Turtle Cove (Caleta Tortuga Negra), Isla Santa Cruz. Between December and June, females crawl ashore on sandy beaches at night and dig pits in which they lay dozens of eggs. After about 60 days, the eggs hatch almost simultaneously and the newborns emerge from the sand and wriggle toward the sea. Those that aren't gobbled up by predators on that fateful first crawl swim out to sea where, if they survive a further gauntlet of predators, they live for years before the survivors return to mate near the same beach where they were hatched.

'Adult green sea turtles are huge and can reach 150kg in weight and 1m in length'

LIZARDS

There are many species of lizard on Galápagos, the most famous of which are the three species of large iguana. There are also a few species of small, drab and nonpoisonous snakes, but you would be very fortunate to see one of these retiring creatures.

Marine Iguana

Yet another of the archipelago's unique and remarkable animals, the marine iguana is the world's only seagoing lizard and is common on the rocky shores of all islands. Its size and coloration varies between islands, with the largest specimens (up to 1.5m) on Isla Fernandina and the most colorful on Isla Española, where resplendent scarlet and aqua tones highlight its otherwise blackish skin. Marine iguanas feed by grazing on seaweed underwater; young animals and females feed close inshore but adult males have been recorded at depths of up to 12m and can remain submerged for over an hour. Diving in cool Galápagos waters means that these 'cold-blooded' animals must spend hours a day basking in the sun to restore their internal temperature and thus maintain their metabolism. You will commonly see them draped over warm boulders, sometimes in rows facing the same way to maximize exposure to the sun, and snorting little puffs of spray into the air as they expel salt ingested during dives.

Land Iguanas

Although the two species of land iguana look almost alike, they can be readily told apart from marine iguanas by their yellowish coloration and because they lack a spiny crest. Both live in the arid zone, where their preferred food is the succulent pads and yellow flowers of prickly pear cactuses (opuntias). Males defend territories that support good stands of opuntia and on islands where land iguanas are present, cactus pads tend to grow higher above the ground than on islands without iguanas. Once abundant on several islands, land iguanas have suffered greatly from the depredations of feral dogs and pigs, and today Galápagos land iguanas are best seen on Islas Isabela, Santa Cruz, Seymour and South Plaza. The slightly larger Santa Fé land iguana is found only on that island.

Lava Lizards

The tortoises and iguanas may be more famous, but the most commonly seen reptiles in the islands are the various species of **lava lizard**, which are frequently seen scurrying across rocks at visitor sites and around towns. These engaging lizards reach their greatest length (30cm) and brightest coloration on Isla Española, and feed on a variety of small animals such as insects. Watch for males keeping an eye on their territory from fence posts and even perched on the back of iguanas.

MARINE LIFE

MARINE MAMMALS

Most visitors are unlikely to see any native mammals, but the two species of sea lion are resident, and many species of whale and dolphin (cetacean) have been recorded in Galápagos waters.

Sea Lions (Pinnipeds)

The native mammal you'll see the most of and just about everybody's favorite is the Galápagos sea lion, of which there are an estimated 50,000 throughout the islands. These delightful animals spend much of their time supine on sandy beaches and even on the landing steps provided at some visitor sites. Underwater they swim with consummate grace and speed, and females and pups will readily approach snorkelers and swim among bathers – they'll often be as curious about you as you are about them.

During the mating season, bulls become highly territorial and dominant males patrol up and down just offshore to keep other males from his harem. Bulls can reach 250kg in weight and can move much faster than you both in and out of the water; treat them with respect and caution at landing sites – don't panic, but do exactly what your guide tells you to. The alpha male has exclusive mating rights to up to 30 females – as long as he's able to keep other males away, which may mean that he goes for days without much food or sleep. Pups (generally one per mother) are usually born around the beginning of the dry season. Great places for snorkeling with Galápagos sea lions are Santa Fé, Bartolomé and Española.

The other pinniped species in the islands is the endemic Galápagos fur seal, a largely nocturnal, deep-diving species less commonly seen because it typically hauls out alone on rock platforms or in sheltered coves. The fur seal is actually another species of sea lion, so-named for its dense, luxuriant insulating layer of fur; sealers decimated its population in the 19th century but under protection it has rebounded and is now almost as abundant as the Galápagos sea lion and numbers some 30,000 animals. The grotto at James Bay, Santiago is a great place to see Galápagos fur seals.

'bottlenose dolphins are often seen surfing the bow waves of boats'

Whales & Dolphins (Cetaceans)

Some 25 species of whale and dolphin have been recorded in Galápagos waters, but many of these have been single records of beach-cast animals and only a few are common. Bottlenose dolphins are often seen surfing the bow waves of boats and could turn up anywhere; large flocks of feeding seabirds may indicate where dolphins are also joining in the feast. At night, the dolphins may cause the ocean to glow around them with bioluminescence as they stir up thousands of tiny phosphorescent creatures that light up when disturbed.

The most commonly seen whales are Bryde's and killer whales, which are regularly spotted in the Bolivar Channel; and sperm whales, a deep-diving species most likely to be seen in offshore waters.

OTHER MARINE LIFE

More than 400 species of marine fish have been recorded in Galápagos waters, of which about 50 are endemic. Snorkeling here is a wonderful experience and schools containing thousands of tropical fish are routinely seen. To name but a few, you might see blue-eyed damselfish, white-banded angelfish, yellow-tailed surgeonfish, Moorish idols, blue parrot-fish and concentric puffers. Marine invertebrates commonly encountered include several species of sea urchin, including slate-pencil urchins with broad, blunt spines and others with long, slender spines. The large, colorful chocolate-chip starfish is another common underwater sight. Excellent places to experience the underwater world include Genovesa and the Devil's Crown, a collapsed caldera at the tip of Isla Floreana.

Despite their fearsome reputation, most shark species are harmless and, in fact, one of the best reasons to snorkel or dive in the Galápagos is that you may be lucky enough to see some small specimens. The most common species are two species of reef shark – the white-tipped and black-tipped reef sharks – but both are small and retiring, and your best chance of seeing one is early in the morning. Hammerheads are regularly seen at Devil's Crown by scuba divers, who also head out to Gordon Rocks (easily arranged through a dive center in Puerto Ayora) to see these amazing predators in safety.

A set of shark fins from one shark caught off the coast of Manta can fetch $100. A bowl of shark-fin soup in Asia can cost up to $200. Hence the dwindling shark population.

Several species of ray are more commonly encountered, the most spectacular of which is the huge manta ray. Large manta rays measure up to 6m across their 'wingtips' and specimens 4m across are not uncommon. These harmless animals swim near the surface, filtering plankton and other tiny animals as they wing through the water and sometimes make spectacular leaps. The similar but smaller spotted eagle ray frequents inshore waters, while large schools of the beautiful golden mustard ray may be seen swimming back and forth just beneath the surface in quiet lagoons as they filter plankton; look out for this one at Genovesa and Caleta Tortuga Negra on Santa Cruz. Stingrays are sometimes visible as they sit motionless on the sandy bottom; these bottom-feeders crush and eat live mollusks in their powerful jaws and can inflict a nasty wound with the spine on their back.

One marine animal stands out for its abundance and spectacular coloration – the Sally Lightfoot crab. These nimble invertebrates adorn the rocks on every island between the waves and high water mark, where they scavenge anything and everything edible washed up on the tide. Other crabs commonly encountered include ghost crabs – fleet-footed scavengers on sandy beaches – and hermit crabs, that use deserted seashells as a home and lumber about on or above the tideline.

WES WALKER

Blue-footed booby (p49)

Greater flamingo (p51)

RALPH LEE HOPKINS

Yellow warbler (p53)

RALPH LEE HOPKINS

WES WALKER

Bull sea lion (p55)

RALPH LEE HOPKINS

Galápagos penguin (p50)

Iguana (p54)

RICHARD I'

ERNEST MANEWAL

Male magnificent frigatebird (p50)

Short-eared owl (p52)

RALPH LEE HOPKINS

Waved albatross (p50)

RALPH LEE HOPKINS

JEFF GREE

Giant tortoises (p53)

RALPH LEE HOPKINS

Lava lizard (p55)

Dolphins (p55)

RALPH LEE H

Food & Drink

Outside its borders, Ecuador's culinary wonders are practically unknown, which is a shame considering the delicacies the country conjures up – and we're not just talking potatoes and corn! From the seafood specialties of Manabí province, to the handmade ice creams of the highlands, to the exotic world of tropical fruits, Ecuadorian food is a marvel for the gourmand in everyone.

STAPLES & SPECIALTIES
Although there's plenty of overlap, Ecuadorian food can generally be divided by region, with the highlands and the coast being the most important – or at least the most diverse. That said, Ecuador is a small country and you'll regularly find seafood in the highlands and corn on the coast.

Highlands
It's impossible to discuss food from the highlands without discussing corn. In its numerous varieties, corn has been the staple of the Andean diet for a millennium, and today it forms the basis of countless highland specialties. Kernels are toasted into *tostada* (toasted corn), popped into *cangil* (popcorn), boiled and treated to make *mote* (hominy) and milled into cornmeal. The latter is flavored or filled and wrapped in corn husks or dark green *achira* leaves and steamed. The results are some of the tastiest treats in the highlands, including tamales (similar to Mexican tamales), *humitas* (a lightly sweetened corn dumpling) and *quimbolitos* (a cakier, sweeter corn dumpling).

Potatoes, of course, originated in the Andes, and are another important highland staple. Besides a vast array of tiny, colorful potatoes, you'll find creations such as *llapingachos*, fried potato-and-cheese pancakes which are often served as a side dish with fried eggs. *Quinoa* is an extremely protein-rich grain that forms a staple of the highland indigenous diet and has made its way into contemporary dishes throughout Ecuador.

The highlands most famous *plato típico* (typical dish) – one that visitors either love or hate to spot in the highland markets – is *cuy* (roasted guinea pig). *Cuy* is an indigenous speciality that dates back to Inca times and is supposedly high in protein and low in cholesterol. They're usually roasted whole on spits, and the sight of the little paws and teeth sticking out can be a bit unnerving, but it's well worth sampling. Cuenca (p195) and Loja (p212) are both good places to try it.

Almost as fun as *cuy*-spotting is rounding a busy corner and bumping into the golden-brown head of a giant, whole roasted pig. Known as *hornado* (literally, 'roasted'), this is one of the highland's most popular dishes. In the markets, the juicy meat is pulled right off the carcass when you order it. *Hornado* is almost as popular as *fritada,* fried chunks of pork that are almost invariably served with *mote*. Latacunga (p155) has a famous take on this dish known as the *chugchucara*, which, aside from raising your cholesterol to dangerous levels, makes for a great weekend event.

As throughout Ecuador, soups are an extremely important part of the highland diet and come in countless varieties, including *caldos* (brothy soups), *sopas* (thicker broth-based soups), *locros* (creamier and generally heartier soups), *sancochos* (stewlike soups) and *secos* (stews that are

Give Ecuadorian cooking a go yourself. Pick up a copy of *The Ecuador Cookbook*, which features vegetarian takes on traditional recipes and some great seafood concoctions to boot. Available at Libri Mundi in Quito (p70).

The International Potato Center (www.cipotato .org) has identified nearly 4000 varieties of potatoes in the Andes, the homeland of the world's potatoes.

Tostada (toasted corn) is sold in little bags scooped from giant mounds of the stuff at streetside vendors. With a little onion and spices thrown on top, it's a favorite highland snack.

usually served over rice). *Locro de papa* is a wonderful, thick potato soup served with avocado and cheese.

The Coast

The coast is where Ecuadorian food really shines. Mention food from Manabí to any Ecuadorian, and they'll begin salivating, their eyes will glaze over, and they'll proceed to tell you it's the best food in all of Ecuador. Actually, the entire coast is a culinary paradise, and it can definitely be healthier than some of the highland dishes.

The staple of coastal cuisine, of course, is seafood. All along the coast it's fresh, cheap and delicious. The most widely found seafood plate is *corvina*, which literally means sea bass but is usually just whatever white fish happens to be available that day. When it's really *corvina*, it's *really* good.

Ceviche is outstanding in Ecuador. This delicious dish consists of uncooked seafood marinated in lemon and seasoned with thinly sliced onion and herbs. It's served cold and, on a hot afternoon, goes down divinely with popcorn and a cold beer. Ceviche can be *de pescado* (fish), *de concha* (shellfish) or *de camarones* (shrimp). Only the latter is cooked before being marinated. Improperly prepared ceviche can make you sick (and even spread cholera), but most restaurants in Ecuador are aware of this and prepare ceviche under sanitary conditions. If the restaurant is popular and looks clean, it will most likely be both delicious and safe.

Esmeraldas province, which has a large Afro-Ecuadorian population, is home to some interesting African-influenced specialties including the downright sublime *encocado*, shrimp or fish cooked in a rich, spiced coconut sauce. Guayas province, and especially the town of Playas (p315), is famous for its crab, which is cooked whole and served in piles as big as your appetite, along with a wooden hammer for cracking open the shells. It's one of the most pleasurable (and messy!) culinary experiences in the country. Guayas is also famous for its *seco de chivo* (goat stew), an Ecuadorian classic. If you're not keen on goat, look for *seco de pollo*, the same dish made with chicken.

Plantains and bananas (see the boxed text, below) play a huge role in coastal cooking. One of the country's most interesting and delicious dishes is *sopa de bolas de verde*, a thick peanut-based soup with seasoned, mashed-plantain balls floating in it. And as you're bussing along the northern coast, kids often board the bus selling *corviche* (a delicious

According to Human Rights Watch (www.hrw .org) Ecuador's banana industry is one of the country's most serious perpetrators of human rights abuses. To reflect on the dark side of bananas, see p342.

GOING BANANAS

Bananas and plantains are a vital part of the Ecuadorian diet – so much so that banana queens are elected in the coastal city of Machala. So get to know your bananas and try whatever you can that's made with them. Here's a little primer.

Plátanos are plantains, *verdes* are green plantains and *maduros* are ripe, yellow plantains. *Guineos* are the yellow sweet bananas that most foreigners are familiar with.

OK, now let's take 'em apart: *chifles* are thinly sliced *guineos* fried into crisps, while *patacones* are thickly sliced, smashed *verdes* fried into chewy fritters. *Maduros* are often sliced lengthwise, fried and served whole as a side dish. In the Oriente, *plátanos con queso* are green plantains split lengthwise, filled with cheese and grilled. Loja is famous for its *empanadas de verde* (empanadas made with plantain 'dough') while the coast is known for its *bolas de verde* (balls of mashed plantains with cheese).

Armed with these basics, you're ready to go…out and eat more bananas.

TRAVEL YOUR TASTEBUDS

Perhaps even more fun than tasting weird (ahem – *different*) foods is telling your friends about it when you get home. Rest assured, you'll find some good story fodder in Ecuador.

- *Cuy* – you can't leave without trying roast guinea pig!
- *Yaguarlocro* – with floating chunks of blood sausage this potato-based soup is a classic.
- *Empanada de viento* – literally 'wind empanada,' these are huge, crispy, air-filled, sugar-dusted empanadas with a thin layer of cheese inside.
- *Guatita* – tripe in a seasoned peanut sauce with avocado. When it's good, it's great.
- *Caldo de tronquit* – bull penis soup…go on, give it a try.
- *Caldo de pata* – another classic, cow-hoof soup is…well…you decide.
- Lemon ants – have your jungle guide point out some of these and eat 'em up. They taste just like lemon!

---

plantain dumpling stuffed with seafood or shrimp) from big baskets dangling from their arms.

Seafood soups are simply outstanding. One of the most popular (and an extremely cheap way to fill the belly) is *encebollado*, a brothy seafood and onion soup poured over yucca and served with *chifles* (fried banana chips) and popcorn. It's usually eaten in the morning or for lunch. Another fabulous soup is *sopa marinera*, a delicious broth – which can range from clear to thick and peanuty – loaded with fish, shellfish, shrimp and sometimes crab.

The Oriente

Food from the Oriente plays a less prominent role in national Ecuadorian cuisine. Some typical Oriente dishes include simple yucca- and plantain-based dishes; river fish (including piranha and catfish); the pulpy fruit of the chonta palm; and hunted jungle animals, including *guanta* (the rabbit-sized rodent agouti), turtle and occasionally monkey. Most of these foods are not part of travelers' everyday dining experience in the Oriente, however. But you will encounter some interesting foods. *Pan de yucca* (yucca bread) is sold all over the Oriente. *Ayampacos* are a southern Oriente speciality consisting of chicken, beef or fish wrapped in *bijao* leaves and cooked on a grill. They're particularly popular in Macas (p259). Also look out for dishes cooked with *ishpingo*, a type of cinnamon native to the Oriente. On the off chance that monkey or turtle (or any other rain forest animal) is offered to you while on a trip in the Oriente, decline – hunting these animals is threatening their existence.

Banana trees (and Ecuador has millions of them) are not trees at all – because their trunks have no wood tissue, they're technically herbs!

DRINKS

For more on special drinks that are whipped up for fiestas, see Celebrations (p64).

Ecuador exports more bananas than any country in the world.

Nonalcoholic Drinks

While traveling in Ecuador it's hardly unusual to stumble upon a pack of gringos erupting with ecstatic descriptions of their first encounter with the Ecuadorian *jugo* (juice): 'Tree-tomato juice? I have *no* idea what it is but it tasted amazing!'

Ecuadorian juices are as exotic as the country's fruit selection and a highlight of any visit. Most juices are either *puro* (with no water) or made with *agua purificada* (boiled or bottled water), although you may want to avoid juices from roadside stands or cheap restaurants, where the water quality is questionable. The most common kinds of juice are *mora* (blackberry), *naranja* (orange), *toronja* (grapefruit), *piña* (pineapple), *maracuyá* (passion fruit), *sandía* (watermelon), *naranjilla* (a local fruit that tastes like a bitter orange) and papaya. But plenty of strange ones pop up, and if one doesn't sound familiar, you'd better try it!

Almost as tasty as juices are *batidos* (fruit shakes), usually made with fruit, milk and sugar. One flavor to look out for is *taxo*, a type of passion fruit that goes especially well with milk. Another fruit best enjoyed in a *batido* is *borojó*. Found mostly in the north, it not only tastes unlike anything else, but reportedly increases blood flow to the male reproductive organ (and we all know what that means!).

Chicha (a fermented corn or yucca drink) is a traditional indigenous beverage still widely consumed. *Chicha de maíz* (corn *chicha*) is the traditional highland variety, while *chicha de yuca* (yucca *chicha*) is the traditional *chicha* of the Oriente (although you'll find both in the Oriente). Traditionally, the yucca variety was made by women who masticated the yucca and spit it into pots, where it was left to ferment with the help of enzymes from the saliva. Today it's rarely made this way, and you should jump on any chance to try it (though it's definitely an acquired taste).

Coffee is available everywhere, but is generally disappointing. *Café con leche* (coffee with milk) simply equates to stirring instant coffee powder into a cup of hot milk. *Café negro* is black coffee. Tea, or *té*, is served black with lemon and sugar unless you order *té de hierbas* (herbal tea).

The nonalcoholic beverage *yamor* is made from seven varieties of corn and consumed in great quantities during Otavalo's Fiesta de Yamor (p119).

Alcoholic Drinks

Alas, the libations. As throughout Latin America, beer is of the light pilsner type – in fact, the national beer is called Pilsener and it's rivaled only by Club, the beer of choice on the coast. Despite the fact that both are low on flavor (imagine US Budweiser), they go down beautifully beneath the hot equatorial sunshine. Local wines are truly terrible and should not be experimented with.

As for the strong stuff, the local firewater is *aguardiente* (sugarcane alcohol), which will induce a serious hangover if you're not careful. *Aguardiente* brands such as Cristal from Cuenca are now marketing their drinks to a younger crowd, offering slicker labeling and variations such as Cristal Limón (lemon Cristal) or mixed down versions such as 'Sexy Apple,' 'Fashion Orange' and 'Extreme Wild.' Rum is widely available, cheap and good.

CELEBRATIONS

Food and feasting are an important part of many Ecuadorian celebrations, but two annual events really stand out: Semana Santa (Holy Week) and Finados, or Día de los Difuntos (Day of the Dead). During the week leading up to Good Friday, Ecuadorians feast on a hearty soup called *fanesca*. The best *fanesca* is made with salt cod and at least a dozen types of grains and flavored with a wild array of ingredients. According to many it's the best of all Ecuadorian soups, but you'll have to time your visit to try it. Its origins are unclear, but its ingredients adhere to a blend of Catholic and indigenous beliefs: fish, to avoid the no-meat rule of Lent, and grains to celebrate the early harvest.

During the weeks leading up to Finados (celebrated November 2) bakeries start selling the delightful *guaguas de pan,* loaves of bread shaped and decorated to look like babies. *Guaguas de pan* are invariably accompanied

---

ECUADOR'S TOP FIVE EATERIES

- **La Red** (p273) Perhaps the best reason to spend an evening in San Lorenzo.
- **El Jardín** (p258) Likely the best darn grub (not grubs!) in the upper Amazon Basin; Puyo.
- **Escalón 69** (p329) Traditional coastal dishes with a haute cuisine twist; Guayaquil.
- **Café Mosaico** (p101) You may never find a view like this again; Quito.
- **La Abuela Rosa** (p184) Join the locals in Riobamba for traditional snacks.

---

by a cup of *colada morada*, a sweet, thick beverage of cornmeal, black-berries and other fruits. On November 2, people take both to the cemetery to eat with their dead in a tradition rooted in pre-Hispanic rituals.

Of course, no fiesta is complete without a little *canelazo* – a shot of *aguardiente* livened up with a dose of hot, fresh fruit cider. During any nighttime festival, it's likely you'll see someone selling shots of it in little plastic cups. Don't miss it!

WHERE TO EAT & DRINK

The standard term for restaurant is *restaurante*, which is where you'll often eat when you eat out. A *comedore* is a cheap restaurant and may offer a more authentic experience both in terms of food and atmosphere. *Cevicherías* are ceviche restaurants, while *parrillas* are steak houses. You can guess what *pizzerías* serve. Nearly every city in Ecuador has a *chifa* (Chinese restaurant), which can be a good break from standard Ecuadorian fare.

Desayuno (breakfast) is served at both *restaurantes* and *comedores* and usually consists of *huevos* (eggs) and tostadas (toast), unless you decide to go the Ecuadorian route and have chicken and lentils or whatever meat-and-grains dish is on the menu. Places that cater to tourists often serve great breakfasts.

Ecuadorians are family-oriented folks, so dragging the kids to all but the fanciest restaurants is generally not a problem. Obviously, solo travelers can eat wherever they please, but they'll most likely find conversation at cheap *comedores*, where Ecuadorians often dine alone as well.

Quick Eats

Street foods and market fare are two of the great culinary experiences of Latin America, and Ecuador is no exception. The primary concern, of course, is hygiene, so always follow the tried-and-true rule – if it's busy, it's probably fine. The exception – and it's a serious one – is the water problem. Even when a stand is busy, if the salad is soaked with tap water, or the glasses pulled from a dirty tub, you'll probably get sick whether the locals do or not. Exercise caution, but by all means, explore!

Whether you like it or not, you'll definitely be inundated with street fare while on the buses. Keep an eye on what's for sale – it's often a great way to try regional food. As a bus passes through Latacunga, women board selling biscuits called *allullas*. In Esmeraldas, children jump on selling *corviche*, and near San Miguel de Salcedo, ice-cream vendors bombard the buses with shouts of '¡Helados!' (Ice cream!).

VEGETARIANS & VEGANS

Ecuador's a vegetarian-friendly country. But memorize this: *arroz con menestra* (rice with lentils or beans). It'll come in handy. Almost every restaurant serves *arroz* or *menestra* as a side dish, but for vegetarians

---

Slice an avocado in half, remove the pit, fill the hole with sugar, grab a spoon and dig in. Known as a *batería* (battery), it'll keep you going – they say – in more ways than one.

The 'grain' Quinoa has been a staple of Andean food for thousands of years. It grows at altitudes of up to 4000m and is classified by the UN as a 'super crop' due to its extremely high-protein content. The Inca called it 'mother grain'.

Ecuadorian food is mild rather than spicy hot, but just about everything is spiced up at the table with the country's countless types of delicious *aji* (hot sauce).

DOS & DON'TS

Do...

- tip 10% if *servicio* (service) isn't included in the bill
- exercise patience when ordering something that's not on the menu
- approach eating with an adventurous attitude!

Don't...

- eat pizza with you hands
- drink tap water
- eat hunted animals during rain forest tours (or anytime)

---

and vegans it can be a delicious main course, especially with some *verduras* (vegetables) ordered as well. *Pizzerías* and *chifas* are both great for vegetarians. Note that asking the wait staff if something contains *carne* (meat), and receiving the answer 'No,' may simply mean it doesn't have red meat or pork. *Pollo* (chicken) is rarely considered *carne*. Be specific. Buying fruits and veggies in the market is an excellent way to get a wholesome, meatless lunch.

HABITS & CUSTOMS

Besides the food, there are only a few major differences between dining out in Ecuador and dining out in San Francisco or Sydney: Ecuadorian wait staff take a more laidback approach to table service, and smoking is allowed almost anywhere. Lingering over a dinner is common so you won't get subliminally ushered out as you might in the USA.

When dining out, breakfast is eaten between 8am and 10am, and only market and bus-terminal cafés open before 8am. Lunch is served between noon and 2pm and dinner starts as early as 5pm, though most Ecuadorians dine between 6pm and 8pm, which is when you should dine if you want a lively meal. For standard opening hours, see p386.

EAT YOUR WORDS
Useful Phrases

Do you have a menu in English?

¿Tienen una carta en inglés? — tye·nen oon·a *kar*·ta en een·*gles*

What do you recommend?

¿Qué me recomienda? — ke me re·ko·*myen*·da

Do you have any vegetarian dishes?

¿Tienen algún plato vegetariano? — tye·nen al·*goon pla*·to ve·khe·ta·*rya*·no

I'd like the set lunch/dinner, please.

Quisiera el almuerzo/la merienda, por favor. — kee·*sye*·ra el al·*mwer*·so/la me·*ryen*·da por fa·*vor*

The bill (check), please.

La cuenta, por favor. — la *kwen*·ta por fa·*vor*

Food Glossary

a la brasa	a la *bra*·sa	grilled
aguardiente	a·gwar·*dyen*·te	sugarcane alcohol
almuerzo	al·*mwer*·so	inexpensive set-lunch menu
arroz	a·*roz*	rice
arvejas	ar·ve·khas	peas
batido	ba·*tee*·do	fruit shake

If you like coffee-table books as much as food, pick up André Obiol's *Aromas Colores y Sabores de un Nuevo Ecuador*; it's a little over-nouveau, but it has a great section on Ecuador's fruits and vegetables.

An old Ecuadorian adage affirms that *'Chocolate sin queso es como amor sin besos'* ('hocolate without cheese is like love without kisses).

caldo	*kal*·do	clear soup
camarones	ka·ma·*ro*·nes	shrimp
canelazo	ka·ne·*la*·zo	*aguardiente* livened up with a dose of hot, fresh fruit cider
cangil	kan·*khil*	popcorn
cangrejo	kan·*gre*·kho	crab
carne	*kar*·ne	meat, usually beef
ceviche	se·*vee*·che	seafood that is 'cooked' by marinating it in lemon juice
chifa	*chee*·fa	Chinese restaurant
chifles	*chee*·fles	crispy fried bananas
chivo	*chee*·vo	goat
churrasco	choo·*ras*·ko	dish of fried beef, rice, fried egg, avocado and potatoes
comedores	ko·me·*do*·res	cheap restaurants
concha	*kon*·cha	shellfish
corvina	kor·*vee*·na	sea bass
cuy	koy	roast guinea pig
encebollado	en·se·bo·*la*·do	seafood, yucca and onion soup garnished with *chifles*
guatita	gwa·*tee*·ta	a tripe and potato stew in a seasoned, peanut-based sauce
helados de paila	e·*la*·dos de *pai*·la	ice cream handmade in large copper bowls
huevos	*hwe*·vos	eggs; *huevos fritos* are fried eggs and *huevos revueltos* are scrambled. Order them *bien cocido* (well cooked) if you don't like them runny.
jugo	*khoo*·go	juice
legumbres	le·*goom*·bres	pulse vegetables
lentejas	len·*te*·khas	lentils
llapingachos	lya·pin·*ga*·chos	fried pancakes of mashed potatoes with cheese
maitos	*mai*·tos	fish cooked in palm leaves
mantequilla	man·te·*kee*·lya	butter
menestra	me·*ne*·stra	mixed grains or beans
merienda	me·*ryen*·da	inexpensive set-dinner
mermelada	mer·me·*la*·da	jam
mistela	mi·*ste*·la	an anise-flavored liqueur
mote	*mo*·te	hominy, served with fried pork, toasted corn and hot sauce
pan	pan	bread
patacones	pa·ta·*ko*·nes	sliced then mashed and fried plantains
pescado	pes·*ka*·do	fish
plátanos	*pla*·ta·nos	plantains
pollo	*po*·lyo	chicken
postre	*pos*·tre	dessert
seco	*se*·ko	stew
tallarines	ta·lya·*ree*·nes	noodles
tortillas de maíz	tor·*tee*·lyas de ma·*ees*	fried corn pancakes
tostada	tos·*ta*·da	toast
trucha	*troo*·cha	trout
verdes	*ver*·des	literally 'greens' but refers to green plantains
verduras	ver·*doo*·ras	vegetables

QUITO

Quito

Spread across a spectacular Andean valley and flanked by volcanic peaks, Quito's setting alone is enough to strike you speechless. The historical center – or 'old town,' as it's called – is a maze of colonial splendor, an Unesco World Heritage Site since 1978. Quito is currently flush with pride after 2006 marked the final installment of a massive restoration project that spruced up buildings and churches, brought historic theaters back to life and made the old town's formerly sketchy streets safe to explore once again.

Despite intensive restoration, the old town retains the vibrant working class and indigenous character that has always defined it. Walking its narrow streets is to wander into another world. Stray dogs saunter past indigenous women carrying impossible loads, past legless guitar strummers, blind accordion players, old men in sailor suits selling ice cream, past giant roast pigs peaking out of doorways and shops selling every odd commodity imaginable. The constant white noise of hollering vendors hangs in the air like chanting in a monastery, and the smells of cooking peanuts, car exhaust fumes, baking bread and who knows what else threaten sensory overload.

Only a 20-minute walk from the old town, Quito's 'new town' is a different world entirely; a mixture of multistory hotels, high-rises and drab government complexes. For travelers, its heart is the colorful Mariscal Sucre, which has trendy cafés, international restaurants, travel agencies, cybercafés, bars and small hotels. The area definitely lives up to its nickname *gringolandia* (gringo land), but quiteños (people from Quito) dig it too, so it keeps its Ecuadorian flair.

HIGHLIGHTS

- Wander the streets of Quito's magnificent **old town** (p73), one of Latin America's finest colonial centers

- Ride the new **telefériQo** (p79) up to 4100m Cruz Loma and marvel at the breathtaking views

- Climb down the stairs to the historic neighborhood of **Guápulo** (p86), a bohemian enclave that 'progress' forgot

- People watch in the **Plaza San Francisco** (p77), one of the country's most beautiful plazas

- Straddle the equator and find out which direction the water drains at **La Mitad del Mundo** (p108) – touristy, but all in good fun

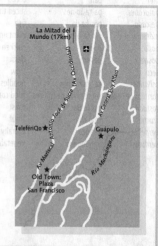

La Mitad del Mundo (17km)

TelefériQo

Guápulo

Old Town:
Plaza San Francisco

Río Machángara

■ TELEPHONE CODE: ☎ 02 ■ AVERAGE TEMPERATURE: 14°C (57°F) ■ RAINIEST MONTH: APRIL

HISTORY

The site of the capital city dates from pre-Hispanic times. The early inhabitants of the area were the peaceful Quitu people, who gave their name to the city. The Quitus integrated with the coastal Caras, giving rise to the indigenous group known as the Shyris. Around AD 1300, the Shyris joined with the Puruhás through marriage, and their descendants fought against the Incas in the late 15th century.

By the time the Spanish arrived in Ecuador in 1526, Quito was a major Inca city. Rather than allowing it to fall into the hands of the Spanish conquerors, Rumiñahui, a general of Atahualpa, razed the city shortly before their arrival. There are no Inca remains. The present capital was founded atop the ruins by Spanish lieutenant Sebastián de Benalcázar on December 6, 1534. Many colonial-era buildings survive in the old town.

ORIENTATION

The country's capital, Quito is Ecuador's second-largest city with 1.4 million people (Guayaquil is the largest). It lies along the floor of a high Andean valley in a roughly north–south direction. The Centro Histórico (historical center) holds nearly all of Quito's famous colonial architecture. Locals call it El Centro, and English-speakers call it the 'old town.'

The north is modern Quito, the 'new town,' with all major businesses and services. Most hotels and restaurants are found here, especially in the travelers' ghetto of the Mariscal Sucre (aka the Mariscal), where many foreigners eat, sleep and drink. The northern end of the city contains the airport and the middle- and upper-class residential areas. Avenida Amazonas is the best-known street, although Avenida 10 de Agosto and Avenida 6 de Diciembre are the most important thoroughfares.

The far south of Quito consists mainly of working-class residential areas. Few travelers venture to this section of the city; it's unsafe and there's little to see.

The surrounding hills and peaks make orienting yourself easy: Cruz Loma and the flanks of Volcán Pichincha are the massive mountains to the west of the city. If you stand facing them, north will be to your right. To the south, you can almost always see the giant hilltop statue of La Virgen de Quito.

The bus terminal is directly south of the old town (about a 10-minute walk from the Plaza Grande). The best way into town from the airport is by taxi (see p107 for details).

Quito's streets are usually one way: Calles Guayaquil and Venezuela head into the old town, and Calles García Moreno and Flores head out of the old town.

QUITO IN...

Two Days

Prepare for exhaustion. Head straight for the **old town** (p73) and start at **Plaza Grande** (p73). Check out the **Centro Cultural Metropolitano** (p75), **La Compañia de Jesus** (p76) and **Plaza San Francisco** (p77). See whatever else you can before a big lunch (save room for that fruit bowl) at **Frutería Monserrate** (p96). Check out the exotic fruits and veggies at the **Mercado Central** (p96) before climbing up to **Parque Itchimbia** (p79). Have a sunset coffee and take in the views at **Café Mosaico** (p101). Rest up for dinner at **La Cueva del Oso** (p97) and a night of live music at **Vox Populi** (p103).

Day two, ride the **telefériQo** (p79) up to Cruz Loma. Visit the **Capilla del Hombre** and nearby **Museo Guayasamín** (p83) before winding down with a **shopping spree** (p104) in the Mariscal Sucre. Close the night with dinner and drinks at **El Pobre Diablo** (p102).

Four Days

To the above itinerary add the requisite daytrip to **La Mitad del Mundo** (p108) to your third day. That evening, take a private **salsa lesson** (p88) and try your new moves at **Seseribó** (p103). Day four, visit the **Museo del Banco Central** (p82) and then see the orchids at the **Jardín Botánico** (p83).

QUITO

ADDRESSES IN QUITO

Several years ago, Quito changed to a new address system based on N, S, W and E quadrants. An old address might be Avenida Amazonas 433, while the new one would be Avenida Amazonas N22-62. The numbers bear no relation to each other. Most buildings now display the new address, but some show the old address, and some have both. In other words, it can be extremely confusing. Both are used in this chapter, depending on the information received from each business. Taxi drivers find places based on cross streets.

Maps

Excellent topographical maps ($2 each) and various tourist highlight maps are available in the map sales room at the **Instituto Geográfico Militar** (IGM; Map pp80-1; ☎ 254 5090, 222 9075/6; 🕑 8am-4pm Mon-Thu, 7am-12:30pm Fri) located on top of a hill, southeast of Parque El Ejido. There are no buses, so you have to either walk or take a taxi. You need to leave your passport at the gate. Aside from the giant map of Quito for sale ($8), city maps are limited.

The most useful maps of Quito are the blue-covered ones by Nelson Gómez, which are available at most bookstores. The Coorporación Metropolitana de Turismo (tourist office; p72) publishes free self-guided walking maps and good city maps ($0.50).

INFORMATION
Bookstores

Abya Yala Bookstore (Map pp80-1; ☎ 250 6247; www.abyayala.org; Av 12 de Octubre 1430 & Wilson; 🕑 8am-6pm Mon-Fri, 9am-1pm Sat) Outstanding selection of books on indigenous culture and anthropology (in Spanish).

Confederate Books (Map p84; ☎ 252 7890; J Calama 410; 🕑 10am-6pm Mon-Sat) Ecuador's largest selection of second-hand books in English and several other languages.

English Bookstore (☎ 254 3996; www.theenglish bookstore.com; cnr J Calama & Av 6 de Diciembre; 🕑 10am-7pm Mon-Sat) Bookstore café with great selection of used books in English.

Libri Mundi (Map p84; ☎ 223 4791; www.librimundi .com in Spanish; JL Mera 851; 🕑 8:30am-7:30pm Mon-Fri, 9am-2pm & 3-6pm Sat) Quito's best bookstore, with

a good selection of titles in English, German, French and Spanish. Lonely Planet guides available.

Libro Express (Map p84; ☎ 254 8113; Av Amazonas 816 & General Veintimilla; 🕑 9:30am-7:30pm Mon-Fri, 10am-6pm Sat) Good for maps, magazines, Lonely Planet guides and Ecuador-related books.

Cultural Centers

Alianza Francesa (Map pp80-1; ☎ 224 9345/50; Av Eloy Alfaro N32-468 near Belgica & Av 6 de Diciembre) French cultural center.

Asociación Humboldt (Map pp80-1; ☎ 254 8480; Vancouver E5-54 at Polonia) German cultural center.

Centro Cultural Afro-Ecuatoriano (Map pp80-1; ☎ 252 2318; JL Tamayo 985) A good information source for black Ecuadorian culture and events in Quito.

Centro Cultural Metropolitano (Map p74; ☎ 295 0272, 258 4363; www.centrocultural-quito.com in Spanish; cnr García Moreno & Espejo; admission $2; 🕑 9am-5pm Tue-Sun, patio until 7:30pm) The hub of cultural events in the old town.

Centro Cultural Mexicano (Map pp80-1; ☎ 256 1548; Orellana 473 at Whymper; cultural@embamex .org.ec; 🕑 9am-2pm & 3-6pm Mon-Fri) Features great monthly exhibits of Mexican artists; inaugurated 2005.

Internet Access

The Mariscal area (especially along J Calama) is bursting with cybercafés, many with Net-to-phone services. Cybercafés are trickier to find in the old town. All charge $0.70 to $1 per hour. The following are a few of the more popular choices:

Friends Web Café (Map p84; ☎ 254 2074; J Calama E6-19; 🕑 7:30am-10:30pm Mon-Fri, 8am-10:30pm Sat & Sun) Cozy little cybercafé with a vibe as good as its juices and snacks.

K'ntuña Net (Map p74; Chile Oe4-22, Pasaje Arzobispal, ground fl, local 14) Located in the back patio.

Papaya Net (Map p84; ☎ 255 6574; J Calama 469 at JL Mera; 🕑 7am-1am) The most popular cybercafé in the Mariscal with groovin' music, alcohol, espresso drinks and snacks.

Sambo.net (Map p84; ☎ 290 1315; JL Mera at J Pinto) Comfy place, fast connection.

Stop 'n' Surf (Map p74; Espejo Shopping, Espejo Oe2-40, Local 64; 🕑 10am-8pm Mon-Sat)

Internet Resources

Corporación Metropolitana de Turismo (www.quito .com.ec)

Gay Guide to Quito (http://gayquitoec.tripod.com)

Municipal website (www.quito.gov.ec in Spanish)

Que Hacer Quito (www.quehacerquito.com in Spanish)

Laundry

There are no laundries in the old town. Most hotels will wash and dry your clothes, but this is expensive. The following places wash and dry clothes within 24 hours (often within five), and all charge between \$0.75 and \$1 per kilo:

Opera de Jabón (Map p84; ☎ 254 3995; J Pinto 325 near JL Mera)

Rainbow Laundry (Map p84; ☎ 223 7128; JL Mera 1337 at L García)

Sun City Laundry (Map p84; ☎ 255 3066; cnr JL Mera & Foch)

Wash & Go (Map p84; ☎ 223 0993; J Pinto 340 at JL Mera)

Medical Services

The following individual doctors have been recommended, many of whom have offices in the Centro Meditropoli (Map p78) near the Hospital Metropolitano.

Clínica de la Mujer (Map p78; ☎ 245 8000; Av Amazonas 4826 & Gaspar de Villarroel) A private clinic specializing in women's medical problems.

Clínica Pichincha (Map p84; ☎ 256 2408, 256 2296; General Veintimilla 1259 & U Páez) Does lab analysis for parasites, dysentery etc.

Dr Alfredo Jijon (Map p78; ☎ 245 6359, 246 6314; Centro Meditropoli, office 215, Mariana de Jesús & Av Occidental) Gynecologist.

Dr John Rosenberg (Map p84; ☎ 252 1104, ext 310, 222 7777, 09-973 9734, pager ☎ 222 7777; Foch 476 & Av 6 de Dicembre) Internist specializing in tropical medicine; speaks English and German, makes house calls and is available for emergencies nearly anytime.

Dr Jorge Cobo Avedaño (Map p78; ☎ 225 6589, 246 3361, ext 222; Centro Meditropoli, office 004) English-speaking dentist.

Dr José A Pitarque (Map p78; ☎ 226 8173; Centro Meditropoli, office 211) English-speaking ophthalmologist.

Dr Silvia Altamirano (☎ 244 4119; Av Amazonas 2689 & Av de la República) Orthodontist and dentist; excellent. Near Parque La Carolina.

Hospital Metropolitano (Map p78; ☎ 226 1520, 226 9030, emergency ☎ 226 5020; Mariana de Jesús & Av Occidental) The best hospital in town.

Hospital Voz Andes (Map p78; ☎ 226 2142; Juan Villalengua 267) American-run hospital with an outpatient department and emergency room near the Iñaquito trolley stop. Fees start at about \$15 for an office visit.

Money

There are several banks and a few *casas de cambio* (currency-exchange bureaus) in the new town along Avenida Amazonas between Avenida Patria and Orellana, and there are dozens of banks throughout town. Banks listed here have ATMs and change traveler's checks.

If you need to change money on a Sunday, head to the Producambios at the airport; the *casa de cambio* in the international arrival area is open for all flight arrivals.

American Express (Map p84; ☎ 256 0488; Av Amazonas 329, 5th fl; ☽ 8:30am-5pm Mon-Fri) Sells Amex traveler's checks to Amex card-holders only. Also replaces lost or stolen checks.

Banco de Guayaquil (Av Amazonas Map p84; ☎ 256 4324; Av Amazonas N22-147 at General Veintimilla; Colón Map p84; Av Cristóbal Colón at Reina Victoria)

Banco del Pacífico (new town Map pp80–1; ☎ 250 1218; 12 de Octubre & Cordero; old town Map p74; ☎ 228 8138; cnr Guayaquil & Chile)

Banco del Pichincha (Map p74; ☎ 258 4149; Guayaquil at Manabí)

MasterCard (Map p78; ☎ 226 2770; Naciones Unidas 8771 at De Los Shyris)

Producambios (airport Map p78; ☽ 6am-9pm; Mariscal ☎ 256 3900; Av Amazonas 350; ☽ 8:30am-6pm Mon-Fri, 9am-2pm Sat)

Visa (Map p78; ☎ 245 9303; De Los Shyris 3147)

Western Union (Av de la República Map pp80-1; ☎ 256 5059; Av de la República 433; Colón Map pp80-1; ☎ 290 1505; Av Cristóbal Colón 1333) For money transfers; charges \$90 for a \$1000 transfer from the USA.

Post

You can mail a package up to 2kg from any post office. Packages exceeding 2kg must be mailed from the **branch post office** (Map p84; ☎ 250 8890; cnr Av Cristóbal Colón & Reina Victoria) in the Mariscal or from the parcel post office (listed here).

Central post office (Map p74; ☎ 228 2175; Espejo 935) In the old town; this is where you pick up your *lista de correos* (general delivery) mail. See p394 for more information.

DHL (Map pp80-1; ☎ 290 1505; Av Cristóbal Colón 1333 at Foch; ☽ 8am-7pm Mon-Fri, 9am-5pm Sat)

Parcel post office (Map pp80-1; ☎ 252 1730; Ulloa 273) If you are mailing a package over 2kg, use this post office, near Dávalos.

'PostOffice' (Map pp80-1; ☎ 290 9209; cnr Av Amazonas & Santa María; ☽ 9:30am-5pm Mon-Fri) Private company offering FedEx, UPS and other international courier services.

Telephone

Quito's area code (telephone code) is ☎ 02. There are also plenty of non-Andinatel phone kiosks around.

Andinatel (Map pp80-1; ☎ 297 7100; Eloy Alfaro 333 near 9 de Octubre) Main office is in the new town.

Andinatel Mariscal offices (JL Mera Map p84; ☎ 290 2756; JL Mera 741 at General Baquedano; Reina Victoria Map p84; Reina Victoria near J Calama) In the Mariscal area.

Andinatel old town office (Map p74; ☎ 261 2112; Benalcázar near Mejía)

Toilets

Public toilets are rare in Quito, but they do exist. In the old town, you'll find some inside the Palacio de Arzobisbal. In the new town, relieve yourself at the bathrooms inside the Mercado Artesenal Mariscal and at the **public toilets** (Map p84; Diego de Almagro near Cordero) behind the Mariscal tourist office. Most restaurants allow you to use their bathrooms.

Tourist Information

South American Explorers (SAE; Map pp80-1; ☎ 222 5228; www.saexplorers.org; Jorge Washington 311 & Leonidas Plaza Gutiérrez; ⏱ 9:30am-5pm Mon-Wed & Fri, 9:30am-6pm Thu, 9am-noon Sat) For more information on this excellent travelers' organization, see p397.

Tourist Information Kiosk (Map p74; cnr Venezuela & Chile, Plaza Grande) Convenient for general questions, directions and maps.

Tourist Offices (Corporación Metropolitana de Turismo; www.quito.com.ec; Centro Histórico office 'El Quinde' Map p74; ☎ 257 0786; García Moreno N12-01 at Mejía; ⏱ 9:30am-6pm Mon-Sat, 10am-4pm Sun; Centro Histórico Palacio Arzobispal office Map p74; ☎ 258 6591; Chile near Venezuela, Plaza Grande; ⏱ 9am-5pm Mon-Sat; Mariscal office Map p84; ☎ 255 1566; Cordero at Reina Victoria; ⏱ 9am-5pm Mon-Fri; airport office Map p78; ☎ 330 0163; Museo del Banco Central office Map pp80-1; ☎ 222 1116; Av Patria at Av 12 de Octubre; ⏱ 9am-5pm Mon-Fri, 10am-4pm Sat & Sun) The El Quinde office in the old town has free Internet service and a great crafts store.

Travel Agencies

Ecuadorian Tours (Map p84; ☎ 256 0488; www .ecuadoriantours.com; Av Amazonas N21-33 near Jorge Washington) Affiliated with Amex, this is a good all-purpose travel agency.

Metropolitan Touring (Av Amazonas Map p84; ☎ 250 6650/1/2; www.metropolitan-touring.com; Av Amazonas N20-39 near 18 de Septiembre; Olmedo Map p74; ☎ 228 9172; Olmedo Oe-548, near García Moreno) Ecuador's biggest travel agency.

DANGERS & ANNOYANCES

Quito has a reputation for being a dangerous city. Fortunately, that danger is easy to avoid by knowing where – and where not – to go.

HIGH ON ALTITUDE

Did the hotel stairs make you breathless? Is your head spinning or achy? Have you got cotton mouth? If so, you're probably suffering the mild symptoms of altitude sickness, which will disappear after a day or two. Quito's elevation of about 2850m can certainly have this affect if you've just arrived from sea level. To minimize symptoms, take things easy upon arrival, eat light and lay off the smokes and alcohol.

Ironically, the area with the most tourist services – the Mariscal Sucre – is one of the most dangerous areas in the city, especially after around 9pm, when you should *take a taxi* even if you have only two blocks to walk. The Mariscal has been plagued by drugs, muggings, assaults and prostitution, and only recently has the city taken even the most token steps to control it (and the police corruption that allows it to continue). In an isolated incident in December, 2005, a German tourist was murdered when she stumbled upon a thief who'd broken into her hotel. While this is out of the ordinary, it illustrates the extent to which rampant crime has gone completely unchecked in the Mariscal. Despite the inconveniences, consider staying in another neighborhood – besides safety issues, you'll have a more authentic experience to boot. Sundays, when no one is around, can also be dodgy in the Mariscal.

All that said, most folks who get mugged could have avoided it simply by taking a taxi. A campaign by local businesses in late 2005 as well as continued public pressure may improve the situation. Foch, between Avenida Amazonas and Diego de Almagro is notoriously bad. Ask your hotel about the current situation.

The old town, once more dangerous than the Mariscal, has been cleaned up and is now entirely safe as late as 10pm during the week and until around midnight on weekends. It's well lit and the city has taken a keen interest in keeping it safe. After dark, do not stray south of Plaza Santo Domingo, east of Plaza San Francisco or north of the Church of La Merced.

The trolley system is plagued with pickpockets; *El Comerico* newspaper reported in 2005 that the Mariscal Trole stop was where you can most likely expect to get pick-pocketed. Either avoid the Trole during rush hour or watch your back.

The steps of García Moreno heading from Ambato to the top of El Panecillo are potentially dangerous. Take a taxi to the top, and flag another to return.

If you get robbed, file a police report, particularly if you wish to make an insurance claim. Do so at the **police station** (Map p74; Mideros & Cuenca), in the old town, between 9am and noon. In the new town, go to the **police station** (Map p84; cnr Reina Victoria & Vicente Ramón Roca).

SIGHTS

If you're short on time head straight to the old town. It's here that Quito distinguishes itself from all other cities in the world. Be certain to see the Plaza and Monastery of San Francisco, the Plaza de la Independencia (Plaza Grande), La Compañía de Jesús and the Museo de Arte Colonial.

Outside the old town, Quito's best museums are the Museo del Banco Central, the Museo Guayasamín and the nearby Capilla del Hombre. Toss the telefériQo and Parque La Carolina into the mix and you'll be busy for days.

Old Town   Map p74

With its narrow streets, restored colonial architecture and lively plazas, Quito's Centro Histórico (aka the old town) is a marvel to wander. Built centuries ago by indigenous

artisans and laborers, Quito's churches, convents, chapels and monasteries are cast in legend and steeped in history. It's a bustling area, full of yelling street vendors, ambling pedestrians, tooting taxis, belching buses and whistle-blowing policemen trying to direct traffic in the narrow, congested one-way streets. The area is magical, and one in which the more you look, the more you find.

Churches are open every day (usually until 6pm) but are crowded with worshippers on Sunday. They regularly close between 1pm and 3pm for lunch.

PLAZA GRANDE

While wandering around colonial Quito, you'll probably pass through the Plaza Grande (formally known as Plaza de la Independencia) several times. The austere white building on the northwest side of the plaza (between Chile and Espejo) with the national flag flying atop is the **Palacio del Gobierno** (Presidential Palace; García Moreno). The president does indeed carry out business in this building, so sightseeing is limited to the entrance. Inside, a mural depicts Francisco de Orellana's descent of the Amazon. The guard at the gate may allow you in to take a look.

On the southwest side of the plaza stands Quito's recently painted **cathedral** (admission $1, Sun services free; ⏰ 10am-4pm Mon-Sat, Sun services hourly 6am-noon & 5-7pm). Although not as rich in decoration as some of the other churches,

---

VIEWS OVER QUITO

Surrounded by mountains, Quito is a city with mind-boggling views. Hitting as many high spots as you can in a day makes for an adventure, and it's a unique way to see the city. Skies are clearest in the morning. Here are some of the best:

- Holiest view – El Panecillo (p77): climb up inside the Virgen de Quito
- Deadliest view – Basílica del Voto Nacional (p75): hold onto your stomach for the hair-raising climb into these gothic towers
- Tastiest view – Café Mosaico (p101): the most amazing balcony in town
- Most patriotic view – Cima de La Libertad (p79): site of Ecuadorian independence, and fantastic views
- Most sweeping view – Parque Itchimbia (p79): kick off your shoes and take in the 360-degree views from the grass
- Most breathtaking view – Cruz Loma and the telefériQo (p79): at 4100m, breathing's made wheezy
- Strangest view – Monastery of Santa Catalina's bell tower (p76): who said church tours can't be fun?

QUITO

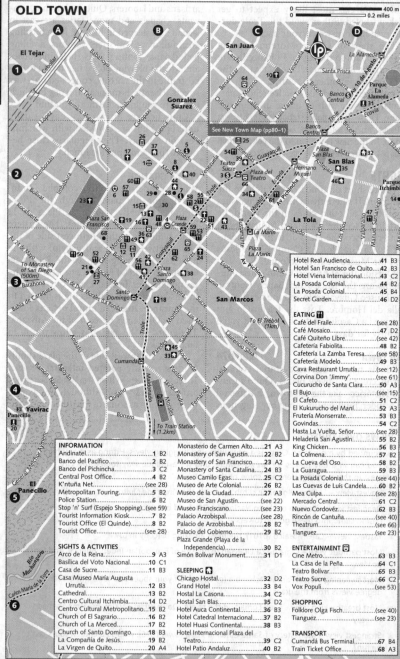

OLD TOWN

INFORMATION
Andinatel..**1** B2
Banco del Pacífico..........................**2** B2
Banco del Pichincha.......................**3** C2
Central Post Office.........................**4** B2
K'ntuña Net..............................(see 28)
Metropolitan Touring......................**5** B2
Police Station..................................**6** B2
Stop 'n' Surf (Espejo Shopping)...(see 59)
Tourist Information Kiosk...............**7** B2
Tourist Office (El Quinde)...............**8** B2
Tourist Office.............................(see 28)

SIGHTS & ACTIVITIES
Arco de la Reina..............................**9** A3
Basílica del Voto Nacional............**10** C1
Casa de Sucre................................**11** B3
Casa Museo María Augusta
    Urrutía......................................**12** B3
Cathedral......................................**13** B2
Centro Cultural Itchimbia..............**14** D2
Centro Cultural Metropolitano.....**15** B2
Church of El Sagrario......................**16** B2
Church of La Merced.....................**17** B2
Church of Santo Domingo..............**18** B3
La Compañía de Jesús...................**19** B3
La Virgen de Quito........................**20** A4
Monasterio de Carmen Alto..........**21** A3
Monastery of San Agustín.............**22** B2
Monastery of San Francisco..........**23** A2
Monastery of Santa Catalina.........**24** B3
Museo Camilo Egas........................**25** B2
Museo de Arte Colonial.................**26** B2
Museo de la Ciudad.......................**27** A3
Museo de San Agustín...............(see 22)
Museo Franciscano....................(see 23)
Palacio Arzobispal....................(see 28)
Palacio de Arzobisbal...................**28** B2
Palacio del Gobierno.....................**29** B2
Plaza Grande (Playa de la
    Independencia).........................**30** B2
Simón Bolívar Monument..............**31** D1

SLEEPING
Chicago Hostal..............................**32** D2
Grand Hotel..................................**33** B4
Hostal La Casona..........................**34** B2
Hostal San Blas.............................**35** B2
Hotel Auca Continental.................**36** B3
Hotel Catedral Internacional........**37** B2
Hotel Huasi Continental................**38** B2
Hotel Internacional Plaza del
    Teatro.......................................**39** C2
Hotel Patio Andaluz......................**40** B2
Hotel Real Audiencia.....................**41** B3
Hotel San Francisco de Quito........**42** B3
Hotel Viena Internacional..............**43** C2
La Posada Colonial........................**44** B2
La Posada Colonial........................**45** B4
Secret Garden...............................**46** D2

EATING
Café del Fraile..........................(see 28)
Café Mosaico.................................**47** D2
Café Quiteño Libre...................(see 42)
Cafetería Fabiolita........................**48** B3
Cafetería La Zamba Teresa.......(see 58)
Cafetería Modelo..........................**49** B3
Cava Restaurant Urrutía...........(see 12)
Corvina Don 'Jimmy'................(see 61)
Cucurucho de Santa Clara.............**50** A3
El Bujo....................................(see 15)
El Cafeto.......................................**51** C2
El Kukurucho del Maní...................**52** A3
Frutería Monserrate......................**53** B3
Govindas.......................................**54** C2
Hasta La Vuelta, Señor.............(see 28)
Heladería San Agustín...................**55** B2
King Chicken.................................**56** B3
La Colmena...................................**57** B2
La Cueva del Oso..........................**58** B2
La Guaragua..................................**59** B3
La Posada Colonial....................(see 44)
Las Cuevas de Luís Candela...........**60** B2
Mea Culpa...............................(see 28)
Mercado Central...........................**61** C2
Nuevo Cordovéz............................**62** B3
Rincón de Cantuña....................(see 40)
Theatrum..................................(see 66)
Tianguez..................................(see 23)

ENTERTAINMENT
Cine Metro....................................**63** B3
La Casa de la Peña........................**64** C1
Teatro Bolívar...............................**65** B2
Teatro Sucre.................................**66** C2
Vox Populi...............................(see 53)

SHOPPING
Folklore Olga Fisch...................(see 40)
Tianguez..................................(see 23)

TRANSPORT
Cumandá Bus Terminal..................**67** B4
Train Ticket Office........................**68** A3

San Juan
San Blas
La Tola
San Marcos
El Panecillo
El Yavirac
El Tejar
Gonzalez
Suarez

See New Town Map (pp80-1)

To Monastery
of San Diego
(500m)

To El Trébol
(1km)

To Train Station
(1.2km)

0   400 m
0   0.2 miles

it's worth popping into for a peak at the religious paintings by several notable artists of the Quito School (also see p38). You'll also see the ornate tomb of Mariscal Sucre, the leading figure of Quito's independence. To the left of the main altar is a statue of Juan José Flores, Ecuador's first president. Situated behind the main altar, on the smaller altar of Nuestra Señora de los Dolores, is a plaque showing where President Gabriel García Moreno died on August 6, 1875. He was hacked up with a machete outside the Palacio del Gobierno (just across the plaza) and was carried, dying, to the cathedral.

On the northeast side of the plaza, the **Palacio Arzobispal** (Archbishop's Palace; Chile) is now a colonnaded row of small shops and restaurants. It's located between García Moreno and Venezuela.

Just off the plaza, the outstanding **Centro Cultural Metropolitano** (☎ 295 0272, 258 4363; www .centrocultural-quito.com; cnr García Moreno & Espejo; admission $2; ☺ 9am-5pm Tue-Sun, patio until 7:30pm) was the first restoration work undertaken in the old town. Opened in 2000, it fast became an island of cultural activity and the impetus behind the old town's renovation. It houses several temporary art exhibits and hosts excellent art shows on the main interior patio. Along with two more interior patios and two beautiful rooftop terraces (all worth seeing), it houses an auditorium, a library and a pleasant café.

The building itself, which you can wander freely, is rich in history. It was supposedly the pre-Hispanic site of one of the Inca Atahualpa's palaces. A Jesuit school from 1597 to 1767, it then became a *cuartel* (army barracks). In 1809 royalist forces imprisoned a group of revolutionaries here and gruesomely murdered them a year later. The grisly act is memorialized in a wax exhibit in the on-site **Museo Alberto Mena Caamaño** (admission additional $1).

NORTH OF PLAZA GRANDE

Two blocks northwest of the Plaza Grande you'll find, **La Merced** (cnr Cuenca & Chile; admission free; ☺ 7am-noon & 2-5pm). Construction of this church began in 1700 and was finished in 1742. At 47m, its tower is the highest in colonial Quito, and it contains the largest bell of Quito's churches. Legend has it that the tower, the only unblessed part of the church, is possessed by the devil.

Supposedly the only person strong enough to resist the devil was a black bell-ringer named Ceferino, and no one has dared enter the tower since he died in 1810. Hence the clock stands still and the bell hangs un-rung.

Myth aside, La Merced has a wealth of fascinating art, including paintings that show volcanoes erupting over the church roofs of colonial Quito and the capital covered with ashes.

One block to the northeast is the excellent **Museo de Arte Colonial** (☎ 221 2297; Mejía 0e6-132; admission $2; ☺ 10am-6pm Tue-Fri, 10am-2pm Sat). In a restored 17th-century building, the museum houses what many consider to be Ecuador's best collection of colonial art. It's surely the best place to see the famous sculptures and paintings of the Quito School, including the works of Miguel de Santiago, Manuel Chili (the indigenous artist known as Caspicara) and Bernardo de Legarda. The museum was closed for restoration in 2005 and 2006.

Several blocks east, inside a beautifully restored colonial home, the **Museo Camilo Egas** (☎ 257 2012; mce@uio.bce.fin.ec; Venezuela 1302 at Esmeraldas; admission $0.50; ☺ 9am-5pm Tue-Fri, 10am-4pm Sat & Sun) houses a small but excellent exhibit of painter Camilo Egas' work. Egas was Ecuador's first *indigenista* (indigenous movement) painter, and his paintings of indigenous people – idealistic as they are – are stunning.

High on a hill in the northeastern part of the old town stands the Gothic **Basílica del Voto Nacional** (☎ 258 3891; cnr Venezuela & Carchi; admission $2; ☺ 9am-5pm), built over several decades beginning in 1926. Rather than gargoyles, however, turtles and iguanas protrude from the church's side. The highlight is the basilica's **towers**, which you can climb to the top of if you have the nerve; the ascent requires crossing a rickety wooden plank inside the main roof and climbing steep stairs and ladders to the top. You can also climb the spiral staircase and three sets of ladders into and above the clock tower. Liability? Pshaw!

EAST OF PLAZA GRANDE

Two blocks from the Plaza Grande, the **Monastery of San Agustín** (Chile & Guayaquil; admission free) is another fine example of 17th-century architecture. Many of the heroes of the battles for Ecuador's independence are buried here, and it is the site of the signing of Ecuador's declaration of independence on August 10, 1809. In the church's convent, the **Museo de San Agustín** (☎ 251 5525, 258 0263; Chile & Guayaquil; ☼ 9am-1pm & 3-6pm) houses many canvases of the Quito School, including a series depicting the life of Saint Augustine, painted by Miguel de Santiago.

Due south of San Agustín stands the **Monastery of Santa Catalina** (Espejo 779 at Flores; admission $1.50; ☼ 8:30am-5:30pm Mon-Sat), which is a fully functioning convent and monastery that opened to the public in 2005. Since its founding in 1592, entering nuns have spent five cloistered years in solitary cells. To this day the 20 nuns inside have only one hour to talk to each other or watch TV. But they make all sorts of natural products (shampoos, nonalcoholic wine, hand cream, elixirs and more), which you can purchase from a rotating door that keeps the nuns hidden.

A tour of the monastery and its interesting museum lasts over an hour – and it's a gruesome hour at that: 18th-century religious paintings depict virgins and saints presiding over the fires of purgatory while devils grind the bodies of sinners on spiked wheels. One painting shows a thirsty flock of sheep slurping up rivers of blood pouring from Jesus' wounds, while another depicts cherubs plucking the flesh from Christ's ribs after a session of brutal self-flagellation.

Supposedly, secret underground tunnels connect Santa Catalina to the church of Santo Domingo three blocks away.

Further northeast, at the junction of Calles Guayaquil and Manabí, is the tiny **Plaza del Teatro**, where you'll find – along with microphone-toting preachers, protesters and hollering newspaper peddlers – the exquisitely restored **Teatro Sucre** (see p103). Built in 1878, it is Quito's most sophisticated theater.

CALLES GARCÍA MORENO & SUCRE

Beside the cathedral on García Moreno stands the 17th-century **Church of El Sagrario** (García Moreno; admission free; ☼ 6am-noon & 3-6pm), originally intended as the main chapel of the cathedral, but now a separate church. Around the corner on Calle Sucre is Ecuador's most ornate church, **La Compañía de Jesús** (admission $2.50; ☼ 9:30-11am & 4-6pm), which

is capped by green-and-gold domes visible from Plaza San Francisco one block away. Seven tons of gold were supposedly used to gild the walls, ceilings and altars of La Compañía, and quiteños proudly call it the most beautiful church in the country. The construction of this Jesuit church began in 1605, the year that the Monastery of San Francisco was completed, and it took 163 years to build.

A block-and-a-half southeast of La Compañía is the beautifully restored **Casa de Sucre** (☎ 295 2860; Venezuela 573 at Sucre; admission $1; ☼ 8:30am-4:30pm Tue-Fri, 10am-4pm Sat & Sun). This is the former home of Mariscal Antonio José de Sucre, the hero of Ecuadorian independence. It is now a small museum, full of early 19th-century furniture.

Back on Calle García Moreno, just southwest of Calle Sucre, you'll find the **Casa Museo María Augusta Urrutía** (☎ 258 0107; García Moreno 760 near Sucre; admission $2.50; ☼ 9am-5pm Tue-Sun). This restored house was once the home of the distinguished philanthropist María Augusta Urrutía. With plenty of period furnishings, it is a good example of a late-19th-century aristocrat's house.

Further south, the 18th-century **Arco de la Reina** (García Moreno at Rocafuerte), a massive arch built in the 18th century to give shelter to churchgoers, spans García Moreno. On one side, the **Museo de la Ciudad** (☎ 228 3882; cnr García Moreno & Rocafuerte; admission $3; ☼ 9:30am-5:30pm Tue-Sun) occupies the beautifully restored San Juan de Dios hospital. Built in 1563, it functioned as a hospital until 1973. The museum depicts daily life in Quito through the centuries with displays including dioramas, model indigenous homes and colonial kitchens. There are also temporary exhibits of Ecuadorian and foreign artists. Guides are available for an additional $2 in Spanish or $4 in English, French or German.

On the other side of the arch stands the **Monasterio de Carmen Alto** (cnr García Moreno & Rocafuerte). Inside this fully functioning convent, cloistered nuns stay busy producing some of the finest, most traditional sweets in the city. One of the tastiest treats of all are the *limones desamargados* (literally 'desoured lemons'), which are made by hollowing out tiny lemons and filling them with a sweetened milk concoction. They sell out quickly, so get there early on a

Tuesday or Thursday morning. Through a revolving contraption that keeps the nuns hidden from view, they also sell traditional baked goods, aromatic waters for nerves and insomnia, bee pollen, honey and bottles of full-strength *mistela* (an anise flavored liqueur).

PLAZA & MONASTERY OF SAN FRANCISCO

Walking from the old town's narrow colonial streets into the open **Plaza San Francisco** reveals one of the finest sights in all of Ecuador – a sweeping cobblestone plaza backed by the long whitewashed walls and twin bell towers of Ecuador's oldest church, the **Monastery of San Francisco** (Cuenca at Sucre; admission free; ☼ 7-11am daily, 3-6pm Mon-Thu). With its giant plaza and its mountainous backdrop of Volcán Pichincha this is surely one of Quito's highlights.

Construction of the monastery began only a few weeks after the founding of Quito in 1534, but the building was not finished until 70 years later. It is the city's largest colonial structure. The founder was the Franciscan missionary Joedco Ricke, who is credited with being the first man to sow wheat in Ecuador. He is commemorated by a **statue** at the far right of the raised terrace in front of the church.

Although much of the church has been rebuilt because of earthquake damage, some of it is original. The **chapel of Señor Jesús del Gran Poder**, to the right of the main altar, has original tilework. The **main altar** itself is a spectacular example of baroque carving, while much of the roof shows Moorish influences.

To the right of the main entrance is the **Museo Franciscano** (☎ 295 2911; www.museofrancis cano.com in Spanish; admission $2; ☼ 9am-1pm & 2-6pm Mon-Sat, 9am-noon Sun), which contains some of the church's finest artwork, including paintings, sculpture and furniture dating to the 16th century. Some of the furniture is fantastically wrought and inlaid with thousands of pieces of mother-of-pearl. The admission fee includes a guided tour, available in English or Spanish. Good guides will point out *mudejar* (Moorish) representations of the eight planets revolving around the sun in the ceiling, and will explain how the light shines through the rear window during the solstices, lighting up the main altar. They'll also demonstrate an odd confessional technique, where two people standing in separate corners can hear each other while whispering into the walls.

To the left of the monastery stands the **Capilla de Cantuña** (Cantuña Chapel), which houses an excellent art collection from the Quito School. It's also shrouded in one of Quito's most famous legends, that of the indigenous builder Cantuña, who supposedly sold his soul to the devil so the devil would help him complete the church on time. But just before midnight of the day of his deadline, Cantuña removed a single stone from the structure, meaning the church was never completed. Thusly he tricked the devil and saved his soul.

PLAZA & CHURCH OF SANTO DOMINGO

Near the southwest end of Calle Guayaquil, Plaza Santo Domingo is a regular haunt for street performers, and crowds of neighborhood quiteños fill the plaza to watch pouting clowns and half-cocked magicians do their stuff. The plaza is especially attractive in the evening when the domes of the 17th-century **Church of Santo Domingo** (Flores & Rocafuerte; admission free; ☼ 7am-1pm & 4:30-7:30pm), on the southeast side of the plaza, are floodlit. In front of the church stands a **statue of Mariscal Sucre**, depicting the marshal pointing toward La Cima de la Libertad (p79), where he won the decisive battle for independence on May 24, 1822.

A fabulous Gothiclike altar dominates the inside of the church. The original wooden floor was only recently replaced. An exquisite **statue of the Virgen del Rosario**, a gift from King Charles V of Spain, is one of the church's main showpieces; it resides in an ornately carved baroque-style side chapel. Construction of the church began in 1581 and continued until 1650.

EL PANECILLO

The small, ever-present hill to the south of the old town is called **El Panecillo** (the Little Bread Loaf) and is a major Quito landmark. It is topped by a huge statue of **La Virgen de Quito** (Virgin of Quito), with a crown of stars, eagle's wings and a chained dragon atop the world.

From the summit, there are marvelous **views** of the whole city stretching out below, as well as of the surrounding volcanoes. The best time for volcano views (particularly in the rainy season) is early morning,

METROPOLITAN QUITO

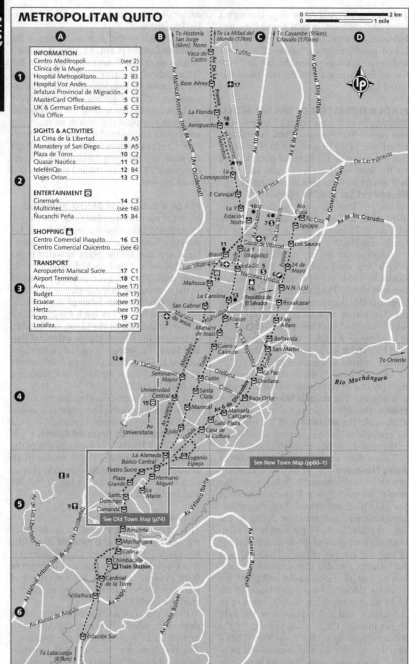

0 —————— 2 km
0 —————— 1 mile

INFORMATION
Centro Meditropoli.....................(see 2)
Clínica de la Mujer...........................1 C3
Hospital Metropolitano......................2 B3
Hospital Voz Andes...........................3 C3
Jefatura Provincial de Migración...........4 C2
MasterCard Office.............................5 C3
UK & German Embassies.....................6 C3
Visa Office...7 C2

SIGHTS & ACTIVITIES
La Cima de la Libertad.......................8 A5
Monastery of San Diego......................9 A5
Plaza de Toros.................................10 C2
Quasar Nautica................................11 C3
telefériQo......................................12 B4
Viajes Orion....................................13 C3

ENTERTAINMENT ☺
Cinemark..14 C3
Multicines....................................(see 16)
Ñucanchi Peña.................................15 B4

SHOPPING 🛍
Centro Comercial Iñaquito................16 C3
Centro Comercial Quicentro............(see 6)

TRANSPORT
Aeropuerto Mariscal Sucre...............17 C1
Airport Terminal..............................18 C1
Avis...(see 17)
Budget...(see 17)
Ecuacar.......................................(see 17)
Hertz...(see 17)
Icaro...19 C2
Localiza.......................................(see 17)

To Hostería San Jorge (6km); Nono
To La Mitad del Mundo (17km)
To Cayambe (55km); Otavalo (170km)

Tufiño
Vaca de Castro
Base Aérea
La Florida
Aeropuerto
La Concepción
E Carvajal
La Y Estación Norte
Gaspar de Villarroel
La Y (Iñaquito)
Brasil
Juan Villalengua
Estadio
Mañosca
La Carolina
República de El Salvador
San Gabriel
Mariana de Jesús
Mariana de Jesús
Cuero y Caicedo
Floron
Eloy Alfaro
Bellavista
San Martin
Orellana
Colón
Colón
La Paz
Orellana
Seminario Mayor
Santa Clara
Universidad Central
Mariscal
Baca Ortiz
Manuela Cañizares
Galo Plaza
Ejido
Casa de la Cultura
La Alameda
Banco Central
Eugenio Espejo
Teatro Sucre
Plaza Grande
Hermano Miguel
Santo Domingo
La Marin
Cumandá
Recoleta
Machangara
Colina
Chimbacalle
Train Station
Cardinal de la Torre
Villaflora
Estación Sur

Vaca de Castro
Av De La Prensa
Av Mariscal Antonio José de Sucre (Av Occidental)
Av Amazonas Metrobus
Av 10 de Agosto
Av 6 de Diciembre
Av General Eloy Alfaro
De Las Palmeras
Av El Inca
Río Coca
Río Coca
Jipijapa
Av de los Granados
Los Sauces
24 de Mayo
Ecovia
N.N.U.U.
Benalcazar
Av General Eloy Alfaro
Av de los Shyris
Naciones Unidas
Trole
Mañalpa
Av de la República
De la Prensa
Metrobus
Av America
Ecovia
Av 6 de Diciembre
Manuela Cañizares
Av La Gasca
Av Universitaria
Av de Los Libertadores
Av Mariscal Antonio José de sucre (Av Occidental)
Av Velasco Ibarra
Av Simón Bolívar
Av General Rumiñahui
Av Napo
Av Alonso de Angulo

Río Machángara
To Oriente

See New Town Map (pp80–1)
See Old Town Map (p74)

To Latacunga (87km)

17
18
19
10
4
7 9
1
11
5
3
14
13
2
15
12
8
9

before the clouds roll in. Definitely don't climb the stairs at the end of Calle García Moreno on the way to the statue – they're unsafe due to muggings. A taxi from the old town costs about $4, and you can hail one at the top for the trip back to town.

Around the Old Town
MONASTERY OF SAN DIEGO
Northwest of El Panecillo, the beautiful 17th-century **Monastery of San Diego** (Map p78; ☎ 295 4026, 295 2516; Calicuchima 117 & Farfán; admission $2; ☺ 9:30am-12:30pm & 2:30-5:30pm) sits in a quiet courtyard behind thick walls above the old town. The only way inside is by tour. Although the tour is recited with the enthusiasm of a mass in Latin, it's worth suffering through to see the wealth of colonial art inside. There are outstanding works from both from the Quito and Cusco schools, including one of Quito's finest pulpits, carved by the notable indigenous woodcarver Juan Bautista Menacho.

There's also a fascinating 18th-century painting by Miguel de Santiago of the Last Supper. The oddest piece of work here is an unidentified painting by **Heronimous Bosch**, titled *Passage from this Life to Eternity*. No one can explain how it got here. At the end of the tour you can climb narrow stairs to the bell tower and walk along the rooftop.

LA CIMA DE LA LIBERTAD
Further up the flanks of Volcán Pichincha, one of the finest views of the city can be had from **La Cima de la Libertad** (Map p78; ☎ 228 8733; Av de los Libertadores s/n; admission $1; ☺ 8:30am-4:30pm Tue-Fri, 9am-1:30pm Sat & Sun). This monument was built at the site of the Batalla de Pichincha (Battle of Pichincha), led by Mariscal Antonio José de Sucre on May 24, 1822. It was the decisive battle in the struggle for independence from Spain.

Less impressive than the battle *or* the view is the military museum housing a collection of military artifacts and a shrine to an unknown soldier. Glass-encased uniforms may not fire you up, but the tiled mural by Eduardo Kingman, which hangs above the building certainly might.

The best way here is by taxi.

PARQUE ITCHIMBIA
High on a hill east of the old town, this newly resurrected green space boasts magnificent views of the city. It's the perfect spot to spread out a picnic lunch, soak up the sun and take in the unobstructed 360-degree views. The park's centerpiece is the **Centro Cultural Itchimbia** (Map p74; ☎ 295 0272), a large glass and iron building modeled after the city's original Mercado Santa Clara. It hosts regular art exhibits and cultural events. The park has cycling paths and walking paths too.

Buses signed 'Pintado' go here from the Centro Histórico, or you can walk up (east) Elizalde, from where signed stairways lead to the park.

TelefériQo
Quito's newest tourist attraction – and a mind-boggling one at that – is the **telefériQo** (Map p78; ☎ 800 835 333 7476, 250 0900; www.teleferiqo .com in Spanish; Av Occidental near Av La Gasca; adult/child under 6/express lane $4/3/7; ☺ 11am-10pm Mon, 9am-10pm Tue-Thu, 9am-midnight Fri & Sat), a multimillion dollar sky tram that takes passengers on a 2.5km ride up the flanks of Volcán Pichincha to the top of Cruz Loma. Once you're at the top (a mere 4100m), you can hike to the summit of Rucu Pichincha (4680m), an approximately three-hour hike for fit walkers (p87 and p111). Don't attempt the hike to Rucu Pichincha until you've acclimatized in Quito for a couple days.

The telefériQo complex is an eyesore of overpriced restaurants, video arcades, a go-kart track, souvenir shops, a dance club and even a theme park (admission $2 to $10). While merry-go-rounds are undeniably fun at high altitudes, the real reason to come up here is for the views and the walking.

To get here, either take a taxi (about $2 from the Mariscal) or take one of the telefériQo shuttles ($1) which depart about every 30 minutes from the Trole's Estación Norte stop, the Río Coca stop of the Ecovía line and Plaza La Marín parking area in the old town.

On weekends the wait can last up to four hours; either pay the $7 express-line fee or (even better) come on a weekday. Also try to visit in the morning, when the views here are best.

New Town   Map pp80–1
PARQUES LA ALAMEDA & EL EJIDO
From the northeast edge of the old town the long, triangular **Parque La Alameda** begins its grassy crawl toward the new town. At

QUITO

NEW TOWN

INFORMATION

Abya Yala Bookstore	1 D5
Alianza Francesa	2 F1
Andinatel	3 D2
Asociación Humboldt	4 D2
Banco del Pacífico	(see 8)
Canadian Embassy	5 F3
Centro Cultural Afro-Ecuatoriano	6 E4
Centro Cultural Mexicano	7 F4
DHL	(see 17)
Dutch Embassy	8 E4
French Embassy	9 E3
Instituto Geográfico Militar	10 D6
Migraciones	11 E1
Parcel Post Office	12 B3
PostOffice (courier)	13 D3
South American Explorers	14 C5
Tourist Office	(see 28)
US Embassy	15 D5
Western Union	16 E2
Western Union	17 D3

SIGHTS & ACTIVITIES

Alta Montaña	18 C5
Bike Stop	19 F1
Capilla del Hombre	20 H2
Casa de la Cultura Ecuatoriana	(see 28)
Church of El Belén	21 B6
Compañía de Guías de Montaña	22 C5
Fundación Golondrinas	(see 54)
Jardín Botánico	23 E1
Legislative Palace	24 C6
Montaña	25 E5
Museo Amazónico	(see 1)
Museo de Ciencias Naturales	26 E1
Museo de Jacinto Jijón y Caamaño	27 D5
Museo del Banco Central	28 C5
Museo Etnográfico de Artesanía de Ecuador	29 E3
Museo Etnográfico de Artesanía de Ecuador	(see 1)
Museo Guayasamín	30 G2
Nuevo Mundo Expeditions	31 C5
Quasar Nautica	32 G1
Quito Observatory	33 C5
Reserva Bellavista Office	34 C5
Rocódromo	35 D6
Sanctuary of El Guápulo	36 G3
Statue of Francisco de Orellana	37 F4
Tropic Ecological Adventures	38 E3
Universidad Católica	(see 27)
Vivarium	39 E1

To Aeropuerto Mariscal Sucre (6km)

To Toa Bed & Breakfast (1km)

See Mariscal Sucre Map (p84)

See Old Town Map (p74)

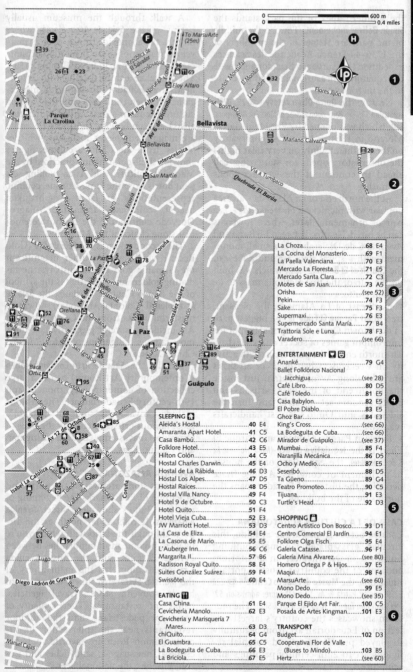

La Choza..**68** E4
La Cocina del Monasterio...........**69** F1
La Paella Valenciana...................**70** E3
Mercado La Floresta....................**71** E5
Mercado Santa Clara...................**72** C3
Motes de San Juan......................**73** A5
Orisha..(see 52)
Pekin..**74** F3
Sake...**75** F3
Supermaxi...................................**76** E3
Supermercado Santa María........**77** B4
Trattoria Sole e Luna.................**78** F3
Varadero.....................................(see 66)

ENTERTAINMENT
Ananké.......................................**79** G4
Ballet Folklórico Nacional
  Jacchigua...............................(see 28)
Café Libro...................................**80** D5
Café Toledo................................**81** E5
Casa Babylon..............................**82** E5
El Pobre Diablo...........................**83** E5
Ghoz Bar....................................**84** E3
King's Cross................................(see 66)
La Bodeguita de Cuba................(see 66)
Mirador de Guápulo...................(see 37)
Mumbai......................................**85** F4
Naranjilla Mecánica....................**86** D5
Ocho y Medio.............................**87** E5
Seseribó......................................**88** D5
Ta Güeno....................................**89** G4
Teatro Promoteo.........................**90** C5
Tijuana.......................................**91** E3
Turtle's Head..............................**92** D3

SHOPPING
Centro Artístico Don Bosco........**93** D1
Centro Comercial El Jardín.........**94** E1
Folklore Olga Fisch.....................**95** E4
Galería Catasse............................**96** F1
Galería Mina Alvarez.................(see 80)
Homero Ortega P & Hijos...........**97** E5
Maqui...**98** F4
MarsuArte...................................(see 60)
Mono Dedo.................................**99** E5
Mono Dedo...............................(see 35)
Parque El Ejido Art Fair............**100** C5
Posada de Artes Kingman.........**101** E3

TRANSPORT
Budget......................................**102** D3
Cooperativa Flor de Valle
  (Buses to Mindo)...................**103** B5
Hertz...(see 60)

SLEEPING
Aleida's Hostal...........................**40** E4
Amaranta Apart Hotel................**41** C5
Casa Bambú................................**42** C6
Folklore Hotel.............................**43** E5
Hilton Colón...............................**44** C5
Hostal Charles Darwin................**45** E4
Hostal de La Rábida....................**46** D3
Hostal Los Alpes.........................**47** D5
Hostal Raices...............................**48** D5
Hostal Villa Nancy......................**49** F4
Hotel 9 de Octubre.....................**50** C3
Hotel Quito................................**51** F4
Hotel Vieja Cuba........................**52** E3
JW Marriott Hotel......................**53** D3
La Casa de Eliza..........................**54** E4
La Casona de Mario....................**55** C5
L'Auberge Inn............................**56** C6
Margarita II................................**57** B6
Radisson Royal Quito.................**58** F4
Suites González Suárez...............**59** F4
Swissôtel....................................**60** E4

EATING
Casa China..................................**61** E4
Cevichería Manolo......................**62** E3
Cevichería y Marisquería 7
  Mares......................................**63** D3
chiQuito.....................................**64** G4
El Guambra.................................**65** C5
La Bodeguita de Cuba................**66** E3
La Briciola..................................**67** E5

the southern apex of the park stands the **Simón Bolívar monument**. Toward the middle of the park are **statues** of the members of the 1736–44 French Académie des Sciences expedition that surveyed Ecuador and made the equatorial measurements that gave rise to the metric system.

Nearby, the **Quito Observatory** (☎ 257 0765; admission $1; ☯ 8am-noon & 3-5pm Mon-Fri, 8am-noon Sat), which was opened by President García Moreno in 1864, is the oldest observatory on the continent. Only on very clear nights the observatory opens for stargazing; call ahead to confirm if the weather looks promising.

At the north end of La Alameda – an area popular with picnickers on weekends – is a pair of ornamental **lakes**, where rowboats can be hired. Nearby, between LF Borja and Avenida 6 de Diciembre, is a small monument with a spiral staircase and a view of the **Church of El Belén** (L Sodir), which was built on the site of the first Catholic mass to be held in Quito.

Northeast of La Alameda, the pleasant, tree-filled **Parque El Ejido** is the biggest park in downtown Quito. It's a popular spot for impromptu games of soccer and volleyball. The north end of the park teems with activity on weekends, when open-air **art shows** are held along Avenida Patria. Just inside the north end of the park, artisans and crafts vendors set up stalls and turn the sidewalks into Quito's largest handicrafts market.

Between Parque Alameda and Parque El Ejido is the **legislative palace** (Montalvo near Av 6 de Diciembre), the equivalent of the houses of parliament or congress. A huge frieze depicting the history of Ecuador spans the north side of the building.

CASA DE LA CULTURA ECUATORIANA

Located across from Parque El Ejido, this circular, glass-plated landmark-building houses a movie theater, an auditorium and one of the country's most important museums, the **Museo del Banco Central** (☎ 222 3259; cnr Av Patria & Av 12 de Octubre; admission $2; ☯ 9am-5pm Tue-Fri, 10am-4pm Sat & Sun). The museum showcases the country's largest collection of Ecuadorian art, from beautifully displayed pre-Hispanic and colonial religious art to 20th-century paintings and sculpture.

A walk through the museum usually begins in the **Sala de Arqueología**, where moody tribal-music drones over a marvelous display of more than 1000 ceramic pieces dating from 12,000 BC to AD 1534. The mazelike exhibit begins with arrowheads from Ecuador's first nomadic hunter-gatherers, then continues with the Valdivia culture (Ecuador's first settled agriculturalists) and ends with the Inca. En route are magnificent pieces including 'whistle-bottles' from the Chorrea culture, figures showing skull-deformation practiced by the Machalilla culture, wild Asian-looking serpent bowls from the Jama-Coaque, ceramic representations of *tzantzas* (shrunken heads), 'coin axes' from the Milagro-Quevedo culture and the famous ceremonial stone chairs of the Manteños.

The second room is the **Sala de Oro** (Gold Room) which, among other magnificent pre-Hispanic gold pieces, displays the radiating golden sun-mask that is the symbol of the Banco Central. Upstairs, the **Sala de Arte Colonial** (Colonial Art Room) showcases masterful works from the Quito School of Art including several pieces by Ecuador's most famous indigenous sculptor, Manuel Chili (Caspicara).

Finally, the **Sala de Arte Contemporáneo** (Contemporary Art Room) boasts a large collection of contemporary, modern and 19th-century Ecuadorian art. The exhibits include canvases by some of Ecuador's most famous artists, including the likes of Oswaldo Guayasamín, Eduardo Kingman and Camilo Egas.

AVENIDA AMAZONAS

A solitary stone archway at the north end of Parque El Ejido marks the beginning of modern Quito's showpiece street, **Avenida Amazonas**. It rolls as far north as the airport, although the strip with which you're likely to become most familiar lies between Parque El Ejido and the busy Avenida Cristóbal Colón. It's the main artery of the **Mariscal Sucre** area, lined with modern hotels, souvenir stores, travel agencies, banks and restaurants. There's plenty of room for pedestrians, and the outdoor restaurants near the intersection of Vicente Ramón Roca are favorite spots for espresso, newspapers, sandwiches and ice-cold Pilsener, the national beer.

MARISCAL SUCRE & AROUND

The Mariscal Sucre area, known simply as the 'Mariscal,' is the neighborhood loosely bound by Avenidas 10 de Agosto, Cristóbal Colón, 12 de Octubre and Patria. All the travel-related services you could possibly need can be found in this area.

On Avenida 12 de Octubre, just south of the Mariscal, are two worthwhile museums.

Above Abya Yala bookstore (p70) the **Museo Amazónico** (☎ 256 2663; Av 12 de Octubre 1436; admission $2; ☽ 8:30am-12:30pm & 2-5pm Mon-Fri) is run by the Salesian Mission and houses an impressive display of indigenous artifacts collected by the missionaries in the Oriente. It's not huge, but it's an interesting exhibit, especially if you plan to head to the jungle.

The **Museo de Jacinto Jijón y Caamaño** (☎ 257 5727/1317, 252 1834; Av 12 de Octubre & Vicente Ramón Roca; admission $0.60; ☽ 8:30am-4pm Mon-Fri) houses an interesting private archaeology collection and an exhibit of colonial art featuring some of the masters of the Quito School. This museum is on the 3rd floor of the library in the **Universidad Católica**, across the traffic circle from the Casa de la Cultura Ecuatoriana. Admission includes a guided tour (in English if you call in advance).

Just north of the Mariscal, the small but worthwhile **Museo Etnográfico de Artesanía de Ecuador** (☎ 223 0609; www.sinchisacha.org; Reina Victoria N26-166 & La Niña; ☽ 8am-6:30pm Mon-Fri, 10am-6pm Sat) exhibits the artwork, clothing and utensils of Ecuador's indigenous people with special emphasis on the peoples of the Oriente. Run by the outstanding Fundación Sinchi Sacha (also see Tianguez, p97 and p104), this museum was closed for remodeling as this book went to print, with plans to reopen in early 2007.

PARQUE LA CAROLINA

North of the Mariscal lies the giant **Parque La Carolina**. On weekends it fills with families who come out to pedal paddleboats, play soccer and volleyball, cycle along the bike paths, skate or simply escape the city's urban chaos.

In 2005, Quito inaugurated the park's newest addition, the **Jardín Botánico** (☎ 246 3197; admission $1.50; ☽ 9am-3pm Mon, 9am-5pm Tue-Sun). With more than 300 plant and tree species from around Ecuador and an out-standing *orquideario* (orchid greenhouse) with nearly 1000 orchid species, it's well worth the admission price. An ethno-botanical garden is also in the works.

To further acquaint yourself with Ecuador's flora and fauna, head next door to the country's best natural-history museum, the **Museo de Ciencias Naturales** (☎ 244 9824; Rumipamba s/n, Parque La Carolina admission $2; ☽ 8:30am-1pm & 1:45-4:30pm Mon-Fri). Contemplating the thousands of dead insects and arachnids on display is a good way to rile your nerves before a trip to the Oriente.

Nearby, you can provide further fodder for your jungle fears with a visit to the **Vivarium** (☎ 227 1799; www.vivarium.org.ec in Spanish; Av Amazonas 3008 at Rumipamba; admission $2.50; ☽ 9:30am-5:30pm Tue-Sun), home to 87 live reptiles and amphibians, including poisonous snakes, boa constrictors, iguanas, turtles, frogs and tortoises. It's a herpetological research and education center, and all but one of the critters (the frightening-looking king cobra) are native to Ecuador.

MUSEO GUAYASAMÍN & THE CAPILLA DEL HOMBRE

In the former home of world-famous painter Oswaldo Guayasamín (1919–99), this wonderful **museum** (☎ 246 5265, 245 2938; Calle Bosmediano 543; admission $2; ☽ 9am-1:30pm & 3-6:30pm Mon-Fri) houses the most complete collection of his work. Guayasamín was also an avid collector, and the museum displays his outstanding collection of more than 4500 pre-Colombian ceramic, bone and metal pieces from throughout Ecuador. The pieces are arranged by theme (bowls, fertility figurines, burial masks etc), rather than by era or cultural group, and the result is one of the most beautifully displayed archeological collections in the country.

The museum also houses Guayasamín's collection of religious art, including a crucifix by the famous indigenous carver Caspicara and a tiny crucifix with a pendulum heart inside that ticks against the chest cavity when touched (or breathed on, according to the caretaker).

If you're moved to take something home with you, there's a jewelry store, a T-shirt store and a gallery with original prints.

A few blocks away stands one of the most important works of art in South America, Guayasamín's **Capilla del Hombre** (Chapel of Man;

MARISCAL SUCRE

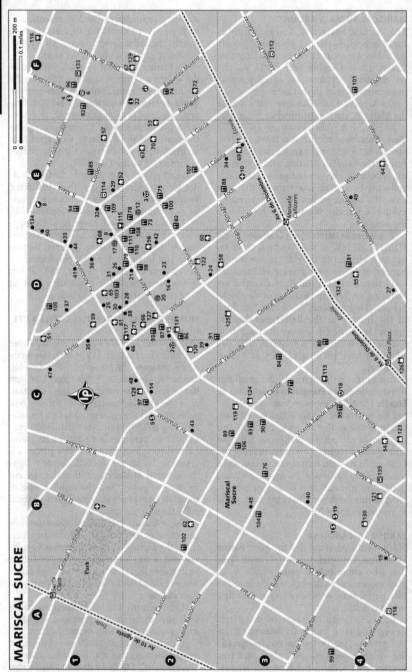

INFORMATION
American Express................................**1** B4
Andinatel (branch).........................**2** C2
Andinatel (branch).........................**3** E2
Banco de Guayaquil.....................**4** F1
Banco de Guayaquil.....................**5** C2
Branch Post Office.........................**6** F1
Clínica Pichincha............................**7** B1
Colombian Embassy......................**8** E1
Confederate Books........................**9** D1
Dr John Rosenberg.....................**10** E3
Ecuadorian Tours...................(see 1)
English Bookstore..........................**11** E3
Friends Web Café...........................**12** E2
Libri Mundi...**13** D2
Libro Express...................................**14** C2
Metropolitan Touring................**15** B4
Opera de Jabón..............................**16** D2
Papaya Net..**17** D1
Police Station...................................**18** C4
Producambios **19** B4
Rainbow Laundry...................(see 32)
Sambo.net...**20** D2
Sun City Laundry...........................**21** D2
Tourist Office...................................**22** F2
Wash & Go **23** D2

SIGHTS & ACTIVITIES
Arie's Bike Company..................**24** D2
Beraca...**25** D1
Biking Dutchman.........................**26** D1
Bipo & Toni's...................................**27** D4
Dracaena..**28** D2
Ecole Idiomas.................................**29** E1
Emerald Forest Expeditions.......**30** D1
Enchanted Expeditions.............**31** D1
Etnotur..**32** E1
Galasam...**33** D1
Guayasamín Spanish School.....**34** E3
Gulliver......................................(see 111)
Kem Pery Tours.............................**35** C1
Moggely Climbing.......................**36** D1
Native Life..**37** D1
Neotropic Turis.............................**38** D2
Pamir..**39** C2
Rainforestur....................................**40** B3
Ritmo Tropical................................**41** D1
River People...........................(see 31)
Safari Tours......................................**42** D2
San Francisco Language
Institute...**43** C2
Sangay Touring..............................**44** D1
Sani Lodge Office.........................**45** B3
Scuba Iguana..................................**46** C2

Sierra Nevada Expeditions........**47** C1
Surtrek..**48** C2
Tropical Dancing School........(see 65)
Vida Verde..**49** E4
Yacu Amu Rafting/Ríos
Ecuador....................................(see 31)
Yuturi Jungle Adventure...........**50** D1

SLEEPING
Albergue El Taxo...........................**51** D1
Alberto's House.............................**52** E1
Antinea Apart Hotel....................**53** E2
Café Cultura...................................**54** C4
Casa Helbling.................................**55** D4
Crossroads.......................................**56** D2
Dagui's.......................................(see 12)
El Cafecito..**57** E1
El Vagabundo.................................**58** D3
Hostal Adventure.........................**59** D1
Hostal Alpa Aligu.........................**60** D2
Hostal Amazonas Inn.................**61** D1
Hostal Dé jà vu..............................**62** B2
Hostal El Arupo..............................**63** E2
Hostal Fuente de Piedra............**64** E4
Hostal Vamara................................**65** D1
Hotel Pickett...................................**66** D2
Hotel Sebastián.............................**67** F2
Iguana Lodge...................................**68** D1
La Casa Sol.......................................**69** E3
Loro Verde..**70** E2
Mansión del Ángel.......................**71** D2
Posada del Maple.........................**72** F2

EATING
Adam's Rib..**73** E2
Aladdin's..**74** F2
Boca del Lobo.................................**75** E2
Café Amazonas.............................**76** B3
Café Galletti.....................................**77** C3
Café Sutra...**78** E2
ChaCha..**79** D2
Chifa Mayflower............................**80** C4
Churrascaría Tropeiro................**81** D4
Coffee Tree......................................**82** E2
Dimmi, di si......................................**83** C3
El Arabe...**84** C3
El Cafecito...............................(see 57)
El Chisme...**85** E1
El Cucurucho..................................**86** D2
El Español..**87** D2
El Maple...**88** E3
Fast Food Restaurants..............**89** C3
Fried Bananas................................**90** C3
Grain de Café.................................**91** D2

Hassan's Café..................................**92** F1
Kallari..**93** D2
La Canoa...**94** E1
La Cocina Quiteña.......................**95** C4
La Jaiba Mariscos.........................**96** F1
Las Redes...**97** C2
Le Arcate....................................(see 91)
Magic Bean......................................**98** D2
Mágico Oriental.............................**99** A4
Mama Clorindas.........................**100** E2
Mare Nostrum..............................**101** F4
Mediterraneo Cevichería........**102** B2
Red Hot Chili Peppers..............**103** D1
Rincón de Francia........................**104** B3
Roble Viejo......................................**105** D1
Sakti..**106** C3
Shorton Grill...................................**107** E2
Siam...**108** D2
Su Cebiche.......................................**109** E1
Texas Ranch...................................**110** D2
Zócalo...**111** D2

ENTERTAINMENT
Humanizarte....................................**112** F3
La Reina Victoria...........................**113** C4
Mayo 68..**114** E1
No Bar...**115** E1
Papillon..**116** F1
Patatu's Bar.....................................**117** D2
Patio de Comedías.......................**118** A4

SHOPPING
Ag..(see 124)
Altar...**119** C3
Centro Artesanal.........................**120** C2
El Aborigen......................................**121** B4
Explorer..**122** D2
Galería Beltrán...............................**123** C4
Galería Latina........................(see 13)
La Bodega...**124** C3
Los Alpes..**125** D3
Mercado Artesanal La
Mariscal.....................................**126** C4
Mythos Shop..................................**127** D2
Pomaire...**128** C2
Productos Andinos......................**129** F2
Taller Alderuti...............................**130** B4
Tatoo..**131** D2

TRANSPORT
Localiza...**132** D4
Panamericana................................**133** F1
TAME..**134** E1
Transportes Ecuador.................**135** B4

☎ 244 6455, 246 5266; www.guayasamin.com; Mariano Calvache at Lorenzo Chávez; admission $3, with purchase of entry to Fundación Guayasamín $2; ☺ 10am-5pm Tue-Sun). The fruit of Guayasamín's greatest vision, this giant monument-cum-museum is a tribute to humankind, to the suffering of Latin America's indigenous poor, and to the undying hope for something better. It's a moving place, and the tours (available in English, French and Spanish and included in the price) are highly recommended. They

usually leave upon request during opening hours.

Mirroring the Inca cultural reverence of the number 'three,' the chapel is broken architecturally and thematically into three: There are three levels to the chapel, the windows are 3 sq meters, and the tiles all around the *capilla* are each 30 sq cm. The exhibits adhere to precolonial, colonial and contemporary themes and follow the three stages of Guayasamín's career.

QUITO

The collection itself, which has numerous murals, is superb. One of the most impressive works is the mural *Los Mutilados,* a meditation on the Spanish Civil War. It's composed of eight separate paintings which can be rotated to create a total of almost three million combinations (you can experiment yourself with the computer next to it and save your creation). Guayasamín studied Da Vinci for eight years and did 470 sketches to get the mural right. The other masterwork is the mural *El condor y el toro,* which represents the forced fight between a condor and a bull during *Yaguar raimi* (blood festival). During the festival, a condor was tied to the bull's neck; if the condor won, it prophesied a good harvest.

The museum and chapel are in the residential district of Bellavista, northeast of downtown. You can walk uphill, or take a bus along Avenida 6 de Diciembre to Avenida Eloy Alfaro and then a Bellavista bus up the hill. A taxi costs about $2.

Guápulo

If you follow Avenida 12 de Octubre up the hill from the Mariscal, you'll reach the Hotel Quito at the top. Behind the hotel, stairs lead steeply down the other side of the hill to the historic neighborhood of Guápulo. The views all the way down here are magnificent. Ramshackle houses stand interspersed among colonial whitewashed homes with terra-cotta-tile roofs, and the odd bohemian café makes for a welcome break.

At the bottom of the hill stands the neighborhood's centerpiece, the **Sanctuary of El Guápulo** (Map pp80-1; 9am-6pm, sometimes closed for lunch), a beautiful church built between 1644 and 1693. The church has an excellent collection of Quito School art and sculpture, and a stunning 18th-century pulpit carved by master wood-carver Juan Bautista Menacho.

The best views of Guápulo are from the lookout behind the Hotel Quito, next to the **statue of Francisco de Orellana** (Map pp80-1; Calle Larrea near González Suárez). The statue depicts Francisco de Orellana looking down into the valley that was the beginning of his epic journey from Quito to the Atlantic – the first descent of the Amazon by a European.

ACTIVITIES
If you're itching to get active, you will find there's plenty to do both within and around the city.

Climbing
Climbers can get a serious fix at the **Rocódromo** (Map pp80-1; 250 8463; Queseras del Medio s/n; admission $1.50; 8am-8pm Mon-Fri, 8am-6pm Sat & Sun), a 25m-high climbing facility across from the Estadio Rumiñahui. There are more than a dozen routes (some as hard as class 5.12; 7C on the French scale) on the three main walls, a four-face bouldering structure, and a rock building. Shoe rental costs $1.50, ropes $2 and harnesses $1. Chalk bags and carabiners are extra. If you rent equipment, the staff will belay you.

The Rocódromo is located just outside the Estadio Rumiñahui (a stadium) and is walking distance from the Mariscal.

Montaña (Map pp80-1; 223 8954; mountain_refugeecuador@yahoo.com; Cordero E12-141 at Toledo; 10am-10pm Mon-Wed, 10am-midnight Thu & Fri, 3-10pm Sat) is a meeting place for climbers from Quito. It's a good source of nonbiased information (no one's trying to sell anything but a cup of coffee) and a good place to meet local climbers. Trips are sometimes arranged and everyone's included. The owner sets up slide shows or chats on weekend evenings.

For information on climbing operators, see p72.

Cycling
On the second and last Sunday of every month, the entire length of Avenida Amazonas and most of the old town are closed to cars, and loads of peddlers take to the street for the bimonthly **ciclopaseo**. The entire ride, which you can cycle part or all of, stretches from the airport, through the old town and into the southern reaches of Quito.

Local mountain-biking companies rent bikes and offer excellent tours including one-day rides through the *páramo* (Andean grasslands) of Parque Nacional Cotopaxi; down-hill descents; trips that incorporate a stop at Papallacta hot springs; two-day trips to Cotopaxi and Chimborazo; and two-day trips to Cotopaxi and Laguna Quilotoa. Single-day trips cost about $45, not including park entrance fees. Check both operators listed here to compare prices and trips.

Biking Dutchman (Map p84; ☎ 256 8323, 254 2806; www.bikingdutchman.com; Foch 714 at JL Mera) is Ecuador's pioneer mountain-biking operator, has good bikes and guides and an outstanding reputation. **Arie's Bike Company** (Map p84; ☎ 290 6052; www.ariesbikecompany.com; Wilson 578 at Reina Victoria) has received great reports from readers.

For high-quality parts and bikes by makers including KHS, Marin and Manitou, stop by **Bike Stop** (Map pp80-1; ☎ 225 5404; www .bikestopecuador.com in Spanish; Av 6 de Diciembre N34-55 at Checoslovaquia; ☆ 10am-7pm Mon-Fri, 9:30am-1:30pm Sat). It's also good source of information.

Hiking

Quito's new telefériQo (Map p74) takes passengers up to Cruz Loma (4100m) from where you can hike to the top of jagged Rucu Pichincha (about 4680m). Beyond the rise of Cruz Loma and past a barbed-wire fence (which no one seems to pay any attention to), well-marked trails lead to Rucu Pichincha. It's approximately three hours to the top, and some scrambling is required. Don't attempt this hike if you've just arrived in Quito; allow yourself a couple days' acclimatization.

Before the telefériQo went in, climbing Rucu Pichincha was dangerous due to armed robberies, but that danger seems to have disappeared entirely. It's easy to assess from the top of the telefériQo, and you can inquire at SAE (p72) if you want to make sure. It's a spectacular hike, best done in the morning before the clouds roll in.

WALKING TOUR

Sundays, when cars are forbidden to enter the old town, are marvelous for a stroll.

The **tourist information kiosk** (Map p74; cnr Venezuela & Chile) on the Plaza Grande offers free maps of walks in the old town with detailed information on the sights seen.

The wonderful **Plaza Grande** (1; p73) is a good starting point; after checking out the **Palacio del Gobierno** (2; p73) and the **cathedral** (3; p76), continue southwest on García Moreno and turn right on Sucre to see **La Compañía de Jesús** (4; p76). From here, walk one block northwest along Sucre to the impressive **Plaza and Monastery of San Francisco** (5; p77). From the plaza, backtrack to García Moreno and then head southwest (right) for three blocks, under the arch at Rocafuerte,

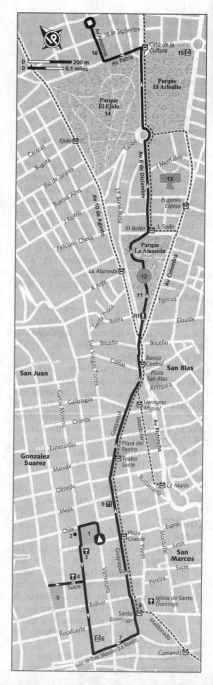

to the **Museo de la Ciudad** (6; p76). If you continue past the museum on García Moreno, you'll hit the historic street Juan de Dios Morales. Turn southeast (left) and after two blocks you'll be on the historic alley of **La Ronda** (7) whose colonial balconied houses are some of the oldest in Quito. The street is notorious for bag snatchers so stay alert. From La Ronda walk up to Calle Guayaquil and turn northeast (left), and you'll pass the **Church and Plaza of Santo Domingo** (8; p77) on your right.

From the Plaza Santo Domingo, head northeast along Calle Guayaquil toward the new town. Between Mejía and Chile you'll pass the hole-in-the-wall **Heladería San Agustín** (9; p97), a 140-year-old ice-cream parlor well worth a stop for a couple of scoops of iced nourishment.

Bear north and you'll soon pass the impressive **Simón Bolívar monument** (10; p79) just inside the southern corner of triangular **Parque La Alameda** (11; p79) and the **Quito Observatory** (12; p82).

As you leave the park, continue north on Avenida 6 de Diciembre. After three blocks, you'll pass the modern **legislative palace** (Legislative Congress Building; 13; p82) on your right. Continuing on Avenida 6 de Diciembre takes you past the popular **Parque El Ejido** (14; p82) on your left and the huge, circular, mirror-walled **Casa de la Cultura Ecuatoriana** (15; p82) on your right. Turn left past the Casa de la Cultura and walk three blocks along Avenida Patria, with Parque El Ejido to your left, until you reach the small stone arch marking the beginning of Quito's most famous modern street, **Avenida Amazonas (16)**.

It is about 3km from the heart of the old town to the beginning of Amazonas.

COURSES
Dance
Learn to dance salsa or you'll spend a lot of time shoe-gazing anytime you hit one of Ecuador's *salsotecas* (salsa clubs). Most schools also offer *merengue* (a ballroom dance originating from Haiti), *cumbia* (a dance originally from Colombia, similar to salsa) and other Latin American dances. The following schools in the new town are both excellent:

Ritmo Tropical (Map p84; ☎ 255 7094; ritmotropical5@hotmail.com; Av Amazonas N24-155 at Calama; ⊙ 9am-8pm Mon-Fri) One-on-one lessons cost $5 per hour, group lessons $4.50 per hour. Offers capoeira too.

Tropical Dancing School (Map p84; ☎ 222 0427; tropicaldancing@hotmail.com; Foch E4-256 at Av Amazonas; ⊙ 10am-8pm Mon-Fri, Sat & Sun by reservation only) One-on-one lessons cost $6 per hour, group lessons $5 per hour.

Language
Studying Spanish is the perfect excuse for a prolonged stay in Quito. There are more than 80 Spanish schools in Quito, with classes for all levels. Courses can last anywhere from a couple of days to months or more. Most schools offer one-on-one instruction and can arrange accommodations with local families. Make sure you get what you want by visiting several schools before deciding. Rates for private lessons vary between $6 and $9 per hour. Some charge an inscription fee (usually around $20).

Beraca (Map p84; ☎ 290 6642; beraca@interactive.net.ec; Av Amazonas 1114) Cheap and well-liked.

Bipo & Toni's (Map p84; ☎ 255 6614, 256 3309; www.bipo.net; J Carrión E8-183 at Leonidas Plaza Gutiérrez)

Ecole Idiomas (Map p84; ☎ 223 1592; info@ecotravel-ecuador.com; L García E6-15 near JL Mera) Volunteer projects available.

Guayasamín Spanish School (Map p84; ☎ 254 4210; www.guayasaminschool.com; J Calama E8-54 near 6 de Diciembre) Ecuadorian owned; lots of reader recommendations.

San Francisco Language Institute (Map p84; ☎ 252 1306; www.sanfranciscospanish.com; Av Amazonas 662, 2nd fl, Office 201) Pricey ($9 per hr, plus $50 inscription fee) but gets high recommendations.

Vida Verde (Map p84; ☎ 222 6635, 256 3110; www.vidaverde.com; Leonidas Plaza Gutiérrez n23-100 near Wilson)

QUITO FOR CHILDREN
Keeping the kiddos happy in Quito might require a bit of effort, but there's definitely plenty to do. **Parque La Carolina** (p83) has loads of fun stuff: after taking them to one of the playgrounds or pedaling them around the lake in a paddleboat, walk through the natural-history museum or – even better – to the **Vivarium**, where the snakes, turtles and lizards will surely dazzle them. Another museum that will likely go over well is the **Museo Amazónico** (p83).

Puppet shows are sometimes staged at Centro Cultural Itchimbia and theaters throughout Quito; you check the entertainment listings and watch for the word *'títeres'* (puppets).

There's a sparkling new **theme park**, complete with bumper cars and other rides, at the telefériQo (p79). Further afield, the **Quito Zoo** (p110) in Guayllabamba will never fail to busy the youngsters for a day.

Tourist-oriented babysitting services are impossible to find in Quito unless you're staying at one of the city's top-end hotels, in which case the hotel will arrange for a sitter.

TOURS

Conventional travel agencies (p72) offer all sorts of standard tours to places such as Mitad del Mundo, Pululahua, rose plantations in Cayambe and more.

City Tours

The Corporación Metropolitana de Turismo offers four different **guided walks** (adults/children under 12 $10/5; ☺ morning & afternoon departures Tue-Sun) in the old town with friendly cop-cum-tourist guides. Called *paseos culturales* (cultural walks), they depart from the tourist office (p72) inside the Palacio Arzobispal.

Outside Quito

Quito is one of the easiest places in Ecuador to arrange a guided tour, be it a Galápagos cruise, climbing trip or jungle tour. Tours, of course, can also be arranged in towns closer to the destination (especially in Riobamba, Baños and Tena), which is sometimes better value. But many find Quito the most convenient. Also see p230 for more information.

For mountain-biking tours near Quito, see p86. Many tour companies that operate in the Oriente or Gálapagos (or anywhere in the country for that matter) have offices in Quito. These offices are included here, but receive more detailed treatment (including prices) in their respective regional chapter.

Alta Montaña (☎ 252 4422, 09-422 9483; Jorge Washington 8-20) Owner Ivan Rojas has been on the Ecuadorian mountain scene for years, and is an invaluable resource for expeditionists. Courses, guide recommendations and equipment rental available.

Compañía de Guías de Montaña (Map pp80-1; ☎ 290 1551, 255 6210; www.companiadeguias.com;

Jorge Washington 425 at Av 6 de Diciembre) A top-notch mountain-climbing operator whose guides are all ASEGUIM (Asociación Ecuatoriana de Guías de Montaña; Ecuadorian Association of Mountain Guides) instructors and speak several languages. Two-day trips cost $224 per person, three days $330, not including park entrance fees. Tailor-made trips are available.

Dracaena (Map p84; ☎ 254 6590; J Pinto E4-453) Offers four- to eight-day tours of Cuyabeno (p236) that have received excellent reviews from our readers. Five-day tours are $200 per person.

Emerald Forest Expeditions (Map p84; ☎ 254 1278; www.emeraldexpeditions.com; J Pinto E4-244 at Av Amazonas) Owned by Luís García, one of the best guides in the northern Oriente, Emerald Forest consistently gets outstanding reports from travelers. Luís bases his trips in Pañacocha just off the Río Napo (see also p238). They're $60 to $80 per person per day.

Enchanted Expeditions (Map p84; ☎ 256 9960; www.enchantedexpeditions.com; Foch 769) Runs some of the best (and priciest) small boats in the Galápagos. Also arranges excursions to the Oriente and the Andes. Located between JL Mera and Av Amazonas.

Etnotur (Map p84; ☎ 256 4565, 223 0552; Cordero 1313 at JL Mera) Mainland and Galápagos tours. English, German, French and Spanish are spoken.

Fundación Golondrinas (Map pp80-1; ☎ 222 6602; www.ecuadorexplorer.com/golondrinas; Isabel La Católica N24-679) Located inside La Casa de Eliza, this conservation project treks in the *páramo* and forests west of Tulcán (see p135).

Galasam (Map p84; ☎ 250 7079/80; www.galasam .com; Av Amazonas 1354 at Cordero) Known for its economical to midrange Galápagos cruises, but reports from customers have been mixed; complaints are frequent.

Gulliver (Map p84; ☎ 252 9297, 09-946 2265; www .gulliver.com.ec; cnr JL Mera & Calama; ☺ 8am-8pm) Well-regarded operator offering trekking, climbing, mountain-biking and horseback-riding trips in the Andes. Excellent prices, daily departures. Does Cotopaxi, Ilinizas, Quilotoa and more. Most daytrips cost $30 to $45 per person. Five- to seven-day Cotopaxi trips with acclimatization programs are based out of its Hostería PapaGayo (p148) and cost $360 to $450 and $500 respectively.

Kem Pery Tours (Map p84; ☎ 222 6583; www .kempery.com; J Pinto 539) Kem Pery does trips to Bataburo Lodge (three/four nights $215/$200), on the edge of Huaorani territory. See also p241.

Moggely Climbing (Map p84; ☎ 255 4984; www .moggely.com; J Calama E4-54) Reputable climbing operator, long in the business. Uses only ASEGUIM guides.

Neotropic Turis (Map p84; ☎ 252 1212, 09-980 3395; www.neotropicturis.com; J Pinto E4-340 near Av Amazonas & Wilson) Neotropic runs the wonderful Cuyabeno Lodge in the Reserva Producción Faunística Cuyabeno (see p237).

A four-day trip costs $200 to $288 per person. Also are excursions to Peru via the Marañon River.

Nuevo Mundo Expeditions (☎ 250 9431; www .nuevomundotravel.com; 18 de Septiembre E4-161) Professional outfit with strong conservation interests, top-end prices, and top-end tours and guides. Organizes Galápagos tours, four- to five-day Río Napo cruises aboard its comfy *Manatee Amazon Explorer* (see p241); and Andean trekking and ethnobotanical trips.

Pamir (Map p84; ☎ 222 0892; info@pamirtravels.com .ec; General Baquedano near JL Mera) Slick operator with very experienced climbing and trekking guides. Also sells Galápagos cruises.

Quasar Nautica (Map p78; ☎ 244 6996; www.quasar nautica.com; Brasil 293 near Granda Centeno, Edificio IACA, 2nd fl) Offers expensive but excellent luxury yacht trips in the Galápagos.

Rainforestur (Map p84; ☎ 223 9822; www.rainforest ur.com; Av Amazonas 420 at F Robles) Offers well-received rafting trips on the Río Pastaza near Baños, and trips to Cuyabeno and elsewhere (for details, see p167). Also offers trekking and indigenous market tours in the Quito area.

River People (☎ 290 6639; www.riverpeoplerafting ecuador.com; Foch 746) Family run, affable and highly professional white-water rafting outfit. Trips start in Tena but go to a variety of rivers.

Safari Tours (Map p84; ☎ 255 2505, 250 8316; JL Mera & J Pinto; ☼ 9am-7pm) Excellent reputation and long in the business. Offers all range of tours and trips, from volcano climbs and jungle trips to local jeep tours and personalized off-the-beaten-track expeditions. It's also a great place to arrange Galápagos trips.

Sangay Touring (Map p84; ☎ 255 0176/80; www .sangay.com; Av Amazonas N24-196 at Cordero) Offers a variety of standardized day tours, including Jeep trips, hiking excursions and visits to cloud forests and volcanoes. Rates range from $25 to $75 per person. Also arranges economically priced Galápagos tours.

Scuba Iguana (Map p84; ☎ 290 6666, 290 7704; www .scubaiguana.com; Av Amazonas 1004 at Wilson) One of the best dive operators for the Galápagos (see p364). It also offers Professional Association of Diving Instructors (PADI) dive courses in Quito.

Sierra Nevada Expeditions (Map p84; ☎ 255 3658; www.hotelsierranevada.com; J Pinto 637 near Cordero) Long in the business, Sierra Nevada offers climbing and river-rafting trips. Owner Freddy Ramirez is well established and a very reputable mountain guide.

Surtrek (Map p84; ☎ 223 1534, 250 0530; www .surtrek.com, www.galapagosyachts.com; Av Amazonas 897) Top-end company with years of experience in trekking and climbing. Personalized tours available. Prices average $130 to $160 per day. Also offers unique 'island hopping' Galápagos tours where you sleep on different islands rather than aboard a cruise ship.

Tropic Ecological Adventures (Map pp80-1; ☎ 222 5907; www.tropiceco.com; Av de la República E7-320) Long-time agency offering numerous three- to six-day tours to the Oriente, Andes and cloud forest. It sells other operators' tours, but it's a good way to compare some of the best on offer, and rates are good.

Yacu Amu Rafting/Ríos Ecuador (Map p84; ☎ 223 6844, 290 4054; www.yacuamu.com; Foch 746) Excellent river-rafting operator with daily departures to the Río Toachi and Río Blanco, and several other Class III-IV options. Located between JL Mera and Avenida Amazonas, rates start around $75 per person. Other trips range from two to eight days. There is also a four-day kayaking school. Owner Steve Nomchong has competed and worked as a judge and safety inspector on the international circuit, so you're in good hands. He now owns Ríos Ecuador, based in Tena (see p249).

FESTIVALS & EVENTS

As throughout Ecuador, people celebrate **New Year's Eve** by burning elaborate, life-sized puppets in the streets at midnight, launching explosives into the sky, and otherwise throwing general public safety to the wind. It's a great time to be here. **Carnaval**, held the weekend before Ash Wednesday (a changing date in February), is celebrated by intense water fights – no one is spared (careful with your camera if it isn't waterproof!). Colorful religious processions are held during **Semana Santa** (Easter Week), the most spectacular being the procession of *cucuruchos* (penitents wearing purple robes and inverted cone masks) on Good Friday.

Throughout the first week of December, the **founding of Quito** is celebrated with bullfights at the **Plaza** (Map p78), just beyond the intersection of Avenida América and Avenida 10 de Agosto. The fiesta reaches its height on the night of December 6, when there is lots of dancing in the streets.

SLEEPING

Most people stay in the new town, preferring to hunker down in the Mariscal's comfortable and traveler-oriented hotels, which offer easy access to international restaurants, cybercafés, travel agencies and nightlife. The downside is that the modern Mariscal could be just about anywhere. It's also dangerous at night (see p72). If you'd like a traditional slice of Quito and don't mind the absence of granola-and-cappuccino breakfasts on every corner, try the old town. Awaking to the area's sights, sounds and smells is an experience unlike any other.

The quiet and increasingly artsy new-town neighborhood of La Floresta is a pleasant (and safer) alternative to the Mariscal, and it's only a few blocks' away from its more popular counterpart.

The rather hazily defined area between the old and new towns, (southeast of Parque El Ejido, near the Instituto Geográfico Militar), has a nontouristy feel and is a 10- to 15-minute walk from both the old town and the Mariscal. It's technically part of the new town.

The area around Guápulo and Hotel Quito (also in the new town) doesn't boast a ton of choices, but it's an interesting area. Guápulo is wonderful at night (and during the day) and the area has a more local, nontouristy feel.

Old Town   Map p74

The hotels between Plaza Santo Domingo and the bus terminal are some of the cheapest, but it's a dodgy area after about 7pm.

BUDGET

Hotel Catedral Internacional (☎ 295 5438; Mejía 638; s/d $7/12) This is an extremely tidy hotel, with old but cared-for decorations, odd furniture and marvelously outdated bedspreads. Those with windows are the best (others can feel a bit gloomy), and there's an inviting little sitting area on the 2nd floor.

Grand Hotel (☎ 228 0192, 295 9411; www.geocities.com/grandhotelquito; Rocafuerte 1001; s/d with shared bathroom $4.50/8, with private bathroom $6.50/12) It's clean and has lots of character, but the street's a little sketchy after dark, and rooms are gloomy if you don't get a window. However, it's a family-run place and an old backpacker haunt – good if you want cheap and nontouristy accommodations.

Hotel Internacional Plaza del Teatro (☎ 295 9462, 295 4293; Guayaquil N8-75; s/d $10/16) Across from the Plaza del Teatro, this old-time hotel maintains a hint of its elegance with its marble staircase, wide hallways and balconied rooms. The off-street rooms lack balconies and character, but are quieter.

Hostal San Blas (☎ 228 1434; Caldas 121, Plaza San Blas; s/d with private bathroom $6.75/10, with shared bathroom $5/6.75) This friendly, family-run hotel on the recently renovated Plaza San Blas is a good deal if you don't mind small rooms. Rooms are dark (windows open onto a small interior patio) but clean and cute. A kitchen and rooftop terrace are in the works.

Hotel Huasi Continental (☎ 295 7327; Flores 332; r per person with shared/private bathroom $4/7) Several readers have recommended this hotel with Spartan but clean, comfortable rooms. Unfortunately, few have windows, but the beds are firm and the staff are professional. Cable TV costs $1 extra.

La Posada Colonial (☎ 228 2859; Paredes 188; r per person with shared/private bathroom $4/5) Although a bit close to the bus terminal, this is still one of the best-value places in the old town. Beds are saggy, but it's extremely well-kept and totally secure. Rooms are bright and cheerful with polished wood floors, and the staff is great.

Chicago Hostal (☎ 228 0224; chicagohostal@panchored.net; Los Ríos 1730; dm $5.50, s/d with shared bathroom $6/12, with private bathroom $9/16; 🖳) On the new town border, this ultra-friendly new hotel is spotless, straightforward rooms with cable TV. There's a dining room and bar for guests and free left-luggage service.

Hostal La Casona (☎ 257 0626, 258 8809; Manabí 255; s/d $6/8) La Casona has three floors of dark, clean, musty rooms opening onto a dimly lit, interior patio. It's the sort of place that has plenty of things (low doorways or strangely placed TV mounts) to hit your head upon.

AUTHOR'S CHOICE

Secret Garden (☎ 295 6704, 316 0949; Antepara E4-60 at Los Ríos; dm $6.75, s or d with shared/private bathroom $17.50/24) With a hostel like this around, you have no excuse for sleeping outside the old town. Owned by an Ecuadorian/Australian couple, this is easily one of the best budget digs in Quito, and no one can compete with the view from the 5th-floor terrace. An all-you-can-eat breakfast (additional $2.50) and nightly dinners (about $3.75) are served. Its five colorful floors are livened up with groovy paintings from past guests. There are three dorm rooms and 11 private rooms, one of which has its own bathroom. The other private rooms have a bathroom for every two rooms. Spanish lessons, travel information and lots of activities are available too.

QUITO

MIDRANGE

Hotel Viena Internacional (☎ 295 4860; Flores 600 at Chile; s/d with bathroom $11/22) Though the 70s, grapevine wallpaper can bug your eyes out, the spotless rooms, top-notch service and cheerful interior patio make this the best hotel deal in the old town. Rooms have hardwood floors, TVs, hot water and good showers. Those with balconies are a bit noisy, but the breeze is nice.

Hotel San Francisco de Quito (☎ 228 7758; www .uio-guided.com/hsfquito; Sucre 217; s/d with bathroom $14/24, s/d mini-apartments with kitchenettes $18/30) One of the old town's finer hotels, this historic converted house boasts spotless rooms with telephone, TV and constant hot water. Some even have lofts. Because it's a colonial building, rooms lack windows, but double doors open onto a lovely balcony over a pretty interior courtyard. Breakfast is included.

Hotel Real Audiencia (☎ 295 2711; www.realau diencia.com; Bolívar Oe3-18; s/d $26/42) Until the old town's recent facelift, this nondescript but immaculately kept hotel was the best in the area. It's still an excellent choice; many rooms have views, and the service is tops. The price includes breakfast in the top-floor restaurant with great views.

La Posada Colonial (☎ 228-0282; posadacolonial@ yahoo.com; García Moreno 1160 near Mejía; s/d $20/35) Though rooms are few (three to be exact) in this newly converted restaurant/hotel, they're spotless and spacious, with hardwood floors, large windows (a rarity in these old colonial houses) and comfortable beds. It certainly qualifies as 'pretty.' Don't confuse this with the other hotel of the same name.

Hotel Auca Continental (☎ 295 4799; aucahotel@ hotmail.com; Sucre Oe4-14; s/d with breakfast $10/20) The modernish Auca is plain and time-tattered but totally fine. It even has an elevator.

TOP END

Hotel Patio Andaluz (☎ 228 0830; www.hotelpatioan daluz.com; García Moreno N6-52; s/d $55/110; ☐) The old town's fanciest hotel is one seriously plush pad. Inside a remodeled 16th-century home, the 30 rooms open onto interior wooden-floor balconies. The woodwork everywhere is beautiful. Doubles have king-size beds and giant TVs to match, and everything has a peaceful feel.

New Town
BUDGET

La Casona de Mario (Map pp80–1; ☎ 254 4036, 223 0129; www.casonademario.com; Andalucía N24-115; r per person $8) In a lovely old house, La Casona de Mario is outstanding value, with homey rooms, shared spotless bathrooms, a garden, a TV lounge and a guest kitchen. Numerous readers have recommended the place for its hospitality, atmosphere, quiet but convenient location, and general all-round value.

Casa Bambú (Map pp80–1; ☎ 222 6738; G Solano 1758 near Av Colombia; dm $4, r per person with shared/private bathroom $5/7) This gem of a place has spacious rooms, a wee garden, a giant rooftop terrace, guest kitchen, a book exchange, laundry facilities and outstanding views from the hammocks on the roof. It's worth the uphill hike to get there.

El Cafecito (Map p84; ☎ 223 4862; www.cafecito .net; Cordero E6-43; dm $6, s/d $9/14) Over the excellent café of the same name (p101), this is an eternally popular budget choice, and for good reason. Rooms are clean, the place has a mellow vibe and the café makes breakfast convenient. All bathrooms are shared.

L'Auberge Inn (Map pp80–1; ☎ 255 2912; www .ioda.net/auberge-inn; Av Colombia N12-200; s/d with shared bathroom $7/13, with private bathroom $10/17) This comfortable *hostal* (small and reasonably priced hotel) offers spotless rooms, a small garden area, an on-site travel agency, a common room with a fireplace, a pool table and an excellent pizzeria.

Montaña (Map pp80–1; ☎ 223 8954; mountain _refugeecuador@yahoo.com; Cordero E12-141 at Toledo; dm $7, s/d $9/15) Opened in 2004 by an avid local climber, Montaña has a welcoming vibe and is an excellent choice for climbers and trekkers on a budget. It's a great place to hook up with local altitude freaks. With one double, two singles, a triple and a quad, it only sleeps 11.

Albergue El Taxo (Map p84; ☎ /fax 222 5593; Foch E4-116; s/d with shared bathroom $7/14, with private bathroom $8/16) Friendly and modest, El Taxo occupies a converted 70s house with pleasant, colorful rooms, most of which have shared bathrooms. The no-frills common area has a fireplace (rarely fired up), and the guest kitchen is well kept.

La Casa de Eliza (Map pp80–1; ☎ 222 6602; manteca@uio.satnet.net; Isabel La Católica N24-679; dm/ d $6/12) Although this old favorite is definitely showing its age, it's still a friendly, homespun place. It occupies a converted house with a big guest kitchen, a sociable common area, a small book exchange and simple rooms.

El Vagabundo (Map p84; ☎ 222 6376; vagabundo ecuador@hotmail.com; Wilson E7-45; r per person $8) 'The Vagabond' offers clean but dull rooms which amount to a fairly good deal thanks, in large part, to its friendly owners and the attached pizzeria.

Hostal Dé jà vu (Map p84; ☎ 222 4483; 9 de Octubre 599; dm $6, s/d with shared bathroom $10/12, with private bathroom $12/15) Colorfully painted walls and old wacky furniture give this slightly run down, but popular, *hostal* a somewhat underground feel.

Margarita I (Map pp80-1; ☎ 295 2599; Elizalde 410; s/d with bathroom $4/8) Just east of Parque La Alameda, this is a no-frills hotel (sometimes used hourly) with several floors of clean, simple rooms with private bathroom and cable TV. And hey, it's the only one in town with 24-hour Playboy channel.

Other hotels offering good value in the new town:

Hostal Adventure (Map p84; ☎ 222 6340; rfcedno@ interactive.net.ec; J Pinto E4-225; r per person with shared/private bathroom $6/7) Basic but clean, carpeted and friendly, with guest kitchen and terrace.

Iguana Lodge (Map p84; ☎ 256 9784; iguanalodge@ yahoo.com; J Calama E4-45; r per person with shared/ private bathroom $8/10) Good, comfy place in the heart of the Mariscal.

Hostal Vamara (Map p84; ☎ 222 6425; hostal vamara@yahoo.com; Foch 753 & Av Amazonas; dm $3, r with shared bathroom per person $6, with private bathroom & TV per person $8) Has some of the cheapest dorm beds in town.

Hostal Alpa Aligu (Map p84; ☎ 256 4012; alpa aligu@yahoo.com; J Pinto 240; dm $4)

Dagui's (☎ 222 8151; davidcando@hotmail.com; J Calama E6-05; dm per person $5)

Hotel Pickett (Map p84; ☎ /fax 541 453, 551 205; Wilson 712; s/d $10/20) Straightforward hotel; perfectly fine for the price.

Hotel 9 de Octubre (Map pp80-1; ☎ 255 2424, 255 2524; 9 de Octubre 1047; s $10-13, d $14-16) Drably institutional but acceptable.

MIDRANGE

Hostal Amazonas Inn (Map p84; ☎ 222 5723, 222 2666; J Pinto E4-324 & Av Amazonas; r per person $9-12) This no-nonsense hotel is excellent value. The rooms are spotless, the showers have

constant hot water, and TVs get 70-plus channels. Rooms on the 1st floor have windows and are by far the best. The staff is friendly, the location is central and there's a great breakfast café downstairs.

Folklore Hotel (Map pp80-1; ☎ 255 4621; www .folklorehotel.com; Madrid 868 near Pontevedra; s/d with breakfast $15/25) This delightfully converted house in La Floresta has spacious, colorful rooms with blue-and-yellow checkered bedspreads that match the house paintjob. It has a small garden and a welcoming family-feel.

La Casa Sol (Map p84; ☎ 223 0798; www.lacasasol .com; J Calama E8-66; s/d $25/42, ste with kitchen $36/60) An immaculate, bright-orange B&B with two floors of small rooms opening onto a tiny courtyard, Casa Sol is a remodeled house that was recently added to the list of Quito's Cultural Heritage sites. Guests rave about the place. Rates include breakfast.

Aleida's Hostal (Map pp80-1; ☎ 223 4570; www .aleidashostal.com.ec; Andalucía 559 at Salazar; s/d with shared bathroom $11/22, with private bathroom $17/34 or $22/39) This friendly three-story guesthouse in La Floresta is family run and has a very spacious feel with lots of light, huge rooms, high wooden ceilings and hardwood floors. The owner welcomes guests with a shot of *punta* (homemade firewater). Breakfast is available for $2 to $4 extra.

Hostal El Arupo (Map p84; ☎ 255 7543; pita emi@ uio.satnet.net; Rodríguez E7-22 near Reina Victoria; s/d $18/26) One of several good guesthouse-cum-hostels on the quietest street in the Mariscal, El Arupo is a spotless and homey converted house with a lovely little front patio. Rooms are a bit dark, but the beds are firm, prices include breakfast, and there's an immaculate communal kitchen.

Crossroads (Map p84; ☎ /fax 223 4735; www.cross roadshostal.com; Foch E5-23; dm $6-7, s/d with shared bathroom $12/18, with private bathroom $15.50/25) This well-kept and popular hotel occupies a converted house and has basic but clean rooms. Facilities include a good café (with homemade granola and waffles), cable TV, kitchen and a patio with a fireplace. Has a friendly vibe and cool staff.

Hostal Raices (Map pp80-1; ☎ 255 9737; JL Tamayo N21-255; s/d $12/20) This small, attractively decorated *hostal* boasts a TV lounge and spacious, well-lit rooms with wood floors and colorful bedspreads. The walls are done up with an almost overbearing, rust-color faux effect, with little birdies and ribbons painted in for additional dazzle, but it's tolerable.

Antinea Apart Hotel (Map p84; ☎ 250 6838; www.hotelantinea.com; Rodríguez E8-20; s $43-70, d 60-85; 🖵) One of Quito's finest boutique hotels, this warmly remodeled mansion is the place to treat yourself. Persian rugs, beautiful art, ceramics, gold-framed mirrors, black porcelain in the bathrooms and great attention to detail give this a deliciously luxurious atmosphere. The priciest rooms have fireplaces. Monthly apartments are available.

Casa Helbling (Map p84; ☎ 222 6013; www.casahelbling.de; General Veintimilla E18-166; s/d with shared bathroom $12/18, with private bathroom $18/26) In a homey, colonial-style house in the Mariscal, Casa Helbling is clean, relaxed, friendly and has a guest kitchen, laundry facilities and plenty of common areas for chilling out.

Toa Bed & Breakfast (Map pp80-1; ☎ 222 4241; www.hostaltoa.ec; F Lizarazu N23-209 near La Gasca; s/d $20/32, apt $50) Although slightly out of the way (about a 15-minute walk from the Mariscal), Toa is a wonderful B&B, with cheery, comfy rooms adorned with handicrafts, a common area with a fireplace, a big communal table and a spotless kitchen. There's a sunny back patio and a fully equipped apartment to boot.

Hostal Charles Darwin (Map pp80-1; ☎ 223 4323; www.chdarwin.com; La Colina 304; s/d incl breakfast $26/36; 🗶 🖵) This intimate hotel in a stylish retro house (think 1960s) sits on a quiet street and has comfortable rooms. Extras include a small garden, kitchen facilities, laundry service and the company of two big dogs. Needless to say, the owners are Darwin fanatics.

Hostal Los Alpes (Map pp80-1; ☎ 256 1110; www.hotellosalpes.com; JL Tamayo 233; s/d with breakfast $48/71) A little on the gaudy side, but a beauty nonetheless, Los Alpes is a restored house filled with art and artifacts that gives the whole place an artsy, alpine feel. Some of the comfortable carpeted rooms have balconies, and the on-site restaurant is excellent.

Hostal de La Rábida (Map pp80-1; ☎ 222 2169; www.hostalrabida.com; La Rábida 227; s/d $51/64) This option occupies a lovely converted house with an immaculate white-wall interior and fresh, carpeted rooms. There's a tiny bar/lounge and a restaurant serving delicacies such as *filet chateaubriand* (thick steak) and *crepes suzette* (crepes with orange liqueur) – for guests only.

Hostal Villa Nancy (Map pp80-1; ☎ 255 0839, 256 2473; npelaez@pi.pro.ec; Muros 146; s/d $39/59, ste $75; 🗶) In an upper-class residential neighborhood, this large, converted house is an excellent choice for those seeking a little refinement. The place has superb staff and there's always a helpful, English-speaking person on duty. There's a sundeck, sauna, small garden, an elegant living room (with chandeliers) and 12 spotless rooms.

Other reliable midrange options:

Hostal Fuente de Piedra (Map p84; ☎ 256 9776, 252 5314; www.ecuahotel.com; Wilson 211 & JL Tamayo; s/d incl breakfast $30/40) The highlight here is the lovely outdoor patio.

Loro Verde (Map p84; ☎ 222 6173; Rodríguez E7-66; s/d $9/18) Simple but comfy; great location.

TOP END

Quito's luxury hotels are popular with businesspeople and tour groups. Most offer cheaper rates to walk-in guests than they do when booked from abroad (provided, of course, there are rooms), so it's worth popping in if you're out for a splurge. Rates at chain hotels are cut by nearly 50% on Saturday and Sunday.

Café Cultura (Map p84; ☎ 222 4271; www.cafecultura.com; F Robles 513; s/d $77/89) This wonderful boutique hotel occupies a converted mansion with a garden. The beautifully painted common rooms have crackling fireplaces, while the bedrooms come decorated with murals painted by different artists. Water is purified throughout the hotel (you can even drink the shower water!). Travelers love this place and reservations are advised. Bring your children at no additional charge.

Mansión del Ángel (Map p84; ☎ 255 7721; Wilson E5-29; s/d with breakfast $65/105) An intimate, attractive boutique hotel in a refurbished colonial-style home, Mansión del Ángel offers elegantly furnished rooms with brass canopy beds. There's a rooftop garden too.

Hotel Vieja Cuba (Map pp80-1; ☎ 290 6729/30/31; viejacuba@andinanet.net; Diego de Almagro 1212; s/d $49/67, ste $85/104) This stunning boutique hotel, masterfully designed in a crisp, colonial Cuban theme, has refreshing rooms and a colorful flair. Two rooms have fireplaces, and the two tower-suites are supremely comfortable. Not a detail is missed.

Suites González Suárez (Map pp80-1; ☎ 223 2003, 222 4417; www.sgshotel.com; San Ignacio 2750 & González

Suárez; s/d $60/72, ste $96; 🖥) This sophisticated little hotel perched on the hill overlooking Guápulo has plush rooms with outstanding views. Nab a suite and you can step from a giant Jacuzzi into your king-size bed or warm up further in your en-suite sauna. It's a quiet, elegant place with a business traveler feel. Buffet breakfast and airport pickup is included.

Hotel Quito (Map pp80-1; 🕿 254 4600; hotel quito@orotels.com; González Suárez N27-142; standard s $67-98, d $79-116, ste $146; 🖥 🛎) A Quito landmark, this handsome luxury hotel is set high on the hill above Guápulo. Although its heyday was in the 1960s (as its minimalist design makes clear), it's still a classy place, and the views from its rooms (and from the bar, the restaurant, the lobby and the outdoor swimming pool) are unbeatable. The hotel has a nostalgic romance that other luxury accommodations lack. In 2006 the hotel inaugurated its swanky new casino.

Hotel Sebastián (Map p84; 🕿 222 2300, 222 2400; hsebast1@hsebastian.com.ec; Diego de Almagro 822; s/d $59/69, ste $74/84; 🖥) Many of Hotel Sebastián's 50 good-sized rooms have balconies, and some have great views. The rooms all feature cable TV, direct-dial phones, room service, desks and attractive furnishings. The water throughout the entire hotel is filtered, so drink up. There is a cozy bar with a fireplace.

Hilton Colón (Map pp80-1; 🕿 256 1333, 256 0666; www.hilton.com; Av Amazonas & Av Patria; s/d low season from $160/190; high season from $195/220; 🛎) Besides its fabulous central location, Quito's original luxury hotel has everything you might need for a luxurious stay – a pool, sauna, massage parlor, exercise room, discotheque, casino, salons, a small shopping mall, a 24-hour coffee shop, several cafés and restaurants, two bars and numerous meeting rooms.

Other luxury chain hotels with all mod cons and the service you'd expect:

Swissôtel (Map pp80-1; 🕿 256 7600, 256 6497; www .swissotel.com; Av 12 de Octubre 1820; r from $150; 🗵 🖥 🛎)

Radisson Royal Quito (Map pp80-1; 🕿 223 3333; www.radisson.com/quitoec; Cordero 444; s/d $150-200, ste from $160)

JW Marriott Hotel (Map pp80-1; 🕿 /fax 297 2000; www.marriott.com; Orellana 1172 & Av Amazonas; r from $150)

Around Quito

Hostería San Jorge (Map p78; 🕿 /fax 256 5964, 223 9287; www.hostsanjorge.com.ec; s/d $50/60, ste $85; 🛎) How about staying in an old hacienda on a mountainside overlooking Quito? This 25-room *hostería* (small hotel), once owned by 19th-century Ecuadorian President Eloy Alfaro, is 4km west of Avenida Occidental, on the road to Nono. With more than 30 hectares on the property, outdoor activities are plentiful. It boasts an indoor pool, sauna, spa and steam room, and a restaurant and fully equipped bar (complete with pool table). All rooms have rustic fireplaces and hot showers. Airport pickup costs $10 and all meals are available at moderate rates. Great for acclimatizing climbers.

Las Cuevas de Alvaro (🕿 222 8902; birdecua@hoy .net; J Carrión 555-C; r per person with 3 meals $61) Here's an odd one: created by Ecuadorian eccentric Alvaro Bustamante, 'Alvaro's Caves' were excavated by hand from a grassy hill in the middle of nowhere. Eventually, they became a series of caves joined by underground passageways. God knows why Alvaro built this structure – something about 'man's ties and dependence on the land,' but they've now been turned into a seven-room underground hotel. The restaurant serves delicious homemade food ($17 for nonguests). The grounds have a children's play area, an artificial lake and lookout towers, and horseback riding and hiking are available. It's about 32km (one hour) east of Quito.

Apartments & Homestays

Visitors wanting to stay for a longer time may want to rent a room, apartment or suite with a kitchen. Many apartments require a one-month minimum stay, although we've listed some here that can be rented daily or weekly as well. The SAE has a notice board full of shared-housing advertisements (see p72). La Casona de Mario (p92) is great for long-term stays, and Toa Bed & Breakfast (opposite) has an excellent apartment.

Alberto's House (Map p84; albertohouse@hotmail .com; García 648; r per week/month $49/150) Alberto's has facilities that include shared hot showers, a laundry room, kitchen privileges, a TV lounge, a pool table and a garden with a barbecue area. He's even building a dance studio! It's popular with volunteers thanks to its welcoming, communal spirit. Rooms are private with shared bathroom (it's a

QUITO

house, after all). Contact Alberto through El Arupo (p93).

The following apartments also offer daily rates.

Amaranta Apart Hotel (Map pp80-1; ☎ 254 3619; www.aparthotelamaranta.com; Leonidas Plaza Gutiérrez N20-32; s/d $50/55, per month $1200/1500; 🖳) The Amaranta sports mini-apartments with dated decor, but kitchens are stocked with all the right utensils. Breakfast is included.

Hotel San Francisco de Quito (Map p74; ☎ 228 7758; hsfquito@andinanet.net; Sucre 217; s/d/tr $18/25/45) This charming old-timer has a few modern apartments over its hotel in the old town. See p92.

If you'd like to stay in a local home, stop by the SAE for their long list of families interested in hosting travelers (see p72). If you are taking Spanish courses, ask at your school. Prices average between $5 and $15 per person per day, and sometimes include meals and laundry service. English is not always spoken.

EATING

As a popular tourist destination and the nation's capital, Quito is laden with international restaurants featuring countless cuisines in every price range. But the real treat here is sampling the many varieties of Ecuadorian cuisine – from landmark mom-and-pop places cooking up a single specialty, to gourmet restaurants offering nouveau Ecuadorian fare in sumptuous colonial dining rooms. It's all food that you won't find anywhere else in the world.

Many restaurants close on Sunday. For more on Ecuadorian cuisine, see p61.

Old Town   Map p74

The historical center is where you'll find Quito's most traditional eateries, places which, unlike in the Mariscal Sucre, have been honing family recipes for generations.

Cafetería Fabiolita (El Buen Sanduche; ☎ 228 4268; Espejo 0e4-17; sandwiches $1, seco de chivo $2.50; ✆ 9am-6pm) For more than 40 years Fabiola Flores and her daughter Margarita have been serving up the city's favorite *secos de chivo* (goat stew), one of Ecuador's most traditional dishes. This immaculate little shop beneath the cathedral is still the most authentic place to try it (9am to 11am only). Its famous *sanduches de pernil* (ham sandwiches) even humble city politicians.

La Colmena (☎ 228 4823; Benalcázar 619; lunch $2.35; ✆ 9am-7:30pm, to 5pm Sun) For 50 years, the Vaca Meza family has been serving one of Ecuador's favorite dishes, *guatita*, a tripe and potato stew in a seasoned, peanut-based sauce. Whether you can stomach tripe or not, it's well worth sampling the original at this old-town landmark.

La Guaragua (☎ 257 2552; Espejo 0e2-40 near Guayaquil; mains $2-6; ✆ 10am-9pm Mon-Thu, 10am-11pm Fri-Sun) The tables are a bit officelike, but the food is excellent at this new café-cum-restaurant with imaginative salads and delicious appetizers such as *tortillas de quinoa* (quinoa patties) and empanadas.

Mercado Central (Pichincha; full meals $1-3; ✆ 8am-4pm, to 3pm Sun) For stall after stall of some of Quito's most traditional (and cheapest) foods, head straight to the Mercado Central, where you'll find everything from *locro de papa* (potato soup with cheese and avocado) and seafood, to *yaguarlocro* (blood sausage soup) and *fritada* (fried pork). Fruits and veggies are available too. Located between Esmeraldas and Manabí.

Corvina Don 'Jimmy' (Mercado Central; Pichincha; ✆ 8am-4pm, to 3pm Sun) Open since 1953, this is the Mercado Central's most famous stall, serving huge portions of corvina (sea bass). Ask for it with rice if you don't want it over a big bowl of ceviche. Everyone from governors to diplomats has eaten here. The Mercado Central is between Esmeraldas and Manabí.

Hasta La Vuelta, Señor (☎ 258 0887; Chile 0e4-22, Palacio Arzobispal, 3rd fl; mains $6-7; ✆ noon-11pm Mon-Sat, to 4pm Sun) Ecuadorian cuisine gets a

---

AUTHOR'S CHOICE

Frutería Monserrate (☎ 258 3408; Espejo 0e2-12; mains $1.50-3; ✆ 8am-8pm) If there's one restaurant in the old town that you don't want to miss, this is it. It's best known for the giant bowls of tropical fruits smothered in raspberry topping and whipped cream, but it also serves delicious soups, sandwiches, Ecuadorian snacks and outstanding breakfasts (complete with huge croissants and bottomless cups of fresh-roasted coffee). Popular with locals and hygienically impeccable, it's the antithesis of the swanky new restaurants popping up in the old town and a welcome stop for all travelers.

gourmet twist at this excellent restaurant with balcony seating. Thursday through Sunday it's a great place to try the highland's two most famous soups: *yaguarlocro* and *caldo de patas* (cow hoof soup). For something unique, try the *empanada de viento* (wind empanada).

Café del Fraile (☎ 251 0113; Chile Oe4-22, Pasaje Arzobispal, 2nd fl; drinks $2-4, sandwiches $4.50; 🕙 10am-midnight Mon-Sat, noon-10pm Sun) Old World atmosphere and balcony seating make this café-cum-bar the perfect spot for evening hot chocolate or a stiff cocktail. Sandwiches, snacks and desserts are quite good too.

Tianguez (Plaza San Francisco; mains $3-5; 🕙 10am-6pm Mon & Tue, to midnight Wed-Sat, to 10:30pm Sun) Tucked into the stone arches beneath the Monastery of San Francisco, Tianguez is one of the city's most perfectly situated cafés. Tables on the plaza are perfect for an evening *canelazo* (Ecuador's favorite hot alcoholic drink – aguardiente livened up with a dose of hot, fresh fruit cider) or an afternoon *te de coca* (coca leaf tea).

Mea Culpa (☎ 295 1190; Chile Oe4-22, Palacio Arzobispal; mains $9-20; 🕙 12:30-3:30pm & 7-11pm Mon-Sat, noon-5pm Sun) An over-the-top Mediterranean menu and a strictly enforced dress code make this one of the old town's premier restaurants. The views and romantic setting reportedly dwarf the food, but why not throw on that party dress and find out for yourself?

El Buho (☎ 228 9877; cnr García Moreno & Espejo; mains $4-7; 🕙 11am-7pm Mon-Wed, to 9pm Fri & Sat, noon-5pm Sun) From the folks that brought you Mea Culpa (but wouldn't let you in wearing jeans), comes El Buho, an excellent café inside the Centro Cultural Metropolitano (p75), with delicious sandwiches, burgers, ceviches, salads and more.

Cava Restaurant Urrutía (☎ 258 4173; García Moreno N2-60 near Sucre; mains $7-16; 🕙 12:30-11pm Tue-Sat, to 5pm Sun) Occupying (ironically enough) what was once the dining room where philanthropist María Augusta Urrutía (p76) fed needy children, this is now one of the Centro Histórico's finest restaurants. Some of the dishes, including the squash blossom soup and lemon ice cream, are based upon Urrutía's recipes.

Cucurucho de Santa Clara (☎ 257 2114; cnr Rocafuerte & Benalcázar; mains $6-10; 🕙 12:30-11pm Tue-Sat, 2:30-4pm Sun) Aimed squarely at tourists and affluent quiteños, this gourmet restaurant occupies the historic Santa Clara market building, with elegant tables interspersed beneath adobe brick arches. It's Ecuadorian cuisine at its finest. Go for the Sunday buffet ($18) for a real treat.

La Cueva del Oso (☎ 258 3826; Chile 1046; mains $7-10; 🕙 noon-midnight Mon-Sat, noon-4pm Sun) Loungelike Cueva del Oso serves exquisitely prepared Ecuadorian specialties. The bar, with its low, round booths, makes for a sultry escape from the noise outside.

Cafetería La Zamba Teresa (☎ 258 3826; Chile 1046; almuerzo $3, mains $4-8; 🕙 8am-5:30pm) Attached to La Cueva del Oso, this is the people's chance to sample some of the restaurant's outstanding cooking. The set lunches are a steal, and the *sopa marisco* (seafood soup; $8) is delicious.

Theatrum (☎ 257 1011; www.theatrum.com.ec; Manabí N8-131; 🕙 12:30-4pm & 7:30-11:30pm Mon-Fri, 7:30-11:30pm Sat, 12:30-4pm Sun) On the 2nd floor of the historic Teatro Sucre, creatively concocted and extravagantly presented prix-fixe meals are served to a well-heeled crowd before the show downstairs. It's one of the city's most elegant dining rooms.

Rincón de Cantuña (☎ 228 0830; García Moreno N6-52; mains $7-12; 🕙 7am-10:30pm) Inside the Hotel Patio Andaluz (p91), this upscale restaurant serves both gourmet Spanish and Ecuadorian fare to a foreign clientele. You could skip the full dinner and just try the *sopa de bolas de verde* (peanut and plantainball soup), a wonderful coastal delicacy that's well worth the $5.

Govindas (☎ 295 1083; Esmeraldas 853; almuerzo $1.20-1.60; 🕙 noon-3pm Mon-Sat) Leave it to the Krishnas to whip out a delicious buffet-style vegetarian lunch in the old town.

Las Cuevas de Luís Candela (☎ 228 7710; Benalcázar 713 & Chile; mains $6-10; 🕙 10am-11pm) Built in the vaulted cellar of an old-time building, this atmospheric and windowless Spanish/Ecuadorian restaurant has been around since 1963. Bullfighting greats Manolo and Manolete both ate here, and the toilet (the first of its kind in the old town) was 'inaugurated' by President Arosemena (be sure to take a…look).

Heladería San Agustín (☎ 228 5082; Guayaquil 1053; ice cream $1.20; 🕙 9am-6pm Mon-Fri, 9am-4pm Sat, 10am-3pm Sun) The Alvarez Andino family has been making *helados de paila* (ice cream handmade in big copper bowls) since 1858, making this Quito's oldest ice-cream parlor and an absolute must for ice-cream fans. Made with real fruit juices, they're more akin to sorbets.

Cafetería Modelo (cnr Sucre & García Moreno; ☺ 8am-8pm) Opened in 1950, Modelo is one of the city's oldest cafés, and a great spot to try traditional snacks such as *empanadas de verde* (plantain empanadas filled with cheese), *quimbolitos* (a sweet cake steamed in a leaf), tamales (cornmeal stuffed with meat and steamed in a banana leaf) and *humitas* (similar to Mexican tamales).

El Cafeto (www.elcafeto.com; Chile 930 & Flores, Convento de San Agustín; coffee $0.75-2; ☺ 10am-6pm Mon-Sat) This outstanding Ecuadorian-owned coffee shop serves coffee made from 100% organic Ecuadorian beans. The espresso is likely the best in town.

El Kukurucho del Maní (☎ 258 5494; Rocafuerte Oe5-02 at García Moreno; prices $0.25-0.50; ☺ 7am-7pm Mon-Sat, 8am-6pm Sun) C'mon, where else do they cook up kilos of sugary nuts, corn kernels and *haba* (peeled fava) beans in a copper kettle big enough to cook a pig in? These are the best of the candied peanuts you see sold everywhere.

For those pinching pennies, you'll find good family-style food and cheap *almuerzos* (set lunches) at:

Café Quiteño Libre (☎ 228 8403; Sucre Oe3-17; almuerzos $2, mains $2-3; ☺ 7am-7pm Mon-Sat) In the brick-wall cellar of the Hotel San Francisco de Quito.

La Posada Colonial (☎ 228-0282; García Moreno 1160 near Mejía; almuerzos $2, mains $2-3; ☺ 8am-4pm Sun-Thu, to 11pm Fri & Sat) Located inside its namesake hotel.

Nuevo Cordovéz (☎ 295 5200; Guayaquil 774; almuerzos $1.40-1.75, mains $2-3; ☺ 8am-8pm Mon-Sat) Colorful booths and a bullfighting theme.

King Chicken (☎ 295 6655; Bolívar 236; mains $2-4; ☺ 10am-9:30pm Mon-Sat) Good fried chicken, big ice-cream sundaes, dinerlike atmosphere.

New Town

If you're willing to splash out a bit, you can have a lot of fun filling your stomach in the new town. On the flipside, most of the Mariscal has succumbed to foreign tastes, making it hard to find anything resembling a local and reasonably priced restaurant. You can still find loads of family-style places that cater to locals by wandering the streets in the area west of Avenida Amazonas and north of Jorge Washington and along Cordero northwest of Amazonas.

ECUADORIAN

La Cocina Quiteña (Map p84; ☎ 09-710 4047; Vicente Ramon Roca E5-86 at Reina Victoria; mains $1.50-4; ☺ 7am-5pm Mon-Fri, 8am-5pm Sat & Sun) Free popcorn and a local crowd make this as authentic as you can get around the Mariscal. Soups, *menestras* (lentils or beans), ceviche, noodle and rice dishes and seafood are all dirt cheap. There are outdoor tables too.

Mama Clorindas (Map p84; ☎ 254 4362; Reina Victoria 1144; meals $3-7; ☺ 11am-10pm Mon-Sat) This modest, friendly restaurant serves delicious national specialties to a mostly foreign clientele. Prices are reasonable.

Motes de San Juan (Map pp80-1; Nicaragua N14-53 at José Riofrío, San Juan; mote dishes $1.50; ☺ 9:30am-2pm) Businessmen, nurses, cops, laborers, families, you name it – everyone comes to this hole-in-the-wall eatery, high on a hill in San Juan. Why? They all swear it's the best *mote* (hominy, served with fried pork, toasted corn and hot sauce) in town. Fifty years cooking Quito's most traditional dish has to mean something! Take a cab or kill your legs hiking up José Riofrío.

El Chisme (Map p84; ☎ 254 5560; Luís Cordero 1204 near JL Mera; almuerzos $2; ☺ 12:30-4pm Mon-Fri) This friendly, locally owned eatery cooks up cheap Ecuadorian meals, and the owner is hip to the pickiness of foreigners. Great set lunch.

La Choza (Map pp80-1; ☎ 223 0839; Av 12 de Octubre N24-551; mains $4-7; ☺ noon-4pm & 7-10pm Mon-Fri, noon-4pm Sat & Sun) Delicious Ecuadorian food is served in colorful, elegant surroundings. Expect to pay about $15 for a complete meal.

La Canoa (Map p84; ☎ 250 1419; Cordero E4-375 near JL Mera; mains $3-6; ☺ 24hr) This highly regarded restaurant from Guayaquil is your best opportunity to try Ecuadorian delicacies without emptying your wallet: there's *sopa de verde* (plantain soup), *caldo de manguera* (tripe soup that's said to be an aphrodisiac), seafood *bandera* (a mixed seafood plate) and other treats.

El Cucurucho (Map p84; ☎ 254 1941; JL Mera N23-84 near Wilson; ☺ 9:30am-7pm Mon-Sat) This drool-inducing *dulcería* (candy shop) sells more than two dozen types of traditional Ecuadorian sweets.

SEAFOOD

Quito has great seafood places around every corner.

Cevichería Manolo (Map pp80-1; ☎ 256 9254; cnr Diego de Almagro & La Niña; mains $4-6; ⏰ 8am-5pm or 6pm) Join the locals at this excellent and affordable seafood restaurant, with several types of Ecuadorian and Peruvian ceviches on the menu, plus great seafood dishes including *camarones al ajillo* (shrimp in garlic sauce) and *sopa marinera* (seafood soup).

Las Redes (Map p84; ☎ 252 5691; Av Amazonas 845; mains $7-17; ⏰ 10am-10pm Mon-Sat) One of the city's best *cevicherías* (ceviche restaurants), Las Redes boasts a friendly staff and a lovely dining room. Try the *gran ceviche mixto* (mixed ceviche); it's huge and delicious and costs about $12.

El Guambra (pp80-1; ☎ 290 6793; Av 6 de Diciembre at Jorge Washington; mains $1.25-4; ⏰ 7:30am-4:30pm Mon-Sat, 7:30am-3:30pm Sun) It doesn't look like much, but this wee restaurant serves knock-out ceviche and seafood dishes at rock-bottom prices. It's owned by a family from Manabí, the land of what's arguably Ecuador's best food.

Su Cebiche (Map p84; ☎ 252 6380; JL Mera N24-200; mains $4-7; ⏰ 9am-5pm) This slick little lunch-time joint serves excellent coastal specialties. Try the *sopa marinera*, a delicious mixed-seafood soup, or one of seven types of ceviches.

Mare Nostrum (Map p84; ☎ 223 7236, 252 8686; Foch 172 at JL Tamayo; mains $10-17; ⏰ noon-10pm Tue-Sat) In a Gothic, castlelike building complete with knights in armor on the walls and giant wood tables and chairs, Mare Nostrum serves exquisite seafood dishes with both Spanish and Ecuadorian influences.

Cevichería y Marisquería 7 Mares (Map pp80-1; La Niña 525; mains $1-5; ⏰ 7:45am-5:30pm) This is the place to go for cheap *encebollado* (a tasty seafood, onion and yucca soup). Bowls – served cafétería-style – are only $1.30 and make an excellent lunch.

Mediterraneo Cevichería (Map p84; ☎ 261 1214; J Carrión 974 at U Páez; mains $3-5; ⏰ 8am-5pm Mon-Sat) In terms of value, it's hard to beat the *almuerzos* here ($2), considering you get an appetizer, soup, main course, dessert and juice. It's a cute little house too, and popular with lunchtime business folks. Good ceviches.

La Jaiba Mariscos (☎ 254 3887; Av Cristóbal Colón 870) Another excellent upscale restaurant specializing in seafood.

LATIN AMERICAN

La Bodeguita de Cuba (Map pp80-1; ☎ 254 2476; Reina Victoria 1721; mains $3-5; ⏰ noon-4pm & 7-10pm Tue-Fri, noon-midnight Sat & Sun) With its wooden tables and graffiti-covered walls, this is a great place for Cuban food and fun. Cuban musicians perform to a standing-room-only crowd on Thursday nights, when the bar stays open till 2am.

Varadero (Map pp80-1; ☎ 254 2575; Reina Victoria 1721; mains $3-4; ⏰ noon-2am Mon-Sat) Owned by the same folks as La Bodeguita, Varadero serves Cuban sandwiches and light meals and has live music on Wednesday, Friday and Saturday nights.

Chacha (Map p84; cnr JL Mera & Foch; mains $1.50-2; ⏰ noon-11pm Mon-Sat) This cheap Argentine eatery serves pizza, pasta and empanadas at outdoor tables. Readers and travelers continually recommend it.

Red Hot Chili Peppers (Map p84; ☎ 255 7575; Foch E4-314; mains $4-6; ⏰ noon-10:30pm Mon-Sat) Think fajitas – the rest of the menu is good, but doesn't quite measure up to that sizzling plate of chicken or beef. Wash 'em down with the excellent piña coladas and you'll be singing Jimmy Buffet all the way home.

Churrascaría Tropeiro (Map p84; ☎ 254 8012; General Veintimilla 546; all you can eat $12; ⏰ 1-3pm & 6-10pm Mon-Sat, 1-4pm Sun) With 10 types of meat, three types of salad and an all-you-can-eat policy, how can you go wrong?

Zócalo (Map p84; ☎ 223 3929; cnr JL Mera & J Calama; mains $4-6; ⏰ 11am-1am) Zócalo is a popular restaurant-cum-bar with a prime, 2nd-floor location, situated right in the hub of the Mariscal Sucre – hence its popularity. The atmosphere is fun, and the food (snacks, Mexican-style dishes etc) is decent.

Orisha (Map pp80-1; ☎ 252 0738; Diego de Almagro 1212; mains $4-7; ⏰ noon-3pm & 7-10pm Mon-Sat) This is a cozy little Cuban restaurant with Yoruba crafts adorning the walls and excellent food on the menu.

ASIAN

Siam (Map p84; ☎ 223 9404; J Calama E5-10; mains $5-8; ⏰ 12:30-4pm & 6-11pm) Siam cooks up delicious Thai food, and, while the portions are bit small, it's a nice break for those fed up with Ecuadorian food.

Sake (Map pp80-1; ☎ 252 4818; P Rivet N30-166; mains $6-12; ⏰ 12:30-3pm & 6:30-11pm Mon-Sat, 6:30-9pm Sun) This is Quito's premier (and most expensive) sushi restaurant, a trendy, upscale place with outstanding food. Reservations are a must on weekends.

Chifa Mayflower (Map p84; ☎ 254 0510; J Carrión 442; meals $3-6; 11am-11pm) Celebrity chef Martin Yan, believe it or not, called this busy Chinese restaurant the best in town (check out his autographed photo by the door), and whether you agree or not, it's definitely a great deal. Lots of veggie options.

Mágico Oriental (Map p84; ☎ 222 6767; U Páez 243; mains $4-12; 12:30-3:30pm & 6-11pm Mon-Fri, 12:30-10:30pm Sat, till 9pm Sun) Elegant, classy and authentic, Mágico Oriental serves delicious Chinese dishes.

Pekin (Map pp80-1; ☎ 223 5273; Whymper N28-42; mains $4.50-8; noon-3pm & 7-10:30pm Mon-Sat, noon-8:30pm Sun) Pekin has a slightly conservative air, but the owners are friendly and the food is good.

Casa China (Map pp80-1; ☎ 252 2115; Cordero E9-242; mains average $4; 11am-3pm & 6:30-10:30pm) Good, reasonably priced Chinese food. The chicken noodle soup is a tasty, grease-free treat.

ITALIAN

Le Arcate (Map p84; ☎ 223 7659; General Baquedano 358; mains $4-6; 12:30-3pm & 6-11pm Mon-Sat, noon-4pm Sun) This Mariscal favorite bakes more than 50 kinds of pizza (likely the best around) in a wood-fired oven and serves reasonably priced lasagna, steak and seafood. Great place.

La Briciola (Map pp80-1; ☎ 254 7138; Toledo 1255; mains $6-10; 12:30-3pm & 7:30-11pm Mon-Sat) This longtime favorite has an outstanding and varied menu. The portions are large and the wine is fairly priced. Make a reservation if you hope to eat before 9:30pm.

Trattoria Sole e Luna (Map pp80-1; ☎ 223 5865; Whymper N31-29 & Coruña; mains $6-8; noon-4pm & 7-10:30pm Mon-Sat) This is an excellent restaurant with a delightful nouveau-Italian atmosphere and friendly service. It's great for lunch, and the risotto is tops.

Dimmi, di si (Map p84; ☎ 252 0466; J Carrión E4-148; mains $2.50; 9am-6pm Mon-Fri,) The owner-chef here cooks up delicious fresh pasta, pizza and other traditional Italian fare. A slice of pizza goes for $1.50. Phone orders weekends only

MIDDLE EASTERN

Quito has a sizable Middle Eastern community and the restaurants to keep them – and visiting *shawarma* (meat sliced off the spit and served in pita bread) aficionados – well fed.

Aladdin's (Map p84; ☎ 222 9435; cnr Diego de Almagro & Baquerizo Moreno; mains $2-4; 10:30am-11pm, to 1am Fri & Sat) This extremely popular souk-themed restaurant serves great falafel and *shawarma* sandwiches, and main courses. Giant hookahs attract the hipsters.

Hassan's Cafe (Map p84; ☎ 223 2564; Reina Victoria near Colón; mains $2-6; 9:30am-8pm Mon-Sat) Lebanese food – *shawarmas,* hummus, kebabs, stuffed eggplant, veggie plates – is good, fresh and cheap at this 10-table restaurant.

STEAKHOUSES & GRILLS

Adam's Rib (Map p84; ☎ 256 3196; J Calama 329; mains $4-6; noon-10:30pm Mon-Fri, noon-9pm Sun) Adam's has been grilling up US-style ribs and barbecued meats since 1986. And with a bar, pool table and satellite TV, it's no wonder there's a faithful stream of expats.

Shorton Grill (Map p84; ☎ 252 3645; J Calama E7-73; mains $8-22; noon-11pm) This excellent, conveniently located grill serves large juicy portions of meat, seafood and poultry *a la brasa* (grilled).

Texas Ranch (Map p84; ☎ 290 6199; JL Mera 1140; mains $4-7; 1pm-midnight) Texas Ranch serves up whopping burgers (that's the Texas part) and Argentine-style grilled meats.

VEGETARIAN

Many of the cafés listed later – especially Grain de Café, Kallari and El Cafecito – offer a variety of vegetarian dishes as well.

El Maple (☎ 290 0000; cnr Foch & Diego del Almagro; mains $3-5; noon-9pm) This well-loved restaurant serves excellent organic vegetarian food. The four-course set lunches ($2.80) are a steal, and the juices are tops.

Sakti (☎ 252 0466; J Carrión 641; almuerzos $2, mains $2-3; 8:30am-6:30pm Mon-Fri) This caféteria-style restaurant serves a range of cheap, wholesome soups, veggies, fruit salads, pastas and lasagna to a faithful crowd of lunchtime locals.

Roble Viejo (Cordero near Av Amazonas; almuerzo $1.40; noon-2:30pm Mon-Fri) Good for cheap vegetarian *almuerzos.*

INTERNATIONAL

Quito's luxury hotels all have excellent international restaurants. The Hilton Colón (p95) and the Swissôtel (p95) both have sumptuous Sunday brunches.

La Cocina del Monasterio (Map pp80-1; ☎ 225 6948; Av Eloy Alfaro N33-231; mains $5-8.50; ☾ noon-9:30pm Mon-Sat) Inside a converted little monastery, this charming restaurant serves outstanding Ecuadorian and international dishes at midrange prices. Try the *costillitas Carmelitas* (barbecued 'Carmelite ribs'). Great for a treat.

Fried Bananas (Map p84; ☎ 256 2003; JL Mera N21-251; mains $2.50-4; ☾ noon-9pm Mon-Sat) This cute little place has a varied menu of steak, seafood, trout, chicken, soups and salads, all creatively prepared and fresh as can be.

Boca del Lobo (Map p84; ☎ 252 2828; J Calama 284; mains $5-9; ☾ 5pm-2am Mon-Sat) Beneath the sonic pitter-patter of ambient grooves, smartly dressed diners order delicacies such as rosemary sea bass, salmon *ishpingo* (an Amazonian cinnamon-like spice), stuffed plantain tortillas, *guanábana* (soursop) cocktails, raclette, focaccias, pizzas and excellent desserts.

Rincón de Francia (Map p84; ☎ 222 5053; Vicente Ramón Roca 779; meals from $20) This is one of the best-known French restaurants in town and has been for decades. A full meal will cost at least $20 and twice that if you dip into the wine.

La Paella Valenciana (Map pp80-1; ☎ 222 8681; Diego de Almagro 1727; mains $10-24; ☾ noon-3pm & 7-9:30pm Mon-Sat, noon-3pm Sun) Serves knockout Spanish seafood plates, including excellent paella. Portions are gigantic.

CAFÉS

Café Amazonas (Map p84; cnr Av Amazonas & Vicente Ramón Roca; coffee $0.60, mains $2-4; ☾ 7am-10pm) An Amazonas classic with outdoor tables, this is a favorite haunt for everyone from *petroleros* (oil industry folks) to travelers.

Café Mosaico (Map p74; ☎ 254 2871; Manuel Samaniego N8-95 near Antepara, Itchimbia; mains $8.50-11, drinks $2.50-5; ☾ 11am-10:30pm, from 4pm Tue) Sure the drinks are overpriced, but you won't find a balcony view like this anywhere else. This is a must for an evening cocktail or a mid-morning coffee (when you'll likely have the balcony, the stunning views and your banana pancakes all to yourself).

Kallari (Map p84; ☎ 223 6009; www.kallari.com; Wilson E4-266 at JL Mera; breakfasts $2, lunches $2.50; ☾ 9am-5pm Mon-Fri, 9am-1pm Sun) Besides the fact that Kallari's chocolate bars induce orgasms on the spot, this Quichua coop serves up some delicious, healthy break-

fasts and lunches as well. For lunch, try the guacamole sandwich and the grilled plantain with cheese.

Café Galletti (Map p84; ☎ 252 7361; J Carrión E5-40 near JL Mera; coffee drinks $0.85-2; ☾ 9am-8pm Mon-Fri) Nuclear-physicist-turned-coffee-roaster might seem like a recipe for disaster. Not here. This Ecuadorian-/US-owned café has excellent organic espresso drinks.

chiQuito (Map pp80-1; ☎ 323 7630; Camino de Orellana 630; ☾ 11am-8pm Wed-Sun) This intimate and artsy café makes for a perfect lunch or coffee break during a leisurely walk down to Guápulo.

Coffee Tree (Map p84; ☎ 252 6957; cnr Reina Victoria & Foch; mains $2-3; ☾ 24hr) This place is fast becoming a Mariscal hit, thanks to its house-roasted coffee, good food and outdoor tables.

Magic Bean (Map p84; ☎ 256 6181; Foch E5-08; mains $4-7; ☾ 7am-10pm) Long the epicenter of the Mariscal, the Magic Bean serves a variety of well-prepared breakfasts, lunches, juices and snacks for the ever-present crowd of hungry travelers.

El Español (Map p84; ☎ 255 3995; cnr JL Mera & Wilson; ☾ 8am-9pm Mon-Fri, 8:30am-6pm Sat & Sun) This Spanish delicatessen is a good place to stock up for picnics.

Café Sutra (Map p84; ☎ 250 9106; J Calama 380; snacks $2-6; ☾ noon-3am Mon-Sat) With its dim lighting, mellow music and cool crowd, Café Sutra is a great place for a snack and a beer before a night out.

El Cafecito (Map p84; ☎ 234 862; Cordero 1124; mains $2-4; ☾ 8am-11pm) Serves inexpensive, mainly vegetarian meals and snacks all day long. Great breakfasts.

Grain de Café (Map p84; ☎ 256 5975; General Baquedano 332; mains $4-7; ☾ 9am-11pm Mon-Fri) Kick back over coffee or order a full meal. This is a laid-back place in the best sense, and there are lots of vegetarian options. Hamburgers too.

GROCERIES

Mercado Santa Clara (Map pp80-1; cnr Dávalos & Versalles; ☾ 8am-5pm) This is the main produce market in the new town. Besides an outstanding produce selection, there are cheap food stalls.

Supermercado Santa María (Map pp80-1; cnr Dávalos & Versalles; ☾ 8:30am-8pm Mon-Sat, 9am-6pm Sun) Huge supermarket conveniently across from Mercado Santa Clara.

Supermaxi (Map pp80-1; cnr La Niña & Y Pinzón; daily) Biggest and best supermarket near the Mariscal.

Mercado La Floresta (Map pp80-1; Galavis at Andalucía; 8am-5pm Fri) This small but lovely fruit and vegetable street market takes place every Friday in its namesake neighborhood.

ENTERTAINMENT

Most of the *farra* (nightlife) in Quito is concentrated in and around the Mariscal, where the line between 'bar' and 'dance club' is blurry indeed. Bars in the Mariscal, for better or worse, are generally raucous and notorious for 'gringo hunting,' when locals of both sexes flirt it up with the tourists (which can be annoying or enjoyable, depending on your state of mind). Dancing on the bar tops is generally de rigueur. Bars with dancing often charge admission, which usually includes a drink. Remember to always take a cab home if you're out in the Mariscal at night (see p72).

For something far more relaxed, sans the pickup scene, head to La Floresta or Guápulo, where drinking is a more cerebral affair.

For movie listings and other events, check the local newspapers *El Comercio* and *Hoy*, or pick up a copy of *Quito Cultura*, a monthly cultural mag available free from the tourist offices. Online, check out www.quehacer quito.com (in Spanish).

Bars

El Pobre Diablo (Map pp80-1; 223 5194; Isabel La Católica E12-06; 12:30pm-2am Mon-Fri, 7pm-2am Sat) El Pobre Diablo makes for an excellent escape from the Mariscal scene. It's a friendly, laid-back place with live jazz Wednesday and Thursday nights, wood tables, a great vibe and a solid cocktail menu. There's a restaurant too, serving delectable dishes such as pork chop in a cilantro sauce, vegetable lasagna and shrimp in coconut sauce.

La Reina Victoria (Map p84; 222 3369; Reina Victoria 530; 5pm-midnight Mon-Sat) If there's one watering hole that's forever and faithfully nurtured the thirsty souls of foreign travelers (since 1982, anyway), it's the Reina Victoria. With a fireplace, dartboard, bumper pool, great food and excellent pub ambience, it's hard to beat this home away from home.

Naranjilla Mecánica (Map pp80-1; JL Tamayo 549 near General Veintimilla; 5pm-12:30am, from 7pm Sat)

One room is covered entirely in red fur and outside, grass abuts the carpet beneath a VIP hammock. Cool art adorns the walls and an ultra hip crowd sips blood-red cocktails to house and techno. In other words, it doesn't get much hipper than this.

Mirador de Guápulo (Map pp80-1; 256 0364; Rafael León Larrea & Pasaje Stübel; mains $4-6; 4pm-12:30am) This cozy café-cum-bar sits on the cliffside overlooking Guápulo. The views are unbeatable, and the snacks – mostly Ecuadorian specialties – are tasty. There's live music Wednesday through Saturday nights, when there is a cover charge of $4.50.

Ta Güeno (Map pp80-1; Camino de Orellana N27-492) A bohemian air, friendly vibe, a wonderful candle-lit terrace overlooking Guápulo and big pitchers of delicious *canelazo* make this the most popular bar in Guápulo.

Ananké (Map pp80-1; Camino de Orellana 781; 6pm-late) This cozy little bar-cum-pizzeria sits perched on the hillside in Guápulo. It has a wee terrace (complete with fireplace) and several good nooks for making out.

No Bar (Map p84; J Calama 380 & JL Mera; admission $3-5; 6pm-3am) This Mariscal institution keeps 'em coming with its four small, dark dance-floors, a chaotic bar (always with dancing on top) and plenty of beer-bonging and spraying of Pilsener. It's mobbed on weekends. Expect high-energy dance pop and lots of pick-up lines.

Mumbai (Map pp80-1; Isabel La Católica N24-685) Quito's only martini bar, Mumbai draws a hip, moneyed crowd with its stylish, modern atmosphere.

On Reina Victoria, around Santa María and Pinta, there are several wildly popular bars with packed weekend dance-floors. The area is flooded with bar-hoppers, taxis and hotdog vendors, but it's a dangerous area after dark, so don't wander far from the club entrances. Inside you're fine. Two favorites near here are **Tijuana** (Map pp80-1; cnr Reina Victoria & Santa María; admission $3-4) and **Papillon** (Map p84; cnr Santa María & Diego de Almagro; admission $3-4), which both blast out a broad mix of international dance music.

English pubs have long been the rave in Quito, and most serve food. The most popular include the following:

Patatu's Bar (Map p84; 222 9302; Wilson E4-229; 11:30am-3am Mon-Fri, 8pm-3am Sat) Great fun.

Turtle's Head (Map pp80-1; 256 5544; La Niña 626) Wickedly raucous; excellent beer and food.

King's Cross (Map pp80-1; ☎ 252 3597; Reina Victoria 1781; ✆ 5:30pm-late Mon-Fri, 6:30pm-late Sat)
Ghoz Bar (Map pp80-1; La Niña 425)

Nightclubs
Hitting the dance floor of one of Quito's *salsotecas* is a must. If you don't know how to salsa, try a few classes first (see p88).

Mayo 68 (Map p84; L García 662) This popular salsa club is smaller (and some say, for that reason, better) than Seseribó.

Live Music
Peñas are usually bars that have traditional *música folklórica* (folk music) shows.

Vox Populi (Map p74; ☎ 228 2263; Espejo Oe2-12 at Flores; ✆ 4-11pm Tue, Wed & Sun, 4pm-2am Thu-Sat) French-owned Vox Populi is the hippest, slickest bar in the Centro Histórico (hell, it's one of the hippest in the city), featuring excellent live music ranging from Cuban *son* (a slow, rhythmic dance) to Latin jazz. The jams begin at 10pm Thursday through Saturday.

Ñucanchi Peña (Map p78; ☎ 254 0967; Universitaria 496; admission $5; ✆ 8pm-2am or 3am Thu-Sat) Popular with students and families, this *peña* is one of the best places to catch a *folklórica* show.

La Casa de la Peña (Map p74; ☎ 228 4179, 243 9073; García Moreno N11-13; admission $3-5; ✆ 7pm-midnight Thu, 7pm-2am Fri & Sat) The setting alone, inside an ancient building in the old town, makes this intimate *peña* a great place to hear Ecuadorian folk music.

Café Libro (Map pp80-1; ☎ 252 6754; J Carrión 243; admission $3-5; ✆ 5pm-1am Mon-Fri, from 6pm Sat) Live music, contemporary dance, tango, jazz and other performances draw an artsy and intellectual crowd to this cozy, bohemian venue. Excellent.

AUTHOR'S CHOICE

Seseribó (Map pp80-1; ☎ 256 3598; General Veintimilla & Av 12 de Octubre, Edificio Girón; admission $7; ✆ 9pm-1am Thu-Sat) Bust out your dancin' shoes and hang on to that rhythm-stick for a night at Seseribó, Quito's best *salsoteca*. The music is tops, the atmosphere is superb, and the dancing is outta sight. The devoted *salseros* (salsa dancers) turn up on Thursdays, which makes it a great night to go. Admission includes drinks.

La Bodeguita de Cuba (Map pp80-1; Reina Victoria 172) This Cuban restaurant features excellent live Cuban music on Thursday nights from about 9pm to 2am. Get there early.

Café Toledo (Map pp80-1; ☎ 255 8086; Toledo 720 at Lérida; admission $5) Small, mellow place for live music.

Casa Babylon (Map pp80-1; cnr Madrid & Toledo; admission $3-5) Casa Babylon is a totally non-touristy place to catch a rock or punk show, usually by local bands.

Theater & Dance
Teatro Sucre (Map p74; ☎ 228 2136, 228 2337; www.teatrosucre.com in Spanish; Manabí N8-131; admission $3-70; ticket office ✆ 10am-1pm & 2-6pm) Recently restored and now standing gloriously over the Plaza del Teatro, this is the city's most historical theater. Performances range from jazz and classical music to ballet, modern dance and opera.

Teatro Bolívar (Map p74; ☎ 258 2486/7; www.teatrobolivar.org; Espejo) Likely the city's most illustrious theater and definitely one of its most important, the Bolívar is currently undergoing restoration work after a fire nearly burnt it to the ground. Performances and tours – everything from theatrical works to international tango-electronica gigs – are still given. It's situated between Flores and Guayaquil.

Humanizarte (Map p84; ☎ 222 6116; www.humanizarte.com; Leonidas Plaza Gutiérrez N24-226; ✆ 5:30pm Wed) This excellent theater and dance group presents Andean dance performances. You can either call or check the website for other performances.

Ballet Folklórico Nacional Jacchigua (Map pp80-1; ☎ 295 2025; www.jacchigua.com in Spanish; cnr Av Patria & Av 12 de Octubre; admission $25) This folkloric ballet is as touristy as it is spectacular. It is presented daily at the Teatro Demetrio Agilera at the Casa de la Cultura Ecuatoriana (p82). It's quite a show. Contact any travel agency or upper-end hotel for tickets or buy them at the door or online.

Teatro Prometeo (Map pp80-1; ☎ 222 6116; Av 6 de Diciembre 794) Affiliated with the Casa de La Cultura Ecuatoriana, this inexpensive venue often has modern-dance performances and other shows that non-Spanish speakers can enjoy.

Patio de Comedías (Map p84; ☎ 256 1902; 18 de Septiembre 457) Presents plays and performances Thursday through Sunday nights, usually at 8pm.

QUITO

Cinemas

Most of the cinemas in Quito show popular English-language films with Spanish subtitles, while cheaper places resort to kung-fu and porn.

Ocho y Medio (Map pp80-1; ☎ 290 4720/21/22; www.ochoymedio.net in Spanish; Valladolid N24-353 & Vizcaya; ☺ café 11am-10:30pm) This Floresta film house shows great art films (often in English) and has occasional dance, theater and live music. There's a small café attached.

The most recent Hollywood blockbusters are shown at **Cinemark** (Map p78; ☎ 226 0301; www.cinemark.com.ec in Spanish; Naciones Unidas & Av América; admission $4) and **Multicines** (Map p78; ☎ 225 9677; www.multicines.com.ec in Spanish; Centro Comercial Iñaquito; admission $4), which are both multiscreen, state-of-the-art cinemas.

SHOPPING
Arts & Crafts

There are loads of excellent crafts stores in the new town along and near Avenida Amazonas. If buying from street stalls, you should bargain. In the fancier stores, prices are normally fixed, although bargaining is not out of the question. Note that souvenirs are a little cheaper outside Quito if you have the time and inclination to search them out.

The following is a list of stores that sell a wide selection of goods at a variety of prices. There are many other stores in the area.

La Bodega (Map p84; ☎ 222 5844; JL Mera N22-24) In business for 30 odd years, La Bodega stocks a wide and wonderful range of high-quality crafts, both old and new.

Ag (Map p84; ☎ 255 0276; JL Mera N22-24) Ag's selection of rare, handmade silver jewelry from throughout South America is outstanding. There are also antiques, including rarities such as *vaca loca* (crazy cow) costumes, perfect for your next indigenous party.

Mercado Artesanal La Mariscal (cnr JL Mera & Jorge Washington) Half a city block is filled with crafts stalls (and the usual hippie bracelets, ponchos and even a couple of body piercing stalls), with good prices and mixed quality. It's great for souvenirs.

Folklore Olga Fisch (Map pp80-1; new town ☎ 254 1315; Av Cristóbal Colón 260; old town Map p74; García Moreno N6-52, Hotel Patio Andaluz) The store of legendary designer Olga Fisch (who died in 1991), this is the place to go for the very best and the most expensive crafts in town. Fisch was a Hungarian artist who immigrated to Ecuador in 1939 and worked with indigenous artists melding traditional crafts with fine art. Her unique designs are stunning.

Productos Andinos (Map p84; ☎ 222 4565; Urbina 111) This two-floor artisans' cooperative is crammed with reasonably priced crafts.

Galería Latina (Map p84; ☎ 254 0380; JL Mera N23-69) Galería Latina sells superb quality Andean textiles, jewelry, sweaters and handicrafts all at high prices.

Centro Artesanal (Map p84; ☎ 254 8235; JL Mera E5-11) This excellent shop is known for canvases painted by local Indian artists.

Tianguez (Map p74; Plaza San Francisco; mains $3-5) Attached to the eponymous café, Tianguez is a member of the Fair Trade Organization and sells outstanding crafts from throughout Ecuador.

El Aborigen (Map p84; ☎ 250 8953; Jorge Washington 614) Talk about an arts and crafts supermarket! Huge selection and good prices too.

Centro Artístico Don Bosco (Map pp80-1; ☎ 252 7105; Mariana de Jesús 0e1-92 near 10 de Agosto) This is the retail outlet for a cooperative of woodworkers from throughout the highlands. The cooperative was formed to give people an alternative to immigrating to cities, so it's an excellent cause. It has mostly furniture, but beautiful boxes, frames and wall hangings too.

Clothing

Maqui (Map pp80-1; ☎ 250 3158, 252 3009; maqui@ecnet.ec; Muros N27-193; ☺ 9am-5:30pm Mon-Fri) If you're interested in a finer 'panama' hat than those you see all over the Mariscal, visit the store of Miriam Kelz, who puts the finishing touches on some of Quito's most stylish straw hats.

Tatoo (Map p84; ☎ 280 4333; JL Mera near Wilson) This is Ecuador's top brand of outdoor-wear, and the prices are as high as the quality.

Mythos Shop (☎ 222 6407; Wilson 712 at JL Mera) Pop into Mythos for killer T-shirts by local designer Cholo Machine (www.cholomachine.com in Spanish), plus the quintessential souvenir T-Shirts as well.

Homero Ortega P & Hijos (Map pp80-1; ☎ 252 6715; www.genuinepanamahat.com; Isabel la Católica N24-100) One of Ecuador's biggest sellers of Ecuadorian straw hats (aka panama hats). Selection is conservative but good.

Galleries

Sadly, over the last few years, most of Quito's fine art galleries have closed due to an unfavorable market. There are a few places, however, that still exhibit and sell local work. The most popular place to purchase paintings is **Parque El Ejido Art Fair** (Map pp80-1; Av Patria at Av Amazonas; 9am-dusk Sat & Sun) during the weekend art fair (see p79). The work here consists mostly of generic imitations of established Ecuadorian artists, but it's cheap and colorful. Also pop into La Bodega (opposite), which usually has some excellent art on hand.

Posada de Artes Kingman (Map pp80-1; 222 2610; Diego de Almagro 1550 at Pradera) This small but well-stocked gallery is dedicated to the works of Ecuadorian painter Eduardo Kingman, the teacher and primary influence on better known artist Guayasamín. Prints, cards, T-shirts, etchings and jewelry line the walls and shelves.

Galería Mina Alvarez (Map pp80-1; 252 0347; www.arteminaalvarez.com in Spanish; J Carrión 243) For a peek at some truly outstanding art, drop by the gallery of Mina Alvarez, whose colorful paintings, mostly of Latin American women, will dazzle even the weariest of critics.

MarsuArte (Map pp80-1; main gallery 245 8616; Av 6 de Diciembre 4475 at Portugal; Swissôtel Map pp80-1; 254 1283; Av 12 de Octubre 1820) This exclusive gallery is extremely expensive, but it's one of the few in town where you can get a look at some of the country's most established artists. The branch inside the Swissôtel (p95) is actually better than the main branch.

Pomaire (Map p84; 254 0074; pomaire@uio .satnet.net; Av Amazonas 863) Long-standing art gallery, café and bookstore with monthly exhibits mostly by contemporary Ecuadorian artists.

Taller Alderuti (Map p84; 254 3639; Jorge Washington near Av Amazonas) The art at Alderuti (a member of the Fair Trade Organization) sits somewhere between handicrafts and fine art, but all of it springs from Ecuador's indigenous cultures, both past and present. Occasionally, the store closes for lunch between 1:30pm and 3pm.

Galería Catasse (Map pp80-1; 224 0538; Av 6 de Diciembre at Checoslovaquia) Chilean-born painter, Carlos Tapia Catasse is one of Quito's premier (if not mainstream) contemporary artists. It's worth a visit if you're an art hound.

Galería Beltrán (Map p84; 222 1732; Reina Victoria 326) With more than 30 years in the art business, this art gallery sells paintings by well-known Ecuadorian artists.

Outdoor Supplies

Mono Dedo (La Floresta Map pp80-1; 09-922 6615; www.monodedo.com in Spanish; Lérida E13-37 near Pontevedra; 2-7:30pm Mon-Fri, 9:30am-12:30pm Sat; Rocódromo Queseras del Medio s/n; 11am-7:30pm Mon-Fri, 9:30am-5pm Sat & Sun) Outstanding climbing store with rock and ice gear, clothing, tents, bags and more. The branch at the Rocódromo (p86) has more gear.

The following stores sell and rent camping and mountaineering equipment:

Altar (Map p84; 290 6029; JL Mera 615)
Explorer (Map p84; 255 0911; Reina Victoria 928)
Los Alpes (Map p84; 223 2362; Reina Victoria N23-45)

Shopping Centers

Centros comerciales (shopping malls) are nearly identical to their North American counterparts and sell international brands. Most stores are closed Sunday, but the following malls are open every day (from about 10am to 8:30pm). They all have fast-food restaurants inside.

Centro Comercial El Jardín (Map pp80-1; 298 0300; Av Amazonas & Av de la República)
Centro Comercial Iñaquito (Map p78; CCI; 225 9444; Av Amazonas & Naciones Unidas)
Centro Comercial Quicentro (Map p78; 246 4512; Av 6 de Diciembre & Naciones Unidas)

GETTING THERE & AWAY
Air

Quito's newly remodeled airport, **Aeropuerto Mariscal Sucre** (Map p78; 294 4900; www.quitoairport .com in Spanish; Av Amazonas at Av de la Prensa) serves all international and domestic flights in and out of the capital. It's located about 10km north of downtown. See p107 for bus and taxi information on getting there. For domestic and international flight and airline information, see p400 and p404. The following are Ecuador's principal domestic airlines, with the widest choice provided by TAME:

AeroGal (225 7301, 225 8086/7; Av Amazonas 7797) Near the airport.
Icaro (Map p78; 245 0928, 245 1499; www.icaro .com.ec in Spanish; Palora 124 at Av Amazonas) Across from the airport runway.
TAME (Map p84; 250 9375/6/7/8, 290 9900; Av Amazonas 1354 at Av Cristobal Colón)

Bus

Quito's main bus terminal is the **Cumandá Bus Terminal** (Map p74; Maldonado at Javier Piedra), located just south of Plaza Santo Domingo, in the old town. It can be reached by walking down the steps from Maldonado, or by taking the Trole (see opposite) to the nearby Cumandá stop. After around 6pm you should take a taxi, as this is an unsafe area at night. Don't take the Trole if you're loaded with luggage; it's notorious for pickpockets.

Several dozen bus companies serve the terminal with connections to just about everywhere in the country. On weekends and vacations, purchase your ticket a day or so in advance. The terminal has a post office, an Andinatel office, ATMs, restaurants and small stores.

Approximate fares and travel times are shown in the following table. There are daily departures for each destination and several departures per day to most. There are numerous buses per hour to popular places such as Ambato or Otavalo. There is a $0.20 departure tax from the bus terminal.

Destination	Cost ($)	Duration (hr)
Ambato	2	2½
Atacames	9	7
Bahía de Caráquez	9	8
Baños	3.50	3
Coca	9	9 (via Loreto)
Cuenca	10	10-12
Esmeraldas	9	5-6
Guayaquil	7	8
Huaquillas	10	12
Ibarra	2.50	2½
Lago Agrio	7	7-8
Latacunga	1.50	2
Loja	15	14-15
Machala	9	10
Manta	8	8-9
Otavalo	2	2¼
Portoviejo	9	9
Puerto López	12	12
Puyo	5	5½
Riobamba	4	4
San Lorenzo	6	6½
Santo Domingo	2.50	3
Tena	6	5-6
Tulcán	5	5

For comfortable buses to Guayaquil from the new town, travel with **Panamericana**

(Map p84; ☎ 255 3690, 255 1839; Av Cristóbal Colón & Reina Victoria), or **Transportes Ecuador** (Map p84; ☎ 222 5315; JL Mera N21-44 near Jorge Washington). Panamericana also has long-distance buses to other towns, including Machala, Loja, Cuenca, Manta and Esmeraldas.

A few buses leave from other places for some destinations in the Pichincha province. **Cooperativa Flor de Valle** (☎ 252 7495; Larrea near Ascunción) goes daily to Mindo. See p143 for departure times.

Car

Car rental in Quito, as with elsewhere in Ecuador, is expensive – taxis and buses are much cheaper and more convenient than renting a car. Rental vehicles are useful for visiting some out-of-the-way areas that don't have frequent bus connections (in which case, a more expensive 4WD vehicle is a good idea). See p408 for more car-rental information.

Avis (☎ 244 0270) At the airport.

Budget (www.budget-ec.com in Spanish) Amazonas (☎ 223 7026; cnr Av Amazonas & Av Cristobal Colón); airport (☎ 224 0763, 245 9052; Av Amazonas at Av de la Prensa)

Ecuacar Av Cristóbal Colón (☎ 252 9781, 254 0000; Av Cristóbal Colón 1280 near Av Amazonas); airport (☎ 224 7298; Av Amazonas at Av de la Prensa)

Hertz Swissôtel (☎ 256 9130; Av 12 de Octubre 1820); airport (☎ 225 4257; Av Amazonas at Av de la Prensa)

Localiza (☎ 250 5974, 250 5986; Av 6 de Diciembre 1570 near Wilson)

Contact Ivan Segovia at **Edivanet** (☎ 264 6460, 09-379 1889, 09-824 5152) who will drive you anywhere in the country (provided there are roads) in a van for up to 10 people. The cost is about $60 per day, plus the price of his hotel room. Split with a group, it's quite affordable.

Train

Although most of Ecuador's train system is in shambles, you can still ride the rails if you're determined. A weekend tourist train leaves Quito and heads south for about 3½ hours to the Area Nacional de Recreación El Boliche, adjoining Parque Nacional Cotopaxi. See p149 for more information.

The **Quito train station** (Map p74; ☎ 265 6142; Sincholagua & Vicente Maldonado) is about 2km south of the old town. Purchase tickets in advance at the **train ticket office** (Map p74;

☎ 258 2927; Bolívar 443 at García Moreno; round-trip per person $4.60; ⏱ 8am-4:30pm Mon-Fri). The trains are old-fashioned with primitive bathroom facilities (all part of the fun), and many passengers ride on the roof.

GETTING AROUND
To/From the Airport

The airport is at the north end of Avenida Amazonas, about 10km north of the old town. Many of the northbound buses on Avenida Amazonas and Avenida 10 de Agosto go to the airport. Some have *Aeropuerto* placards, and others say *Quito Norte*. If you're going from the airport into town, you will find bus stops on Avenida 10 de Agosto, about 150m away from the front entrance of the terminal.

A taxi from the new town costs about $4 (more from the old town). From the airport into town, taxi drivers will invariably charge you more if you hail them within the airport driveway. To save a couple of dollars, catch a cab just outside the airport on either side of Avenida Amazonas.

Car

Driving in Quito can be a hectic experience, especially in the old town. Remember, most streets are one-way. Leaving your car (or a rental car) on the street over night is asking to have it stolen. There are private garages throughout town where you can park overnight for around $10; inquire at your hotel for the nearest one.

Public Transportation
BUS

Local buses all cost $0.25; pay as you board. They are safe and convenient, but watch your bags and pockets on crowded buses. There are various bus types, each identified by color. The blue *Bus Tipos* are the most common and allow standing. The red *ejecutivo* buses don't allow standing passengers and are therefore less crowded, but are more infrequent.

Buses have destination placards in their windows (not route numbers), and drivers will usually gladly tell you which bus to take if you flag the wrong one.

TROLE, ECOVÍA & METROBUS

Quito has three electric bus routes – the Trole, the Ecovía and the Metrobus. Each runs north–south along one of Quito's three main thoroughfares. Each line has designated stations and car-free lanes, making them speedy and efficient. As the fastest form of public transport, they're also crowded and notorious for pickpockets. They run about every 10 minutes from 6am to 12:30am (more often in rush hours), and the fare is $0.25.

The Trole runs along Maldonado and Avenida 10 de Agosto. In the old town, southbound trolleys take the west route (along Guayaquil), while northbound trolleys take the east route (along Montúfar and Pichincha).

The Ecovía, runs along Avenida 6 de Diciembre between Río Coca in the north and La Marin in the south.

The newest line is the Metrobus, which runs along Avenida América, from the Universidad Central del Ecuador (northeast of Parque El Ejido) to north of the airport.

Taxi

Cabs are all yellow and have red 'taxi' stickers in the window. Usually there are plenty available, but rush hour, Sundays and rainy days can leave you waiting 10 minutes for an empty cab.

Cabs are legally required to use their *taxímetros* (meters), and most drivers do; many however charge a flat rate of $2 between the old and new towns, about $0.25 to $0.50 more than if the meter was on. Whether the extra quarter is worth haggling over is up to you. When a driver tells you the meter is broken, flag down another cab.

Late at night and on Sundays, drivers will ask for a higher fare, but it should never be more than twice the metered rate.

The minimum fare is $1. Short journeys will start at that and climb to about $4 for a longer trip.

You can also hire a cab for about $8 per hour, which is a great way to see outer city sites. If you bargain hard and don't plan on going very far, you could hire a cab for a day for about $60.

AROUND QUITO

☎ 02

There are numerous excellent daytrips from the capital. Aside from the destinations covered in this section, Otavalo (p116) can easily be visited in a day from Quito. The train ride to El Boliche recreation area in Parque Nacional Cotopaxi makes for a wonderful outing (see p106 and p149), as do the magnificent hot springs of Termas de Papallacta (p231).

Getting There & Away

Destinations in this section can all be reached by public bus in less than two hours. Taxi is also an option if you have between $30 and $60 to spare. Travel agencies in Quito (p72) also offer daytrips to most of the places covered here.

LA MITAD DEL MUNDO

Ecuador's biggest claim to fame (and name) is its location right on the equator. **La Mitad del Mundo** (The Middle of the World; admission $2.50; 9am-6pm Mon-Fri, 9am-7pm Sat & Sun) is the place where Charles-Marie de La Condamine made the measurements in 1736 showing that this was indeed the equatorial line. His expedition's measurements gave rise to the metric system and proved that the world is not perfectly round, but that it bulges at the equator. Despite the touristy nature of the equator monument that now sits here, there is simply no excuse to come this far and not see it. You just have to get into the spirit of things.

Sundays are busy with quiteño families, but, if you don't mind the crowds, they can be great days to visit because of the live music on the outdoor stage between 1pm and 6pm. Listening to a nine-piece salsa band rip up the equatorial line beneath the bright Andean sunshine can be quite an experience.

At the center of La Mitad del Mundo stands a 30m-high stone trapezoidal **monument** topped by a brass globe. It's the centerpiece of the park, which itself is modeled after a colonial village. You can take an elevator to the top of the monument, where there is a lookout.

Also at La Mitad del Mundo is an impressive 1:200 scale model of colonial Quito, housed in the **Museo del Quito en Miniatura** (admission $1.50; 9am-5:30pm). A light show takes you from dawn in the miniature city to late at night. Nearby, the **planetarium** (admission $1.50; 9am-5:30pm) presents a variety of astronomy shows. Of course, there are plenty of gift shops selling postcards and cheap souvenirs.

Calima Tours (239 4796/7) arranges inexpensive hikes ($8 per person) around the crater rim of nearby Pululahua. It's a good price, considering it includes the $5 park entrance fee. It also goes to Rumicucho archaeological site (see opposite).

Outside and a few hundred meters east of La Mitad del Mundo complex is the excellent **Museo Solar Inti Ñan** (239 5122; adult/child under 12 $2/1; 9:30am-5:30pm), supposedly the site of the real equator. Definitely more interesting than the official complex next door, it's a meandering outdoor exhibition, with fascinating exhibits of astronomical geography and explanations of the importance of Ecuador's geographical location. One of the highlights is the 'solar chronometer,' an

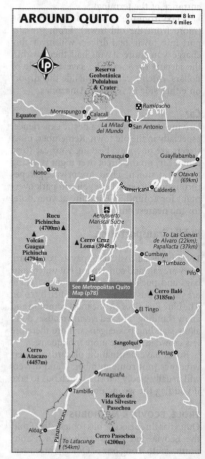

MYTHS FROM THE MIDDLE OF THE EARTH

The idea of standing with one foot in each hemisphere is an intriguing one, and the closer you get to the equator, the more you hear about the equator's mysterious energy. But what is fact and what is fiction?

There's no point in starting softly, so let's debunk the biggest one first. La Mitad del Mundo is not on the equator. But it's close enough. Global Positioning System (GPS) devices show that it's only about 240m off the mark. And no one who sees the photos of you straddling the equator has to know this, right?

Another tough one to swallow is the myth of the flushing toilet. One of the highlights of the Museo Inti Ñan is the demonstration of water draining counterclockwise north of the equator and clockwise 3m away, south of the equator. Researchers claim it's a crock. The Coriolos Force – which causes weather systems to veer right in the northern hemisphere and left in the southern hemisphere – has no effect on small bodies of water like those in a sink or a toilet. Draining water spins the way it does due to plumbing, eddies in the water, the shape of the basin and other factors. (Why winds and weather systems end up rotating the opposite direction of the Coriolis Force is another subject altogether.)

How about some truth: you do weigh less on the equator. This is due to greater centrifugal force on the equator than at the poles. But the difference between here and at the poles is only about 0.3%, not the approximately 1.5% to 2% the scales at the monument imply.

It is true that the spring and autumn equinoxes are the only days when the sun shines directly overhead at the equator. In fact, that's what defines an equinox. But that doesn't mean the days and night are equal in length, as many would have you believe – this happens just before the spring equinox and just after the autumn equinox, and the day depends on where you are on the planet.

If all this myth-debunking has brought on a spell of the doldrums, rest assured – it comes with the territory: the Doldrums was the name given by sailors to the regional lack of winds along the equatorial belt caused by the intense heating of the earth's surface at the equator. The heating causes air to rise, rather than blow, and rising air doesn't sail a ship. But that's all part of the fun on the equator.

unique instrument made in 1865 that shows precise astronomical and conventional time, as well as the month, day and season – all by using the rays of the sun. But the real reason to come, of course, are the water and energy demonstrations. You'll have to decide for yourself if they're hoaxes. Either way, they're fascinating.

Getting There & Away

La Mitad del Mundo is 22km north of Quito near the village of San Antonio. From Quito, take the Metrobus ($0.25) north to the Cotocollao stop. At Cotocollao, transfer to the green Mitad del Mundo bus (they're clearly marked) *without* leaving the platform. The transfer costs an additional $0.15 (pay on the bus), and the entire trip takes one to 1½ hours. Don't make the mistake of getting off at the Centro de Exposiciones Mitad del Mundo, which is about 10 minutes too early. The bus drops you right in front of the entrance.

RUMICUCHO

About 5km north of La Mitad del Mundo, this small, pre-Columbian **archaeological site** (admission $1.50; 9am-3pm Mon-Fri, 8am-4pm Sat & Sun) was built around 500 BC by the Quitu-Cara culture and used principally as a ceremonial site during the equinoxes. The site is officially open during the hours listed above, but you can walk in at anytime. It's not Ecuador's most impressive site, but there are good views of Quito in the distance, and there probably won't be anyone else around. Walk all the way through; the best views are from the side furthest from the entrance.

Taxis to Rumicucho are available in San Antonio (the town near La Mitad del Mundo); the round-trip fare, including waiting time, is between $5 and $8.

RESERVA GEOBOTÁNICA PULULAHUA

This small, 3383-hectare reserve lies about 4km northwest of La Mitad del Mundo. The most interesting part of the reserve is the

QUITO

volcanic crater of the extinct Pululahua. This was apparently formed in ancient times, when the cone of the volcano collapsed, leaving a huge crater some 400m deep and 5km across. The crater's flat and fertile bottom is used for agriculture. Within the crater there are two small cones – the larger Loma Pondoña (2975m) and the smaller Loma El Chivo.

The crater is open to the west side, through which moisture-laden winds from the Pacific Ocean blow dramatically. It is sometimes difficult to see the crater because of the swirling clouds and mist. The moist winds, combined with the crater's steep walls, create a variety of microclimates, and the vegetation on the fertile volcanic slopes is both rampant and diverse. Because the walls are much too steep to farm, the vegetation grows undisturbed and protected. There are many flowers and a variety of bird species.

The crater can be entered on foot by a steep trail from the **Mirador de Ventanillas** viewpoint on its southeast side (easily reached by bus from La Mitad del Mundo). The steep trail is the best way to see the birds and plants, because most of the flat bottom is farmed. There is also an unpaved road on the southwest side via Moraspungo.

In the colorful village of Calacalí, the (much smaller) **original equatorial monument** can be seen; it was moved there after being replaced by the enlarged replica now at La Mitad del Mundo.

Information
The official entrance fee for the reserve is $5 which you must pay before you hike down into the crater or as you enter by car via Moraspungo; there are no charges for viewing from the Ventanillas viewpoint.

See p108 for information on inexpensive tours from there.

Sleeping & Eating
Near Moraspungo are some cabins in the upper-budget price range. **El Crater Restaurant** (☎ 243 9254; ☼ Sat & Sun), near the Ventanillas viewpoint, is perched on the crater's edge, serves good food and has superb views.

Getting There & Away
From La Mitad del Mundo, a paved road continues to the village of Calacalí, about 7.5km away. There are occasional buses

from San Antonio to Calacalí, particularly on weekends. About 4km beyond La Mitad del Mundo on the road to Calacalí is the first paved road to the right. Ask the driver to drop you off there. About 1km along this road, there is a small parking area at the viewpoint.

Alternatively, continue on the road to Calacalí for 3km, which brings you to a sign for Moraspungo to the right. From the turnoff, it's 3km to Moraspungo and about 12km more into the crater. You pay the entry fee of $5 per person at Moraspungo.

CALDERÓN
This village is about 10km northeast of Quito on the Panamericana (not the road to La Mitad del Mundo). Calderón is a famous center of unique Ecuadorian folk art: the people make bread-dough decorations, ranging from small statuettes to colorful Christmas tree ornaments such as stars, parrots, Santas, tortoises, candles and tropical fish. The ornaments make practical gifts as they are small, unusual and cheap (buy a handful for $2). These decorative figures are inedible – preservatives are added so that they'll last many years. There are many stores selling the crafts on the main street.

From Quito, take an *interparroquial* bus from Plaza La Marín in the old town, or the intersection of Avenida Cristóbal Colón and Avenida América in the new town.

GUAYLLABAMBA & AROUND
If you follow the Panamericana another 15km beyond Calderón you will hit **Guayllabamba**, a small town set in a fertile river valley of the same name that is famous for its produce. Try to stop off at the roadside stands selling enormous avocados and bumpy green *chirimoya*, a fruit whose creamy center is slightly tart and pure ecstasy. About 3km before you reach Guayllabamba, you'll pass the **Quito Zoo** (☎ 236 8900, 236 8898; admission $3; ☼ 9am-5pm Tue-Sun). There are a few African and Asian species but the highlight is the Ecuadorian animals including the rare Andean spectacled bear and Galápagos turtles. Buses from Quito's Plaza Italia to Guayllabamba cost $0.55.

Some 3km beyond Guayllabamba, the road forks, and both routes end at Cayambe (p115). About 10km along the right fork, you pass a turnoff that leads back to Quito via **El Quinche**, whose impressive church and Virgin of El Quinche draws crowds from Quito during its November festival. The road passes through countryside and tiny hamlets to the town of **Pifo**. The road will eventually lead you back to Quito via the town of **Tumbaco**.

SANGOLQUÍ

Sangolquí's bustling Sunday-morning market is Quito's nearest indigenous market. The market actually runs all week (though to a much smaller extent), with the second-biggest day on Thursday. Sundays are the best day to visit. Local buses head here from Plaza La Marín in Quito's old town. Sangolquí is about 20km southeast of Quito's old town.

Situated 2.5km southwest of Sangolquí on the road to Amaguaña, **Hostería La Carriona** (☎ 233 1974, 233 2004; www.lacarriona.com; s/d $85/98;) is a 200-year-old colonial hacienda that is a delightful place to stay. The old architecture is fronted by a cobbled courtyard and is surrounded by flower-filled gardens. It also has a pool, sauna, steam bath, Jacuzzi, games area and a large restaurant. The 30 units vary distinctly in character, from the cozy rural rooms to lavish suites. It is a 30-minute drive from Quito.

REFUGIO DE VIDA SILVESTRE PASOCHOA

This small but beautiful **wildlife reserve** (admission $7; dawn-dusk) stands on the northern flanks of the extinct Pasochoa volcano, at elevations between 2900m and 4200m. It has one of the central valley's last remaining stands of humid Andean forest, with more than 100 species of birds. The luxuriant forest contains a wide range of highland trees and shrubs, including the Podocarpaceae, the Ecuadorian Andes' only native conifer (the pines seen elsewhere are introduced). Orchids, bromeliads, ferns, lichens and other epiphytic plants also contribute to the beauty.

There are several trails, from easy half-hour loops to fairly strenuous all-day hikes. The shorter trails are self-guided; guides are available for the longer walks. One trail, which takes about eight hours, leads out of the reserve and to the summit of Pasochoa (4200m).

The park ranger will give you a small trail map. **Fundación Natura** (☎ 250 3385/6/7, 250 3394, 250 3202/3; Av República 481 & Diego de Almagro; 9am-1pm & 2-5pm Mon-Fri) in Quito has trail maps and information and can make overnight reservations.

Sleeping & Eating

Overnight **camping** (per person $3) is permitted in designated areas. There are latrines, picnic areas, barbecue grills and water. There is also a simple **shelter** (dm $5) with 20 bunk beds, hot showers and kitchen facilities; bring your own sleeping bag. On weekends, when the place is usually crowded with locals, a small restaurant is open; otherwise, bring your own food.

Getting There & Away

This is the tricky part. The reserve lies approximately 30km south of Quito. Buses leave from Plaza La Marín in Quito's old town about twice an hour for the village of Amaguaña ($1, one hour). Ask the driver to let you off near Parque El Ejido. From the church nearby, there is a signed cobblestone road to the reserve, which is about 7km away. Walking is the only option. Alternatively, you can go all the way into Amaguaña (about 1km beyond El Ejido) and hire a truck to the reserve's entrance and information center for about $10 (the truck can take several people).

VOLCÁN PICHINCHA

Quito's closest volcano is Pichincha, looming over the western side of the city. The volcano has two main summits – the closer, dormant **Rucu Pichincha** (4680m) and the higher **Guagua Pichincha** (4794m), which is currently very active and is monitored by volcanologists. A major eruption in 1660 covered Quito in 40cm of ash; there were three minor eruptions in the 19th century. A few puffs of smoke occurred in 1981, but in 1999 the volcano rumbled into serious action, coughing up an 18km-high mushroom cloud and blanketing the city in ash.

Climbing either of the summits is strenuous but technically straightforward, and no special equipment is required. Rucu Pichincha is now easily climbed from the top of the telefériQo (see p79).

Climbing the smoking Guagua Pichincha is a longer trip. It is accessible from the village of Lloa, located southeast of Quito. From the village, it's about eight hours by foot to the **refugio** (hikers refuge; dm $5). It is then a further short but strenuous hike from the *refugio* to the summit. Reaching the summit will take you two days if you walk from Lloa. There are numerous agencies in Quito (Safari Tours is a good one, p90) that offer this as a daytrip from town.

Dangers & Annoyances

Before the telefériQo was built, Rucu Pichincha was plagued with crime. At the close of this edition, the trail from Cruz Loma (at the top of the telefériQo) to Rucu Pichincha was safe, but consider checking with SAE (p72) to see if it's remained so. It likely has.

As for Guagua Pichincha, stay up to date on the volcano's activity either by dropping into SAE or checking the website of the **Instituo Geofísico** (www.igepn.edu.ec).

Northern Highlands

The steep green hills, dust-blown villages, busy cities and flower plantations of the north are a stone's throw from the capital. Strong indigenous cultures, Afro-Ecuadorian communities, colonial descendants and mestizos all inhabit this highland region. The famous Otavalo market, with its cacophony of color, dates back to pre-Inca days. While many foreign visitors flock north for the Otavalo market, the humbler byways of this region offer much more.

The massive glaciated Volcán Cayambe, the third-highest peak in the country, stands sentinel at the gateway to the north. Beyond it lies the diverse geography of volcanoes, lakes and hot springs, the harsh and misty beauty of the *páramo* (Andean grasslands), and humid green valleys growing bananas, papaya and coffee.

Between the cities of Otavalo and Ibarra, small indigenous villages continue their traditional weaving, woodcarving and leatherwork, a process perfected through the centuries. Some of these small hamlets make an excellent base for hiking the steep surrounding slopes, Volcán Cotacachi or the revered Taita (father) Imbabura.

Ibarra, a busy town with ashen colonial facades, marks the beginning of the Ibarra–San Lorenzo route to the north coast. Further north you'll find the lowland Afro-Ecuadorian communities of the Chota Valley, famous for their marimba beats and soccer stars.

A wobbly road out of Quito whisks you to the cloud forests of the western Andean slopes. Excellent bird-watching, hiking and tubing entertain visitors through lazy days in Mindo. The Intag region offers a glimpse of a very remote life in lush pointed hills.

HIGHLIGHTS

- Browse and haggle in Otavalo's colorful world-famous **crafts market** (p118)
- Spot some of the hundreds of bird species darting around the western Andean slopes **cloud forest reserves** (p139)
- Spend a rainy weekend sipping whiskey by the fire in a **colonial hacienda** (p124)
- Mountaineer on **Volcán Cayambe**'s (p116) massive chalk-blue glacier
- Stake out the elusive spectacled bear at the **wildlife protection program** (p127) near Santa Rosa

Colonial Hacienda ★

Otavalo ★

Santa Rosa ★
Cloud Forest Reserves ★

Volcán Cayambe ★

- AVERAGE TEMPERATURE IN TULCAN: 10°C (50°F)
- RAINIEST MONTH IN TULCAN: OCTOBER & NOVEMBER

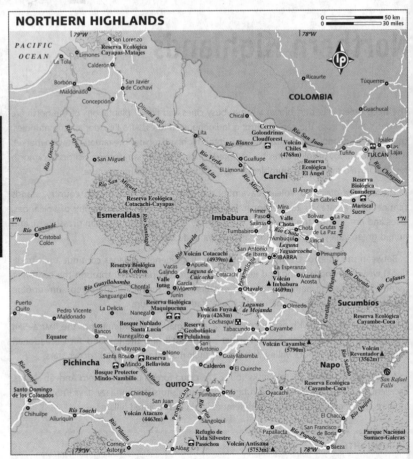

National Parks

At 403,103 hectares **Reserva Ecológica Cayambe-Coca** encompasses an enormous territory leading from alpine tundra to rain forest. Volcáns Reventador and Cayambe sit within its bounds. Also straddling rain forest is 204,420-hectare **Reserva Ecológica Cotacachi-Cayapas**; its most accessible point is Cotacachi. The comparatively tiny 15,715-hectare **Reserva Ecológica El Ángel** is a *páramo* treasure harboring condors and foxes.

COCHASQUÍ ARCHAEOLOGICAL SITE

Arid skins of dirt and dust cover these pillowy remnants of the ancient Cara civilization (see p24). The site is searing and shadeless, but the sweeping views of valleys and ridgetops merit a visit. It takes imagination to understand this place, with so much of it having been whittled away by the elements.

Declared a national archaeological site in 1977, the area has hosted intermittent investigations, but with funding being low, much of the site remains unexcavated. It is thought to have been a military stronghold and religious center before the Inca conquest. Visitors will see 15 low, truncated, grass-covered pyramids (up to 100m long) and about 30 smaller mounds. While the site is interesting, it is not as dramatic as other well-known early Andean archaeological sites. The pyramids were created around AD 900.

Local Spanish-speaking guides provide tours of the **museum** and **site** (free; ⏱ 9am-4pm

Tue-Sun). Guides earn little and would be well-thanked with a tip. There is no public transportation. Some buses (try Transportes Otavalo/Lagos) take the Tabacundo road between Quito and Otavalo and can drop you off at the turnoff. From there, a cobbled road climbs 9km to the site. Try to grab a lift from Cochasquí workers and guides arriving around 9am. Taxis from nearby Cayambe charge about $8 per hour for the service.

CAYAMBE TO OYACACHI
☎ 02 / pop 30,473

The snow-dusted peak of Cayambe looms over the rolling farmland that leads into town. Cayambe, about 64km north of Quito along the Panamericana, is considered Ecuador's flower capital (see below). Swatches of color and enormous white tents set the backdrop coming into town. Local homemade cheese and *bizcochos* (salt crackers) are also produced there. Most buses between Quito and Otavalo can drop you in Cayambe.

Archaeological sites dating as far back as 1300 BC have been discovered in Cayambe's outskirts. If you're interested in local **archaeology** and history of the Caras and other na-

tive cultures, contact local historian Marco Sandoval (☎ 236 3237).

About 2km north of town on the Panamericana you'll find **Hostería Napoles** (☎ 236 0231; s/d $10/15), where you can stay in comfortable brick cabins and try local cheese at its popular restaurant. For an option in town try **Hotel Crystal** (☎ 236 1460; 9 de Octubre 215; s/d $6/10) where rooms are adequate but basic.

Squeeze in among the student crowd to use Internet at **Andinanet** (☎ 236 4126; Bolívar & Ascazubi) or grab a slab of cake at **Aroma** (Bolívar & Rocafuerte; lunch $2; ☾ 7am-9pm, closed Wed) with gossiping locals. At the confectionary ovens of **Bizcochos San Pedro** (Olmedo 035) you can snap hot sugar cookies fresh out of the oven. It is located off the street behind an interior courtyard in front of the cemetery.

Headed towards the volcano you'll pass the little village of Oyacachi, known for its indulgent community-run **hot springs** ($2). Some basic hostels and camping by permission are your options for overnighting.

On the road to Oyacachi is **Hacienda Guachala** (☎ 236 3042, 09-814 6688; www.guachala.com; s/d $31/37; ☒), a gorgeous retreat with red-tile roofs and a sunny stone courtyard. The oldest hacienda in Ecuador, Guachala was

A ROSE BY ANY OTHER NAME

Flower farms are considered the star industry of the highlands, employing 60,000 people in small communities with few other job opportunities. The flower boom brings prosperity to the average Ecuadorian, it cuts rural unemployment and discourages migration. With the heart of the industry centered on Cayambe, the local income level has risen to match Chile's national average. So, this is good news, right?

It turns out that the cost of a rose is high – for the environment, that is. There is simply no way to grow plump, flawless roses other than to douse the hell out of them with chemical pesticides, some of which are banned in the US and other countries. The worst farms cut corners on proper precautions such as fumigation suits, leaving their handlers to deal with the fallout, which ranges from rashes to cancer – a dear price to pay for employment.

The German Flower Label Program (www.flp-ecuador.com) is working to educate farms about proper procedure and certify environmentally friendly farms with a green seal. In turn, those farms will receive free advertising in Germany and a stamp so consumers can choose to support safe environmental practices and social policies. A major beneficiary of this program will be the women who make up 60% to 70% of flower industry employees.

The US lags far behind in any kind of certification program for several reasons according to Ramiro Peñaherra, president of flower company Latinflor. One is that half of all flowers are sold in supermarkets, which can demand the lowest industry prices to sell in quantity. Farms that invest in expensive environmental safeguards are forced to sell low, can't turn a profit and eventually fold. Some growers are uniting and working toward a (yet to be governmentally approved) US-based green label called Veriflora. The next challenge will be to make US consumers savvy about choosing their valentine bouquets. For now, Americans don't shop for greener flowers, they shop for the reddest rose.

founded in 1580. Seven kilometers south of Cayambe, it's a great base for the hot springs, hiking or horseback riding. White-washed rooms are adorned with Andean textiles and blankets. There is a spring-fed enclosed pool, restaurant and bar.

A bus leaves for Oyacachi from near the Cayambe plaza at 8am on Saturday and Sunday and it returns around 3pm. Oyacachi has no phone service.

VOLCÁN CAYAMBE

At 5790m the extinct Volcán Cayambe is Ecuador's third-highest peak and the highest point in the world through which the equator directly passes – at about 4600m on the south side. There is a **climbing refuge** (per person $17), but you need a 4WD to reach it. The climb is more difficult than the more frequently ascended peak of Cotopaxi. To get vertical, contact **Safari Tours** (☎ 255 2505; admin@safari.com.ec; Foch E5-39) or **Oswaldo Freire** (☎ 254 8206; ossy@uio.telconet.net); both offer reputable guiding and four-day **glacier schools**, so you can learn to swing that ice axe just right. Guide services average $70 per day.

OTAVALO

☎ 06 / pop 31,000 / elevation 2550m

Otavalo has been an Andean crossroads since pre-Inca times, when jungle traders would journey here on foot. Today's market is a hyperbolic version of the same tradition: buses arrive from Quito delivering droves of visitors from around the globe. While the tourists bargain for rugs and sweaters, the local artisans take their market earnings to fill up on staples such as rice and meat.

Visitors will find Otavalo a friendly and prosperous place that takes pride in its heritage. The population consists of those of European descent, mestizos and *indígenas* (indigenous people). The *indígenas*, who mostly live in nearby villages, dress primarily in traditional attire. Men wear dark felt hats, short cotton pants, blue ponchos and long ponytails. Women braid their hair and wear frilly, embroidered white blouses, long black skirts, *fachalinas* (headcloths) and bright layered necklaces.

Otavaleños (people from Otavalo) receive international recognition for their weaving (see p125) and craftsmanship but their achievement has been the result of centuries of hardship. Exploited first by co-

lonialists and then the sweatshops of Ecuadorian landowners, this population found a possibility to prosper for itself only after the Agrarian Reform of 1964. That success is relative: even today a number of artisans live on a meager income and struggle to profit from their weavings and crafts in a system where only intermediaries can bring merchandise to market.

Otavaleños are the wealthiest and most commercially successful *indígenas* in Ecuador – a status which translates to owning hotels and Ford Rangers and having an indigenous mayor. This juxtaposition of savvy and tradition may seem like a contradiction but in reality it illuminates how marginalized the rest of Latin America's native populations are in comparison.

Although Otavalo is probably Ecuador's most cliché destination outside of the Galápagos, there are ways to scratch beneath its colorful, commercial surface. For a more fulfilling encounter take the time to converse with vendors, participate in community tourism and visit the outlying communities which are the creative source and soul of the merchandise at the market.

For detailed cultural information about the people of Otavalo, read Lynn Meisch's *Otavalo: Weaving, Costume and the Market* (Libri Mundi, Quito, 1987), available only in Ecuador.

Information

Locally recommended doctors (both making house visits) include: **Dr Leonardo Suarez** (☎ 292 0057, 09-779 1206) who speaks some English and is available in emergencies; and **Dr Klaus Fay** (☎ 292 1203; Sucre near Morales; ☽ Tue-Sat), who speaks German and English.

Andinatel Calderón (near Modesto Jaramillo); Salinas (at Plaza de Ponchos)

Banco del Pacífico (Bolívar at García Moreno) Has an ATM.

Banco del Pichincha (Bolívar) Located between García Moreno and Piedrahita. Changes traveler's checks and has an ATM.

Book Market (Roca; ☽ Mon-Sat) The place to buy, sell and trade books in English, German, French and other languages. On Roca between García Moreno and Montalvo.

Hospital (☎ 292 0444, 292 3566; Sucre) Some 400m northeast of downtown.

Native C@ffé Net (☎ 292 0193; Sucre near Colón; per hr $1; ☽ 8am-10pm Mon-Sat, Sun 9am-9pm) Fast satellite connection, fax and phone service.

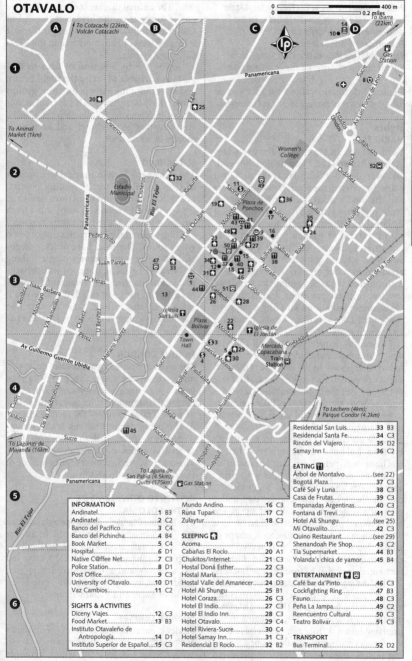

OTAVALO

0   400 m
0   0.2 miles

To Cotacachi (22km);
Volcán Cotacachi

To Ibarra
(22km)

Gas
Station

Panamericana

To Animal
Market (1km)

Women's
College

Estadio
Municipal

Plaza de
Ponchos

Iglesia
San Luis

Plaza
Bolívar

Town
Hall

Iglesia de
El Jordán

Mercado
Copacabana
Train
Station

Av Guillermo Guerrón Ubidia

To Lechero (4km);
Parque Condor (4.2km)

To Lagunas de
Mojanda (16km)

To Laguna de
San Pablo (4.5km);
Quito (175km)

Gas Station

Panamericana

NORTHERN HIGHLANDS

INFORMATION	
Andinatel................................**1** B3	
Andinatel................................**2** C2	
Banco del Pacífico................**3** C4	
Banco del Pichincha.............**4** B4	
Book Market.........................**5** C4	
Hospital.................................**6** D1	
Native C@ffee Net...............**7** C3	
Police Station.......................**8** D1	
Post Office............................**9** C3	
University of Otavalo...........**10** D1	
Vaz Cambios.........................**11** C2	

SIGHTS & ACTIVITIES	
Diceny Viajes.......................**12** C3	
Food Market........................**13** B3	
Instituto Otavaleño de	
Antropología.....................**14** D1	
Instituto Superior de Español...**15** C3	

Mundo Andino......................**16** C3	
Runa Tupari.........................**17** C3	
Zulaytur...............................**18** C3	

SLEEPING	
Acoma..................................**19** C2	
Cabañas El Rocío.................**20** A1	
Chukitos/Internet.................**21** C3	
Hostal Doña Esther..............**22** C3	
Hostal María........................**23** C3	
Hostal Valle del Amanecer....**24** D3	
Hotel Ali Shungu.................**25** B1	
Hotel Coraza........................**26** C3	
Hotel El Indio......................**27** C3	
Hotel El Indio Inn.................**28** C3	
Hotel Otavalo......................**29** C4	
Hotel Riviera-Sucre..............**30** C4	
Hotel Samay Inn..................**31** C4	
Residencial El Rocío............**32** B2	

Residencial San Luis............**33** B3	
Residencial Santa Fe............**34** C3	
Rincón del Viajero................**35** D2	
Samay Inn I.........................**36** C2	

EATING	
Árbol de Montalvo..............(see 22)	
Bogotá Plaza......................**37** C3	
Café Sol y Luna..................**38** C3	
Casa de Frutas....................**39** C3	
Empanadas Argentinas........**40** C3	
Fontana di Trevi..................**41** C2	
Hotel Ali Shungu................(see 25)	
Mi Otavalito......................**42** C3	
Quino Restaurant................(see 29)	
Shenandoah Pie Shop.........**43** C2	
Tía Supermarket.................**44** B3	
Yolanda's chica y amor.......**45** B4	

ENTERTAINMENT	
Café bar da'Pinto...............**46** C3	
Cockfighting Ring...............**47** B3	
Fauno.................................**48** C3	
Peña La Jampa...................**49** C2	
Reencuentro Cultural..........**50** C3	
Teatro Bolívar....................**51** C3	

TRANSPORT	
Bus Terminal......................**52** D2	

Police station (☎ 101; Av Luis Ponce de Leon) At the northeastern end of town, now authorized to process replacements for lost identity documents.
Post office (2nd fl, Sucre at Salinas)
Vaz Cambios (cnr Modesto Jaramillo & Saona) This exchange house has good rates and changes traveler's checks.

General information about the city can be found at www.otavalo.gov.ec (in Spanish).

Sights
MARKETS

Vendors hock an astounding array of wares at the **crafts market** on Plaza de Ponchos each and everyday, but Saturday is the principal market day, when the roads jam with visitors and the food market and household goods stalls overflow into adjacent streets. Plaza de Ponchos is the nucleus of tourist activity, with its staple of woolen goods – such as tapestries, blankets, ponchos, thick hooded sweaters, scarves, gloves, hats and alpaca goods from other regions – in addition to embroidered blouses, hammocks, carvings, jewelry, original paintings and struggling Guayasamín imitations, knit finger puppets, clay pipes, fake shrunken heads, handbags and woven mats.

The mostly female vendors will call you *amigo* or *amiga* and chide you, their friend, to buy *their* goods. In the first hours there's a slight pressure to be vendors' lucky first sale of the day. But the options can be dizzying – numerous yet similar at once. Take your time to browse the tables and check out pricing first. Bargaining is expected, especially with multiple purchases. Don't be shy about asking for a deal but don't be ruthless either.

The action peters out midafternoon as groups of men gather in corners to drink and vendors lose interest and begin visiting one another while their toddlers nap under piles of sweaters. Food stalls set up at the northern end proffer vats of chicken or tripe soup roiling on portable stovetops, scraps of whole flop-eared suckling pigs served with *mote* (maize) kernels, and scoops of *chicha* (a fermented corn drink) from plastic buckets.

The **food market** (cnr Modesto Jaramillo & Montalvo; ☉ 7am-1pm) sells produce and household goods for the locals, and there is an **animal market** (Map p123; ☉ 6-10am) that begins in the predawn hours. While you might have little use for an enormous cauliflower or screaming piglets, these are interesting places to

visit. The animal market is over a kilometer out of town; cross the bridge at the end of Colón and follow the crowds to get there. It is located west of Panamericana in the Viejo Colegio Agrícola.

During the high season of June to August it's advisable to arrive the night before and start shopping early before tour groups choke the passageways. The market is not free of pickpockets. While shopping, leave any valuables at the hotel and keep your money in a safe spot.

EL LECHERO

The **Lechero** is a famous magical tree outside of Otavalo known for its healing powers. Locals hike or drive up from town to visit it. It's worth a hike up if you want some fresh air, great views of town or a little magic.

To get there take Piedrahita out of town going south. The road here quickly steepens. Look for some arrows painted along the way. Hike some unpaved switchbacks and follow the road past a fragrant Eucalyptus grove to the crest of a hill where you'll see a lone, stubby tree. You can continue the hilltop going north to get to Parque Condor. It's 4km one-way.

PARQUE CONDOR

The recently opened **Parque Condor** (☎ 292 4429; condor@accessinter.net; admission $2.25; ☉ 9:30am-5pm Tue-Sun) is a Dutch-owned foundation which rehabilitates raptors, vultures and other birds of prey. Trained raptors fly several times a day for public demonstrations. It's a great opportunity to see an Andean condor up close, as well as eagles, owls, falcons and hawks. The center is perched on the steep hillside of Pucara Alto, 4km from town.

INSTITUTO OTAVELEÑO DE ANTROPOLOGÍA

The **Instituto Otavaleño de Antropología** (admission free; ☉ 8:30am-noon & 2:30-6pm Tue-Fri, 8:30am-noon Sat) is a small archaeological and ethnographical museum with a local focus, and has a library and a bookstore. It's located inside the University of Otavalo, one block north of Sucre and Panamericana.

Spanish Courses

Students enthusiastically recommend **Mundo Andino** (☎ 292 1864; espanol@interactive.net.ec; cnr Salinas & Bolívar 4-04; per hr $4), which arranges homestays with local families and organizes student activities and long-term volunteer opportunities.

Instituto Superíor de Español (☎ 292 2414; www .instituto-superior.net; Sucre 11-10; groups/individuals per hr $3.50/5) also receives high marks from readers. They can also arrange family homestays. The main branch is in Quito.

Tours

Anthropologist Rodrigo Mora is an invaluable source of local information and his company **Zulaytur** (☎ 09-814 6483, 09-944 0004; www.geocities.com/zulaytur; 2nd fl, cnr Sucre & Colón) has many reader recommendations. Guided bilingual tours to village indigenous homes offer a rare opportunity to glimpse the conditions of working artisans and interact with them while learning about the weaving process. Tours cost $16 per person. Zulaytur also offers trips to hike to Lagunas de Mojanda and Laguna de Cuicocha. Don't mistake similarly named operations.

Runa Tupari (☎ 292 5985; www.runatupari.com; Sucre & Quiroga) partners with local indigenous communities for sightseeing, hiking, horseback riding and biking trips. Rural homestays are $22 per night. Offbeat options include a bumpy 2000m mountain-bike descent into the Intag's tropical cloud forest and a round-trip 10-hour hike up 'Mama' Volcán Cotacachi (4939m). They also sell Intag coffee and local crafts.

Readers give kudos to **Diceny Viajes** (☎ 292 1217; Sucre 10-11) for good guiding and friendly attention.

Festivals & Events

Otavalo's best-known celebration, the **Fiesta del Yamor**, occurs in the first two weeks of September. An elected queen oversees processions, live music and dancing, fireworks displays and cockfights. Revelers consume copious amounts of *yamor*. Seven varieties of corn are slowly simmered together to produce this unusual nonalcoholic drink (longer-fermented versions are alcoholic). It's available only during fiesta time from Yolanda's (p121).

June 24 is **St John the Baptist Day** (especially celebrated in its namesake suburb near the intersection of Cisneros with the Panamericana), known locally as *La Fiesta de San Juan* or its pagan name *Inti Raymi*, the summer equinox. It is said that local *in-*

dígenas live and die to celebrate this event. During the whole year money is saved and chores are done so at this opportunity everyone can don their best finery, make expensive contributions of food and drink, and wildly participate. The festivities continue through June 29, the **Day of St Peter & St Paul**. Look for the bullfight in Otavalo and the boating regatta on Laguna de San Pablo, as well as celebrations in nearby Ilumán.

Some small village fiestas date back to pre-Columbian rituals and can last up to two weeks. Revelers process from the church through neighborhoods, where homes offer the dancers food and alcohol. As drunkenness sets in, dancers get sloppier and the resulting collisions between rivals can escalate into full-out brawls. These fights have occasionally led to deaths, to which the authorities, perhaps for their own safety, turn a blind eye. Given this, outsiders should exercise caution around these events. In general they are considered OK to attend and well-worth viewing, but keep your distance from wild revelers and exit in the sober stages.

A fiesta called **Corazas** is celebrated a few kilometers southeast of Otavalo on the southern shores of Laguna de San Pablo in the villages around San Rafael. Some south-shore villages also celebrate the **Pendoneros Fiesta** on October 15.

The precise dates of these celebrations vary from year to year, but they are usually well publicized, with posters announcing events. For up-to-date information, check out www.otovalo.gov.ec.

Sleeping

Otavalo's perennial popularity has brought a good selection of well-priced accommodations to town. Make sure your bargain hotel has hot water and adequate bed covers. If you're picky, try to reserve in advance or arrive before the weekend rush.

BUDGET

Hotel Riviera-Sucre (☎ 292 0241; www.rivierasucre .com; García Moreno 3-80 & Roca; r per person with shared/ private bathroom $7/15) A Belgian-owned hotel in a sprawling, charming home with large, colorful rooms and hot-water bathrooms. Endless nooks reveal a garden, fireplaces, a library, laundry facilities and a small café.

Rincón del Viajero (☎ 292 1741; www.rincondel viajero.org; Roca 11-07; r per person incl breakfast with shared/private bathroom $7.50/10) A great choice for its warm hospitality and homey, snug rooms. After artwork was stolen by guests, the owners had landscapes painted directly on the walls. English is spoken and there's a restaurant, TV lounge with fireplace, hot water and a rooftop terrace. Ask about their camping facilities outside of town.

Hostal Valle del Amanecer (☎ 292 0990; amanacer@uio.satnet.net; cnr Roca & Quiroga; r per person incl breakfast with shared/private bathroom $7/9) A very popular choice among travelers, its best feature is the shady courtyard strewn with hammocks. While rooms are on the small side, and hospitality is seriously flagging, the atmosphere and tasty breakfasts still lure visitors in. Bike rentals are available and there's a laundry service.

Residencial El Rocío (☎ 292 0584; Morales 11-70; r per person with shared/private bathroom $4/5) Friendly, simple accommodations on the quieter side of downtown with hot water and roof views of the hilltops. The family also owns **Cabañas El Rocío** (r per person $10), a comfortable garden escape in the San Juan neighborhood on the other side of the Panamericana.

Hotel El Indio (☎ 292 0060; Sucre 12-14, s/d with bathroom $10/15) While the inadvertent 1970s mod ambience could be fun, there are better-value options out there for the price. Cable TV provides the Charlie's Angels reruns.

Chukitos (☎ 292 4959; www.chukitoshostal.4t.com; Bolívar 10-13 & Morales; s/d with bathroom $7/14; 🖳) Run by friendly staff, the best perk of this place is the Internet call-center downstairs. The slightly dusty rooms have narrow twin beds and Andean folk decor, cable TV and hot water.

Other reasonable and cheap spots include **Residencial San Luis** (☎ 292 0614; Calderón 6-02; r per person with shared/private bathroom $4/5), **Residencial Santa Fe** (☎ 292 0171; Colon near Sucre; r per person $5) and the very basic **Hostal María** (☎ 292 0672; Modesto Jaramillo near Colón; r per person $3).

MIDRANGE

Acoma (☎ 292 6570; Salinas 7-57; s/d with shared bathroom $15/20, s/d with private bathroom & cable TV $20/30, ste $50) This gorgeous new Santa Fe-style hotel seems out of place in Otavalo, but it's great value. The modern design includes cedar floors, mosaic tiles and skylights sculpted into the adobe. Ignore the baubles and trinkets at the gift shop and head straight to the slick on-site bar and

restaurant to relax. Breakfast is included and kids stay free.

Hostal Doña Esther (☎ 292 0739; www.otavalohotel.com; Montalvo 4-44; s/d $21/29) This small colonial-style hotel is a cozy fit with its red-tile floors and attractive rooms surrounding a courtyard draped with ferns. Owned by a Dutch family, the service is personable and there's an attached restaurant, Árbol de Montalvo (see opposite).

Hotel Otavalo (☎ 292 3712, 292 4999; hotovalo@im.pro.ec; Roca 5-04; s/d $18/26) A chipper yellow colonial decked out with polished hardwood floors and a bright covered courtyard. Its petite rooms are well cared for. The upstairs restaurant, serves traditional hearty fare (see Quino's, opposite).

Hotel Ali Shungu (☎ 292 0750; www.alishungu.com; cnr Egas & Quito; s/d with bathroom $37/49, apt $98-134; 🗙) Once the crown jewel of Otavalo, this classic has lost some of its sparkle. Rooms decorated with Andean designs are well-worn but clean, and have hot water. Two family apartments come complete with VCR and stereo system. The best feature is the sprawling patio which overlooks the garden and Volcán Imbabura. Try the excellent on-site restaurant (opposite). The American owners have started a new lodge outside of town in Yanbiro, ask for details.

Hotel Samay Inn (☎ 292 1826; samayinnhotel@hotmail.com; Sucre 1009 near Colon; r per person with bathroom $12, ste $36) A stiff and starchy remodel in the heart of the main strip. Attractive rooms have stucco and tile decor, comfortable beds, solid furniture and cable TV. Balconies offer prime people watching, but it's a noisy spot.

Samay Inn I (☎ 292 2871; samayinnhotel@hotmail.com; Sucre 14-14 near Quito; r per person with bathroom $9, suite $36) Not to be confused with its newer version. A dated mega-motel whose uncluttered and clean tiled rooms are nonetheless good value. Kids get discounted rates.

Hotel El Indio Inn (☎ 292 0922, fax 292 2324; Bolívar 9-04; s/d incl breakfast $28/40) A modern hotel, well lit but somewhat generic, featuring large carpeted rooms, a restaurant and a game room. Rooms have cable TV and telephones. Not to be confused with its budget version Hotel El Indio, mentioned earlier. Breakfast and tax are included in the price.

Hotel Coraza (☎ 292 1225; www.ecuahotel.com; coraza@andinanet.net; cnr Sucre & Calderón; s/d $25/35) This large hotel appeals more to Ecuadorian nationals. Spacious, carpeted rooms are set off with glass and mirrors and touches of kitsch. In addition to TV and telephone there's also a restaurant and laundry service.

Eating

Restaurants are plentiful; especially if you like pizza, but you may find the Mexican food regrettable.

Mi Otavalito (☎ 292 0176; Sucre 11-19; mains $2-4; ☯ 8am-11pm) Offers Ecuadorian dishes that are of good quality in a family atmosphere. Try the *almuerzo*, a four-course set lunch with grilled meat or fresh trout alongside a hearty soup.

Bogotá Plaza (☎ 292 0359; Sucre near Colon; mains $1.50-3; ☯ 8am-4pm) Try this tiny family-run place for a filling set lunch and cups of wonderfully robust Colombian coffee.

Café Sol y Luna (Bolívar 11-10; mains $5-6; ☯ 8:30am-10pm Tue-Sun) A small Belgian-owned café with a cozy dining patio and warm interior. Food is more healthy than exciting; the slim menu board offers crisp organic salads, home-style pastas and veggie burgers.

Quino (Roca near García Moreno; mains $5; ☯ 10am-11pm) This popular locale with bright, citrus-colored walls and a homey atmosphere is the place if you're hankering for seafood in the mountains. Try the grilled fish or shrimp ceviche with lots of lime.

Árbol de Montalvo (☎ 292 0739; Montalvo 4-44; mains $5-8; ☯ noon-10pm Fri-Sun, 6-9pm Mon-Thu) Cooks satisfying thin-crust pizzas with organic toppings.

Hotel Ali Shungu (☎ 292 0750; cnr Egas & Quito; meals $5-12; ☯ 7:30am-8:30pm) Food with gourmet touches is served up in an ambient setting overlooking the garden. The menu caters to homesick visitors, with waffles in raspberry syrup, roast beef sandwiches, salads and New York cheesecake. The coffee and some of the produce is organic.

Fontana di Trevi (Sucre near Salinas; meals $5-6; ☯ noon-10pm) Try the original pizza joint which created the copycat craze. It's located on the 2nd floor, half a block off Plaza de Ponchos. Top picks include the basil and tomato salad and vegetarian pizza.

Empanadas Argentinas (Sucre 2-02 near Morales; $0.50; ☯ 8am-9pm Mon-Sat) Join the student crowd with their uniforms askew for a slice of pizza or salty beef or cheese empanadas. The *choclo* (corn) and pineapple ones add an Ecuadorian twist.

Shenandoah Pie Shop (☎ 292 1465; Salinas 5-15; pie slices $1; ☯ 7:30am-9pm) Famous for its deep-dish pies stuffed with sugary fruit, and is best with a vanilla milkshake.

Casa de Frutas (Sucre near Salinas; mains $3-5; ☯ 8:30am-10pm) Located in an eclectic and somewhat disheveled courtyard, this spot serves satisfying granola and fruit bowls and omelette breakfasts. Lunch includes salad and soy burgers, juices and Intag coffee.

Yolanda's Chicha de Yamor (green house at Sucre & Mora) Open late August to mid-September during festival time, Yolanda Cabrera serves delicious local fare such as *tortillas de maiz* (corn tortillas), *mote* (hominy), *empanaditas* (Spanish pies) and the local favorite of *fritada* (fried pork). Of course, the real attraction is her *chicha de yamor* (see p119).

Tía (Sucre near Calderón; ☯ 9am-8pm) Don't expect much meat or produce at this grocery store, whose specialty is all things canned, but you will find an ATM.

Entertainment

Peñas are lively folk venues common to the high Andes; of which Otavalo has a few good ones. It's not a party town per se, but on weekend nights after 10pm the disco scene can simmer into something sweaty and festive.

Peña La Jampa (☎ 292 2988; Modesto Jaramillo; admission $2-3; ☯ 10pm-3am Fri & Sat) Offers a mix of live salsa, merengue, *rock en español* (Spanish rock) and *folklórica* (folk music) in its new location on Modesto Jaramillo between Quito and Quiroga.

Café bar da'Pinto (Colon; 4pm-2am) This cozy club is good spot to check out live *folklórica*. Between Bolívar and Sucre.

Fauno (Morales; ☯ 2pm-3am Tue-Sun) A slicker three-level club attracting the younger crowd with Latin rock on weekends. Find it between Sucre and Modesto Jaramillo.

Reencuentro Cultural (☎ 292 2241; Sucre 11-59 5-10) This new locale hosts live music, exhibitions and cultural events but is only open sporadically.

Teatro Bolívar (Bolívar 9-03; admission $0.50) This cinema presents two showings daily, one's usually a kid flick, the other a Jean Claude Van Damme. In the block between Calderón and Colon.

There's a weekly **cockfight** (31 de Octubre; admission $0.50; ☯ 7pm Sat) that one local argues is not about the gamecocks, but the passionate audience, whose faces 'express the full range of each human emotion.'

Getting There & Away
BUS
Buses depart Quito's main terminal every 20 minutes or so and charge $2 for the two- to three-hour ride to Otavalo. Transportes Otavalo and Transportes Los Lagos used to race each other on the highway until they merged into Transportos Otavalo/Los Lagos. It is the only bus company allowed into Otavalo's bus terminal. The others drop passengers off on the Panamericana, from where they have to hoof it six to eight blocks to downtown.

From the terminals of northern towns of Ibarra ($0.45, 35 minutes) or Tulcán ($3.00, three hours), buses leave for Otavalo every hour or so. Buses from Tulcán drop you on the Panamericana.

In Otavalo, the **main bus terminal** (Atahualpa) is at the northern end of town, from where you can take a taxi to most hotels for $1. From this terminal, Transportes Otavalo/Los Lagos leave for Quito and Ibarra every 10 minutes.

Both Transportos Otavalo/Los Lagos and Transportes 6 de Junio travel to the remote Intag valley hamlets of Apuela ($3, 2½ hours) and García Moreno ($4, 3½ hours). The screeching rollercoaster ride over sheer drops through spectacular scenery is somewhat of an event. Old local buses, with fares roughly $1 per hour of travel, drive the route south of Otavalo to San Pablo del Lago (20 minutes) and Araque (two hours). Cooperativa Imbaburapac has buses from Otavalo to Ilumán (30 minutes), Agato (two hours), San Pablo del Lago (15 minutes), Ibarra (45 minutes) and Cayambe (35 minutes) every hour or so. The bus to Ibarra passes through the small indigenous villages en route to the north. Transportes Cotacachi goes to Cotacachi via the longer route (through Quiroga), and Transportes 6 de Junio takes the shorter route ($0.25, 25 minutes), via the Panamericana. Intrepid travelers could brave these lesser-known areas in a daytrip, although, as most villages lack in accommodations, plans should be made for an early return.

For the villages of Calderón, Guayllabamba and Cayambe, take an Otavalo–Quito bus (most frequent on Saturday afternoons). The buses stop at the turnoff from the main

road in Cayambe, a walk of several hundred meters into town.

TAXI & SHUTTLE
Taxis charge a minimum of $1 per ride and $7 per hour.

For door-to-door van service contact **Hotel Ali Shungu** (292 0750), their shuttle goes back and forth between Quito and your hotel for $7 per person one-way (see p121). New licensing regulations may curtail this service in the future.

AROUND OTAVALO
 06
Outside Otavalo you'll see planted fields checkered onto steep hills; their sharp contours translate to strenuous hikes with rewarding views. The adventurous should hit the trails to mountain lakes and visit indigenous villages where time crawls by. Tucked away from view are the old haciendas, once-grandiose epicenters of colonial society, now serving as romantic hideaways. Visitors who have had enough shopping can reach these places within a short bus or taxi ride from downtown.

Hikers shouldn't miss the spectacular Lagunas de Mojanda, southwest of Otavalo. Ecuador's largest lake, Laguna de San Pablo, provides a more domesticated setting, with ferry trips and paddleboats available from shoreline hosterías (small hotels). Each September an international swimming competition has competitors swimming 3800 cold meters across the lake. The village of San Pablo del Lago sits at the southeast end.

The Panamericana heads northeast out of Otavalo, passing by the indigenous villages of **Peguche**, **Agato** and **Ilumán**. Explore them by bus, taxi or with a tour. The villages southwest of Laguna de San Pablo manufacture fireworks, totora mats and other reed products. Other otavaleño villages are nearby, consult the tourist agencies in Otavalo for suggestions. Tour prices are not far off a long taxi rental and the added value is well worth it.

Las Palmeras (292 2607; www.laspalmerasinn .com; dm/s/d $15/40/50) offers pretty cottages set in the rural hills, and is friendly and keyed into travelers. Try the neighbor's Hawaiian energy massages, rent a bike or go horseback riding with an expert trainer who specializes in horse therapy and natural horsemanship. Spanish lessons, laundry and movies are available on-site. Meals cost extra and security deposits are required. German and English are spoken.

Lagunas de Mojanda

A crumbling cobbled road leads high up in the *páramo* to three turquoise lakes set like gemstones into the hills. Located 17km south of Otavalo, the area acquired protected status in 2002 and since has become a safer and better-protected destination. If you have come to camp, set up on the south side of the biggest lake, **Laguna Grande** or in the basic stone refuge (bring a sleeping bag and food). The jagged peak of **Fuya Fuya**, an extinct volcano (4263m), looms nearby. If

you want to hoof it from the closest lodgings (listed below), bring lots of water. Taxis charge extra (about $12 each way plus $8 per hour to wait) for wear and tear. To save a few bucks, stay at a nearby inn or taxi out early from Otavalo and hike back the same day. Both Casa Mojanda and Zulaytur (see p119) offer guided hikes which include transportation for about $30. For information about the lakes see the **Mojanda Foundation/Pachamama Association** (☎ 292 2986, www.casamojanda.com/foundation.html) across from Casa Mojanda on the road in.

A brisk, scenic walk across the *páramo* drops into the archaeological site of Cochasquí, 20km due south. Bring a 1:50,000 topographical map of the Mojanda area,

NORTHERN HIGHLANDS

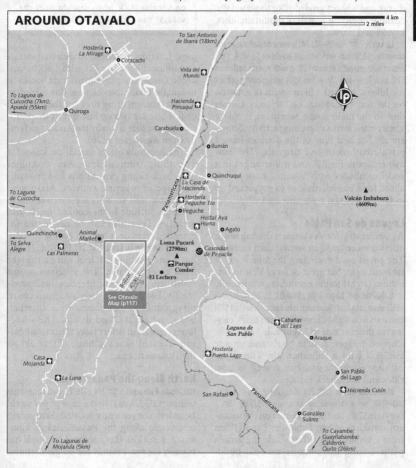

AROUND OTAVALO

0 — 4 km
0 — 2 miles

To San Antonio de Ibarra (18km)

Hostería La Mirage
Cotacachi

Vista del Mundo

Hacienda Pinsaquí

To Laguna de Cuicocha (7km); Apuela (55km)
Quiroga

Carabuela

To Laguna de Cuicocha

Ilumán

Quinchuquí
La Casa de Hacienda
Hostería Peguche Tío
Peguche
Hostal Aya Huma
Agato

Volcán Imbabura (4609m)

To Selva Alegre
Quinchinche
Las Palmeras
Animal Market

Loma Pucará (2790m)
Cascadas de Peguche

Parque Condor
El Lechero

See Otavalo Map (p117)

Bolívar

Laguna de San Pablo

Cabañas del Lago
Araque

Hostería Puerto Lago

San Pablo del Lago
Hacienda Cusín

Casa Mojanda
La Luna

San Rafael

Panamericana

González Suárez

To Lagunas de Mojanda (5km)

To Cayambe; Guayllabamba; Calderón; Quito (26km)

numbered ÑII-F1, 3994-III, available from the IGM in Quito (p70).

Consummate relaxation can be found at **Casa Mojanda** (☎ 292 2986, 09-973 1737; www.casamo janda.com; s low/high season $75/90, d year-round $124), a lovely inn 4km south of Otavalo. It's on the road to Lagunas de Mojanda, with views of steep Andean farmland. Cheerful cottages are equipped with electric heaters and hot-water bathrooms; some have fireplaces. Slip into the outdoor Japanese-style hot tub after a long day of hiking. The grounds include horse stables, an organic garden and a library and mini-theatre. The American-Ecuadorian owners are active in local nature preservation and community projects. Rates include breakfast and dinner with fresh garden ingredients and a short guided hike to waterfalls. Arrange ahead for rentals of mountain bikes, kayaks and horses.

La Luna (☎ /fax 09-973 7415; www.hostallaluna.com; campsites $2.50, dm with/without breakfast $5.50/4, r per person with shared bathroom $9, d with private bathroom $20) is a low-key, low budget getaway perfect for hikers, located 4.5km south of Otavalo on the way to Lagunas de Mojanda. Guests dine in the main house, where the fireplace games is the nexus of evening activity. Showers are hot and four of the doubles have a private bathroom and fireplace. The new owners speak English and will arrange hikes and lunchboxes with advance notice. Call ahead for a bus schedule or to get picked up in Otavalo. A taxi costs about $4.

Laguna de San Pablo

A popular stop for weekenders driving north offers a more tranquil setting than Otavalo. The paved road encircling the lake is never far from sight, but great views of Volcán Imbabura (right) to the northeast compensate.

Cabañas del Lago (☎ 291 8001, Quito ☎ 02-243 5936; www.cabañasdellago.com; cabañas incl breakfast $73) consists of a tight cluster of prim brick cabins on the east side of Laguna de San Pablo. Clipped hedges, paddle boats and on-site minigolf lend a suburban air. There's an on-site restaurant and bar as well as boat rides and horseback riding.

Hacienda Cusín (☎ 291 8013, 291 8316, USA 800-683-8148; www.haciendacusin.com; s/d $75/105) is a fairytale 17th-century hacienda on the southern outskirts of San Pablo del Lago (10km from Otavalo). Tall cedars shade the garden paths linking the cottages and old build-

ings. Interiors combine Andean tapestries and unusual church relics with old colonial decor. Guests can play squash, ride horses or mountain bikes, then cap the day cozied to the bar where roaring fires cut the highland chill. There are two exclusive craft shops, including one that is run by the Andrango family from Agato (see p126).

The hacienda offers special packages for everything from weddings to overnight horseback-riding expeditions and Spanish-language or weaving courses. Make sure you book well in advance for weekends. Packages include home-cooked meals and activities. Discounts can be negotiated for extended stays or if booked online.

Hostería Puerto Lago (☎ 292 1901/2; d $79; ✗) has Austere cabins that look out on the lake from a perfect lawn. The spacious rooms sport firm mattresses, fireplaces and satellite TV. For diversion there's a tennis court, playground, games room, wi-fi Internet, boats and kayaks, and llamas. The white-linen restaurant offers tasty traditional cuisine. Located 5km southeast of Otavalo on the Panamericana.

North Along the Panamericana

Hacienda Pinsaquí (☎ 294 6116/7; www.haciendapin saqui.com; r $72-120, ste $144) is a taste of old world Ecuador, conveniently located 5km north of Otavalo along the Panamericana. Constructed in 1790, this purebred hacienda has been in the same family for six generations.

History just seeps from the decor, which includes antique French washbasins and gaunt portraits. South American liberator Simón Bolívar used to stay in room one on his travels north to Bogota. It includes 28 luxury rooms and suites ideal for families, some with Jacuzzi. If the hot tub is full, check out the reading room with fireplace, the on-site chapel or the cozy low-lit bar, ideal for sipping *canelazos* (a cinnamon-flavored liqueur) and hatching revolutionary plans. Guests can mountain bike or go horseback riding with a pick from the renowned stables. A stay includes an American breakfast, and lunch or dinner is $15.

Vista del Mundo (☎ 294 6112; www.sparesortvistadelmundo.com, s/d cabins incl breakfast & dinner $81/90) has an unhinged Vegas quality, and is likely the only spa resort in the world whose restaurant specializes in *fritada* (fried pork). Round brick cabins are roofed in the hats of different nations (fedora, fez and turban to name a few). Inside, elaborate cartoonish murals represent each nationality. Dubbed 'The only place in the world you'll see Jews and Arabs side-by-side,' by its Israeli owner. Peace begins with the wide variety of treatments and hydromassage offered in the spa.

Peguche

The drone of electric looms penetrates the landscape of this small weaving village. Traditional products can still be found at **Tejidos Mimahuasi** in the home of weavers José María

Cotacachi and Luz María Fichabamba. Ask locals for directions.

On the central plaza of Peguche, the **Centro Pachakutik** occasionally features *folklórica* concerts.

From the railway line in Peguche, a trail leads about 2km southeast to the waterfalls known as **Cascada de Peguche**. These falls are sacred to the locals and visitors should stay away during the Fiesta de San Juan, when men use them for ritual cleansing baths. Near the falls is a pre-Columbian archaeological site in poor condition. Ask locals in town for directions and advice.

Guests come to **Hostal Aya Huma** (☎ 292 1255; www.ayahuma.com; s/d with shared bathroom $8/12, with private bathroom $14/20) for a quiet village retreat. The real estate is wonderful but it could use combing over. Its café serves hearty breakfasts and vegetarian food; if you're lucky there's live music.

On the other side of town **Hostería Peguche Tío** (☎ 292 2619; peguchetio@mail.com; r per person $10) has adequate bunkrooms and a lounge has billiards and weekend entertainment. You won't find guinea pigs under the bed at **La Casa de Hacienda** (☎ 294 6336; www.casadehacienda .com; r per person incl breakfast $22) but if you order in advance the local delicacy of *cuy asado* (roasted guinea pig) can be on your plate. This hotel/restaurant has gracious hosts and tidy brick cabins with fireplaces and rocking chairs. It's located 1km north of Peguche.

NORTHERN HIGHLANDS

A TIGHTLY WOVEN CULTURE

Behind the broad and bountiful selection of the woolens stalls at the Otavalo market is a living, breathing industry with a culture unto itself. Small indigenous villages outside Otavalo are home to weaving families. The activity starts before dawn in many households. Weavers gather in a small dirt-floor room to do their swift, silent work. Production starts with washing, carding, spinning and dyeing the wool. Children observe in corners, play with yarn instead of Legos, practicing to one day join in. Four thousand years ago, the ancestors of *otavaleño* weavers were using the backstrap loom. They sat on the cold ground, like their modern counterparts, holding the loom between their bare feet, and interlaced threads into complex and dazzling designs.

'There's beauty in the artistry handed down from the generations,' comments anthropologist and guide Rodrigo Mora. 'It is the one thing the children do not need from school because it is who they are.'

This identity faces its own challenges as the use of electric looms continues to rise. And as trade beyond borders shoots up, so has the incursion of foreign products. That means visitors who travel the length of the Andes begin to spot the same stuff everywhere, and stop buying.

Otavalo addressed this by placing stricter controls on goods sold in its market. These days 80% to 90% of the artistry sold is local. Buyers who want to support traditional industry should focus on purchasing handmade goods, even though their bulk is murder on the luggage.

Cooperativa Imbaburapac (Av Atahualpa or bus terminal) has some buses that go through Peguche en route to Agato.

Agato

Agato, 2km east of Peguche, is home to the **Tahuantinsuyo Weaving Workshop** where master weaver Miguel Andrango demonstrates traditional weavings on backstrap looms. These high-quality textiles are geared toward aficionados. The family runs an outlet at the Hacienda Cusín on weekends (see p124). Ask locals for directions.

Ilumán

Weavers work in this village off the Panamericana about 7km northeast of Otavalo. It is also famous for its shamans; the local shamans' association has around 120 members. Members advertise by scrawling their name in large letters on their homes. Feel free to try it out, but remember that cleansings, involving raw egg and spittle, can get messy. The easiest way to get here from Otavalo is on the Imbaburapac bus.

Cotacachi

Unesco benighted this town 'City of Peace.' *Otavaleños*, uninspired by the resident tranquility, say, '*Mil veces preso en Otavalo que suelto en Cotacachi*,' which translates roughly to, 'prison in Otavalo is a thousand times better than being let loose in Cotacachi.' With the natural attractions of Lago de Cuicocha and Volcán Cotacachi, this mannered and mellow colonial town may some day give Otavalo a run for its money.

Cotacachi is famous for its leatherwork. Stores lining 10 de Agosto sell everything from handbags and wallets to designer jackets. Highland Ambato (see p165) undercuts Cotacachi's leather market with more competitive pricing.

For information about community tourism, horseback-riding and hiking tours, go to the municipal tourism office upstairs in the new **Casa de las Culturas** (☎ 291 5140; cotacachi@turismoaventura.net; Eloy Alfaro N32-300; ♡ 11am-7pm Wed-Sun). This refurbished colonial has a rotating exhibit with Guayasamín paintings on loan and an upstairs library/Internet center. It also serves organic coffee.

The **Museo de las Culturas** (García Moreno 13-41; admission $1; ♡ 9am-noon & 2-5pm Mon-Fri, 2-5pm Sat, 10am-1pm Sun), located in the neoclassical old municipal palace, gives the ethnohistory of the region, from 8500 BC through colonial and republican periods. Don't miss the exhibit of indigenous religious festivals.

Market day is Sunday.

SLEEPING & EATING

El Mesón de las Flores (☎ 291 5264; García Moreno & Sucre; s/d $20/36) This bone-white colonial waxes romantic with flowerboxes, old brass trumpets and guitars. High-ceiling rooms have older fixtures but are freshly painted and well kept. Balconies have views of the convent. The bar is well stocked and the courtyard restaurant (mains $4 to $6; open 7am to 8pm) offers local and international cuisine; chicken in wine sauce and *llapingachos* (fried pancakes of mashed potatoes with cheese) are particularly nice.

Hostal Plaza Bolívar (☎ 291 5755; cotacachi@turismoaventura.net; 3rd fl, Bolívar 12-26 at 10 de Agosto; r per person with shared/private bathroom $4/6) These dogeared budget rooms are spick and span. The entrance is hidden by an archway into a courtyard.

Hostería La Mirage (☎ 291 5237, 291 5077, USA ☎ 800-327-3573; www.mirage.com.ec; d $250-280, ste $300-600; ☒) This toney version of heaven may actually have outdone the original. Beyond the locked iron gates, peacocks stroll the green past white cupolas and columned entrances. Part of the exclusive Relais & Chateaux association, La Mirage counts among its distinguished guests the Queen of Spain. The decor is exquisite and romantic with its original paintings, canopy beds, flower bouquets and antique accents. Highlights include the glass-roofed indoor swimming pool and Jacuzzi. Tennis, horseback riding and mountain biking are offered. The spa is a throwback to Roman decadence, featuring treatments ranging from milk-and-rose-petal baths in the Cleopatra room to shamanic cleansings in a stone-slab candlelit nook. Plain old massages start at $30. Rates include dinner and breakfast but not taxes.

A leisurely meal at the restaurant (mains $13 for nonguests) guarantees a memorable experience in fusion (Ecua-International) cuisine. Quail in a fig sauce or a hearty goat stew with yuca and green banana dumplings are a few of the savory offerings. For dessert try ice cream infused with fragrant lavender. The glassed-in restaurant fills up on Saturday with shoppers from the Otavalo market.

Reserve ahead for both meals and accommodations.

El Leñador (☎ 291 5083; Sucre 10-12 & Juan Montalvo) Argentine-style grill specializing in *carne colorado,* a regional meat speciality. While the food is decent the chop-chop service by serious waiters is great. A leisurely lunch here inevitably leads to a siesta.

La Tola (☎ 291 5509; 9 de Octubre & Rocafuerte) A large dining hall dressed in ferns and bamboo decor and specializing in grilled meats and trout. It fills up on weekends when there is occasional live music.

GETTING THERE & AWAY
Cotacachi is west of the Panamericana and 15km north of Otavalo. From Otavalo's bus terminal there are buses at least every hour ($0.25, 25 minutes). In Cotacachi, *camionetas* (pickups or light trucks) can be hired from the bus terminal by the market at the far end of town to take you to Laguna de Cuicocha ($12 round-trip, including half-hour waiting time). A more economical option is to take a Transportes Cotacachi bus (from Otavalo or Cotacachi) to Quiroga where you can grab a taxi from the plaza.

RESERVA ECOLÓGICA COTACACHI-CAYAPAS
This huge **reserve** (lake admission $1, entire park $5) protects western Andean habitats ranging from Volcán Cotacachi down to the northwestern coastal lowlands. Travel from the highland to lowland areas of the reserve is nearly impossible (how's your bushwhacking?). Most visitors either visit the lowlands from San Miguel on Río Cayapas (see p275) or the highlands around Laguna de Cuicocha, which are described here. From Cotacachi, just before arriving at Laguna de Cuicocha, you will pass the rangers' booth and entrance point to the Reserva Ecológica Cotacachi-Cayapas.

Sights
Drive 18km west on the rattling road from Cotacachi and you'll come upon **Laguna de Cuicocha**, a stunning dark lagoon cradled in a collapsed volcanic crater. Some 3km wide and 200m deep, the lagoon also features cone-shaped islands that shot up in later eruptions. Savor this stunning landscape by hiking the trail which skirts the perimeter. The path follows the shore, edging inland

when cliffs lean up to the shore. Hummingbirds, attracted by abundant flowers and orchids, flit about. The trail begins near the reserve's entrance booth and circles the lake counterclockwise, a circuit of six hours. If the mist clears, you'll see the spire of Volcán Cotacachi. Boats for hire make short trips around the islands. There have been robberies here. Never go alone and check the current situation with the local guards at the park entrance.

Sleeping & Eating
Hostería Los Pinos de Cuicocha (☎ 09-614 939, 09-621 4711; www.lospinosdecuicocha.com; road to Intag km 4; s/d $69/92) Snug and down-to-earth accommodations with handmade furniture and electric heaters in rooms, set on 40 hectares. Having Laguna de Cuicocha in your backyard isn't cheap but it is lovely. A full-service restaurant/bar serves sustenance by the hearth. The property has direct access to the Cuicocha loop. Owners are an affable German-Ecuadorian couple who speak English as well.

Getting There & Away
A group can hire a taxi or pickup from Cotacachi for around $20; be sure to pay after returning so you don't get ditched! One-way fares by taxi or truck cost about $8 from Cotacachi. A two-day hike leads from Laguna Cuicocha to Laguna Mojanda via a southern trail through the village of Ugshapungu. The 1:50,000 Otavalo map numbered NII-F1, 3994-IV is recommended; look for it at IGM in Quito (p70).

INTAG VALLEY
The crumbly gravel road into Intag presents the drama and suspense of a Russian overture. After chugging to dry and scrabbled heights, the road then scissors and plunges, only to crawl out of mountain gutters and climb again. Sometimes mudslides block this road but drivers seem to have an uncanny talent for its narrow dimensions and ghastly conditions.

Upon entering the sector of Intag you'll find the **Andean Bear Conservation Project** (www.espiritudelbosque.com; volunteers per month $100), which trains volunteers as bear trackers. Part of the job is hiking through remote cloud forest in search of the elusive spectacled bear, whose predilection for sweet corn is altering its wild

NORTHERN HIGHLANDS

SOLIDARITY IN THE STICKS

The rural Intag valley is home to modest subsistence farmers. In these humid hills the trees are weighted in tropical fruit and kids ride horses bridled with a scrap of rope. It's hard to believe this community is a hotbed of environmental activism.

It started with the burning of a mining camp on May 15, 1997. The vigilante act was a reaction to seven years of copper mining which had left the Río Junin polluted with waste and toxic substances from the camps which caused skin infections. No one was stepping in. With the government providing incentives for mining companies, local residents found themselves powerless to defend their farms and health, never mind the environment.

The lack of communication was a major obstacle to resolving local issues, so in December, 2000, residents founded *Periodico Intag*, a rural newspaper with community-based reporters. Part of the paper's mission is to 'promote literacy in Intag by providing something to read and a reason to write.' The paper, with an English translation online at www.intagnewspaper.org, relies on local contributors, many of whom have had only a sixth-grade education, to tell it like it is.

Local women became the bedrock of community activism. They include Silvia Quilumbango, the president of DECOIN (Intag Defense and Ecological Conservation), who started with doing committee drudge work with a baby in tow; Elvira Haro, a campesina (peasant) activist who saw the mining devastation in Peru and keeps the tailings in her pocket as a reminder; and 'the women of Junin, who,' states Maryellen Fiewiger, a founder of the newspaper, 'have kept mining company personnel out of the reserve, simply blocking the way with their bodies.'

---

behavior. Field research has the end goal of improving preservation decisions in the future. Volunteers can sign up for a week but a month is better.

Get off just before Santa Rosa for the two-hour walk into **Siempre Verde** (USA ☎ 404-262-3032, ext 1486; www.siempreverde.org), a small community-run research station supporting tropical conservation education. There's excellent hiking and bird-watching. Students and researchers are welcome with prior arrangement.

An hour's walk from Santa Rosa you'll find the **Intag Cloud Forest Reserve**, a primary cloud forest reserve run by the founder of the Defense and Ecological Conservation for Intag (DECOIN). The best way to set up a visit is through Safari Tours in Quito (see p90).

Apuela
☎ 06

From a distance Apuela appears as a scattering of Monopoly-game homes, balanced on a mountain shelf. On Sundays locals flood the center to play soccer and browse the market for provisions and blue jeans. Coffee addicts should visit Café Río Intag, a cooperative coffee factory. The beans are produced by **Asociacion Río Intag** (☎ 664 8489; aacri@andinanet.net; near plaza), a group of local farmers and artists. They also sell handbags

woven with agave fibers, handmade soaps and crafts made by local women.

The office of **DECOIN** (Otavalo ☎ 264 8509; www.decoin.org), a long-standing environmental organization, is located uphill from the plaza.

Pradera Tropical (☎ 264 8557; cabins per person $4) has decent cabins near the school. It's a good deal but you won't find hot water here, or nearly anyplace else. The long-standing **Residencial Don Luís** (r per person $4), a lesser bargain, is a couple of blocks uphill from the plaza.

You'll find a complex of tidy wood cabins called **Cabañas Río Grande** (☎ 264 8296; r per person $4) right next to the hot springs. It boasts the softest beds in town and also has a pretty good restaurant. Zulaytur in Otavalo can make a reservation (see p116).

Nangulví thermal springs (admission $16; ⊙ 6am-9pm) have recently added a collection of three-person cabins ($20) to maximize on-site soaking. Tucked between steep valley walls, these tiled pools next to the Intag River offer a welcome rest. These hot (35°C; 98°F) and cold (18°C; 64°F) pools fill up on weekends.

Transportes Otavalo and 6 de Julio have buses from Otavalo ($3, 2½ hours) at 8am, 10am, noon, 2pm and 3pm daily. Ask which buses continue to more remote villages, going past Vacas Galindo to García Moreno and Junín. At 3pm daily there is a round trip to Otavalo from Apuela.

Junín
☎ 06

The road to Junín is gnarled and stunning, with its visual apex near the farming village of García Moreno. Here it squeezes across a narrow ridge rimmed with banana trees, which below hills lap into the distance.

The highly recommended **Junín Community Reserve** (☎ 664 8593; ecojunin@yahoo.es; r per person incl 3 meals $25; volunteers per day $15) operates from a three-story bamboo base lodge. Birdwatching from the hammock-strewn terrace isn't bad for starters, and you can hike to vistas and waterfalls with attentive Spanish-speaking guides. Bunkrooms are plain but snug and vegetarian meal options and robust cups of Intag coffee are included.

The reserve not only offers a great opportunity to meet the locals, but also is part of a larger program to develop sustainable income for community members without contributing to further environmental degradation. The area is under considerable pressure to open up to mining but so far a cohesive grass-roots opposition has thwarted attempts (see the boxed text, opposite).

Contact the center in advance to volunteer or visit. From Junín the reserve is a 20-minute uphill walk. In the rainy season bus services are limited and you must arrange transportation with the reserve or a guide for the two-hour approach.

Volunteers can help by farming, doing biological research or teaching in the community. Donations of used books for the children are happily received.

RESERVA BIOLÓGICA LOS CEDROS

This fantastic, remote reserve is set in 6400 hectares of primary forest contiguous with the Reserva Ecológica Cotacachi-Cayapas. It is one of the only access points to the Southern Chocó, a forest ecosystem considered to be one of the most diverse bioregions of the planet. Living treasures include more than 240 species of birds, 400 types of orchids and more than 960 nocturnal moths.

Guests arrive at the village of Chontal and undertake a rugged four- to six-hour hike through the Magdalena River valley into the Cordillera de la Plata. Contact the reserve in advance to arrange for a guide, pack animals and accommodations. If you want to ride, a mule runs $10 extra. Facilities include a scientific research station, dining and cooking facilities, accommodations in dorms or private rooms, hot water and electricity. The price includes all meals and guide services. Communication with **Los Cedros** (www.reserva loscedros.org, loscedros@ecuanex.net.ec; r per person $30) is via email only. Volunteering may be arranged ($300 per month, one month minimum).

If you're coming from Otavalo, check which Intag buses have services to Chontal. From Quito **Transportes Minas** (☎ 06-286 8039; Calle Los Ríos) goes to Chontal (3½ hours) at 6am every day from near the Ayora Maternity Hospital. In Chontal you can get breakfast at Ramiro and Alicia's *hostal* while waiting for your pack mules (and guide).

SAN ANTONIO DE IBARRA
☎ 06

Woodcarving is the fame of this small village near Ibarra. Artisans whittle cedar and walnut from the jungle lowlands into Virgin Marys, Don Quixotes and nursing mothers. Several craft stores crowd the main square of the Parque Central but if you're looking for artists at work you might be disappointed. Most of the actual work takes place out of sight. The most renowned gallery is **Galería Luís Potosí** (☎ 293 2056; Parque Central; admission free; ☾ 8am-6pm), whose namesake has achieved fame throughout Ecuador and abroad.

Hostal Los Nogales (☎ 293 2000; Sucre 3-64; r per person $5) is the only hotel in town and has basic rooms. Most visitors stay in Ibarra or Otavalo.

Buses from Ibarra ($0.18, 15 minutes) are frequent throughout the day. Get off at the main plaza. A taxi costs around $3.

IBARRA
☎ 06 / pop 108,535 / elevation 2225m

Ibarra, with its choked streets and colonial charm weathered to a weary gray, is neither the provincial backwater it once was, nor a thriving draw for tourism. With commerce picking up, it's unclear whether it will embrace its cobbled foundations or pave over them. The fast-growing capital of Imababura province lies just 22km northeast of Otavalo. To properly enjoy the architectural beauty of *la ciudad blanca* (the white city), take an evening walk or ride through its peaceful well-lit streets in order to admire the narrow wooden balconies, sculpted facades and palm-lined parks. In the daytime it is far too hectic and gritty to get the same effect.

NORTHERN HIGHLANDS

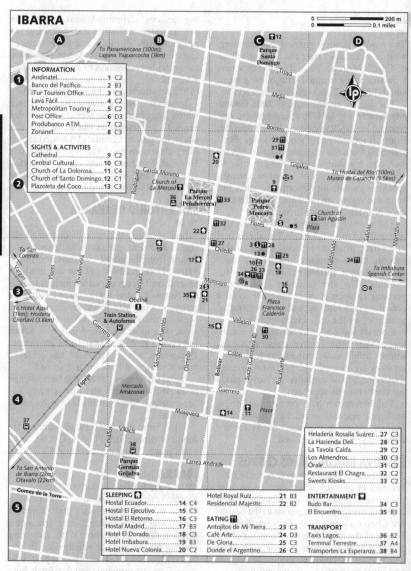

IBARRA

0 — 200 m
0 — 0.1 miles

INFORMATION	
Andinatel................................1	C2
Banco del Pacífico.................2	B3
iTur Tourism Office...............3	C3
Lava Fácil..............................4	C2
Metropolitan Touring...........5	C2
Post Office............................6	D3
Produbanco ATM..................7	C2
Zonanet................................8	C3

SIGHTS & ACTIVITIES	
Cathedral..............................9	C2
Central Cultural...................10	C3
Church of La Dolorosa.........11	C4
Church of Santo Domingo....12	C1
Plazoleta del Coco...............13	C3

To Panamericana (300m);
Laguna Yaguarcocha (3km)

Parque Santo Domingo

Troya

Mejía

Borrero

García Moreno

Church of La Merced

Parque La Merced (Peñaherrera)

Rodríguez

Grijalva

Parque Pedro Moncayo

To Hostal del Río (100m);
Museo de Caranchi (3.5km)

Church of San Agustín

Flores

Plaza

Salinas

Montalvo

To San Lorenzo

Vargas

Rivadeneira

Borja

Narváez

Oviedo

Moncayo

Maldonado

To Imbabura Spanish Center

Obelisk

Train Station & Autoferros

Guerrero

Sánchez Cifuentes

Olmedo

Bolívar

Velasco

Plaza Francisco Calderón

To Hotel Ajaví (1km); Hostería Chorlaví (3.8km)

Colón

Sucre (Carretera 8)

Rocafuerte

Espejo

Mercado Amazonas

Cevallos

Guerrero

Mosquera

Plaza

To San Antonio de Ibarra (2km);
Otavalo (22km)

Villacís

Parque Germán Grijalva

Larrea Andrade

Gomez de la Torre

Heladería Rosalía Suárez...27	C3
La Hacienda Deli.................28	C3
La Tavola Calda..................29	C2
Los Almendros....................30	C3
Órale...................................31	C2
Restaurant El Chagra..........32	C2
Sweets Kiosks.....................33	C2

SLEEPING			Hotel Royal Ruíz..................21	B3
Hostal Ecuador....................14	C4		Residencial Majestic............22	B2
Hostal El Ejecutivo...............15	C3			
Hostal El Retorno................16	C3		EATING	
Hostal Madrid......................17	B3		Antojitos de Mi Tierra.........23	C3
Hotel El Dorado...................18	C3		Café Arte.............................24	D3
Hotel Imbabura...................19	B3		De Gloria.............................25	C3
Hotel Nueva Colonia...........20	C2		Donde el Argentino.............26	C3

ENTERTAINMENT	
Budo Bar.............................34	C3
El Encuentro.......................35	B3

TRANSPORT	
Taxis Lagos.........................36	B2
Terminal Terrestre...............37	A4
Transportes La Esperanza....38	B4

Ibarra offers diversity atypical of a highland town, with students, mestizos, indigenous groups and Afro-Ecuadorians. The mild climate is ideal for hoofing it around the ice-cream shops (p132) and green plazas. Ibarra occupies a crossroads pointing to the coast, Otavalo, the tropical valley of Chota and the *páramo* villages to the northeast.

Hotels fill up quickly during the last week of September for Ibarra's annual fiesta, but it is a fun time with lots of live music and activities.

Orientation

Ibarra's old architecture and shady plazas sit north of the center. The area around

Mercado las Amazonas and Sanchez and Cifuentes are unsafe at night.

Information

Andinatel (Sucre 4-48)

Banco del Pacífico (☎ 295 7714; cnr Olmedo & Moncayo) The only place in town that changes traveler's checks; it has an ATM too.

Hostal El Ejecutivo (☎ 295 6575; Bolívar 9-69; per hr $1; ☑ 7am-late) Internet café.

iTur Tourism Office (☎ 260 8409; www.turismoibarra .com; Oveido & Sucre; ☑ 8:30am-1pm & 2-5pm Mon-Fri) Staff can help direct you to community tourism.

Lava Fácil (Sucre near Grijalva) Laundry service in about a day.

Metropolitan Touring (☎ 295 6239; Flores near Sucre; ☑ 8:30am-6:30pm Mon-Fri, 9am-noon Sat) A reliable, all-purpose travel agency which handles international flights as well as local tours.

Post office (☎ 264 3135; Salinas 6-64)

Produbanco ATM (cnr Sucre & Flores)

Zonanet (☎ 225 8858; Moncayo 5-74; per hr $1; ☑ 8:30am-9pm) Internet access.

Sights & Activities

You can't miss **Parque La Merced**, also known as Peñaherrera, an oversized statue of the Virgin tops its church. Built at the beginning of the 19th century, the main feature of the Church of La Merced is an ornate altar with the Virgin of La Merced, patron saint of armed forces.

The gorgeous palm-filled plaza of **Parque Pedro Moncayo** is dominated by the baroque-influenced **cathedral**. The altars are covered in gold leaf and Troya's paintings of the 12 apostles adorn the pillars. The park itself is named after native son Pedro Moncayo (1807–88), a journalist and diplomat.

Take a walk out to the north end of Bolívar where you'll find the quaint **Parque Santo Domingo**. Behind this small park, the Dominican **Church of Santo Domingo** houses La Virgin del Rosarío, a painting by famous artist Diego de Robles, on its altar. The church also has a **museum of religious art** (admission $0.50; ☑ 9am-noon & 3-6pm Mon-Sat).

On the corner of Oveido and Sucre you'll find a tiled patch not bigger than a parking space called **Plazoleta del Coco** by the locals. Here you'll find the tourist office. The **Centro Cultural** (☎ 264 4087; cnr Oveido & Sucre; admission $0.50; ☑ 8:30am-4:30pm Mon-Sat) houses an archaeology museum featuring prehistoric ceramics and gold artifacts from Pimam-

piro, with signs in English. There's also a local historical archive and library.

Locals are fond of **Laguna Yaguarcocha**, a lake encircled by an auto racetrack 3km north ·of town on the Panamericana. Its name 'blood lake' was coined by the Inca defeat of the Caras here when the Incas dumped thousands of Caras bodies into the lake. Buzzing cars and boats, along with the litter, make it an unlikely destination for visitors seeking refuge in nature.

Courses

The **Imbabura Spanish Center** (☎ 295 9429; Casa 10, Manzana 33, Urbanización La Victoria) offers one-on-one tuition for $5 an hour and homestays with meals for about $15 a day. The school is in a private house away from downtown.

Sleeping
BUDGET

Ibarra's cheapies tend toward old and outdated. Make sure there's hot water.

Hostal del Río (☎ 261 1885, 09-944 2792; Juan Montalvo 4-55 & Flores; s/d $12/15) Fusing modern art deco with regional colonial style, this excellent option starts with a curved staircase leading to rooms with red hardwood floors, snug fluffy beds and bright accents. For pampering, ask for the room with Jacuzzi. Located in a quiet neighborhood a few blocks east of downtown.

Hostal El Ejecutivo (☎ 295 6575; Bolívar 9-69; s/d $7/12; ▣) Old plaids dominate the ample rooms and lend a retro feel. Rooms have hot baths, telephone and TV. The 1st floor is a busy Internet café.

Hostal Ecuador (☎ 295 6425; Mosquera 5-54; r per person $5) Bare, bright rooms give the effect of a sanitarium but the attention is sincere.

Hostal El Retorno (☎ 295 7722; Moncayo 4-32; r per person with shared/private bathroom $6/7) A cheery little place with pint-sized beds and TVs. Request a room with windows; the interior rooms are dark.

Hotel Nueva Colonia (☎ 295 2918; fax 295 5543; Olmedo 5-19; r per person $8) A happy, swept courtyard is betrayed by dark rooms with lumpy beds. Rooms include TV and telephone and there's a restaurant and roof patio.

Hotel Imbabura (☎ 295 0155, 295 8522; hotel _imbabura@hotmail.com; Oviedo 9-33; r per person $5) This slanting colonial's pastel courtyard is filled with tables and a popular corner bar. While communal bathrooms are clean,

NORTHERN HIGHLANDS

rooms are drab, with chipped walls and droopy mattresses.

Hotel El Dorado (☎ 295 8700; Oviedo 5-74; r per person incl breakfast $8) A generic experience; has cable TV. The on-site restaurant serves for a quick bite.

Residencial Majestic (☎ 295 0052; Olmedo 7-63; r per person with shared/private bathroom $4/6) A 2nd-floor hotel whose windowless, narrow cells are at least squeaky clean.

MIDRANGE
Hostal Madrid (☎ 264 4918; Olmedo 8-69; r per person $10) Offers sharp rooms with private bathroom, cable TV and telephone.

Hotel Royal Ruíz (☎ 264 4644/53; hroyalruiz@ andinet.net; Olmedo 9-40; r per person $10) A popular modern hotel with friendly desk staff. Beds are firm and cheery rooms come with cable TV and telephone.

The best hotels are west of town, near the Panamericana. They're often booked well in advance, particularly on weekends.

Hostería Chorlaví (☎ 293 2222; chorlavi@andinanet .net; s/d incl breakfast about $45/50; 🏊) Weekenders flock to this classic, converted hacienda 4km west of Ibarra to enjoy the swimming pool and tennis courts. It is considered the best hotel in the area. If you're looking for a quiet getaway, this probably isn't it. Live music on weekends draws tour groups and shoppers from Otavalo. Lunch and dinners are about $8, and the buffet breakfast is $7 for nonguests.

Hotel Ajaví (☎ 295 5640, 295 5221; h-ajavi@imbanet .net; Av Maríano Acosta 16-38; s/d $27/47; 🏊) Large carpeted rooms and king-sized beds create a comfortable yet generic atmosphere. There's also a restaurant, bar, heated swim-ming pool and sauna ($5 extra). Doubles have TV, telephone and minifridge.

Eating
The city is famous for its sweets, *nogadas* (nougat) made with nuts and *arrope de mora* (thick blackberry syrup), sold in kiosks.

Antojitos de Mi Tierra (☎ 295 0592; Plaza Francisco Calderón, Sucre; ⏰ noon-10pm Tue-Sun) The place to go for traditional snacks such as *chicha de arroz* (a sweetened rice drink) and tamales, *humitas* (small tamales wrapped in corn husks) and *quimbolitos* (different corn dumplings steamed in corn husks or leaves). Owner Marta Jduregi is a well-known local historian and chef.

Café Arte (☎ 295 0806; Salinas 5-43; mains $6; ⏰ 9am-midnight) A funky and relaxed artist-owned gathering spot, it's a good place to meet locals and check out local bands. Rotating art graces the walls and there's an adjoining exhibit space. Tasty offerings lead toward Mexican, with added staples of sandwiches, pizzas and espresso. The owners let out a few extra rooms to guests – call ahead if you're interested and ask for Magdalena or Olmedo.

Órale (☎ 295 0850; Sucre; mains $4; ⏰ 3:30-9:30pm Mon-Sat) Authentic Mexican in a casual atmosphere with tiled floors and varnished green tabletops. Lightly spiced enchiladas and *flautas* (meat and cheese roll-ups) are served with margaritas or a delicious hibiscus punch. In the block between Grijalva and Borrero.

La Hacienda (☎ 09-502 8493; Oveido & Sucre; sandwiches $3; ⏰ 8am-9pm) A busy deli and cheery atmosphere. Baguette sandwiches are the speciality. Try *El Español*, Serrano ham and

---

THE CONE OF ETERNAL YOUTH

Teenage boredom inspired Rosalía Suárez to invent ice creams in the kitchen back in 1897, when she was just 17. Her experimentation led to a discovery – the best ice cream had no cream at all. With this knowledge, Rosalía turned entrepreneurial and her shop **Heladería Rosalía Suárez** (☎ 06-295 8722; Oviedo 7-82) has been a sensation for more than a century. *Helados de paila* are actually sorbets stirred with a wooden spoon in a large copper pail (the *paila*) and cooled on a bed of straw and ice. The shop, now run by her grandson, claims the recipe requires pure juice from tropical fruits and egg whites. It's not entirely possible to imitate – ice from the first versions was brought down from the glacier of Volcán Imbabura, which has since disappeared.

Doña Rosalía lived until the age of 105, which speaks something to the restorative qualities of a good *helado*. It's a theory worth testing, anyway. *Guanábana* (similar to soursop) is the shop's most popular flavor. The tart *naranjilla* (known as lulo) and *maracuyá* (passion fruit) are also worth a lick.

tomatoes with escarole, balsamic vinegar and olive oil.

Los Almendros (☎ 295 7631; Velasco 5-59 & Sucre; lunch $2.25; ⏱ noon-3:30pm) Customers line up out the door for well-prepared Ecuadorian comfort food in a bland but bustling setting. Lunch is a daily menu with three delicious courses.

La Tavola Calda (☎ 09-962 2560; Sucre 3-37; pizzas $4-6; ⏱ 4-10pm, Mon-Sat) A cozy nook next to the dance school serving brick-oven pizzas with a variety of toppings, wine and sangria. Owner Ruben can help arrange community tourism.

Donde el Argentino (☎ 09-945 9004; Plaza Francisco Calderón, Sucre; mains $4-5; ⏱ noon-6pm) This matchbox-sized café specializes in thick slabs of steak and fries. The quality is decent and outdoor tables on the square provide a dose of atmosphere.

De Gloria (☎ 260 4118; Olveido 67-2; desserts or mains $2-3; ⏱ 8:30am-8pm) A dessert café with an open, friendly flour-spattered kitchen. Creamy *tres leche* (butter cake) and pies are the main event but lasagna, crepes and salads are also recommendable.

El Chagra (☎ 295 2114; Olmedo 7-48; mains $3; ⏱ 8am-10pm) Slip into a high-backed leather booth for some stew or trout. There's something comforting about the plastic table cloths and droning telenovelas.

Drinking & Entertainment

Ibarra is a quiet city, but it has a few places worth popping into for a mellow evening.

Café Arte (☎ 295 0806; Salinas 5-43; ⏱ 4pm-midnight Mon-Fri, 4pm-3am Fri & Sat) One of the best modern music venues in Ecuador, bringing acts from as far as Cuba and Spain. Music varies from jazz and flamenco to rock. Shows start Fridays and Saturdays at 10pm. On Mondays and Wednesdays there's art-house cinema at 4pm.

El Encuentro (☎ 295 9520; Olmedo 9-35) Locals enjoy this cowboy-themed bar and its roundup of antiques and oddities.

Budo Bar (Plaza Francisco Calderón; ⏱ 4pm-midnight Wed-Sat, 10am-4pm Sun) A place to cozy up to the long bar for a beer.

Getting There & Away
BUS

Ibarra's new bus terminal, Terminal Terrestre, is located at the end of Avenida Teodoro Gomez de la Torre. You can grab a taxi

to/from downtown for $1. The following (apart from Transportes La Esperanza) depart from here:

Aerotaxi (☎ 295 5200) goes to Quito, Guayaquil ($9, 10 hours), Esmeraldas ($8, nine hours), Atacames ($9, nine hours) and San Lorenzo ($4, 3½ to four hours).

Cita Express (☎ 295 5627) goes to Ambato ($5, five hours) via El Quinche.

Expreso Turismo (☎ 295 5730) goes to Tulcán every 45 minutes and Quito ($2, 2½ hours).

Flota Imbabura (☎ 295 1094) goes to Quito ($2, 2½ hours), Tulcán ($2, 2½ hours), Guayaquil ($10, 11 hours), Cuenca ($14, 12 hours) and Manta ($10, 12 hours).

Transportes Andina (☎ 295 0833) At the same terminal as Flota Imbabura, goes to Quito ($2.50, 2½ hours) every 10 minutes and Santo Domingo ($4, six hours) every half-hour.

Transportes del Valle Goes four times daily to Chota Valley. It also goes to Lago Agrío at 9:45am ($8, eight hours) and San Lorenzo.

Transportes Espejo (☎ 295 9917) Serves Quito, San Lorenzo and has a service to El Ángel ($1.25, 1½ hours) seven times a day.

Transportes La Esperanza (Parque Grijalva near Sanchez y Cifuentes) Goes to the village of La Esperanza ($0.20, 20 minutes).

Transportes Otavalo/Los Lagos (☎ 295 5593) Heads regularly to Otavalo ($0.35, 35 minutes).

For San Antonio de Ibarra, see p134.

TAXI

If you're rushing to Quito, try **Taxis Lagos** (☎ 295 5150; Flores 9-24). Six passengers can cram into a large taxi and get dropped off wherever they want in Quito ($8, 2¼ hours).

TRAIN

Since the road opened to the coastal town of San Lorenzo, the train service on the Ibarra–San Lorenzo line has been suspended. There are, *autoferros* (buses mounted on a train chassis) that go as far as the point known as Primer Paso ($3.80 one way, 1¾ hours), less than a quarter of the way from Ibarra to San Lorenzo. The short ride is now essentially a round-trip tourist attraction. Alternatively, you can get off at Primer Paso and wait for a passing bus to San Lorenzo.

The *autoferro* only leaves Ibarra with a minimum of 16 passengers. It leaves the train station at Ibarra at 7am Monday through Friday and at 8am on Saturday and Sunday. The return ride departs Primer Paso at 2pm. In tourist low-season

NORTHERN HIGHLANDS

cancelled departures are the norm. Call the **train station** (☎ 295 0390) or check out www .imbaburaturismo.gov.ec (in Spanish) for the latest information.

Getting Around

Local buses with the companies 28 de Septiembre and San Miguel de Ibarra provide service around town and some continue to San Antonio de Ibarra. The best place to catch a San Antonio de Ibarra bus is on Sanchez y Cifuentes near Guerrero. Different buses leave from near the same intersection for several other local destinations.

NORTH OF IBARRA
☎ 06

The winding Panamericana is a favorite of spandex-clad cyclists, who pound up this punishing route on weekends. Entering the **Río Chota valley**, at 1565m, the road drops sharply. The hills turn squat and lush green spreads across the valley floor. The valley is inhabited by Afro-Ecuadorians descended from 17th-century plantation slaves. They make their living growing sugarcane and fruit, which can be scooped up in great bundles at roadside stands. Within an hour's drive from Ibarra, the valley is within arm's reach for daytrips.

A token of this unique Afro-Andean culture is *bomba* music, a blend of driving African drums and plaintive highland notes. Fiestas and concerts are irregular in schedule but sometimes advertised in Ibarra.

Palm-lined hotels with swimming pools make **Ambuquí** a popular weekend destination for highlanders seeking a little warmth. One is **Oasis** (☎ 294 1192; www.oasishosteria.com; r per person $37; ☒), whose bougainvillea, swimming pools with slides and lush gardens mask the fact that you're vacationing next to the highway. Cabañas are tidy and modern, with all meals included. The food is quite good. A day pass is $5. On weekends you can hop a *chiva* (a festive bus with wooden benches) for tours of Chota valley with local music and food.

Next door, the basic **Aruba Hostería** (☎ 294 1146; r per person $10; ☒) has helpful staff and a swimming pool filling the courtyard. Along the road there are open-air eateries serving *sancocho* (stew).

Juncal, the breeding ground for the World Cup soccer team, is next up. This hot, dusty village is the turn off for the road which climbs to **Pimampiro**. Adventurers eager to chart new territory should come here. This button-sized village sits on a steep hillside utterly removed. **Pensión Jose Alveiro** (☎ 29. 7070; Olmedo & Flores; r per person $3.50) is the only hotel in town. Its decrepit rooms and mottled shared bathrooms earn visitors extra points for endurance. A block away, restaurant **El Forastero** (meals $1.25; ☒ 8am-8pm) has a neat appearance and offers rice with *seco* (meat in sauce) made of chicken or beef.

This area borders the backside of Reserva Ecologicá Cayambe-Coca. Hikers should head to the village of Mariana Acosta where guides lead four-hour walks from Nueva America to **Laguna Puruhanta**, a peaceful lake ringed by high peaks.

Back on the Panamericana, the Carchi province marks a return to high Andean landscape and cooler temperatures. **Bolívar** is a large hill town without much tourism. Further on you'll come to **Grutas de la Paz**, a grotto converted to a chapel whose famous Virgin sparkles under the stalactites. Nearby **thermal springs** and **waterfalls** round out the attractions. Take a bus to the springs from Tulcán, or walk the 5km southeast of the Panamericana from La Paz on the road marked 'Las Grutas.' The complex is open Thursday to Sunday.

About 38km south of Tulcán is the small town of **San Gabriel**, at an elevation of 2900m, which has a couple of basic hotels. Five kilometers east is **Bosque de los Arreyanes** (☒ 8:30am-4:30pm), which has a lovely myrtle forest ideal for bird-watching. The waterfalls **Las Cascadas de Paluz** are found on Río San Gabriel 3km to 4km north of San Gabriel (head north on Calle Bolívar and keep going).

LA ESPERANZA
☎ 06

This picturesque village is set against the sloping flanks of Volcán Imababura, 7km due south of Ibarra. It's respite for the road-weary and the best spot to climb **Volcán Imababura** (4609m). To climb it, start off in the early morning and follow the steepening ridge 2000m to the summit, 8km southwest. The last stretch is a scramble over loose rock. If you're not experienced, it is best to hire a local guide. Allow about 10 hours for the round trip.

Those of middling ambition can try **Loma Cubilche** (3836m). This hill south of La Esperanza is an easier climb with lovely views. Walkers can hoof the scenic cobbled road which leaves town headed south.

Wake up to a stack of pancakes at the affable **Casa Aida** (☎ 264 2020; Calle Gallo Plaza s/n; per person $4), the only place to stay in town. Rooms are simple and hot water is sporadic. The friendly family is a great source of local information.

You can walk here from Ibarra or take one of the frequent buses ($0.20, 20 minutes).

RÍO BLANCO AREA
☎ 06

Ditch your highland woolen clothing for the twisty, scenic ride to the steamy tropic lowlands abutting the northern coast. Afro-Ecuadorian farmers tend crops of sugar-cane, bananas and tropical fruits on the steep slopes of the 1000m valley. You'll find a laid-back air and inviting, hilly walks.

Bospas Forest Farm (bospas@hotmail.com; r per person shared/private bathroom $8/10; volunteers per month $190), on the outskirts of **Limonal**, is run by a friendly Ecuadorian-Belgian couple. Comfortable lodge accommodations are in a lush setting a 15-minute walk from the bus. The food is wonderful (tending toward coastal specialities) and guided hikes ($10) are offered. Owner Piet enthusiastically imparts his knowledge of tropical plants and preservation. The farm promotes reforestation, organic pest-control and farming in this highly deforested area. Located 1½ hours from Ibarra.

Guallupe is the entry point to the **Cerro Golondrinas Project** (Quito ☎ 02-222 6602; www.funda ciongolondrinas.org, 4-day packages per person $200), one of Ecuador's best grassroots conservation efforts. Nongovernment organization (NGO) Fundación Golondrinas works locally to promote sustainable farming techniques and curb rampant deforestation. The project aims to conserve some of the remaining forests while improving local living standards and providing a sustainable source of income. Its reserve occupies some 1600 hectares between Reserva Ecológica El Ángel and the Colombian border, in stunning habitats ranging from *páramo* to temperate and subtropical montane cloud forest. Depending on weather conditions, arrangements can also be made to hike into the reserve via El Ángel.

Local hosts provide warm hospitality to visitors, volunteers and researchers. Four-day treks or horseback-riding trips include all food, accommodations and local guiding services. The best time to go is in the dry season between June and September although the *páramo* region may be visited anytime of year.

Fundación Golondrinas, which won the Rolex Award (prestigious international award for enterprise) in 2000, has current priorities to invest in education and raise funding to train locals as naturalist guides. Headquarters are in a popular budget travelers' hostal in Quito, La Casa de Eliza (p92).

EL ÁNGEL
☎ 06

Tufts of ocher grasses ripple surrounding hillsides and entertainment means drag races on the main strip. The stark-still Andean village of El Ángel is the entry point to Páramos El Ángel, a misty wilderness favored by foxes and condors. It's part of the 16,000-hectare **Reserva Ecológica El Ángel** (admission $10). You can arrange *páramo* visits with Cerro Golondrinas (left) or with local hotels.

The village springs to life with the Monday market.

El Ángel Hostería (☎ 297 7584; hwy & Av Espejo 1302; r per person $12) has snuggly high-ceiling cabins with comfortable beds and modern bathrooms. The well-run *hostería* offers guided hikes and city tours in English or German. It's a 10-minute walk to town.

Blas Ángel (☎ 297 7189, 297 7346; hwy & traffic circle; r per person shared/private bathroom $6/8), located behind a gravel lot, has cheerful but bare-bones rooms, with tile floor and patched walls. The host is attentive and the common space offers a TV room with a well-enjoyed, rumpled couch.

Simple restaurants are found in town. Transportes Espejo, on the main plaza, goes to Quito ($3.50, four hours) via Ibarra ($1.20, 1½ hours) every hour. Buses to Tulcán leave early in the morning. At the plaza you'll find shared taxis going to and from the Bolívar crossroads ($0.70), where frequent buses go north or south.

RESERVA BIOLÓGICA GUANDERA

This 1000-hectare, tropical, wet, montane forest reserve was founded in 1994 by Fundación Jatun Sacha (see p253). The reserve lies between 3100m and 3600m on a transitional ridge (forest to *páramo*) 11km east of San Gabriel. Projects include reforestation and finding alternatives to chemical-intensive potato production. Andean spectacled bears (rarely glimpsed), high-altitude parrots and toucans are among the attractions. Jatun Sacha operates a **refuge** (dm $15). Reservations are required and fees must be paid in advance at the **Jatun Sacha office** (Quito ☎ 02-243 2240, 243 2173; www.jatunsacha.org; Pasaje Eugenio de Santillán N34-248 & Maurián, Urbanización Rumipamba) in Quito. Researchers and volunteers are welcome.

From the village of San Gabriel it is 1½ hours on foot to the reserve. Otherwise, you can hop on the 1pm school bus to Mariscal Sucre from San Gabriel's main plaza. Saturday morning buses and cars also go to the Mariscal Sucre market. A taxi from there is about $10 one way.

TULCÁN
☎ 06 / pop 47,359 / elevation 3000m

Tulcán is a chilly highland city steeped in grit and bustle, a narrow urban causeway linking with Colombia. The provincial capital of Carchi used to attract Colombians bargain hunting with the Ecuadorian sucre, but these days the best deals are with Colombian imports. The Sunday street market provides goods and clothing but few handicrafts. The main attraction for foreign visitors is heading overland to Colombia.

Orientation

The town is a long strip with action primarily on Bolívar and Sucre. These parallel streets host shops stacked with brick-a-brac, cheap sneakers and electronics. Visitors should take taxis from the bus station to downtown or to the border, but otherwise the city is walkable. Addresses are numbered in two different ways. To prevent confusion, the nearest intersections, rather than the numbers, are used here.

Information

Exchanging money (between US dollars and Colombian pesos) is slightly better in Tulcán than at the border. If the currency-exchange centers are closed you can try the street moneychangers in front of the banks. They are associated and each has an ID number you can record in case of later problems.

Andinatel (Olmedo near Junín) Branches are both at the bus terminal and at the border.

Banco del Pichincha (cnr 10 de Agosto & Sucre) Will change currency and traveler's checks Monday through Friday only; it has a Visa ATM. There are other banks nearby.

Café Net (Olmedo & Ayacucho; Internet per hr $0.50; ☻ 8am-10pm)

Casa de Cambio (☎ 298 5731; Ayacucho at Sucre; ☻ 7am-6pm)

Clínica Metropolitana (Bolívar & Panamá; ☻ 24hr) A better hospital is in Ipiales, 2km north of the border.

Colombian Consulate (☎ 298 0559; Av Manabi 58-087; ☻ 8:30am-1pm, 2:30-3:30pm Mon-Fri) In a new location in front of Parque Isidro Ayora.

Ecctur (☎ 298 0468, 298 0368; Sucre at 10 de Agosto) Sells tours and airline tickets.

iTur Tourist Information (☎ 298 5760; Cotopaxi; ☻ 8am-6pm Mon-Fri) In a new location at the cemetery entrance. Staff are friendly and helpful.

Post office (☎ 298 0552; Bolívar near Junín) Centrally located.

Sights & Activities

Tulcán's best feature is its cemetery; a big tourist attraction where mourners are prone to stumble upon young lovers in the labyrinth of greenery. Check out its **topiary garden** where bushes and hedges are sculpted into pre-Columbian totems, animals and geometric shapes. The gardens are trimmed by the son of the original artist, who now resides permanently on the grounds.

On the weekends you might find locals behind the cemetery playing an Ecuadorian paddleball game called **pelota de guante**, which uses a soft ball and large, spiked paddles. Walk south from the cemetery one block to the new, mural-covered **Museo Herman Bastidas Vaca**, housing pre-Columbian artifacts and ceramics.

Hot springs are within the reach of daytrippers. Cooperativa 11 de Abril buses depart 8am on Saturdays to the somewhat lukewarm **La Paz thermal springs**. On Sundays at 8am they also make the pilgrimage to **Aguas Hediondas** ($1). These 'stinking waters' are very hot high-sulphur thermal baths. Many of the pools are on the Colombian side; you can cross the border on a day pass to soak in the pools, but those who want to stay on have to enter via the Tulcán border crossing. On Mondays through Fridays Cooperativa Transportes Norte can take you to the turn off for the hot springs at 6am and 12:30pm. Ask locally about the safety

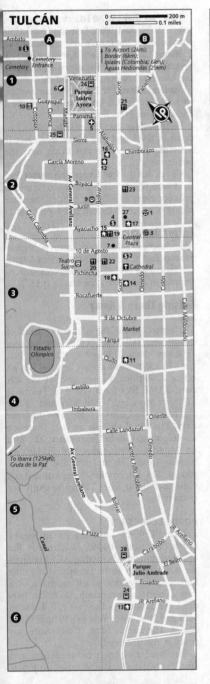

INFORMATION

Andinatel	1 B2
Banco del Pichincha	2 B3
Café Net	3 B2
Casa de Cambio	4 B2
Clínica Metropolitana	5 A1
Colombian Consulate	6 A1
Ecctur	7 B3
iTur	8 A1
Post Office	9 A2

SIGHTS & ACTIVITIES

Museo Herman Bastidas Vaca	10 A1

SLEEPING

Hotel Alejandra	11 B4
Hotel Azteca Internacional	12 B2
Hotel Los Alpes	13 B6
Hotel Lumar	14 B3
Hotel Machado	15 B2
Hotel San Francisco	16 B2
Hotel Sara Espindola	17 B2
Hotel Unicornio	18 B3

EATING

Asadero La Brasa	19 B2
Chifa Pack Choy	(see 18)
El Patio	20 A3
Mama Rosita	21 B1
Restaurant Los Alpes	(see 13)
Tekila	22 B3
Wimpy	23 B2

ENTERTAINMENT

Crazy	(see 17)

TRANSPORT

Bus Terminal	24 B6
Cooperativa Transportes Norte	25 A2
Minibuses to Airport & Border	26 A1
TAME Airline	27 B2
Transportes Velotaxi	28 B5

of travel in this remote border region – due to the conflict in Colombia, it may not be advised.

Sleeping

Tulcán has no shortage of hotels, but most are lackluster.

Hotel Machado (298 4221; cnr Ayacucho & Bolívar; r per person incl breakfast $13) A fresh coat of paint and gleaming bathrooms create a welcome haven. Rooms have cable TV and phone.

Hotel Sara Espindola (298 5925; cnr Sucre & Ayacucho; r per person $16) The staff is eager and rooms are snug, handsomely furnished and provide cable TV. On the central plaza, this is considered the town's best hotel. There's an on-site restaurant, minicasino and disco too.

Hotel San Francisco (298 0760; Bolívar near Atahualpa; r per person $4) While comparisons to the bay city are scant, this hotel is one of the

NORTHERN HIGHLANDS

better options in town. Rooms are brighter and better kept than those next door at Hotel Azteca Internacional, and include hot water and TV. Ask for a window, the interior rooms can be dark and stuffy.

Hotel Azteca Internacional (☎ 298 0481, 298 1447; Bolívar near García Moreno; r per person $5) Dark-paneled and cavernous, the carpeted rooms are a wee bit better than one might expect. Beds are firm and there's TV and phone. The disco downstairs can either be a pro or con. Weekends get pretty loud.

Hotel Alejandra (☎ 298 1784; cnr Sucre & Quito; r per person $5) This member of Hostelling International offers musty but passable rooms with cable TV. On the upside, it is quieter than most.

Hotel Unicornio (☎ 298 0638; cnr Pichincha & Sucre; r per person $6) Offers a variety of carpeted rooms of good and poor quality conveniently located over a good Chinese restaurant. Rooms have TV and telephone.

Hotel Lumar (☎ 298 0402, 298 7137; Sucre near Pichincha; r per person $7) A modern hotel with good service. There's a parking garage and the carpeted rooms have soft beds, cable TV and phone.

Hotel Los Alpes (☎ 298 2235; JR Arellano near Bolívar; r per person $5) The bus terminal has a dodgy reputation but late arrivals can consider this option. Rooms sport limp mattresses but there's hot water and a decent restaurant.

Eating

Tulcán's Colombian restaurants provide a welcome alternative to the Ecuadorian staples.

Mama Rosita (☎ 298 5192; Sucre at Chimborazo; mains $1-2; ☽ 9am-10pm) Famous for its *fritada* and other *comida típica* (traditional Ecuadorian food).

Tekila (☎ 298 6346; Bolívar; mains $2; ☽ 9am-11pm) A cafeteria-style joint featuring Colombian food that is popular with locals. Mild beef with fries and rice or *mondongo* (tripe stew) are the specialities. Located in the block between 10 de Agosto and Pinchincha.

El Patio (☎ 298 4872; Bolívar near 10 de Agosto; mains $3; ☽ 8am-9pm Mon-Sat, 8am-5pm Sun) The dust has settled on the horse stables decor, but the Colombian food is tasty and popular. Try their *bandeja paisa*, which includes no less than four fried foods (pork skins, sausage, egg and banana) in addition to rice, tender smoky beans and avocado. Portions are enormous.

Chifa Pack Choy (☎ 298 2713; cnr Pichincha & Sucre; mains $2-3; ☽ noon-11:30pm) Beneath Hotel Unicornio; serves the town's best Chinese food.

Wimpy (☎ 298 3218; Sucre & Boyacá; mains $2-3; ☽ 6:30am-11pm) A popular greasy spoon serving burgers, hot dogs and fried chicken.

Asadero La Brasa (☎ 298 0968; Ayacucho near Bolívar; mains $1.50; ☽ 8am-9pm) The spot for roast chicken with French fries.

Restaurant Los Alpes (JR Arellano near Bolívar) Located in the Hotel Los Alpes, this place is a simple, inexpensive restaurant near the bus terminal.

Check out the **fruit & vegetable market** (Panamá & Sucre) where horse-drawn carts unload produce every day. By the border, there are plenty of snack stalls and fast-food carts.

Entertainment

Kaleidoscope colors and Latin pop greet movers and shakers at **Crazy** (cnr Sucre & Ayacucho; ☽ 9pm-late Thu-Sat), the *discoteca* (discotheque) in Hotel Sara Espindola (p137).

Getting There & Away

AIR

The **airport** (☎ 298 2850) is 2km northeast of downtown. **TAME** (☎ 298 0675; Sucre near Junín; ☽ 8:30am-9:30am, 11:30am-2:30pm & 3-5pm Mon, Wed & Fri, 8:30am-1:30pm & 3-6pm Tue & Thu) has an office downtown and another at the airport. TAME flies from Quito to Tulcán at 11:15am Monday, Wednesday and Friday and returns to Quito at 3:30pm on the same days. The $30 flight fills up fast. There are also flights to Cali in Colombia at 12:30pm on Monday, Wednesday and Friday, returning from Cali at 2pm ($68 one way, plus a $25 international departure tax). Note that flights from Tulcán to Quito are often full.

BORDER CROSSING

Entering Colombia via the Panamericana north of Tulcán (p136), is currently the only recommended crossing. All formalities are taken care of at the Ecuador–Colombia border crossing known as Rumichaca, 6km away. Fourteen-seat minibuses to the border leave as soon as they are full, between 6am and 7pm, from Tulcán's Parque Isidro Ayora. The fare is $0.80 (Colombian currency is also accepted).

The border is open between 6am and 8pm every day. Taxis and buses drop passengers off before the bridge where you cross on foot. Daytrippers to Ipiales will still need their passport stamped.

On the Colombian side, entrance formalities are straightforward. Check with a Colombian consulate (p136) to make sure your nationality doesn't require a visa. Visas are good for 30 to 90 days. Try for the latter if you want some flexibility later on.

From the border, there is frequent transportation to Ipiales, the first town in Colombia, 2km away. There you'll find plenty of hotels and onward connections; see Lonely Planet's *Colombia* or *South America on a shoestring* for more information.

Upon entering Ecuador, be absolutely certain that your papers are in order. With the conflict in Colombia, drug and weapons searches on the Ecuadorian side are very thorough. Taxis between the bus terminal and the border are about $4 and charge $3 from Parque Ayora.

BUS
Buses traveling to and from Ibarra ($2.50, 2½ hours) and Quito ($5, five hours) leave and arrive via the bus terminal. There are frequent departures, but the selection of times is better in the mornings. Long-distance buses go to Cuenca ($16, 17 hours, once a day), Guayaquil ($13, 13 hours), Ambato ($6, eight hours), Ríobamba ($7, 10 hours) and San Lorenzo ($6, six hours).

Transportes Velotaxi (Carabobo near Bolívar), two blocks north of the bus terminal, has small, fast buses to Quito at least every hour from 2:25am to 10:30pm.

Note that there can be a very thorough customs/immigration check between Tulcán and Ibarra even though they are in the same country.

Cooperativa Transportes Norte (☎ 298 0675; Sierra & Manabí) goes west of Tulcán along the border to Tufiño, Maldonado and Chical. Buses leave from Sierra between Manabí and Cuenca. There is a bus to Tufiño ($1, one hour) every couple of hours until mid-afternoon. At least one bus departs daily around 11am to Maldonado ($2.50, 4½ hours) and Chical ($2.75, five hours) via Tufiño.

Cooperativa 11 de Abril buses leave from a stop in front of the cathedral – these buses go to the thermal springs (see p136) as well as many other nearby destinations.

Getting Around
To get to the airport take a shared minibus from the Parque Isidoro Ayora for $1.50, which takes under 10 minutes. A taxi will cost about $3, or it's a 2km walk from downtown. If flying into Tulcán, you can take a taxi or shared minibus for $1.50.

Shared taxis and minibuses heading to the border leave from the Parque Isidoro Ayora. Either should cost $0.80. The taxis wait until enough passengers cram in to make the trip.

The **bus terminal** (JR Arellano & Bolívar) is inconveniently located 2.5km southwest of downtown. City buses ($0.10) run southwest from downtown along Bolívar and will deposit you at the terminal. To get downtown from here, take a taxi for $1 or cross the street in front of the terminal and take the bus there.

WESTERN ANDEAN SLOPES

The old road to Santo Domingo is a sketchy and beautiful affair, traipsing through some of the last misty stands of cloud forest on the western Andean slopes. Mindo is the most popular of many fine destinations for hiking, mountain biking, horseback riding and just relaxing. It is a bird-watcher's delight. The lodges, reserves and villages listed in this section allow you to explore this unique and spectacular region, often in style. Many of these places are only a few hours' bus ride from Quito.

CLOUD FOREST LODGES
☎ 02
Nanegalito
This village is little more than a bus stop with sidewalk kitchens, sizzling vats of pork and a call center brimming with patrons. A couple of hours northwest of Quito, the junction of Nanegalito heads straight to Bosque Protector Mindo-Nambillo, Reserva Bellavista or right to Reserva Biológica Maquipucuna and Santa Lucía.

Tandayapa
Tandayapa Bird Lodge (☎ 224 1038, 09-923 1314; www .tandayapa.com; s/d incl 3 meals $90/155) is a serious birder's paradise, with highlights such as the

Andean cock-of-the-rock, scaled fruiteater and golden-headed and crested quetzals. The full bird list is online. The lodge offers multilingual bird-watching guides, a comfortable lodge in the cloud forest, a canopy platform and a number of trails for daytrips. From 32km into the journey, a road branches south (left) to Tandayapa, 6km away.

Nanegal

A pleasant town of whitewashed homes dipped in pastels, Nanegal has little fanfare beyond the weekend market and occasional brass band. It's the departure point for Santa Lucía and Maquipucuna Reserves. Transportes San José de Minas ($1.60, two hours) leaves Quito from Anteparra and Plaza San Blas (near El Ejido). Buses have three morning departures on Monday through Friday to Quito and leave at 9am, 1pm and 3pm on weekends from the center of Nanegal.

SANTA LUCÍA

A foray into **Bosque Nublado Santa Lucía** (☎ 02-215 7242; www.santaluciaecuador.com; r per person incl 3 meals $45) inspires wonder. This is a trip for the adventurous. The rustic lodge, a steep one- to two-hour hike from the road, rests on the tip of a peak with commanding 360-degree views of lush hills and valleys. Birding and hiking opportunities are excellent. A predawn hike arrives at a remote cock-of-the-rock lek, active with strutting males. Rooms here are basic but comfortable, with mostly twin beds, and there's shared bathrooms and composting toilets as well. You'll get local flavor from the friendly administrator and chef, who cooks up excellent meals which include salad, potato pancakes and hearty soups.

The reserve is owned and run by a group of 10 families who, looking for a more sustainable future, stopped farming *naranjilla* (tart tropical fruit) with pesticides and deforesting the land, to work with tourism and preservation. Considered one of the country's best examples of community tourism, Santa Lucía won 'Best Poverty Reduction' in the 2004 Responsible Tourism Awards.

A minimum stay of three days is recommended, with entry into the reserve and a guide service for the first and last day included in the price. Certified guides from the local families speak basic English and know the scientific names for plants and

birds. Guests should bring warm clothes for the evening as well as rain gear. Four-wheeled drive transportation from Nanegal is $20 for the half-hour round-trip (for singles or groups); transportation from Quito is $60 one-way for a car full of passengers.

RESERVA BIOLÓGICA MAQUIPUCUNA

Preserving a large swath of the important Chocó-Andean bioregion, this 14,000-hectare reserve is a spot to relax, hike and bird-watch. Its territory covers a variety of premontane and montane cloud forests in the headwaters of Río Guayllabamba at elevations ranging from about 1200m to 2800m. The area is truly wonderful and it's only 50km northwest of Quito.

About 80% of the reserve is primary forest – the remainder is secondary growth and includes a research station and ecotourism lodge. In the reserve, 330 species of birds (a bird list is available), 240 species of butterflies, 45 species of mammals and thousands of plants have been documented. The Nature Conservancy purchased the reserve in 1987 and it is now administered by the nonprofit Fundación Maquipucuna.

Guests stay at a rustic **lodge** (www.maqui .org; r per person incl 3 meals with shared/private bathroom $45/65). The lodge has great deck views from the hammocks and tasty, healthy meals at the restaurant. There's one room with a double bed; the rest have bunks and shared bathrooms with hot showers. Day guests pay a $5 entry fee and can hire a guide for $15. Trails range from an easy 1km walk to a demanding 5.5km hike.

More information on the reserve is available from **Fundación Maquipucuna** (Quito ☎ 02-250 7200; root@maqui.ecx.ec; Baquerizo E9-153 & Tamayo, La Floresta, Quito). In the USA, contact the **Chocó Andean Rainforest Corridor** (USA ☎ 706-542-2968; Institute of Ecology, University of Georgia, Athens, GA 30602-2202). In Quito, **Tropic Ecological Adventures** (Quito ☎ 02-999 000; www.tropiceco.com) can help arrange your visit.

Fundación Maquipucuna can arrange a private vehicle from Quito (about $75 total). If you are driving, a 4WD is recommended from Nanegal to the reserve (19km).

RESERVA BELLAVISTA

This 700-hectare reserve is in the same western Andean slopes as Maquipucuna, at about 2000m above sea level. About 25%

is primary forest and the rest has been selectively or completely logged, but is being allowed to regenerate. Various conservation projects are under way. There are 8km of well-marked trails and the area is highly recommended by bird-watchers (320 species of birds have been recorded).

The main **lodge** (☎ 02-211 6232, Quito 02-223 2313; www.bellavistacloudforest.com; Jorge Washington E7-23 & Reina Victoria; dm $39, s/d/tr with private bathroom incl 3 meals $69/118/171) is a wooden geodesic dome with a jaw-dropping panoramic view. There's a library/restaurant/bar on the ground floor, over which are five small rooms, topped by a two-story dormitory area with a shared bathroom, a restaurant and balcony. Light pours into these cozy rooms, but if you prefer privacy there are larger private cabins a short walk from the main lodge. About a kilometer from the main lodge is a research station with a kitchen and *hostal*-type accommodations.

Guided hikes and horseback riding are offered, as well as multiday packages. Transportation from Quito and meals are optional. Hiring a truck in Nanegalito (56km along on the road to Puerto Quito) is $15. Trucks are lined up on the left side where a small sign says 'Bellavista transport.'

MINDO

☎ 02 / pop 2430 / elevation 1250m

Hikers, backpackers and birders all flock to this welcoming, mellow town snuggled in the hills. Highly walkable and teeming with activities, it's a good place for visitors new to Ecuador to get their sea legs. With road improvements, Mindo is now only 2½ hours west of Quito. Visitors should stay a few days to explore the waterfalls, rivers and gorgeous premontane cloud forest nearby called **Bosque Protector Mindo-Nambillo** (admission $3).

Information

Amigos de la Naturaleza-Mindo (☎ 276 5463; amigosmindo@hotmail.com) is a local conservation organization with an office near Parque Central in Mindo. It provides information about reserves, activities and hiking. For Internet connections try **Café Net** (Av Quito; per hr $1.50; ☻ 10:30am-8:30pm).

British bird-watcher Simon Allen has written *A Birder's Guide to Mindo*. You can contact him by emailing spm_allen@ hotmail.com or writing to 63 Goldstone Crescent, Hove, BN3 6LR, UK.

Sights & Activities

Zing across the treetops on the new **tarabita** (Rd to Cascada de Nambillo; $2; ☻ 8:30am-4pm, closed Mon), a perfectly safe wire basket hooked to steel cables that cruises at 152m high across a river basin and joins with trails in the Bosque Protector Mindo-Narambillo on the other side. It's a 4km walk from town, crossing over a metal bridge, or you can take a taxi. Well-marked trails in the reserve lead to a series of seven waterfalls.

To sweat or get wet there's a myriad of options. **Tubing** ($4) is best in the rainy season, when the rapids on the Río Mindo get a little feisty. A slew of places rent inner tubes on Avenida Quito; most mandate that you hire a guide for safety. If you want to pedal around the countryside, look up Efrain Silva, who guides and rents mountain bikes at **Bicistar** (9 de Octubre; per day $6). If you prefer riding horses, call **Oscar Espinoza** (☎ 09-180 8352) for a guided ride. On the main strip **La Isla** (☎ 09-327 2190; Av Quito; canyoning per person $10) offers camping and canyoning, but adventurous guests are advised to look before they leap; there have been injuries from jumping off waterfalls.

Check out the blooms at **Armonía Orchid Garden** (☎ 276 5471; admission $1; ☻ 7am-6pm), which boasts a collection of more than 200 orchids. It's behind the soccer field.

Mindo has several butterfly farms. **Mariposas de Mindo** (Quito ☎ 02-244 0360; www.mariposasde mindo.com, admission $3; ☻ 9am-6:30pm) is usually better in the morning, when cocoons hatch, but the gorgeous Owl's Eyes predictably take wing at 6pm. It also has a restaurant and comfortable lodging.

If you're interested in the flirting behavior of the dashing crimson cock-of-the-rock, grab a local guide or inquire at your hostel about the **cock-of-the-rock lek** (☻ 09-751 1988; admission $8) 4km south of Mindo, facing the El Monte Sustainable Lodge entrance.

Finally, you can perk up with a tour to **Vivero Mindo** (☎ 390 0445; admission free; ☎ weekends only), a tiny organic coffee plantation that won 'Best Coffee in Ecuador' in a local competition. Coffee is free afterwards.

BIRD-WATCHING

With more than 400 species of birds recorded, Mindo has become a major center

NORTHERN HIGHLANDS

for birders. Locally there is a good selection of competent, professional guides. Although many speak only Spanish, all know the bird names in English and can guide non-Spanish speakers without a snag. Most charge between $70 and $140 per day.

Danny Humbolt (☎ 09-328 0769) Comes recommended.

Irman Arias (Quito ☎ 02-229 9475) An excellent guide. His brother, Marcelo Arias (at Hostal Rubbi), comes highly recommended as well.

Juan Carlos Calvachi (☎ 09-966 4503, 286 5213; calvachi@uio.satnet.net) Juan speaks perfect English, is a top guide and charges about $130 to guide two people for a day (including transportation).

Julia Patiño (☎ 390 0419) A vivacious, highly recommended guide.

Pablo Leon A biologist and owner of Séptimo Paraíso (opposite); he speaks English, charges about $70 per day and is reportedly very good.

Sandra Patiño (☎ 09-935 9361) Provides excellent guiding and companionship.

Sleeping & Eating

The village has mostly basic accommodations while the fancier places lie out of town. Most hotel owners can conform to 3am birders' breakfasts with advance notice. These days everyone and their brother has converted their home into a hostel, and visitors will find no lack of choices. Don't be shy to ask locals directions since there are no street signs.

La Casa de Cecilia (☎ 09-334 5393; casadececilia@yahoo.com; r per person $5) Cecilia's warm reception spruces up these basic lodgings. You'll find an outdoor fireplace on the hammock deck and an open-air kitchen on the river. On nice days take advantage of the lovely swimming hole and sunbathing platform. An adjacent Internet café is being installed, and breakfast or camping is $2. Ask about long-term discounts and work exchanges.

Hospedaje el Madroño (☎ 09-947 3571; 9 de Octubre & Marquesa de Soloada; r per person $5) These snug, pint-sized varnished wood rooms are let by a friendly and active family.

Jardín de los Pájaros (☎ 09-175 6688; Barrío El Progreso; r per person $8) This new *hostal* lacks some finishing touches, but the carpeted rooms are ample and comfortable and there's a large shaded deck.

Hospedaje el Rocío (☎ 390 0041; Rd to Nambillo; r per person $8) A rustic artists' retreat with colorful, cozy group spaces, hammocks looking out on the wild garden and stacks of old *National Geographics* in the hall. A short walk to town.

La Regatta (Barrío El Progreso; r per person $12) A muscle camp retreat with weight-training machines, sauna and Jacuzzi (closes at 9pm). Rooms are welcoming with white brick walls and spongy carpets. For non-jocks the garden is lined with torch lamps and benches for reading.

Cabañas Armonía (☎ 390 0431, 09-943 5098; www.orchids-birding.com; r with shared/private bathroom incl breakfast $7/$14) Tucked away in tousled, unkempt gardens, the accommodations here are in quiet, rustic cabins or dorm-style rooms in the main house. Attached is Armonía Orchid Garden (p141).

El Descanso (☎ 390 0443; www.eldescanso.net; private r per person $16) A large wooden house with a great semicircular deck. There are also cabins on this spacious property encircled by gardens and hummingbird feeders. The wooden rooms are cozy but you'll find the beds a little saggy.

Other perfectly acceptable crash pads include the spotless and central **Hostal Arco Iris** (☎ 390 0405; main plaza; r per person with shared/private bathroom $5/8) and the cabin-style **Hostal Bijao** (☎ 390 0430; r per person $7.50); the latter also serves meals for $3 to $4.50. English is spoken at **Rubbi Hostal** (☎ 235 0461; marceloguideofbirds@yahoo.com; r per person $5), and its owner Marcelo is a known birding guide.

There are several restaurants along the main street leading up to the plaza.

Café El Monte (☎ 390 0402; ⏰ 10am-9pm Fri-Sun, 4-9pm Mon-Thu) The whole-wheat pizza with zucchini and tomatoes simply sizzles. The café is also popular for its homemade baked goods, garden salads and organic coffee.

Fuera de Babylonia (☎ 09-475 7768; Calle los Ríos; ⏰ 7:30am-9:30pm) A woodsy ambience and an original menu make this an interesting choice. Try the steamed trout or beet soup. Located one block off the plaza.

Los Colibris (⏰ 8am-5pm Mon-Thu, 8am-8pm Fri-Sun) Dine on a thatched patio draped with bougainvillea and surrounded by darting hummingbirds. Serves everything from breakfast, with pancakes and eggs, to dinner, offering trout cooked six ways and mushroom fettuccini, which is delectable. An enjoyable 30-minute walk from town or you can get here by taxi. Go 1km out of Mindo on the road to Nambillo, then turn left after 400m for Los Colibris.

OUTSIDE OF TOWN

El Monte Sustainable Lodge (☎ 390 0402, 09-380 4675; www.ecuadorcloudforest.com; r per person incl 3 meals & activities $86) The perfect place to unplug. Run by a warmhearted and knowledgeable young American-Ecuadorian couple, El Monte is a wooded retreat with three lovely, private riverside cabins. The aesthetic is contemporary and comfortable, with lots of wood and subtle natural tones. The three cabins sleep up to four people and have hot showers and bathtubs. Located 4km south of Mindo along a winding dirt road, it's reached by a *tarabita* (hand-powered cable car) over Río Mindo. The communal lodge has rustic, oversized furniture and excellent candlelit dinners. The food is delicious and mostly vegetarian, with options such as tamales, curry and salads from the organic garden. There are on-site trails and guided activities, including bird-watching, hiking and tubing. Reserve ahead so the owners can meet you in Mindo. A two-night minimum is suggested.

Séptimo Paraíso (☎ 09-368 4417, Quito ☺ 02-243 4163; www.septimoparaiso.com; standard/superior r $65/92, ste $110) In 'seventh heaven' there are elegant rooms with a woodsy flavor and the heated pool and Jacuzzi are indeed divine. Just off the road into Mindo (2km below the 'Y'), these two lodges have room for 72 people in a private 300-hectare reserve with great bird-watching. Rates include breakfast. Its excellent restaurant, La Chorrera (mains $7 to $13), is open to the public, and there's also a bar and wine cellar.

Mindo Gardens Lodge (Quito ☎ 02-225 2489/90; info@mindogarden.com; s/d incl breakfast $43/61) Attractive two-story cabins with hand painted cupboards and river views. About a kilometer north of El Monte Sustainable Lodge, it's reached by car or a 45-minute walk from town. Pathways lead through wooded gardens to the main lodge, which has a dining room (meals $8) with additional patio seating and a family-friendly games room upstairs. The lodge offers attentive service and can arrange local tours. A trail on the property leads to the new *tarabita* and waterfalls.

Bambu Hostal (Quito ☎ 02-229 0423; elbambumindo@hotmail.com; campsite $3, r per person $8-10) A barnlike *hostal* with a rough hewn charm, river access and lovely quiet meadows. Breakfast is included. Go 1km out of Mindo on the road to Nambillo, and turn left after 400m for Bambu.

Getting There & Away

From Quito, **Cooperativa Flor de Valle** (Quito ☎ 02-252 7495) goes to Mindo ($2.50, 2½ hours) Monday through Friday at 8am and 3:45pm. On weekends buses leave at 7:20am, 8am, 9am, and 3:45pm. The cooperative is located on M Larrea just west of Ascunción, near Parque El Ejido. The bus returns from Mindo to Quito daily at 6:30am and 2pm. Saturday and Sunday buses leave at 2pm, 3pm and 4pm. On Sunday there's an extra trip at 5pm.

There is also a Mindo bus from the Santo Domingo de los Colorados bus terminal at 2pm daily with Cooperativa Kennedy (five hours). There are buses from Mindo to Santo Domingo at 7am and 1pm (3½ hours).

Getting Around

A taxi cooperative runs from the plaza. Prices are higher than in other areas. A trip to the 'Y' intersection with the main road costs $3, from where there are a number of buses headed to Quito, and some going to Santo Domingo or the coast.

WEST OF MINDO

This beautiful and out-of-the-way route links Quito to the western lowlands and coast. After passing the road to Mindo, the road drops and flattens near **Puerto Quito** before intersecting with the main road between Santo Domingo de los Colorados and the north-coast port of Esmeraldas.

Pedro Vicente Maldonado

Low hills flatten into ruffles and the village is a strip of squat cement buildings fringed by jungle. At the far edge of town you'll find **Arashá Rainforest Resort & Spa** (☎ 09-924 008, Quito ☎ 02-224 9881; www.arasharesort.com; r per person incl 3 meals $69; ☒), nuzzling visitors in the lap of cloud forest luxury. The poshest spot on the western Andean slope, accommodations are in stilted thatched huts set in the undulating hills. In addition to bird-watching, hiking and wildlife-watching excursions, the resort offers an excellent spa, a pool, whirlpool, waterfalls, a kids' swimming area, rafting, minigolf and an international restaurant. The hotel is 3km outside the village of Pedro Vicente Maldonado on the old road to Santo Domingo and about 200m off the main road to Puerto Quito.

Puerto Quito

Not much goes on in Puerto Quito and that's the charm. It's a relaxing place to see birds and waterfalls and swim in lazy rivers. There are frequent buses from Quito's bus terminal (use Transportes Kennedy, San Pedrito or Alóag) and Santo Domingo. Accommodations listed are without hot water.

In the center, **Hotel Macallares** (☎ 215 6088; Av 18 de Mayo 313; r per person $12) has firm beds and neat citrus-sherbet-colored rooms.

Ítapoa Reserve (☎ 09-478 4992; r per person incl 3 meals $25) is a small pocket of primary and secondary forest which has an old farmhouse where guests are able to stay. The owner Raul is an affable biologist who gives engaging presentations of area flora and fauna. It is both a wonderful introduction to cloud forests and a relaxing trip. Activities here include tubing, making chocolate and tagua rings. English is spoken here.

Central Highlands

As poetic monikers go, few can top the sound of 'The Avenue of the Volcanoes,' the nickname coined by German explorer (and unwitting wordsmith) Alexander von Humboldt when he traveled through Ecuador's central Andean valley in 1802. Not surprisingly, the name stuck. South of Quito the Panamericana winds past eight of the country's 10 highest peaks, including the picture-perfect snowcapped cone of Volcán Cotopaxi (5897m) and the glaciated behemoth, Volcán Chimborazo (6310m).

For trekkers and climbers, the central highlands are a paradise, and even inexperienced (but acclimatized and extremely fit) climbers can have a go at summiting the country's highest peaks. Those who are happier *off* the hill will find the region just as thrilling. The central highlands are home to scores of tiny indigenous villages, some of which are so remote you can only get there on foot, and where people lead lives that have changed little over the centuries.

The region is also home to many of the country's most traditional markets. Wandering through these outdoor markets, where you'll find the most unimaginable and interesting goods is one of the country's most memorable experiences.

Riobamba and Baños are two of the best towns in the country for adventure sports. There's ample opportunity for climbing, hiking, mountain biking, rafting, canyoning and more.

CENTRAL HIGHLANDS

HIGHLIGHTS

- Hike the **Quilotoa loop** (p156) and experience magnificent Andean scenery, indigenous villages and the awesome crater lake of Laguna Quilotoa

- Whiz through Andean cloud forest, past stunning waterfalls and into the tropical lowlands on a bike ride from **Baños to Puyo** (p175)

- Climb to the most distant point from the center of the Earth – the snowcapped peak of **Volcán Chimborazo** (p187), Ecuador's highest mountain

- Ride the roof of the train down the hair-raising descent of **La Nariz del Diablo** (p186), one of the world's greatest train rides

- Trek beneath the majestic volcanic peaks of **Parque Nacional Cotopaxi** (p149), crowned by the perfect cone of Ecuador's second highest peak, Volcán Cotopaxi

Parque Nacional Cotopaxi

Quilotoa loop

Volcán Chimborazo

Puyo

Baños

La Nariz del Diablo

■ AVERAGE TEMPERATURE IN RIOBAMBA: 12°C (53°F)　　■ RAINIEST MONTH IN RIOBAMBA: MARCH

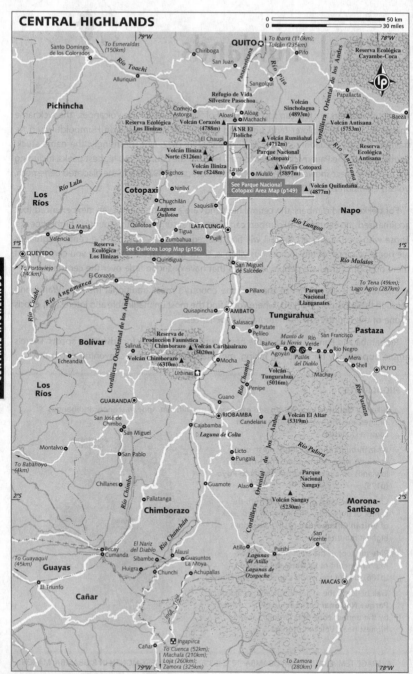

CENTRAL HIGHLANDS

Climate

December and January are considered the best months to visit, and March to May the worst. Bad months just mean you'll get wet and miss the views, thanks to the clouds. Climbing is possible year-round, but there are two primary seasons: June through September is the dry season, and November through January is the snow season (we're talking about high elevation climbs here). August gets windy.

National Parks

Parque Nacional Cotopaxi (p149) is one of the country's most visited national parks. Volcán Chimborazo (p187) is the primary reason to visit the **Reserva de Producción Faunística Chimborazo**. **Parque Nacional Llanganates** (p165) is most easy accessed from around Baños, but access in general is extremely difficult. **Parque Nacional Sangay** (p176) is the largest park in the central highlands.

Getting There & Around

No towns in the central highlands have public airports. You'll have to get around by bus. Buses, of course, go just about everywhere. The most important transportation hubs are Latacunga, Ambato, Baños, Riobamba and Guaranda.

MACHACHI & ALOASÍ

☎ 02

About 35km south of Quito, Machachi (population 12,469) is a humdrum little mountain town that explodes to life during its sprawling **Sunday market**, one of the biggest in the highlands. It fills half the town, with sections dedicated to meat, seafood, fruit and vegetables, wholesale items, used farm equipment and small animals. A cacophonous animal market simultaneously occurs on the south side of town, outside the Estadio El Chan; it starts around 5am and finishes around 10am.

The town's traditional attraction is the **Güitig mineral-water bottling plant** (admission $2; ☼ daily), which has an ice-cold swimming pool. It's about 4km from town (taxi $2).

Aloasí (population 6855) is a village almost opposite Machachi, on the west side of the Panamericana. It's a tiny place, beautifully and conveniently situated at the base of **Volcán Corazón** (4788m), an extinct volcano that makes for a straightforward but strenuous acclimatization hike before tackling nearby Cotopaxi.

Sleeping & Eating

La Estación de Machachi (☎ 230 9246; s $30-34, d $34-46) This charming little inn in Aloasí sits directly outside the old train station and is beautifully decorated with antiques and farm gadgets. It has a pleasant garden, a good restaurant, 10 rooms and a cabin that sleeps four. Breakfast costs $4 to $5, and other meals run about $8.

Hotel Estancia Real (☎ 231 5760; Luis Cordero; r $10) One of several low-budget hotels across from the Plaza Mayorista in Machachi, this one takes hourly guests too, but the rooms are acceptable.

The best places to eat are on the Panamericana south of Machachi.

El Café de la Vaca (☎ 231 5012; Panamericana; almuerzo $5.50, mains $3-8; ☼ 8am-5:30pm) About 3km south of Machachi, this is by far the best restaurant in the area and a favorite weekend stop for quiteños (people from Quito). You can't miss it; the building is painted to look like a black-and-white dairy cow. The restaurant serves good local food, as well as sandwiches and huge burgers. The almuerzo (set-lunch menu) is good value but available Monday through Friday only.

Getting There & Away

Buses depart from Quito's bus terminal en route to Latacunga and can drop you in Machachi ($0.75, one hour). Direct buses to Machachi leave from the small Villaflora terminal near the Villaflora Trole stop in southern Quito.

From Machachi, Transportes La Dolorosa buses leave at least every hour during the day to nearby Aloasí. Stay on until the end of the line to reach the train station, which is approximately 3km from the Panamericana.

THE ILINIZAS

☎ 02

The Panamericana winds its way south from Machachi through open pastureland hemmed in by volcanic peaks. To the west stands Cerro Rumiñahui, just inside the border of Parque Nacional Cotopaxi. To the east you'll see the two sharp peaks of the Ilinizas. The jagged sawtooth ridge of **Iliniza Sur** (5248m), occasionally dusted in snow, is Ecuador's sixth-highest peak. It's one of Ecuador's most difficult climbs, suitable only for experienced mountaineers with technical ice and climbing equipment. **Iliniza Norte** (5126m), on the other hand, is a rough scramble, suitable for fit, acclimatized and experienced hikers. It's Ecuador's eighth-highest peak. The mountains lie about 25km southwest of Machachi as the condor flies.

Many climbers stay in one of the several simple *hostales* (small and reasonably priced hotels) in the El Chaupi area. From El Chaupi you can continue on foot (or try to hire a pickup to take you) another 9km to the parking area where the climb begins; be sure your driver takes you to the parking area with the shrine to La Virgen. From the parking area, it is a three- to four-hour climb to the **refuge** (dm $10) where you can spend the night.

Fit hikers could leave Quito at dawn, catch an early bus from Machachi to El Chaupi and walk hard to reach the refuge by nightfall.

The refuge is at 4650m, just east of and below a saddle between the two mountains, and has bunks (bring a sleeping bag), cooking facilities, a fireplace (although not much fuel) and a caretaker. The generator only occasionally provides lighting, so bring candles. Water has to be carried from a nearby stream and boiled. You could camp for free, but campsites are exposed to the weather and have no facilities, and you should not leave your gear unattended. From the refuge, it is a three-hour climb to Iliniza Norte along a fairly well-defined – but at times narrow, steep and slippery – trail.

El Chaupi Area

Most folks who come to the tiny village of El Chaupi (population 1322), about 7km southwest off the Panamericana, are on their way to climb the Ilinizas. There are several *hostales* in the area which are all good for acclimatizing before tackling nearby Cotopaxi. El Chaupi itself has a **phone** (☎ 286 0830) and a store with minimal supplies.

Sleeping & Eating

Hostería PapaGayo (☎ 231 0002, 09-990 3524; www .hosteria-papagayo.com; Panamericana Sur Km 43; camping/dm $3/6, r with private bathroom $8-12) This stunningly converted, 150-year-old farmhouse is the perfect base for acclimatizing, climbing

and trekking in and around the Ilinizas, Cotopaxi and nearby Corazón. Both dorm beds and private rooms are available, making it an excellent budget option for cash-strapped climbers. Rooms are straightforward but colorful, some have private bathrooms, and some even have fireplaces. It boasts an excellent restaurant, a bar and a sort of 'disco barn' (haa-aay!) for weekly parties. There are lots of animals around (outside), and hiking and climbing information (inside). Tours, guides and horseback riding can be arranged. It's 500m west of the Panamericana and about 2km north of the El Chaupi turn-off (or 1km south of the Machachi toll booth). Bus drivers know the spot.

Hostal Llovizna (☎ 09-969 9068; iliniza_blady@ yahoo.com; dm incl breakfast $10) About 500m from El Chaupi on the road to Ilinizas, Llovizna is owned by Vladimir Gallo, the manager of the Ilinizas climbers' refuge. It's the best of the simple accommodations in town, with several beds and a guest kitchen.

Hacienda San José (☎ 09-973 7986, Quito ☎ 02-289 1547; dm $10) Situated 3km from El Chaupi, this farm has two cabins with bunks, fireplaces and hot showers. In the main house, there's a kitchen and a sitting room. Maps are available, and the climbers' refuge can be reached in a few hours of walking. Very fit hikers could reach Iliniza Norte and return in one long day. This place has been recommended by climbers.

Hostel Valhalla (☎ 255 4984; www.hostelvalhalla .com; Panamericana Km 19; camping/dm $5/9, d $14-19, r with bathroom $34) This new hostel, owned by Moggely Climbing in Quito (p89), is still coming into its own, but its location, with views of more than a dozen peaks, is hard to beat. It's a three-story unembellished cement structure with a rooftop terrace and nine double rooms with shared bathrooms. Three of them have wood-burning stoves, and one has a private bathroom. It has two dorm rooms, and is popular with groups. The owners will provide transportation to the base any peaks in the area.

GETTING THERE & AWAY

To get to El Chaupi from Machachi, take one of the blue-and-white buses signed 'El Chaupi,' which leave about every hour during the day from Avenida Amazonas at 11 de Noviembre; because they stop to pick everyone up, the ride takes about 40 minutes. If you're driving, take the unsigned turn-off from the Panamericana about 7km south of Machachi and continue along a cobbled road another 7km to El Chaupi. From El Chaupi the road turns to dirt and continues another 9km to the Ilinizas parking area, identified by a small shrine to the Virgin. You can also hire a pickup in Machachi (ask around the plaza) to take you directly to the parking area for about $30.

PARQUE NACIONAL COTOPAXI

☎ 03

The centerpiece of Ecuador's most popular **national park** (admission $10) is the snowcapped and downright picture-perfect **Volcán Cotopaxi** (5897m), Ecuador's second-highest peak. Within the 33,393 hectares of national park that surround the volcano, you'll find outstanding hiking and trekking opportunities, as well as a handful of fabulous old haciendas offering everything from horseback riding to guided climbs of Cotopaxi itself. The park offers a good look at the *páramo* (Andean grasslands) and the views everywhere are sublime.

Volcán Cotopaxi is an active volcano, though present activity is limited to a few gently smoking fumaroles that cannot be seen except by mountaineers who climb up to the icy crater and peer within. There have, however, been many violent eruptions in the past few centuries – three of which wiped out the town of Latacunga. There are also several other peaks within the park, of which **Volcán Rumiñahui** (4712m) is the most important.

The park's wildlife is unusual and interesting. Although rarely seen, the Andean condor is one of many of the park's bird species. The most frequently seen mammals are white-tailed deer and rabbits. Little red brocket deer are also present; they are only about 35cm high at the shoulder. With luck, you may glimpse a *colpeo* (Andean fox) or puma. The rare Andean spectacled bear lives on the remote and infrequently visited eastern slopes of the park.

Although Cotopaxi park has the most well-developed infrastructure of the mainland parks (there are rangers, a small museum and information center, a climbers'

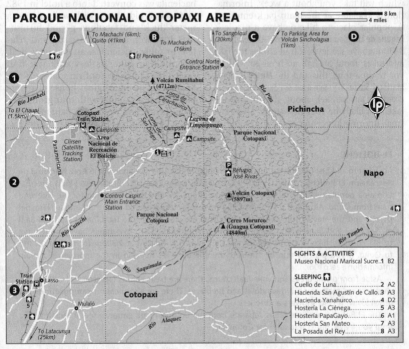

PARQUE NACIONAL COTOPAXI AREA

0 ____ 8 km
0 ____ 4 miles

To Machachi (6km); Quito (41km)
To Machachi (16km)
To Sangolqui (30km)
To Parking Area for Volcán Sincholagua (1km)

El Porvenir
Control Norte Entrance Station
▲ Volcán Rumiñahui (4712m)
Loma de Carachaurco
Cotopaxi Train Station
Río Jambeli
To El Chaupi (1.5km)
Loma de San Diego
Campsite
Laguna de Limpiopungo
Campsite
Campsite
Pichincha
Río Pita
Panamericana
Clirsen (Satellite Tracking Station)
Area Nacional de Recreación El Boliche
Parque Nacional Cotopaxi
Control Caspi Main Entrance Station
Refugio José Rivas
▲ Volcán Cotopaxi (5897m)
Napo
Parque Nacional Cotopaxi
Río Cutuchi
Cerro Morurco (Guagua Cotopaxi) (4840m)
Río Tambo
Río Saquimala
Train Station
Lasso
Cotopaxi
Mulaló
Río Alaquez
To Latacunga (25km)

SIGHTS & ACTIVITIES
Museo Nacional Mariscal Sucre..1 B2

SLEEPING 🛏
Cuello de Luna.....................2 A2
Hacienda San Agustín de Callo..3 A3
Hacienda Yanahurco................4 D2
Hostería La Ciénega..............5 A3
Hostería PapaGayo................6 A1
Hostería San Mateo..............7 A3
La Posada del Rey................8 A3

refuge, and camping and picnicking areas), facilities are basic. Most nonclimbers visit on daytrips.

Information

The Cotopaxi entrance fee ($10) does not include the overnight refuge fees or camping fees. The main entrance is officially open 7am to 3pm, but drivers can get *out* until about 6:30pm. Hikers can get in or out at anytime. Altitude sickness is a very real danger – acclimatize for several days in Quito before attempting to walk in.

If you plan to take a guided climb or tour, you're best off doing so from Quito (p89) or Riobamba (p183), which have the best climbing operators. Both towns also have mountain-biking operators that have great cycling tours within the park.

Activities

HIKING & CLIMBING

The hiking and mountaineering possibilities within the national park are outstanding. You can camp for a night, or bring plenty of food and hike all the way around Cotopaxi, which will take you about a week. Information is available at the main park entrance. A popular place to hike or have a picnic is **Laguna de Limpiopungo**, a shallow Andean lake 3830m above sea level; a trail circles the lake and takes about an half an hour to walk. If you're on a tour, this and the **Museo Nacional Mariscal Sucre** (☑ 8am-noon & 1-5pm; admission included with park entry fee), about 4km before the lake, will likely be your first stops. There is a small information center at the museum.

Both mountaineers and the curious hike up to **Refugio José Rivas** (dm $17) at about 4800m on the northern slopes of Cotopaxi, and some 12km from the lake. Bunk beds and cooking facilities are available, but bring a warm sleeping bag. There is a guardian on duty who can show you where you can leave your gear if you need to do so; bring a padlock. Climbing beyond the refuge requires stamina, experience and snow- and ice-climbing gear; it's not a climb for beginners, although it is relatively straightforward for experienced climbers. See p183 and p89 for information on hiring mountaineering guides.

Sleeping

Although listed in the Ilinizas area (p148), both Hostería Papagayo and Hostel Valhalla make excellent bases for climbing and trekking in Cotopaxi. The following are comfortable accommodations in the area surrounding the park.

Hostería La Ciénega (☎ 271 9052, 271 9093, Quito ☎ 02-254 9126, 254 1337; hcienega@uio.satnet.net; s/d $38/56, ste $74-98) This exquisite 400-year-old hacienda was converted into a hotel in 1982 and has 16 old rooms with walls almost a meter thick and fabulous period furnishings. It's a wonderful place to stay and, relative to other haciendas, an excellent deal. The modern annex is less attractive (but priced the same), so confirm that your reservation is in the original house. The restaurant/bar is popular with tour groups. La Ciénega is 1.5km west of the Panamericana, about 2km south of the village of Lasso. Bus

---

EL BOLICHE

Adjacent to and just outside Parque Nacional Cotopaxi's western boundary, the **Area Nacional de Recreación El Boliche** (☎ 02-315 1802/03/04, ext 237; Panamericana, Km 20.3; admission $10) is a recreation area popular with quiteños on weekend outings. It's also the destination for the weekend train from Quito. Although it's touristy, the train is far less crowded than the famous Nariz del Diablo, and the views (from the roof, of course!) are wonderful. The train leaves Quito at 8am on Saturday and Sunday and arrives at El Boliche around 11am. Passengers have about three to 3½ hours to hike or picnic before the train leaves El Boliche at 2:30pm for the return trip to Quito. If you plan to ride on the roof, bundle up – it's freezing in the morning. For train information see p106.

Aside from picnic areas and volleyball courts, there are basic **cabins** (per person $5) with bunks, sheetless old mattresses, big windows and fireplaces. There are also pleasant **campgrounds** (per person $3) with cold showers and toilets.

The El Boliche entrance fee is separate from the Cotopaxi park entrance fee; it remains valid until you leave, but is not valid for Cotopaxi.

WHERE HAVE ALL THE FROGS GONE?

Until the 1990s, *Atelopus* frogs, which have a distinctive orange belly and a jet-black back, were a common sight around Laguna Limpiopungo. Disturbingly, beginning in the 1990s, sightings of these colorful creatures decreased to the occasional glimpse, and today they're nearly gone.

The disappearance of frogs is not unique to Limpiopungo. In fact, the journal *Nature* reported in 2006 that an estimated two-thirds of tropical America's 110 harlequin frog species (a member of the genus *Atelopus*) have disappeared entirely. Herpetologists have been puzzling the loss of frog and toad species all over the world for nearly two decades, and have been unable to agree upon an explanation for their alarming demise.

One of several theories holds that worldwide air quality has degenerated to the extent that amphibians, which breathe both with primitive lungs and through their perpetually moist skin, are exposed to lethal doses of airborne toxins. Another theory suggests that frog skin gives little protection against UV light, and that the world's increasing UV-light levels has proven deadly. The most convincing study, however, was the one released in 2006 in *Nature,* and it largely squelched disagreement among scientists. The study showed that it was a fungus that was wiping out frogs, and that the fungus multiplied in the 1980s as a result of global warming. It became, in essence, a frog epidemic in tropical America's highlands. It wasn't the first study to link the decline in amphibian species to global warming, but it was the first to explain *how* they were linked.

Perhaps frogs are the modern-day canaries in the coalmine. Should we heed the sign, or keep on digging?

drivers will drop you at the sign and you can walk from there.

El Porvenir (Quito ☎ 02-223 1806; www.volcanoland .com; r per person with shared/private bathroom $20/35, with full board & activities $69/89) On the northern flanks of Cotopaxi, about 4km from the northern entrance to the park, El Porvenir is a wonderful, fully functioning hacienda with a divinely cozy common area kept warm by a crackling fireplace. Delicious traditional food is served in a rustic dining room, and the bedrooms are simple but supremely comfortable. The setting, high in the *páramo* with nothing but views of Cotopaxi for company, is spectacular. Horseback riding, mountain biking and other activities are available, and the staff is outstanding. The hacienda is run by Tierra del Volcán (see Web page), an excellent, ecoconscious company with two other haciendas and loads of activities. The owners provide jeep transportation to the hacienda via a dirt road.

Hacienda San Agustín de Callo (☎ 271 9160, 271 9510, Quito ☎ 02-290 6157/8; www.incahacienda .com; r/ste $275/317) Not only is this Ecuador's best-known hacienda, it's also the site of the best-preserved northernmost remains of the Inca empire (those further north are poorly maintained). In fact, many of the hacienda walls, including those forming three of the bedrooms, were built by the Incas. The hacienda was used by the French Geodesic mis-

sion to measure the equator in 1748, and by the expeditions of Alexander von Humboldt in 1802 and climber Edward Whymper in 1880. Today, the owner is the warm-hearted Mignon Plaza, whose grandfather and uncle were once presidents of Ecuador. In 1998, *National Geographic* funded research on the site, and excavations and investigations are slowly progressing. It's a marvelous place to stay, with five double rooms and two suites. All the rooms have at least two fireplaces, one in the bedroom and one in the bathroom. Rates include breakfast, dinner and guided activities such as fishing, trekking and mountain biking, two hours of horseback riding and a visit to a rose plantation.

Cuello de Luna (☎ 09-970 0330, Quito ☎ 02-224 2744; www.cuellodeluna.com; dm from $11, s/d/tr without bathroom $20/26/36, s/d/tr/q with bathroom $23/34/45/53) This is a great budget choice, located almost 2km northwest of the main entrance to the national park. At 3125m, it is a good place to acclimatize and hike before heading into Cotopaxi. There are dorm beds, a few rooms with shared hot showers and 16 rooms with private hot showers (many with fireplaces). Breakfast ($4) and other meals ($7 to $10) are available. Several of our readers have recommended this.

Hostería San Mateo (☎ 271 9015; www.hosteriasan mateo.com; s/d $36/44) Further south, near Km 75 on the Panamericana, this is a centuries-old place in attractive rural surroundings with distant views of Cotopaxi. There are five comfortable doubles with private hot bathroom, and a private cottage (which costs a little more). The owners are hospitable and run a good restaurant.

Hacienda Yanahurco (Quito ☎ 02-254 5472; 2-day packages per person $295) A remote place beyond the far east side of the park, Yahahurco has seven rooms with private bathroom and affords you the opportunity to visit some of the lesser-known eastern slopes of the Andes. Rates include all meals, horseback riding, fishing, rain gear and rubber boots.

La Posada del Rey (☎ 271 9319; s/d $24/31; 🐾) This modernish place located just north of La Ciénega and southwest of Lasso is nothing to write home about, but – with perfectly adequate rooms with fireplace and TV – definitely does the trick.

Getting There & Away

All of the haciendas provide transportation from Quito, usually at no additional cost.

There are three entrances to the park. The main entrance is via a turnoff about 22km south of Machachi (or roughly 30km north of Latacunga). From the turnoff, it's 6km northwest from the Panamericana to **Control Caspi**, the park's main entrance. Any Quito–Latacunga bus will let you off at the turnoff. Follow the main dirt roads (also signed) to the entrance. It's another 9km or so to the museum.

It's also possible to reach the park from the north, via Machachi, but you'll need to hire a vehicle and a guide who knows the route; the 21km road in is usually passable only during December to January. This northern route (known as **Control Norte**) is signed at the turnoff to Machachi.

The third entrance, rarely used to access the national park itself, is the entrance to El Boliche. This turnoff is about 16km south of Machachi. The road is paved as far as the Clirsen Satellite Tracking Station (once operated by NASA), about 2km from the Panamericana. Nearby is the Cotopaxi train station, where the Sunday train excursion from Quito stops (see the boxed text El Boliche, p150). From here, the road becomes dirt and is closed to vehicles. It eventually reaches the unattended entrance to Cotopaxi.

On weekends, local tourists visit the park, and there is a good chance of getting

a lift from the turnoff to the main entrance and on to Laguna Limpiopungo. Midweek the park is almost deserted and you'll probably end up walking.

From Latacunga you can hire a pickup (about $20 to $30 to the refuge), but you should bargain and be specific if you want to go all the way to Refugio José Rivas. You can arrange for the pickup to return for you on a particular day for another $20 to $30. It is almost an hour's walk uphill (at 4800m) from the parking lot to the refuge, which looks as if it's only about a 10-minute stroll away.

Any car will get you into the park to visit the museum, see the llamas and picnic by Limpiopungo, where excellent views of the mountain are possible if the weather permits. You could camp here and continue on foot.

LATACUNGA

☎ 03 / pop 51,700 / elevation 2800m

A bustling market town and the capital of Cotopaxi province, Latacunga appears rather dull from the Panamericana. But once you cross the bridge over the swift Río Cutuchi and head toward the main plaza, the buildings get older, terra-cotta-tiled roofs appear, and old Latacunga starts to looks pretty damn cool. The town is famous for its Mamá Negra festivals and seems to have more barber shops per capita than any town in Ecuador. It's a good base for transportation to Cotopaxi, it's the starting point for the Quilotoa loop (p156), and it's the best point from which to visit the Thursday morning market in Saquisilí.

Latacunga's name originates from the indigenous words *llacta cunani,* which translate charmingly into 'land of my choice.' Latacunga was once an important colonial center, but today there is little evidence of its long history, thanks to nearby Cotopaxi. The volcano, which dominates the town on a clear day, erupted violently in 1742 and destroyed the town. Latacunga was rebuilt but destroyed by another eruption 26 years later. The indomitable (or foolhardy) survivors rebuilt the town again, only to have an immense eruption in 1877 destroy it a third time. Proving that history repeats itself, Latacunga was rebuilt on the same site. Fortunately, at present, Cotopaxi's activity is extremely minor.

Information

AJ Cyber Café (Quito 16-19; per hr $1) Fast Internet access.

Andinatel (Quevedo near Maldonado; ☑ 8am-10pm) Telephone center.

Banco de Guayaquil (Maldonado 7-20) Bank with ATM; changes traveler's checks.

Banco del Pichincha (Quito near Salcedo) Bank with ATM.

Captur (☎ 281 4968; cnr Orellana & Guayaquil; ☑ 8am-noon & 2-6pm) Moderately helpful tourist information.

Discovery Net (☎ 280 6557; Salcedo 4-16; per hr $1; ☑ 8am-9:30pm Mon-Sat, 8am-noon Sun) Internet access.

Hospital (Hermanas Páez near 2 de Mayo)

Post office (Quevedo near Maldonado)

Tourist Information (☑ 8am-6pm daily; Bus Terminal, Panamericana) Friendly tourist information office run by local high school students; inside the bus terminal.

Sights & Activities

There's far more to do *around* Latacunga than there is to do *in* it, partly because most of the historic buildings have been wiped out by volcanic eruptions.

The well-tended **Parque Vicente León** is the main plaza and has some interesting topiary work enclosed by pretty cast-iron fences. At the southeast corner of the plaza stands the **town hall** (cnr Maldonado & Orellana), topped by a pair of stone condors. On the south side stands the **cathedral** (Maldonado near Sanchez de Orellana). Behind the cathedral, the little arcade of **Pasaje Catedral** is worth a quick peek.

Latacunga's **markets** are likely the town's most interesting sights. The three sweeping plazas around the intersection of JA

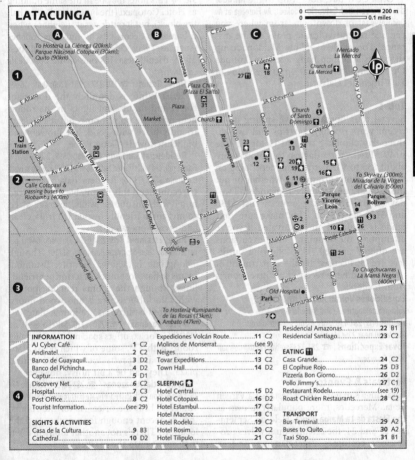

INFORMATION	
AJ Cyber Café	1 C2
Andinatel	2 C2
Banco de Guayaquil	3 D2
Banco del Pichincha	4 D2
Captur	5 D1
Discovery Net	6 C2
Hospital	7 C3
Post Office	8 C2
Tourist Information	(see 29)

SIGHTS & ACTIVITIES	
Casa de la Cultura	9 B3
Cathedral	10 D2
Expediciones Volcán Route	11 C2
Molinos de Monserrat	(see 9)
Neiges	12 C2
Tovar Expeditions	13 C2
Town Hall	14 D2

SLEEPING	
Hotel Central	15 D2
Hotel Cotopaxi	16 C2
Hotel Estambul	17 C2
Hotel Macroz	18 C1
Hotel Rodelu	19 C2
Hotel Rosim	20 C2
Hotel Tilipulo	21 C2
Residencial Amazonas	22 B1
Residencial Santiago	23 C2

EATING	
Casa Grande	24 C2
El Copihue Rojo	25 D3
Pizzería Bon Giorno	26 D2
Pollo Jimmy's	27 C1
Restaurant Rodelu	(see 19)
Roast Chicken Restaurants	28 C2

TRANSPORT	
Bus Terminal	29 A2
Buses to Quito	30 A2
Taxi Stop	31 B1

CENTRAL HIGHLANDS

Echevería and Amazonas are alive with action every day (but especially on Tuesday and Saturday market days) and are particularly photogenic on clear days with Cotopaxi visible in the distance. They're completely nontouristy, and just about the only crafts you'll find that are worth their own thread are the locally made string bags known as *shigras*.

If you have more time to kill, wander on down to the **Casa de la Cultura** (☎ 281 3247; Vela 3-49; admission $0.50; ✆ 8am-noon & 2-6pm Tue-Sat), built on the site of a former Jesuit watermill known as **Molinos de Monserrat**. It houses a small ethnography and art museum, and hanging out on the stone steps above the river is a fine enough way to pass an hour in the sun.

On a clear day, hoof it up to the **Mirador de la Virgen del Calvario** (lookout; Av Floreana at Av Oriente) east of downtown, from where you can see several volcanic peaks in the distance. To get there follow Maldonado up the stairs and then hang a left on Avenida Oriente and follow that up to the statue of La Virgen del Calvario.

Tours

Several tour operators have sprung up in recent years offering daytrips and two- to three-day climbing trips to Cotopaxi (see p149). Prices for a daytrip to Cotopaxi are about $35 to $45 per person, depending on the size of your group, and whether or not the $10 park entrance fee is included. Two-day summit trips to Cotopaxi cost $130 and $150 per person – but make sure your guide is qualified and motivated if you're attempting the summit. Other excursions are offered as well. The following outfitters are all licensed by the department of tourism and have received positive reports from readers:

Expediciones Volcán Route (☎ 281 2452; volcanroute@hotmail.com; Salcedo 4-49)
Neiges (☎ 281 1199; neigestours@hotmail.com; Guayaquil near 2 de Mayo)
Tovar Expeditions (☎ 281 1333; reivajg1980@hotmail.com; Guayaquil 5-38)

Festivals & Events

Latacunga's major annual fiesta is La Virgen de las Mercedes, more popularly known as the **Fiesta de La Mamá Negra**. Held on September 23 and 24, the celebration involves processions, costumes, street dancing, Andean music and fireworks. This is one of those festivals that, although outwardly Christian, has much pagan indigenous influence and is well worth seeing. A big parade in honor of La Mamá Negra is held during the **Independence of Latacunga**, which is celebrated on November 11 with parades and a bullfight.

Sleeping

Hotels fill up fast on Wednesday with people staying the night for the Thursday-morning market at Saquisilí. Try to arrive early. Prices can double during the hugely popular Fiesta de La Mamá Negra.

BUDGET

Hotel Central (☎ 280 2912; Orellana at Salcedo; s/d $10/14) This hotel may be in the same building as Hotel Cotopaxi (the building takes up half the block), but it outdraws its neighbor when it comes to decor, kitschy finishing touches (such as 1960s ceramic ashtrays) and, best of all, friendliness. It's one of the best deals in town.

Hotel Rosim (☎ 280 2172, 281 3200; Quito 16-49; s/d $8/16) White is definitely the dominant color, and fluorescent lights in the rooms help drive the point home, but it's a clean, friendly place with good, hot showers and big white towels. Good value.

Residencial Santiago (☎ 280 0899; 2 de Mayo & Guayaquil; s/d with shared bathroom $5.50/11, with private bathroom $6.75/13.50) Readers have written in to recommend this hospitable, fairly priced hotel with turquoise walls, average-sized rooms and a friendly owner. No frills, clean and owner-operated.

Hotel Estambul (☎ 280 0354; Quevedo 644; r per person with shared/private bathroom $8/10) Though a longtime Latacunga favorite, Estambul seems to have lost much of its former friendliness, though the rooms remain spotless with colorful bedspreads and wood floors. The shared bathrooms are immaculate.

Hotel Cotopaxi (☎ 280 1310; Salcedo 5-61; s/d $10/16) Cotopaxi offers spacious, comfortable rooms with TV, some of which boast giant windows and pretty views of the central plaza. They can be a bit noisy, however.

Residencial Amazonas (☎ 281 2673; F Valencia 47-36; r per person with shared/private bathroom $3/5) Well, you can't beat the price. As for the rooms, they're decent enough for a night. And the location? There's not another lobby in town that opens onto the market.

MIDRANGE

Hotel Macroz (☎ 280 0907, 280 7274; hotelmakroz@ latinmail.com; F Valencia 8-56; s/d $15/25, 2 beds $30) With boom-box stereos (some rooms only), TVs, fridges, hairdryers and a flashy, black-and-gold 1980s decor, this is the swankiest place in Latacunga. Breakfast is included and the service is tops.

Hotel Rodelu (☎ 280 0956, 281 1264; www.rodelu .com.ec; Quito 16-31; s/d $18/27, ste s/d $30/40) Just off the Parque Vicente León, Hotel Rodelu is the sharpest hotel in town. The rooms are comfy, with lots of wood paneling, indigenous motifs adorning the walls, TV and telephone. There's a pleasant restaurant downstairs.

Hotel Tilipulo (☎ 281 0611; hoteltilipulo@hotmail .com; cnr Guayaquil & Quevedo; s/d $9/18) The almost log-cabin feel to this place lends a touch of charm to otherwise totally bland rooms with low ceilings, TV and telephone.

Eating

The classic dish of Latacunga is the *chugchu-cara* – a tasty, heart-attack-inducing plate of *fritada* (fried chunks of pork), *mote* (hominy), *chicharrón* (fried bits of pork skin), potatoes, fried banana, *tostado* (toasted corn), popcorn, and cheese empanadas. There are several *chugchucara* restaurants on Quijano y Ordoñez, a few blocks south of downtown. They're busiest on weekends, when families fill the tables and musicians stroll door to door. **Chugchucaras La Mamá Negra** (☎ 280 5401; Quijano y Ordoñez 1-67; chugchucara $4; ☺ 10am-7pm Tue-Sun) is one of the best.

The Latacunga area is also famous for its *allullas* (pronounced 'azhiuzhias'), which are dry biscuits made of flour and pork fat, as well as its *queso de hoja* – unpasteurized cheese wrapped in banana leaves. Both are available in the stores along the Panamericana directly north of the main pedestrian bridge (Avenida 9 de Julio).

El Copihue Rojo (☎ 280 1725; Quito 14-38; mains $3-5, almuerzos $2; ☺ 12:30-3pm & 6-9pm Mon-Sat) Probably the prettiest little restaurant in Latacunga, the Copihue Rojo dishes out delicious daily *almuerzos*, plus meats, pastas and five types of soup.

Pizzería Bon Giorno (☎ 280 4924; cnr Orellana & Maldonado; mains $4-7; ☺ 1-11pm Tue-Sat, 11am-11pm Sun) Giant portions of hearty lasagna slide down wonderfully after a few days in the hills. Good pizzas ($5 to $10) and pastas ($3.50 to $5) too.

Restaurant Rodelu (☎ 280 0956; Quito 16-31; mains $4-7; ☺ 7:15am-9:30pm Mon-Sat) In its name-sake hotel, Rodelu serves darn good pizza, delicious breakfasts and passable espresso drinks.

Pollos Jimmy's (☎ 280 1922; Quevedo 8-85 near Valencia; mains $2.25-2.50; ☺ 10am-10pm) Pop in for delicious rotisserie chicken served with rice, potatoes and chicken soup. The place stays busy for a reason.

Casa Grande (☎ 09 822 4242; cnr Quito & Guayaquil; almuerzos $1.30; ☺ 7am-5pm Mon-Sat) Tiny, family-run place serving cheap *almuerzos*.

There are many cheap roast chicken restaurants along Amazonas between Salcedo and Guayaquil.

Entertainment

Latacunga is pretty quiet, but if you want to see what the local youth get up to on a weekend night, pop into **Skyway** (☎ 281 3016; Av Oriente 137 at Napo), where karaoke is free on Friday nights; Saturdays it's all about the dance floors.

Getting There & Away

BUS

From Quito ($1.50, two hours) buses will drop you at the **bus terminal** (Panamericana) if Latacunga is their final destination. If you're taking a bus that's continuing to Ambato or Riobamba it'll drop you on the corner of 5 de Junio and Cotopaxi, about five blocks west of the Panamericana. From there it's a 10-minute walk downtown. Buses to Ambato ($1, 45 minutes) leave from the bus terminal. If heading south to Riobamba, it's easiest to catch a passing bus from the corner of 5 de Junio and Cotopaxi, although these can be full during vacations. Otherwise, bus to Ambato and change there.

Slower Quito-bound buses leave the terminal, while faster long-distance buses can be flagged on the Panamericana near 5 de Junio.

Transportes Cotopaxi has hourly buses to Quevedo ($3.75, 5½ hours) in the western lowlands. The road is paved as far as Zumbahua, beyond which it deteriorates. This is one of the roughest, least-traveled and perhaps most spectacular bus routes joining the highlands with the western lowlands. The bus climbs to Zumbahua, at 3500m, and then drops to Quevedo at only 150m above sea level.

For buses to villages along the Quilotoa loop, see the boxed text, p160.

TAXI

Plaza Chile (Plaza El Salto) is the place to go to hire taxis and pickup trucks for visits to Parque Nacional Cotopaxi and remote villages (pickups double as taxis on many of the rough roads in the highlands). Rates depend on your bargaining ability.

THE QUILOTOA LOOP
☎ 03

Bumping along the spectacular dirt roads of the Quilotoa loop and hiking between the area's Andean villages is one of Ecuador's most exhilarating adventures. Transportation is tricky but the rewards are abundant: highland markets, the breathtaking crater lake of Laguna Quilotoa, splendid hikes and traditional highland villages. Most of the villages along the loop have only basic accommodations, but you can base yourself in Chugchilán, which has good lodging options for all wallet sizes. (Tigua is another option.) One of the best parts of the loop

is the fact that you'll have many chances, especially in Quilotoa, to interact with indigenous folks. They can seem somewhat withdrawn at first, but are friendly and talkative once the ice is broken, especially if you speak some Spanish or – even better – Quichua.

Transportation is infrequent, and you may have to walk for long distances or wait for hours, so always carry warm clothes, a water bottle, some snacks and maybe even a sleeping bag.

The loop is explained heading clockwise from Latacunga, although you can travel in reverse with no problems.

Pujilí
pop 6185 / elevation 2900m

Pujilí, 10km west of Latacunga, is easily recognized by the bright blue and yellow stairway climbing the hillside to a lookout above the village. Most people zip through without stopping, but if you're not pressed for time it's worth a peek, if only to see the stunning interior of the church. The main market day is Sunday and there is a smaller

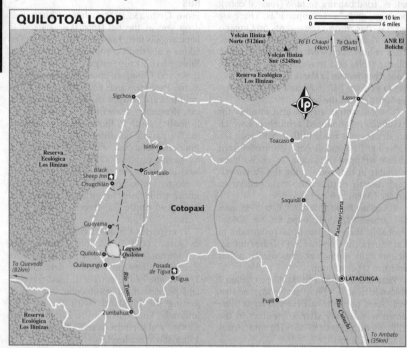

QUILOTOA LOOP

market on Wednesday. Pujilí is famous for its **Corpus Christi** celebrations (a movable date in June), when the colorful **El Danzante** festival takes place and costumed dancers parade around on stilts. **All Souls' Day** festivities (November 2) are also interesting.

Pujilí has a basic cheap hotel just off the main plaza and a couple of simple restaurants. There are frequent public buses from Latacunga.

Tigua
elevation 3500m

From Pujilí, the road begins to climb. It winds into the upper reaches of the *páramo*, and soon the peaks of Cotopaxi, Rumiñahui and the Ilinizas appear in the distance. Traditional *chozas* (indigenous grass houses) pop up now and again, and the patchwork mountainsides become impossibly steep.

About 43km after Pujilí you arrive in Tigua, a community that's known for the bright paintings of Andean life that are locally made on sheepskin canvases mounted on wooden frames. Originally used to decorate drum skins, this indigenous art form is now known internationally but still takes its name from the village. In Tigua, at Km 53 on the Latacunga–Zumbahua road, you'll find the outstanding Galería Tigua-Chimbacucho, which sells beautiful paintings and masks at prices that are better than *anything* you'll find in Quito. The priciest are the paintings by Alfredo Toaquiza, whose father, Julio, was a progenitor of the Tigua art form. If the gallery is closed (which it usually is), ask around the village and the caretaker will open it up.

Posada de Tigua (Hacienda Agrícola-Ganadera Tigua Chimbacucho; ☎ 281 3682, 280 0454; laposadadetigua@latinmail.com; Vía Latacunga-Zumbahua Km 49; r per person with half/full board $17/23) is part of a working dairy ranch, and this family-operated farmhouse-turned-inn is a rustic but delightfully cozy place to stay. Six rooms share one bathroom, there's one room outside the house, and a wood-burning stove stays roaring 24 hours a day. Three meals are included and horses can be hired for rides to Quilotoa. It's 3km before Tigua and about 500m below the road. It's signed, but tell the bus driver if you want to get off here.

Samana Huasi (☎ 281 4868, Quito ☎ 02-256 3175; www.tigua.org; Km 53; dm, r & board per person $19) is a lovely new community-run lodge with two comfortable dorm rooms and three private doubles. All the rooms have shared bathrooms (the toilets are self-composting), and stay cozy and warm at night. The restaurant is upstairs and has wonderful views over the valley. The lodge was started with the help of Jean Colvin from the USA, who is the author of a beautiful book on Tigua art that's usually available at the lodge and at bookstores in Quito. Located just below the gallery, Samana Huasi is the only orange building in the village; it's easily found.

Zumbahua
pop 11,895 / elevation 3800m

Some 15km west of Tigua, the tiny village of Zumbahua is surrounded by green patchwork peaks that seem to jut up from nowhere, a spectacular setting that makes for great hiking. Locals will point you to trails that lead to the mountaintops. The village has a wonderfully unspoiled **Saturday market** that draws indigenous people from the mountains, often hauling their goods with llamas. On Friday nights, Zumbahua is hoppin' – traditional Andean music, dancing and heavy drinking carry on so late the action sometimes spills over to market day. It's not a tourist event.

If you want to check out the market without spending the night, you can pay Condor Matzi $1 or so to watch your bags, which is better than lugging them around the market.

There are a few small and very basic *residenciales* (cheap hotels) around the main plaza. They fill up fast on Fridays.

Condor Matzi (☎ 281 4611; r per person $5), in an old building with a wooden balcony, is arguably the best *residencial* in town. It's a simple place but has handsome woodwork and Tigua paintings that give it a cheerful feel. Call ahead or ask at the store two doors down to be let in.

Hotel Quilotoa (r with shared/private bathroom $5/7), directly across the market plaza from Condor Matzi, is a modernish but simple place run by a friendly Quichua woman. It's clean, and the rooftop terrace (drag a chair up there) has great views.

Laguna Quilotoa
elevation 3854m

About 14km north of Zumbahua, the famous volcanic-crater lake of **Quilotoa** (admission to crater & village per person $1) is one of Ecuador's most staggering sights. From the precipitous crater rim there are stunning views of the mirror-green lake some 400m below, and the snowcapped peaks of Cotopaxi and Iliniza Sur tower in the distance. Fit walkers can hike around the crater rim in four to five hours, and another trail leads down to the water. The latter takes about a half-hour down and over twice that to get back up. The alkaline lake has no inflow or outlet, and you must not drink the water.

On the southwest side of the crater, the tiny village of Quilotoa has sprung up over the years in response to tourism. Accommodations are available in ramshackle little places along the single road that constitutes the settlement. They're just about the only accommodations you'll find in Ecuador actually run by local indigenous people. Although far from luxurious (they're extremely basic), they offer a unique chance to spend time with Quichua families and support indigenous businesses. Most have grass roofs typical of traditional homes in the *páramo*, and can be freezing at night, so bring warm clothes and a sleeping bag if you plan on staying.

All prices quoted here (which change frequently) include a simple breakfast and dinner. If you're just up for the day, *almuerzos* are available at nearly every house in the village for about $2.

The longest running, biggest (although not necessarily best) place up here is **Hostal Cabañas Quilotoa** (Latacunga ☎ 03-281 4625; r per person $8), operated by renowned Tigua artist Humberto Latacunga. The new rooms downstairs are probably the most comfortable in the village, but again, at this altitude and at this level, they're all pretty much a matter of personal preference. Humberto's place, unlike the others, has an electrically heated shower.

Princesa Toa (r per person $8) is the only community-run place in the village. It's a little more refined than the others (which is saying little), but the two sleeping rooms are communal.

The smaller places tend to be slightly more personal and homey, yet also more basic. The best way to choose a place is to walk around and check each one out and decide which one feels best to you. Some visitors prefer the intimacy that the bigger

---

HIKING FROM LAGUNA QUILOTOA TO CHUGCHILÁN

Prospective guides offer their services (sometimes a bit persistently) for the excellent hike from Quilotoa to Chugchilán, but you can do it yourself if you trust your sense of direction. The walk takes about five hours with breaks. Never leave after 2pm.

From the parking area, climb to the crater rim and look left across the crater for the lowest and most obvious sandy area, which lies about a quarter of the way around. You must first hike for about an hour to reach that spot. As you're hiking around the rim, it's the third low sandy spot. It's very important to identify the low sandy spot before starting the hike in order to avoid the *most common mistake*: leaving the crater rim too soon. Once you peg the sandy spot, you're good.

After reaching the low sandy spot, look just west of north and you'll see the village of Guayama. Beyond Guayama and across a canyon you can see Chugchilán. Walk down along a row of eucalyptus trees and head toward Guayama. Eventually, you'll hit the road to Guayama, which you should follow to Guayama and not Guayama Grande (which, oddly enough, is actually smaller). In Guayama, you can usually find a drink.

From Guayama it's another two hours to Chugchilán. As you're leaving Guayama, walk past the cemetery counting the right turns: the first is at the cemetery and the second one leads to a house. The third right turn follows the top of a gully. Follow the path above the gully without dropping into it. After about 20 minutes, you'll reach the edge of the canyon, where you'll encounter a tunnel-like trail that leads all the way to Chugchilán. En route, you'll cross two footbridges. After crossing the cement footbridge over the Río Sihui, you then climb the second hour to Chugchilán.

The Black Sheep Inn (opposite) put up signs to mark the trail, but prospective guides at Quilotoa have removed those near the crater. Once you're off the crater, you should be able to follow the signs that remain posted.

places lack. They all have smoky fireplaces, communal sleeping areas and charge about $5 to $8 per person.

Chugchilán

pop 6356 / elevation 3200m

After the turnoff to Laguna Quilotoa, the road turns to dirt, and the bumping begins. The road zigs and zags through 22km of breathtaking Andean scenery before passing through the wee village of Chugchilán. Built into the mountainside overlooking the spectacular Río Toachi canyon, Chugchilán is an excellent base for hikes in the area, and many people end up staying for days. You can hike Quilotoa, walk to nearby villages, visit a cheese factory or ride horses into the nearby cloud forest. There are three excellent places to stay on the northern edge of town, and all of them arrange horseback-riding trips and provide local hiking information.

Black Sheep Inn (☎ 281 4587; www.blacksheepinn .com; dm/s/d/tr/q $22.50/48/67/91/112; ☒ 🖳), barely 1km north of town, is an international award–winning ecolodge that's a truly special place to unwind. If you're interested in ecotourism you'll fall in love with it. Owned by a North American couple, it's a friendly place that practices high-altitude permaculture and participates in community projects. It has self-composting toilets (bedecked with lovely flowers), an organic vegetable garden and a combination chicken/greenhouse for fresh eggs and salads. The inn provides detailed hiking information for its guests and arranges horseback-riding and jeep trips. There is a good music collection, a lending library and free purified water, coffee and tea. Cold beer, cheese, brownies and cookies are always on hand. Outside there's a zipline and a wooden sauna ($10 extra per group). A beautiful three-story bunkhouse sleeps 10, and the private rooms sleep up to four. Each private room has a loft, a wood-burning stove, comfy beds and a homey feel. All bathrooms are shared and have blazing-hot showers. Rates include delicious, wholesome vegetarian breakfasts and dinners. Credit cards are not accepted.

Hostal Cloud Forest (☎ 281 4808; jose_cloudforest@ hotmail.com; r per person incl breakfast & dinner with shared/ private bathroom $6/8), the cheapest and simplest of Chugchilán's lodgings, is clean and friendly and serves excellent food. Travelers

dig it despite the fact that the rooms with shared bathrooms are bit cramped (although they do open onto a balcony). Rooms with private bathrooms are bigger.

Hostal Mama Hilda (☎ 281 4814, Quito ☎ 02-258 2957; r per person incl breakfast & dinner with shared/ private bathroom $13/16) Mama Hilda is an attractive place with cozy, brick-wall rooms with lofts, hammocks outside the rooms, and good views. The shared bathrooms are spotless. It's popular both with backpackers and tour groups from Quito, and it's very friendly.

Sigchos

pop 1272 / elevation 2800m

From Chugchilán, it's 23 muddy, bumpy kilometers to the town of Sigchos, which has a small Sunday market, and…that's about it. You can hike here in about five hours from Chugchilán via either the road or the Río Toachi canyon, and then get the 2pm bus back or the bus east toward Saquisilí and Latacunga. It's 52km from here to Saquisilí. There are a couple of basic places to stay and a small Sunday market.

Restaurant y Hotel La Posada (☎ 271 4224; cnr Galo Atiaga & Las Ilinizas; r per person $3) is a good choice. It has private bathrooms, and the rooms are small but they're respectable. It has a good restaurant downstairs (*almuerzos* $1.50; open 6am to 9pm). Also try the three-story **Hostal Tungurahua** (Calle Tungurahua; r per person $5) or the smaller **Pensión Sigchos** (r per person $4.50).

Isinliví

pop 3310 / elevation 2900m

Some 14km southeast of Sigchos, and just off the Quilotoa loop, the village of Isinliví makes a good hike from either Sigchos or Chugchilán. There's an interesting woodworking/cabinetry shop here, a small handicrafts center and nearby *pucarás* (pre-Inca hill fortresses). A popular day hike is to the Monday market at nearby Guantualo.

Lovely accommodations are available at **Llullu Llama** (☎ 281 4790, 281 4570; www.isinlivi.safari .com.ec; dm from $5, r per person from $8), a renovated, old adobe farmhouse with meter-thick walls and a wood-burning stove. There's a sauna (fired up for an additional cost), and food is available (including veggie options) for $3 to $5 per meal. The place is owned by Safari Tours (see p90) in Quito.

CENTRAL HIGHLANDS

TRANSPORTATION ON THE QUILOTOA LOOP

Most people get around the Quilotoa loop by public transportation, which is fun but takes patience. No buses go all the way around the loop. From Latacunga, they only go as far as Chugchilán, and they either go clockwise (via Zumbahua and Quilotoa) or counterclockwise (via Saquisilí and Sigchos). Tigua is served by passing buses.

If you don't wish to take public transportation, you could hire a taxi in Latacunga. They'll do the whole route in a long day starting at around $50. The road is the worst between Quilotoa and Sigchos; it's now paved from Latacunga to Quilotoa.

The following schedule lists public transportation going both directions on the loop. The times listed here are rough (like the road) so always be ready a little early.

Bear with us – if you think transportation on the loop is confusing, try squeezing the myriad details into a boxed text!

CLOCKWISE

Latacunga–Chugchilán (direct)
The bus via Zumbahua departs daily from Latacunga at noon, passing Zumbahua at around 1:30pm, Laguna Quilotoa at around 2pm and arriving in Chugchilán at about 4pm ($4).

Latacunga–Zumbahua
Transportes Cotopaxi buses ($2, two hours) bound for Quevedo depart hourly from Latacunga's bus terminal, and drop passengers a short walk from Zumbahua.

Zumbahua–Laguna Quilotoa
Trucks can be hired for $5; the rate goes up if there's more than two of you. The Latacunga–Chugchilán bus passes around 1:30pm, and the trip from Zumbahua to Laguna Quilotoa takes approximately 45 minutes.

Laguna Quilotoa–Chugchilán
To get from Laguna Quilotoa to Chugchilán take the Latacunga–Chugchilán bus between 2pm and 2:30pm ($2, two hours).

Chugchilán–Latacunga (direct)
Good morning! Buses via Sigchos leave Monday through Friday at 3am, passing Sigchos at around 4am, Saquisilí at around 7am and arriving in Latacunga around 8am. On Saturday this bus departs at 7am. On Sunday you must switch buses in Sigchos. You can also return via Zumbahua ($4) (see Counterclockwise).

There are direct buses to Isinliví from Latacunga's bus terminal at 1pm on Monday, Tuesday, Wednesday and Friday, and at 10:30am or 11am on Saturday and Sunday. Buses leave Saquisilí to Isinliví on Thursday between 10:30am and 11am. There are two daily buses from Sigchos.

Saquisilí
pop 5234

Each and every Thursday morning, Saquisilí takes the idea of 'market day' to exultant heights. Ecuadorian economists consider the **Thursday morning market** the most impor-

tant indigenous village market in the country, and many travelers rate it as the best they've seen in Ecuador. It's not a tourist-oriented event, although there are the usual few *otavaleños* (people from Otavalo) selling their sweaters and weavings. This market is for the inhabitants of remote indigenous villages who flood into town to buy or sell everything from bananas to homemade shotguns and from herbal remedies to strings of piglets.

There are eight different plazas, each of which sell specific goods. Especially interesting is the **animal market**, a cacophonous

Chugchilán–Sigchos

A daily milk truck ($1) leaves Chugchilán between 8:30am and 9am taking about one hour to reach Sigchos, allowing you to avoid the 3am Chugchilán–Latacunga bus. Two other buses go to Sigchos on Thursday afternoon. Sunday departures are at 4am, 5am, noon and between 1pm to 3pm and 7pm to 9pm.

Sigchos–Latacunga

The bus from Sigchos to Latacunga ($1.50, two hours) departs daily at 2:30pm from beside the church. Additional buses leave on Wednesday, Saturday and Sunday. Otherwise catch the passing bus from Chugchilán at around 7am. Both stop in Saquisilí.

Saquisilí–Latacunga

Buses ($0.25, 20 minutes) depart Plaza Concordia in Saquisilí every 10 minutes.

COUNTERCLOCKWISE

Latacunga–Chugchilán

The bus via Sigchos departs daily at 11:30am, passing Saquisilí just before noon and Sigchos at around 2pm, arriving in Chugchilán around 3:30pm. This bus leaves Latacunga's bus terminal an hour earlier (10:30am) on Saturdays ($4).

Latacunga–Saquisilí

Buses ($0.25, 20 minutes) depart from Latacunga's bus terminal every 10 minutes.

Latacunga–Sigchos

Transportes Nacional Saquisilí buses leave Latacunga's bus terminal at 9am daily Friday to Wednesday. On Sunday, an additional bus ($1.50, 2½ hours) leaves at 3:30am.

Sigchos–Chugchilán

Take the passing bus from Latacunga ($2, leaves around 2pm or the daily milk truck ($1), which leaves Sigchos daily at 7:30am; the trip takes about one hour.

Chugchilán–Latacunga (direct)

Buses to Latacunga via Zumbahua leave Chugchilán Monday through Friday at 4am, passing Quilotoa (two hours) at around 6am, Zumbahua (about 2½ hours) at around 6:30am and arriving in Latacunga (about four hours) around 8am. On Saturday this bus leaves at 3am, and on Sunday it leaves at 6am and 10am ($4).

affair with screaming pigs playing a major role. It's almost 1km out of town – go early and ask for directions.

In September, 2005 the municipality decided to ban vendors from the street, limiting selling to the market plazas and dramatically reducing the size and scope of the market. On our visit, the market was a fraction of its former self, though still well worth visiting. Whether short-sighted city officials continue the policy remains to be seen.

Most travelers find it best to stay in Latacunga; the bus service begins at dawn, so you won't miss anything. Otherwise, you can stay at **Hotel San Carlos** (☎ 272 1981; Bolívar & Sucre; s/d $7/12), a friendly little place right on the main plaza with large windows and fuzzy red velvet headboards.

There are plenty of hole-in-the-wall places to eat.

SAN MIGUEL DE SALCEDO
☎ 03 / pop 9850

Salcedo's claim to fame is its multilayer, fruity ice-cream bars, sold on sticks at nearly every store in town. It's almost comical how much ice cream this place produces. Located 14km south of Latacunga, it also has a Sunday market. The town holds a **Mamá Negra fiesta** around November 1, but outside this time, there's little reason to hang about. There are a couple of basic hotels in the town center.

Hostería Rumibamba de las Rosas (☎ 272 6128, 272 6306, 272 7309; rumipamba@rumipamba.com; d $60; 🏊) is on the northern outskirts of town. With a small private zoo, a duck pond, pony and llama rides, tennis courts and game rooms, it has a rather Disneyland atmosphere.

AMBATO

☎ 03 / pop 154,100 / elevation 2577m

Ambato takes a little warming up to. Compared with nearby Baños, it offers little for the traveler, except the chance to experience a totally nontouristy Ecuadorian city. And it's actually an interesting place. The **Monday market**, which fills the streets downtown, is one of the biggest in Ecuador. Above town, there are fabulous views of the puffing Volcán Tungurahua (5016m), and Ambato's parks and quintas (historic country homes converted into parks) are lovely. The *ambateños* (people from Ambato) themselves must be some of the best-dressed folks in Ecuador.

The city is proud of its cultural heritage, and nicknames itself 'Tierra de Los Tres Juanes' (Land of the Three Juans), after the writers Juan Montalvo and Juan León Mera (see p39), and lawyer/journalist Juan Benigno Malo. All three are immortalized in Ambato's parks, museums and buildings.

The city lies 47km south of Latacunga (136km south of Quito) and is the capital of Tungurahua province. It was badly damaged in a 1949 earthquake, but a modern city was soon rebuilt.

Information

Andinatel (Castillo near Rocafuerte) Telephone center.

Banco de Guayaquil (cnr Mera & Sucre) Bank with ATM.

Banco del Pacífico (cnr Lalama & Cevallos) Bank with ATM.

Banco del Pichincha (Lalama near Sucre) Bank with ATM.

Cambiato (☎ 282 1008; Calle Bolívar 686) Changes traveler's checks.

Compunet (Cevallos 15-57; per hr $1; 🕙 9am-9pm Mon-Sat) Internet access; inside the Asociación de Empleados building.

Net Place (Montalvo 05-58 near Cevallos; per hr $1) Internet access.

Post office (Castillo at Bolívar)

TAME (☎ 282 6601, 282 0322, 282 2595; Calle Bolívar 20-17) Airline office for flight reservations from other cities.

Tourist office (☎ 282 1800; Guayaquil & Rocafuerte; 🕙 8am-2pm & 3-5pm Mon-Fri)

Sights & Activities

LAS QUINTAS

Because the 1949 earthquake destroyed most of the old buildings downtown, you'll have to wander out of it to get some history. Several famous *ambateños* had quintas that survived the earthquake and are now open to the public. They're well worth visiting.

La Quinta de Juan León Mera (☎ 282 0419; Av Los Capulíes s/n; admission $1; 🕙 9:30am-5:30pm Wed-Sun) is set in a lush, meandering botanical garden in the suburb of Atocha. Set on the banks of the Río Ambato, it's the perfect spot to escape the city. You can wander through the gardens, down a trail through the trees, and out to the grassy riverside – a perfect spot for a picnic.

Across from and just past La Quinta de Juan León Mera, the **Parque Infantil** (Children's Park) is a sight to see on Sunday afternoons, when it seems half the city is hanging around sucking down ice creams, riding the amusement train and chasing their children around.

Close by is **La Quinta de la Liria**, the country home of the mountaineer Nicolás Martínez. Also set in a pleasant garden, the quinta underwent some needed restoration and reopened in November, 2005.

All of the previous are in the suburb of Atocha, about 2km northeast of downtown. To get there by foot, walk northwest on Montalvo, cross the river, and turn right on Capulíes.

Another pleasant walk takes you along Calle Bolívar, southwest of downtown, to the modern suburb of Miraflores. The river can be crossed about 2km away from town on Avenida Los Guaytambos, which soon leads to **La Quinta de Juan Montalvo** (admission $1; 🕙 9:30am-5:30pm Fri-Sun), where that writer's former villa stands.

MONUMENTO A LA PRIMERA IMPRENTA

For wonderful views of billowing Volcán Tungurahua, head up to the **Monumento a La Primera Imprenta**, on the northwest side of town. On a day of high volcanic activity, seeing the volcano spew clouds of steam with Ambato in the foreground is magnifi-

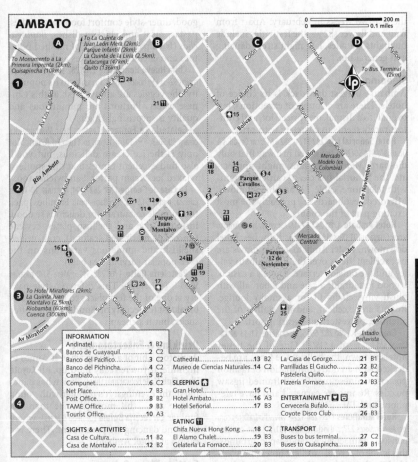

AMBATO

0   200 m
0   0.1 miles

To Monumento a La Primera Imprenta (2km); Quisapincha (10km)

To La Quinta de Juan León Mera (2km); Parque Infantil (2km); La Quinta de la Liria (2.5km); Latacunga (47km); Quito (135km)

To Bus Terminal (2km)

To Hotel Miraflores (2km); La Quinta Juan Montalvo (2.5km); Riobamba (60km); Cuenca (300km)

Estadio Bellavista

INFORMATION

Andinatel	1 B2
Banco de Guayaquil	2 C2
Banco del Pacífico	3 C2
Banco del Pichincha	4 C2
Cambiato	5 B2
Compunet	6 C2
Net Place	7 B3
Post Office	8 B2
TAME Office	9 B3
Tourist Office	10 A3

SIGHTS & ACTIVITIES

Casa de Cultura	11 B2
Casa de Montalvo	12 B2
Cathedral	13 B2
Museo de Ciencias Naturales	14 C2

SLEEPING

Gran Hotel	15 C1
Hotel Ambato	16 A3
Hotel Señorial	17 B3

EATING

Chifa Nueva Hong Kong	18 C2
El Alamo Chalet	19 B3
Gelatería La Fornace	20 B3

La Casa de George	21 B1
Parrilladas El Gaucho	22 B2
Pastelería Quito	23 C2
Pizzería Fornace	24 B3

ENTERTAINMENT

Cervecería Bufalo	25 C3
Coyote Disco Club	26 B3

TRANSPORT

Buses to bus terminal	27 C2
Buses to Quisapincha	28 B1

CENTRAL HIGHLANDS

cent. A taxi up to the top should cost no more than $2, and you can walk down to the bus stop to return downtown.

PARQUE JUAN MONTALVO

Ambato's main plaza is surprisingly beautiful, with handsome stone entryways, sculpted juniper bushes shading wooden benches, flowering trees and a giant statue of Juan Montalvo in the center. On the northwest side of the plaza, you can visit his former house, **Casa de Montalvo** (☎ 282 4248; admission $0.50; ❤ 9am-noon & 2-6pm Mon-Sat). Next door the **Casa de Cultura** (☎ 282 0338, 282 4248; admission free; ❤ 9am-noon & 3-6pm Mon-Fri) has an art gallery. On the northeast side of this plaza is the modern and rather bleak **cathedral**.

MUSEO DE CIENCIAS NATURALES

This **natural-history museum** (☎ 282 1958; Sucre & Lalama; admission $2; ❤ 8:30am-12:30pm & 2:30-5:30pm Mon-Fri, 9am-5pm Sat), in the Colegio Bolívar, houses hundreds of stuffed birds, mammals and reptiles. There's also a rather gruesome display of freaks, such as two-headed calves and six-legged lambs, an archaeological collection with Inca pieces, traditional Ecuadorian clothing, a coin collection and other displays.

Festivals & Events

Ambato is famous for its **Fiesta de Frutas y Flores** (Festival of Fruit and Flowers), which is an annual festival that's supposed to coincide with Carnaval but is usually held during the last two weeks in February. Apart from fruit and flower shows, the festivities include bullfights, parades, late-night street dancing and general fun.

Sleeping

Ambato's biggest drawback is its choice of hotels. There are a couple of exceptions, but overall it's a dismal, overpriced lot, and comfort rarely seems to correlate with price.

Hotel Señorial (☎ 282 5124, 282 6249; cnr Cevallos & Quito; s/d $14.50/29) Decorated in a way that only die-hard *Miami Vice* fans might appreciate, the Señorial has clean, carpeted rooms with telephone, cable TV and big windows. Mirrored headboards are probably the most exciting part of the rooms.

Hotel Ambato (☎ 242 1791/2/3; www.hotelambato .com; Guayaquil 01-08; s/d $48/62) Easily the best hotel downtown, Hotel Ambato's main draws are its excellent views over the Río Ambato valley and the outside terrace. There's a casino, a good restaurant, a café and a bar, all with plush vinyl chairs fit for a smoky lounge. Rooms are excellent, and the staff is of the attentive, polyester suit–wearing sort.

Gran Hotel (☎ 282 5915; Rocafuerte 11-33 at Lalama; s/d incl breakfast $15/21) One of the better hotels in town, the halls of the Gran are bedecked with an odd combination of fashion posters, Chinese motifs and framed jigsaw puzzles. Rooms are carpeted and have telephone and TV.

Hotel Miraflores (☎ 284 3224; www.hmiraflores .ec; Av Miraflores 227; s/d incl breakfast $31/51) Set on expansive, immaculately landscaped grounds, this is one of several excellent hotels on Avenida Miraflores, about 2km from downtown.

Eating

Pizzería Fornace (☎ 282 3244; Cevallos 17-28; pizzas $3-5; noon-10pm) Thanks to the roaring, wood-fired brick oven, thin crusts and fresh ingredients, this is easily the best pizza in town. Plenty of pasta dishes adorn the menu as well.

Parrilladas El Gaucho (☎ 282 8969; Calle Bolívar near Quito; mains $6-8; noon-11pm Mon-Sat, noon-4pm Sun) This steak-house fires up delicious Argentinean-style *parrillada* (grilled meats), including juicy steaks or combo plates brought sizzling on a tabletop grill.

El Alamo Chalet (☎ 282 4704; Cevallos 17-19; mains $3-6; 8am-10pm) Easily identified by it's chalet-style wooden facade, El Alamo serves

good, diner-style comfort food: sandwiches, pastas, meat and chicken dishes, *llapingachos* (fried pancakes made of mashed potatoes and cheese), milkshakes and more.

Chifa Nueva Hong Kong (☎ 282 3796; Bolívar 768; mains $2-3; noon-11pm) Thanks to its popularity, the veggies are always fresh at this Chinese eatery. Portions are humungous and quality is surprisingly high.

Gelatería La Fornace (Cevallos near Montalvo; ice cream $0.50-3; 10am-10pm, to 11pm Fri & Sat) Not only is the ice cream delicious, but you'll also find excellent espresso at this spotless, relaxed ice-cream parlor. Sandwiches too.

La Casa de George (☎ 282 4494; Martínez 10-150 at Cuenca; mains $4.50-6; 8am-4pm) Families pack this humble restaurant for delicious seafood, including rice and shellfish plates, ceviche (uncooked marinated seafood), crab, grilled shellfish and numerous variations on the ever-popular *corvina* (sea bass).

Pastelería Quito (☎ 282 5475; Mera 514; pastries $0.50-1; 7am-9pm) This cafeteria-style bakery is one of the few places to grab an early breakfast (especially on Sunday). The coffee sucks, but it's cheap.

Drinking & Entertainment

Ambato's a bit of a snorer when it comes to nightlife. If you're really hard up, hit **Coyote Disco Club** (Calle Bolívar near Quito), which has dancing in the evenings. It's popular with young people and a bit more upscale than the funkier **Cervecería Bufalo** (Olmedo & Mera), where beer and dancing are paramount. There is a casino at Hotel Ambato.

Getting There & Away
BUS
The **bus terminal** (☎ 282 1481; Av de las Américas at Av Colombia) is 2km northeast of downtown. Get there by heading northeast on 12 de Noviembre to the traffic circle, and then turn right on Avenida de las Américas.

For destinations north of Quito, you can easily take a bus to Quito and change at the terminal there.

Getting Around

The most important local bus for travelers is the route between the bus terminal and downtown. From the terminal, climb the exit ramp to Avenida de las Américas, which crosses the train tracks on a bridge. On this bridge is a bus stop, where a westbound (to

BUSES FROM AMBATO

Destination	Cost (US$)	Duration (hr)
Baños	1	1
Cuenca	7	7
Esmeraldas	6	8
Guaranda	2	2
Guayaquil	6	6
Ibarra	5	5
Lago Agrio	6	11
Latacunga	1	¾
Loja	9-13	11
Machala	6	8
Manta	7	10
Otavalo	3.50	4½
Puyo	2.50	3
Quito	2	2½
Riobamba	1	1
Santo Domingo	3	4
Tena	4-5	6

your right) bus, usually signed 'Centro,' will take you to Parque Cevallos for $0.20.

Buses marked 'Terminal' leave from the Martínez side of Parque Cevallos. Buses to the suburb of Ficoa also leave from this park. A block away is Bolívar, which has buses to the suburb of Miraflores running along it. Buses to the Atocha suburb (for more quintas) leave from 12 de Noviembre and Sevilla or Espejo.

AROUND AMBATO

☎ 03

Salasaca and Pelileo are the most frequently visited villages near Ambato because they lie on the good main road to Baños. Other villages are off the main road but are interesting to visit on daytrips. With the exception of Patate, none of the following villages have accommodations.

Buses to Salasaca ($0.35, 25 minutes), Pelileo ($0.40, 28 minutes) and Patate ($0.70, one hour) leave every 20 minutes or so from Plaza La Dolorosa in the neighborhood known as Ferroviaria, which is a $1 cab ride from downtown.

Quisapincha
elevation 3120m

Famous for its leather, Quisapincha is a tiny town with more leather jackets, handbags, wallets, shoes and soccer balls than the town

can hold – which is why everything is so cheap. The best part is that there's no hard sell; you can browse the leather in the myriad of shops along the main drag without any pressure at all. If you do decide to buy, you'll pay about $30 to $45 for a fine leather jacket, provided you can find a cut you like.

It's also a town of crumbling old adobe buildings that amazingly still serve their purposes as buildings. Part of the joy of visiting Quisapincha is the 10km bus ride from Ambato, which gives you spectacular views of the city and the smoking, steaming Volcán Tungurahua.

Buses ($0.30, 25 minutes) to Quisapincha leave from the northwest end of Martínez (at the corner of Perez de Anda) in Ambato.

Parque Nacional Llanganates & Píllaro

Created in 1996, **Parque Nacional Llanganates** encompasses 219,719 hectares of *páramo*, cloud forest and lowland forest and is home to deer, mountain tapirs, Amazonian tapirs, pumas, jaguars and the Andean spectacled bear. It's also rich in bird life and orchids. However merciless rain and fog, impenetrable forest, impassable peaks and complete lack of infrastructure make it the most difficult park to visit in Ecuador.

The park is also shrouded in legend. Rumiñahui, Atahualpa's war general, supposedly buried the treasure he was carrying as a ransom to the Spanish for the release of the captive Inca ruler. When the Spanish killed Atahualpa, despite being promised the gold they demanded, Rumiñahui supposedly hid the treasure – said to be a 'roomful' of gold – in the impenetrable Llanganates. Many bonafide expeditions have searched for it using ancient maps, but nobody has found it!

The village of **Píllaro**, about 20km northeast of Ambato, is the main entry point for the park. Here you can hire guides ($10 to $20 per day, plus food for the guide) and mules. There are almost no trails. Few tour operators will go here; the exception is Rainbow Expeditions (p171) in Baños.

Píllaro itself is an interesting village. It's famous for its bulls, and during July and August fiestas are celebrated with bullfights, highland food and parades. Quito's Independence Day, on August 10, is also vigorously celebrated with a bullfight and a bull run, in which the bulls charge through the streets; everybody participates.

Salasaca

As you head southeast from Ambato on the Baños road, the first place of interest is Salasaca, about 14km away. The town and its environs are home to some 2000 indigenous Salasaca who are famous for their high-quality woven tapestries.

The Salasaca are also known for their typical dress, especially in the men, who often wear broad-brimmed white hats, black ponchos and white shirts and trousers. Originally, the Salasaca came from Bolivia, but they were conquered by the Inca in the 15th century and relocated here. One of the ways in which the Inca controlled the peoples they conquered was to move them en masse to an area that the Inca had long dominated.

There is a **craft market** held every Sunday morning near the church on the Ambato–Baños road. Also along this road are several craft stores that are open daily. One of these is a women artisans' cooperative. Nearby is **Alonso Pilla's house** (☎ 09-984 0125; 7am-6pm). Pilla gives weaving demonstrations on a backstrap loom using traditional techniques, and sells weavings.

On the Sunday after Easter, a magnificent indigenous street dance takes place on the road between Salasaca and Pelileo, and on June 15, the Salasacas dress up in animal costumes for **Santo Vintio**. Both **Corpus Christi** (which takes place on a movable date in June) and the **feast of St Anthony** (end of November) are colorfully celebrated.

Pelileo

Some 6km beyond Salasaca on the Baños road, the larger and unimpressive village of Pelileo is famous for its blue jeans. Despite the town's 400-year history, the Pelileo of today is a very modern village. Pelileo celebrates its **cantonization** on July 22 with the usual highland festivities: bullfights, parades and plenty of food and drink.

Baños is only 24km away, but the road drops some 850m from Pelileo. The descent along the Río Pastaza gorge is spectacular, and some of the best views of erupting Tungurahua are to be seen on this drive.

Patate & Around

Nicknamed the 'City of Eternal Spring,' Patate is a tranquil village with a beautiful climate and an ideal location on Río Patate. About 20km northeast of Pelileo, it became a popular destination for volcano watchers after nearby Volcán Tungurahua erupted back to life (see opposite). The village is known for its *arepas* (a spice cake wrapped and cooked in leaves), *chicha de uva* (a nonalcoholic, fermented grape beverage) and its *aguardiente* (sugarcane alcohol), allegedly some of the best in the highlands. Once you're drunk and full of cake, there's little left to do except doze in the newly remodeled main plaza, chat with the locals or relax in one of the nearby resorts.

Although Patate may suffer from light ashfall in the event of a major eruption, it is considered safer than Pelileo and Baños.

Jardín del Valle (☎ 287 0209, 287 0508; Soria at Calderón; s/d $8/16) is the best option for accommodations in town – a simple but comfy little place with a dense green garden in back and friendly owners. It's a block off the main plaza.

At **Hospedaje Altamira** (☎ 287 0339; Ambato 26-13; s/d $3/6), basic is an understatement (think plywood dividers turning one room into three), but Doña Leticia Tamayo is wonderfully friendly and keeps the place clean enough that it's easy to forget just how ramshackle the place is. There's a shared hot shower and a garden out back.

Down by the river, **Hostería Viña del Río** (☎ 287 0143, 287 0139; r per person incl breakfast $21, cabañas per person $23;) is best midweek and low season, when you'll likely have the three swimming pools, sauna, steam room and Jacuzzis all to yourself. It's mobbed on weekends when facilities are open to the public ($4 per person).

A former family farm, nestled into the mountains at 2900m, **Hacienda Manteles** (☎ / fax 285 9474, 287 0123, Quito ☎ 02-250 4902, 255 0791; www.haciendamanteles.com; s/d incl breakfast $57/69) was converted into a beautiful country inn in 1992. It's about 15km from Patate. From the leafy front lawn, there are lovely views of the Río Patate valley and of puffing Volcán Tungurahua in the distance. It's a wonderful place to relax, and you can hike, explore the nearby cloud forest on horseback and even fish. Dinner is available. Guests with reservations can arrange to be picked up from the bus station in Patate at no extra charge.

About 5km or so from Patate, the handsome **Hacienda Leito** (☎ 285 9328/9; www.hacienda leito.com; s/d/ste $85/115/170) is the swankiest place in the area. The eclectic common area is adorned with big chairs and random art and has a warmly welcoming ranch-style feel.

BAÑOS
☎ 03 / pop 12,300 / elevation 1800m

Hemmed in by luxuriant green peaks, blessed with steaming thermal baths and adorned by a beautiful waterfall, Baños is one of Ecuador's most enticing and popular tourist destinations. Ecuadorians and foreigners alike flock to this idyllically set town to hike, soak in the baths, ride mountain bikes, zip around on rented quad-runners, volcano-watch, party and break their molars on the town's famous *milcocha* (taffy). Touristy as it is, it's a wonderful place to hang out for a few days, complementing outdoor-activity days with excellent dining out.

Baños is also the gateway town into the jungle via Puyo and Misahuallí. East of Baños, the road drops spectacularly, and exceptional views of the upper Amazon Basin stretch out below. They're best taken in over the handlebars of a mountain bike, which you can rent in town for the downhill ride.

Although Baños suffered a major setback in 1999 due to the erupting Tungurahua (see the boxed text Life on the Slopes of 'Little Hell', below), volcanic activity has decreased to a few insignificantly steaming fumaroles (as of early 2006), and the town is as hopping as ever. It is, however, an unpredictable area and you must keep yourself apprised of potential dangers.

Orientation
Baños is tiny, and with the mountains towering over town making for easy reference it's impossible to get lost. Everything is walking distance from the bus terminal. Few buildings in Baños have street numbers or addresses.

Information
Baños has loads of cybercafés, but they appear and disappear frequently. Ask your hotel staff

---

LIFE ON THE SLOPES OF 'LITTLE HELL'

Set in a lush green valley on the slopes of Volcán Tungurahua, Baños has been synonymous with relaxation and tourism for decades. This suddenly changed in 1998, when increased seismic activity from Tungurahua was detected. The volcano was placed on yellow alert, meaning it was being monitored and showing signs of activity, but that dangers of a major eruption were not imminent. Seismologists then changed it to orange alert after an Australian climber and his Ecuadorian guide were burned by a gaseous eruption on October 5, 1999.

Over the next two weeks, Tungurahua, which means 'little hell' in Quichua, pumped clouds of steam and ash into aerial columns kilometers high, and ashfall was a regular occurrence in the surrounding area. At night, streams of glowing lava cascaded down the sides of the volcano. By October 17, authorities ordered the evacuation of more than 20,000 inhabitants of Baños and nearby villages, and the roads between Ambato and Puyo and between Riobamba and Puyo were closed. With the volcano erupting almost daily, tour operators in Quito and Ambato began offering trips to see the volcanic wonders from a safe distance.

Weeks turned into months, and by January 2000 there still had not been an eruption large enough to cause substantial damage to Baños. The inhabitants, desperate to return to their homes and their livelihoods, defied government orders and clashed with troops at a military checkpoint, resulting in several injuries and the death of one woman. Soon afterward, an agreement was reached, and about 3000 people were allowed back into Baños.

Slowly, curious daytrippers and tourists began to trickle into Baños, and week after week more residents began to return and reopen their tourism businesses. The town was kept on orange alert until September 5 2002, when it was demoted to yellow alert.

At the time of research, the volcano was still active, burping ash, smoke and steam, but the threat of an eruption was no longer considered imminent. Tourism and daily life were entirely back to normal. The roads between Baños and Riobamba and between Ambato and Puyo were both open.

For daily volcano updates in Spanish, visit the website of the Instituto Geofísico (www.igepn.edu.ec). Weekly updates are given in English on the Smithsonian Institute's Global Volcanism Program (www.volcano.si.edu).

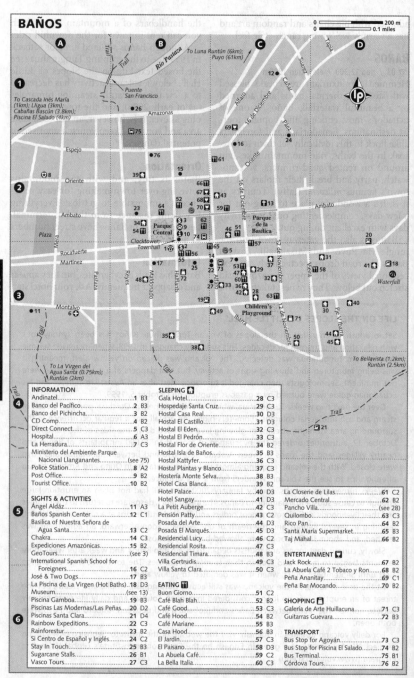

BAÑOS

To Luna Runtún (6km);
Puyo (61km)

To Cascada Inés María
(1km); Lligua (3km);
Cabañas Bascún (3.8km);
Piscina El Salado (4km)

Río Pastaza

Puente
San Francisco

Amazonas

Espejo

Oriente

Ambato

Plaza

Rocafuerte

Martínez

Montalvo

Parque
Central

Clocktower,
Townhall

Parque
de la
Basílica

Ambato

Children's
Playground

Waterfall

To La Virgen del
Agua Santa (0.75km);
Runtún (2km)

To Bellavista (1.2km);
Runtún (2.5km)

Trail

INFORMATION
Andinatel..1 B3
Banco del Pacífico............................2 B3
Banco del Pichincha..........................3 B3
CD Comp...4 B2
Direct Connect..................................5 C3
Hospital..6 A3
La Herradura.....................................7 C3
Ministerio del Ambiente Parque
Nacional Llanganantes...............(see 75)
Police Station....................................8 A2
Post Office...9 B2
Tourist Office....................................10 B2

SIGHTS & ACTIVITIES
Ángel Aldáz.....................................11 A3
Baños Spanish Center......................12 C1
Basílica of Nuestra Señora de
Agua Santa..................................13 C2
Chakra...14 C3
Expediciones Amazónicas................15 B2
GeoTours...................................(see 3)
International Spanish School for
Foreigners...................................16 C2
José & Two Dogs..............................17 B3
La Piscina de La Virgen (Hot Baths)..18 D3
Museum.....................................(see 13)
Piscina Gamboa...............................19 B3
Piscinas Las Modernas/Las Peñas....20 C2
Piscinas Santa Clara.........................21 D4
Rainbow Expeditions.......................22 C3
Rainforestur.....................................23 B2
Si Centro de Español y Inglés...........24 C2
Stay In Touch...................................25 B3
Sugarcane Stalls..............................26 B1
Vasco Tours.....................................27 C3

SLEEPING
Gala Hotel.......................................28 C3
Hospedaje Santa Cruz.....................29 C3
Hostal Casa Real.............................30 D3
Hostal El Castillo.............................31 D3
Hostal El Eden.................................32 C3
Hostal El Pedrón.............................33 C3
Hostal Flor de Oriente.....................34 C3
Hostal Isla de Baños........................35 B3
Hostal Kattyfer...............................36 C3
Hostal Plantas y Blanco...................37 C3
Hostería Monte Selva......................38 C3
Hotel Casa Blanca...........................39 B2
Hotel Palace....................................40 D3
Hotel Sangay...................................41 D3
La Petit Auberge..............................42 C3
Pensión Patty..................................43 C3
Posada del Arte...............................44 D3
Posada El Marqués..........................45 D3
Residencial Lucy..............................46 C3
Residencial Rosita...........................47 C3
Residencial Timara..........................48 B3
Villa Gertrudis................................49 C3
Villa Santa Clara.............................50 C3

EATING
Buon Giorno....................................51 C2
Café Blah Blah.................................52 B3
Café Good..53 C3
Café Hood..54 C3
Café Mariane...................................55 B3
Casa Hood.......................................56 B3
El Jardín...57 C2
El Paisano..58 D3
La Abuela Café.................................59 C2
La Bella Italia...................................60 C3

La Closerie de Lilas..........................61 C2
Mercado Central..............................62 B2
Pancho Villa..............................(see 28)
Quilombo..63 C3
Rico Pan..64 C2
Santa María Supermarket.................65 B3
Taj Mahal..66 B2

ENTERTAINMENT
Jack Rock...67 B2
La Abuela Café 2 Tobaco y Ron........68 B2
Peña Ananitay..................................69 C1
Peña Bar Mocando..........................70 B2

SHOPPING
Galería de Arte Huillacuna...............71 D3
Guitarras Guevara...........................72 B3

TRANSPORT
Bus Stop for Agoyán........................73 C3
Bus Stop for Piscina El Salado...........74 B2
Bus Terminal....................................75 B1
Córdova Tours.................................76 B2

about emergency-evacuation procedures in the event of an eruption.

Andinatel (☎ 274 0411; cnr Rocafuerte & Halflants) Telephone center.

Banco del Pacífico (cnr Halflants & Rocafuerte) Bank with ATM; changes traveler's checks.

Banco del Pichincha (cnr Ambato & Halflants) Bank with ATM; changes traveler's checks.

CD Comp (Ambato near Alfaro; per hr $2; ☽ 8am-11pm) Internet access.

Direct Connect (Martínez near Alfaro; per hr $2; ☽ 9am-10pm) Internet access.

Hospital (☎ 274 0443, 274 0301; Montalvo near Pastaza) The small, local hospital. Pharmacies are along Ambato.

La Herradura (Martínez near Alfaro; per kg $1; ☽ 8am-12:30pm & 2-7pm) Same-day laundry service.

Ministerio del Ambiente Parque Nacional Llanganates (☎ 274 1662; bus terminal; ☽ sporadic hours Mon-Fri) Administration office for Llanganates; has small, photocopied topo maps and lots of information.

Police station (☎ 274 0251; Oriente near Mera)

Post office (☎ 274 0901; Halflants near Ambato)

Tourist office (☎ 274 0483; mun_banos@andinanet .net; Halflants near Rocafuerte; ☽ 8am-12:30pm & 2-5:30pm Mon-Fri) Guidebooks to Baños are sold here; basic maps are free.

Sights & Activities

Baños offers lots of jungle trips, but the best things here are rafting, cycling and horseback riding. Most of the agencies offering jungle tours end up sending you through Quito anyway.

The latest addition to fun in Baños is swing-jumping (or *puenting* or pendulum jumping, or whatever whoever you're with decides to call it). It's similar to bungee jumping only you don't bounce. You jump from one bridge with a rope fastened to another bridge, and swing like a pendulum. Any agency in town can set you up.

Motorcycles, 4WDs and dune buggies are rented at numerous shops around town, all for about $10 per hour.

BATHS

Baños means 'baths,' which is precisely what the town is famous for, and precisely what you should get into at least once while you're here. Most of them are fed by thermal springs burbling from the base of the active Volcán Tungurahua. The water in the pools is constantly being recycled and only looks murky because of its mineral content, which is

touted for its restorative and healthful properties. Chlorates, sulfates and magnesium are among the principal chemicals found in the baths.

There are four municipal baths. Three are in Baños (only one is hot), and the fourth is out of town. All have changing rooms and clothing storage. Towels are available for rent, but generally not until after 8am, so bring your own if you're going for a crack-o'-dawn dip. Everyone is supposed to shower and put on a bathing suit before entering the pools. (Sorry, nudies!)

The best-known bath in Baños is **La Piscina de La Virgen** (Montalvo; admission daytime/night $1/1.20; ☽ 4:30am-5pm & 6-10pm), the only hot pools in town. It has three pools: one is cold, another is warm and a third reaches nearly 48°C (118°F), making it a scalding experience indeed. The best time to hit the pools is in the early morning, when there are fewer people and – because they can't seem to drag themselves out of bed before 9am – almost no tourists. It's a lovely experience. If you're curious, ask the basket woman to show you the *ojo del agua*, where the water, heated by the volcano, gushes from the earth at a scorching 50°C (122°F).

Piscinas Santa Clara (admission $1; ☽ 8am-5pm Sat & Sun) has two cooler pools (about 22°C or 72°F), which are higher in minerals than La Virgen.

With a waterslide, a swing set, water toys and cool pools, **Piscinas Las Modernas/Las Peñas** (Martínez; admission children/adults $0.50/1; ☽ 8am-5pm Fri-Sun) is a place where you can take the kids for the day.

If you walk up the hill and past the cemetery on Martínez, you'll end up on a track that crosses a stream (Quebrada de Naguasco) on a small wooden footbridge. The trail continues on the other side to a road in front of Cabañas Bascun, where you turn left to reach **Piscina El Salado**, (☽ 4:30am-5pm; admission $1). These are the only other hot pools, and because they're 2.5km out of town, they're usually less crowded. The setting isn't quite as pretty as La Virgen, but the baths are outstanding; the hot pool is just cool enough to enjoy (unlike the scalding water at La Virgen), and the water burbles straight from the ground of the pools. There's also an ice-cold creek to dip into if you're the masochistic sort. Buses come out here ($0.20, 10 minutes), departing from the stop on Rocafuerte.

Numerous private baths have sprung up in town, though none of them are mineral baths. Still, they're relaxing. One of the best is **Piscina Gamboa** (☎ 274 0441; cnr Montalvo & Alfaro; admission $3-12; ☒ 8am-9pm), which has an indoor lap pool, *baños de cajón* (steam boxes), hot tub, mud masks and massages. The basic $3 fee covers the pool only.

MASSAGES

For excellent full-body massages and herbal facials, make an appointment or drop by **Stay In Touch** (☎ 274 2138; Martínez near Alfaro; ☒ by appointment or walk-in), the massage practice of a friendly and skilled US-Ecuadorian couple. One-hour massages are $25 and facials are $20.

For Swedish massage and reflexology, visit Carmen Sánchez at **Chakra** (☎ 09-255 6698; cnr Alfaro & Martínez; per hr $20; ☒ 9am-6pm Wed-Mon).

BASILICA DE NUESTRA SEÑORA DE AGUA SANTA

Within the town itself, the **Basílica de Nuestra Señora de Agua Santa** (Ambato at 12 de Noviembre; admission free; ☒ 7am-4pm) is worth seeing. The church is dedicated to the Virgin of the Holy Water, who is credited with several miracles in the Baños area. Inside the church, paintings depict her miracles and have explanations in Spanish along the lines of: 'On January 30, 1904, Señor X fell off his horse as he was crossing the Río Pastaza bridge. As he fell 70m to the torrents below, he yelled "Holy Mother of the Holy Water" and was miraculously saved!' Other paintings show people being miraculously saved from exploding volcanoes, burning hotels, transit accidents and other misfortunes.

Just above the church is a **museum** (admission $0.50; ☒ 8am-5pm) with an eclectic display of taxidermic animals, religious paintings, church vestments and local handicrafts.

VOLCANO WATCHING

For a while, the attraction of watching the erupting Volcán Tungurahua practically dwarfed the town's baths. Although not as dramatic as it was, the volcano still puffs smoke and ash and seeing it is an unforgettable experience. The crater cannot be seen from the town itself. You have to walk either to Runtún (see Hiking, right), to the northern edge of town, near the Puente San Francisco, or to other spots outside town.

The tourist office provides free maps that pinpoint the best places. Tour companies offer night tours that are totally worthless unless the volcano is more active than it was in 2005 and 2006. Find out first.

MOUNTAIN BIKING

Several companies rent out mountain bikes starting at about $5 per day, but check the equipment carefully as maintenance is sometimes poor. The most popular ride is the dramatic descent to Puyo (see p175), which is about 61km to the east on the edge of the Oriente. You pass the spectacular Pailón del Diablo waterfall on the way. There is a passport control at Mera, and again at Shell, so carry your documents. From Puyo (or anytime before), you can simply take a bus back to Baños, putting your bike on the roof. Various other mountain-biking options are available, and the outfitters will be happy to tell you about them.

HIKING

Baños has some great hiking. The tourist office provides a crude but useful map showing some of the trails around town.

The walk down to Río Pastaza is easy and popular. Just behind the **sugarcane stalls** by the bus station, a short trail leads to the **Puente San Francisco**, the bridge that crosses the river. You can continue on trails up the other side as far as you want.

Going south on Maldonado takes you to a path that climbs to **Bellavista**, where a white cross stands high over Baños. The path then continues to the settlement of **Runtún**, some two hours away. The views are outstanding. You can then loop around and back down to Baños, ending up at the southern end of JL Mera. This takes you via the statue of **La Virgen del Agua Santa** about half an hour from town. The whole walk takes four to five hours.

West of town, turn right by a religious shrine and walk down to Puente San Martín and visit the impressive falls of **Cascada Inés María**, a few hundred meters to the right of the bridge. You can also cross the bridge and continue to the village of **Lligua**, about three hours away. From this road, trails climb up the hills to your right.

JUNGLE TRIPS

Loads of jungle trips from Baños are advertised, but not all guides are experienced.

For more information on jungle tours, see 'Visiting the Oriente,' p227.

Three- to seven-day jungle tours cost about $30 to $50 per person per day, depending on the destination (there is usually a three- or four-person minimum). Baños is always full of travelers and is a good town in which to organize a group if you are not already with one. Most trips now go through Quito.

Rainbow Expeditions (☎ 274 2957, 09-895 7786; rainbowexpeditions2005@hotmail.com; Alfaro at Martínez) is owned by Germán Shacay, a member of the Shuar indigenous community from the southern Oriente. It's an extremely well-run operation with interesting trips into several areas of the Oriente, including Shuar communities outside of Macas. Trips have an interesting cultural slant.

Other recommended operators are **Rainforestur** (☎ 274 0743; www.rainforestur.com.ec; Ambato 800) and **Vasco Tours** (☎ 274 1017; www.vascotours .banios.com; Alfaro near Martínez), a professionally run outfit whose guide and owner, Juan Medina, knows the business very well.

CLIMBING & TREKKING

Climbers are advised not to ascend the currently erupting Volcán Tungurahua (5016m). The refuge on that volcano has been destroyed – although some people still climb up to it, it is not recommended. For detailed information about these volcanoes in Parque Nacional Sangay, see p176.

Climbs of Cotopaxi and Chimborazo can also be arranged. A reputable climbing outfitter is **Expediciones Amazónicas** (☎ 274 0506; amazonicas2002@yahoo.com; Oriente 11-68 near Halflants). It has rental equipment and can arrange licensed guides. Rainforestur (see above) has rental equipment and licensed climbing guides, and can tailor your itinerary to include acclimatization. The going rate for climbs with a minimum of two people is $65 to $80 per person per day, plus park fees.

HORSEBACK RIDING

Horse rentals cost around $5 per hour or $35 per day. Many half- or full-day trips start with a long jeep ride out of town, and the actual riding time is short. Inquire carefully to get what you want. **Ángel Aldáz** (☎ 274 0175; Montalvo & Mera) and **José & Two Dogs** (☎ 274 0746; josebalu_99@yahoo.com; cnr Maldonado & Martínez) are both good. Christián, at Hostal Isla de Baños (p172), arranges guided horseback-

riding trips that last a half day, a full day, or from two to nine days. Christián speaks English and German.

RAFTING

Long in the business, **GeoTours** (☎ 274 1344; www.ecuadorexplorer.com/geotours; Ambato at Halflants; ☼ daily) offers half-day trips on the Río Patate for $30. Trips last four hours (only two hours are spent on the river) and a snack is included. Also available is a full-day trip to Río Pastaza for $100. This trip is 10 hours, with four hours on the river, and lunch is included. Complete gear is provided. Experience is necessary only for the full-day Class IV to V run. It also offers a three-day kayaking course ($150).

Rainforestur (left) also offers excellent rafting trips.

Courses

One-on-one or small-group Spanish classes start around $4.50 and are offered by the following schools:

International Spanish School for Foreigners (☎ 274 0612; 16 de Diciembre & Espejo)

Si Centro de Español y Inglés (☎ 274 0360; Paez near Oriente)

Baños Spanish Center (☎ 274 0632; www.spanish center.banios.com; Oriente 8-20 near Cañar)

Tours

Several companies around town, particularly around the intersection of Martínez and 16 de Diciembre, offer *chiva* tours (tours in traditional open-sided buses). They all charge $3 to $5 per person and are pretty damn goofy; you have to get in the spirit. *Chivas* also drive around town looking for people to pick up, so you could just jump on. Night tours to the volcano are not worth it unless volcanic activity is up.

Festivals & Events

Baños became the seat of its canton on December 16, 1944, and an annual fiesta is celebrated on this and the preceding days. There are the usual processions, fireworks, music and a great deal of street dancing and drinking at night. Fun! Also, there are processions and fireworks during the entire month of October as the various *barrios* (neighborhoods) of Baños take turns paying homage to the local icon, Nuestra Señora de Agua Santa.

CENTRAL HIGHLANDS

Sleeping

There are scores of excellent hotels in Baños, and competition is stiff, so prices are low. Rates are highest on weekends and during vacations. During the latter, every hotel in town can fill up.

BUDGET

Hostal Plantas y Blanco (☎ 274 0044; option3@hotmail .com; Martínez near 12 de Noviembre; r per person $4.50-7.50; 🖳) Attractively decorated and eternally popular 'Plants and White' (you figure it out) scores big points with travelers for its rooftop terrace, outstanding breakfasts, on-site steam bath and overall value. Single rooms are cramped but fine. It's an excellent, traveler-friendly hotel, with beers available on the honor system from the terrace upstairs.

Hospedaje Santa Cruz (☎ 274 0648; santacruz hostal@yahoo.com; 16 de Diciembre; r per person $5-7) Brought to you by the same owners as Plantas y Blanca, this is a great value for spacious rooms with bathroom and hot water. They're a bit low on light, but no matter – there's an overgrown garden with plastic tables where you can get all the sun you need.

La Petit Auberge (☎ 274 0936; reservation_banos@ hotmail.com; 16 de Diciembre; dm/s/d $6/10/16, s/d with fireplace $12/20) With a rustic, cozy cabinlike feel, this is a fabulous deal and especially homey if you nab one of the pricier rooms with a fireplace. No worries if you don't get a hearth – you can lounge around the big one in the common area. Breakfast is included.

Hostal El Pedrón (☎ 274 0701; www.elpedron .banos.com; Alfaro near Martínez; r per person with shared/ private bathroom $9/13.50) Rustic old El Pedrón's highlight is its giant, tree-filled garden with hammocks and chairs. There's no other hotel garden this size in town. Random touches such as pink Chinese lampshades, vintage bedspreads and dusty antiques give add character. Snag room eight if you can.

Residencial Timara (☎ 274 0599; www.timara.ba nios.com; Maldonado; r per person with shared/private bathroom $4/8) Timara's the best of the super-cheapies, assuming you go for the shared bathroom. It's friendly, everything is spotless and the rooms get lots of light. There are guest kitchen facilities too.

Hostal El Castillo (☎ 274 0285; Martínez 2-55; r per person $7) Though it hardly lives up to a name like 'The Castle,' El Castillo is a fair deal for friendliness and clean, run-of-the-mill rooms with TVs. The attached restaurant offers good cheap breakfasts and lunches at discounts to guests.

Pensión Patty (☎ 274 0202; Alfaro 5-56; r per person $4.50) Well known, family-run, dark and funky, this is an old, old climbers' favorite. Showers are shared.

Residencial Lucy (☎ 274 0466; Rocafuerte 2-40; r per person with shared/private bathroom $3/5) The inside of this three-story, motel-like structure is surprisingly cleaner than it's dilapidated exterior suggests. Just fine for a night or two.

Other long-standing and acceptable hotels include:

Residencial Rosita (☎ 274 0396; 16 de Diciembre near Martínez; r per person with shared/private bathroom $4/5) Big rooms, shared bathrooms. Also two apartments ($5 per person).

Hostal Kattyfer (☎ 274 1559; hostalkattyfer@hotmail .com; 16 de Diciembre near Martínez; r per person $5) Large, simple rooms and a guest kitchen.

Hostal Flor de Oriente (☎ 274 0418, 274 0717; www .flordeoriente.banios.com; cnr Ambato & Maldonado; r per person incl breakfast $12) Spotless rooms; decent restaurant.

Hotel Casa Blanca (☎ /fax 274 0092; hcasablanca@ latinmail.com; cnr Maldonado & Oriente; r per person $12-15) Clean and modern; some rooms are slightly cramped.

MIDRANGE

Posada El Marqués (☎ 274 0053; Pje V Ibarra; www .marquesbanios.com; r per person $8.50) Colorfully painted indigenous motifs adorn the rooms of this comfortable, friendly hotel at the end of a quiet street. Most of the rooms are giant and well lit, and a few rooms have views of the falls. The family that owns the place is as friendly as they come. It's also conveniently close to the Piscina de La Virgen baths.

Villa Santa Clara (☎ 274 0349; www.hotelvilla santaclara.com; 12 de Noviembre; s/d $10/20; 🥋) Considering the swimming pool, this is a good deal for simple motel-style rooms opening on to a sparse concrete patio area. You get kitchen privileges, and there's a restaurant to boot. Rooms in the old house are slightly cheaper than those in the newer sector.

Hostal Isla de Baños (☎ /fax 274 0609, 274 1511; islabanos@andinanet.net; Halflants 1-31; s/d incl breakfast $14.50/24.50) This quiet, German-run *hostal* is set in attractive gardens and boasts cheerful, clean rooms with brick walls and lots of Andean art. The pricier rooms have balconies. In all, it's one of the loveliest places in town.

The owner offers horseback-riding and jeep tours, and there's lots of good travel information around.

Posada del Arte (☎ 274 0083; www.posadadelarte .com; Pje V Ibarra; s $19-22, d $34-38) One of the coziest places in town, Posada del Arte is an exquisite little guesthouse with colorful rooms, firm beds, handsomely carved wooden headboards, a rooftop terrace and a relaxing common room. The US owners have filled it with beautiful Ecuadorian paintings, making it a unique place to stay. The midrange rooms have views, as do the priciest rooms, which also have fireplaces. The restaurant serves delicious, traveler-friendly meals.

Hostal El Eden (☎ 274 0616; 12 de Noviembre; r per person $8) El Eden has clean, pleasant, motel-like rooms with 1970s decor, brick walls and TVs. It's a comfortable place offering modern comfort without being overbearing or cold and, with a good restaurant attached, it's solid value.

Hotel Palace (☎ 274 0470; hotelpalace@hotmail .com; Montalvo 20-03; s/d $28/39; ☒) Down by the waterfall and conveniently close to La Virgen hot baths, Hotel Palace is clean and pleasant with a mix of old-fashioned and modern rooms, all of which are comfortable and classy. There's a garden, a pool, a sauna, a spa, a Turkish bath and a games room (with darts and table tennis). It's a great place to treat yourself, especially during off-season when it's quiet.

Villa Gertrudis (☎ 274 0441; www.villagertrudis .com; Montalvo 20-75; s/d incl breakfast $15/30; ☒) Low-key and quiet, Villa Gertrudis has a beautiful garden, 1960s wood furniture, hardwood floors and a relaxing vacationy feel. It's inside a grand chalet-style home and has been around for decades. Prices include use of the indoor pool across the street.

Hotel Sangay (☎ 274 0490, 270 0917; www.sangay spahotel.com; Montalvo near Martínez; standard s/d $21/34, cabin s/d $34/44; executive s/d $49/61; ☒) The resortlike Hotel Sangay boasts squash and tennis courts, a Jacuzzi and sauna, and a restaurant and bar. All rooms have telephone and cable TV. It's the kind of place you'd stay if you're looking for traditional four-star service. All rates include continental breakfast and use of the facilities.

Other perfectly comfortable options:

Hostería Monte Selva (☎ 274 0566, 274 0244; www .hosteriamonteselva.com; Halflants; s/d $29/49; ☒) Swanky, with wooden cabins. Sauna facilities too.

Gala Hotel (☎ 274 2870; cnr 16 de Diciembre & Montalvo; s/d $12/24) Brand spankin' new. Comfortable, modern.

Hostal Casa Real (☎ 274 0215; hcasareal@hotmail .com; Montalvo near Pje V Ibarra; r per person $9-10) Great if you snag a room with a balcony and hammock.

AROUND BAÑOS

Luna Runtún (☎ 274 0882/3, 274 0835; www.lunarun tun.com; superior/deluxe d $207/268; ☒) Perched on the edge of an impossibly steep mountainside overlooking Baños, Swiss/Ecuadorian-owned Luna Runtún is one of the country's most luxurious hotels. It's in the style of a traditional hacienda, with a giant garden that supplies the kitchen with fresh vegetables. Views from the bay windows of the deluxe rooms almost make your stomach drop. The spa itself, filled with the scent of fresh roses and eucalyptus, is stunning. Rates include the hot tub and sauna, but massages and treatments cost extra. Spa services are available to nonguests. It's 6km beyond Baños via the road to Puyo. It can also be reached on foot by climbing up from Baños for about 3km along either of the main trails.

Cabañas Bascún (☎ 274 0334; Vía a Piscina El Salado s/n; s/d $37/49; ☒) Just outside town, near Piscina El Salado, Bascún has a hot and a cold pool, a water slide, a sauna, a tennis court and a restaurant. The pool facilities are open only on weekends and during vacations. The place is popular as a family weekend getaway, but the surroundings are pleasant. Nonguests can use the pool and sauna for about $4.

Eating

Ambato – Baños' busy pedestrian street – is lined with restaurants. Their outdoor tables make for good people watching, but as a whole they're generally unexceptional. The best restaurants are on side streets.

Baños is famous for its *milcocha*, a delicious chewy taffy that's softened and blended by swinging it onto wooden pegs, usually mounted in the doorways of the town's shops. Pieces of chewable *caña de azucar* (sugarcane) are sold at the stands across from the bus terminal. You shouldn't leave Baños without trying both.

On certain days (particularly during fiestas), you can buy *cuy* (roast guinea pig) at some of the market restaurants or along Ambato. Go on, give it a shot.

La Abuela Café (☎ 09-965 4365; www.abuelacafé .banios.com; Ambato near 16 de Diciembre; mains $2-4; ☺ 7:30am-11pm) When it comes to atmosphere, La Abuela's the best on the strip. (How can you beat the swinging saloon doors and balcony tables?) Plus, it's friendly, the food's good and the *almuerzos* are cheap and wholesome. Pastas, chicken dishes, steaks, Mexican plates and veggie options make for a varied menu.

Quilombo (☎ 274 2880; cnr Montalvo & 12 de Noviembre; mains $3-6; ☺ Wed-Sun) With a hilarious menu and a decor as eccentric as its owner, Quilombo (which means 'mess' or 'insanity' in Argentine slang) is an excellent Argentine barbecue with outstanding grilled chicken and plenty of huge steak dishes.

El Paisano (☎ 274 2134; Vieira near Martínez; mains $2.50-4.50; ☺ 8am-10:30pm) Despite the bright florescent lighting and faint smell of paint (it doubles as the owner's art studio), El Paisano serves up some of the most nurturing veggie food in town. Try the wholesome veggie surprise known as 'Concierto en A major from Belegum de su Secreto,' one of several oddly named dishes.

Casa Hood (☎ 274 2668; Martínez at Halflants; mains $3-4; ☺ 8am-10:15pm Wed-Mon) It just doesn't get much cozier than Casa Hood, where a giant hearth warms the dining room, and funky art hangs everywhere. The book exchange is probably the best in town, and the food – Mexican dishes, lasagna, blackened sea bass, pad Thai, veggie plates, falafel and a long list of cocktails – is delicious.

Café Hood (☎ 274 0537; Maldonado near Parque Central; mains $3-6; ☺ 10am-10pm) Of all the Hoods and Goods in Baños, this *might* just be the best. Some of the dishes, such as the soft tacos or the chickpeas and spinach in curry sauce with yogurt and cucumbers, are simply excellent. The menu is mostly Tex-Mex with a splash of Thai, Greek and Indian thrown in.

Café Good (☎ 274 0592; 16 de Diciembre; mains $2-4, almuerzos $2; ☺ 8am-10pm) Café Good serves vegetarian food, curries, pastas and chicken dishes. Both the veggies with peanut sauce and veggies in coconut curry are tasty and wholesome.

Buon Giorno (☎ 274 1724; Rocafuerte at 16 de Diciembre; mains $3-6; ☺ 11:30am-11:30pm) This warm little Italian restaurant serves delicious dishes from the mother country including pastas (of course), lasagna, risotto and numerous fish, chicken and meat dishes. Candles and good music make for a romantic evening.

Café Mariane (☎ 274 0911; Halflants at Rocafuerte; mains $4-6; ☺ 11am-11pm) This colorful restaurant serves excellent French-Mediterranean cuisine at reasonable prices.

La Closerie de Lilas (☎ 274 1430; Alfaro 6-20; mains $3-5; ☺ 9am-10pm) A great little family-run place (kids included) serving steaks, delicious trout dishes and pastas. Some dishes have a French flair.

La Bella Italia (☎ 274 0121; 16 de Diciembre; mains $3-5; ☺ 7am-9pm) Little and friendly Bella Italia serves delicious Italian food, but the 9-year-old girl who often runs the front of the house is the real star of the show.

El Jardín (☎ 09-418 3069; 16 de Diciembre at Rocafuerte; mains $3-6) Deservedly popular for it's leafy garden and good food, El Jardín is a great hangout with a variety of meat and fish dishes and sandwiches that can be enjoyed al fresco.

Pancho Villa (☎ 274 2870; Montalvo at 16 de Diciembre; mains $3.50-4; ☺ 12:30-9:30pm Mon-Sat, Mexican food fanatics will find these tacos, enchiladas and burritos a very loose interpretation of the real thing, but it's the perfect spot when you're jonesin' for tortillas and mariachi music.

Taj Mahal (Alfaro near Oriente; mains $1.50-2, ☺ 4pm-midnight Tue-Sun) Hooka pipes and maroon vinyl booths complement cheap *shawarmas* (spiced lamb in pita) and falafel.

Rico Pan (☎ 274 0387; Ambato near Maldonado; ☺ 7am-8pm Mon-Sat, 7am-noon Sun) This is the place to go if you need an early breakfast, plus it sells some of the best bread in town.

Café Blah Blah (☎ 09-867 2300; Halflants near Ambato; mains $2-3; ☺ 7:30am-7pm Tue-Sun) This tiny café serves big breakfasts (omelets, pancakes and fruit plates).

Santa María Supermarket (☎ 274 1641; cnr Alfaro & Rocafuerte; ☺ 8:30am-8pm) Stock up on picnic supplies and the like at this modern supermarket.

Mercado Central (Alfaro & Rocafuerte) For fresh fruits and vegetables and cheap, cheap *almuerzos* and breakfasts, visit the town's central market.

Entertainment

Nightlife in Baños means dancing in local *peñas* (small venues that feature live folk music), hanging out in bars or simply windng down the night in a restaurant with friends after a day's mountain biking and soaking in the pools.

Peña Ananitay (16 de Diciembre near Espejo; 9pm-3am) This is the best place in town to catch live *folklórica* (Andean folk music). It can get packed, but that's part of the fun.

The best place to barhop is the two-block strip along Alfaro, north of Ambato.

Peña Bar Mocando (☎ 274 0923; Alfaro near Ambato; 4pm-2am) Always popular thanks to its sidewalk bar, party atmosphere and upstairs rock and dance room.

La Abuela Café 2 Tobaco y Ron (☎ 09-965 4365; www.tabacoyron.banios.com; 4pm-2am) Wee place with karaoke and a great little balcony overlooking Alfaro (get there early to snag it).

Jack Rock (Alfaro 5-41; 7pm-2am) Jack Rock boasts a rock-and-roll theme and the best pub atmosphere in town. It plays classic rock during the week and salsa, merengue, *reggaetón* (a blend of reggae and Latin) and *cumbia* (a dance originally from Colombia, similar to salsa) on weekends, when people dance it up good.

Shopping

Souvenir shopping can be fun in Baños. One local craft is *tagua* nut carving. *Taguas* are hard, white, golfball-sized nuts that resemble ivory and are carved into all sorts of interesting little figurines.

Galería de Arte Huillacuna (☎ 274 0187; yojaira tour@yahoo.com; 12 de Noviembre near Montalvo; 8:30am-9pm) The best art in town is exhibited (and sold) here; it's well worth checking out even if you don't intend to buy. All artists are Ecuadorian.

Guitarras Guevara (☎ 274 0941; Halflants 284) For more than 50 years Jacinto Guevara has been hand-making guitars. Pick one up for anywhere from $50 to $300.

Getting There & Away

Buses from Ambato's bus terminal leave about every half-hour for Baños. The fare is under $1 and the ride is about an hour. To and from Quito and many other towns, it's sometimes quicker to catch a bus to Ambato and change rather than wait for the less frequent direct buses.

The Baños **bus terminal** (Amazonas) is within easy walking distance of most hotels. Buses for Quito ($3.50, 3½ hours) leave almost every hour. The road to Riobamba ($1, one hour) via Penipe ($0.50, 30 minutes) recently reopened, so buses no longer need to drive via Ambato. To the Oriente, buses depart regularly for Puyo ($2, two hours), Tena ($4, five hours) and Coca ($10, 10 hours).

There are also daily buses to Guayaquil ($7, seven hours) and Otavalo ($5, five hours).

Getting Around

Westbound buses leave from Rocafuerte, behind the market. Marked 'El Salado,' they go as far as Piscinas El Salado ($0.20, 10 minutes). Eastbound buses that go as far as the dam at Agoyán leave from Alfaro at Martínez. Cars and jeeps can be rented through **Córdova Tours** (☎ 274 0923, 09-965 4365; www.cordova tours.banios.com; cnr Espejo & Maldonado).

FROM BAÑOS TO PUYO
☎ 03

When it comes to views of the upper Amazon Basin, it just doesn't get much better than the road from Baños to Puyo. Nicknamed 'La Ruta de las Cascadas' (Highway of the Waterfalls), it follows the Río Pastaza canyon as it drops steadily from Baños, at 1800m, to Puyo, at 950m, passing more than a dozen waterfalls on the way. The bus ride is great, but zipping down on a mountain bike is even better. It's mostly downhill, but there are some definite climbs, so ready those legs (it's about 61km if you do the whole thing). For info on mountain-bike rentals, see p170.

Most people go only as far as the spectacular Pailón del Diablo waterfalls, about 18km from Baños, but if you make the grunt beyond the falls, it's pretty smooth sailing as far as Río Negro, with only a couple of climbs and lots more to see. It's worth making it to Río Negro, if only to see the change in ecology as you head into the lower elevations. To get back to Baños hail a bus anytime and throw the bike on top.

Baños to Río Verde

Before the first tunnel, you'll pass the Agoyán hydroelectric project. After the tunnel, you'll catch a little spray from the first waterfall, and about 40 minutes' riding time from Baños you'll pass the spectacular **Manto de La Novia** waterfalls. For a closer look at the falls, take the *tarabita* (cable car; $2), which transports you 500m across the river gorge at the hair-raising height of 100m.

From Manto de La Novia, it's about 25 minutes' ride to the village of **Río Verde**, the access point for the 15-minute downhill hike to the spectacular **Pailón del Diablo** (Devil's Cauldron), Ecuador's most famous falls. People in Baños tell you it takes three hours to ride to Río Verde, but unless you're riding a tricycle with flat tires, it's only about 1½ hours. There are two views of the falls – one from the suspension bridge (maximum capacity five people!) and an up-close view from the lookout (admission $0.50) run by the Pailón del Diablo snack bar. Both are worth seeing.

Río Verde to Puyo

Shortly after leaving Río Verde, the road starts to climb. About a half an hour (riding time) uphill from Río Verde you come to **Machay**, the perfect place to stop for a picnic lunch and a dip in the river. A 2.5km trail leads into the cloud forest and past **eight waterfalls**, which range from wee tumblers to the beautiful Manantial del Dorado, 2.5km in. You can safely lock your bike at the start of the trail.

After Machay, you have two good climbs, then it's downhill nearly all the way to Río Negro, 15km from Río Verde. As the road drops, the vegetation rapidly becomes more tropical, and the walls of the Río Pastaza canyon are covered with bromeliads, giant tree ferns, orchids and flowering trees. Before you hit Río Negro, you'll pass through the village of **San Francisco**, which has a dirt plaza, a few simple eateries and places to buy water or beer.

After San Francisco, it's only another 10 to 15 minutes to **Río Negro**, a funky little town built up along the main road. There are restaurants (some of which are surprisingly slick) and plenty of places to buy refreshments. There's even a hotel.

After Río Negro, you start really feeling tropical. After 17km you pass **Mera**, which has a police checkpoint (have your passport ready) and some 7km further you pass **Shell** where there is another police checkpoint. At the end of the descent, 61km from Baños, you arrive the mellow jungle town of Puyo (see p256).

PARQUE NACIONAL SANGAY

Stretching for about 70km south and southeast of Baños, the 517,765-hectare **Parque Nacional Sangay** (admission $10) contains some of the most remote and inaccessible area in Ecuador. The park was established ir 1979 and became a World Heritage Site ir 1983, protecting an incredible variety of ter rain. Its western boundary is marked by the Cordillera Oriental, and three of Ecuador' highest volcanoes are within the park. The northernmost, Tungurahua, used to be accessed easily from Baños (although it is cur rently not accessible because of eruptions) while the more southerly volcanoes, El Alta and Sangay, require a much greater effort The area around the park's namesake, Volcán Sangay, is particularly rugged and remote. Nevertheless, the routes to the three volcanoes provide the most frequently usec accesses to the park.

From the park's western areas, which climb to over 5000m around each of the three volcanoes, the terrain plunges from the high *páramos* down the eastern slopes o the Andes to elevations barely above 1000m at the park's eastern boundaries. In between is terrain so steep, rugged and wet (over 400cm of rain is recorded annually in some eastern areas) that it remains a wilderness in the truest sense. The thickly vegetated slopes east of the mountains are the haunts of very rarely seen mammals, such as Andean spectacled bears, mountain tapirs, pumas, ocelots, jaguarondis and porcupines. Nobody lives in these parts.

Only two roads of importance enter the park. One goes from Riobamba to Alao (the main access point to Volcán Sangay) and peters out in the *páramos* to the east. The second is the newly completed Guamote-Macas road, which links the highlands to the Oriente. Construction of this road prompted Unesco to place the park on its 'National Parks in Peril' list. Though it was removed from this list in 2005, colonization will likely follow in the wake of the road, and is the greatest future threat to the park. The road was almost fully paved by 2006.

Volcán Tungurahua

With a (pre-eruption) elevation of 5016m, Tungurahua is Ecuador's 10th-highest peak. It was a beautiful, cone-shaped volcano with a cap of snow perched jauntily atop its lush, green slopes. Since the many eruptions beginning in late 1999, the snow has melted, and the cone and crater have changed in shape.

Until 1999, travelers liked to walk part of the way up the volcano, perhaps as far as the village of Pondoa, or to the (now destroyed) refuge at 3800m. Beyond the refuge, it gets steep, but the mountain was considered one of Ecuador's easier 5000m peaks to climb. As of early 2006 people were ascending as far as the refuge, although this is extremely risky at best and therefore not advised. Ask in Baños about the current situation.

Volcán El Altar

At 5319m, this jagged and long-extinct volcano is the fifth-highest mountain in Ecuador. It has nine peaks and is widely considered the most beautiful and most technically difficult of Ecuador's mountains. The wild *páramo* surrounding the mountain and the greenish lake of Laguna Amarilla (Yellow Lagoon) within the blown-away crater are targets for adventurous backpackers with both experience and complete camping gear.

To get to El Altar, take a bus from Riobamba or Baños to **Penipe**, a village halfway between Riobamba and Baños. From Penipe, take a bus or hire the occasional truck to **Candelaria**, about 15km to the southeast. From Candelaria (which has a very simple store), it's about 2km to Hacienda Releche (not a place to stay) and the nearby ranger station, where you pay the park fee. You can stay the night here for another $2. You can also sleep at nearby **Campamento Collanes** (r per person $12) owned by Oswaldo Cedeño, a local guide; inquire in Candelaria before heading out. Cedeño also has mules. He or other guides can be hired for $20 to $30 per day.

There are many trails in the area, and it is worth having a guide to at least show you the beginning of the main trail to El Altar, which is less than an hour away from the station. Once you're on the main trail, the going is fairly obvious.

The best times to go are September to March. The wettest months in the Oriente are July and August, which means that El Altar is frequently clouded in at that time. El Altar is far enough south of Tungurahua that even a massive explosion should not affect hikers in the area.

Volcán Sangay

This 5230m-high volcano is one of the most active in the Andes – it is constantly spewing out rocks, smoke and ash. The volcanological situation changes from hour to hour and year to year. The mountain is not technically difficult to climb, but people attempting it run the risk of being killed by explosions, so climbing attempts are rare. You can hike to the base if you wish, although the approach is long and tedious, and the best views are from afar.

To get there, take a bus from Plaza San Francisco in Riobamba to the villages of **Licto** or **Pungalá**, which are next to one another; buses leave daily. From there, occasional trucks (which leave early in the morning on most days) go another 20km (one hour) to the village of **Alao**, where there is a national-park ranger station. There, you pay the park fee, get information, can hire guides and are allowed to sleep for a nominal fee.

Lagunas de Atillo

With the opening of the Guamote–Macas road, the spectacular *páramo* lakes region of Lagunas de Atillo is suddenly easily accessible. The area is excellent for trekking and still gets very few visitors. About 79km from Riobamba, the road passes through the village of **Atillo**. From here you can hike six to eight hours over a nearby ridge to the **Lagunas de Ozogoche**. In the village of Atillo itself, a woman named Dora Paña offers basic lodging and meals. Otherwise, bring everything from Riobamba, and pick up a topo map at the Instituto Geográfico Militar (IGM; p70) in Quito. People in Atillo can give you loose hiking information. You should make sure to first visit the park office in Riobamba.

From Atillo the road winds its way down the eastern slopes of the Andes to the village of **San Vicente**, passing through the easternmost extremity of the national park, before ending in Macas in the southern Oriente (see p262 for details of tours and park access from Macas).

From Riobamba, the Cooperativa Unidos buses to Atillo leave at 5:45am and 3pm from near Plaza San Francisco. The morning bus leaves from the corner of Velasco and Olmedo, while the afternoon bus leaves from 10 de Agosto near Benalcazar, across from the plaza. Drivers and buses are always hanging around the corner of Benalcazar and Guayaquil if you have questions.

GUARANDA

☎ 03 / pop 20,474 / elevation 2670m

Despite being the capital of Bolívar province, Guaranda is small enough and removed enough that residents still take to staring at foreigners when they roll into town. It's a dignified, provincial place with beautiful old adobe buildings, crumbling wooden balconies, Spanish tiled roofs and a handsome central plaza. It's surrounded by pretty hills – seven to be exact – which inspires locals to call their town 'the Rome of the Andes.' Despite the fact that there's nothing do besides wandering around, it's worth visiting to get off the beaten track. It's also the access point for Salinas, described next.

Information

Andinatel (Rocafuerte near Pichincha) Telephone center.
Banco del Pichincha (Azuay near 7 de Mayo) Bank with an ATM; does not change traveler's checks.
Clínica Bolívar (☎ 298 1278) One of several clinics and pharmacies near Plaza Roja, south of the hospital.
Hospital (Cisneros s/n)
Post office (Azuay near Pichincha)

Sights & Activities

The main market day is Saturday, and there's a smaller market on Wednesday. The best place for the market is **Plaza 15 de Mayo** (Selva Alegre at 7 de Mayo), which is worth visiting even on ordinary days for its pleasantly quiet, forgotten colonial air. The market at Mercado 10 de Noviembre is held in a modern, ugly concrete building.

Guaranda takes its name from a 16th-century indigenous chief named Guaranga, who is immortalized in a 5m-high monument, **El Indio Guaranga**, which is situated about 3km west of town on the top of a hill ($2.50 by taxi). The views of Volcán Chimborazo and the surrounding countryside from here are splendid. The monument is clearly visible from the northwest end of town.

Festivals & Events

Guaranda is famous for its February/March **Carnaval** celebrations, when people stream in from all over for such rural festivities as water fights, dances and parades. The local drink of choice during the celebration is

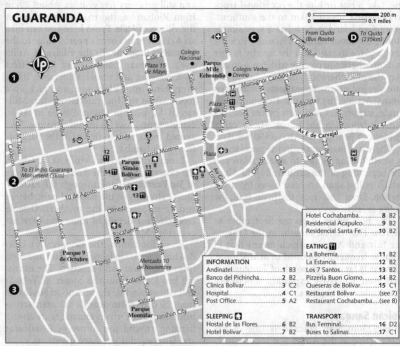

Hotel Cochabamba.................**8** B2	
Residencial Acapulco...............**9** B2	
Residencial Santa Fe...............**10** B2	

EATING 🍴
La Bohemia............................**11** B2	
La Estancia............................**12** B2	
Los 7 Santos..........................**13** B2	
Pizzería Buon Giorno...............**14** B2	
Queseras de Bolívar................**15** C1	
Restaurant Bolívar..................(see 7)	
Restaurant Cochabamba..........(see 8)	

INFORMATION
Andinatel...............................**1** B3	
Banco del Pichincha................**2** B2	
Clínica Bolívar........................**3** C2	
Hospital.................................**4** C1	
Post Office.............................**5** A2	

SLEEPING 🛏
Hostal de las Flores................**6** B2	
Hotel Bolívar..........................**7** B2	

TRANSPORT
Bus Terminal..........................**16** D2	
Buses to Salinas.....................**17** C1	

'Pájaro Azul' (Blue Bird), an *aguardiente* flavored with local herbs (one *guarandeño* – person from Guaranda – said chicken is used to flavor the drink!).

Sleeping

Hostal de las Flores (☎ 298 0644; Pichincha 4-02; r per person with shared/private bathroom $8/9) This is Guaranda's most traveler-oriented hotel, a pretty place in a nicely refurbished old building. The rooms are cheerful and open onto a small interior courtyard, and have cable TV, firm beds and telephones.

Hotel Bolívar (☎ 298 0547; Sucre 7-04; s/d $8/16) Along with Hostal de las Flores, this is one of the best in town, with two stories of pleasant simple rooms around a central courtyard. There's a good restaurant and a great café attached.

Hostal Marquez (☎ 298 1306; 10 de Agosto at Alfaro; s/d with shared bathroom $6/12, r with private bathroom $15) Bright sunny rooms, multi-colored walls, cable TV and 'guaranteed' hot water (except when Guaranda turns off the water, of course!) make for a good-value hotel.

Hotel Cochabamba (☎ 298 1958, 298 2124; vviteriv@gu.pro.ec; García Moreno 5-21; s with shared/private bathroom $5/15, d $10/20) Time has taken its toll on what was once the town's best hotel. Rooms are bright but (unlike the prices) have gone downhill. It's fine if others in this range are full. Rooms with shared bathroom look better than those with private.

The cheapest hotels in town are ratty as hell, but **Residencial Acapulco** (☎ 298 1953; 10 de Agosto 8-06; r per person with shared/private bathroom $3/6) and **Residencial Santa Fé** (☎ 298 1526; 10 de Agosto; r per person with shared/private bathroom $5/7) are just passable. Both have restaurants.

Eating

Los 7 Santos (☎ 298 0612; Convención de 1884 near 10 de Agosto; mains $1-3; ☾ 10am-11pm Mon-Sat) Quite possibly the best reason to come to Guaranda, Los 7 Santos is the town's one traveler refuge, an artsy bar-café with three generations – grandma, mother and son – at the helm. Tons of plants and an eccentric art collection make it hard to leave. The food is mostly snacks, light meals and breakfast.

La Bohemia (☎ 298 4368; cnr Convención de 1884 & 10 de Agosto; mains $2-4; ☾ 8am-9pm Mon-Sat) Cozied up with grain sacks on the ceilings and serving both delicious and cheap *almuerzos* ($2), this family-run joint is easily one of the best places in town. Chase your meal down with one of the giant *batidos* (fruit shakes).

Restaurant Cochabamba (García Moreno; ☾ 7am-9pm Mon-Fri, 7am-3pm Sat) Below its namesake hotel, this is the slickest restaurant in town, and although it's good, comfortable and very friendly, it's a bit overpriced.

La Estancia (☎ 298 3157; García Moreno near Sucre; mains $3-4.50; ☾ noon-10pm Tue-Sat, till 4pm Mon) Restaurant by day, bar by night, La Estancia is a cool little place with an old-fashioned sign, wooden tables and friendly staff. Most of the menu is meat-oriented (steaks, breaded steaks, chicken) or pasta.

Restaurant Bolívar (Sucre 7-04; mains $1.50-3) Comfortable and recently remodeled, Bolívar serves a reasonable selection of food, cheap *almuerzos* and has a friendly atmosphere.

Pizzería Buon Giorno (☎ 298 5406; Sucre at García Moreno; pizzas $3.50-7; ☾ noon-10pm Tue-Sun) Good little pizza parlor serving fluffy-crust pizzas, lasagna and burgers.

Queseras de Bolívar (☎ 298 2205; Av Gral Enriquez; ☾ 8:30am-1pm & 2:30-6pm Mon-Sat, 8:30am-noon Sun) Stock up here on the province's famous cheeses, chocolate and other treats.

Drinking & Entertainment

Two restaurants double as bars: Los 7 Santos has a fireplace in the back and is easily the best place in town to bump into midnight. La Estancia transforms into a low-key bar after dinner. You'll find a few bars and even a *discoteca* or two along 10 de Agosto just west of Eloy Alfaro.

Getting There & Away

Guaranda's bus terminal is on the east side of town. It's a solid 15-minute walk or a $1 cab ride downtown. Afternoon buses can get booked up in advance, so plan ahead.

Buses depart hourly for Ambato ($2, two hours) and Quito ($4.50, five hours). Almost as frequently, there are buses for Babahoyo ($2.50, 2½ hours) and Guayaquil ($4, four hours). There are numerous daily buses to Riobamba ($2, two hours) via El Arenal; this passes the Chimborazo park entrance and access road to the mountain refuges.

BUS RIDES TO BLOW YOUR MIND

The bus rides to and from Guaranda are some of the most spectacular in the country. The 99km road from Ambato to Guaranda is the highest-paved road in Ecuador, climbing to well over 4000m in the bleak *páramo* before dropping down to Guaranda, at 2650m. The road passes within 10km of Volcanes Chimborazo (6310m) and Carihuairazo (5020m), affording mind-boggling views of these snowcapped giants. If going to Guaranda, sit on the left side for the best views. In addition to the mountains, you get a good look at the harsh and inhospitable *páramo*.

From Guaranda you can head due east to Riobamba on a dizzying 61km dirt road that skirts the southern flanks of Chimborazo and provides fantastic views that are not for the faint of heart (sit on the left side of the bus). Most buses now take the new road to Riobamba via El Arenal, which gets you even closer to Chimborazo and avoids the steep drop-offs of the older route.

Finally, you can head down the western slopes of the Andes to Babahoyo and the coast – a spectacular route that was once the most important connection between Quito and Guayaquil, although it is now infrequently used.

For information on buses to Salinas, see right.

SALINAS

☎ 03 / pop 1000 / elevation 3550m

About 35km north of Guaranda, the remote village of Salinas is set in wild, beautiful countryside and is famous for its cheeses, salamis, divine chocolate, dried mushrooms and rough-spun sweaters. Everything is made in cooperative factories, which are open to visitors Monday through Saturday. Spending a day or two here makes for a fascinating and educational visit to a remote area of Ecuador. The countryside around offers pleasant walks, and everything is *muy tranquilo* (very mellow). Market day is Tuesday.

The **tourist office** (☎ 239 0022; www.salinerito.com; 9am-5pm) faces the main plaza. If it's not open, there's usually a friendly young kid around to help with information. There are no banks or other tourist services in the village. Guides can be hired here for tours of the factories and for the many hikes around town.

Tienda El Salinerito (Plaza Central; 9am-5pm daily) is Salina's local outlet for all the natural products made by the communities. If you don't visit the factories, you can buy everything here for the same price.

Sleeping & Eating

El Refugio (☎ 239 0024; dm $6, r with bathroom per person $8) Two blocks above the plaza, El Refugio is a simple, clean, comfortable place run by the local youth cooperative. It's nothing fancy, but does the trick for these parts. Hot showers are available.

Hostal Samilagua (sadehm2@latinmail.com; r per person $6) Directly across from El Refugio, the privately run Samilagua is as simple as its competition and just as friendly. Rooms are cement, rather than wood, but they're colorfully painted and comfortable.

La Minga Café (☎ 239 0042; lamingacafé@hotmail.com; El Salinerito at Guayamas; mains $1.50-3; 7:30am-10pm) Facing the main plaza, this café is an excellent spot for breakfast after that early morning bus ride, or for a beer and dinner after a long hike.

Getting There & Away

Queseras de Bolívar (p179) cheese shop in Guaranda has information about getting to Salinas. But it's easy: take a bus from near the Plaza Roja in Guaranda; they leave at 6am and 7am and hourly from 10am to 4pm Monday through Friday, and on weekends at 6am and 7am only. Buses return to Guaranda at 11am and at 1pm and 3pm daily. There are additional returns during the week. The drive is spectacular.

RIOBAMBA

☎ 03 / pop 126,100 / elevation 2750m

Deemed 'the Sultan of the Andes,' Riobamba is a traditional, old-fashioned city that both bores and delights travelers. It's sedate yet handsome, with wide avenues and random mismatched shops tucked into imposing 18th- and 19th-century stone buildings. It lies at the heart of an extensive scenic road network and is the starting point for the spectacular train ride down the Nariz del Diablo (see Train, p186, and the boxed text The Devil's Nose, p186). Thanks to Riobamba's proximity to Chimborazo, the country's highest peak, the city is home to some of the country's best climbing operators.

Riobamba is also an important commercial center for the central highlands. Except on Sundays – when it seems you could easily starve searching for somewhere to buy food – the city hums with activity. Saturday is market day, when indigenous people pour into town. The trading that goes on, in everything from bootleg CDs and bloomers to donkey butter, grain mills and chickens, easily rivals the markets at Saquisilí and Machachi, making Saturday one of the best days to be in town.

Information

Other banks with ATMs are around town.

Andinatel (Tarqui at Veloz; 8am-10pm) Telephone center.

Banco de Guayaquil (Primera Constituyente) Bank with ATM; changes traveler's checks.

Banco del Pichincha (cnr García Moreno & Primera Constituyente) Bank with ATM; changes traveler's checks.

Café Digital (Rocafuerte near 10 de Agosto; per hr $0.70; 9am-10pm Mon-Sat) Internet access.

Clínica Metropolitana (294 1930; Junín 25-28) Locally recommended clinic.

Hospital Policlínico (296 1705, 296 5725, 296 8232; Olmedo 11-01) Hospital, southeast of downtown.

Lavandería Donini (Villaroel near Larrea; per kg $0.80; 9am-1pm & 3-6pm Mon-Sat) Same-day laundry service.

Metropolitan Touring (296 9600/601; mtrioopr@andinanet.net; cnr Av León Borja & Francia) Local office of Ecuador's biggest travel agency.

Parque Nacional Sangay Office (295 3041; parquesangay@andinanet.net; Av 9 de Octubre near Duchicela; 8am-1pm & 2-5pm Mon-Fri) West of downtown; get information and pay entry fees to Parque Nacional Sangay here.

Police station (296 1913, 296 9300; Av León Borja)

Post office (cnr Espejo & 10 de Agosto)

Sights

MUSEUMS

Inside the beautifully restored Monasterio de las Conceptas, Riobamba's **Museo de Arte Religioso** (296 5212; Argentinos; admission $2; 9am-noon & 3-6pm Tue-Sat) houses one of the country's finest collections of both 17th- and 18th-century religious art. The museum's signature piece is a priceless, meter-tall monstrance inlaid with more than 1500 precious stones, including emeralds, pearls, diamonds, rubies amethysts and aquama-

rines. Made of solid gold with a solid silver base, it weighs over 360kg (making it incredibly difficult to steal). Within the monstrance are three inlaid glass hearts, each containing – according to the caretakers – blood of the three craftsmen who made it. Look closely. Thirteen other rooms display paintings and sculptures of saints and sinners, with all the blood and morbidity typical of Ecuador's religious art.

If you're just trying to kill some time, pop into the **Museo de la Ciudad** (295 1906; Primera Constituyente at Espejo; admission free; 8:30am-12:30pm & 2:30-6:30pm Mon-Fri, 8am-4pm Sat). Opened in 2004, it occupies a beautifully restored building from 1910, once inhabited by a woman who was both Riobamba's best hair stylist and possessed by the devil. Slightly less interesting than its previous inhabitant, the museum's exhibits include a permanent national park display, historical photos of Riobamba and temporary visual-art exhibits on the 2nd floor.

PARKS

The handsome, tree-filled **Parque Maldonado** (Primera Constituyente at Espejo) is flanked by Riobamba's **cathedral** on the northeastern side. A few blocks southeast, **Parque La Libertad** (Primera Constituyente at Alvarado) is anchored by its neoclassical **basilica** (Veloz near Alvarado), famous for being the only round church in Ecuador. It was designed, built and decorated mainly by locals, making it a great source of civic pride. It's often closed; try Sundays and evenings after 6pm. Just north of downtown, the **Parque 21 de Abril** (Orozco at Ángel León) has an observation platform with excellent views of the surrounding mountains.

MARKETS

The Saturday market transforms Riobamba into a hive of commercial activity, when thousands of people from surrounding villages come to barter, buy and sell. They flood into town by truck, cart, donkey and foot, unloading impossibly giant loads and spreading out their wares along the streets northeast of Parque de la Concepción. Every plaza in the city fills with vendors. Needless to say, it's a colorful affair, though it's tourist appeal lies in people watching and gadget-spotting more than in buying. The only place with handicrafts is **Parque de la Concepción** (Orozco & Colón).

CENTRAL HIGHLANDS

RIOBAMBA

0	400 m
0	0.2 miles

INFORMATION
Andinatel..........................1 D4
Banco de Guayaquil............2 C3
Banco del Pichincha..........(see 2)
Café Digital.........................3 C3
Clinica Metropolitana..........4 D2
Lavandería Donini................5 C4
Metropolitan Touring...........6 B2
Police Station.....................7 B3
Post Office..........................8 D4

SIGHTS & ACTIVITIES
Alta Montaña......................9 B2
Andes-trek........................10 C4

Basílica...............................11 D4
Cathedral...........................12 D3
Expediciones Julio Verne....13 B3
Museo de Arte Religioso.....14 D3
Museo de la Ciudad............15 D4
Pro Bici.............................16 D3
Pro Bici (annex)................17 C3
Veloz Coronado Expeditions.18 B3

SLEEPING
Hostal Montecarlo..............19 C3
Hostal Oasis.......................20 E4
Hotel Glamour....................21 B2
Hotel Imperial....................22 C3
Hotel Los Shyris.................23 C3
Hotel Riobamba Inn...........24 C3
Hotel Segovia....................25 D3
Hotel Tren Dorado.............26 C3
Hotel Whymper..................27 B2
Hotel Zeus........................28 A2
La Estación........................29 B3
Residencial Nuca Huasi......30 C3

EATING
Chifa Pekin........................31 B2
El Chacarero......................32 D4
El Delirio Restaurant..........33 C3
El Rey del Burrito...............34 B2
El VIP................................35 C3
La Abuela Rosa..................36 A3
La Cabaña Montecarlo........37 C3
La Parrillada de Fausto.......38 B2
Mercado La Merced...........39 C4
Natural Food......................40 D4
Pizzería San Valentín.........41 B2
Sierra Nevada....................42 C3

ENTERTAINMENT
Tentadero..........................43 B2

SHOPPING
Tagua Shop.....................(see 9)

TRANSPORT
Buses to Atillo (afternoon)...44 D4
Buses to Atillo (morning)....45 D4
Guano & Teresita Bus Stop..46 D2
Oriente Bus Terminal...........47 E2

As you're walking around, keep your eyes peeled for locally made *shigras*. Also look out for baskets and mats woven by the indigenous Colta from the reeds lining the shores of nearby Laguna de Colta.

Tours

Riobamba is an excellent base for climbing Chimborazo (and many other nearby peaks) and is home to several of Ecuador's top mountain guides. For more information on climbing Chimborazo, see p187, and always keep in mind that there is no guarantee you'll reach the summit. Two-day summit trips start around $140 per person for Chimborazo ($160 for Cotopaxi) and include guides, climbing gear, transportation and meals. Rates rarely include park entrance fees ($10).

One-day mountain-biking trips start at $35 per person. Downhill descents from the refuge on Chimborazo – an exhilarating way to take in the views – are very popular.

A pioneer in Ecuadorian mountaineering, Enrique Veloz is the senior advisor of the Asociación de Andinismo de Chimborazo and owner of **Veloz Coronado Expeditions** (☎ 296 0916; www.velozexpediciones.com; Chile 33-21 at Francia), an outstanding guide business he owns with his two sons. His sons are both certified with ASEGUIM (Asociación Ecuatoriana de Guias de Montaña; Ecuadorian Mountain Guides Association). Veloz himself has climbed Chimborazo some 500 times. Whether his sons guide or someone else guides, you can count on their certification and training.

Many readers have written and raved about **Expediciones Julio Verne** (☎ 296 3436; after 6pm 296 0398; www.julioverne-travel.com; Espectador 22-25), a recommended Ecuadorian/Dutch-owned operator offering affordable two-day summit trips to Chimborazo, Cotopaxi and other peaks. The company arranges guided treks, rents out climbing and trekking gear and offers transfers to trailheads for climbers without a guide. It also offers downhill mountain biking on Chimborazo. It's also a good place to set up tours to the Oriente.

Alta Montaña (☎ 295 0651; aventurag@laserinter .net; Av León Borja 35-17) is run by friendly Rodrigo Donoso, an accomplished mountaineer and photographer who speaks English. Apart from arranging guided climbs of the highest mountains in Ecuador, Alta Montaña manages three mountain refuges on Volcán Chimborazo and arranges acclimatization and training days before ascents.

Two other excellent guides (both ASEGUIM certified) are Marcelo Puruncajas and his son Pablo, who speak Spanish, English and German. Both can be found at Marcelo's **Andes-trek** (☎ 295 1275, 09-929 8076; www .andes-trek.com; Colón 22-25; ⏰ 9am-8pm). They can also be hired for trekking trips anywhere in Ecuador.

Pro Bici (☎ 295 1759; Primera Constituyente 23-51 & 23-40) is one of the country's best mountain-bike operators, with more than 11 years of experience. It offers mountain bike rentals and day tours, and the owner, Galo Brito, speaks English. If you don't want a guide, bikes are available for rent ($10 to $25 per day, depending on the bike); the staff will provide you with maps. It's especially good if you want off-the-beaten-track biking experiences.

Festivals & Events

Riobamba's annual fiesta celebrates the **Independence Battle of Tapi** of April 21, 1822. On and around that date, there is a large agricultural fair with the usual highland events – street parades, dancing and plenty of traditional food and drink.

Sleeping

Though a bit less majestic than names such as 'Golden Train,' 'Zeus,' 'Imperial,' and 'Glamour' might imply, Riobamba has some decent lodging options. Most are downtown, 2km from the bus terminal and within walking distance of the train station.

BUDGET & MIDRANGE

Hotel Tren Dorado (☎ 296 4890; htrendorado@hotmail .com; Carabobo 22-35; r per person $9) Conveniently near the train station, the friendly Tren Dorado has spotless, comfortable, flowery rooms that would make Martha Stewart proud. A self-serve breakfast ($3 extra) is served at 5:30am on train days so you can fill up before the ride. The hot water seems infallible, and the TVs are big.

Hostal Oasis (☎ 296 1210; Veloz 15-32; r per person $7) When it comes to friendliness, value and down-home cutesiness, it's hard to beat Oasis, a gem of a guesthouse behind the owners' home. Rooms (and two apartments) are grouped around a garden, complete with a llama and two squawking parrots. There's free transportation to/from train and bus stations, and camping is available.

La Estación (☎ 295 5226; Unidad Nacional 29-15 near Carabobo; s/d $10/20) Colorful rooms make for a cheerful stay at this friendly hotel across the street from the train station. There's a restaurant downstairs and fake archeological souvenirs for sale in the lobby.

Hotel Glamour (☎ 294 4406; www.hotelglamour.com.ec; Primera Constituyente 37-85; r per person $12-25) Futuristic in a 1960s *Star Trek* sort of way, Hotel Glamour has a decor that might just drive you cultured earthlings nuts. But it's a relatively quiet area, there's a restaurant, rooms are clean and heated (a rarity in town), and there's cable TV – complete with remote control, Mr Spock.

Hotel Los Shyris (☎ 296 0323; Rocafuerte 21-60 & 10 de Agosto; r per person with shared/private bathroom $6/7) The large and modernish Shyris is a great value for its central location and clean rooms with TV. It's a bit slim on character, but most of the rooms get tons of sunlight, and the beds, although a tad saggy, do the trick.

Residencial Ñuca Huasi (☎ 296 6669; 10 de Agosto 10-24; r per person with shared/private bathroom $3/5) Once Riobamba's most popular backpacker crash-pad, Ñuca Huasi has gotten a bit grimy over the years, but it's fine if you're pinching pennies. The building itself is a beauty.

Hostal Montecarlo (☎ 296 0557, 296 1577; montecarlo@andinanet.net; 10 de Agosto 25-41; s/d $15/29) The best hotel downtown, the Montecarlo occupies an attractively restored, turn-of-the-20th-century house. The use of blue (blue couches, blue carpet, blue trim and blue plaid bedspreads) can be a bit overbearing, but it's a lovely place nonetheless. Breakfast is available from 5am on train days.

Hotel Zeus (☎ 296 8036/7/8; www.hotelzeus.com.ec; Av León Borja 41-29; s/d $24/37, executive s/d $37/49, ste $55-80) Between the bus terminal and downtown, Hotel Zeus is a seven-story hotel with varying rooms. The standards are pretty worn out, but the pricier rooms are excellent, and some have outstanding views.

Hotel Riobamba Inn (☎ 296 1696, 294 0958; Carabobo 23-20; s/d $13.50/23.50) Though the rooms are a bit dark (brightened mostly by the painfully orange plaid bedspreads), they're comfortable and spacious and have TV and telephone. There's is a restaurant with limited hours.

If everything else is full, you'll be fine at the following:

Hotel Whymper (☎ 296 4575; Ángel León 23-10; s/d $9/18) Pricey for what's on offer, but comfy. Some rooms have views.

Hotel Imperial (☎ 296 0429; Rocafuerte 22-15; r per person with shared/private bathroom $5/6) Clean, friendly and noisy.

Hotel Segovia (☎ 09-445 9626; Primera Constituyente 22-26; r per person $6) Drab and impersonal, but secure and clean.

AROUND RIOBAMBA

Albergue Abraspungo (☎ 294 0820; www.abraspungo.com; s/d $40/50) Situated 3.5km northeast of town on the road to Guano, Abraspungo is an attractive inn built around a traditional hacienda. Spacious rooms, a restaurant and bar, and horseback riding are all available here. Climbing expeditions can also be arranged here.

Hostería La Andaluza (☎ 290 4223, 290 4248; www.hosteria-andaluza.com; s $45-61, d $55-73) About 15km north of Riobamba on the Panamericana, this colonial hacienda has been lovingly restored and is now perhaps the best hotel in Chimborazo province. There are two restaurants, a small exercise room and sauna, and a bar with a fireplace. Nearly all the antique-furnished rooms have fireplaces, as well as cable TV and telephones. If you take a chance and just arrive, much lower rates can be negotiated.

Eating

On train days, early-bird breakfasts are available from 5am at Hotel Tren Dorado and Hostal Montecarlo; arrange the day before.

Sierra Nevada (☎ 295 1542; Constituyente 27-38; mains $3-4; ☉ 8-11am, noon-4pm & 6-10pm Mon-Sat) Serving excellent seafood, Ecuadorian dishes and out-of-nowhere concoctions like goulash, Sierra Nevada is a sure shot for any meal. It also whips out what are likely the best *almuerzos* in town ($3).

La Abuela Rosa (☎ 294 5888; Brasil 37-57 at Esmeraldas; mains $0.80-1.50; ☉ 4pm-9:30pm Mon-Fri) Drop by Grandma Rosa's for *comida típica* (traditional Ecuadorian food) and tasty snacks including sandwiches, chocolate and cheese. Friendly, cozy and popular with locals.

Pizzería San Valentin (☎ 296 3137; Av León Borja & Torres; mains $2-5; ☉ 5pm-midnight Mon-Sat) The cornerstone of Riobamba's nightlife, San Valentin is a lively place, great for both eating and socializing. Order at the counter (pizza, hamburgers or Tex Mex) and eat at the tables.

El Chacarero (☎ 296 9292; 5 de Junio 21-46; mains $3.50-5; ☾ 3-10:30pm) The delicious pizza, big wooden booths and a great atmosphere make this dimly lit pizzeria an excellent choice. Skip the spaghetti dishes.

El Rey del Burrito (☎ 295 3230; Av León Borja 38-36; mains $3-5; ☾ 11am-11pm Mon-Sat, till 4pm Sun) 'The King of the Burrito' serves classics like burritos, tacos and enchiladas. It's a festive place on the ground floor of a converted house.

Natural Food (☎ 295 5195; Tarqui near Primera Constituyente; almuerzos $1.50; ☾ noon-2:30pm) Herbivores, beeline it to Natural Food for delicious, hearty (and cheap!) vegetarian *almuerzos*. You can bring your meat-eating mate, since they do meat too.

El VIP (☎ 295 1553; Pichincha near Primera Constituyente; almuerzos $1.70; ☾ noon-3pm Mon-Fri, 6pm-late Thu-Sat) Cheap and tasty vegetarian *almuerzos* are served in an Asian-esque café atmosphere.

Chifa Pekin (☎ 296 0325; Av León Borja near Brasil; mains $2-3; ☾ 11am-11pm) It's just your standard *chifa* (Chinese restaurant), but when you have the hankering, it does the trick. Veggie options too.

Mercado La Merced (Mercado M Borja; Guayaquil; ☾ 7am-6pm) Even if you don't like Ecuador's classic *hornado* (whole roast pig), it's worth wandering into this surprisingly clean market, where giant roasted-brown pig carcasses lay draped across dozens of countertops. Almost as fun as trying the pork is hearing what the women yell out to get your attention (like 'Hey handsome, try *this* pork!'). Best on Saturdays. It's located between Espejo and Colón on Guayaquil.

La Cabaña Montecarlo (☎ 296 2844; García Moreno 24-10; mains $4-6; ☾ noon-9:30pm Mon-Sat, noon-3:30pm Sun) This one's pricey by Riobamba standards, but the service and food (seafood, trout, soups, filet mignon and other takes on steak) are good.

La Parrillada de Fausto (☎ 296 7876; Uruguay 20-38; mains $4-6; ☾ noon-3pm & 6-10:30pm Mon-Sat) This fun, Argentine-style grill serves great barbecued steaks, trout and chicken in a ranch-style setting. Don't miss the cool, cavelike bar in back.

El Delirio Restaurant (☎ 296 6441; Primera Constituyente 28-16; mains $6-9; ☾ noon-10pm Tue-Sun) Riobamba's most atmospheric eatery is a lovely place to dine, but the food and service are a bit hit and miss.

Entertainment

Nightlife, limited as it is, centers on the intersection of Avenida León Borja and Torres and northwest along León Borja toward Duchicela. On weekends the area turns into a teen madhouse, and even if you don't join 'em, it's fun to walk around and watch 'em. **Pizzería San Valentin** (☎ 296 3137; Av León Borja & Torres; ☾ 5pm-midnight Mon-Sat) is an eternally popular hangout in the area. Nearby, **Tentadero** (Av Leon Borja near Ángel Leon; admission $3; ☾ 8pm-late Fri & Sat) is the town's hottest (both in terms of popularity and temperature) *discoteca*, spinning electronica and salsa well into the night.

Shopping

Riobamba is known for it's *tagua* carvings (see Shopping p175) and the **Tagua Shop** (Av León Borja 35-17; ☾ 9am-7pm Mon-Sat, 10am-5pm Sun) has the best selection.

For Ecuadorian textiles, head to **Parque de la Concepción** (Orozco & Colón). Although it's best on Saturday, there are vendors there throughout the week.

Getting There & Away
BUS

Riobamba has two bus terminals. The **main bus terminal** (☎ 296 2005; Av León Borja at Av de la Prensa) is almost 2km northwest of downtown. Buses bound for Quito ($4, four hours) and intermediate points are frequent, as are the buses for Guayaquil ($5, 4½ hours). Transportes Patria has a Machala bus at 9:45am ($6, six to seven hours) and there are several buses a day for Cuenca ($6, six hours). Buses for Alausí leave 20 times a day between 5am and 8pm with CTA ($1.50, two hours). Flota Bolívar has seven daily buses to Guaranda ($2, two hours). Some continue on to Babahoyo; all buses now take the El Arenal route, which also passes the access road to Chimborazo and the mountain refuges.

For buses to Baños and the Oriente, you have to go to the **Oriente bus terminal** (Espejo & Luz Elisa Borja), northeast of downtown. The road to Baños reopened in 2005, making the ride just under an hour (as opposed to two hours via Ambato). If Tungurahua's volcanic activity increases, this road could close again.

Buses to Atillo in Parque Nacional Sangay (see p177) leave from different corners just southwest of Plaza San Francisco.

CENTRAL HIGHLANDS

TRAIN

The only service out of Riobamba is the famous ride down La Nariz del Diablo (see the boxed text, below). The schedule changes somewhat regularly, so inquire locally for the latest information. Your best bet is to call the **train station** (☎ 296 1909; Av León Borja at Unidad Nacional), which is also where you buy your tickets either the day before, or the morning of (starting at 6am) the departure. You must have your passport to purchase a ticket; if you're buying tickets for friends, bring their passports as well.

The train ($11) leaves Riobamba at 7am Wednesday, Friday and Sunday. It picks up more passengers in Alausí and goes only as far as Sibambe, immediately below La Nariz del Diablo, where there are no services. From Sibambe, the train ascends La Nariz del Diablo and returns to Alausí, where passengers can spend the night, continue on to Cuenca by bus or return to Riobamba by bus. Riding on the roof is, of course, allowed.

Getting Around

North of the main bus terminal, behind the Church of Santa Faz (the one with a blue dome), is a local bus stop with buses to downtown, nearly 2km away. These buses run along Avenida León Borja, which turns into 10 de Agosto near the train station. To return to the bus terminal, take any bus marked 'Terminal' on Primera Constituyente; the fare is $0.25.

Three long blocks south of the main bus terminal (turn left out of the front entrance), off Unidad Nacional, is a smaller terminal with frequent local buses for Cajabamba, Laguna de Colta and the chapel of La Balbanera. Buses for Guamote also leave from there.

To visit the villages of Guano and Santa Teresita, take the local bus from the stop at Pichincha and New York.

GUANO & SANTA TERESITA

☎ 03

These small villages are a few kilometers north of Riobamba and are easily reached by bus. **Guano** (population 6872) is an important carpet-making center, and although most travelers won't have room in their packs for a couple of souvenir carpets, it's interesting to see this cottage industry. To see some carpet stores, get off the bus in Guano's central plaza, and then walk down Avenida García Moreno. There are no hotels and only a few restaurants. Look for the

---

THE DEVIL'S NOSE

The most exciting part of the train ride south of Riobamba is the hair-raising descent from Alausí to Sibambe, down a death-defying stretch of track called La Nariz del Diablo (The Devil's Nose). The run is the only section of track still functioning of the once spectacular Ferrocarril Transandino (Trans-Andean Railway), which ran from Guayaquil to Quito.

Construction of this historic line began in Guayaquil in 1899 and made it as far as Sibambe, where it met a steep Andean slope of nearly solid rock, no less intimidating than the devil's nose itself. To reach Alausí a series of switchbacks was carved into the rock (and many lives were lost in the process) that would allow the train, by advancing and reversing, to ascend nearly 1000m to Alausí at 2607m. The completion and first ascent of the Nariz del Diablo in 1902 was the most incredible feat of railway engineering the world had seen.

The Ferrocarril Transandino reached Riobamba in 1905, later crossed its highest point at Urbina (3618m) and finally reached Quito, after its magnificent wind through the Avenue of the Volcanoes, in 1908.

Landslides caused by the torrential rains of the 1982–83 El Niño, and further damage during the 1997–98 El Niño, effectively closed the entire run, and only the stretch from Riobamba to Sibambe has been repaired.

The steep descent after Alausí is still accomplished by a series of switchbacks down the steep mountainside. Occasional rickety-looking bridges cross steep ravines, the train regularly derails (a minor annoyance and part of the fun), and everyone rides on the roof. Actually, the greatest hazard is probably the train's emission of steam, soot and cinders during the ride, so wear clothes that you don't mind getting dirty. Dress warmly and bring a spare dollar to rent a cushion. See above.

topiary garden with El Altar rising in the background – a pretty sight.

From the main plaza, you can continue by bus to **Santa Teresita**, a few kilometers away. At the end of the bus ride, turn right and head down the hill for about 20 minutes to the *balneario* (spa), where swimming pools are fed by natural springs. The water is quite cool (22°C or 72°F), but the views of Tungurahua and El Altar are marvelous. There is a basic cafeteria and camping is permitted.

Local buses to Guano and Santa Teresita leave Riobamba from the stop at Pichincha and New York.

SOUTH OF RIOBAMBA

☎ 03

About 17km south of Riobamba, the Panamericana rolls through the wee village of **Cajabamba**, the original site of Riobamba until it was devastated by an earthquake in 1797. The quake started a landslide that leveled the town and killed most of the several thousand who died in the disaster. You can still see a huge scar on the hillside as you arrive.

Every Sunday morning, just south of town, one of the highland's most traditional rural **markets** takes place in the open fields just off the highway. Indigenous traders lay out their wares in neat rows, transforming the bare fields into a bustling but surprisingly orderly throng of people who buy, sell and barter produce.

Further south, and just off the Panamericana, you'll pass the little chapel of **La Balbanera**. Built on the site of the earliest church in Ecuador, the chapel site dates from 1534, although only a few stones at the front survived the 1797 earthquake. Inside, disaster paintings immortalize the event.

About 4km south of Cajabamba is **Laguna de Colta**, whose blue waters are often choked with reeds. The reeds form an important crop for the indigenous Colta who use them to make their famous mats and baskets. Traditional Colta women dye the fringes of their hair a startling golden color. If you have the time or inclination, you could walk around the lake in a couple of hours and take in the fabulous views of Chimborazo.

You can easily visit this area on a day excursion from Riobamba by taking local buses or by hiring a taxi. Most of the buses from Riobamba head down the Panamericana through Cajabamba, stopping at the

junction on the main highway. They then continue to Laguna de Colta, passing La Balbanera en route.

VOLCÁN CHIMBORAZO

Not only is the extinct Volcán Chimborazo the highest mountain in Ecuador, but its peak (6310m), due to the earth's equatorial bulge, is also the furthest point from the center of the earth – tell that to your K2-climbing buddies. For insatiable trivia buffs, it is higher than any mountain in the Americas north of it.

Nearby is the ninth-highest mountain in Ecuador, the 5020m **Volcán Carihuairazo**. Climbing either mountain is an adventure only for experienced mountaineers with snow- and ice-climbing gear (contact the guides listed under Riobamba or Quito), but reaching the refuge on Chimborazo is as simple as hiring a car in Riobamba.

Chimborazo and Carihuairazo are both within the Reserva de Producción Faunística Chimborazo (admission $10). It's called a 'fauna-production reserve' because hundreds of vicuñas (a wild relative of the llama) live and breed here. They're easy to spot on the bus ride between Guaranda and Riobamba, and you'll surely see them if you're doing any trekking in the park.

Activities
CLIMBING

Most climbers acclimatize at a lower elevation (Riobamba or Quito are just adequate; higher lodges are a better choice) and arrive at Chimborazo's climbing refuges ready to climb. After a short sleep (more like a restless nap), climbers set out around midnight, when the snow is hard. There are several

> **THE PANAMERI-WHAT**
>
> Right around Cajabamba, the Panamericana splits – the easternmost branch is the Ecuadorian Panamericana, which becomes a regular road when it hits the border with Peru, and the westernmost branch is the international Panamericana, which is still referred to as such once it hits the Peruvian border. Throughout the rest of this chapter, references to the Panamericana should be understood as the Ecuadorian, not international, Panamericana.

CENTRAL HIGHLANDS

THE ICEMEN COMETH

Wander over to Riobamba's Mercado La Merced (p185) on a Wednesday or Saturday morning, and you'll discover a whole row of juice stalls. You'll see glass pitchers of red, yellow, white, pink, green and orange fruit juices standing atop shiny silver blender bases. The stall owners pile minimountains of passion fruit, papayas, berries and other exotic fruits onto the shelves in alluring displays. If you look closely, you'll notice something else: blocks of ice wrapped in grass. But that aint just *any* ice. That's glacial ice from Chimborazo.

Two brothers, Juan and Baltazar Ushca, chop the ice from the glaciers by hand before wrapping the blocks in *páramo* grass to keep it from melting during its long journey to market, strapped to the back of a mule. Locals will tell you that the ice makes far tastier juice than any ice from a freezer – and who could argue with that? Surely no ice could taste as good as that pulled from ice mines located at 4700m on the slopes of an Andean volcano. Who knows, maybe it's just the romance of it. But one thing's for certain; it's a living piece of history.

The Ushca brothers are the last of the famous *hieleros de Chimborazo* – the icemen of Chimborazo. Indigenous Ecuadorians have been hacking blocks of ice from the glaciers of Ecuadorian peaks and lugging it down from the mountains since long before the Spaniards arrived. The ice trade from Chimborazo itself throve well into the 20th century and slowed only in the 1970s, after the first ice factory was built in Riobamba. Until then Pedro Jaya, the most famous *hielero* of all, was in charge of bringing some 80 mule-loads of ice down to market twice each week. But Jaya died in 1993 and the Ushca brothers are the last of a dying breed.

It's possible to hike the routes that the *hieleros* take by contacting a climbing operator in Riobamba. Or you could hunt down the movie *Los Hieleros del Chimborazo* (1980), a sort of Ecuadorian cult classic directed by Igor and Gustavo Guayasamín. Or you could just settle for an icy juice in Mercado La Merced and know just how much went into that glass of fruity goodness before you slug it down.

---

routes, but most parties these days take the **Normal Route**, which takes eight to 10 hours to the summit and two to four to return.

Just below the summit is a large bowl of snow that must be crossed; this gets notoriously soft during the day and is the main reason climbers leave the refuge at midnight. Because many climb this route, wands marking the way are often found. The sunrise high up on the mountain is unforgettable.

The previously popular **Whymper Route** is currently unsafe.

There are no proper refuges on Carihuairazo, so climbers usually set up a base camp on the south side of the mountain. When climbing, do not leave anything unattended, as it could get stolen. The climb is relatively straightforward for experienced climbers, but the usual ice-climbing gear is needed. Skiers and snowboarders have made some descents on this mountain.

HIKING

The area around these mountains is also suitable for backpacking trips – the walk from Mocha (on the Panamericana north of Riobamba) or Urbina (see opposite) over

the pass between the two mountains and emerging at the Ambato–Guaranda road is as good a choice as any. Allow three days for this hike and bring plenty of warm clothes. June to September is the dry season in this region. Maps are available at the IGM (p70) in Quito, or from the Tagua Shop (p185), in Riobamba.

Sleeping

There are three small lodges on the lower slopes of Chimborazo, which are suitable for acclimatization, and two high climbing refuges, which are suitable as bases for climbing the volcano. Note that all of these places are very cold at night, so bring appropriate clothing. Blankets are provided in the lower lodges, but most people use their sleeping bags as well.

The cheapest place to stay in the area is **La Casa del Condor** (beds $3), in the small indigenous community of **Pulingue San Pablo**, on the left just after crossing over the boundary into the reserve on the Riobamba–El Arenal road. Although within the reserve, the community owns the surrounding land, and the ecotourism project **Proyecto El Cóndor** (Condor

Project; www.interconnection.org/condor) is helping them to improve their livelihoods in this harsh environment. Families still live in the small, rounded, thatched-roof huts typical of the area, but La Casa del Condor is a stone building with rooms for a weaving cooperative and two bedrooms, each with two bunk beds for travelers. There's a gas-heated shower and basic kitchen facilities. The altitude here is over 3900m – perfect for acclimatization. Locals provide basic guiding services, and there are fine hikes in the area. Information can be obtained from Riobamba resident **Tom Walsh** (☎ 03-294 1481; twalsh@ch.pro.ec), who has been instrumental in helping the villagers set up the project.

Just outside of the reserve's boundary, southeast of Chimborazo, is **Urbina**, which at 3618m was the highest point on the Trans-Andean Railway. It now consists of nothing more than the former train station, built in 1905. This historic building was turned into **Posada La Estación** (in Riobamba ☎ 294 2215; beds $7), a simple but comfortable *hostal* operated by Alta Montaña (see p183). There are eight rooms, a hot shower, a fully equipped kitchen and meals. Good acclimatization, or simply scenic hikes, can be achieved from here as well.

Alta Montaña also operates the two climbers' refuges. The lower one is **Refugio Hermanos Carrel** (beds $10) at 4800m, and the upper one is **Refugio Whymper** (beds $10) at 5000m. The latter was named after Edward Whymper, the British climber who in 1880 made the first ascent of Chimborazo with the Swiss Carrel brothers as guides. The lower refuge has 14 beds, while the upper one has 70 and is better suited for a summit attempt. Both have caretakers, equipped kitchens, storage facilities and limited food supplies (soups and sandwiches). At 5000m, Refugio Whymper is Ecuador's highest, and altitude sickness is a very real danger. It is essential to spend several days acclimatizing at the elevation of Riobamba or even higher before going on to the refuge.

Getting There & Away

Several buses a day go from Riobamba to Guaranda via the now-paved El Arenal route. About 45 minutes from Riobamba, it passes Pulingue San Pablo. About 7km further you pass the signed turn-off for the Chimborazo refuges. The elevation here is 4370m. This is the cheapest access route.

From the turn-off it is 8km by road to the parking lot at Refugio Hermanos Carrel; you have to walk this road (or hitchhike if you are lucky). Because of the altitude, allow several hours for this walk. Refugio Whymper is almost 1km further, and you have to walk (allow another hour if you are carrying a heavy pack). Bus drivers will drop you at the turnoff.

Most hotels in Riobamba can arrange a taxi service (about $25 round trip) to Refugio Hermanos Carrel via this route.

To reach Posada La Estación *hostal*, take a bus along the Panamericana and ask the driver for the Urbina road, almost 30km north of Riobamba. It's about 1km from the Panamericana by road to Urbina.

GUAMOTE

☎ 03 / pop 1920 / elevation 3050m

After roughly following the train tracks south from Riobamba, the Panamericana passes through the village of Guamote, some 47km south of Riobamba. The town's fascinating and unspoiled **Thursday market** is one of the largest rural markets in Ecuador. Spending a night here – especially on a Wednesday before the market – offers a glimpse into life in a small and mostly indigenous highland town. You can stay at **Inti Sisa** (☎ 291 6319; www.intisisa .org; JM Plaza at Garcia Moreno; r per person $12), which is part of a community tourist project run by a Belgian-Ecuadorian. It's a cozy, well-run place that also offers mountain-biking and horseback-riding trips.

Guamote is on the Riobamba–Cuenca route, which has several services per day. However, unless your bus is actually going to Guamote (usually only on Thursdays), you will be dropped off on the Panamericana and will have to walk about 1km in.

ALAUSÍ

☎ 03 / pop 5570 / elevation 2350m

Set on the edge of Río Chanchán gorge and presided over by a giant statue of St Peter, the busy little railroad town of Alausí is the last place the train passes through before its descent down the famous Nariz del Diablo. Many jump on the train here, rather than in Riobamba, though you're more likely to score a good seat in Riobamba. Parts of Alausí are wonderfully picturesque, especially near the train station and around the main plaza where cobbled streets and old adobe buildings with wooden balconies take you back in time.

Alausí lies about 97km south of Riobamba and has a busy **Sunday market**. The train station is at the north end of 5 de Junio.

Sleeping & Eating

The town has several unexciting hotels, most of which are on Avenida 5 de Junio, the main street. Places fill up on Saturday nights with Sunday market-goers and weekend visitors.

Hotel Europa (☎ 293 0200; 5 de Junio 175 at Orozco; s with shared/private bathroom $5/8, d $8/14) Recently remodeled and spotlessly clean, the Europa is one of the best in town, offering modest but comfy rooms and a decent restaurant.

Hotel Americano (☎ 293 0159; García Moreno 159; r per person $5) A block east of 5 de Junio, near the train station, Hotel Americano is showing its years, but its clean doubles are still a fair option.

Residencial Alausí (☎ 293 0361; 5 de Junio 142 at Orozco; r per person with shared/private bathroom $3/5) Just off the south end of 5 de Junio, Alausí is a friendly place with clean, straightforward rooms.

Hotel Tequendama (☎ 293 0123; 5 de Junio 152; s/d $5/10) Clean, family-run hotel with shared bathrooms only. Breakfast is available.

Hotel Panamericano (☎ 293 0156; 5 de Junio & 9 de Octubre; r per person with shared/private bathroom $5/8) and **Hotel Gampala** (☎ 293 0138; 5 de Junio 122; s/d $8/16) are both passable as well.

Apart from the hotel restaurants, several basic restaurants offer standard fare along the main street.

Getting There & Away

BUS

Buses arrive and depart from Avenida 5 de Junio. The buses from Riobamba ($1.50, two hours) arrive every hour or so. Buses for Cuenca ($4, four hours) depart several times daily. Most buses between Riobamba and Cuenca enter town – if not, it's a 1km walk into town from the Panamericana.

Old buses (or pickup trucks acting as buses) leave from 5 de Junio for nearby destinations. Some of the bus rides can be quite spectacular, especially the one to Achupallas, about 23km by road to the southeast.

TRAIN

Alausí used to be a major railroad junction, but services are now limited to the Nariz del Diablo Riobamba–Sibambe run (see p185 for more details). The train leaves Alausí on Wednesday, Friday and Sunday at 9:30am, and tickets go on sale at 8am. The fare is $11. The trip takes around two hours to go over the famous Nariz del Diablo (see the boxed text The Devil's Nose, p186). Roof-riding is allowed, but the roof is often full with riders from Riobamba or tour groups who pile on while their guide stands in line to buy tickets.

Southern Highlands

As you roll further south along the Panamericana, the giant snowcapped peaks of the central highlands fade from the rearview mirror. The climate gets warmer, distances between towns become greater and the decades clunk down by the wayside. Although few peaks top 4000m here, the topography is rugged – so rugged in fact that not until the 1960s did the first paved road reach Cuenca, Ecuador's third-largest city and the southern highland's main urban center.

The region's isolation has given it a rich and tangible history. Many villages have cobbled streets and old houses with balconies, and the tradition of handicrafts is still very strong. In and around Cuenca, women wear white straw hats and colorful skirts, while further south the striking jet-black clothing and white felt hats identify the indigenous Saraguro.

Although you won't be out scaling glaciers down here, outdoor activities are abundant. The lake-studded Parque Nacional Cajas offers great hiking and camping, and superb trout fishing. Parque Nacional Podocarpus offers magnificent hikes through cloud forest, tropical humid forest and *páramo* (Andean grasslands). From the laid-back gringo hangout of Vilcabamba you can spend days walking or horse riding through the mysterious mountainside.

If the southern highland colonial towns don't take you far enough into the past, there's always Ingapirca, Ecuador's most important Inca ruins. They're just a two-hour bus ride north of Cuenca.

SOUTHERN HIGHLANDS

HIGHLIGHTS

- Explore the colonial streets of **Cuenca** (p195), Ecuador's most stunning city
- Hike the Miradores loop trail and the Huigerones trail in the magnificent **Parque Nacional Podocarpus** (p216)
- Hunker down in mellow **Vilcabamba** (p219) and treat yourself to massages and hot tubbing after hiking the hills around town
- Bundle up and head into the moor-like, lake-studded hills of the splendid **Parque Nacional Cajas** (p208)
- Visit **Ingapirca** (p194), Ecuador's best Inca ruins and home to some of the Inca's finest mortarless stonework

- AVERAGE TEMPERATURE IN CUENCA: 14°C (57°F)
- RAINIEST MONTH IN CUENCA: APRIL & MAY & MAY

SOUTHERN HIGHLANDS

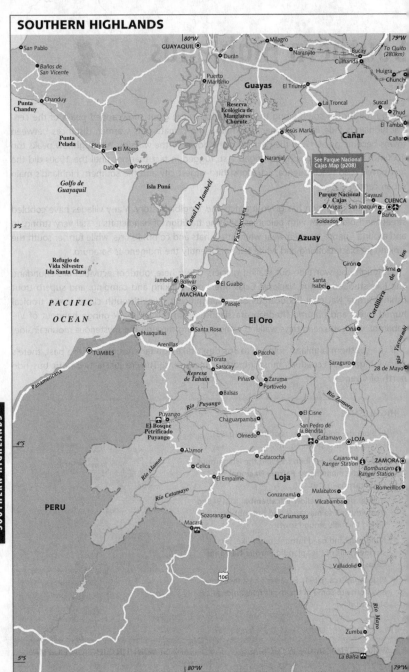

See Parque Nacional
Cajas Map (p208)

SOUTHERN HIGHLANDS

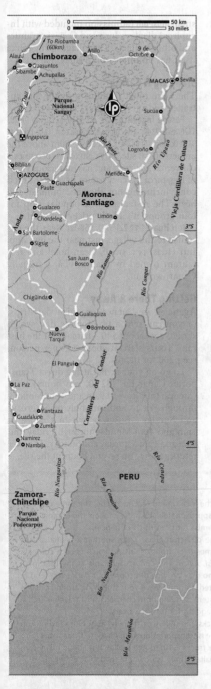

History

The southern highlands had a colorful history even before the Spanish conquest. These were the lands of the Cañari, an independent culture with exceptional skill in producing ceramics, fine weavings, gold jewelry and other metalwork.

In the late-15th century the Cañari were conquered by the Inca, who built several major centers. These included the city of Tomebamba at present-day Cuenca, and the fortress of Ingapirca, the best-preserved pre-colonial ruin found in Ecuador today. The Inca influence was short lived, however, and the Spanish conquistadors under Francisco Pizarro took control by the 1530s. Cuenca was (re)founded relatively late, in 1557. Several other important towns of the region were established earlier, such as Loja in 1548.

Climate

South of Cuenca, altitudes diminish enough that the temperatures, especially around Loja and Vilcabamba, remain comfortably warm year-round. It's even a bit humid at times. The rainy season, when it can be cold and wet (but almost always with several hours of sunshine in the morning), is October to early May.

National Parks

Southern highlands' two national parks – **Parque Nacional Cajas** (p208) situtated near Cuenca, and **Parque Nacional Podocarpus** (p216) near Loja – are easily accessible and offer wonderful hiking and backpacking opportunities. Be sure to visit both sectors of Podocarpus to really experience the park. Note that part of Parque Nacional Sangay falls within this region, but its access primary points are further north (see p176).

Getting There & Away

There are regular flights between Quito and Cuenca, and Quito and Loja. If you are coming from the north, Cuenca is six hours south of Riobamba by bus and the first logical stop. Loja is four hours further south and the best departure point for Peru, either via Macará or via Vilcabamba and the infrequently used crossing near Zumba. Guayaquil, on the southern coast, is only about 3½ hours by bus from Cuenca.

INGAPIRCA

☎ 07 / elevation 3230m

The most important Inca site in Ecuador, Ingapirca (which means 'Wall of the Inca') was built toward the end of the 15th century during the Inca expansion into present-day Ecuador. The **site** (admission $6; ☯ 8am-6pm) was sacred to the indigenous Cañari (whose descendants, ironically, administer the site today) for centuries before the Inca conquered them.

Opinions are mixed about both the significance and function of Ingapirca. The main structure, an elliptical platform known as the Temple of the Sun, was used for ceremonial and religious purposes and perhaps as a solar observatory. It boasts some of the Inca's finest mortarless stonework, including several of the trapezoidal niches and doorways that are hallmarks of Inca construction. The less-preserved buildings were probably storehouses, and the complex may have been used as a *tambo* (stopping place) along the royal Inca road that ran from Cuzco to Quito.

Unfortunately, the ruins were well known and lacked protection, so many of the dressed stones that were used for the buildings were stolen over the centuries. Ingapirca's precise history may be forever lost, but its importance is now recognized and the site is officially protected.

The site is about 1km away from the village of Ingapirca and is easily visited on a day trip from Cuenca. A few signs in English and French explain the site, and local guides are available for a nominal charge. Next to the archaeological site a

small **museum** (admission included with Ingapirca) displays Inca and Cañari ceramics and other artifacts. The village of Ingapirca itself has an interesting Friday market.

Sleeping & Eating

There are toilet facilities near the site entrance and camping (free) is allowed.

Posada Ingapirca (☎ 221 5116, in Cuenca 07-283 1120/8508/2340; www.grupo-santaana.com; Calle Larga 6-93 at Borrero; s/d $37/43) Located 500m above the archeological site, this deluxe inn occupies a converted *hacienda* and has marvelous views of Ingapirca. Its cozy rooms have all the mod cons, including hot showers, minibar and heat. The restaurant is a popular stop for tour groups; it's a little pricey but good.

Inti Huasi (☎ 221 5171; r $8-12) Near the entrance to the village, just near the bus stop, Inti Huasi is a small, clean hotel and restaurant owned by Mamá Julia, a friendly Cañari woman.

Getting There & Away

Agencies in Cuenca organize day trips, or you can rent a taxi for the day, which should cost about $40 – bargain for the best rate. Tours start at about $35 per person; see p200 for details.

To go on your own, catch a direct Transportes Cañar bus ($2.50, two hours) from Cuenca; they leave at 9am and 1pm Monday through Friday, and 9am only on Saturdays and Sundays. Buses return to Cuenca at 1pm and 4pm Monday through Friday and 9am and 1pm Saturday and Sunday. The later returns allow you several hours at the site.

THE INCA TRAIL TO INGAPIRCA

Though it sees only a fraction of the traffic of the Inca trail to Machu Picchu, the three-day hike to Ingapirca is still a popular trek. Parts of this approximately 40km hike follow the original royal road that linked Cuzco with Quito and Tomebamba (at present-day Cuenca).

The starting point for the hike is the village of **Achupallas**, 23km southeast of Alausí (see p189). The route is faint in places and sometimes even nonexistent, so you'll need a compass and three 1:50,000 topographical maps – *Alausí*, *Juncal* and *Cañar* – available at the IGM (p70) in Quito. There are sometimes locals around who may provide directions, but pack extra food in case you get lost. The area is remote but inhabited, so don't leave your stuff lying around outside your tent. Also be prepared for extremely persistent begging from children; most travelers refuse to hand anything out in order to discourage begging for future walkers.

To get to Achupallas, take one of the daily trucks from Alausí or, more reliably, hire a taxi-pickup for about $10 to $15 one way. Alternatively, there is transportation from Alausí to **Guasuntos** (also known as La Moya), from where you can wait for trucks ($10) to Achupallas. It is about 10km from Alausí to La Moya and another 15km to Achupallas. There is nowhere to stay at either place.

Buses also leave every half hour from Cuenca to the town of El Tambo, 8km from Ingapirca. From El Tambo, buses leave about every hour to Ingapirca.

CAÑAR

☎ 07 / pop 11,200 / elevation 3104m

The small town of Cañar, 66km north of Cuenca on the Ecuadorian Panamericana, has a colorful local market every Sunday, which is visited by indigenous Cañari who come down from the remote villages in the surrounding mountains.

Cañari men wear distinctive belts made by an unusual weaving method that gives rise to designs and motifs appearing on both sides of the belt. These may be available in the market. They are also woven by the local prisoners and if you head down to the jail, you will be allowed in to make purchases.

Hostal Ingapirca (☎ 223 5201; Calle Sucre at 5 de Junio; s/d $8/10) has decent rooms with TV. On the corner of the main plaza **Residencial Mónica** (☎ 223 5486; r per person $5) has small, modest rooms.

Cañar's hardly a culinary center, but it has plenty of simple, adequate restaurants, most of which serve standard *almuerzos* (set lunches) and *meriendas* (set dinners).

There are frequent buses to Cañar from Cuenca's bus terminal ($1.50, 1½ hours).

BIBLIÁN

☎ 07 / pop 4370

The wee village of Biblián, about 26km south of Cañar, is famous for one thing: its neogothic **Santuario de la Virgen del Rocío** (Sanctuary of the Virgin of the Dew), perched high on a hillside above the Panamericana. The building is highly visible to the east of the main highway and looks more like a fairytale princess's palace than it does a church. It was originally a small colonial shrine built into a cliff, but in the 1940s it was enlarged into a church with the altar built into the rock where the shrine was. There is a huge pilgrimage here on September 8 (see p224) and a lesser one on Good Friday.

AZOGUES

☎ 07 / pop 27,900 / elevation 2500m

The bustling capital of Cañar Province, Azogues lies about 35km north of Cuenca on the Panamericana. It's a handsome colonial center with steep, narrow streets and balconied adobe houses. The Pacifictel and post office are on the main plaza.

Azogues is an important producer of panama hats, which are finished and sold in Cuenca. Except on Saturdays, when it jumps to life for its weekly market, Azogues is generally a *tranquilo* (relaxed) place, good for a few hours of wandering around.

Azogues' principal sight is the **Church of San Francisco**, which dominates the town from a hill to the southeast. It's a half-hour climb up here, but worth it for the sweeping views of the town and the surrounding countryside.

Sleeping & Eating

Hostal Rivera (☎ 224 8113; 24 de Mayo & 10 de Agosto; s/d $14/20) By far the best hotel in town, Hotel Rivera has an attached restaurant (mains run $3 to $7) and 24 clean rooms with carpeting, TV, telephone and private hot-showers.

Hotel Santa María (☎ 224 1883; cnr Serrano & Emilio Abad; s/d $8/16) Near the main plaza, the Santa María is clean and nondescript – fine for a night if the Rivera's too pricey.

Several inexpensive restaurants around town serve the usual Ecuadorian fare. The best of the lot is likely **El Padrino** (Bolivar 609 near 10 de Agosto; mains $3-6; ⏰ daily), which has a pleasant dining room and a lengthy menu.

Getting There & Away

The main bus-stop area is just off the Panamericana, which is renamed 24 de Mayo as it goes through Azogues. There are daily departures to Quito ($9, eight hours) and Guayaquil ($6, four hours). Buses to Cuenca ($0.60, 45 minutes) leave from the local bus terminal on Rivera, about three blocks south of the main market.

CUENCA

☎ 07 / pop 417,000 / elevation 2530m

Debating the relative beauty of Cuenca and Quito is a favorite pastime in these parts, but an impossible issue to resolve. In terms of grandeur, Quito wins hands down. But Cuenca – that colonial jewel of the south – takes the cake when it comes to beauty. Its narrow cobblestone streets and whitewashed red-tiled buildings, its handsome plazas and domed churches, and its setting above the grassy banks of the Río Tomebamba, where women still dry clothes in the sun, all create a city that's supremely impressive. Though firmly anchored in its colonial past, Ecuador's third-largest city also has a modern edge, with international restaurants, art galleries, cool cafés and welcoming bars tucked into its magnificent architecture. It has a large student population and (unsurprisingly) is popular with foreigners.

Barely half a century before the arrival of the Spaniards, the powerful Inca Tupac-Yupanqui, after conquering the Cañari, began construction of a major city at the site of present-day Cuenca. Its splendor and importance were to rival that of the imperial capital of Cuzco. The indigenous people told of sun temples covered with gold sheets and palaces built using the most skilled *cuzqueño* stonemasons, but what happened to Tomebamba, as the city was called, is shrouded in mystery.

By the time Spanish chronicler Cieza de León passed through in 1547, Tomebamba lay largely in ruins. Today it is difficult to imagine Tomebamba's splendor, as all that remains are a few recently excavated Inca walls by the river.

In 1999 Cuenca was honored by Unesco, which declared its center a World Cultural Heritage Site.

Information
EMERGENCY
Police station (☎ 281 0068; Luís Cordero near Presidente Córdova) The migraciones (immigration) office is also here.

INTERNET ACCESS
There are numerous cybercafés in town, and new ones open regularly. All charge $0.80 to $1 per hour and most are open daily.
Bapu Net (Presidente Córdova 9-21)
Cuenca Net (cnr Calle Larga & Hermano Miguel)
Cybercom (cnr Presidente Córdova & Borrero)
Dot Com (Hermano Miguel near Presidente Córdova)

INTERNET RESOURCES
www.cuenca.gov.ec Cuenca's municipal website.
www.cuencanos.com Loads of Cuenca information, mostly in Spanish.

LAUNDRY
Fast Klín (☎ 282 3473; Hermano Miguel 4-21; per kg $1; ⏰ 8am-7pm Mon-Sat)
La Química (Borrero near Presidente Córdova; per kg $1; ⏰ 9am-1pm & 3-6:30pm Mon-Sat)

Lavahora (☎ 282 3042; Honorato Vásquez 6-76; per kg $0.75; ⏰ 9am-1pm & 3-6:30pm Mon-Sat)

MEDICAL SERVICES
The following are excellent clinics and have some English-speaking staff. Consultations cost about $20.
Clínica Hospital Monte Sinai (☎ 288 5595; Miguel Cordero 6-111)
Clínica Santa Inés (☎ 281 7888; Daniel Córdova 2-113)

MONEY
Banco de Guayaquil (Mariscal Sucre near Borrero) Bank with ATM; changes traveler's checks.
Banco del Pacífico (cnr Gran Colombia & Tarqui) Bank with ATM.
Banco del Pichincha (cnr Solano & 12 de Abril) Bank with ATM; changes traveler's checks.
Vaz Corp (☎ 283 3434; cnr Gran Colombia & Luís Cordero; ⏰ 8:30am-1pm & 2:30-5:45pm Mon-Fri, 9am-12:45pm Sat) Changes traveler's checks and foreign currency.

POST
Post office (cnr Gran Colombia & Borrero)

TELEPHONE
Etapa (Benigno Malo 726; ⏰ 7am-10pm) Telephone call center.

TOURIST INFORMATION
Bus Terminal Information office (☎ 284 3888) In the bus terminal.
Tourist information (iTur; ☎ 282 1035; i_tur@cuenca .gov.ec; Mariscal Sucre at Luís Cordero; ⏰ 8am-8pm Mon-Fri, 9am-3pm Sat) Extremely friendly and helpful; English is spoken.

TRAVEL AGENCIES
Metropolitan Touring (☎ 283 1185, 283 1463; www .metropolitan-touring.com; Mariscal Sucre 6-62) Good all-purpose travel agency.

Sights & Activities
PARQUE CALDERÓN
Parque Calderón is the city's main plaza, dominated by Catedral de la Inmaculada Concepción, the '**new cathedral**,' whose giant sky-blue domes are visible mainly from the rear of the church. Inside, the marbled interior is rather stark. Construction began in 1885, and the cathedral was supposed to be much taller than it is – an error in design meant that the intended bell towers could not be supported by the building.

Almost unnoticed on the other side of the park stands the stark-white **old cathedral** (also known as El Sagrario), which was renovated for the 1985 visit of Pope John Paul II to Ecuador. Construction of this building began in 1557, the year that Cuenca was founded. In 1739, it was used as a triangulation point by La Condamine's expedition to measure the shape of the earth.

PLAZAS & CHURCHES
While Parque Calderón is, without a doubt, Cuenca's showpiece plaza, the city has plenty of other fine plazas, each crowned by its own church. Cuenca's churches have unpredictable hours; generally, they are open 6:30am to 5pm Friday and Saturday, and often until 8pm on Sunday. When they're open, admission is free.

Once marking the western edge of the historical center, the quiet **Plaza de San Sebastián** (Parque Miguel León; cnr Mariscal Sucre & Talbot) is anchored by the 17th-century **Church of San Sebastián** (cnr Bolívar & Talbot), one of the city's oldest churches. In 1739, the Frenchman Juan Seniergues, a member of La Condamine's geodesic expedition, was violently murdered in this plaza during a fiesta, apparently because of an affair with a local woman. The south side of the plaza is flanked by the **Museo de Arte Moderno** (☎ 283 1027; cnr Mariscal Sucre & Talbot; admission by donation; ☻ 9am-1pm & 3-6:30pm Mon-Fri, 9am-1pm Sat & Sun), which now houses a small but strong collection of local and Latin American art.

Two blocks east of Plaza de San Sebastián stands the bare, 19th-century **Church of San Cenáculo** (cnr Bolívar & Montalvo). One block north of the church is **Gran Colombia**, the main handicraft and shopping street in Cuenca. The street's landmark building is the **Church of Santo Domingo** (cnr Gran Colombia & Padre Aguirre), which has some fine carved wooden doors and colonial paintings inside. Although it looks older, the church was built in the early 20th-century.

Although its doors are rarely open to the public, the **Church of El Carmen de la Asunción** (Mariscal Sucre near Padre Aguirre), founded in 1682, is one of Cuenca's prettiest sights, thanks to the colorful **flower market** (☻ daily) held on the small **Plazoleta del Carmen** out front. A few paces south along Padre Aguirre brings you to the 19th-century **Church of San Francisco**, which towers handsomely above the

not-so-handsome (but still very interesting) **Plaza de San Francisco**. The plaza is flanked by old arcaded buildings with wooden balconies and is crowded with a permanent ramshackle street market.

On the western side of the historical center, the **Church of San Blas**, on the plaza of the same name, was once the western boundary of colonial Cuenca. Originally built in the late 16th-century, the small colonial church has since been replaced by an early 20th-century building. The modern church is one of the city's largest and is the only one in Cuenca built in the form of a Latin cross.

RÍO TOMEBAMBA & CALLE LARGA
The swift, rock-strewn Río Tomebamba is attractively lined with old colonial buildings that tower above the grassy riverside. The buildings themselves open onto the street of Calle Larga, which runs parallel to – and directly above – the river. From Calle Larga, three attractive stone stairways lead down to Avenida 3 de Noviembre, which follows the river's northern bank and makes for a pleasant walk. The largest staircase, at Hermano Miguel, is known as **La Escalinata**.

One of the river's landmark features is the **Puente Roto** (Broken Bridge), the remaining third of an old stone bridge that once spanned the river.

Inside one of Calle Larga's historical buildings, the **Museo Remigio Crespo Toral** (☎ 283 3208; Calle Larga 7-27 near Borrero) contains religious sculptures, colonial furniture, paintings and a fine selection of indigenous artifacts. It has been under restoration for some years and was scheduled to reopen in late 2006.

A block away, on the stairs down to the river, the **Centro Interamericano de Artes Populares** (Cidap; ☎ 284 0919, 282 9451; Hermano Miguel 3-23; admission free; ☻ 9:30am-1pm & 2-6pm Mon-Fri, 10am-1pm Sat) displays changing exhibits of traditional indigenous costumes, handicrafts and artwork from around Latin America. It has an outstanding crafts store and promotes many of its featured artists and artisans by selling their work.

Further along Calle Larga, the **Museo de las Culturas Aborígenes** (☎ 283 9181; Calle Larga 5-24; museoarq@etapaonline.net.ec; admission $2; ☻ 9am-6:30pm Mon-Fri, 9am-1pm Sat) houses an outstanding collection of about 5000 archaeological pieces representing some 20 pre-Hispanic cultures of Ecuador and reaching as far back as 13,000

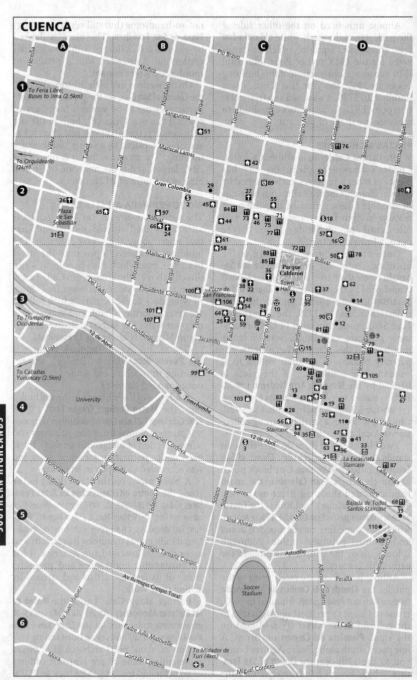

CUENCA

INFORMATION

Banco de Guayaquil	**1** D3
Banco del Pacífico	**2** B2
Banco del Pichincha	**3** C4
Bapu Net	**4** D3
Bus Terminal Information Office	(see 108)
Clínica Hospital Monte Sinai	**5** B6
Clínica Santa Inés	**6** B4
Cuenca Net	**7** D4
Cybercom	**8** D3
Dot Com	**9** D3
Etapa	**10** C3
Fast Klín	**11** D4
La Química	**12** D3
Lavahora	**13** C4
Metropolitan Touring	**14** D3
Migraciones	(see 15)
Police Station	**15** C3
Post Office	**16** D2
Tourist Information	**17** C3
Vaz Corp	**18** D2

SIGHTS & ACTIVITIES

Abraham Lincoln Cultural Center	**19** D4
Amazing Grace	**20** D2
Centro de Estudios Interamericanos	(see 29)
Centro Interamericano de Artes Populares	**21** D4
Church of El Carmen de la Asunción	**22** C3
Church of San Blás	**23** F3
Church of San Cenáculo	**24** B2
Church of San Francisco	**25** C3
Church of San Sebastián	**26** A2
Church of Santo Domingo	**27** C3
Ecotrek	**28** C4
Expediciones Apullacta	**29** B2
Flower Market	(see 38)
Inca Ruins (Museo Manuel Agustín Landivar)	**30** E5
Mamá Kinua Cultural Center	(see 100)
Museo de Arte Moderno	**31** A2
Museo de las Conceptas	**32** D4
Museo de las Culturas Aborígenes	**33** D4
Museo del Banco Central 'Pumapungo'	**34** F5
Museo Remigio Crespo Toral	**35** C4
New Cathedral (Catedral de la Inmaculada Concepción)	**36** C3
Old Cathedral	**37** D3
Plaza Rotary Market	(see 60)
Plazoleta del Carmen	**38** C3
Puente Roto	**39** D5
Sampere	(see 21)
Sí Centro de Español e Inglés	**40** C4
Terra Diversa/The Travel Center	**41** D4

SLEEPING

Casa Naranja	**42** C2
El Cafecito	**43** D4
Gran Hotel	**44** C2
Hostal Chordeleg	**45** B2
Hostal Colonial	**46** C2
Hostal El Capitolio	**47** D4
Hostal El Monarca	**48** D4
Hostal El Monasterio	**49** C3
Hostal La Orquídea	**50** D3
Hostal Macondo	**51** B1
Hostal Paredes	**52** D2
Hostal Santa Fe	**53** D4
Hotel Allí Tiana	**54** C3
Hotel Carvallo	**55** C2
Hotel Crespo	**56** C4
Hotel El Dorado	**57** D2
Hotel Inca Real	**58** C3
Hotel Milan	**59** C3
Hotel Norte	**60** D2
Hotel Pichincha	**61** C2
Hotel Santa Lucia	**62** D3
Hotel Victoria	**63** D4
La Cofradía del Monje	**64** C3
La Posada del Angel	**65** A2
Mansión Alcazar	**66** B2
Verde Limón	**67** D4

EATING

Aguacolla Café	**68** D5
Cacao & Canela	**69** D4
Café Austria	**70** C4
Café Eucalyptus	**71** C4
El Cántaro	**72** C3
El Pedregal Azteca	**73** C4
Goura	**74** C4
Grecia	**75** C3
Guajibamba	**76** D2
Heladería Holanda	**77** C4
La Barraca	**78** D3
La Olla Mágica	**79** D3
Las Brasas de San Juan	**80** C4
Los Capulies	**81** D3
Mamá Kinua Cultural Center	(see 100)
Moliendo Café	**82** C4
Monday Blue	**83** C4
New York Pizza	**84** C2
Raymipampa	**85** C3
Restaurant El Paraíso	**86** E3
Tres Estrellas	**87** D5
Tutto Freddo	**88** C3

ENTERTAINMENT

Bar San Ángel	(see 79)
Café Eucalyptus	(see 71)
Cine Cuenca	**89** C2
Del Tranquilo	**90** D3
Fuzzión	**91** D4
Kaos	**92** D4
La Mesa	**93** D4
Multicines	(see 109)
Tal Cual	**94** C4
Teatro Casa de Cultura	**95** C3
WunderBar	**96** D4

SHOPPING

Acción	**97** B2
Artículos Deportivos	**98** C3
Barranco	**99** B4
Casa de la Mujer	**100** B3
Casa del Sombrero Alberto Pulla	**101** B3
Crafts Market	**102** E2
Explorador Andino	**103** C4
Homero Ortega P & Hijos	**104** G1
La Paja Toquilla	**105** D2
Plaza San Francisco Market	**106** C3
Sombreros Don Migui	**107** B3

TRANSPORT

Bus Terminal	**108** G1
Icaro	**109** D5
TAME	**110** D5

SOUTHERN HIGHLANDS

BC. The layout is very attractive, and there's a small gift shop and bookstore.

Continuing east, you finally come to some small (almost nonexistent) **Inca ruins** at the Museo Manuel Agustín Landivar on Calle Larga, beside the Río Tomebamba. Unfortunately the site and the museum were closed indefinitely in early 2006, but you can still see the ruins from the outside.

MUSEO DEL BANCO CENTRAL 'PUMAPUNGO'

Considered Cuenca's most important museum, **Museo Pumapungo** (☎ 283 1255; www.museo pumapungo.com; Calle Larga near Huayna Capac; adult/child under 12 $3/1.50; ☺ 9am-6pm Mon-Fri, 9am-1pm Sat) merits a visit for the maze-like ethnographic exhibit alone. An entire floor of colorfully animated dioramas displays the traditional costumes of Ecuador's many cultures, including Afro-Ecuadorians from Esmeraldas province, the cowboy-like *montubios* of the western lowlands, several rainforest groups and all the major highland groups. The climax of the exhibit are five stunningly displayed *tsantsas* (shrunken heads) from the Shuar culture of the southern Oriente.

The other major aspect of the museum is the **archaeological site** out back, which is believed to have been the actual location of the Inca site of Tomebamba. All that's left to see, however, are the foundations of a few buildings spread around a landscaped park.

MUSEO DE LAS CONCEPTAS

Cuenca's best **religious museum** (☎ 283 0625; Hermano Miguel 6-33; admission $1; ☺ 9am-5pm Tue-Fri, 10am-1pm Sat) is housed in the Convent of the Immaculate Conception, which was founded in 1599. The chapel of the infirmary has a display of crucifixes by the noted 19th-century local sculptor Gaspar Sangurima. Other parts of the building display a variety of religious paintings, carvings, statuettes, nativity scenes and other art.

MARKETS

Thursday is the main market day and there's a smaller market on Saturday. The two main market areas are **Plaza de San Francisco** (Presidente Córdova at Padre Aguirre) and **Plaza Rotary** (Mariscal Lamar at Hermano Miguel). The San Francisco market is mainly for locals, though there's a row of stalls on the north side with weavings and sweaters from Otavalo. The market at Plaza Rotary is mainly fruits and vegetables. Both markets are lively and interesting, and continue on a smaller scale throughout the week.

ORQUIDEARIO

If you've any interest in the world's most outrageous and beautiful plant species, you'll love the Universidad de Cuenca's **Orquideario** (☎ 284 2893; Quinta de Balsaín; admission free; ☺ 8am-noon & 2-6pm Mon-Fri), 2km west of downtown. With over 400 species of orchids, it's one of the country's best. Between December and May, when most of the plants are in flower, it's truly a sight to see. It's still worth visiting the rest of the year. To get there, take bus 1B ($0.25) from Muñoz. A taxi will cost about $2.

MIRADOR DE TURI

For a lovely view of Cuenca, take a taxi (about $4) south of town along Avenida Solano to the stark white Church of Turi, perched high on a hillside in the southern suburb of Turi. The views are especially splendid on the occasional evenings (usually around holidays) when all of the churches' steeples and domes are lit throughout town. It's about 4km from the center.

Courses

Cuenca's a wonderful place to study Spanish. Most language schools charge $5 to $7 per hour for one-to-one classes.

Abraham Lincoln Cultural Center (☎ 282 3898; rboroto@cena.or.ec; Borrero 5-18)

Amazing Grace (☎ 283 5003; Mariscal Lamar 6-56). Especially good for advanced students.

Centro de Estudios Interamericanos (Cedei; ☎ 283 9003, 282 3452; info@cedei.org; Gran Colombia 11-02) A nonprofit school offering drop-in and/or long-term courses in Spanish, Quichua, Portuguese, Latin American literature and indigenous culture.

Sampere (☎ 282 3960; www.sampere.com/cuenca; Hermano Miguel 3-43)

Sí Centro de Español e Inglés (☎ 284 6932; Jaramillo 7-27; www.sicentrospanishschool.com; ☺ morning & afternoon classes) Twenty-hour/one-week ($140) minimum.

Tours

Local tour operators offer day trips to Ingapirca (p194), Parque Nacional Cajas (p208), nearby villages and markets, and other local

MAMÁ KINUA'S CULTURAL TOURS

Mamá Kinua Cultural Center (☎ 284 0610; Torres 7-45, Casa de la Mujer; ☻ 8am-5:30pm Mon-Fri) is a Quichua-run café, bookstore, gift shop, cultural center and community-tourist project all rolled into one. Not only can you get some of the best, healthiest, down-home indigenous cooking around, but you can set yourself up on one of Cuenca's most interesting tours.

The tours side of the operation is called **Kushi Waira**, and offers daily guided visits to the indigenous communities of Tarqui, 40 minutes outside of Cuenca. After hiking to different indigenous communities, you're treated to a traditional *pampamesa* (community feast) lunch. They also show crafts and give demonstrations on daily projects like spinning wool, milling grains, planting crops or harvesting. Horseback rides are also available with a guide from the community who explains local traditional forest uses and medicinal plants along the way. Both of these are day trips and cost $35 per person.

Those who would like to plunge deeper into community life can stay at the community cabañas for $11 per night. You can usually help out with daily chores, eat with families and learn about life in a small Ecuadorian community.

The best part about these trips is that every penny you spend goes directly to the indigenous community of Tarqui, about 20km south of Cuenca. The money helps fund a health center and provide economic alternatives to migration (which has been alarmingly high since the economic crisis in 1999). Stop by the cultural center for more information (and a bite to eat!).

ttractions. Prices average $35 to $40 per person. Note that entrance fees are generally not included in many tours – ask when you book.

Terra Diversa/The Travel Center (☎ 282 3782; www.terradiversa.com; Hermano Miguel 5-42) is an aliance between Monta Runa, a company hat offers well-received horse-riding trips, and Biketa, which offers mountain-biking rips. Both cost about $48 per person per day, including guide, transportation, lunch and your bike or horse. They offer two- to four-day horse-riding trips, overnighting in haciendas. The office has a small library, reference maps, luggage storage and a notice board. Cajas and Ingapirca tours are both offered. A three-hour Cuenca city tour costs $15.

Expediciones Apullacta (☎ 283 7815, 283 7681, 09-977 1605; www.apullacta.com; Gran Colombia 11-02) also offers day tours to Ingapirca, Cajas and other places, and has received good reports.

Ecotrek (☎ 284 1927, 283 4677; ecotrex@az.pro.ec; Calle Larga 7-108) is recommended for trekking, mountaineering (rock and ice) and Amazon travel – especially to the southern Oriente. It also goes to the Galápagos.

English-speaking Humberto Chica, at Cabañas Yanuncay guesthouse (p202), organizes day trips and overnight tours to Cajas, the southern Oriente and other areas. Tours are small and personal.

Mamá Kinua Cultural Center (see the boxed text, above) is an indigenous organization offering some very interesting cultural tours.

Festivals & Events

Cuenca's **Independence Day** is November 3, which combines with November 1 and 2 (All Saints' Day and All Souls' Day) to form an important vacation period for the city. The markets are in full swing, and music, dancing, parades and drinking round out the fun. April 12, the anniversary of Cuenca's foundation, is similarly celebrated for several days around that date.

Carnaval, as in other parts of Ecuador, is celebrated with boisterous water fights in which *no one* is spared.

Cuenca's colorful Pase del Niño **Christmas Eve procession**, which starts in the suburbs in the morning and emerges, finally, near the cathedral in the afternoon, is one of the most spectacular parades in the country. **Corpus Christi** (usually the ninth Thursday after Easter) is also colorfully celebrated for several days.

Sleeping

Cuenca has a great selection of hotels in all price categories, but prices are a tad higher than elsewhere. During vacation periods, and especially on long weekends, be sure to book ahead as Cuenca is a popular destination.

SOUTHERN HIGHLANDS

BUDGET

Casa Naranja (Naranja Lodging; ☎ 282 5415, 288 3820; www.casanaranja.galeon.com; Mariscal Lamar 10-38 near Padre Aguirre; s $8-15, d $12-18) With stunning results, a local *cuencana* artist turned her 100-year-old family home into a modest but delightfully artsy guesthouse. Rooms are simple, and some have private bathrooms. Communal kitchen, too.

Hostal Paredes (☎ 283 5674; Luís Cordero 11-29; r per person with shared/private bath $4/6) Supposedly Cuenca's first hotel, Paredes is a wacky, friendly place in an early 20th-century building. Dali-esque paintings adorn the walls, plants fill the balconied lobby and a few caged parakeets complement the quirkiness. Beds are saggy but it's a great deal.

Verde Limón (☎ 283 1509, 282 0300; www.verdelimonhostal.com; Jaramillo 4-89 near Ceuva; dm $6, r per person $7; 🖳) 'Green Lime' refers to the neon-green walls that make this little hostel almost blindingly vibrant. The wood floors creak, the back balcony's crooked and the common room in front makes a perfect lounge. Private rooms are quite nice, though the kitchen could use some sprucing up. A great deal.

Hostal El Monarca (☎ 283 6462; hostalmonarca@hotmail.com; Borrero 5-47; s/d $7/14) Earthy orange walls, wild art and groovy wood carvings make the sunlit patio of this new, family-run *hostal* all the more lively. Baths are all shared, and the life-is-good-let's-turn-up-the-music vibe is just what some of us road monkeys need.

El Cafecito (☎ 283 2337; www.cafécito.net; Honorato Vásquez 7-36; dm $5, r with private bath $15) As popular for its restaurant/bar as for its rooms, El Cafecito is a favorite for the travelin' social crowd and local hipsters alike. Modest, comfortable rooms have clean white walls and open onto a garden out back, and things get lively every night.

Hostal El Monasterio (☎ 282 4457; Padre Aguirre 7-24; r per person shared/private bath $6/8) On the 6th floor of a building across from Plaza San Francisco, this unique hotel boasts fabulous views from the communal kitchen and eating area. You have to climb six floors when the elevator isn't working (which is often).

Hotel Pichincha (☎ 282 3868; karolina7a@hotmail.com; Torres 8-82; r per person $4.50) Mammoth by Cuenca standards, this impersonal 60-room hotel is a fair value and popular with backpackers and Ecuadorians alike. The rooms are clean, but shared bathrooms are pretty shabby.

Hotel Norte (☎ 282 7881; Cueva 11-63; r per person with shared/private bath $4/6) Of the cheap hotels around the Plaza Rotary market, this is the best.

Also fine options:

Hostal El Capitolio (☎ 282 4446; Hermano Miguel 4-19; s/d $4.50/9) Totally acceptable for the price – seven rooms, shared baths.

Hostal Santa Fe (☎ 282 2025; alezamsar@yahoo.com; Borrero 5-57; s/d $8/16) Spotless, windowless rooms with TV; a new place and a fair deal.

MIDRANGE

La Posada del Angel (☎ 284 0695; www.hostalposadadelangel.com; Bolívar 14-11; s/d incl breakfast $31/46; 🖳) Color, character, history, you name it – Posada del Angel has all the ingredients of the perfect B&B. Sunlight floods the multicolored lobby, itself lovingly adorned with squishy couches and a sculpture of the Virgin. Rooms open onto interior balconies, and several others are reached by an impossibly narrow wooden staircase.

Hostal Macondo (☎ 284 0697, 283 0836; www.hostalmacondo.com; Tarqui 11-64; s/d with shared bath $13.50/20, with private bath $19/26) The splendid, colonial-style Hostal Macondo keeps travelers pouring in with its sunny back garden, cheerful indoor sitting areas, artisanal decor and excellent breakfasts. If you spend a little extra on the latter, you can gorge yourself on the cook's knock-out cornmeal pancakes. Kitchen privileges and continental breakfast included.

Hotel Milan (☎ 283 1104, 283 5351; Presidente Córdova 9-89; r per person $9) The eternally reliable Milan offers good, comfortable rooms with firm beds and consistent hot water. It 'broadcasts' movies into rooms each night at 9pm. Some rooms have balconies with good views, and there's a pool table and a 4th-floor café serving breakfast (included).

La Cofradía del Monje (☎ 283 1251; cofradiadelmonje@hotmail.com; Presidente Córova 10-33; s/d $18/32) In a unique location across from the lively Plaza San Francisco, this is a stunning new B&B in a refurbished century-old home. All but one of the seven rooms have giant windows, and all are superbly comfortable. Faux-painted walls, blonde wood floors and flowing curtains add to the elegance.

Cabañas Yanuncay (☎ 288 3716, 281 9681; yanuncay@etapa.com.ec; Calle Canton Gualaceo 2-149; r per person $12) This quiet guesthouse, 3km southwest of downtown, offers rooms in a private house or in two cabins in the owner's garden. There are good walks in the area, and rates include breakfast, kitchen privileges and the use of a sauna and whirlpool. Dinners cost $6 and are made with organic products from the on-site farm. The owner, Humberto, speaks English and German and arranges local tours.

Hostal La Orquídea (☎ 282 4511, 283 5844; Borrero 9-31; s/d/apt $23/31/98) In a beautifully refurbished colonial building, La Orquídea has comfortable, immaculate rooms featuring handsome hardwood floors, gold detailing, eclectic paintings and (more importantly) cable TV and telephone. One apartment sleeps five.

Hotel Inca Real (☎ 282 3636; incareal@cue.satnet.net; Torres 8-40; s/d incl breakfast $37/45) The Inca Real is a charmingly renovated hotel with a classical feel and a bright interior courtyard. Rooms are carpeted and the bedspreads are a bit over-flowery, but you can distract yourself from that fact with cable TV. There's a beautiful new tapas bar attached.

Hotel Carvallo (☎ 283 2063; Gran Colombia 9-52; www.hotelcarvallo.com; s/d with breakfast $53/77, ste $122-146) This handsome hotel occupies a splendidly refurbished, century-old, three-story building and has 30 immaculate, carpeted rooms with mini-bar and cable TV. They open onto balconies over an open interior, and some still have their original pressed-tin ceilings.

Hotel Victoria (☎ 282 7401; www.grupo-santaana .com; Calle Larga 6-93; s/d with breakfast $43/55; 🖳) In an exquisitely remodeled building overlooking the river, Hotel Victoria offers 23 immaculate rooms with stark white walls and wood finishings. Two suites have giant terraces over the river, and everything smells fresh. There's a cozy, dimly lit bar and an excellent restaurant, too.

Hostal Colonial (☎ 282 3793; hcolonia@cue.satnet .net; Gran Colombia 10-13; s/d incl breakfast $16/26) Blue carpeted rooms detract a bit from the 'colonial' atmosphere, but this longtime hotel with cozy rooms and crooked interior balconies is good value nonetheless.

Cuenca has plenty of other good hotel options:

Hostal Chordeleg (☎ 282 2536; hostalfm@etapaonline .com.ec; Gran Colombia 11-15; s/d $18/28)

Gran Hotel (☎ 283 1934, 283 5154; Torres 9-70; s/d $12/18)

Hotel Alli Tiana (☎ 283 1844, 282 1955; Presidente Córdova & Padre Aguirre; s/d $16/22)

TOP END

Mansión Alcazar (☎ 282 3918, 282 3889; www.man sionalcazar.com; Bolívar 12-55; s/d $79/122; 🖳 ✗) Mansión Alcazar occupies a century-old building and has a beautiful garden out back. Inside, below interior balconies, a water fountain spills over with freshly picked sunflowers. There's a 'champagne lounge' bedecked with period furniture, a library and a TV room, all perfect for luxurious evenings inside. Each of the 14 rooms is unique, and all are divinely comfortable.

Hotel Santa Lucia (☎ 282 8000; www.santalucia hotel.com; Borrero 8-44; s/d $79/92; 🖳) Plush burgundy fabrics hang from the walls, and giant heavy curtains adorn the doorways of this magnificently remodeled building dating from 1859. With a Spanish-style interior courtyard, detailed woodwork, chandeliers, Oriental rugs and a relentless attention to details, Hotel Santa Lucia is both decadent and refined – surely one of Cuenca's top five.

Hotel Crespo (☎ 284 2571; www.hotelcrespo.com; Calle Larga 7-93; s/d $73/85; 🖳) In a lovely, century-old building overlooking Río Tomebamba, Hotel Crespo is a traditional top-end hotel with suited bellhops and spacious rooms with high, molded ceilings, wood-paneled walls and classical furnishings.

Hotel El Dorado (☎ 283 1390; www.eldoradohotel .com.ec; Gran Colombia 7-87; r $110; 🖳 🖳) Downtown's most traditional luxury hotel – a seven-floor, 92-room giant – seems a bit out of place in this old city, but it sure is comfy. Rates include a buffet breakfast.

Eating

On Sundays, most restaurants are closed, so start your search *before* your blood-sugar crashes. The rest of the week you'll find plenty of great restaurants to choose from.

Café Eucalyptus (☎ 284 9157; www.caféeucalyptus .com; Gran Colombia 9-41; plates $2-6; 🕓 5-11pm Mon & Tue, 5pm-midnight Wed & Thu, 5pm-1am Fri, 7pm-4am Sat) In a remodeled, colonial-style building with two crackling fireplaces, two big couches, two floors of tables, one beautiful bar, 30 wines, several microbrews and 100 small-plate dishes ('international tapas' if you will), Café Eucalyptus is *the* place to treat yourself.

Cacao & Canela (☎ 282 0945; cnr Jaramillo & Borrero; ☽ 4-11pm Mon-Wed, 4pm-midnight Thu-Sat) This excellent little café-cum-bar serves cheap, wholesome sandwiches and good coffee in a warm, dimly lit atmosphere.

Guajibamba (☎ 283 1016, 09-845 8015; Luis Cordero 12-32; mains $4-6; ☽ noon-3pm & 6-11pm Mon-Sat) This atmospheric restaurant has a small menu of traditional plates like *seco de chivo* (similar to goat stew) and gourmet *fritada* (fried pork with hominy, avocado and other garnishings). It's also one of the best places to try *cuy* (roast guinea pig); if you're game, call an hour before you go for prep time ($17 for two).

Moliendo Café (☎ 282 8710; Honorato Vásquez 6-24; light meals $1-3; ☽ 9am-9pm Mon-Sat) Moliendo Café serves delicious Colombian *antojitos* (appetizers) at prices that make everyone happy. The *arepa mixta* (a sort of corn pancake smothered with seasoned beans, chicken, peas and beef) is a delicious meal in itself – and you can't beat it for the price.

Monday Blue (☎ 282 3182; cnr Calle Larga & Luís Cordero; mains $2.50-4; ☽ 4:30pm-midnight) The festive Mexican atmosphere is more Cancún than Cuenca, but it's undeniably fun wolfing down sandwiches, Mexican food, *shawarmas* and pizza in this restaurant-cum-bar.

Tres Estrellas (☎ 282 2340, 282 6968; Calle Larga 1-174; most mains $4-5; ☽ 11:30am-3pm & 5:30pm-1am Tue-Sat) Long in the business, Tres Estrellas receives rave reviews for its gourmet *cuy* ($16.50, serves two). If you're not up for that squeaky delicacy, there's outstanding grilled beef, chicken and pork on the menu too.

Mamá Kinua Cultural Center (☎ 284 0610; Torres 7-45, Casa de la Mujer; ☽ 8am-5:30pm Mon-Fri) Pop into this women-run restaurant for some of the tastiest *almuerzos* around. It's mostly vegetarian and always wholesome and filling. For $1.80, you can't go wrong. Also see the boxed text on p201.

Raymipampa (☎ 283 4159; Benigno Malo 8-59; mains $3-5; ☽ 8:30am-11pm Mon-Sat, 9:30am-10pm Sun) Recently remodeled and as friendly as ever, this Cuenca institution makes a great hangout for locals and travelers alike. The food hangs somewhere between Ecuadorian comfort food and diner fare.

Aguacolla Café (☎ 282 4029; Bajada de Todos Santos; almuerzos $2; ☽ 11am-10pm Mon-Fri) You're best off trying the artificial rock-climbing cave *before* you fill your belly with a vegetarian *almuerzo*. Think peace, love and organics.

La Olla Mágica (☎ 245 2222; Hermano Miguel 6-70; mains $1.50-2.50; ☽ 9am-9pm Mon-Sat) It's hard to beat pork chops at this price ($2.50), served on a wooden platter with potatoes and salad.

Las Brasas de San Juan (☎ 282 1801; Jaramillo 7-34; mains $3-9; ☽ 4-10pm Mon-Sat) Though a hair on the pricey side, one reader claimed they're the best steaks in Ecuador. This grill house is lovely, the owners are friendly and you definitely get what you pay for. Pizzas and pastas too.

El Pedregal Azteca (☎ 282 3652; Gran Colombia 10-33; mains $5-9; ☽ noon-3pm & 6-10:30pm Mon-Sat, to 11:30pm Fri & Sat) El Pedregal serves delicious Mexican food (probably because it is Mexican-run), and the atmosphere follows suit. The portions can be a bit small, however, so fill up on the free corn chips. Live music Friday nights.

La Barraca (☎ 284 2967, 282 5094; Borrero 9-68; mains $3-4; ☽ noon-midnight, till late Fri & Sat) Casual atmosphere and great music complement excellent snacks (guacamole and chips, popcorn and the like), which all make perfect bedmates with an ice-cold beer. The 'international' mains, however, leave plenty to be desired.

Los Capulies (☎ 284 5887; cnr Presidente Córdova & Borrero; mains $3.50-5.50; ☽ 9am-4pm & 6pm-late Mon-Sat) Los Capulies serves delicious, reasonably priced, traditional Ecuadorian meals and livens things up with entertainment on weekends. The cantina out back provides after-dinner fun. Popular with tour groups.

Café Austria (☎ 284 0899; Benigno Malo 5-45; light meals $1-3; ☽ 9am-11pm) This classy but casual café pulls an excellent espresso and serves tasty Austrian-style cakes to go with it. Sandwiches on wholegrain bread make for a good lunch.

Tutto Freddo (cnr Benigno Malo & Bolívar; ice cream $0.75-3; ☽ 9am-11pm, to 10pm Sun) Across from the main plaza, this is likely the best (and most popular) spot in town for a mammoth banana split or a towering milkshake. And the upstairs booths are great.

Heladería Holanda (☎ 283 1449; Benigno Malo 9-55; snacks $1-2.50; ☽ 9am-7:30pm, to 6:30pm Sun) Serves up excellent coffee, ice cream, cakes, yogurt and fruit salads.

New York Pizza (☎ 284 2792, 282 5674; Gran Colombia 10-43; mains $1.50-3.50; ☽ 9:30am-11pm Mon-Sat, 11am-10pm Sun) Pop in here for thin-crust pizza starting at $1.10 a slice.

The following all serve straightforward Ecuadorian fare and are best for their cheap *almuerzos*. You'll find more locals than tourists at most.

Restaurant El Paraíso (Bolívar near Vega; almuerzos & merienda $2, mains $1.50-2; 8am-10pm Mon-Sat) All vegetarian; ice cream too.

Grecia (282 4869; Gran Colombia 9-69; almuerzos $1.50, mains $3-4; 8am-5pm Mon-Sat) Excellent *almuerzos* (hence the crowd).

Goura (245 0531; Jaramillo 7-27; almuerzos $2, mains $2-4; 8:30am-3pm Mon-Sat) Hearty vegetarian, organic *almuerzos*. Pizzas and curries too.

El Cántaro (282 3989; Bolívar 8-50; mains $3-4, almuerzos $2.20; 8am-10pm Mon-Sat) Big *almuerzos*, convenient location.

Entertainment
BARS & NIGHTCLUBS
Cuenca is Ecuador's third-largest city, so you'll always find something to do on the weekend. Midweek, however, the place can be as dead as Pizarro. Discos are open Thursday through Saturday nights – doors open around 10pm but things don't really get moving until around midnight. Bars are generally open nightly, often as early as 5pm.

There are numerous cozy and welcoming little bars along Honorato Vásquez, near El Cafecito (p101). They change owners and names regularly, but they usually keep the same vibe – which is generally great for a few stiff ones among friends. East of Hermano Miguel along Presidente Córdova, there are several wildly popular (and equally loud) bars with dance floors.

Tal Cual (285 0207; Calle Larga 7-57; 5:30pm-midnight Tue-Thu, 5:30pm-2am Fri & Sat) Tucked in beside a narrow stairway, this bar attracts a friendly local crowd, especially Thursdays through Saturdays when there's live music. Friday and Saturday it's salsa and *merengue*, and the chairs are cleared for dancing.

La Mesa (Gran Colombia 3-55) If you *really* want to salsa, hit this longtime favorite, where locals and tourists shake their groove-things on a small, friendly and always hot dance floor. The tiny sign out front is easy to miss.

Café Eucalyptus (284 9157; www.caféeucalyptus .com; Gran Colombia 9-41) This is an excellent spot for a relaxed drink with a mostly gringo crowd. Wednesday nights, women drink free from 6pm to 10pm. On Saturdays, live salsa music or DJs keep the crowd jumping into the wee hours.

Del Tranquilo (284 3418; deltranquilo@hotmail .com; Borrero near Mariscal Sucre) This one's a fun but tame bar in an old converted house. People go for the live music Thursday through Saturday nights.

Bar San Ángel (283 9090; cnr Hermano Miguel & Presidente Córdova; admission $3; 9am-2am Wed-Sat) On the 2nd floor of an old building, San Ángel is too small to be a nightclub, but the atmosphere sure pushes in that direction. It's popular with locals who come for the live music Thursday through Saturday nights.

WunderBar (283 1274; Hermano Miguel at Calle Larga) This hip, hoppin' German-owned hangout near the river is always good for a fun night. Food is served.

Kaos (Honorato Vásquez 6-11) The laid-back and British-owned Kaos has couches, pool tables and snacks – great for a good night out.

Fuzzión (Presidente Córdova near Cueva drink minimum $2) Of the bars located along Presidente Córdova, this is one of the busiest. It's a hypertrendy place, and the table-talk stops after midnight when the music gets loud and the dancing kicks in.

CINEMAS
Movies cost about $4 per person. Check Cuenca's newspaper *El Mercurio* for cinema listings. **Teatro Casa de Cultura** (Luís Cordero at Mariscal Sucre) screens good movies, and for blockbuster Hollywood flicks in English (with Spanish subtitles) head to **Cine Cuenca** (Padre Aguirre near Mariscal Lamar) or **Multicines** (Milenium Plaza, Astudillo s/n).

Shopping
Cuenca is the center of the *paja toquilla* (or 'panama') hat trade (see the boxed text on p206). The region also produces many other fine handicrafts, including *ikat* textiles, which are made with threads that are tie-dyed before weaving – a method dating from pre-Columbian times. Typical *cuencano* baskets are huge. Gold and silver-filigreed jewelry from the nearby village of Chordeleg can sometimes be found too.

HATS
Cuenca is the center of the panama hat industry and one of the best places to buy straw hats. Cuenca's hat tradition – and its haberdasheries – can be roughly divided into two types: hats for export (panama hats) and hats made for and used by local

IT'S NOT A PANAMA, IT'S A MONTECRISTI!

For well over a century, Ecuador has endured the world mistakenly crediting another country with its most famous export – the panama hat. To any Ecuadorian worth his or her salt, the panama hat is a *sombrero de paja toquilla* (toquilla-straw hat), and to the connoisseur it's a Montecristi, named after the most famous hat-making town of all. It's certainly not a paaa…

The origin of this misnomer – surely one of the world's greatest – dates to the 1800s, when Spanish entrepreneurs, quick to recognize the unrivaled quality of *paja toquilla,* began exporting them via Panama. During the 19th century, workers on the Panama Canal used these light and extremely durable hats to protect themselves from the tropical sun and helped solidify the association with Panama.

Paja toquilla hats are made from the fibrous fronds of the *toquilla* palm *(Carludovica palmata),* which grows in the humid, hilly inland regions of the central Ecuadorian coast, particularly around Montecristi (p298) and Jipijapa (p299). A few Asian and several South American countries have tried to grow the palm to compete with the Ecuadorian hat trade, but none could duplicate the quality of the fronds grown here.

The work that goes into these hats is astonishing. First the palms are harvested for their shoots, which are ready just before they open into leaves. Bundles of shoots are then transported by donkey and truck to coastal villages where the fibers are prepared.

The preparation process begins with beating the shoots on the ground and then splitting them by hand to remove the long, thin, flat, cream-colored leaves. The leaves are tied into bundles and boiled in huge vats of water for about 20 minutes before being hung to dry for three days. Some are soaked in sulfur for bleaching. As the split leaves dry, they shrink and roll up into the round strands that are used for weaving.

Some of the finished straw stays on the coast, but most is purchased by buyers from Cuenca and surrounding areas, where the straw is woven into hats. Indeed, you'll see more panama hats in and around Cuenca than you'll see anywhere in Ecuador.

The weaving process itself is arduous, and the best weavers work only in the evening and early in the morning, before the heat causes their fingers to sweat. Some work only by moonlight. Weaves vary from a loose crochet (characteristic of the hats you see sold everywhere) to a tighter 'Brisa' weave, which is used for most quality panama hats.

Hats are then graded by the density of their weaves, which generally fall into four categories: standard, superior, *fino* (fine) and *superfino* (superfine). Most hats you see are standard or superior. If you hold a real *superfino* up to the light, you shouldn't see a single hole. The best of them will hold water and some are so finely woven and so pliable that they can supposedly be rolled up and pulled through a man's ring!

After the hats are woven, they still need to be trimmed, bleached (if they're to be white), blocked and banded. Then they're ready to sell. Although standard grade hats start around $15 in Ecuador, a *superfino* can cost anywhere between $100 and $500. While it may seem expensive, the same hat will easily fetch three times that amount on shelves in North America and Europe. And considering the work that goes into a *superfino,* it rightly should.

indigenous people. Visit one of Cuenca's traditional hatters on Tarqui and you'll see hundreds of refurbished white straw hats, tagged for their owners and hanging everywhere. They usually have a few top-quality hats for sale, too. Other hat shops are tourist oriented.

Casa del Sombrero Alberto Pulla (☎ 282 9399; Tarqui 6-91; ☉ 6am-6pm) This is the shop of Cuenca's most famous hatter, 78-year-old Alberto Pulla, who has been refurbishing hats since he was six. After he shows you

the many hats he has for sale (upstairs), he'll show you all the magazine articles written about him around the world.

Sombreros Don Migui (Tarqui near Calle Larga) Another hatter that works more with the local market, this old place has some excellent *superfinos* for sale.

Barranco (☎ 283 1569; Calle Larga 10-41; ☉ 9am-12:30pm & 1:30-6pm Mon-Fri) Barranco has been finishing panama hats since the 1950s, and its factory is now open to visitors. There's a small museum showing the history of panama hats, and someone will walk you through the factory explaining the entire process of finishing hats. There's plenty of pretty hats for sale too.

Homero Ortega P & Hijos (☎ 280 9000; www .homeroortega.com; Gil Ramirez Davalos) More akin to a hat emporium, this is Ecuador's best-known hat seller. The company exports around the world and has a huge selection of quality men's and women's straw hats.

La Paja Toquilla (☎ 282 0058; cnr Hermano Miguel & Jaramillo) This small store sells some stylish straw hats in both men's and women's styles.

CRAFTS

There are several good craft stores on Gran Colombia and on the blocks just north of Parque Calderón. The best place for a serious spree, however, is the **Casa de la Mujer** (☎ 284 5854; Torres 7-33; ☷ 9:30am-1pm & 3-6:30pm Mon-Fri, 9am-3pm Sat), which houses over 100 craft stalls and makes for hours of shopping fun.

The Thursday **Plaza Rotary market** (Mariscal Lamar & Hermano Miguel) is mainly for locals (which means pigs and polyester, fruit and furniture), but there are a few craft stalls. You're best off heading to the nearby **craft market** (cnr Sangurima & Machuca; ☷ 8am-5pm), which has an odd but interesting combination of basketry, ceramics, iron-work, kitchen utensils, bright plastic animals, gaudy religious paraphernalia and guinea pig roasters (great gift for mom, but tough to get home).

OUTDOOR EQUIPMENT

For outdoor supplies:

Acción (☎ 283 3526; Bolívar 12-70; ☷ 9am-1pm & 3-8pm Mon-Sat) Camping, fishing, mountaineering, knives and more.

Artículos Deportivos (cnr Presidente Córdova & Benigno Malo) Sells butane for stoves and a few other supplies.

Explorador Andino (☎ 284 7320; cnr Calle Larga & Benigno Malo) Sells knives, sleeping pads and bags and is worth a peek.

Getting There & Away
AIR

Cuenca's **Aeropuerto Mariscal Lamar** (☎ 286 2203; Av España) is conveniently located 2km from the heart of town.

TAME (airport ☎ 286 2400; downtown ☎ 288 9097, 288 9581; Astudillo 2-22; ☷ 8:30am-1pm & 2-6:30pm Mon-Fri, 9:30am-12:30pm Sat) flies daily to Quito ($63) and Guayaquil ($49). **Icaro** (☎ 281 1450; Milenium Plaza,

Astudillo s/n; ☷ 10am-8pm Mon-Sat, to 7pm Sun) flies to both destinations for the same price.

BUS

Located about 1.5km from downtown, Cuenca's **bus terminal** (☎ 284 3888; Av España) is served by dozens of different bus companies, many with two or three buses every hour.

There are daily buses to Ingapirca (p194), Jima (p210), and Gualaceo, Chordeleg and Sígsig (p209). Buses to Parque Nacional Cajas leave from the Transporte Occidental stop, west of the center; see p209 for complete information.

There are two routes to Guayaquil, the shorter one via Parque Nacional Cajas and Molleturo ($8, 3½ to four hours), and the longer one via La Troncal and Cañar ($8, 5½ hours). Buses leave hourly for Machala ($4.50, four hours); a few continue to Huaquillas ($8, seven hours).

Buses for Azogues ($0.60, 45 minutes) leave every 15 minutes, many continuing to Cañar ($1.50, 1½ hours) and Alausí ($4, four hours).

For Quito ($10, 10 to 12 hours), there are buses about every hour. There's several departures each day to Riobamba ($6, six hours), Ambato ($7, seven hours) and Latacunga ($9, 8½ hours).

There are buses every hour from 6am to 10pm to Loja ($7, five hours) via Saraguro ($5, 3½ hours).

For the southern Oriente, daily buses go to Macas via Guarumales ($8.50, eight hours) or via Limón ($8.50, 10 hours). There are two daily departures (at 11am and 2pm) with **Cooperativa 16 de Agosto** (☎ 283 2703) to Gualaquiza ($7, six hours) along the rough and scenic road via Sígsig.

CAR

For car rental, try **Localiza** (airport ☎ 280 3198/3; España ☎ 286 3902, 286 0174; España 1485 near Granada), which has a branch at the airport and another some 400m northeast of the airport.

Getting Around

Taxis cost about $2 between downtown and either the airport or the bus terminal. From the front of the bus terminal, buses depart regularly to downtown ($0.25). To get to the bus terminal from downtown, use the bus stop on Padre Aguirre, near the flower market. Most buses are marked 'Terminal.'

Local buses for Turi ($0.25), 4km south of the center, go along Avenida Solano.

AROUND CUENCA

☎ 07

From small indigenous villages to hot springs and hiking, there's ample opportunity for excursions from Cuenca. A thorough visit to the city accounts for a couple days worth of day trips to outlying areas. You can easily visit Gualaceo, Chordeleg and Sígsig in one day, and hit Parque Nacional Cajas the next. The ruins of Ingapirca (p194) also make a good day trip from town.

Baños

Not to be confused with the Baños described in the Central Highlands chapter, this Baños (essentially a suburb of Cuenca) has sulfurous hot springs that are popular with weekending *cuencanos*. It's debatable whether it's worth the 5km trip from town – unless you stay or play at **Hostería Durán** (☎ 289 2485/6; www.hosteriaduran.com; r with breakfast $56). This is by far the best complex in Baños, with a private thermal swimming pool, hot pools, steam rooms, pleasant gardens, lovely hotel rooms and the best restaurant in the area. Nonguests can use the private thermal tubs (simple, tiled, square tubs fed by a hose) for $3.50 per person. The swimming pools cost an additional $3.50 per person.

Use of other thermal pools around town costs $1 to $2. Several simple restaurants in the area serve inexpensive Ecuadorian food.

A taxi to Baños costs $4, or you can take a bus ($0.25) from Avenida Torres by the Plaza San Francisco market.

Parque Nacional Cajas

Only 30km west of Cuenca, **Parque Nacional Cajas** (admission $10) encompasses 288 sq km of stunning moor-like *páramo* dotted with more than 200 chilly lakes that shine like jewels against a bleak, rough countryside. An easy day trip from Cuenca, the park has excellent hiking, great trout fishing, unique bird-watching and rugged camping.

Most of the park sits between 4000m and 4500m, so it doesn't normally snow, but the winds and rains can make it very cold. Be

well prepared with warm, windproof gear and plenty of energy.

In sheltered hollows and natural depressions of the terrain, small forests of the *Polylepis* (quenua) tree are seen. This tree grows at the highest altitudes of any tree in the world, and forcing your way into one of these dense dwarf forests is like entering a scene from a Brothers Grimm fairytale.

The driest months are August to January, but it can rain anytime. Night temperatures can drop below freezing, especially in the dry season. Water temperatures are usually about or below 5°C (40°F) – you can leave your swimming suit at home.

INFORMATION
The Laguna Toreadora **ranger station** is on the northern side of the park, a few hundred meters from the park **entrance station**, where you pay your entry fee. The ranger station provides free glossy topographical trail maps. These maps are *sometimes* available at the tourist information office (p196) in Cuenca.

ACTIVITIES
There are a number of signed trails in the most popular area (around Laguna Toreadora) that are suitable for **hikes** of a few hours. Also near the lake is a trail signed for Mirador Ajahuaico, which goes to the top of a nearby mountain and offers impressive views. Multiday treks are possible all the way across the park – the two most popular trails are shown on the map but are poorly signposted, so compass skills are important.

SLEEPING
You can usually sleep at the ranger station (but don't rely on it, as there are only eight beds), which also has a kitchen. Beds have mattresses only, so bring a sleeping bag. Camping is allowed anywhere in the recreation area for $4 per person per night. The bus passes within a few hundred meters of the ranger station.

GETTING THERE & AWAY
Guayaquil-bound buses pass through the park and directly in front of the ranger station and entrance, but unfortunately drivers refuse to sell reduced-fare tickets for the one-hour ride. To avoid paying the full $8 fare to Guayaquil, take a Transporte Occi-

dental bus ($1.25, one hour) in Cuenca from Ricardo Darque between Av de las Américas and Victor Manuel Albornoz. This bus stop is west of the center, so you're best off taking a taxi ($2) there. It still comes out cheaper. The buses depart daily at 6:15am, 7am and 10:20am and at noon, 2pm, 4pm and 5pm. To return to Cuenca, flag any passing Cuenca-bound bus.

A southern road passes the park at the villages of Soldados and Angas, where there are small ranger stations but almost no facilities. These tiny and remote villages are rarely used as access points, but it's possible. The earlier mentioned Transporte Occidental buses go to both Soldados ($1.25, one hour, 34km) and Angas ($1.75, 1¾ hours, 56km).

Apart from the bus, you can take a taxi (about $45) or go on a day trip with one of the tour agencies in Cuenca.

Gualaceo, Chordeleg & Sígsig
Famous for their **Sunday markets**, these three villages together make a great day trip from Cuenca. If you start out early, you could easily visit all three markets and be back in Cuenca for happy hour. Gualaceo has the biggest market (mainly produce, animals and household goods) and the best hotel selection. Chordeleg's market is smaller but good for textiles and jewelry. Sígsig is an important center for 'panama' hats, and its market is the least touristy of all.

GETTING THERE & AWAY
From Cuenca's bus terminal, buses leave every half hour to Gualaceo ($0.80, 50 minutes), Chordeleg ($1, one hour) and Sígsig ($1.25, 1½ hours). You can visit Gualaceo and then walk the approximate 5km to Chordeleg; there are plenty of buses, but the stroll is nice. Buses pass Chordeleg's plaza for Sígsig ($0.50) at least once an hour. Buses return from Sígsig to Cuenca about every hour for $1.

GUALACEO
Gualaceo's pretty location by Río Gualaceo makes the town a popular weekend destination for *cuencanos*, many who have weekend homes here. It is 25km due east of Cuenca, at about 2370m above sea level. There are several restaurants by the river, and a stroll along the banks is a nice way to spend an afternoon.

The Sunday market is several blocks from the bus terminal. There is also an animal market across the covered bridge, on the east bank of the river. The market is not geared towards tourists (there are very few crafts for sale), but is colorful and fun to visit.

There's little reason to spend the night, but if you decide to, you'll find acceptable budget rooms at the family-run **Residencial Gualaceo** (☎ 225 5006; Gran Colombia 3-02; r per person with shared/private bath $5/8). For more comfort, try **Parador Turístico Gualaceo** (☎ 255 110/126; Gran Colombia; s/d $16/22; 🏊), about 1km south of town.

CHORDELEG

About 5km south of Gualaceo, Chordeleg is a pretty little crafts town, known throughout Ecuador for its gold and silver filigree jewelry. The quality has definitely dropped over the decades, but you can still pick up an interesting piece if you search. But beware of low-grade pieces masquerading as 24-karat.

Chordeleg also produces wood carvings, pottery, textiles, embroidered clothing and plenty of 'panama' hats. On the central plaza, a small **museum** (admission free; 🕙 8am-5pm Tue-Sun) details the history and techniques of many of these local handicrafts. Some of the locally made work is for sale.

The tiny village of **San Bartolomé** is off the road between Chordeleg and Sígsig and is famed for its guitar makers.

SÍGSIG

A pleasant colonial village, little happens in Sígsig apart from the Sunday market. It is about 25km south of Gualaceo and is the center of an important hat-making region. On the outskirts of the village, in the old hospital, the **Asociación de Toquilleras Maria Auxiliadora** (ATMA; ☎ 226 6014, 226 6377; Vía Sígsig-Chigüinda, Río Santa Barbara; 🕙 8:30am-4:30pm Mon-Fri) is a women's hat-making cooperative that sells hats far more cheaply than in Cuenca or Quito and provides more direct income for the hat makers.

There are a couple of restaurants on the main market plaza and several basic *residenciales* (cheap hotels) in town.

JIMA

☎ 07 / pop 3500 / elevation 2630m

Just above the Río Moya and surrounded by gentle green hills, Jima (spelled Gima on some maps) is the heart of apple country. It's a quiet, dirt-road village with as many horses as cars, the kind of place where school kids stop and giggle at the odd foreigner who happens through. Besides being a good base for hiking, it's a fine place to unwind and experience rural Ecuador.

With the help of Peace Corps volunteers and Projects for Peace (www.projectsforpeace.org), Jima fired up a community tourism project to provide alternative and sustainable income to project members. One component is the **Centro de Informes** (Information Center; ☎ 241 8270), where you can hire local guides (about $10/19 for two people for a half/full day) to take you on hikes ranging from shorter orchid-spotting jaunts to three-day tramps into the Oriente. You can also pop in for trail information.

Also part of the project, **Hostal Chacapamba** (☎ 241 8035; r per person $4) offers simple but spotless lodging in private rooms with very comfortable beds and kitschy bedspreads.

Buses from Cuenca ($1, 1½ hours) leave from across the Feria Libre, west of the center. To get to the Feria Libre, take a cab ($2), or bus from either Presidente Córdova or Mariscal Lamar; these are signed 'Feria Libre.' There are daily morning departures at 6am, 8:30am and 11am (7am, 8am and 8:30am on Sundays) with **Transportes Jima** (☎ 241 8011).

FROM CUENCA TO MACHALA

☎ 07

The road to the coast passes through impressive mountain scenery. Some 43km from Cuenca it runs through the small town of **Girón**, whose claim to fame is the **Chorro de Girón** waterfall. The town is easily recognizable from the road above by the red-tiled roofs. There's a cheap hotel in town, but no real need to stay. Many operators visit the falls as a $30 day trip from Cuenca, though you can do it yourself for about $5. Simply bus to Girón and hire a pickup truck (about $4.50) to take you the 5km to the entrance to the falls. The walk takes about two hours.

About 37km beyond Girón is **Santa Isabel**, where buses often stop for a meal break. Just below Santa Isabel, the scenery changes both suddenly and dramatically as the road winds through completely barren mountains with no signs of life. Just as suddenly, a forest of *columnar* cacti appears, which soon gives way to cloud forest mixed with tropical agriculture.

About 45km beyond Santa Isabel is the town of **Pasaje**, and 25km further is Machala (p339).

SARAGURO

About 110km south of Cuenca, after passing through scenic pastureland that is criss-crossed by broken fences and spotted with black-and-white cows, the Panamericana crosses the provincial line into Loja. The road continues through eerie *páramo* with spectacular views until it reaches Saraguro, 165km south of Cuenca.

The region of Saraguro, which means 'land of corn' in Quichua, is home to the indigenous Saraguro, the most successful indigenous group in the southern highlands. The Saraguro originally lived in the Lake Titicaca region of Peru, but were forcibly relocated through the empire's system of colonization, known as *mitimaes*.

Today, the Saraguro are readily identifiable by their traditional dress. Both men and women (but especially the women) wear striking flat white felt hats with wide brims that are often spotted on the underside. The men sport a single ponytail and wear a black poncho and knee-length black shorts, occasionally covered with a small white apron. They often carry *alfajoras*: double shoulder bags with one pouch in front and one behind. The women wear heavy, pleated jet-black skirts and shawls fastened with ornate silver pins called *tupus*, which are highly prized and often passed down from mother to daughter as heirlooms.

The Saraguro were well known for their jewelry, but this craft is dying out. Today, cattle-raising is their main occupation.

The best day to be in Saraguro is Sunday, when the **local market** draws Saraguros – dressed finely for the occasion – from the surrounding countryside.

Sleeping & Eating

Residencial Saraguro (☎ 220 0286; cnr Loja & Antonio Castro; r per person $4) As basic as it is, this is still a great little place to crash, considering the

---

MOTHER SPOON

As you roll into Saraguro, one thing becomes clear: it's not a tourist town. It's a market town, where indigenous Saraguro spill in every weekend from outlying communities to buy and sell and go to church bedecked in their traditional black-and-white clothing. There's little set up for the curious visitor. And there's definitely no veggie burgers. But you will find a hearty, healthy meal at Mamá Cuchara (p212). The best part is, your money will be going to a good cause.

Mamá Cuchara – 'Mother Spoon' – is part of the Asociación de Mujeres Indígenas Saraguros (Asomis), an association of indigenous women between ages 18 and 65, working for the equal treatment of Saraguro women. Association president Laura Quizhpe, who is usually at the restaurant register or carrying out plates to customers, explains that Saraguro women face double discrimination – from society *and* from men. According to Quizhpe, the goal of Asomis is to educate Saraguro women, to provide economic alternatives and to raise consciousness at the family level.

The first step began in 1992 with the creation of Mamá Cuchara (p212). A restaurant made sense, says Quizhpe, because the only thing the women really knew how to do was cook. Now the restaurant is the cornerstone of the association. Mamá Cuchara purchases all of its food directly from indigenous women in the region, putting money directly into the hands of Saraguro families. The fresh, often organic products are then used in the restaurant. The money the restaurant makes goes into the association 'bank' to provide loans to women who need it.

There are currently 103 members (not counting the daughters of the members) from 18 outlying Saraguro communities. The women come to town once a month, sometimes walking over an hour to get there, to attend meetings at Mamá Cuchara. They discuss ways to incorporate the family, educate their children, gain support from the men, and provide education and training for the women.

Market day in Saraguro is one of Ecuador's special experiences, offering a glimpse into one of the country's most successful and most distinctive indigenous cultures. Eating at Mamá Cuchara offers the visitor the chance to give something back. And the food, modest as it may be, sure feels good goin' down.

friendliness of the owners, the little interior garden and the well-kept rooms. All have shared baths.

Hostal Samana Wasi (☎ 220 0315; 10 de Marzo near the Panamericana; s/d $8/16) Four blocks from the plaza, this is the most comfortable hotel in town. Conveniently, there's an attached Internet café.

Mamá Cuchara (Parque Central; mains $1.50-2.50; ☻ 7am-10pm Sun-Fri) 'Mother Spoon,' as the name aptly means, serves up hearty, tasty *almuerzos* and dinners, always depending on what's available. Money goes to the indigenous women's association that runs it (see the boxed text on p211). Breakfasts are available.

There are several other restaurants facing the plaza that serve reliable food.

Getting There & Away

Any Loja-bound bus from Cuenca will drop you a block from the main plaza ($5, 3½ hours). Buses to Loja ($2, 1½ hours, 62km) leave hourly during the day. The bus office is a block from the main plaza.

LOJA

☎ 07 / pop 170,000 / elevation 2100m

From Saraguro, the road drops steadily to Loja, whose elevation and proximity to the Oriente gives the town a delightfully temperate climate. Despite Loja's isolation (the nearest town of any importance is five hours to the north), Loja is one of the county's most cultured cities. Founded in 1548, it's one of the oldest towns in Ecuador and is home to a nationally renowned university, an important conservatory and a law school. The city is famous for its musicians (it seems like everyone in town plays something) and its award-winning parks. Despite all this, and the fact that it's the provincial capital, it's still a small town at heart – so much so that you'll find a day or two here plenty of time. Loja is a good base for visiting nearby Parque Nacional Podocarpus and the main stop before heading south to Vilcabamba and (if you're roaming that far) Peru.

Information

EMERGENCY

Police Station (☎ 257 3600; Argentina near Bolivia) Southwest of the center.

Red Cross ambulance (☎ 257 0200)

INTERNET ACCESS

Cybersat (Rocafuerte near Bolívar; per hr $1; ☻ 7:30am-7:30pm)

Jungle Net (☎ 257 5212; Miguel Riofrío 13-64; per hr $1)

World Net (Colón 14-69; per hr $1; ☻ 9am-9pm Mon-Sat, 10am-8pm Sun) Great computers and net-to-phone services.

MEDICAL SERVICES

Clínica San Agustín (☎ 257 0314; cnr 18 de Noviembre & Azuay) Clinic with a good reputation.

Hospital (☎ 257 0540; cnr Samaniego & San Juan de Diós)

MONEY

Banco de Guayaquil (Eguiguren near Valdivieso) Bank with ATM; changes traveler's checks. There are plenty of other banks around town.

POST

Post office (cnr Colón & Sucre)

TELEPHONE

Pacifictel (Eguiguren near Olmedo) Telephone call center.

TOURIST INFORMATION

Ministerio del Medio Ambiente (☎ 258 5421, 257 1534; podocam@impsat.net.ec; Sucre 4-35) Responsible for administering Parque Nacional Podocarpus; provides information and simple maps.

Tourist office (iTur; ☎ 258 1251; cnr Bolívar & Eguiguren; ☻ 8:30am-1pm & 3-6:30pm Mon-Fri, 9am-noon Sat) Helpful, with some maps available.

Sights & Activities

There's no denying that Loja's a relatively uneventful place, nor the fact that after an afternoon of exploration you'll have seen just about everything downtown. Once you do, hit the parks – they're what really make Loja unique.

DOWNTOWN

Loja's main plaza is the lively Parque Central, where hordes of people – office workers, cab drivers, newspaper vendors – gather to start the day. Walk over to the east side of the plaza and check out the ornate interior of the **cathedral** (Parque Central). On the south side of the plaza, the **Museo del Banco Central** (10 de Agosto; admission $0.25; ☻ 9am-4pm Mon-Fri) has a small exhibit of local archaeology, ethnography and art.

Two blocks south, the **Church of Santo Domingo** (cnr Bolívar & Rocafuerte) is worth a peek for a

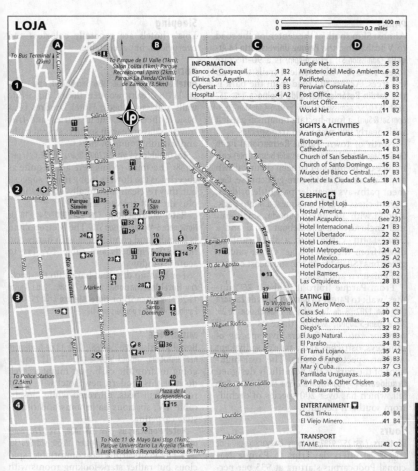

LOJA

INFORMATION	
Banco de Guayaquil	1 B2
Clínica San Agustín	2 A4
Cybersat	3 B3
Hospital	4 A2
Jungle Net	5 B3
Ministerio del Medio Ambiente	6 B2
Pacifictel	7 B3
Peruvian Consulate	8 B3
Post Office	9 B2
Tourist Office	10 B2
World Net	11 B2

SIGHTS & ACTIVITIES	
Aratinga Aventuras	12 B4
Biotours	13 C3
Cathedral	14 B3
Church of San Sebastián	15 B4
Church of Santo Domingo	16 B3
Museo del Banco Central	17 B3
Puerta de la Ciudad & Café	18 A1

SLEEPING	
Grand Hotel Loja	19 A3
Hostal America	20 A2
Hotel Acapulco	(see 23)
Hotel Internacional	21 B3
Hotel Libertador	22 B2
Hotel Londres	23 B3
Hotel Metropolitan	24 A2
Hotel Mexico	25 A2
Hotel Podocarpus	26 A3
Hotel Ramses	27 B2
Las Orquídeas	28 B3

EATING	
A lo Mero Mero	29 B2
Casa Sol	30 C3
Cebichería 200 Millas	31 C3
Diego's	32 B3
El Jugo Natural	33 B3
El Paraíso	34 B2
El Tamal Lojano	35 A2
Forno di Fango	36 B3
Mar y Cuba	37 C3
Parrillada Uruguayas	38 A1
Pavi Pollo & Other Chicken Restaurants	39 B4

ENTERTAINMENT	
Casa Tinku	40 B4
El Viejo Minero	41 B4

TRANSPORT	
TAME	42 C2

glimpse of the religious paintings inside. Two blocks north of the Parque Central, **Plaza San Francisco** (Bolívar & Colón) is crowned by a statue of the city's founder astride his horse.

Be sure to walk over to **Plaza de la Independencia** (cnr Alonso de Mercadillo & Valdivieso), where the citizens of Loja gathered on November 18, 1820 to declare their independence from Spain. It's a lovely plaza, flanked by old, wooden, colonial-era buildings with pillared overhangs and little shuttered balconies. On the plaza's southern side stands the wooden, baby-blue and white **Church of San Sebastián**, resembling something off a movie set. Walk south of the plaza and turn right on narrow **Lourdes**, the best preserved and oldest colonial street in Loja.

AROUND TOWN

North of downtown, the **Puerta de la Ciudad** (Door to the City; 258 7122; admission free; 10am-10pm Mon-Fri, 11am-10pm Sat & Sun) is a giant castle with an arched doorway spanning Sucre, the entrance to downtown. Inside the castle are two floors of art galleries, a **café** (258 7194; 10am-noon & 3-10pm Mon-Fri, 2-10pm Sat, 2-9pm Sun) and several lookouts over town.

For a pleasant walk, head east from the center on Rocafuerte and cross Río Zamora. From there, climb the small hill to the statue of the **Virgin of Loja**, lovely city views.

Just north of downtown, **Parque de El Valle** is the heart of the neighborhood of El Valle. It's worth a visit to see the old church and the wooden buildings surrounding the plaza.

PARKS

Almost 5km south of the center, on the road to Vilcabamba, the **Parque Universitario La Argelia** (admission $1; ☼ 9am-4pm) is a 90-hectare forest reserve with excellent trails through the trees. Across the road from the park is the **Jardín Botánico Reynaldo Espinosa** (☎ 257 1841, 257 0252; admission $0.60; ☼ 9am-4pm Mon-Fri, 1-6pm Sat & Sun), a four-hectare botanical garden with nearly 900 plant and tree species.

North of town, **Parque Recreacional Jipiro** (Av Santiago de las Montañas at Salvador Bustamante) can induce the feeling you've been shrunk down and tossed into a miniature-golf course. Cement pathways meander past little bridges, a giant chess board, mosques, a skate park, a pond with a Chinese pagoda, small animal enclosures, a paddleboat pond and a 'Euro-Latin' castle with a slide running down from the top. To get there, catch a green bus ($0.25) from the southeast corner of Eguiguren and Peña.

From Parque Jipiro it is about 25 minutes' walk to **Parque La Banda/Orillas de Zamora** (☎ 254 1202; 8 de Diciembre s/n; admission $0.25; ☼ 8:30am-5:30pm), where there is a small outdoor zoo that shelters five species of monkeys, ostriches and a pair of sadly kept Andean spectacled bears. The real highlight of the park is the beautifully designed **Orquideario** (☼ 8am-1pm & 2-6pm Mon-Fri, 8am-6pm Sat), which has over 200 species of orchids from southern Ecuador.

Tours

Biotours (☎ 257 9387; biotours_ec@yahoo.es; 24 de Mayo 08-28) offers day trips to Parque Nacional Podocarpus starting at $35 per person (minimum two), including lunch.

Aratinga Aventuras (☎ 258 2434; Lourdes 14-80; ☼ closed for lunch) is great for bird-watching tours and guides. Both have received good reports.

Festivals & Events

El Día de La Virgen del Cisne (see the boxed text on p224) is celebrated in Loja on September 8 with huge processions.

An important fiesta celebrating the **Independence of Loja** takes place on November 18. Festivities may go on for a week, featuring parades and cultural events. The feast of **San Sebastián**, which coincides with the foundation of Loja, is celebrated annually on December 8.

Sleeping

Loja's hotels are generally colorless and overpriced, but acceptable.

BUDGET

Hotel Londres (☎ 256 1936; Sucre 07-51; r per person $4) With creaky wooden floors, big white walls and saggy beds, Hotel Londres is as basic as they come, but it's a tried-and-true travelers' favorite with spotless shared baths and friendly young owners.

Las Orquideas (☎ 258 7008; Bolívar 08-59; r per person $8) The small rooms here aren't quite as cheerful as the flowery lobby might suggest, but they're clean and totally acceptable – plus the staff are very friendly.

Hotel Metropolitan (☎ 257 0007/244; 18 de Noviembre 6-41; r per person $10) The Metropolitan is friendly and comfortable with hardwood floors, decent beds and cable TV. Try to score a window.

For beat-up digs that barely do the trick, try **Hotel Internacional** (☎ 257 8486; 10 de Agosto 15-28; r per person $7) or **Hotel Mexico** (☎ 257 0581; Eguiguren 15-89; r per person $4).

MIDRANGE

Hostal America (☎ 256 2887; Calle 18 de Noviembre near Imbabura; s/d incl breakfast $20/27) If you're going to drop the cash, you might as well do it at this modern new hotel with giant rooms, firm beds, mirrored white closets, cable TV, spacious bathrooms and office-style carpeting.

Hotel Podocarpus (☎ 258 1428, 257 9776; hotel podocarpus@hotmail.com; Eguiguren 16-50; s/d $23/30; ▣) The Podocarpus has comfortable, spacious but rather stark-looking rooms with cable TV and telephone. Each has a coffee table with armchairs, and the staff are extremely courteous.

Hotel Acapulco (☎ 257 0651; www.hotelacapulco .com.ec; Sucre 07-61; s/d incl breakfast $16/26) If you don't mind a windowless abode, the small rooms here do the trick. Bedroom doors open onto the interior, and potato chips and sodas are set out on the wooden dressers.

Grand Hotel Loja (☎ 258 6600/1; ghloja@hotmail .com; cnr Aguirre & Rocafuerte; s/d incl breakfast $36/60; ▣) Helpful and friendly, this large, modern hotel has comfortable rooms with 1970s-style golden bedspreads and incongruous decorations like mounted Guayasamín prints. It's a posh place for Loja, but do your best to get a room with a window.

Hotel Ramses (☎ 257 1402, 257 9868; www.ho
elramses.webjump.com; Colón 14-31; s/d incl breakfast
625/36) The multifloor Ramses has nice, big
carpeted rooms that has huge writing desks
with lamps, as well as the usual cable TV
and telephone. It is a bit worn but pleasant
and a good value.

Hotel Libertador (☎ 256 0779, 257 8278; www.ho
ellibertador.com.ec; Colón 14-30; s/d $43/55; ☎ ▯) The
highlights at Loja's most upscale hotel are
the buffet breakfast (included in the price),
hot and dry saunas, and a 4th-floor swimming pool with views. It's a traditional place
with suited-up staff and formal service.

Eating

On Sundays, families head out to the *comedores* (cheap restaurants) around Parque de
El Valle, many of which serve *cuy*. Loja specialties include *tamales lojanos* (a savory corn
dumpling steamed in a corn husk), *cecina*
(salty fried pork served with yucca) and some
of the country's best *humitas* (a lightly sweetened corn dumpling with cheese, steamed in
a corn husk).

El Tamal Lojano (☎ 258 2977; 18 de Noviembre
5-12; light items $0.70-1, almuerzos $2; ☒ 9am-2pm
& 4-8pm Mon-Sat) The *almuerzos* are good,
but the real reason to come is for the delicious *quimbolitos* (a sweet cake-like corn
dumpling wrapped in *achira* leaves), *humitas, empanadas de verde* (a plantain pastry
stuffed with seasoned chicken) and *tamales
lojanos*. Try them all!

Mar y Cuba (☎ 258 5154; Rocafuerte 09-00 at 24 de
Mayo; mains $4-5; ☒ 10am-4:30pm & 6:30-10pm Tue-Sat,
10am-4pm Sun) Along with commie-island clas-
sics like *ropa vieja* (a sort of shredded beef
stew), this Cuban restaurant serves excellent
seafood and several types of ceviche.

A lo Mero Mero (Sucre 06-22; mains $3-4, almuerzos
2; ☒ 9:30am-9pm Mon-Sat) It's not quite up to
Mexico City standards, but if you've a han-
kering for refried beans and tortillas, it's the
only place you'll get them.

Forno di Fango (☎ 258 2905; Bolívar 10-98; pizzas
4.50-13; ☒ noon-10:30pm) This spic-and-span
pizzería serves tasty pizzas pulled from an
adobe oven smack in the middle of the dining room. Lasagna too.

El Jugo Natural (☎ 257 5256; Eguiguren 14-20; light
meals $1-2; ☒ 7am-8pm) Pure, all-natural juices,
yogurt shakes, fruit salads and personalized
pizzas make up the menu at this small café.
It's great for a fruit-and-yogurt breakfast.

Diego's (☎ 256 0245; Colón 14-88; mains $3-5; ☒ 8am-
10pm Mon-Sat, 8am-3pm Sun) Formal waiters, faded
wallpaper and a casual clientele make this
Loja classic a surreal place. Plates include garlic chicken, pastas and filet mignon.

Salon Lolita (☎ 257 5603; Salvador Bustamante Celi
at Guayaquil, El Valle; mains $3-8; ☒ 11am-11pm) North
of downtown, this is *the* place for traditional
food from Loja. *Cuy* comes roasted whole
in $8, $10 or $12 sizes. They also serve a
traditional chicken dish called *gallina cuy-
ada* and *cecina*. Take an 'El Valle' bus from
Avenida Universitaria at Parque Bolívar.

Cebichería 200 Millas (☎ 257 3563; Peña 07-41;
mains $3.50-6; ☒ 9am-3pm) The place to go (with
everyone else) for good, reasonably priced
seafood lunches.

Parrillada Uruguayas (☎ 257 0260; Salinas 16-56;
mains $4-8; ☒ 5pm-2am) Serves whopping por-
tions of delicious grilled meats.

Casa Sol (☎ 258 8597; 24 de Mayo 07-04; snacks
$0.80-1.50; ☒ 9am-11pm) This cute new family
place serves traditional snacks at balcony
tables. Best in the evening.

El Paraíso (☎ 257 6977; Quito 14-50; set meal $2;
☒ 7am-9:30pm) Pop in here for good wholesome set vegetarian lunches and dinners at
$2 a pop. Good deal.

There are numerous grilled-chicken joints
along Alonso de Mercadillo, west of Bolívar,
where you can pick up a quarter-chicken
with soup and fries for about $2. **Pavi Pollo**
(Alonso de Mercadillo 14-99; ☒ 9am-11pm Mon-Sat, 9am-
8:30pm Sun) is a good one.

Entertainment

Although *lojanos* (people from Loja) are
known as good singers and guitar players,
nightlife in the town is fairly low key. On
Sunday nights from 8pm to 9pm, in the
Parque Central, the local military marching
band rips into what are likely the liveliest
drum-and-brass tunes you'll ever hear.

El Viejo Minero (Sucre 10-76) This rustic old
watering hole is the perfect place for a relaxed beer and snacks in a friendly pub-like
environment.

Casa Tinku (Alonso de Mercadillo near Valdivieso) Casa
Tinku is a spirited little bar with a great vibe;
there's usually live music on weekends.

Getting There & Away

AIR

Loja is served by La Toma airport, in Catamayo (see p223), some 30km to the west.

TAME flies to/from Quito ($49) Monday to Saturday and Guayaquil ($36) Tuesday through Thursday. Tickets can be purchased in Loja at **TAME** (☎ 257 0248; Av Ortega near 24 de Mayo; ⏰ 8:30am-1pm & 2:30-6pm Mon-Fri, 9am-1pm Sat).

For transport to the airport, call **Aerotaxi** (☎ 257 1327, 258 4423), which charges $4 per person for the 40-minute shuttle service to the airport or catch a bus to Catamayo ($1, 45 minutes) from the bus terminal.

BUS & TAXI

Almost all buses leave from the **bus terminal** (☎ 257 9592; Av Cuxibamba s/n), about 2km north of downtown. There are daily departures to the following places:

Destination	Cost (US$)	Duration (hr)
Ambato	$13	11
Catamayo	$1	¾
Cuenca	$7	5
Gualaquiza	$6	6
Guayaquil	$9	8-9
Macará	$6	6
Machala	$5	5
Quito	$15	14-15
Riobamba	$12	10
Zamora	$2.50	2

Huaquillas, on the main route to Peru, can also be reached by a night bus in about seven hours, thus avoiding having to backtrack to Machala.

Transportes Sur-Oriente has buses to Vilcabamba ($1, 1½ hours) once an hour, and Vilcabambaturis runs faster ($1, one hour) minibuses every half hour from 6:15am to 9:15pm. Fastest of all are the *taxis colectivos* (shared taxis; $1.20, 45 minutes), which leave from Av Universitaria, about 10 blocks south of Mercadillo in Loja; ask a local taxi driver to take you to the Ruta 11 de Mayo taxi stop.

Loja is also the departure point for buses to both southern border crossings into Peru: Macará (see p225 for details) and Zumba (see p223).

PARQUE NACIONAL PODOCARPUS

Easily accessed from Loja and Zamora (and to a lesser extent from Vilcabamba), Ecuador's southernmost **national park** (admission $10) spans altitudes ranging from over 3600m to about 900m, from the *páramo* and lake-covered mountains southeast of Loja to the rainforests south of Zamora (p218) in the southern Oriente. Between these extremes the countryside is wild and rugged, and home to rare animal and plant species.

QUININE: MIRACULOUS CURE, MAGIC INGREDIENT

Podocarpus might be the namesake tree of Ecuador's southernmost national park, but the region's most famous tree is *Cinchona succirubra,* the tree from which quinine, the drug that treats malaria, is extracted. Known locally as *cascarilla,* the tree is now seldom seen outside the park, as demand for quinine has left few of them standing.

Though quinine was first isolated in 1820 by the French chemists Pierre Joseph Pelletier and Joseph Caventou, the curative properties of the tree's bark were known long before. Indigenous South Americans used the bark medicinally for ages and later taught Jesuit missionaries its properties as a fever breaker. It finally became world famous in the mid-1600s after a local monk used extracts from the bark to cure the dying Countess of Cinchón, the wife of a Peruvian viceroy. After her recovery from malaria, fame of the tree's 'miraculous' properties spread throughout the world. A century later European scientists named the tree *Cinchona succirubra* after the countess. For 300 years, until effective synthetic medicines were invented, quinine would be the world's only treatment for malaria.

Even if you've never taken malaria meds, you've probably ingested quinine. It is, after all, the magic ingredient in tonic water. Tonic water was originally just that – a tonic that contained a high amount of quinine. It was consumed heavily by the British in India as a prevention against malaria. Legend has it that the only way the Brits could get the stuff down was to tailor the bitterly flavored 'tonic' with gin and a bit of lime. Hence the gin and tonic.

Unfortunately, because so little quinine is used in tonic today, malaria prevention cannot be used as an excuse for slugging successive rounds of gin and tonic. But you can stand back and admire the *Cinchona* tree during a visit to Podocarpus.

SOUTHERN HIGHLANDS

Scientists have found a high degree of endemism (species found nowhere else) here, apparently because the complex topography combines with the junction of Andean and Amazonian weather patterns to cause unique microclimates throughout the park. The result is incredible biodiversity. Up to 90 different tree species have been recorded in just a single hectare – apparently a world record. Some of the most important plants here include three species of the park's namesake genus, *Podocarpus*, Ecuador's only native conifer.

Animals include the Andean spectacled bear, mountain tapirs, puma, two species of deer and the Andean fox. All of these animals are hard to see and prized by local poachers. Birds are abundant and include such exotic-sounding species as the lachrymose mountain-tanager, streaked tuftedcheek, superciliaried hemispingus and pearled treerunner.

Although it's a national park, Podocarpus faces huge problems. Legal boundaries are not respected by local colonists, and logging often occurs within park limits. But despite these problems, there are wonderful day-hiking opportunities from both Loja and Zamora – in fact, the best way to see the park is to visit the Highlands sector (from Loja) one day and the lowlands sector (from Zamora) the next. The park entry fee is valid for five days, so you can use the ticket to visit both areas of the park.

You can also visit the park on a guided tour (usually by horseback) from the village of Vilcabamba (p219).

Podocarpus receives a lot of rainfall, so be prepared for it. October through December are the driest months.

Highlands Sector

The main entrance to the highland sector is **Cajanuma**, about 10km south of Loja. From the Cajanuma entrance, a dirt road leads 8.5km uphill to the **Cajanuma ranger station** (overnight fee per person in tent/cabaña $5/2). From here several short, self-guided trails wander through the cloud forest.

The best option for a day hike is the 5km **Los Miradores loop trail**, a strenuous four-hour hike through the cloud forest and into the *páramo*. The views from the ridge-top are spectacular. Another trail leads 14.5km to the highland lakes of **Lagunas del Compadre**,

which for most hikers requires a minimum of three days: one in, one on the lakes and one out. There is no water between the trailhead and the lakes.

At the Cajanuma ranger station there are seven basic **cabañas** (per person $5), three of which have beds. None have blankets. There's also a **camping area** (per tent $3).

For more information on the western and central parts of the park, visit the Ministerio del Medio Ambiente in Loja (p212). Verbal information is available at the park.

GETTING THERE & AWAY

If you're coming out for the day from Loja, the best way to deal with transport is to take a taxi ($8 to $10) from town all the way up to the ranger station. Set out early and you can hike for several hours before walking the 8.5km back to the Loja–Vilcabamba road. Then flag a passing bus back to Loja. The two-hour walk from the station to the main road is an enjoyable walk itself. You could also arrange for the taxi to pick you up at a later time. There are rarely cars on the park road, so don't expect to hitch.

Lowlands Sector

The lush tropical forests of Podocarpus' lowlands are easily accessible from Zamora, meaning the area is an easy day trip from both Zamora and Loja. The climate is hot and humid but beautiful, and the rainiest months are May through July. May and June are the best months for orchids.

The main access to this area of the park is the **Bombuscaro entrance** (8am-5pm or 6pm), 6km south of Zamora by a rough road. From the parking area at the end of the road it's a half-hour walk on an uphill trail to the ranger station where you pay the entry fee. The park rangers are friendly and helpful and can suggest places to **camp** (per person $2). There are two basic **cabañas** (per person $5), but you'll need a sleeping bag and pad. For a small fee to help pay for gas, you can usually use the kitchen.

From the Bombuscaro ranger station, there are several short, maintained (but sometimes muddy) trails through the forest. One goes to a waterfall. The longest is the 6km **Los Huigerones trail**, which is the only trail that will really get you into some primary forest. Another trail leads to a deep (but very swift) swimming hole called the *área fotográfico,* on the Río Bombuscaro. The bird-watching is excellent.

There's another infrequently used entrance to the park at the tiny village of **Romerillos**, about 25km south of Zamora by a different road. Because of illegal mining in the area, park rangers only recommend visiting with a local guide, as it can be dangerous accidentally stumbling across a miner's gold claim.

GETTING THERE & AWAY

The easiest way to get to the Bombuscaro entrance is by taxi from Zamora; they hang out behind the bus terminal and charge $4 for the ride. You can have the driver return to pick you up at the end of the day (additional $4) or you can walk back. Buses to Romerillos ($1.50, two hours) leave at 6am and 2pm from Zamora's bus terminal.

ZAMORA

☎ 07 / pop 16,074 / elevation 970m

The tranquil, humid and easygoing town of Zamora is the best base for exploring the verdant lowlands sector of Parque Nacional Podocarpus. Though geographically part of the Oriente, Zamora is closer to Loja by bus (two hours) than to jungle towns, most of which are a long way north.

The bus ride from the highlands is beautiful. As you descend toward the Oriente, the scenery becomes tropical and the vegetation thicker, and you begin seeing strange plants, such as the giant tree fern.

In 1953, Zamora became the provincial capital when the province of Zamora-Chinchipe was created.

Orientation

Central streets are signed, but few buildings use numbers.

Information

Zamora has no ATMs and none of the banks change traveler's checks. Bring cash.

Hospital (Sevilla de Oro near Pio Jaramillo Alvarado)

Ministerio del Ambiente (☎ 260 6606; vía Zamora-Loja s/n; ☉ 8am-4:30pm Mon-Fri) Northwest of town; information on Parque Nacional Podocarpus.

Pacifictel (cnr Amazonas & José Luis Tamayo; branch Francisco de Orellana near Sevilla de Oro) Telephone call-centers.

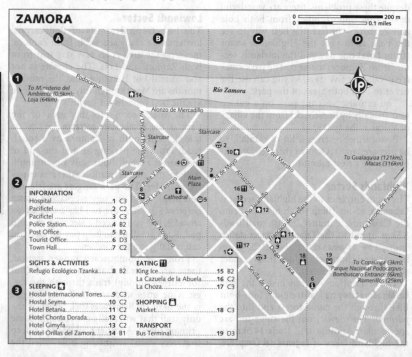

ZAMORA

0 — 200 m
0 — 0.1 miles

INFORMATION
Hospital..........................1 C3
Pacifictel........................2 C2
Pacifictel........................3 C3
Police Station..................4 B2
Post Office......................5 B2
Tourist Office...................6 D3
Town Hall........................7 C2

SIGHTS & ACTIVITIES
Refugio Ecológico Tzanka....8 B2

SLEEPING 🏠
Hostal Internacional Torres....9 C3
Hostal Seyma...................10 C2
Hotel Betania...................11 C2
Hotel Chonta Dorada..........12 C2
Hotel Gimyfa...................13 C2
Hotel Orillas del Zamora......14 B1

EATING 🍴
King Ice.........................15 B2
La Cazuela de la Abuela......16 C2
La Choza........................17 C3

SHOPPING 🛍
Market...........................18 C3

TRANSPORT
Bus Terminal....................19 D3

Police station (cnr Diego de Vaca & José Luis Tamayo)

Post office (cnr 24 de Mayo & Sevilla de Oro)

Tourist Office (iTur; ☎ 260 5996; cnr Diego de Vaca & Av Heroes de Paquisha) Zamora's first official tourist office was due to open at the close of this edition; it's located beside the market. Until then it was on the 3rd floor of the *municipio* (town hall).

Sights & Activities

Zamora's main attraction is nearby Parque Nacional Podocarpus (p216). Spotting animals in the park is difficult, but you can do it in town at the **Refugio Ecológico Tzanka** (☎ 260 5692; refugioecologicotzanka@yahoo.es; Jorge Mosquero at José Luis Tamayo; admission $2; ☻ 9am-5pm), a wildlife rescue center that's more a zoo than anything else. It's a ramshackle place with raptors, parrots, monkeys and a friendly tapir. Taking pictures costs an extra $5 per camera.

The covered indoor **market** (Diego de Vaca at Av Heroes de Paquisha) is worth a browse to kill a little time.

Sleeping

Zamora's hotels are a nondescript bunch, but there are several decent places to choose from. Water is generally warm to mildly cold.

Copalinga (☎ 09-347 7013; www.copalinga.com; Km 3, road to Bombuscaro; d $20-80) In a beautiful spot halfway between Zamora and the national park, this Belgium-owned hideaway opened in 2005 and has two 'rustic' cabins and six 'deluxe' cabins. They're all comfortable, and the deluxe cabins have giant windows and balconies. It's on 75 hectares with several trails into the forest. Rates depend on the service and type of food you want.

Hotel Orillas del Zamora (☎ 260 5704, 260 5565; hotel_o_zamora@hotmail.net; Podocarpus; s/d incl breakfast $12/15) Next to the river, this is a spiffy, modern place with four floors of comfortable rooms. They're worth the price if you get one with a view over the river. Bottled water is included in the rate.

Hotel Betania (☎ 260 7030/32; hotelbetaniaz@ hotmail.com; Francisco de Orellana; s/d incl breakfast $12/17) The Betania is a comfortable and modern new hotel with firm beds and an attached restaurant. It's one of the best in town.

Hostal Internacional Torres (☎ 260 5195; Francisco de Orellana; r per person $5.75) Of international stature, definitely not. In fact, the flowered bedspreads, saggy beds and Catholic posters make for a much more provincial feel. Rooms have cable TV, telephones and fans.

Hostal Seyma (☎ 260 5583; 24 de Mayo near Amazonas; s/d $3/6) Seyma is clean and friendly, but it can be noisy if you don't choose your room carefully. With flowery wallpaper and tiny twin beds, it's sort of like sleeping in a dollhouse.

Also try the **Hotel Chonta Dorada** (☎ 260 6384, 260 7055; hotelchontadorada@hotmail.com; Pío Jaramillo near Amazonas; s/d $7/11.50) and the modern, comfortable **Hotel Gimyfa** (☎ 260 6103; Diego de Vaca near Pio Jaramillo; s/d $7/14).

Eating

Food is hardly Zamora's forte, and restaurants serve only the standard Ecuadorian fare, along with burgers and hotdogs. The better hotels (such as Chonta Dorada) have decent restaurants, and there are numerous cheap eateries inside and around the market.

La Choza (☎ 260 5504; Sevilla de Oro; mains $2.50-5) Named for the thatched-roof bar inside, this is one of the best options in town. Choose from burgers, ceviches and traditional plates like *churrasco* (steak with eggs, rice and garnishing) and the local specialty, *ancas de rana* (frogs' legs).

King Ice (cnr Diego de Vaca & José Luis Tamayo; food $1.50-2.50; ☻ 8am-midnight) Zamora's best ice-cream parlor serves surprisingly tasty burgers and hot dogs too.

La Cazuela de la Abuela (☎ 260 7492; Amazonas near Pio Jaramillo; mains $2-4; ☻ 6am-9pm Mon-Fri, 6am-3pm Sat) It's just your standard place, but *corvina* (technically sea bass, but usually just a white fish here) and chicken are both done well.

Getting There & Away

The **bus terminal** (Av Heroes de Paquisha at Amazonas) is at the southeast end of downtown.

Buses leave almost hourly to Loja ($2.50, two hours) between 3am and 8pm. There are five daily buses heading north to Gualaquiza ($5, five hours), and at least one departure daily to Cuenca ($8, seven hours), Quito ($15, 15 to 18 hours) and Guayaquil ($10, 11 hours). See opposite for details of transport to Parque Nacional Podocarpus.

VILCABAMBA

☎ 07 / pop 4200 / elevation 1500m

People come to Vilcabamba to relax – which is an easy task once you're here, considering the tranquility of the village and its stunning mountainous surroundings. The

SOUTHERN HIGHLANDS

slightly surreal peaks that practically engulf Vilcabamba make for some excellent day hikes from town. Furthermore, nearly every other building (and there aren't many) has a sign out front advertising massages and facials, a trend started by a few hotels and later picked up by the rest of the resident population, a large percentage of whom are foreigners who couldn't bring themselves to leave. Most of those who stayed, as well as a handful of locals, now own cafés, offer horse-riding tours or own rustic little hotels offering travelers ample opportunity to do what you do in Vilcabamba: kick back. The town offers access to remote sections of Podocarpus and is a good stopping point en route to or from Peru via Zumba.

Vilcabamba has for many years been famous as the 'valley of longevity.' Inhabitants supposedly live to be 100 or more, and some claim to be 120 years old. This has been attributed to their simple, hard-working lifestyle, their diet of nonfatty foods and the excellent climate. Scientific investigation has been unable to substantiate these beliefs, but the legend persists.

Orientation & Information

Most of the town surrounds the plaza, and addresses are rarely used. Everything closes for an hour or so from 1pm.

Craig's Book Exchange (1-5pm) Great book exchange 1.5km east of town on road to Cabañas Río Yambala.

Hospital (267 3188; Av Eterna Juventud near Miguel Carpio)

Lavalisto (Fernando de la Vega near Valle Sagrado; laundry per kg $0.80; 8-11am & 1-4:30pm) Same-day laundry service.

Pacifictel (Sucre near Fernando de la Vega) One of several telephone centers in town.

Pepe Net (Fernando de la Vega near Sucre; per hr $1; 9am-9pm) Internet access.

Police station (264 0896; Agua de Hierro near Bolívar) By the post office.

Post office (Agua de Hierro near Bolívar)

Shanta's Bar (laundry $2.50 for 1-3kg) Two-hour turnaround on laundry.

Tourist office (264 0090; cnr Bolívar & Diego Vaca de la Vega; 8am-1pm & 3-6pm)

Vilcanet (Huilco Pamba near Juan Montalvo; per hr $1; 9am-9pm) Outdoor cybercafé; above Hotel Mandango.

Sights & Activities

There are wonderful hikes in the mountains around Vilcabamba, and most hotel staff

can point out trails. The most popular hike is up to the ragged mountaintop of Mandango or to the lookout just below.

Orlando Falco is a passionate, interesting and experienced English-speaking naturalist guide. He conducts walking tours to Podocarpus and other areas for about $20 to $35 per person (plus the $10 park fee). Contact him at Primavera Arts (p223) or at the Rumi-Wilco Ecolodge or Pole House (p222).

Several readers and numerous locals have recommended local guide Jorge Mendieta of **Caminatas Andes Sureños** (673 147; jorgeluis 222@latinmail.com; central plaza) for his guided hikes. He knows the area well and is especially versed in medicinal plants. A hike with him costs $6 to $15 per person, depending on the length of the walk. Two-day walks are also possible for $25 per day.

The folks at **Cabañas Río Yambala** (09-106 2762; www.vilcabamba.cwc.net) arrange two- and three-day hiking and horse-riding trips into their private Las Palmas nature reserve on the edge of Podocarpus, where they have a simple lodge (bunk beds, toilet, shower and kitchen facilities). Hiking trips cost $70/105 per person for two/three days, and riding trips are $25 to $40 per person per day. Prices drop for groups of three or more.

Caballos Gavilan (264 0281; gavilanhorse@yahoo .com; Sucre), run by the friendly Gavin, a New Zealander who has lived here for years, offers guided two- to three-day horse treks with overnights in his refuge near the park. These cost $35 per day and include everything. It's an excellent operation and his horses are very well cared for.

Across from the tourist office, **Centro Ecuestre** (267 3151; Diego Vaca de la Vega) is a cooperative of several local horse and mule owners offering tours lasting from two hours to three days. Most speak only Spanish. It's a good way of helping the local economy.

Horseback-riding trips are also offered by the friendly René León at **La Tasca Tours** (09-152 3118, 09-184 1287; latascourts@yahoo.ec; Diego Vaca de la Vega) and the French-owned **Monta Tours** (267 3186; solomaco@hotmail.com; Sucre).

About 1.5km east of town, the **Centro Recreacional Yamburara** (admission $0.30) has a small zoo with local animals, an excellent collection of orchids, a swimming pool and a playground for the youngsters.

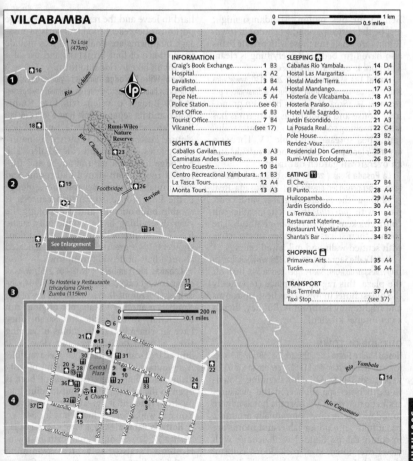

VILCABAMBA

INFORMATION	
Craig's Book Exchange	1 B3
Hospital	2 A2
Lavalisto	3 B4
Pacifictel	4 A4
Pepe Net	5 A4
Police Station	(see 6)
Post Office	6 B3
Tourist Office	7 B4
Vilcanet	(see 17)

SIGHTS & ACTIVITIES	
Caballos Gavilan	8 A3
Caminatas Andes Sureños	9 B4
Centro Ecuestre	10 B4
Centro Recreacional Yambura..	11 B3
La Tasca Tours	12 A4
Monta Tours	13 A3

SLEEPING	
Cabañas Río Yambala	14 D4
Hostal Las Margaritas	15 A4
Hostal Madre Tierra	16 A1
Hostal Mandango	17 A3
Hostería de Vilcabamba	18 A1
Hostería Paraíso	19 A2
Hotel Valle Sagrado	20 A4
Jardín Escondido	21 A3
La Posada Real	22 C4
Pole House	23 B2
Rendez-Vouz	24 B4
Residencial Don German	25 B4
Rumi-Wilco Ecolodge	26 B2

EATING	
El Che	27 B4
El Punto	28 A4
Huilcopamba	29 A4
Jardín Escondido	30 A4
La Terraza	31 B4
Restaurant Katerine	32 B4
Restaurant Vegetariano	33 B4
Shanta's Bar	34 B2

SHOPPING	
Primavera Arts	35 A4
Tucán	36 A4

TRANSPORT	
Bus Terminal	37 A4
Taxi Stop	(see 37)

Sleeping

CENTRAL

Vilcabamba has wonderful hotels with outstanding prices. Those outside the village can be marvelously quiet and relaxing, while those in town are generally cheaper (but still quite comfortable).

Rendez-Vous (☎ 09-2191180; rendezvousecuador@ yahoo.com; Diego Vaca de Vega 06-43; s/d $8/16; ☐ wifi connection $3) French-owned Rendez-Vous is a lovely place near the river with immaculate rooms with whitewashed brick walls, firm beds and a soft fragrance of eucalyptus wood. Each room opens onto the beautiful garden and has a hammock out front. Breakfast with homemade bread included.

Jardín Escondido (Hidden Garden; ☎ 264 0281; www .vilcabamba.org/jardinescondido.html; Sucre; dm $8, r per person $10-15; ☑) Recently remodeled, colorful Jardín Escondido is the slickest in the center, and it really does have a garden hidden within its doors. It's a relaxing place, cheerfully painted with yellow and blue walls. The priciest rooms are quite luxurious.

Residencial Don German (☎ 264 0130, 09-132 4669; Jaramillo; r per person $4) Run by the friendly Libia Toledo Cueva, these simple digs have clean cheerful rooms with shared hot-showers. There's a tiny, well-lit common area and a communal kitchen. It's basic, but totally acceptable.

Hostal Mandango (☎ 09-370 5266; Huilco Pamba near Juan Montalvo; r per person shared/private bath $3/5; ☑)

Behind the bus station, Mandango might just be the best super-budget choice in town. Rooms are small, but those with private baths also have firm beds and everything is clean. The pool is occasionally filled.

Hostal Las Margaritas (☎ 267 3130; www.vilca bamba.org/lasmargaritas.html; cnr Sucre & Jaramillo; r per person $8; ☒) Sort of a cross between grandma's house and a hotel, Las Margaritas has fresh-smelling rooms with stark white walls, satiny bed spreads and cable TV. There's a crystal-clear two-lane lap pool outside and an overgrown garden out front.

La Posada Real (☎ 264 0904; cnr Agua de Hierro & La Paz; r per person incl breakfast $6) La Posada Real is all about the expansive grassy yard, complete with *parrilla* (barbecue), volleyball court, chickens and an outdoor bathtub. The rooms themselves are rather unattractive with scuffed walls and mildewed ceilings.

Hotel Valle Sagrado (☎ 264 0386; www.vilcabamba .org/vallesagrado.html; Sucre; r per person $4) Just off the plaza, this ragtag old place (reportedly the oldest hotel in town) has beat-up rooms and frightening bathrooms. But hey, there's a communal kitchen!

OUTSIDE OF TOWN

Hostal Madre Tierra (☎ 258 0269, 258 0687, 09-309 6665; www.madretierra1.com; dm $13.50, r per person $13.50-25, ste per person $34; ☒ 🖳) This stunning, down-to-earth hotel-spa pioneered the pleasure-aesthetic that most Vilcabamba hotels adhere to today. Guests dine communally around a beautifully set outdoor table, and rooms are in comfy cabins. Suites have balconies with views over town, inset rock floors, colorful tiles, batik bead spreads and ceramic decorations. Prices include organic breakfasts and dinners, and paying a little more will include massages as well. Local hiking and riding information, a café/bar, book exchange, video room and table games are all included. It's a fantastic deal. The full-service spa (treatments $16 to $40) is open to nonguests. It's 2km from town (a 15-minute walk).

Hostería y Restaurante Izhcayluma (☎ 264 0095; www.izhcayluma.com; dm $7, s $13-20, d $20-30; ☒) Located 2km south of town on the Zumba road, German-owned Izhcayluma is one of Vilcabamba's best. Highlights are its sweeping views over the valley and a swimming pool that's fed by a burbling fountain trickling through the hillside garden. The rooms are supremely comfortable, the hammocks are hard to leave and the restaurant serves huge portions of excellent food. All sorts of massage treatments are available. Prices include your choice of four breakfasts and use of a mountain bike to ride into town.

Rumi-Wilco Ecolodge (rumiwilco@yahoo.com; http://koberpress.home.mindspring.com/vilcabamba; r per person $4-4.50) Budget travelers will love Rumi-Wilco and its separate **Pole House** (d/tr $16/18). Both are within the private Rumi-Wilco Nature Reserve, which is owned by naturalist guides Orlando and Alicia Falco. The ecolodge has eight natural adobe and tile-roofed rooms with shared bathrooms and communal kitchens. Beyond the ecolodge is the Pole House, so called because it is a cabin built on stilts and overlooking the river. Everything has a wonderfully rustic feel, with hammocks around and outdoor showers. It's a great place to relax. Located about a half-hour walk from town.

Cabañas Río Yambala (☎ 09-106 2762; www.vil cabamba.cwc.net; cabins per person with 2 meals $10-14, without meals $5-9) About 4km southeast of town, Río Yambala is another Vilcabamba original, run by friendly Brits Charlie and Sarah. They have six charming, rustic cabins of varying sizes, all with hot-showers and views, and limited self-catering facilities are available. A restaurant serving a small menu of tasty dishes, including vegetarian food and beer, is open to the public. There's outstanding hiking from here and it's great for nature lovers. You can walk there or hire a taxi for $4.

Hostería Paraíso (☎ 258 0266; r per person incl breakfast $9; ☒) About 1km north of town, Hostería Paraíso has a great swimming pool, friendly owners, a restaurant, a flower-filled garden crowned by a stuffy, pyramid-shaped bioenergetic meditation room (now *that's* entertainment) and rooms that don't quite measure up to everything else. Rates include use of the pool and spa facilities. It's not a bad deal midweek off-season when you'll have the place to yourself.

Hostería de Vilcabamba (☎ 264 0271/72/73; info@ vilcabamba.org; s/d/bungalow $24/34/40; ☒) Further out on the Loja road, this is Vilcabamba's most traditional place to stay, with a giant manicured lawn, plastic chaise longues and rather cold but immaculate rooms.

Eating

The restaurant at Izhcayluma *hosteria* (left) is outstanding and well worth the trip up.

Several restaurants along Diego Vaca de la Vega, just west of the plaza, serve cheap Ecuadorian-style *almuerzos*.

La Terraza (cnr Diego Vaca de la Vega & Bolívar; mains $2.50-4; ☾ 8am-9pm) On the northeast corner of the plaza, La Terraza has a small menu of Italian-, Mexican- and Thai-influenced plates with plenty of vegetarian options. Coffee is brewed by the cup. It's especially good if you snag an outdoor table.

Jardín Escondido (cnr Sucre & Agua de Hierro; mains $3-5; ☾ Wed-Mon) Inside its namesake hotel, Jardín Escondido serves good but pricey Mexican food in a lovely garden setting. It's mostly tacos, enchiladas and nachos, but a little *mole* (a spicy sauce made from chocolate and other surprise ingredients) is thrown in for authenticity's sake. Breakfasts are big.

Restaurant Vegetariano (Valle Salgado at Diego Vaca de la Vega; mains $2-3; ☾ 8:30am-8:30pm) This modest eatery is a solid vegetarian option, serving salads, soups, lasagna and $2.60 *almuerzos*.

Shanta's Bar (mains $3-6; ☾ noon-3am) On the road to Río Yambala, Shanta's serves great trout, pizza and frogs' legs in a laid-back, open-air, rustic setting with saddle seats at the bar. It's a great place to chill.

El Punto (cnr Sucre & Fernando de la Vega; ☾ 8am-6:30pm) This friendly little café whips out tasty treats and good breakfasts.

El Che (Bolívar; mains $3-4; ☾ Tue-Sun) Hit this one for Argentinean food, steaks, pizzas and pastas.

Huilcopamba (cnr Sucre & Diego Vaca de la Vega; mains $2.50-4; ☾ 8am-9pm) and **Restaurant Katerine** (Sucre at Jaramillo; mains $2.50-4) are reliable Ecuadorian-owned places.

Shopping

Primavera Arts (Diego Vaca de la Vega near Sucre; ☾ irregular) On the north side of the plaza, Primavera has lovely, hand-painted T-shirts and crafts.

Tucán (Fernando de la Vega near Sucre; ☾ 10am-1pm & 2-6pm) Tucán stocks loads of souvenirs, postcards, jewelry and T-shirts. It also sells crude but helpful maps.

Getting There & Around

Buses, taxis and mini-vans all leave from the tiny **bus terminal** (cnr Av Eterna Juventud & Jaramillo). Shared taxis depart frequently to Loja ($1.20, 45 minutes) after five people cram in; there are also buses ($1, 1½ hours) and Vilcabambaturis minibuses ($1, 1¼ hours).

Buses from Loja head south to Zumba ($6, six hours) and on to the Peruvian border (see below for details).

Vilcabambaturis (at the bus terminal) also sells tickets for the Loja–Piura (Peru) bus ride, which goes via Macará (see p225 for details). It doesn't come through Vilcabamba, but it's good to purchase your ticket a day in advance if you're heading that way.

Transportes Mixtos is a cooperative of 15 taxi-trucks, which charge $1.50 to $4 for getting to nearby places (most within the $2 range); they hang out around the plaza.

ZUMBA & THE PERUVIAN BORDER

☎ 07

The border crossing south of Zumba is the most remote of the formal crossings between Ecuador and Peru. It's an outpost in the truest sense. From Loja or Vilcabamba, it's an all-day journey to San Ignacio, Peru – the best place to spend the night. An all-weather road heads south via Vilcabamba and continues through beautiful countryside before hitting the town of Zumba, 115km south of Vilcabamba and 10km north of the border.

From Loja, Transportes Nambija ($7.50, six hours) buses leave for Zumba at noon and midnight, and **Sur Oriente** (☎ 256 1649) services go at 5am, 8am, 5:30pm and 9:30pm. All stop in Vilcabamba for just over an hour after leaving Loja.

Zumba has a basic *pensión* (cheap hotel), though there's little reason to stay. From Zumba, *rancheras* (open-sided trucks) leave at 2:30pm to the border at **La Balsa** ($1.75, 1½ hours) where you get your exit stamp (or entry stamp if coming from Peru). Over the bridge there are *taxi colectivos* (shared taxis) to **San Ignacio** ($3, 1½ hours) where you can spend the night. Most travelers recommend La Posada, which also changes money.

From San Ignacio, there are regular mini buses to **Jaén** ($3.50, three hours) beginning at 4am. Once you're in Jaén, take a *mototaxi* (motorcycle taxi) to the *colectivo* stop and then get a *colectivo* to **Bagua Grande** (one hour). From Bagua Grande you then get a bus to **Chachapoyas** (three hours), the first town of any real size.

CATAMAYO & AROUND

☎ 07

Loja was founded twice. The first time was in 1546, on what is now **Catamayo**; the

LA VIRGEN DEL CISNE

Throughout Ecuador, but especially in Loja province, you'll see stickers and shrines, pendants and figurines dedicated to La Virgen del Cisne. The original statue of the virgin is housed in El Cisne, in an enormous, Gothic-style church (called El Santuario) that stands in sharp contrast to the humble houses of traditional *campesinos* (country people) that surround it.

According to local lore, the ancestors of these *campesinos* made the long and difficult journey to Quito in the late-16th century in search of a fitting religious statue. They returned in 1594 with the carving of La Virgen del Cisne and installed it in a small shrine. Since then, the icon has been the 'Queen' of the *campesinos*, and her devotees are responsible for the biggest religious procession in Ecuador.

A huge festival is held in her honor on August 15, after which thousands of pilgrims from Ecuador and northern Peru carry the statue on their shoulders to Loja (70km away), with many of the pilgrims walking the entire way. The Virgin finally arrives in Loja on August 20, where she is ceremoniously installed in the cathedral. On November 1, the process is repeated in reverse, and the Virgin rests in El Cisne until the following August. There is another major (if smaller) festival in El Cisne on May 30.

For most of the year, tours and buses make day trips to the village from Loja and Catamayo to see the sanctuary and statue. But on procession days, forget it! You walk like everybody else – the road is so full of pilgrims that vehicles can't get through. If you're lucky enough to be here around procession dates, this is truly a sight to see.

second time was on its present site, two years later. Despite its long history, Catamayo is a totally unremarkable town except for its airport, La Toma, which serves Loja 30km away.

About 15km west of Catamayo, the Panamericana passes through the village of **San Pedro de la Bendita**. From here, a road runs north for another 22km to the village of **El Cisne**, home to the famous Virgin del Cisne (see the boxed text, above).

About 40km south of Catamayo, **Gonzanamá** is noted for its weavers and for the production of *alforjas* (saddlebags). There are basic places to stay. From Gonzanamá, the road continues to the villages of **Cariamanga** and **Sozoranga**, which both have basic *pensiones* (cheap hotels), before ending in Macará at the border. This road is the southernmost of two roads to Macará and passes through a remote area seldom visited by gringos.

All of these places are served regularly from Loja's bus terminal.

CATACOCHA

☎ 07 / elevation 1800m / pop 5369

Catacocha's 19th-century adobe houses and multicolored sun-bleached doors, its Spanish-tile roofs and its beautiful location over the sweeping Valle de Casanga make it the prettiest town southwest of Loja. It lies

on the northernmost of two roads between Loja and Macará, a road that passes through spectacular countryside that grows continually drier as it approaches the coastal lowlands. Whether you're heading to Macará or not, the town is worth a visit.

Besides being deemed a National Cultural Heritage Site in 1994, Catacocha's claim to fame is its **Mirador de Shiriculapo**, a lookout perched atop a 150m-high rock wall over the Valle de Casanga. Also called Balcón del Inca ('Inca's Balcony'), it was supposedly a sacred site for the pre-Inca indigenous Palta. It's also a legendary lovers' leap, and locals will tell you about couples who took the plunge. To get to the lookout, walk back towards the highway from the plaza and through the hospital gates (they're open during daylight hours).

There are few tourist services, though information is available at the **municipio** (town hall; ☎ 268 3157; ☼ Mon-Fri).

The best hotel in town is **Hotel Tambococha** (☎ 268 3551; cnr 25 de Junio & Lauro Guerrero; s/d $8/12), right on the main plaza. It's a great little hotel, with immaculate rooms with colorful walls, plenty of light and electrically heated showers.

There are several restaurants around town, none of which stand out.

Buses from Loja ($2.30, two hours) stop here en route to Macará.

MACARÁ

☎ 07 / **elevation** 450m / **pop** 11,500

As the road drops in elevation from Catacocha to Macará it snakes through some of South America's largest remaining stands of tropical dry forest, a landscape that has a definitive feature – the giant bottle-trunk Ceiba. Scattered over otherwise barren mountainsides, these majestic and usually leafless trees have massively swollen trunks and produce a seasonal white fruit that give the trees a striking Dr Seussian character.

By the time you get to Macará, it's hot. This small, unimportant town 3km from the Peruvian border receives little international traffic compared with the more convenient coastal route via Huaquillas. The main advantage to the Macará route is the ease of crossing and the scenic descent from Loja.

Macará itself is an odd little town of high curb sides and unfinished buildings, where residents lounge around in hammocks in front of their shops along the main drag. Almost everything happens between the central intersection of Bolívar and Rengel and the city hall.

Information

The bank in Macará does not have foreign-exchange facilities, but you can change money informally at Parque Carlos Román (where the taxi ranks are); look for the conspicuous guy in mirrored sunglasses with the black briefcase. Change only what you need as rates are poor.

Internet is available for $1 per hour at **Robles Net** (Abdón Calderón near Bolívar; 🕑 8am-10:30pm) and **Computo** (Bolívar at Rengel).

Sleeping & Eating

Unless you like dusty border towns (and Macará definitely qualifies), there's little reason to even get off the bus, let alone spend the night. If you do, accommodation is plentiful and cheap.

Hostal El Conquistador (☎ 269 4057; Bolívar at Abdón Calderón; s/d $8/14) This is a modern, comfortable and friendly hotel with an oddly designed interior stairway and comfortable tile-floor rooms with cable TV and remote control fans.

Hostal Santigyn (☎ 269 4539; Bolívar at Rengel; s/d incl breakfast $7/14) Santigyn has small but light and airy rooms with miniscule bathrooms. It's a good place. Dig the painting of the joint-smoking Mona Lisa beside the stairs.

Hotel Karina (☎ 269 4764; kari_20_08@hotmail.com; cnr 10 de Agosto & Antonio Ante; s $8-12, d $14-18; ❄) Opened in 2005, this is the only place in town with air-conditioning. The rooms are no better than others in town, but the cool air can be nice when things are hot. It's across from the market.

Bekalus (☎ 269 4136; Valdivieso btwn 10 de Agosto & Rengel; r per person with shared/private bath $3/5) Get a room in the new sector and you're set – they're bright, clean and comfortable. Those in the older sector are dull and depressing.

There are a few simple restaurants around the intersection of Bolívar and Rengel. Most are open only at meal times and have limited menus.

D'Marcos (Jaime Roldos near Amazonas; mains $5-6) This is the town's best restaurant, and the only place with a menu exceeding three items. It's mostly seafood and all priced by season.

Getting There & Away

Transportes Loja Internacional (Lázaro Vaca at Juvenal Jaramilla) buses leave six times a day to Loja ($6, five hours) and take the Catacocha route. **Union Cariamanga** (☎ 269 4047; cnr Loja & Manuel E Rengel) has several buses a day to Loja ($6, six hours) via Cariamanga, a longer ride.

TO/FROM PERU

The crossing via Macará is much quieter than the crossing at Huaquillas. Macará is 3km from the border. Most people buy tickets direct to Piura (Peru) from Loja. The service is offered at 7am, 1pm, 10:30pm and 11pm with **Loja International** (☎ 257 9014, 257 0505), and the bus stops at the border, waits for passengers to take care of exits and entries, and then continues to Piura. The entire ride is eight hours (and costs $8). It's advisable to buy your tickets at least a day before you travel. Some people have recommended the night bus for the sake of convenience, but you'll miss the beautiful bus ride. If you want to break the journey from Loja, do so at Catacocha (opposite). If you're in Catacocha, buses leave from the **Transportes Loja Internacional terminal** (Lázaro Vaca at Juvenal Jaramilla).

SOUTHERN HIGHLANDS

The Oriente

You can't help but feel the rub of the first world chafing against the ancient in the Oriente, Ecuador's Amazon Basin. Consider the Tagaeri and Taromenani, who refuse all contact with the modern world but inhabit the same forest where oil exploitation grows day by day. These worlds will one day meet. The Oriente is an intense place with clenching stakes for everyone involved. Its earliest inhabitants lobbed heads for it, and politicians, colonists, environmentalists, indigenous groups and big industry continue the battle today.

For visitors the pull is mega-biodiversity. Beyond the cloud forests of the eastern Andean foothills, it's all rain forest, home to 50% of Ecuador's mammals, 5% of the earth's plant species and prolific bird life. Slip on your rubber boots to tread its forested hills, wetland marshes, big rivers and black-water lagoons. You'll be sharing real estate with tapirs, manatees, freshwater dolphins, anacondas, caimans, monkeys, sloths, peccaries and seldom-seen jaguars.

Equally fascinating is the human geography of the Oriente. The Achuar, Cofan, Huaorani, Quichua, Secoya, Shuar, Siona and Zaparo all call it home. These ancient cultures joined the 20th century at rocket speed, when, in the 1960s, oil exploration threw roads and colonists into areas few explorers reached. Ecuador's native population is a panorama as diverse and discordant as any modern population. Adaptation has not made their history or cultures any less interesting.

HIGHLIGHTS

- Float the blackwater paradise of Reserva Producción Faunística Cuyabeno's **flooded forest** (p236)
- Mountain bike the winding backroads of **Gualaquiza** (p264)
- Climb the lookout towers of a **jungle lodge** (p241 and p253) in Upper and Lower Río Napo for dizzying views of the rain forest canopy
- Journey to the heart of **Huaorani village** (p238) life with a native guide
- Ride the rolling rapids with some **river rafting** (p247) along the Río Jondachi
- Dance and feast at the Chonta festival in **Shuar territory** (p260)
- Dine on piping-hot *maitos* (fish grilled in palm leaves) in **Coca** (p240)

Reserva Producción Faunística Cuyabeno
Coca
Jungle Lodges
Río Jondachi
Huaorani Village
Shuar Territory
Gualaquiza

- AVERAGE TEMPERATURE IN NUEVO ROCAFUERTE: 10°C (50°F)
- RAINIEST MONTH IN NUEVO ROCAFUERTE: JULY

THE ORIENTE

Climate

The Oriente loves rain and gets plenty of it from April to July, its wettest months. Afternoon and evening rains are common throughout the year. Rubber boots are essential raingear and provide protection against snake bites as well. The driest months are August and between December and March. In some areas lagoons will dry up, tumbling waterfalls turn into trickles and long distance canoe rides turn epic because the river runs that much slower. Small rivers may become impassable when water levels decrease.

You'll find a contrast between the sweltering flatlands (from the Coca area north toward Colombia and east to Peru) and cooler upland hills (around Tena, Misahuallí and Puyo). Damp jungle nights can feel downright chilly. Don't forget a sweater, although you can probably leave the woolen poncho back in Otavalo!

Orientation

The Río Pastaza divides the Oriente (population: 433,013) into north and south. The northern Oriente is well connected with the capital and frequently visited. With a long day's travel from Quito, you can reach Lago Agrio (the access point for Cuyabeno reserve); Coca (the access point for Parque Nacional Yasuní and jungle lodges on the lower Río Napo); the white-water rafting mecca of Tena; or the village of Misahuallí, departure point for jungle lodges on the upper Río Napo. If you're short on time, the northern Oriente is your best bet for a quick introduction to Ecuador's Amazon Basin.

The southern Oriente is the least visited part of Ecuador. It is more difficult to explore but tantalizing nonetheless; you can find guides for hire in Macas, or visit Kapawi, Ecuador's most isolated jungle lodge. The south has less oil drilling, yet mining and cattle ranching have taken a toll.

National Parks

The impenetrable and remote **Parque Nacional Sumaco-Galeras** has 205,249 hectares of high peaks and dense tropical forest where jaguars and tapirs run wild. One of the few ways in is a white-water trip, rafting the stunning Río Hollín. South of the Río Napo is **Parque Nacional Yasuní**, a 9620-sq-km expanse of diverse wildlife (with 500 bird species), native populations, scientific stations and, astonishingly, oil exploration. Access is exclusively through tour operators. Further south, **Parque Nacional Sangay** straddles highlands and Amazon Basin. Volcanoes Sangay, Tungurahua and El Altar sit within its 517,765 hectares. The peaks are best accessed via the highland side, but Macas is a good base for a strenuous hike to the upper lakes.

Visiting the Oriente

If you had envisioned yourself running naked with the locals, you're probably about 50 years too late. Ecuador's rain forest is the most accessible of all Amazon Basin countries. It's easy to scratch its surface but takes some work to research its dizzying options. Independent travel into the forest is locally discouraged and often impossible. The independently minded are better off hiring a reputable independent guide or opting for community tourism. The easiest way to see the rain forest is by taking an organized tour (see the boxed text, p230) or by staying at a jungle lodge. These trips will cut down the time you whittle away coordinating logistics and get you into the heart of the forest more quickly, where there's a better – although never guaranteed – chance of seeing bigger mammals.

Jungle lodges are often exquisite settings with comfort, relaxation, excellent food and daily excursions into the forest. Many lodges have canopy towers, which substantially aid bird-viewing, and they're usually staffed by multilingual naturalist guides. For details on some of the best lodges, see p241 and p253.

Those interested in 'cultural tours' should choose their guide or tour with extra care. While *curanderos* are generally healers who offer natural medicine, shamans are spiritual advisors whose work is informed by a complex system of beliefs that the visitor may not be privy to. It pays to do research on these cultures and traditions before diving in. Some unscrupulous outfitters see ayahuasca or other psychotropics used ritually in indigenous cultures, as a good-time replacement for cocktails or whatever, when in reality these illegal substances would best be regarded with respect and caution. For more information see p251.

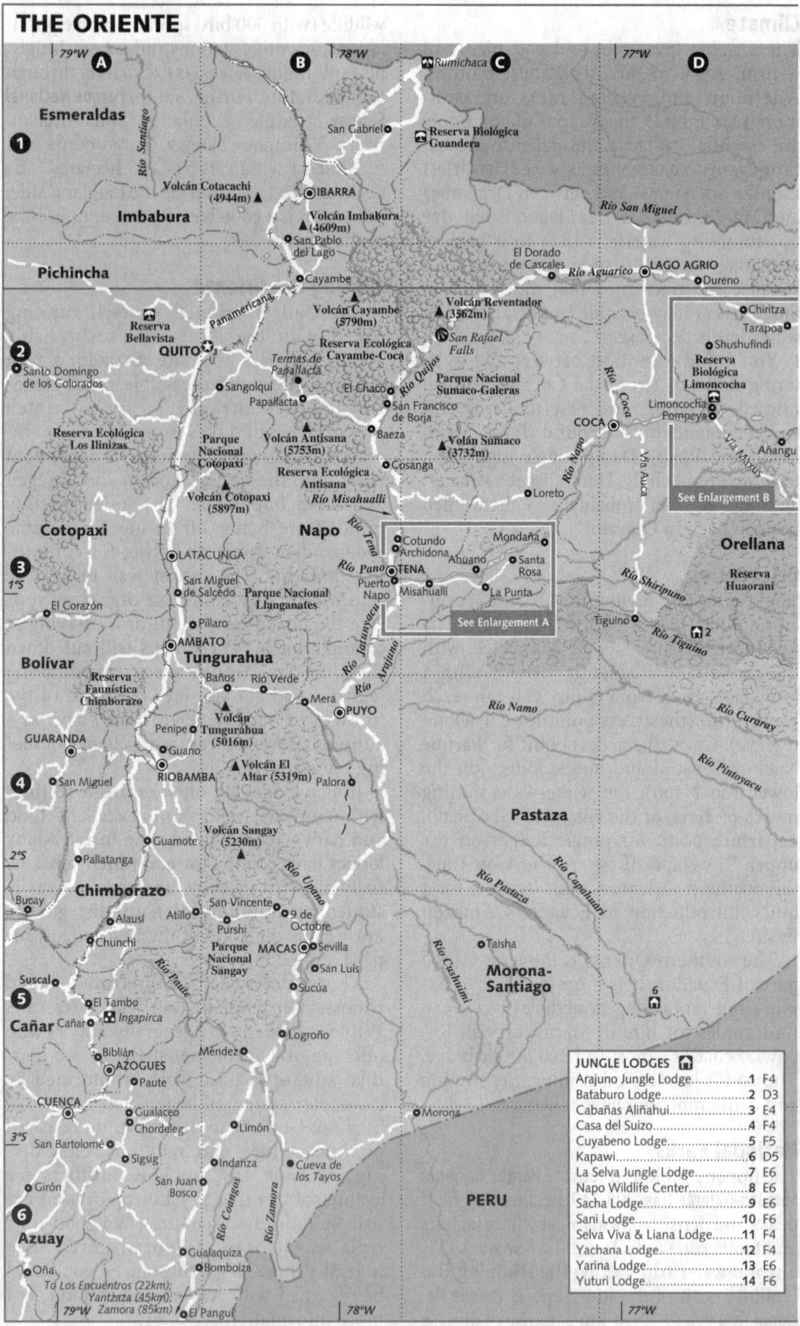

THE ORIENTE
79°W
78°W
77°W
A
B
C
D
1
2
3
4
5
6
1°S
2°S
3°S
Esmeraldas
Imbabura
Pichincha
Cotopaxi
Bolívar
Tungurahua
Napo
Chimborazo
Cañar
Azuay
Orellana
Pastaza
Morona-Santiago
PERU
Rumichaca
San Gabriel
Reserva Biológica Guandera
Río Santiago
Volcán Cotacachi (4944m)
IBARRA
Volcán Imbabura (4609m)
San Pablo del Lago
Cayambe
Panamericana
Reserva Bellavista
QUITO
Volcán Cayambe (5790m)
Volcán Reventador (3562m)
San Rafael Falls
Reserva Ecológica Cayambe-Coca
Termas de Papallacta
Santo Domingo de los Colorados
Sangolquí
Papallacta
El Chaco
Río Quijos
San Francisco de Borja
Parque Nacional Sumaco-Galeras
Baeza
Volán Sumaco (3732m)
Reserva Ecológica Los Ilinizas
Parque Nacional Cotopaxi
Volcán Antisana (5753m)
Reserva Ecológica Antisana
Cosanga
Volcán Cotopaxi (5897m)
Río Misahualli
El Dorado de Cascales
Río Aguarico
LAGO AGRIO
Dureno
Río San Miguel
Chiritza
Tarapoa
Shushufindi
Reserva Biológica Limoncocha
Limoncocha
Pompeya
Vía Maxus
Añangu
See Enlargement B
Río Coca
COCA
Río Napo
Vía Auca
Loreto
Río Tena
Cotundo
Archidona
Mondaña
Ahuano
Santa Rosa
Río Pano
TENA
Puerto Napo
Misahuallí
La Punta
See Enlargement A
LATACUNGA
San Miguel de Salcedo
Parque Nacional Llanganates
El Corazón
Pillaro
AMBATO
Río Jatunyacu
Río Arajuno
Río Shiripuno
Reserva Huaorani
Tiguino
2
Río Tiguino
Reserva Faunística Chimborazo
Baños
Río Verde
Mera
PUYO
Río Namo
Río Curaray
Volcán Tungurahua (5016m)
Penipe
GUARANDA
Guano
RIOBAMBA
Volcán El Altar (5319m)
Palora
San Miguel
Río Pintoyacu
Volcán Sangay (5230m)
Guamote
Pallatanga
Río Upano
Río Pastaza
Río Capahuari
Bucay
Alausí
Atillo
San Vincente
9 de Octobre
Purshi
Chunchi
Parque Nacional Sangay
MACAS
Sevilla
Río Cushuimi
Taisha
Río Paute
San Luís
Suscal
Sucúa
El Tambo
Ingapirca
6
Cañar
Logroño
Biblián
Méndez
AZOGUES
Paute
CUENCA
Gualaceo
Chordeleg
Morona
Limón
San Bartolomé
Sígsig
Indanza
Cueva de los Tayos
Girón
San Juan Bosco
Río Coangos
Río Zamora
Gualaquiza
Bomboiza
Oña
To Los Encuentros (22km); Yantzaza (45km); Zamora (85km)
El Pangui
JUNGLE LODGES
Arajuno Jungle Lodge.....1 F4
Bataburo Lodge.....2 D3
Cabañas Aliñahui.....3 E4
Casa del Suizo.....4 F4
Cuyabeno Lodge.....5 F5
Kapawi.....6 D5
La Selva Jungle Lodge.....7 E6
Napo Wildlife Center.....8 E6
Sacha Lodge.....9 E6
Sani Lodge.....10 F6
Selva Viva & Liana Lodge.....11 F4
Yachana Lodge.....12 F4
Yarina Lodge.....13 E6
Yuturi Lodge.....14 F6

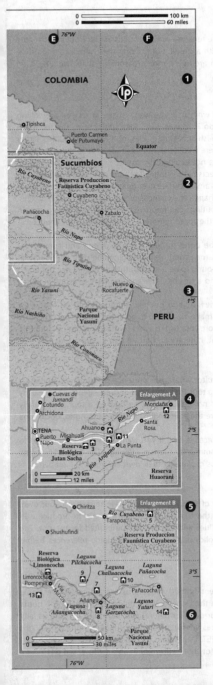

THE NORTHERN ORIENTE

Oil platforms, jungle lodges, indigenous villages, park lands and the white-water rivers and grey cities in between comprise the modern mosaic of the northern Oriente. With so much frontier development, it would be tempting to write off this area as tainted – except there is so much of it, and its biodiversity is mind-boggling and inspiring. You won't find wild animals near the main towns of Lago Agrio, Coca, Tena and Puyo, but that gives the perfect excuse to take your explorations further.

A paved road from Quito splits at Baeza; the north fork heads to Lago Agrio, the south fork goes to Tena. The other main road zips from highland Baños to Puyo in under two hours. In the rainiest months (June to August) roads can wash out and airports can close. Always allow an extra day or two between important connections in Quito.

FROM QUITO TO LAGO AGRIO
☎ 06

The road climbs from the Quito Valley over the eastern Cordillera via a pass nearly 4100m high. From the shivering heights of *páramo* (Andean grasslands) you descend into the Amazon Basin through remnant cloud forest, past waterfalls and into the humid lowlands of the Oriente. Two hours from Quito you'll pass Ecuador's best thermal baths, Papallacta, to your left. A half-hour later the road forks at Baeza; Tena is to the right, Lago Agrio 170km to the left. This latter road parallels the trans-Andean oil pipeline (which removes hundreds of thousands of barrels of oil each day), its visual impact so searing that one Ecuadorian said, 'Every time I see it I see the wealth sucked out of the jungle.' Some 95km before Lago Agrio, San Rafael Falls is next to the road on the right. At 145m high, these are Ecuador's biggest falls. Here to the left stands the (usually cloud-covered) 3562m Volcán El Reventador, which erupted spectacularly in November, 2002.

Papallacta
elevation 3300m

After a sweaty jungle expedition or arduous hike, a soak in these celestial hot springs is

THE ORIENTE

PREPARING FOR A JUNGLE TRIP

Because access is difficult, indigenous areas are sensitive and directions are far from intuitive, the jungle is best observed either in a tour or with a guide. Considering the complicated logistics, many tours and lodges offer packages which are as, or more, reasonable than swinging it on your own.

Types of Tours

The first step in trip planning is figuring out what it is you want to see, what you are willing to spend and how much time you have to do it. Lower costs may translate to the following conditions: more basic accommodations, Spanish-speaking guides, non-naturalist guides, larger group sizes and treading the beaten path where wildlife sightings are few. In some cases, tours may be cutting corners with practices that are not ecologically sound.

Different operators emphasize different aspects of the jungle. They can advise you on the probability of seeing wildlife, although no sightings anywhere are ever guaranteed (if they were, you'd be at the zoo). Observation towers greatly enhance the chances of sighting birds and monkeys. Early morning, late afternoon and nighttime outings can improve the chances of seeing certain species. Basically, the longer your trip is and the more remote it is, the better your chances of sighting birds and other wildlife.

Seeing how indigenous cultures live can be done through both high-end and community tourism. The high-end options will offer translators, comfortable lodging and may run beneficial community programs. Community tourism is bound to be a more authentic experience but much easier if you at least speak Spanish, don't mind a flexible itinerary, and have a strong stomach and sense of adventure.

Independent travelers can boat to Peru on the Río Napo, but hiking around alone is not advised (it is a jungle out there). Whatever choices you make, be sure to tread lightly and respect the local communities. Work the details out carefully before your trip to avoid confusion or disappointment, and thoroughly discuss costs, food, equipment, itinerary and group size before a tour.

Booking a Tour

The most likely place to book your tour is Quito, where the presence of numerous operators allows you to shop quickly and thoroughly for a tour that suits your desires. Agencies can usually get you into the jungle with only a few days' notice. Once you've booked a tour, you usually have to make your own way to the town where the tour begins (usually Lago Agrio, Coca, Tena or Misahuallí).

Booking a tour from Tena, Coca, Puyo or Macas is best if you want a guide for short trips to a nearby reserve or to try one of the many community tourism offerings. The Cofan, Huaorani, Quechua, Shuar and other groups all offer trips guided by their own community members.

Guides

A good guide will be able to show you a lot of things you would have missed on your own, whereas an inadequate guide will likely spoil the trip. Guides should be able to produce a license on request. Find out the guide's specialities and if game will be hunted for the pot. The rain forest is overhunted, and a no-hunting policy is a must. Seek out guide references before you pony up.

What to Bring

Most jungle towns have only very basic equipment. Bottled water, tarps (for rain) and rubber boots (up to about size 45) are all readily available in the Oriente. Many guided tours loan both boots and raingear, but make sure to check with your outfitter beforehand. Mosquito nets are usually provided in most places that need them. Besides your general travel supplies, bring a flashlight with extra batteries and sunblock with 30% DEET. Depending on the time of year and your destination, you may need to bring malaria pills (for more information about these, see p415).

medicine for weary bones. Termas de Papallacta is Ecuador's most luxurious, best-kept and probably most scenic thermal baths. The complex, which has more than three-dozen pools, is about 3km outside the village of Papallacta itself. It's also a good daytrip from Quito, 67km (two hours) away. Be prepared for the on-off chilly rains.

TERMAS DE PAPALLACTA

About 1.5km before the village, on the left as you approach from Quito, a signed dirt road leads 2km uphill to Termas de Papallacta. The setting is grand: beyond the lush hillsides you can see the snowcapped **Volcán Antisana** (5753m), 15km south, on a clear day. Be aware that the hot springs are a poorly kept secret and weekend crowds can swell to 2000 people! It's really best to go during the week. There are two sets of pools: the **Balneario** (admission $6, free for hotel guests; 7am-9pm) and the **Spa** (admission $15). The Balneario is a Roman holiday with more than 25 sparkling pools of varying temperatures surrounded by plush grass and red-orange blossoms. The nearby Río Loreto-Papallacta makes for an exhilarating plunge. Towels and lockers (both $0.50) are available. There's little reason to spend the extra money on the spa, although it is less crowded, smaller, has nicer changing facilities and extra sauna facilities. Pool water is changed daily.

SLEEPING & EATING

Hotel Termas de Papallacta (Quito 02-250 4747, 256 8989; www.termaspapallacta.com; Foch E7-38 & Reina Victoria, 4th fl; s/d $66/90, 6-person cabins $205;) A posh retreat of thatched adobe cabins with smart wood-panel rooms. The surrounding outdoor hot-springs are exclusively for hotel guests. All accommodations have private bathrooms, heating, hot showers and tubs. An array of spa treatments ($10 to $36) will knead and pat your muscles into oblivion. Weekends must be reserved well in advance.

There are two restaurants (mains $5 to $8; both open 8am to 8pm) – one in the hotel and another at the Balneario. Both serve delicious local trout.

Hostal Antisana (232 0626; r per person $10) This scruffy *hostal* (small, reasonably-priced hotel) sits longingly outside Termas de Papallacta. It's friendly and has a cheap restaurant, but bring warm clothes if you spend the

night. Is located north off the Quito–Baeza road.

Hostería La Pampa de Papallacta (232 0624; r per person $8) The Spartan adobe cabins could use some sprucing up but their location (at the entrance to the springs off the Quito–Baeza road) is convenient.

Coturpa (232 0640; r per person shared/private bathroom $7.50/10; 7am-5pm) Simple community-run accommodations located in the village of Papallacta offer cement-slab hot springs on-site (admission $2; a far cry from Termas de Papallacta). Bring your own towel.

La Choza de Don Wilson (232 0627; mains $3.50) Almost everyone comes to this honky-tonk restaurant for an excellent fillet of trout and shots of *aguardiente* (sugarcane alcohol) to beat off the chills. You'll find it at the juncture with the road to Termas de Papallacta. Cement-floor rooms out back are plain but clean (single/double rooms $10 to $16) with views of the village below. Situated 40km along the Quito–Baeza road.

GETTING THERE & AWAY

Any of the buses from Quito heading toward Baeza, Tena or Lago Agrio can drop you off in Papallacta, as can the occasional Papallacta bus. Leaving Quito you can opt to flag down a bus at the intersection known as El Trébol (ask your taxi driver) to avoid the bus terminal. To go to the Termas de Papallacta complex, make sure that the driver lets you off on the road to the baths, 1.5km before the village. To leave Papallacta, flag down a bus on the main road. Weekend buses are standing-room only.

Baeza & Around

Weathered but friendly, this old Spanish missionary and trading outpost, first founded in 1548, makes a quiet base for walks in the surrounding foothills. Plant and bird life are outstanding and, since Baeza hosted the world rafting championships in 2005, white-water culture is gaining momentum.

A half-hour beyond Papallacta the road splits. The northerly road goes to Lago Agrio and the other reaches Baeza 2km from the junction and continues toward Tena.

SLEEPING & EATING

Samay Inn (232 0170; Nueva Andalucía; shared/private bathroom $4/5) Rooms in this friendly clapboard home come in all the colors of the rainbow. There's TV and hot water.

Hostal Bambu's (☎ 232 0219; Nueva Andalucía; r per person $10) Cool interiors have tile floors and flannel bedspreads. There's table tennis and an enclosed thermal pool for kicks. Located at the east end of the strip, toward Tena.

Oro Negro (☎ 232 0016; r per person without bathroom $6) A well-kept little truck stop with a gas station, restaurant and direct TV in the rooms where beds are stacked on concrete slabs. It's at the junction of the roads to Lago Agrio and Tena.

El Viejo (☎ 232 0442; Nueva Andalucía; mains $6; ☻ 7am-9pm) A two-tier dining room with bright sunflower walls and tasty trout and ceviche.

Cabañas San Isidro (Quito ☎ 02-254 7403; www .ecuadorexplorer.com/sanisidro; Carrión 555, Quito; s/d incl 3 meals $97/170) In a spectacular setting at 2000m, this former cattle ranch offers first-class birding. Its co-owner Mitch Lsinger is one of the top birders of South America. Comfortable cabins have decks with fine views of forest. Rooms have hot-water bathrooms and there are sturdy hiking trails nearby. Advance reservation is required. To get there go 17km on the road to Tena (mileage starts from the juncture before Baeza), the turn-off is just before the village of Cosanga.

About 10km away on the road to Lago Agrio you reach the village of San Francisco de Borja and **Cabañas Tres Ríos** (☎ 09-792 0120; r per person incl breakfast & dinner $30), a group of lovely cabins east of the village and across Río Quijos. They can also arrange Spanish classes and area tours, hikes, rafting and biking. Catering mainly to kayakers, the cabins are often full from November to February. Contact **Small World Adventures** (USA ☎ 1-800-585-2925; www.smallworldadventures.com) for more information.

GETTING THERE & AWAY
Flag down one of the many buses going to and from Lago Agrio, Tena and Quito and hope there's room. Coming from Quito, take a Tena-bound bus from the main terminal.

San Rafael Falls
Beyond Baeza you will pass by thick patches of cloud forest harboring strange species of birds and plants. **San Rafael Falls** (admission $10) and a sash of Río Quijos can be glimpsed

from the road. The entrance fee is steep, but waterfall fanatics earn bragging rights to Ecuador's largest falls. To visit the falls, ask the bus driver to let you off just before at the *puente* (bridge) crossing Río Reventador (not the community of the same name). You'll see a concrete-block hut on the right side of the road. From the hut, it's about 2.5km down a steep trail to the falls. Back on the main road, flag a bus down when you want to move on.

Volcán El Reventador
Until this volcano erupted in 2002 it was possible to hike to its summit. Due to continuing volcanic activity, hiking is allowed only to the *refugio* (basic shelter) at 2400m. Given that lava flows have wiped out the already faint trail, it's easy to get lost and no one would think to come and find you. Contracting a local guide would be most prudent. **Victor Cansino** (☎ 09-357 7143; turismo volcanreventador@yahoo.com; per day $30) has extensive experience leading vulcanologists up the mountain and can teach you about the medicinal uses of native plants. A hike to the straw-hut refuge is six hours round-trip. It's also possible to sleep there and return the next day. If activity eventually calms, the hike to the crater is six hours one-way. For updates consult the **Instituto Geofísico** (☎ 02-222 5655; www.igepn.edu.ec).

You can stay overnight at **Hostería San Rafael** (☎ 281 8221; r per person $10; ☻), a friendly, if run-down, concrete lodge where you may also find Victor serving up fish and chips in the restaurant. The volcano is within the eastern boundaries of **Reserva Ecológica Cayambe-Coca**, which includes **Volcán Cayambe** (for more information see p116). There are no signs or entrance stations. The guard station is in the village of **El Chaco**, about 20km beyond the Río Reventador bridge on the way to Baeza.

Bus drivers on the Quito–Lago Agrio run can let you off at the San Rafael falls, opposite the *hostería* (small hotel), which is a good starting point for the hike).

LAGO AGRIO
☎ 06 / pop 34,100
The first oil workers nicknamed Lago Agrio 'bitter lake,' after Sour Lake, Texas, the former home of Texaco, which pioneered local drilling (see p235). The city's official name is Nueva Loja, although no one will bother

call it that. Locals settle for 'Lago.' What-
ver you call it, this unkempt oil town is
ot high on tourists' lists. It takes a certain
reed to navigate the platform sandal shops
nd street grills serving *guanta* (agouti).
eedy bars, prostitutes and fugitives share
eal estate with high-spending oil workers
hile hard-working locals keep their heads
own and mind their own business (as visi-
ors should too).

The provincial capital of Sucumbíos, La-
o's real attraction is as the entry point to
he spectacular and singular Cuyabeno re-
erve. For most travelers, Lago is simply an
vernight stop on the way to the reserve.

nformation

ago Agrio has very few street signs and
cant building numbers. *Casas de cambio*
currency-exchange services) on Avenida
Quito near Avenida Colombia can change
Colombian pesos.

ndinatel (cnr Orellana & 18 de Noviembre)
anco de Guayaquil (cnr Quito & 12 de Febrero;
⏰ 8am-4pm Mon-Fri, 9am-noon Sat) Changes traveler's
necks; has an ATM.

Banco del Pichincha (12 de Febrero) Has an ATM.
Casa de Cultura (☎ 283 2505; 2nd fl, cnr Manabí &
Av Quito; ⏰ 2-9:30pm Mon-Fri) Offers movie viewings.
Contact Manual Silva for local indigenous and environ-
mental affairs.
Clínica González (☎ 283 0728, 283 1691; cnr Av Quito
& 12 de Febrero) The best medical attention.
Frente de Defensa de la Amazonia (☎ 283 1930;
admin@fda.ecuanex.net.ec; Eloy Alfaro 352) Contact with
Cofan indigenous guides; active in environmental issues.
Interactive (☎ 283 0529; Río Amazonas; per hr $3)
Internet access, inside the entrance to Hotel La Cascada.
Migraciones (Immigration Office; 18 de Noviembre)
Police station (Av Quito)
Post office (Rocafuerte)
World System Internet (Av Quito 522 near Orellana; per
hr $1.50; ⏰ 9:30am-7pm Mon-Sat, 9:30am-noon Sun)

Dangers & Annoyances

The ongoing conflict in neighboring Colombia has made border towns such as
Lago Agrio havens for Colombian guer-
rillas, antirebel paramilitaries and drug
smugglers. Suffice it to say, it is not recommended to cross into Colombia here.
In town, bars can be risky and side-streets

LAGO AGRIO

0   200 m
0   0.1 miles

INFORMATION
Andinatel............................1 B2
Banco de Guayaquil.........2 B3
Banco del Pichincha.........3 B2
Casa de Cultura................4 C3
Casas de Cambio..............5 C2
Clínica González...............6 B3
Colombian Consulate.......7 C2
Frente de Defensa de la
   Amazonía......................8 C2
Interactive...............(see 18)
Migraciones......................9 C2
Police Station..................10 B3
Post Office......................11 B3
TAME Airline Office.........12 B1
World System Internet.....13 B3

SLEEPING
Araza Hotel.....................14 A3
Hotel Casablanca............15 C2
Hotel D'Mario.................16 C3
Hotel Gran Colombia.......17 C3
Hotel La Cascada............18 C3

EATING
Pizzería D'Mario............(see 16)

TRANSPORT
Taxis-Trucks to La Punta...19 C2
Transportes Putumayo.....20 B3

THE ORIENTE

unsafe, so stick to the main drag, especially at night, or take a taxi to the restaurants further out. Tourists rarely have problems.

Armed robberies have taken place near the entry to the Cuyabeno reserve. At this time, ranger presence is increasing and lodges are coordinating to keep the area safer. At the time of research many lodges were reconsidering their presence.

Sights & Activities

You might find Cofan (see p236) selling their handicrafts at the Sunday morning **market**.

Sleeping

There are decent hotels along Avenida Quito. Mosquitoes can be a problem, especially in the rainy months (June to August), so look for fans or mosquito nets in the rooms. Most lack hot water, or charge steeply for it.

Hotel Casablanca (☎ 283 0181; Av Quito 228; s/d $10/15) The best value in town, even if the colorful Biblical references feel a little preachy. Whitewashed, ample rooms have fans and there are Bible verses scattered throughout.

Hotel Gran Colombia (☎ 283 1032; Av Quito 265; s/d with fan $10/12, s/d with air-con $15/18; 🛄) Country decor rooms seem puny in this megalith, but it's secure and decent value. The restaurant is popular and most rooms have phones, minibar and cable TV.

Hotel D'Mario (☎ 283 0172; Av Quito 1-171; hotel mario@andinanet.net; s $15-32, d $17-40; 🛄 🖳 🖵) Tour groups favor this midstrip staple. While the service is somewhat indifferent, there's free Internet for guests and the rooms, though cramped, make cozy efforts. All rooms have private bathroom and fan or air-conditioning; some come with fridges and drinks.

Araza Hotel (☎ 283 0223, 283 1247; arazahot@andinanet.net; Av Quito 610; s/d incl breakfast $36/46; 🖵 🖳) Gauzy curtains and firm beds create an ambient refuge. Rooms in the posterior building are larger but less cozy. All are sparkling clean with hot water, TV and minifridge. If you have time, check out the gym and swimming pool.

Hotel La Cascada (☎ 283 2229; aliarco@yahoo.com; Av Quito 291; s/d incl breakfast $25/35; 🛄 🖳) Offstreet rooms are small yet snug, insulating guests from the gritty streets. The swimming pool sparkles and all rooms have TVs

and recessed lighting. Breakfast is serve in the restaurant, which is also open fo other meals.

Eating

Because oil workers end work on Sun day it's the busiest night for eating out o traveling. Most restaurants are closed Mon day and Tuesday.

Maytos (☎ 283 0641; Av Quito; mains $5; 🕑 2-11pr Mon-Sat) Serves fish *(maitos)* Huaorani-style but with a garlicky twist. Wrapped in banan leaves and steamed over hot coals, the flavor steam right into the moist, flaky fish, serve alongside *patacones* (sliced and then mashe and fried plantains) and rice. Perfect with tall, cold brew. Next to the Texaco station.

Pizzería D'Mario (Av Quito; mains $5; 🕑 6:30am midnight) Opt for grilled meats or pasta ove the pizza, whose gloppy aspect is amateu This outdoor café is the social hub fo travelers and tour groups passing throug Lago. Located inside Hotel D'Mario.

Freedom (☎ 283 1180; Av Quito & Circubalacíon dinner $8; 🕑 6:30-11pm, closed Mon & Tue) Thi thatched-hut outdoor grill has tasty side of homemade salsa, salad and yuca.

Other eateries, including chicken rotis serie stalls and fast-food vendors line Ave nida Quito.

Getting There & Away

AIR

Flying isn't that expensive and it avoids a trying bus trip on a corkscrew mountair road. Reservations fill up fast with jungle lodge guests and oil workers traveling home for the weekend; so make reservations early If you can't, it is worth getting on the wait ing list and going to the airport in the hope of cancellations. Tour companies sometimes book up more seats than they can use.

TAME (☎ 283 0113; Orellana near 9 de Octubre) ha flights from Quito at 10:30am Monday to Saturday. Flights return to Quito at 11:30am on the same days. On Mondays and Fridays flights leave Quito at 4:30pm and return from Lago Agrio at 5:30pm ($43, 30 minutes).

Icaro (☎ 283 2370/1, 288 0546; www.icaro.com.ec airport) flies from Quito Monday, Wednesday and Friday at 10:25am and returns at 11:20am.

The airport is about 3km east of town (a 10-minute trip), and taxis (yellow or white pickup trucks) cost about $2.

THE ORIENTE

ORDER CROSSING

'he Colombian border is less than 20km
orth of town but it is best to avoid it. The
rea is notorious for smugglers, and in early
000, FARC (Revolutionary Armed Forces
f Colombia) rebels crossed the border and
idnapped a group of tourists and oil work-
rs, who were later released.

The most frequently used route from
,ago Agrio is to La Punta (about 1½ hours),
n Río San Miguel. Taxi-trucks leave Lago
Agrio from the corner of Alfaro and Co-
ombia and go to La Punta during the day.
'rom La Punta you cross to Puerto Colón,
n the Colombian side of the river, and
hen get a bus to Puerto Asis (about six

hours by unpaved road), where there are
hotels and transportation by road, air and
river to other parts of Colombia.

BUS

The drive from the jungle up into the Andes
(and vice versa) is beautiful, and it's worth
doing in daylight. Night buses have had
occasional robberies.

The bus terminal, about 2km northwest of the center, has a wide selection of
routes and options. Buses depart for Quito
($8, eight hours) almost every hour until
11:45pm. Cooperativo Loja and Cooperativo Esmeraldas have better *ejecutivo* buses.
Putumayo goes to Tulcán via a new route

A CRUDE LEGACY

The damage oil companies have wreaked on the Ecuadorian Amazon – both naturally and cultur-
ally – is extreme. According to environmentalists, one of the greatest oil-related disasters of all
time lies at the feet of the Texaco oil corporation (now Chevron), which, in partnership with state-
owned Petroecuador, extracted some 5.3 billion liters of oil from the northern Oriente between
1964 and 1992. The US-based company now faces accusations that it knowingly dumped more
than 30 times the amount of oil that was spilled by the *Exxon Valdez* in 1989 in Alaska.

In early 2005, ChevronTexaco was embroiled as a defendant in a historic class-action trial
filed against the company in the USA on behalf of some 30,000 Ecuadorians. The main claim
is that Texaco designed and operated a system that intentionally dumped 70.1 billion liters of
toxic waste water and 60.6 million liters of raw crude into the rain forest; was racist in its disregard for the industry-wide standards practiced in developed nations; decimated the indigenous
populations (especially the Cofan and Secoya) and the fragile rain forest ecosystems in the region where it drilled; and created a toxic environment resulting in cancer rates up several times
higher than the norm. The company is now accused of committing a crime against humanity
by subjecting the indigenous groups to risk of extinction due to its intentional contamination.
Sounds major? It is.

The lawsuit is the first ever class-action environmental suit brought against an American multinational oil by rain forest dwellers, or for that matter any party, on their home turf. United States
federal courts earlier had removed the case to Ecuador, arguing that was a more convenient forum
for the trial. Chevron says that Texaco complied with Ecuadorian law while operating in Ecuador
and adhered to industry-wide standards. It also says health problems are caused largely by fecal
matter in the water, not petroleum contamination. The $40 million Chevron spent in 1995 to
clean up is less than 1% of the $6 billion the plaintiffs estimate a comprehensive environmental
clean-up to cost (not including individual damages).

Judicial inspections of the area examine toxic contamination at the sites Texaco claims to have
remediated. Although Texaco closed shop in the northern Oriente in 1992, there are reportedly
more than 600 open-air pits still leeching toxins into local ecosystems. Many of the pits are the
size of a football field, and they are certainly worth a visit if your idea of a vacation is to see
firsthand the ugly impact of the oil industry in a pristine ecosystem. Amazon Watch estimates the
contaminated area of rain forest to be roughly the size of Rhode Island. For a 'toxic tour,' you can
contact the **Front for the Defense of the Amazon** (www.texacotoxico.com) in Lago Agrio.

To learn more about the case and how to get involved check out the websites of **Amazon
Watch** (www.amazonwatch.org), **ChevronToxico** (www.chevrontoxico.com) or **Texaco Rainforest** (www
.texacorainforest.org). You can read ChevronTexaco's side of the story on the **Texaco website** (www
.texaco.com).

THE ORIENTE

($7, seven hours). If you want to cross the border, this is the best option. Ruta Costa has seven departures daily for Guayaquil ($14, 14 hours) There are one or two daily departures, mainly overnight, to Tena, Puyo, Ambato, Riobamba, Cuenca and Machala.

Buses to Coca aren't usually found in the bus terminal; catch a Petroleras Rancheras ($3, 2½ hours) open-air bus on Avenida Quito in the center. They leave every 20 minutes until 6pm. Transportes Putumayo buses go through the jungle towns of Dureno and Tarapoa and have access to the Cuyabeno reserve.

ALONG RÍO AGUARICO
☎ 06
This is one of the few regions within the Cuyabeno reserve that travelers can visit on their own. It's off the beaten track, so come prepared.

The Cofans have well-organized **ecotourism** (www.cofan.org) with detailed information available in English on the website. Given the rapid environmental degradation of the area around Lago Agrio, these trips start at Chiritza but head to remote Zábalo.

The Cofan are related to the Secoya people, and they numbered in the tens of thousands before early contact with whites decimated them (mainly by disease). Before the discovery of oil, most Cofans' exposure to non-Indigenous people was limited to the occasional missionary, and they still remain reticent.

The Cofans are excellent wilderness guides with broad knowledge about the medicinal and practical uses of jungle plants. A tour costs $65 per day with a native guide and $100 per day with an English-speaking naturalist. Guides Delfín Criollo and Lauriano Quenama have been recommended by readers. Contact them via the www.cofan .org website or by asking around in Dureno. They speak Cofan, with Spanish as their second language, but they do not understand English. The normal tour lasts six days but tours can be tailored to individual requests with previous notice.

Dureno
This is off-the-beaten-path tourism and is not for those expecting creature comforts. Although you won't see much wildlife, a local guide can show and explain jungle

plants to you; these trips are more for th cultural experience.

With river transportation infrequen take a Transportes Putumayo bus (there a several a day) to Tarapoa or Tipishca. The pass the Dureno (Cofan village) turnof 23km from Lago Agrio. It is poorly marke so ask your driver for the indigenous villag known as Comuna Cofan Dureno. From th turnoff, follow the path to Río Aguaric 100m away. If you didn't call ahead by radi to arrange for transportation across the rive you can holler, mime and whistle to attra the attention of the villagers on the othe side, although this might not always work

Caution! There are two Durenos. Th Cofan village is 23km east of Lago Agri if you miss the turnoff, you will end up the colonists' village of Dureno, 4km fu ther east.

Zábalo
This is a small Cofan community on R Aguarico near the confluence with th smaller Río Zábalo. Across the river fro the village there is an interpretive cente with a Cofan guide. Souvenirs are sold, an a rain forest walk to see medicinal and othe plants, accompanied by the guide, is part the program. Visiting the village witho advance notice is discouraged and takin photographs is not allowed.

For information and to make reserva tions contact **Randy Borman** (Quito ☎ 02-247 094 randy@cofan.org). The son of American mission aries who came to the Oriente in the 1950 Randy was raised among Cofan, and fo mally educated in Quito. He later founde the settlement of Zábalo, where he still live with his Cofan wife and family, along with handful of other Cofan families. He is high respected and the chief of the most trad itional remaining group of Cofan. Rand guides occasional groups but spends muc of his time in Quito working to preserve th Cofan culture and the rain forest.

RESERVA PRODUCCIÓN FAUNÍSTICA CUYABENO
This beautiful **reserve** (admission $20) is unique flooded rain forest covering 6034 s km around Río Cuyabeno in northeaster Ecuador. Seasonally inundated, the floode forest provides a home to diverse aquati species and bird life. Macrolobium an

ceiba treetops thrust out from the underwater forest, creating a stunning visual effect. The blackwater rivers, rich in tannins from decomposing foliage, form a maze of waterways which feed the lagoons.

The boundaries of the reserve shift with the political winds, but it is now substantially larger than it was originally.

The reserve was created in 1979 with the goals of protecting this area of rain forest, conserving its wildlife and providing a sanctuary in which the indigenous inhabitants of the area – the Siona, Secoya, Cofan, Quechua and Shuar – could lead their customary way of life. The numerous lakes and swamps are home to fascinating aquatic species, such as freshwater dolphins, manatees, caimans and anacondas. Monkeys abound, and tapirs, peccaries, agoutis and several cat species have been recorded. The bird life is abundant.

Its protected status notwithstanding, Cuyabeno was opened to oil exploitation almost immediately after its creation. The new oil towns of Tarapoa and Cuyabeno and parts of the trans-Ecuadorian oil pipeline were within the reserve's boundaries. Roads were built, colonists followed, and tens of thousands of hectares of the reserve became logged or degraded by oil spills and toxic waste. At least six oil spills were recorded between 1984 and 1989, and others occurred unnoticed. Many of the contaminants entered Río Cuyabeno itself.

Various international and local agencies set to work to try to protect the area, which although legally protected was, in reality, open to development. Conservation International funded projects to establish more guard stations in Cuyabeno, train local Siona and Secoya to work in wildlife management, and support Cordavi, an Ecuadorian environmental-law group that challenged the legality of allowing oil exploitation in protected areas.

Finally, in late 1991 the government shifted the borders of the reserve further east and south and enlarged the area it covered. The new reserve is both remoter and better protected. Vocal local indigenous groups – which are supported by Ecuadorian and international nongovernmental organizations (NGOs), tourists, travel agencies and conservation groups – are proving to be its best stewards.

Due to its remoteness, and to protect the communities within it, travelers are recommended to visit only with a guided tour.

Tours

Agencies in Quito offer Cuyabeno tours that are actually run by a handful of operators on location. The tour camps and lodges are nearby each other on the river, with a few not far away around the vast lagoon. There is no location significantly privileged; all are relatively close and have similar chances to see wildlife. Travel is mainly by canoe and on foot – except between the drier months of December to February, when low water levels may limit the areas accessible by canoe. Most visitors come during the wetter months of March to September. Annual rainfall is between 2000mm and 4000mm, depending on the location, and humidity is often between 90% to 100%.

The best rates, especially for solo travelers, are obtained by squeezing into an existing trip. When booking a tour, check to see if transportation to and from Lago Agrio is included, if the travel day is considered a tour day in the price, if there is boiled or purified water and whether you can expect naturalist or native guides. The entry fee to Cuyabeno reserve is usually added on top of the cost of any tour. In Tarapoa, there is a guard post where you can pay the fee and ask for information.

Neotropic Turis (Quito ☎ 02-252 1212, 09-980 3395; www.neotropicturis.com) runs the comfortable and recommended **Cuyabeno Lodge** (packages per person for 4 days/3 nights $200-288, 5 days/4 nights $250-360) on Laguna Grande. Thatched huts spread out over a hillside offer a bit of privacy, and most have private bathroom and hot water. Rooms are rustic but comfortable with firm beds and mosquito nets. Bilingual naturalist guides get top reviews from guests and the food and attention are excellent. Prices include transfers from Lago Agrio, guide, drinking-water, coffee and tea. Canoes and kayaks are available to paddle around the lake.

SOUTH FROM LAGO AGRIO
☎ 06

The dusty, naked strips of brush, oil fires and banged-up villages between Lago Agrio and Coca exemplify the impact of oil on a recently pristine jungle. In the early 1970s communications were limited to mission airstrips and river travel but today this area sees a seamless stream of trucks and buses. The bus crosses the Río Aguarico a few kilometers outside Lago and passes occasional small communities. Shortly before reaching Coca, the bus goes through the small town of **La Joya de las Sachas**, where Hotel America is the best of a few poor options, and then passes the belching wells of the Sacha oil works. The road is narrow but in good condition and almost entirely paved.

COCA

☎ 06 / pop 18,300

Not long ago Coca was a cluster of lean-tos on dirt roads. Growth means concrete, lots of it, paved roads and ubiquitous hairdressing shops. The capital of the Orellana province since 1999 (and officially known as Puerto Francisco de Orellana), Coca embraces the fallout of oil exploration. Executives from 'the company,' as it's called (any oil company) are easily recognizable breakfasting in the best hotels in crisp shirts and leather boots. Throw into the mix the soldiers and sailors, urbanized indigenous and colonists. If you're traveling on to a jungle lodge on the lower Napo or to Peru, Coca is a lackluster but strangely compelling stop along the way.

Information

Andinatel office (cnr Eloy Alfaro & 6 de Diciembre)

Banco del Pinchincha (cnr Bolívar & 9 de Octubre) Has an ATM.

Casa de Cambio 3R (☎ 288 1229; cnr Napo & García Moreno; ☼ 8am-8pm Mon-Sat) Charges 4% commission to cash traveler's checks.

Clínica Sinai (cnr Napo & García Moreno) This clinic is preferred to the hospital.

Imperial Net (García Moreno; per hr $1.80; ☼ 9am-10pm) Internet service.

Post office (Napo near Cuenca)

Tourist information office (García Moreno; ☼ 8:30am-1pm & 2-5:30pm Mon-Fri) Information about Coca and the province of Orellana.

Tours

Tours which start in Coca may actually be better booked in Quito, due to a dearth of local operators. It's worth stopping by Luís García's **Emerald Forest Expeditions** (Quito ☎ 02-882 309; www.emeraldexpeditions.com; cnr Quito & Espejo, Coca, next to bar) if only to see the photo

of the 8m anaconda on the wall. With 20 in the business, Luís is a warm and engaging tour operator/guide with vast knowledge of his subject. His speciality is snakes. He loves them and has the charisma to make you love them too.

Tailored tours are $50 per day. Options include three-day camping trips to Pañacocha, a cloud and dryland forest where you can see dolphins, macaws and toucans. A new offering is an exciting 10-day journey (one-way) to Iquitos, Peru, via the Río Napo, guided by Fausto Andi. It requires four passengers minimum. All food and transportation are included in trips and guides speak English. Trips deeper into the jungle (to Ríos Shiripuno and Cononaco or to the Río Tiputini in Parque Nacional Yasuní) can also be arranged. It's best to make prior arrangements in Quito; see p89 for more details. However, you might get in with another group by stopping by the Coca office.

River Dolphin Expeditions (☎ 09-917 7529; Guayaquil near Napo) has extremely mixed reader reviews. Randy Smith, the former owner, has returned to Canada and his former partner Ramiro Viteri is now running the outfit. Expeditions run $60 per day or $750 for a 10-day trip to Iquitos, Peru (with a four-person minimum).

Tropic Ecological Adventures (Quito ☎ 02-225 907; www.tropiceco.com; Av República E7-320, apt 1A, Quito) also does tours to Huaorani territory. See p90 and p241.

Kem Pery Tours (Quito ☎ 02-226 583; www.kempery.com; Ramirez Dávalos 117 & Amazonas, Quito; lodge 3/4 nights $215/$255) does tours to Bataburo Lodge, on the edge of Huaorani territory, about nine hours from Coca by boat and bus. Canoes motor into the remote Ríos Tiguino and Cononaco and tours combine wildlife viewing with cultural visits. There is a $20 fee to enter Huaorani territory. Guides are both bilingual and native. See p241.

Independent guides who are recommended include **Oscar Tapuy** (☎ 288 1486; oscarta23@yahoo.com), one of the country's top birdguides and **Jarol Fernando Vaca** (Quito ☎ 02-224 1918; shiripuno2004@yahoo.com), a Quito-based naturalist and butterfly specialist who can take adventurous visitors into the Shiripuno area and is authorized by Huaorani to guide in their territory. Both speak English.

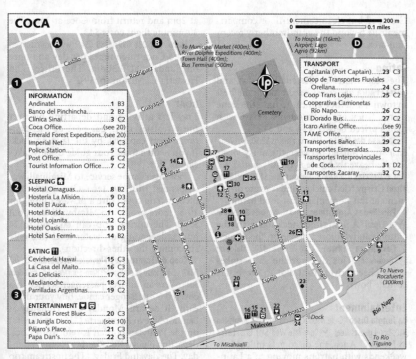

COCA

To Municipal Market (400m);
River Dolphin Expeditions (400m);
Town Hall (400m);
Bus Terminal (500m)

To Hospital (16km);
Airport; Lago
Agrio (92km)

To Nuevo
Rocafuerte
(300km)

To Misahuallí

To Río
Tiguino

INFORMATION	
Andinatel......................1	B3
Banco del Pinchincha..........2	B2
Clínica Sinaí...................3	C2
Coca Office...............(see 20)	
Emerald Forest Expeditions..(see 20)	
Imperial Net...................4	C3
Police Station.................5	C2
Post Office....................6	C2
Tourist Information Office......7	C2

SLEEPING	
Hostal Omaguas.................8	B2
Hostería La Misión.............9	D3
Hotel El Auca.................10	C2
Hotel Florida.................11	C2
Hotel Lojanita................12	C2
Hotel Oasis..................13	D3
Hotel San Fermin.............14	B2

EATING	
Cevichería Hawai..............15	C3
La Casa del Maito.............16	C3
Las Delicias..................17	C3
Medianoche...................18	C2
Parrilladas Argentinas........19	C2

ENTERTAINMENT	
Emerald Forest Blues..........20	C3
La Jungla Disco...........(see 10)	
Pájaro's Place...............21	C3
Papa Dan's...................22	C3

TRANSPORT	
Capitanía (Port Captain)......23	C3
Coop de Transportes Fluviales	
Orellana....................24	C3
Coop Trans Lojas.............25	C2
Cooperativa Camionetas	
Río Napo...................26	C2
El Dorado Bus................27	C2
Icaro Airline Office........(see 9)	
TAME Office..................28	C2
Transportes Baños............29	C2
Transportes Esmeraldas.......30	C2
Transportes Interprovinciales	
de Coca....................31	D2
Transportes Zacaray..........32	C2

Sleeping

Hotel San Fermin (☎ 288 1848; Quito & Bolívar; s/d with fan $9/17, with air-con $18/28; ⊠) The best new addition to town is this large, well-furnished house. Ample-sized rooms have polished hardwood or tile floors, comfortable beds and new fixtures. All have private bathroom and cable TV. Can arrange community tourism trips.

Hotel El Auca (☎ 288 0127, 288 0600; helauca@ecuanex.net.ec; Napo; s $12-35, d $20-50) Paca (*guatusas*) overrun the grounds, but if you don't mind furry creatures (there are monkeys too) this hotel is the most upscale in town, catering to tour groups and oil workers alike. Accommodations range from rustic wood cabins out back (with the critters) to luxurious and immaculate (if a bit frigid) hotel rooms upstairs in the main building. The cheapest rooms have fans and electric hot-water showers and the hotel rooms have air-conditioning. The restaurant here is a good place to dial into the local scene and there's patio seating surrounded by luxuriant gardens.

Hostería La Misión (☎ 288 0260, 288 0544; fax 880 263; Camilo de Torrano s/n; s/d with fan $17/25, with air-con $20/29; ⊠ 🖳) Small peach- or papaya-colored rooms fill this concrete monolith on the river. There's an enormous swimming pool and all rooms have hot water and cable TV. The riverside restaurant and bar are the place to be on a warm evening (mains $6 to $12), with good service and specialities such as tender steaks and *pollo española* (chicken in a garlicky fresh tomato sauce).

Hostal Omaguas (☎ 288 0136; cnr Quito & Cuenca; s/d $17/28) Brightly tiled and barely broken-in, this welcoming spot has cool, sparsely furnished rooms. It also includes cable TV, hot water and a restaurant.

Hotel Oasis (☎ 288 0206; yuturilodge@yahoo.com; Camilo de Torrano s/n; r per person $8) Rooms are run down, with cracked walls and electrical wires peeking out, but you're away from the fray with a nice deck view of the river. The staff arranges trips to the Yuturi and Yarina Lodges further down Río Napo (see p241).

Hotel Lojanita (☎ 288 0032; cnr Napo & Cuenca; r per person with fan/air-con $8/12; ⊠) Slightly musty but comfortable rooms are near the bus station.

Hotel Florida (☎ 288 0177; Alejandro Labaka; s/d shared bathroom $6/10, with private bathroom $10/15)

THE ORIENTE

Cramped but clean cement-floor compartments lie beyond the grandmotherly reception area.

Eating

The restaurants at **Hostería La Misión** and **Hotel El Auca** are considered among the best in town – and they appear to have the same menu. They are both open all day, with mains priced between $6 and $12.

La Casa del Maito (Malecón; mains $2.50; ☺ 7am-6pm) Stuff yourself between the noisy locals for the heavenly house speciality *maito*.

Las Delicias (cnr Napo & Cuenca; mains $1.50; ☺ 8am-11pm) Crispy fried chicken and fries are on the menu at this homemade fast-food haunt.

Parrilladas Argentinas (2nd fl, cnr Inés & Cuenca; ☺ 6-11pm) A longtime steakhouse in the cotton-candy-colored house on the corner.

Cevichería Hawai (☎ 09-342 320; Malecón; ☺ 8am-noon) This tiny ceviche shop stakes out a cheery river-front slot to serve tart ceviche bowls.

Entertainment

La Jungla Disco (Calle Napo & García Moreno; admission $10, hotel guests free; ☺ 9pm-late Wed-Sat) Upstairs at Hotel El Auca, the disco gets mileage on weekends with patrons moving to a Latin-rock mix and downing the *cuba libres* (rum cocktails) and beers that are included in the admission.

Emerald Forest Blues (☎ 288 2280; Quito; ☺ 9am-late) An '80s soundtrack fills the background of this friendly little bar run by Luís García of Emerald Forest Expeditions.

Papa Dan's (cnr Chimborazo & Napo; ☺ 4pm-2am) A rickety bamboo hangout popular with locals.

Pájaro's Place (cnr Chimborazo & Napo; ☺ 8pm-2am) Mixes *reggaetón* (dance music blending reggae and dancehall with hip-hop) with tropical for steamy jungle nights.

Getting There & Away

AIR

The airport terminal is almost 2km north of town on the left-hand side of the road to Lago Agrio. A 10-minute taxi ride there costs about $1.

TAME (☎ 288 1078; cnr Napo & Rocafuerte; ☺ 7:30am-7pm Mon-Sat, 8am-6pm Sun) flies from Quito to Coca 9:35am on Monday through Saturday, departing at 10:35am. On Tuesday, Thursday and Sunday flights from Quito leave

at 2pm and return from Coca at 3pm. The 30-minute flight costs $43.

Icaro (☎ 288 0997, 288 0546; www.icaro.com.ec) flies to Coca three times per day and once on Sundays at 2:30pm. The office is in Hostería La Misión (p239).

BOAT

Travelers arriving and departing by river must register their passport at the *capitanía* (port captain), by the landing dock. If you're on a tour, your guide usually takes care of this.

Passenger canoe service to Misahuallí was suspended with the Tena–Coca road completion. You could hire a private canoe (for 10 or more people) to Misahuallí for about $250. The upriver trip can take up to 14 hours, depending on water level (it's only six coming the other direction).

Coop de Transportes Fluviales Orellana (☎ 288 0087; Chimborazo at docks; ☺ 8am-5pm Mon-Fri, 2:30-6pm Sun) offers an upriver passenger service in a covered 60-passenger canoe. Buy your ticket early. It departs Monday and Thursday at 8am for Nuevo Rocafuerte ($15, nine hours) on the Peruvian border. It returns to Coca, departing Nuevo Rocafuerte at 5am on Sunday, Tuesday and Friday. (The upstream trip is 12 to 14 hours). Although there's usually a stop for lunch, be sure to bring food and water for the long trip. For information on crossing to Peru by river and continuing to Iquitos in Peru, see p245. Canoes with an 18-passenger capacity can be rented for $60 per hour.

BUS

For most departures it isn't necessary to go to the bus terminal at the north end of town, but still check where to board your bus at purchase time.

Transportes Baños (☎ 288 0182; cnr Napo & Bolívar) has several buses daily to Quito ($10, eight to 10 hours). The trip by Vía Loreto is fastest. **Transportes Esmeraldas** (☎ 288 1077; cnr Napo & Cuenca) has two night buses to Quito. Both companies have buses to Lago Agrio ($3, two hours). **Transportes Zacaray** (☎ 288 0286; cnr Napo & Bolívar) heads daily to Guayaquil ($16, 16 hours). **El Dorado** goes to Tena ($6, six hours), continuing to Puyo ($7, nine hours). **Coop Trans Loja** (☎ 288 0272; cnr Cuenca & Amazonas) goes to Machala ($20, 22 hours) and Loja ($25, 27 hours).

At the bus terminal, 500m north of town, Transportes Jumandy has several buses a day to Tena. Transportes Loja, at the terminal, has evening departures to Santo Domingo, Quevedo, Babahoyo, Machala and Loja. Transportes Interprovinciales de Coca, at the bus terminal and on Alejandro Labaka, has buses that go south to Río Tiguino.

Open-sided trucks called rancheras or *chivas* leave from the terminal for various destinations between Coca and Lago Agrio, and to Río Tiputini to the south. Pickup trucks and taxis at **Cooperativa Camionetas Río Napo** (Eloy Alfaro) provide service in town and out.

VÍA AUCA
☎ 06

This road from Coca crosses Río Napo and continues south across Río Tiputini and Río Shiripuno, ending near the small community of **Tiguino**, on Río Tiguino. Daily rancheras go as far as Tiguino. This used to be Huaorani territory and virgin jungle but the Huaorani were pushed eastward (some groups went westward) into a new reserve when this oil-exploitation road was built in the 1980s. The area is being colonized, and cattle ranches and oil rigs are replacing the jungle in spite of conservationist efforts.

The rivers crossed by the road provide access to remote parts of both the Huaorani Reserve and Yasuní, but you should seek the local advice of authorized guides about the advisability of travel. While some operators have long-standing relationships with the Huaorani, others do not and the Huaorani insist on managing tourism on their own terms to protect their best interests. A daytrip from Coca is still probably OK. The trip takes about three or four hours and costs about $3.

Three to four hours downriver on Río Tiguino is the remote and simple **Bataburo Lodge** (r per person 4 days/3 nights $215), which is sometimes inaccessible during very high or low water levels. There is only river transportation on Monday and Friday. The lodge has rooms with shared bathroom, and there are two rooms with private bathroom; rates include meals, guiding and transportation from Coca. It's in a remote area, and upkeep of the trails is erratic. Safari Tours and Kem Pery Tours (p238) have information about this lodge.

LOWER RÍO NAPO
☎ 06

East of Coca, the Río Napo flows steadily toward Peru and the Amazon River. Villages dot the route, between the tufts of forest and lone fishermen casting nets for *pargo* (fish). The river widens, its jade tint muddied to chocolate brown. This long, lonesome stretch of river contains some of Ecuador's best jungle lodges. East of the settlements of Pompeya and Limoncocha, the river flows just outside the northern border of Parque Nacional Yasuní and finally enters Peru at Nuevo Rocafuerte.

Pompeya & Limoncocha Area

Pompeya is a Catholic mission about two hours downriver from Coca on Río Napo near the **Reserva Biológica Limoncocha**. Now that there is road access and nearby oil drilling, the area is rather depressing and not ideal for spotting wildlife. Pompeya's small **museum**, part of the Capuchin mission, houses a fine collection of indigenous artifacts from the Río Napo area as well as pre-Columbian ceramics, and may be of interest. The area is easily accessed by buses from the oil town of **Shushufindi**, one hour from either Coca or Lago Agrio.

Manatee Riverboat

For sailors at heart, the *Manatee Amazon Explorer* cruise vessel offers a new and completely different way to see the jungle. Guests stay aboard the comfortable flat-bottom river boat and make daytrips to Yasuní National Park, Limoncocha, Tiputini and other tributaries off the Río Napo. It's an interesting idea offering a wider range of habitats and efficient use of motor time (while guests are off on excursion with motor canoes the boat advances to its next destination). The outfitter is **Nuevo Mundo Expeditions** (Quito ☎ 02-250 9431, 256 5261; www.nuevomundotravel.com; 8 de Septiembre E4-161; packages per person 4/5 nights $461/615), well-reputed for combining creature comforts with high-quality natural history and cultural interaction. Trips depart from Coca and run either from Monday to Friday or Friday to Monday.

Yarina Lodge

The small tributary Río Manduro meets the Napo an hour downstream from Coca. Navigate up this narrow green corridor to find

Yarina Lodge (Map pp228-9; packages per person for 3 nights $200), a hillside camp of 20 immaculate bamboo cabañas. Yarina gears toward budget travelers but provides good services. Meals, with vegetarian options, are well-prepared and cabins come equipped with mosquito nets, private bathrooms and hot water. The lodge doesn't feel remote, but its pleasant surroundings offer river views, short trails and the opportunity to watch birds and paddle canoes. A collection of caged exotic animals in 'transition rehabilitation' leaves uneasy impressions. Rates include meals and tours with Spanish- and English-speaking local guides. Information and reservations can be obtained at Hotel Oasis (p239) or **Yuturi Jungle Adventure** (Quito ☎ 250 4037, 250 3225; www.yuturilodge.com; Amazonas N24-236 & Colón). Discounts are available for South American Explorers (SAE) members (see p397).

Sacha Lodge

The setting is magnificent, the hospitality is meticulous and guides are well-informed and fun. Opened in 1992, this Swiss-run **lodge** (Map pp228-9; s/d $840/1290) enjoys broad popularity. Sacha Lodge is built on the banks of Laguna El Pilche, a lake about 1km north of Río Napo. Getting there is an adventure in itself – a three-hour ride in motor-canoe from Coca is followed by a walk through the forest on an elevated boardwalk and then a 15-minute paddle up a blackwater stream in a dugout canoe to the lodge.

The central lodge is a circular two-story thatched hut with a restaurant, bar and small library. Its boardwalks tentacle out to 10 woodsy cabins, each has a modern, stylish bathroom, hot water and a hammock deck for shady siestas. All rooms are screened and have electric lights and ceiling fans. Buffet-style meals are plentiful and varied. There's tasty options for vegetarians and meat-eaters alike.

Sacha is hopping with guests and after-dinner drinks can be as lively as a Mariscal bar. That may be good or bad, depending on your taste. In any case, small trips are the rule for excursions. Guests are divided into groups based on their interests. Hikes and canoe trips typically consist of about five tourists and with a bilingual naturalist and local guide. The terrain includes flat and hilly rain forest, various lakes, coiling little rivers and swamps. The 800 hectares are visited by six kinds of monkey, toucans, poison dart frogs, peccaries, sloths, anacondas, caimans and black agoutis. You may see all of these or none, but keep your eyes peeled.

More cherished than the Eiffel Tower (and ganglier) is the lodge's showpiece – a 60m-high and 290m-long triple-platform canopy walk. It floats you above the forest canopy for rippling views into the distance and peeping-tom privileges with nearby monkeys and birds. A 43m-high wooden observation deck atop a huge ceiba tree is another way to get high.

Most guests come either on a four-day/three-night or a five-day/four-night package – the first option is Friday to Monday, and the second is Monday to Friday. Once you arrive, you won't be disturbed by a new influx of guests until it's time to leave. Airfare is an additional $120 round trip from Quito to Coca, or you can travel by bus. Special interests, such as bird-watching, photography, plants or fishing, can be catered to with advance request and a bird-watching list is available.

Reservations should be made at the Quito office of **Sacha Lodge** (☎ 02-256 6090, 250 9504, 250 9115; www.sachalodge.com; Zaldumbide 375 & Toledo).

Napo Wildlife Center

Paradisaical and pristine describe this **lodge** (Map pp228-9; Cumbaya ☎ 02-897 316; www.napowildlifecenter.com; packages per person for 3/4 nights $595/795), the latest to open on the lower Napo and the only jungle lodge in the boundaries of Parque Nacional Yasuní. The ecotourism project is jointly owned between the Quechua community of Añangu and the US-based nonprofit Tropical Nature.

Guests hike in or paddle up a small tributary from the south banks of the Río Napo. The cluster of thatched circular cabañas huddle on the far side of Laguna Añangucocha like an emerald vision from a Gauguin painting. The central hut is a spacious open construction with azure walls, a lovely wooden deck and a small library. Occasionally you'll hear the calls of red howler monkeys knocking about.

Trips are guided by local Añangans trained as Yasuní park rangers and bilingual naturalist guides. The focus and physicality of the outings are tailored to the interests of guests. Two parrot clay licks on the property are a major attraction for birders, who also come from surrounding lodges. Between late October and early April you are guaranteed to see between eight and 10 species of parrot – sometimes numbering in the thousands. A 36m steel tower in the middle of the forest offers a spectacular canopy panorama and bird life is prolific at sunrise and sunset. The rare zigzag heron is also reportedly seen on the property. Renowned bird-watching guide Jiovanny Rivandeneyra works here.

Perhaps the center is most proud of its environmentally sustainable sewage system, the only of its kind on the Napo, which should set the standard for future lodges (there is growing concern about what the rest of the lodges are doing with their waste). Composting latrines have been installed in the community to increase the village sanitation level. Napo Wildlife Center has received accolades from many environmentalists and avid birders for its quality guiding and sound environmental practices.

Departures to the lodge are on Monday (for the four-night stay) and Friday (for the three-night stay). Rates include lodging, meals, guided excursions and canoe transport from Coca. For reservations contact a Quito travel agency or try to negotiate Tropical Nature's labyrinthine website (www.tropicalnaturetravel.com).

Sani Lodge

Founded and owned by the local Sani community, **Sani Lodge** (Map pp228-9; packages per person for 3/4/7 nights $285/380/665) hopes to be the future of jungle lodges. All profits from tourism go back into the lodge or Quechua community, in the form of scholarships for students to study in Quito, a community store to ease local hunting, emergency medical funds and other projects. The enchanted backdrop of the lodge is a beautiful oxbow lake connected to a small tributary of Río Napo.

This 20-person lodge will appeal to those who want a more intimate experience. Eight circular thatched cabins each sleep two to three people and have private cold-water bathrooms, comfortable beds, mosquito screens and a small porch. Oil lamps provide the light at night, except in the lodge which has solar electricity.

Wildlife viewing is excellent. Monkeys, sloths and black caimans are regularly spotted, and the lodge's bird list records more

than 550 species of birds in the area (the 30m-high tree tower will help you find them). Nocturnal mammals such as tapirs and capybaras live in the area, but are rarely seen. Even jaguar tracks have been spotted on the property – some 160 sq km of land.

Tours are for three, four or seven nights, and the very reasonable rates include three meals a day, canoe transport to/from Coca (four hours upstream from the lodge), and daily excursions with both a native guide and an English-speaking naturalist guide. Readers have rated the lodge and guiding fantastic.

The tourism side of the business is managed – with conservation, community and comfort all in mind – by the North American/Ecuadorian owners of El Monte Sustainable Lodge (see p143). Employees are all members of the community.

Reservations can be made online, by phone or at the Quito office of **Sani Lodge** (☎ 02-255 8881; www.sanilodge.com; Roca 736 & Amazonas, Pasaje Chantilly).

La Selva Jungle Lodge

This North American-run **lodge** (Map pp228-9; packages per person for five days, four nights $750) on the shores of Laguna Garzacocha provides a high-quality, responsible tourism experience. The quality of the guiding is excellent, with many biologist guides, as well as locals employed. In 1992 the lodge won the 'World Congress on Tourism and the Environment' award.

Kerosene lanterns set the rustic ambience. There are 16 double cabins and one family cabin (three rooms), each with private hot bathroom and mosquito screens. Meals, well-prepared and in a wide variety, are outstanding by any standard.

With more than 500 bird species, bird-watching is a major attraction. Group excursions go out on foot and by dugout canoe. A 35m-high canopy platform, a 20-minute walk from the lodge, affords even better viewing. Look out for the rare zigzag heron, which bird-watchers from all over the world come to see. About half of Ecuador's 44 species of parrots have been recorded near here, as well as a host of other exotic tropical birds. Monkeys and other mammals are frequently seen and there are tens of thousands of plant and insect species.

A small research facility offers project space for scientists and students by advance arrangement. Butterfly breeding is one successful operation that visitors can visit to photograph rain forest butterflies and learn about their life cycles.

The lodge is five hours downriver from Coca by regular passenger canoe, but La Selva's private launches make the trip in about half that time. Stays have a four-day/three-night minimum, and prices include river travel from Coca, accommodations, all meals and all guide services. The bar tab, laundry service and airfare ($120 round trip) are all extra. Even the most pampered campers can consider the one-week 'Light Brigade' tour, which involves jungle overnights in deluxe style with pillows and platforms.

Information and reservations are available from the Quito office of **La Selva** (☎ 02-232 730, 556 293; www.laselvajunglelodge.com; San Salvador E7-85 & Carrión).

Pañacocha

If a campfire dinner of piranha reeled in by your own trembling mitts sounds appealing, head to Pañacocha, which means 'Lake of Piranhas' in Quechua. You'll find a gorgeous black-water lake with mirror reflections of dewy clouds. The biodiversity here is incredible – there are 251 plant species counted in a hectare and the backdrop is cloud forest and dry forest. To arrive, hire a local canoe to take you north up the Río Pañayacu from the Río Napo. Tours from Coca go here but you can also take the public canoe slated for Nueva Rocafuerte (see p240) for added adventure and local flavor. There is a small community near the shore where you can stay.

Cheap accommodations are available at **Pensión Las Palmas** (riverfront; r per person $3) but you might be more comfortable camping. *Comedores* (cheap restaurants), including El-sita and Delicia, are within view of the boat landing.

Pañacocha is four to five hours downstream from Coca (depending on your motor), or about halfway to Nuevo Rocafuerte.

Yuturi Lodge

This **lodge** (Map pp228-9; packages per person for 4 nights $350) is built on Río Yuturi, a southern tributary of Río Napo about 20 minutes beyond Pañacocha and five hours from Coca. Surrounded by three lagoons teeming with bird life, the setting is utterly spectacular, with lavender tones of light saturating the lake in the wee morning hours. Cabin rooms are rough-hewn but attractive, with private cold showers and mosquito nets. Guided trips through the forest with both an indigenous and an English-speaking guide are included in the price, as are meals and transport from Coca to the lodge. Night outings on the river search for caimans. The last night of the trip is spent at Yarina Lodge so guests don't have to get up two hours before dawn to meet their flights out of Coca. Readers recommend it. Reservations can be made at Hotel Oasis (p239) or in Quito at **Yuturi Jungle Adventure** (☎ 02-250 4037, 250 3225; www .yuturilodge.com; Amazonas N24-236 & Colón). The four-day/three-night trips depart Friday; the five-day/four-night trips depart Monday.

Nuevo Rocafuerte

A distant dot on the map for most, Nuevo Rocafuerte is in no danger of losing its mystery. While backpackers may bubble with excitement at the idea of floating the Napo all the way to the Amazon River, only the most intrepid should rise to the occasion. In this truly off-piste adventure, aspiring 'Survivors' may have to endure cramped and wet travel, as well as the possibility of seeing their next meal slaughtered.

Nueva Rocafuerte is on the Peruvian border about 12 hours (depending) from Coca along Río Napo. This is a legal border crossing with Peru, albeit a highly independent one. Basic infrastructure such as regular boats and simple hotels are lacking. In the absence of cars, long tufts of grass sprout in the road and nighttime means outdoor barbecues with the TV hauled out to the sidewalk.

If you are continuing to Peru try to make arrangements well in advance. If you don't time it right you could be stuck here (changing light bulbs and watching Charlie's Angels reruns, no doubt) for some time. Bring adequate supplies of water-purification tablets, insect repellent and food. Emerald Forest Expeditions in Coca (p238) offers a jungle tour which ends in Iquitos, Peru.

The very basic **Parador Turístico** (☎ 238 2133; r per person with shared bathroom $3-5), located behind the national police office, fills up fast, since it's the only lodging in town. The fans are fried and you'll need to check that there's actually a bulb in the light socket. Along the strip a few two-shelf stores sell basic provisions; for a hot meal ask around and get your request in a few hours in advance.

For local information, local tours or to hire a boat contact Juan Carlos 'Chuso' Cuenca (☎ 238 2182). His house is the second after the marina. The town has an Andinatel phone office behind the marina.

Electricity is only available from 6pm to 11pm. Make sure you bring a flashlight for the early-morning departure.

GETTING THERE & AWAY

Passenger canoes to Coca depart at 5am on Sunday, Tuesday and Friday mornings. The trip is 12 to 14 hours with a lunch stop in Pañacocha. The canoe is covered but you should still bring rain gear, food and water. Low water conditions may prolong the trip. The fare is $15 each way.

To/From Peru

Exit and entry formalities on the Ecuador side are taken care of in Nuevo Rocafuerte; in Peru they're settled in Iquitos. The official border crossing is at Pantoja, a short ride downstream from Nuevo Rocafuerte. Boats from Nueva Rocafuerte charge $50 minimum to Pantoja. Timing is the key: a **cargo boat** (☎ 65-242 082; $20-35) travels once a month from Pantoja to Iquitos (a four- to six-day trip). Call its owner Camilo to confirm dates. A hammock and 19L of water, in addition to food, are necessary. Be warned that there is only one bathroom and a lot of livestock on board.

Part of the logistical problem is the lack of transportation options in Pantoja. Further downriver in Peru, the village of Santa Clotilde has boats to Iquitos on Tuesday, Thursday and Saturday for $25. But chartering a boat to Santa Clotilde from Nueva Rocafuerte will set you back $200. It's worth asking around at the marina for other options.

PARQUE NACIONAL YASUNÍ

Yasuní (admission $20) is Ecuador's largest mainland park, a massive 9620-sq-km swath of wetlands, marshes, swamps, lakes, rivers and tropical rain forest. Its staggering biodiversity led Unesco to declare it an international biosphere reserve and it was established as a national park shortly after, in 1979. With this pocket untouched by the last ice age, a diverse pool of species has thrived here through the ages; including more than 500 bird species, some previously unknown elsewhere. Resident animals include some of the rarer and more difficult to see jungle wildlife, such as jaguars, harpy eagles, pumas and tapirs.

Yasuní stands today as one of the last true wildernesses in Ecuador. Its inaccessibility has served to preserve it in ways that active protection sometimes cannot. Bordered by Río Napo to the north and the Río Cururay to the south east, the park encompasses most of the watersheds of Ríos Yasuní and Nashiño, as well as substantial parts of Río Tiputini. Its diverse habitats consist of 'terra firma' or forested hills, which are never inundated even by the highest floods; *varzea* or lowlands, which are periodically inundated by flooding rivers; and *igapó*, semipermanently inundated lowlands.

A small but not negligible number of Tagaeri Taromenani indigenous live within the park (see p246). Park territory was altered in 1990 and 1992 to protect this traditional population of hunters and gatherers who vehemently resist contact with the outside world. The nearby Reserva Huaorani contributes as an ecological buffer zone for the national park.

Oil discovery within the park has put a sinister spin on this modern conservation success story. In 1991, despite Yasuní's protected status, the Ecuadorian government gave the US-based oil company Conoco the right to begin oil exploitation. Since then the concession has changed hands several times. Conoco was soon replaced by the Maxus Oil Consortium, whose legacy is the Maxus road, slicing through the park like a 150km coronary incision. While this 'ecological' road can be lifted up and removed (presumably when all the oil is gone), the forest cut in its wake and the subsequent link to the interior for outsiders causes a secondary degradation often worse than the drilling itself.

Oil and the waste products associated with oil exploitation contaminate soil and drainage systems, while noise pollution and vegetation destruction causes an exodus of wildlife. There are claims that this degradation has so far been reasonably well contained, and wildlife is reportedly very abundant – but you can't go there to see it unless you're a researcher or an oil worker!

THE ORIENTE

NO MAN'S LAND RECONSIDERED

The Tagaeri and Taromenani have a history of violent encounters with the outside world, which ultimately led to the withdrawal and self-imposed isolation of these subgroups of the Huaorani. In 1999, a presidential decree from the Ecuadorian government set up Intangible Zones to 'prevent more irreversible damage to indigenous communities and their environment in order to protect life in all forms.' They delineated 700,000 hectares overlapping Yasuní National Park and Huaorani territory where these groups could hunt and live as they have for centuries without threat of contact with outsiders.

Mining, logging and oil exploration are forbidden in these areas which also protect an estimated 500 species of birds, along with jaguars, pumas and manatees and other diverse species. But with evidence surfacing of illegal logging, there is pressure to delineate the exact boundaries of the Intangible Zone, a process inviting keen observation by nearby oil operations. Who will represent the Tagaeri and Taromenani peoples if this happens remains a question, since they are, in fact, unreachable for comment.

Various international organizations – such as the Nature Conservancy (www.nature .org), Conservation International (www.con servation.org) and the Natural Resources Defense Council (www.nrdc.org) – in coalition with Ecuadorian groups such as Fundación Natura (www.fnatura.org) and local grassroots conservation groups, have worked hard to minimize the oil company's impact in Yasuní. Although Parque Nacional Yasuní remains menaced by oil exploitation, hope remains that the threat will not develop into as destructive a pattern as has occurred in other parts of the Amazon.

Recent logging within the Huaorani territory by Colombian lumber companies, which purchase trees (primarily cedar) from the Huaorani, is another way the park buffer zone is being denigrated.

Like most of Ecuador's preserved areas, Yasuní is woefully understaffed. At present, the only permanently staffed ranger station is at Nuevo Rocafuerte, with some other seasonal stations on the southern boundaries of the park. Some of the guides in Coca can take you on trips into the park (see p90).

The annual rainfall is about 3500mm, depending on which part of the park you are in. May to July are the wettest months; January to March are the driest.

PARQUE NACIONAL SUMACO-GALERAS

One of Ecuador's most-remote areas, the little-explored **Parque Nacional Sumaco-Galeras** consists of 205,249 hectares of thick rain forest, hidden caves and cliffs. The park's centerpiece is the 3732m Volcán Sumaco, often plagued by wet weather. The volcano is dormant at this time, although vulcanologists believe it could become active. It lies about 27km north of the Coca–Tena road, from where it takes five or six days round trip to climb it.

The starting point for the climb is the village of **Huamaní**. To get there, take the Coca–Tena road 20km east of the Tena–Baeza road. A short dirt road leading north accesses the village. Here guides can be hired for the climb to the summit, and involves bushwhacking through poorly marked trails tangled in vegetation. Without a guide, it is terribly easy to get lost. Facilities in Huamaní are minimal, so bring food and equipment from Tena (see opposite). The rainiest months (May to August) turn the trail into a mud bath, and clouds cap the mountain views. The driest months are October to December and this is the best time to go.

For more information (in Spanish) on the area, go to www.sumaco.org. Along the roadside in the park you will see road stands selling dried oyster mushrooms harvested in the area. It's a good opportunity to stop and chat with locals and the project funds sustainable agro-forestry.

ARCHIDONA
☎ 06

The faded pastel facades and manicured palm plaza make this yawning village an agreeable stop. A mission founded in 1560 (the same year as Tena, which is 10km to the south), Archidona maintains its smallness and tranquility. Sundays are choice for milling around, seeing the rural folk (including indigenous Quijos) coming into the market and checking out the zebra-striped concrete-block church near the plaza.

Driving from Baeza you'll see **Residencial Regina** (☎ 288 9144; r per person with shared/private bathroom $6/8) before the plaza. Regina has inviting, cool rooms and a covered patio outside. Another good option is **Hotel Palmar del Rio** (☎ 288 9274; Av Napo; r per person $6). Tiled rooms are clean and bright with cable TV; it's located on the south end of the center. There are a few simple and inexpensive places to eat.

From the plaza, you can take a bus to Cotundo and ask to be dropped at the entrance to the **Cuevas de Jumandí** (admission $2), about 4km north of Archidona. Forgo the snack bar and amusement park and tread slowly (with a flashlight) to see the stalactites, stalagmites and odd formations. The cave system, the best known in the area, has three main branches that remain partly unexplored. Rubber boots and old clothes will serve you well in the mud and sludge. For thorough exploration, you'll need a local guide (found in Tena) and equipment.

TENA
☎ 06 / pop 16,670 / elevation 518m
Tena has evolved as the ambassador of the jungle, a cheerful hodgepodge with two fat rivers intersecting at its heart. White-water paddlers get giddy in the rafting and kayaking capital of Ecuador; there are so many rafting options and a cold beer and toasty bed back in town. Even if the river's not your cup of tea, this is a good place to kick back and visit nearby waterfalls and indigenous communities. Breezes off the Río Tena and Río Pano keep the climate comfortable.

The capital of Napo province, Tena was founded in 1560 and plagued by early indigenous uprisings. Jumandy, chief of the Quijos, led a fierce but unsuccessful revolt against the Spaniards in 1578. Today, the area is largely agricultural – cattle ranches and coffee and banana plantations abound.

The anniversary of Tena's foundation is celebrated on November 15, when live music and community events take place the entire week.

Information
Andinatel (Olmedo) Northwest of the footbridge.
Banco del Austro (15 de Noviembre) Changes traveler's checks in the mornings only. Has an ATM.

Banco del Pinchincha (cnr Mera & Amazonas) Has a second branch on the corner of 15 de Noviembre and Tena. Both have ATMs.
Centro Comercial Moscoso (☎ 288 6029; Amazonas; ☿ 8am-8pm Mon-Sat, 8am-2pm Sun) Will also change traveler's checks if there's sufficient cash on hand.
Clínica Amazonas (☎ 288 6495; Santa Rosa; ☿ 24hr)
Cucupanet (per hr $1.20; ☿ 8am-9:30pm) Broadband Internet; located in main plaza.
Electrolava (☿ 8am-7pm) Laundry service; located next to the police station.
Hospital (☎ 288 6302/4) South of town on the road to Puerto Napo.
Police station (☎ 288 6101) On the main plaza.
Post office (cnr Olmedo & García Moreno) Northwest of the footbridge.
Tourism office (☎ 288 8046; Agusto Rueda; ☿ 7am-5pm Mon-Fri) Can give useful information on local hikes and waterfalls.

Sights & Activities
On a clear day, visitors to Tena are sometimes puzzled by the sight of a volcano looming up out of the jungle some 50km away to the north-northeast – this is Volcán Sumaco (opposite).

Take a stroll over the river bridge to **Parque Amazónico** (btwn Río Pano & Río Tena; admission $2; ☿ 8am-5pm), a 27-hectare island with a self-guided trail passing labeled local plants and animal enclosures. Picnic areas, a swimming beach and a bathroom are available.

Market days are Friday and Saturday.

RIVER RAFTING
Packed with rivers and mountains, Ecuador is a white-water paradise and Tena is the capital. Trips range from scenic floats to bone-chattering white water and offer flash panoramas of beautiful jungle, cloud forest, canyons and mountains. Serious outfitters will have everything you would expect back home – decent life jackets, professional guides, first aid and throw bags. Make sure you sign up with one offering these. Kayakers can hire guides or arrange for transport and put-ins through the places mentioned here. For a list of rafting events in Ecuador, go to www.raftingecuador.org.

The most popular river is the Jatunyacu, where rafters tackle a fun 25km stretch of Class III+ (all levels) white water. For more excitement, the Río Misahuallí has wild Class IV+ rapids and includes a portage around a waterfall.

THE ORIENTE

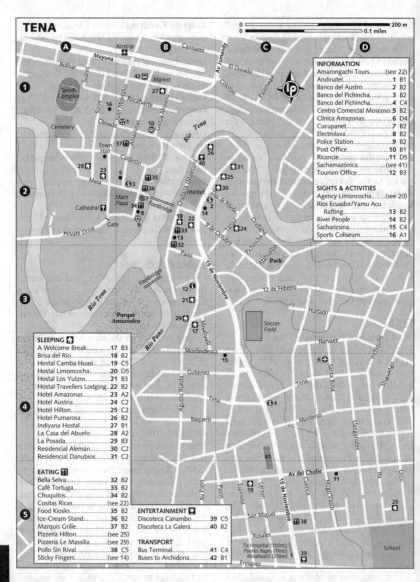

TENA

0 _____ 200 m
0 _____ 0.1 miles

INFORMATION
Amarongachi Tours..........(see 22)
Andinatel.....................1 B1
Banco del Austro...............2 B2
Banco del Pichincha............3 B2
Banco del Pichincha............4 C4
Centro Comercial Moscoso.5 B2
Clinica Amazonas..............6 D4
Cucupanet....................7 B2
Electrolava....................8 B2
Police Station.................9 B2
Post Office...................10 B1
Ricancie.....................11 D5
Sachamazónica..............(see 41)
Tourism Office...............12 B3

SIGHTS & ACTIVITIES
Agency Limoncocha..........(see 20)
Ríos Ecuador/Yamu Acu
   Rafting....................13 B2
River People.................14 B2
Sacharicsina.................15 C4
Sports Coliseum..............16 A1

SLEEPING
A Welcome Break.............17 B3
Brisa del Río.................18 B2
Hostal Camba Huasi..........19 C5
Hostal Limoncocha...........20 D5
Hostal Los Yutzos............21 B3
Hostal Travellers Lodging....22 B2
Hotel Amazonas..............23 A2
Hotel Austria.................24 C2
Hotel Hilton.................25 C2
Hotel Pumarosa..............26 B2
Indiyana Hostal..............27 B1
La Casa del Abuelo...........28 A2
La Posada...................29 B3
Residencial Alemán...........30 C2
Residencial Danubios.........31 C2

EATING
Bella Selva..................32 B2
Café Tortuga................33 B2
Chuquitos..................34 B2
Cositas Ricas...............(see 22)
Food Kiosks.................35 B2
Ice-Cream Stand.............36 B2
Marquis Grille...............37 B2
Pizzería Hilton..............(see 25)
Pizzería Le Massilia.........(see 29)
Pollo Sin Rival...............38 C5
Sticky Fingers..............(see 14)

ENTERTAINMENT
Discoteca Canambo..........39 C5
Discoteca La Galera..........40 B2

TRANSPORT
Bus Terminal................41 C4
Buses to Archidona..........42 B1

River People (Tena ☎ 288 8384, Quito ☎ 02-290 6639; www.riverpeopleraftingecuador.com; 15 de Noviembre & 9 de Octubre) is run by English guide Gary Dent and his sons; it's a top-notch outfitter with rave reviews pouring in. Daytrips to the Jatunyacu are $50. It also guides the Quijos (a Class IV river), the spectacular Jondachi and the very remote Hollin (in Sumaco-Galera). Guides have a minimum of eight years' experience, speak English and flip pancakes (well, sometimes). Jungle camping, kayaking instruction and other tailor-made trips are possible. Seasonally they run the Class III and IV Intag River. Check out breakfast in their upstairs café, Sticky Fingers (p251).

THE ORIENTE

Ríos Ecuador/Yacu Amu (Tena ☎ 288 6727; Quito ☎ 02-223 6844, 290 4054; www.riosecuador.com; Orellana) is a popular outfitter that offers trips for all tastes. Their most popular is a $55 daytrip down the Upper Napo (Class III), suitable for all levels of experience. If you're alone there are guaranteed departures every Saturday. Trips down the Misahuallí (November to March) promise more thrills, with Class-IV rapids and a waterfall portage, which cost $65 per person. Ask about other rivers and multiday trips (see p89).

If you're itchy to get in the driver's seat, a four-day white-water kayaking school (suitable for beginners) is offered for $250. Experienced kayakers can rent equipment. The company is owned by a professional kayaker and the head guide, Gynner Coronel, is certified by the Ecuadorian White-Water Guides Association (AGAR; Asociación de Guías de Aguas Rapidas del Ecuador) and has competed internationally. English and other languages are spoken.

Agency Limoncocha (right) also runs the Río Napo for $40 and rents kayaks for $15 per day. Solo rafters can usually get on a boat on Fridays during high season. See below for more details.

CAVING
For waterfall and caving tours, guide **Manuel Moreta** (☎ 288 9185; manuel.moreta@eudoramail.com) is recommended. He can also arrange tours of Cuevas de Jumandí (see p247) and accommodations by the caves. Don't forget to carry your own flashlights (torches) – including a backup light and extra batteries.

Tours
Amarongachi Tours (☎ 288 6372; www.amarongachi.com; 15 de Noviembre 438) offers various good-time jungle excursions. During its tours (which cost about $40 per person per day), you can stay with a family in the jungle, eat good local food, go for nature hikes, rappel down waterfalls, pan for gold, swim in the rivers and get a look at the rain forest. Amarongachi also operates the lovely Amarongachi and Shangrila cabins; the latter are on a bluff 100m above Río Anzu (a tributary of Río Napo) and feature great views of the river and forest.

Also recommended are the local guides listed with **Ricancie** (Indigenous Network of Upper Napo Communities for Cultural Coexistence & Ecotour-

ism; ☎ 288 8479; ricancie.nativeweb.org; Av El Chofer & Cuenca; ☻ 8am-6pm). Eight Quechua communities band together to offer adventure tours, bird- and animal-watching, demonstrations of healing plants and cultural activities. Although almost all guides speak Quechua and/or Spanish, it is rare that they speak English. The staff can arrange stays in local villages, and know the caves and petroglyphs found in the Tena region. Stays cost $38 per person per day.

Sacharicsina (☎ 288 6839; sacharicsinatour@yahoo.com; Montesdeoca 110) is also recommended. It's run by Olmedo, Oswaldo and Fausto Cerda – a knowledgeable and friendly local Quechua family. They have eight different tours, and rates are generally in the range of $25 to $40 per person per day, depending on group size and the length of the trip. Solo travelers and those who prefer a female guide can be accommodated.

Agency Limoncocha (☎ 288 7583; limoncocha@andinanet.net; Sangay 533), run out of Hostal Limoncocha (below), offers tours to nearby forest around the Río Jatanyacu for $33, as well as rafting. German and English are spoken.

You'll find **Sachamazónica** (☎ 288 7979) in the bus terminal. Indigenous guides and owners, Domingo and Lirio Andy, have worked in Misahuallí and Coca for years and have substantial experience.

Sleeping
BUDGET
Brisa del Río (☎ 288 6444/6208; Orellana; dm/s $6/10) A brand new hostel with pastel dorm rooms, row-showers, all spanking clean and central. Singles have private bathrooms.

Hostal Limoncocha (☎ 288 7583; limoncocha@andinanet.net; Ita 533; r per person with shared/private bathroom $4/6) Backpackers frequent this spot on the hill. Rooms are chipper with hand-painted murals and clean private bathrooms. It is to your right as you arrive from the south. Breakfast and beer (not necessarily together) are available, and there's a guest kitchen and onsite tour operator. German owned.

Residencial Danubios (☎ 288 6378; 15 de Noviembre; r per person $4-6) An outdoor kitchen patio with bamboo walls welcomes visitors for breakfast, the bright white rooms are plain and bathrooms are dated but clean. Showers are cold and rooms with TV cost extra. Not a bad-value option. Located next to the Hilton.

Hotel Hilton (☎ 288 6329; 15 de Noviembre; r per person $6) A tidy little spot with cramped doubles and some crumbly structure – room quality varies. Upstairs rooms have hot water and the owners are very welcoming. Has a popular thatched-hut pizzeria next door.

A Welcome Break (☎ 288 6301; cofanes@hotmail.com; Agusto Rueda 331; r per person $4) The charm wears thin in these cramped lime rooms with bare concrete floors, but the resident family is embracing. Shared showers are clean and there's a guest kitchen, as well as laundry facilities and fenced yard.

Indiyana Hostal (☎ 288 8837; Bolívar 349; r per person $8) The tidy velour sectional sofa, plastic-covered chairs and worn orange carpets transport travelers back to the 70s. Spacious bedrooms have old furniture, fans, hot showers and cable TV.

Hostal Travellers Lodging (15 de Noviembre; r per person $6, with views $12) Forgo the claustrophobic dungeon rooms for their airy upstairs counterparts with good city views. All have hot water. The lodge is run by Amarongachi Tours (p249).

Hostal Camba Huasi (☎ 288 7429; Av de Chofer & Lerzon; r per person $5) OK for its bus station convenience, but rooms sit under a husk of dust. With cold water and cable TV.

Hotel Amazonas (☎ 288 6439; cnr Juan Montalvo & Mera; r per person $3) For $3, what more did you expect?

MIDRANGE

La Casa del Abuelo (☎ 286 6318; Sucre 432; s/d $15/20) An ample refurbished country-style home with large, medieval doors and comfortable bright rooms. There's hot water and fans, and tour arrangements can be made here. On the roof there's a nice mirador with hammocks. Friendly and well-kept, it's a great new option. Ask the owners about their rural guesthouse on the river, 5km away.

Hostal Los Yutzos (☎ 288 6717/6769; www.geocities.com/losyutzos; Agusto Rueda 190; s/d $31/37; ✂ 🖵) This riverside gem has spacious and tasteful rooms. The tiled balcony with wooden loungers has sweeping views of the gurgling river and the city's northern bank. The garden area is thick with green. Internet, cable TV, hot water and breakfast are some of the additional perks.

La Posada (☎ 288 7897; Agusto Rueda; r per person $11; 🖵) A more budget version of its sister hotel Los Yutzos, La Posada asserts its own

charm, with tidy motel-style rooms over the river and wi-fi connection. Wine-colored tiles, modern bathrooms and thick bedding make the rooms inviting. Breakfast is extra and there's an excellent pizzeria on-site.

Hotel Austria (☎ 288 7205; Tarqui; r per person $9) Guarded by two innocuous poodles, this large gated house has clipped shrubbery and Adirondack chairs. Recommended for its bright, high-ceiling rooms with fans and hot water.

Hotel Pumarosa (☎ /fax 288 6320; Orellana; s/d $15/25; ✂) Inviting lilac rooms have high wooden ceilings, large armoires and modern white-tile bathrooms. There is reliable hot water, cable TV and a telephone in every room, and billiards in the lobby. The disco and roller rink right next door mean noisy weekends.

Residencial Alemán (☎ 288 6409; 15 de Noviembre 210; r per person $9-11) Motel-style rooms run dingy from wear and tear, but the quiet, enclosed lawn area is good for reading.

Eating

Café Tortuga (☎ 09-529 5419; Orellana s/n; snacks $2; ⏰ 7:30am-2:30pm Tue-Sat, 4:30-8:30pm Tue-Sun) A new Swiss-run riverfront spot. Try the chicken empanadas, with green banana crust. The tasty fruit frappes and cappuccinos, as well as breakfast, make this an obligatory stop.

Bella Selva (☎ 288 7964; pizzas $2-7; Orellana; mains $2-6; ⏰ 5-11pm) A friendly riverfront pizza parlor with tropical tunes and tasty veggie pizzas, or – for dessert – pizza with peaches and pineapples. Curious?

Chuquitos (☎ 288 7630; main plaza; mains $3-5; ⏰ 7:30am-9pm Mon-Sat) An old favorite over the wide ribbon of the Río Tena with an à la carte menu; the fish is excellent.

Marquis Grille (☎ 288 6513; Amazonas 251; full dinners $12; ⏰ noon-3pm & 6-11pm Mon-Sat) An upscale restaurant with thatched-roof-folkloric ambience. It's family run, with a great chef who turns out delicious smoked trout served with yuca Spanish tortilla. Also recommended are the homemade raviolis and filet mignon. Dinner includes salad, wine and dessert.

Pizzería Le Massilia (☎ 288 7897; Agusto Rueda; pizzas $4-6; ⏰ 5-11pm) If you are still in the mood for pizza, try these sizzling versions served riverside under candlelight. Cheese nachos appetizers are recommended too. The thatched restaurant is attached to La Posada.

Sticky Fingers (15 de Noviembre & 9 de Octubre; breakfast $3-5; ☺ 7:30am-noon) Serves wonderful crepes with fruit and bottomless cups of coffee, among other treats.

Pollo Sin Rival (15 de Noviembre; mains $1.50-3; ☺ Mon-Sat) 'The Chicken Without Rival' is a Tena classic. If you're hankering for roasted bird, head to this popular haunt two blocks south of the bus terminal.

Cositas Ricas (15 de Noviembre; mains $3-6; ☺ 7:30am-9:30pm) Next to Amarongachi Tours in the Hostal Travellers Lodging complex, this favorite of travelers serves vegetarian and Ecuadorian plates, crisp salads and fresh juices.

For the adventurous there are grills by the pedestrian bridge cooking up sausages, chicken and *guanta*. In addition you'll find cheap food kiosks and cafés with patio seating and cold beer.

Drinking & Entertainment

Kids are spinning like bobbins on the dance floors each weekend; it is not necessarily graceful so slip into the mix. Discos open 8pm to 2am, or until 3am Thursday through Saturday. *Reggaetón* rages at **Discoteca Canambo** (Enriquez & 15 de Noviembre; admission $2) but you'll find rock and Latin classics too. Next to Hotel Pumarosa, **Discoteca La Galera** (admission $2) has a fun, slightly more grown-up atmosphere and there's a roller rink attached.

Getting There & Away

The **bus terminal** (15 de Noviembre) is in the southern end of town. There are numerous departures a day for Quito ($5, five hours) via Baeza, and to Coca ($7, six hours). There are regular departures to Puyo ($2.50, three hours), Ambato ($5, six hours) and Baños ($4, five hours). Jumandy has a night bus to Lago Agrio ($7, eight hours). Most of these main routes are paved, but unpaved sections, old buses and inclement weather still make trip lengths in the Oriente notoriously unpredictable.

Getting Around

The local buses for Archidona ($0.25, 15 minutes) leave about every half hour during daylight hours from the west side of the market. Buses for Misahuallí ($1, 45 minutes) leave about every hour from 15 de Noviembre, outside the bus terminal. There are about nine buses a day from the terminal to La Punta ($1.50, 1½ hours), from where boats cross the river to Ahuano. Other local destinations are also served.

MISAHUALLÍ

☎ 06

The sleepiest of all jungle towns, Misahuallí (Mee-sah-wah-YEE) sits swathed in greenery on the junction of two major rivers. On Saturday night, lights blink on and off the main square (more shortages) and a waitress from the coast longs for the thrill of a steamy *salsoteca* (salsa nightclub). Locals may be bored but many a traveler is attracted to this very inertia, of swirling river currents and sunny sandbanks. The proverbial end of the road, Misahuallí (also called Puerto Misahuallí) is still boxed off by water but across the river a dirt road links small villages as far as Bellavista.

WHAT KIND OF TRIP IS THIS? *Oswaldo Muñoz*

Think twice if your jungle tour offers ayahuasca, a psychotropic plant used ritually in Amazon cultures, as part of the authentic experience. Only a professional shaman (not necessarily 'dressed-up' for the occasion) has the trained ability to carry out 'readings' for patients as part of his diagnostic arts. And it is only on rare occasions and with due preparation on the part of the patient, that the intake of this psychotropic plant should be considered.

Given that, there are many serious and complex factors involved prior to taking ayahuasca, such as dietary preparation, professional supervision, menstrual cycles etc, and true professional supervision and guidance is highly recommended. Dangerous side effects from ayahuasca, either due to medication you might be taking at that time or negligent preparation of the plant, could ruin your trip.

There are a number of books available on the subject. Your tour operator should be capable of providing you with these, for a deep-rooted, preliminary understanding what a genuine ayahuasca ritual entails. That, in itself, is a good means of screening your operator before selecting your tour.

This used to be a bustling connection for jungle tours, but nowadays most trips are booked in Quito. The surrounding area has been colonized for decades, and most mammals have been either hunted out or had their habitats encroached upon to the point where they cannot survive. What you can see, if you keep your eyes open – or better still, with a local guide – is a variety of jungle birds, tropical flowers, army ants, dazzling butterflies and other insects.

Misahuallí still offers good guide services and most of them will go further afoot to Parque Nacional Yasuní or Cuyabeno for big jungle adventures. While setting up a trip, enjoy the rolling and rugged physical geography of Misahuallí's outskirts and the hospitable village life.

Information

There is no bank or post office. Internet facilities are slated for 2006. Be sure to carry your passport on buses, boats and tours in the region.

Sights & Activities

Pack a picnic and hit the dirt roads on foot, by bicycle or bus and visit the surrounding villages.

The nearby **waterfall** is a sweet spot for a swim. Local one-day tours often include it, but you can easily reach it on your own. Take a Misahuallí–Puerto Napo bus and ask the driver to drop you off at Río Latas, about 15 or 20 minutes away from Misahuallí. All the drivers know *el camino a las cascadas* ('the trail to the falls'). Follow the river upstream to the falls, passing several swimming holes en route. Be prepared to wade. It takes about an hour to reach the falls, depending on how fast you walk.

Dazzling giant morphos sputter about the **butterfly farm** (Centro de Reproducción de Mariposas; admission $2; ☉ 9am-4pm), located a block off the plaza. It's run by Pepe and Margarita of Ecoselva (see right), and offers a close look at the developing stages of rain forest butterflies. Mature ones are released into the forest. Volunteers are needed.

Tours

With most tours arranged in Quito, independent travelers to jungle-entry points such as Misahuallí have a harder time organizing a group on-site. The perk is a slightly cheaper rate. You'll find an accommodating guide (and price) far more quickly if you already have a small group together (four or more) when you arrive in Misahuallí.

Guides will approach you in the main plaza offering tours – most of these are inexperienced and unlicensed, and you're best off hiring a guide recommended here or by other travelers. The tours range from one to 10 days in duration and prices should include the guide, food, water, accommodations (from jungle camping to comfortable lodges) and rubber boots.

Aventuras Amazónicas (☎ 289 0031; on the plaza) Carlos and María del Carmen Santander run tours for $25 per day. Based in La Posada.

Douglas Clarke's Expeditions (☎ 288 8848; douglas clarkeexpediciones@yahoo.com) Readers recommend this longtime operator with one- to 10-day tours available for $35 per day. Most overnights involve camping and some English is spoken. Contact the Hostal Marena Internacional.

Ecoselva (☎ 289 0019; on the plaza; ecoselva@yahoo .es) Pepe Tapia González takes visitors on fun one- to 10-day tours with overnights at his rustic lodge or jungle camps. He speaks English, has a biology background and is extremely knowledgeable about plants and insects. Rates for four are $25 or $40 (in National Parks) per person per day.

Fluvial River Tours (Quito ☎ 02-228 2859) Owner Hector Fiallos, a respected long-term guide, may be found in Quito or try to contact at the Sacha Hostal on the beach.

Independent guides Recommended guides include Luis Zapata (☎ 289 0084; zorrozz_2000@yahoo.com), who speaks English, and Marco Coro (☎ 890 058; cachitours@hotmail.com), who speaks German and English.

Sleeping & Eating

Misahuallí has frequent water and electricity failures and the lot of its offerings are beat-up and frayed but secure.

France Amazonia (☎ 288 7570; www.france-ama zonia.com; Av Principal s/n; r per person incl breakfast $16; ☒) The best accommodations in town, shady thatched huts set around a sparkling pool and connected by stone pathways. There's also a fire pit perched over the river. Some beds are narrow but rooms are cozy; there's always water because the hotel has its own water tank. Breakfast is included and meals may be ordered ahead. Owners speak French and English.

CRE (☎ 289 0061; Av Principal s/n; r per person $8) Tidy and informal installations include motel-rooms and a collection of varnished cabins in a lemon grove and there's a reliable motorized canoe service. Rooms have hot water and firm mattresses. Located one block from the plaza.

Hostal Marena Internacional (☎ 289 0002; Av Principal s/n; r per person $5-8) The upper levels of this multistory have a delicious breeze. Half a block from the plaza, tiled rooms are neat, with hot-water bathrooms, and TV and refrigerators in the better ones. It's owned by Douglas Clarke's Expeditions.

El Paisano (☎ 289 0027; Rivadeneyra s/n; s/d $7/11) This backpacker haunt is remodeling its stagnant rooms; cement squares with tiny bathrooms, fans and mosquito nets. Staff is friendly and provide laundry service and vegetarian dishes at the open-air restaurant. It's just off the plaza.

Residencial La Posada (☎ 289 0005; on the plaza; r per person $7) Basic rooms with hot water and fans are found above the rambling, corner restaurant.

Hostal Shaw (☎ 289 0019; on the plaza; r per person $5) Situated above, and run by, Ecoselva (opposite). Has simple rooms with fan and shared bathrooms. You'll find espresso at the downstairs café, as well as morning pancakes and vegetarian dishes.

Hostería Misahuallí (☎ 289 0063; www.Misahualli jungle.com; across the Río Misahuallí; r per person with 3 meals $63; ≋) A bit fussy and manicured for a jungle camp, the *hostería* distracts guests with a swimming pool, tennis court, upscale restaurant and bar. The stilted cabins are equipped with hot showers. It's across Río Misahuallí, on the north side of Río Napo. Reservations can be arranged through its **Quito office** (☎ 02-252 0043; miltour@accessinter.net; Ramírez Dávalos 251). It also offers jungle tours.

Restaurant Nico (☎ 289 0088; Calle Santander; mains $2-4; ⏱ 7am-9pm) Nico is the best option in town for filling $1.75 *meriendas* (lunches). Good options include steamed tilapia with rice and banana chips or fresh juices (made with purified water). In keeping with regional decor of bare-butt calendar girls and garlands of plastic fruit.

Getting There & Away

Buses leave from the plaza approximately every hour during daylight hours; the last bus is at 6pm. The main destination is Tena ($1, one hour), where you can make connections to other places. Cooperativos Amazonas has a direct bus from Quito at 11:30am, returning from Misahuallí at 8:30am ($7, six hours).

Since the opening of the Tena–Coca road and the construction of roads east along Río Napo, river traffic has dwindled to the point that passenger canoes are no longer available. Canoe rentals cost $25 per hour (up to 12 passengers). Instead of arranging your trip with drivers on the beach, go to a nearby agency (if the boat has problems they will back you up). If you're staying at a lodge on the Río Napo, transport will be arranged by the lodge.

UPPER RÍO NAPO

☎ 06

The chocolaty waters of the Río Napo flow northeast from Misahuallí toward Coca, broadening in scope as it passes nature reserves, small jungle communities, oil rigs and lodges along its verdant shores. Public canoe transportation down the Napo to Coca has been completely replaced by transportation on the Tena–Coca road. Road construction means development, and however insubstantial it may be, wildlife viewing is less prolific along this corridor than it was in the past. The road along the south bank of the Río Napo to La Punta passes some of the places described below.

Reserva Biológica Jatun Sacha

In Quechua **Jatun Sacha** (admission $6) means 'Big Forest,' and guests will find the diversity spectacular. There are 850 butterfly species, 535 bird species and unquantifiable but nonetheless thrilling quantities of fungi. This 2500-hectare biological station and rain forest reserve is located on the south side of Río Napo, 23km east of Puerto Napo. It is run by **Fundación Jatun Sacha** (Quito ☎ 02-243 2240, 243 2173; www.jatunsacha.org; Pasaje Eugenio de Santillán N34-248 & Maurián, Urbanización Rumipamba), an Ecuadorian nonprofit organization founded in 1985 with the goal of promoting rain forest research, conservation and education.

With neighboring areas being rapidly cleared for logging and agriculture, it is not known how long the incredible biodiversity of Jatun Sacha will remain. Besides taking count of local species, the foundation develops reforestation initiatives and agro-forestry alternatives with local farming communities and indigenous groups. Volunteers (who pay $300 for a minimum one-month stay) are welcome to apply for a variety of projects. One new initiative is to bring Internet access to rural schools that generally don't have libraries.

Guests of the Jatun Sacha biostation stay in **Cabañas Aliñahui** (r per person incl 3 meals $34), high up on the bluff with excellent bird's-eye views. Situated amid a 2-hectare tropical garden, eight cabins provide screened comfort with breezy verandas, solar-heated showers, double rooms and a private bathroom. The restaurant serves healthy Ecuadorian and international meals. Bird-watching and forest walks are some of the activities you can enjoy on-site. Definitely have a peek at the plant conservation center and botanical garden. Discounts for groups and students; contact Jatun Sacha (p253).

Reservations can be made at the Quito office of **Jatun Sacha** (Quito ☎ 02-243 2240, 243 2173; www.jatunsacha.org). To get to either Jatun Sacha or Cabañas Aliñahui from Tena, take an Ahuano or Santa Rosa bus and ask the driver to drop you at either entrance. Aliñahui is about 3km east of the Jatun Sacha research station, or 27km east of Tena on the road to Santa Rosa.

Ahuano

Uniformed schoolchildren skip through the puddles and gape at visitors in this small village, a half-hour downriver from Misahuallí. Poking around the folksy mission church and sloped streets might be interesting but there's not much to do. Buses from Tena to La Punta also arrive here (with the trip followed by a river crossing). On this side of the river this is the end of the road. Boating to Coca is expensive and difficult to arrange, so you're best off returning to Tena and going there by bus.

The friendly **Casa de Doña Maruja** (☎ 09-130 4668; r per person with 3 meals $5) offers bare-bones rooms with split-plank floors beside the gurgling river. Bathrooms are shared and meals are out on the patio with the family. They also have a canoe that can be rented for excursions.

By far the finest digs in town is **Casa del Suizo** (Map pp228-9; Quito ☎ 02-256 6090, 250 9504; www.casadelsuizo.com; Zaldumbide 375 & Toledo; r per person $70, packages per person for 4 days & 3 nights s/d $273/210; ☑). The Swiss-owned lodge stacked up on the bluff proffers a pampered glimpse at the jungle tropics. A maze of covered boardwalks link thatched rooms with high-

ceilings and pale adobe walls. Comfortable rooms are decked out with electricity (yes, in these parts it is a feature), hot showers, terraces gazing out at the river and hammocks. The turquoise pool kisses the lip of the overhang, you can cavort in its crystalline waters with an eye to the murky ribbon of the Napo just below. Included in the daily rate are meals and excursions; which include river trips, jungle hikes, community and mission visits, an on-site butterfly house and wildlife walks. Guides are bilingual.

Guests at the lodge pay $15 per boatload for canoe transport from Misahuallí. For independent travelers, buses from Tena run eight times a day to La Punta, about 28km east of Puerto Napo on the south side of Río Misahuallí. Although the bus doesn't actually go to Ahuano, it's still called the Ahuano bus locally, since most passengers transfer in dugout canoes across the river to Ahuano. Boats are frequent and the fare is about $1 per person. You can ask to be left at Casa del Suizo. Chartering your own boat costs more.

Selva Viva & Liana Lodge

You're guaranteed to see all manner of critters at **AmaZOOnico** (☎ 09-980 0463; www.amazoonico .org; admission $2.50), a well-known animal-rehabilitation center. It is located on the grounds of Selva Viva, a 13-sq-km reserve of primary forest on Río Arajuno, a narrow tributary of the Napo about 3km east of Ahuano. Angelika Raimann and Remigio Canelos (a Swiss/Quechua couple) founded the center in 1994 to care for confiscated or displaced rain forest animals.

Animals ranging from toucans to capybara fill the premises. While cages may not be the ideal setting for your first glimpse of jungle wildlife, the circumstances belie the ugly reality. The displacement of these animals is inherently tied to the destruction of their surrounding habitat and the ease at which illegal traffickers can make a quick buck on their sale. The center has its critics (who see it more as a zoo than a stepping stone to the wild), but an unfortunate number of animals that arrive here, particularly monkeys, are already too domesticated to be re-released. The costs of maintaining them with appropriate food and medicine are astronomical. Healthy animals are released back into the rain forest but these number in the minority. A landmark project plans to release spider monkeys (which are now extinct in the area) into nearby rain forest in 2006.

The center is always looking for volunteers ($80 per month living expenses), especially with veterinary backgrounds, and generally requires a two-month minimum for proper training and experience. Those interested should see the webpage for more information.

A stay in the **Liana Lodge** (Map pp228-9; ☎ 09-980 0463; r per person $16; packages per person for 3 days/2 nights $87, 4 days/3 nights $138) helps fund both the rehab center and the new reserve. Six cabins are scattered throughout a forested hillside, each with crafty touches such as bamboo beds and hand-carved clothes hangers. Rooms were built with remnant wood left over from road-building, and each has two double rooms and a hot shower. It's a carefree riverside atmosphere of bonfires and walks through the woods. Package rates include meals, taxes and local tours.

If you reserve ahead the lodge can send a canoe for you. Otherwise, take a Tena bus to Santa Rosa and get off at the Selva Viva entrance. It's a 2km downstream hike to the lodge, but trails are unmarked and may be difficult to follow. Quechua, English, Spanish, German and French are spoken here.

Arajuno Jungle Lodge

If small and out of the way sounds your speed, check out former Peace Corps volunteer Thomas Larson's new lodge (Map pp228-9; tlarson@pi.pro.ec; packages for 3/4 nights $224/314), slung in a bend of the Río Arajuno. A handful of hillside cabins are snug and screened. The thatched main lodge has a sprawling wood deck and dining area perched over the river. Guests can roam around the 80 hectares of forest, hike, canoe and visit the nearby AmaZOOnico. The chef cooks up locally inspired gourmet such as smoked *cachama maitos* (fish grilled in palm leaves) and *tortilla de yuca* (manioc bread). Grown-up kids will love the rope swing launching over the river (and in!) as well as the flying trapeze. Services are bilingual.

Yachana Lodge

Yachana delights its guest simply by taking ecotourism seriously. Birding, hikes and community visits are all here but with a strong bent toward interaction on the local level.

The parent NGO, Funedesin, was created to find workable solutions in the struggle between the ideals of rain forest preservation and the realities of life in the Ecuadorian Amazon. Rain forest residents can't live on preservation – unless they develop sustainable

---

YACHANA HIGH

In the remote Amazon Basin only 5% of kids finish high school. This dismal figure contributes substantially to this beautiful and biologically rich area's ongoing struggles with poverty and environmental degradation. In the small Río Napo community of Mondaña a program is working to reverse the cycle. Yachana High School offers an innovative learning program to mestizo and indigenous kids from rural areas of the Amazon. According to **FUNEDESIN** (Foundation for Integrated Education & Development; ☎ 02-223 7278, 223 7133, 222 2584; www.funedesin.org), the parent foundation, 'Meaningful education is the key to reversing generations of poverty, raising environmental awareness and ensuring the sustainable use of the region's natural resources.' Fees paid by visitors to Yachana Lodge are a major source of funding for the high school.

Its director, Douglas McMeekin, a former academic flunky, designed the program to engage kids who weren't classroom stars. Students learn by working in responsible farming practices, natural resources management, financial management, guiding, hospitality skills and English, among other things. Students participate in micro-enterprises (one produces organic chocolate for export with local cacao crops), which provide the opportunity to both earn money and bank it, teaching accountability with real greenbacks. The idea is to take students out of their dusty grammars and into relevant situations. Courses rotate three weeks on/three weeks off so kids with farm responsibilities won't have to drop out come planting or harvest time.

So far it appears to be a success, but there is plenty of work to be done before the fledgling class earn diplomas in Ecotourism and Sustainable Development. The program has been approved by the Ecuadorian Ministry of Education and accepts volunteers on a long-term basis.

THE ORIENTE

alternatives. At Yachana training is geared toward training indigenous and colonists alike in organic agriculture, sustainable farming techniques, health awareness, beekeeping, food processing and secondary education (see p255).

The **lodge** (Map pp228-9; packages for 3/4 nights $345/460) is located halfway between Misahuallí and Coca on Río Napo. Its campus of stilted wooden buildings, groomed grounds and gardens are upriver from the tiny community of Mondaña. The lodge has 11 rooms (each room sleeping two or three people), and three family cabins come with a double and a triple room. Each spacious tiled room has a hot shower and a balcony, and solar-power lighting. In addition you'll find a conference center, library and sun deck. The restaurant serves hearty meals, mostly vegetarian. Visitors typically stay for three or four nights, with set departures from Quito on Tuesdays and Fridays. Children aged 12 and under are charged half price. Costs include everything except alcohol, soft drinks, personal expenses and (optional) air transportation from Quito to Coca. From Coca, it's a 1½-hour motorized canoe ride to the lodge.

Visitors can take part in a traditional healing ceremony, go on guided hikes along 20km of trails, take day or night rides in a canoe, check out the butterfly house, visit with the local community or just relax in a hammock. Shuar and Quechua indigenous guides speak English and provide treasure troves of information about the forest

This project is heaped with accolades; it won the Conde Naste award in 2004 for Best Example of Ecotourism. Reservations should be made in Quito at **Funedesin/Yachana Lodge** (☎ 02-252 3777, 250 3275; www.yachana .com; Vicente Solano E12-61 & Av Oriental).

PUYO

☎ 03 / pop 24,432

This small wood-and-concrete sprawl with a river slinking through it represents the juncture between northern and southern Oriente. The capital of Pastaza, Puyo is Ecuador's largest jungle town, though in the absence of oil and the presence of so many highlanders, it doesn't quite feel like it. Visitors will find it to be a busy commercial center obsessed with jeans and the Internet, taming back the verdant swaths of jungle sprouting from its ears. It is also

a hop and a skip to indigenous villages and their attractions.

Fiestas de Fundación de Puyo, the weeklong celebrations of Puyo's founding day, take place in early May.

Information

Amazonía Touring (☎ 288 3064; Atahualpa; ☷ 9am-8pm Mon-Sat, 9am-noon Sun) The only place to change traveler's checks. It charges a 3% commission.

Andinatel (Orellana) Telephone services are available.

Banco del Austro (Atahualpa) Has an ATM.

Banco Internacional (Villamil) Beware – the ATM only takes four-digit pins.

Cámara de Turismo (☎ 288 6737; 2nd fl, Marín, Centro Commercial Zuñiga; ☷ 8:30am-12:30pm & 3-6pm Mon-Fri) Of minimal assistance.

Centro de Información de Turismo Responsable (CITR; ☎ 288 6048; www.amazoniaecuador.net; 9 de Octubre at Bolívar; Internet per hr $0.75; ☷ 8:30am-12:30pm & 3-6pm Mon-Fri) Internet café and information on community tourism. Sells indigenous crafts and serves coffee, juices and popcorn.

Lavandaria La Mocita (☎ 288 5346; cnr Marín & Bolívar; ☷ 7am-5pm) Cheap and efficient laundry service.

Post office (27 de Febrero) Northwest of the market.

Red Cross (☎ 288 5214) Is on the north side of the main plaza.

Voz Andes mission hospital (☎ 279 5172; Shell s/n) In Shell, this is the best bet for medical emergencies.

Tours

Papangu-Atacapi Tours (☎ 288 3875; 27 de Febrero & Sucre; ☷ 8am-12:30pm, 2-6pm Mon-Sat) An indigenous-run agency with a focus on community tourism. Trips go to Sarayacu (a Quechua community), Chareras (Quechua) and Cueva de los Tayos (Shuar). Sarayacu (www .sarayacu.com/tourism) requires a rural charter flight ($300 round-trip) and the cost is $45 per day. Other trips cost $40 per day. Guides are indigenous and 30% of fees go to participating communities.

ONHAE (☎ 288 6148) Not a tour agency, this Huaorani political body still authorizes any access to Huaorani territory. Current director Penti Baihua can guide or arrange three- to eight-day trips; a fascinating seat-of-your-pants kind of journey with very basic accommodations and food.

Local guides include German- and English-speaking Byron Soria (☎ 09-318 8597; www.amazoniajungle.com) and Luis Reyes (☎ 09-970 2209; reylui_05@yahoo.es), a licensed guide with some English offering trips to Reserva Hola Vida or Cuyabeno reserve for $35 to $45 per day.

Sights & Activities

Early risers may sneak views of the jagged peak of **El Altar** (5319m), the fifth-highest

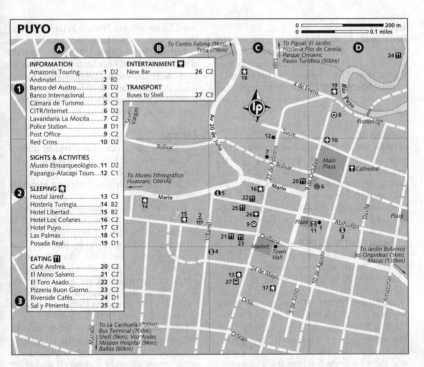

PUYO

0 ————— 200 m
0 ————— 0.1 miles

INFORMATION		ENTERTAINMENT 🎭	
Amazonía Touring	1 D2	New Bar	26 C2
Andinatel	2 B2		
Banco del Austro	3 D2	TRANSPORT	
Banco Internacional	4 C3	Buses to Shell	27 C3
Cámara de Turismo	5 C2		
CITR/Internet	6 C2		
Lavandaria La Mocita	7 C2		
Police Station	8 D1		
Post Office	9 C2		
Red Cross	10 D2		

SIGHTS & ACTIVITIES	
Museo Etnoarqueológico	11 D2
Papangu-Atacapi Tours	12 C1

SLEEPING 🏠	
Hostal Jared	13 D2
Hostería Turingia	14 B2
Hotel Libertad	15 B2
Hotel Los Cofanes	16 C2
Hotel Puyo	17 C2
Las Palmas	18 C1
Posada Real	19 D1

EATING 🍴	
Café Andrea	20 C2
El Mono Salsero	21 C2
El Toro Asado	22 C2
Pizzería Buon Giorno	23 C2
Riverside Cafés	24 D1
Sal y Pimienta	25 C2

To Centro Fatima (9km);
Tena (79km)

To Pigual; El Jardín;
Hostería Flor de Canela;
Parque Omaere;
Paseo Turístico (500m)

To Museo Etnográfico
Huaorani; ONHAE

To La Carihuela (700m);
Bus Terminal (700m);
Shell (9km); Voz Andes
Mission Hospital (9km);
Baños (60km)

To Jardín Botánico
las Orquídeas (3km);
Macas (130km)

mountain in Ecuador, about 50km south-east of Puyo. On clear days look southwest to see **Sangay** (5230m) from the main plaza.

Walk along the river path past the pleasant cafés and kids plunging from the bridge into Río Puyo to **Parque Omaere** (☎ 288 5605; www .omaere.net; admission $3; ☼ 10am-12:30pm, 1-4:30pm Mon-Fri), less than 1km north of the center. The ethnobotanical park offers guided tours (free with admission) of rain forest plants and indigenous dwellings given by indigenous guides. The center is now run by Chris Canady, an ornithologist, author of *Common Birds of the Ecuadorian Amazon*, and a fountain of jungle knowledge. Get there by following Loja north of town for about half a kilometer, until you reach the bridge over the river, and follow the sign.

A pleasant **trail** (locally called the *paseo turístico*) continues past Omaere for 2.5km along the river to the Puyo–Tena road, where you can flag a bus back into town every 20 minutes, or walk back along the trail.

Visitors rave about the **Jardín Botánico las Orquídeas** (☎ 288 4855; admission $5; ☼ 8am-6pm), located 15 minutes south from Puyo on the road to Macas. Enthusiastic owner Omar Taeyu guides visitors through hills of lush foliage and fishponds to see gorgeous plants and countless rare orchids. Call ahead.

The new **Museo Etnográfico Huaorani** (☎ 288 6148; Severo Vargas s/n; admission $3; ☼ 10am-5pm) has a small exhibit and guided tour. Take a taxi there from the center for $1. Perhaps more engaging than the artifacts themselves is the Huaorani's take of their culture and problems. Upstairs is ONHAE, the political body of the Huaorani.

The **Museo Etnoarqueológico** (☎ 288 5605; Atahualpa & 9 de Octubre; admission $1; ☼ noon-6pm) has ceramics, artifacts and an excellent map showing distribution of native populations.

Mountain bikers can make a beautiful 65km downhill **ride** from the central highlands town of Baños to Puyo, via Podunk hamlet of **Shell**. Throw the bike on the roof of a bus in Puyo for the round trip.

Sleeping

An explosion in cheaper midrange offerings means Puyo's grubby dives are a thing of the past – unless you insist.

BUDGET

Hostal Jared (☎ 288 5670; 27 de Febrero; r per person $6) Bright, crisp rooms with ruffled bedcovers and new installations make this friendly spot a great deal. There's dining on the terrace.

Hotel Libertad (☎ 288 3681; Orellana; r per person $6) This tranquil spot offers cramped but spotless singles.

MIDRANGE

El Jardin (☎ 288 6101; www.eljardin.pastaza.net; r per person incl breakfast $15) A welcoming spot set behind a large garden, this rustic wooden house has hammock balconies and plain but comfortable rooms with firm beds and thick comforters. Breakfast is fruit and yogurt and is served in the excellent attached restaurant.

Posada Real (☎ 288 5887; www.posadareal.pastaza .net; 4 de Enero at 9 de Octubre stairs; r per person $15) A beautiful house with a warm, formal atmosphere. Beds have plush spreads and thick pillows and rooms are elegant and tasteful.

Las Palmas (☎ 288 4832; www.laspalmas.pastaza .net; cnr 20 de Julio & 4 de Enero; r per person incl breakfast $10) You'll find this big yellow colonial with attractive gardens and chattering parrot great value. The rooms are neat and simple and there's on-site Internet and a café serving wine and coffee . It is a few blocks' walk to the center.

Hostería Turingia (☎ 288 5180; turingia@andinatel .net; Marín 294; s/d $18/32; 🏊) This Tyrolean outpost on the fringes of Puyo offers wood-paneled cabins with firm double beds and a full-service restaurant. There's patio seating under the bougainvillea and a tiny plunge pool. The accommodations include fans, TVs, telephones and hot water.

Hotel Los Cofanes (☎ 288 5560; loscofanes@yahoo .com; 27 de Febrero 629; r per person $13) The hush corridors of this modern hotel lead to bright and ample tiled rooms. The attention is very good and rooms include phone, fan and cable TV.

Hotel Puyo (☎ 288 4497; hotelpuyo@yahoo.es; 9 de Octubre; r per person $10) Petite, fastidious rooms with stiff Naugahyde furniture are still pretty comfortable. Has TV, telephone and hot water.

Pigual (☎ 288 7972; www.elpigualecuador.com; end of Tuguragua; s/d incl breakfast & dinner $25/50; 🏊) The expansive grounds of this former farm are manicured green with a pool and volleyball court, and quiet cement-and-wooden cab-

ins. The owners are French-Ecuadorian and the restaurant on-site is quite good.

Hostería Flor de Canela (☎ 288 5265; hosteriaflo rdecanela@hotmail.com; Paseo Turístico, Barrio Obrero; s/d $31/53; 🏊) Part-wooded getaway, part Disneyland, this complex of elaborate stone and hardwood cabañas sits near the Río Puyo, next door to Parque Omaere (p257).

Eating

Try the riverside cafés for a typical dish of *ceviche boquetero*, literally 'dumptruck ceviche,' combining corn, toasted kernels and banana chips with a can of tuna elegantly dumped on top.

El Jardín (☎ 288 6101; Paseo Turístico, Barrio Obrero; mains $4-5; ☾ noon-10pm Tue-Sat, noon-5pm Sun) The best grub in the Oriente may be at this ambient house with gardens by the river. The award-winning chef Sofia, also the owner, prepares fragrant *pollo ishpingo* (*ishpingo* is a type of cinnamon native to the Oriente) whose decadent, delicate flavors awake the palate. It's just across the footbridge leading to Parque Omaere (p257).

Café Andrea (9 de Octubre & Bolívar; snacks $2; ☾ 8am-10pm) A cozy spot on the plaza serving cappuccinos and delicious *empanadas de verde* (green plantain turnovers) and other snacks.

Pizzería Buon Giorno (☎ 288 3841; Orellana; pizzas $4.50-6; ☾ 1-10pm Mon-Sat) A happy atmosphere to down cheese-heavy thick-crust pizza and beer.

Sal y Pimienta (☎ 288 5821; Atahualpa; almuerzos $2; ☾ 7am-11pm) A steak joint which is packed with locals for cheap, fast meals.

El Mono Salsero (Orellana s/n; mains $2; ☾ 6:30am-3pm) A cheery street-shack where you can pull up a stool and chow hotdogs and ceviche with the locals.

El Toro Asado (☎ 09-537 8481; Atahualpa & 27 de Febrero; mains $4; ☾ 7am-11pm) In addition to heaping pastas and meats this elegant grill house serves *guanta a la plancha*, an Amazonian…er, rodent. The owner swears it tastes like pork, but we'll leave it to you to find out.

Drinking & Entertainment

Twilight's frenetic buzz concludes around 9:30pm when most good citizens and Internet addicts head for home. If you're still in the mood try **New Bar** (27 de Febrero; ☾ 6pm-2am Mon-Sat), whose dim ambience encourages karaoke on a good night. The back-alley disco **La Matrix** (🕐 Thu-Sat) is popular with the young ones and plays a gaudy mix of rock and Latin faves.

Getting There & Away

Charter flights from the provincial airstrip in Shell charge around $100 per hour, but chances are if you're headed into the deep green yonder, it will be on a tour.

The bus terminal is about 1km southwest of town. There are buses via Baños ($2, 1½ hours) to Ambato ($2.50, 2½ hours). Buses to Quito ($5, 5½ hours) leave about every hour and go either via Baños or Baeza. Buses to Tena ($2.50, three hours) also leave hourly. Flota Pelileo has one bus daily to Guayaquil ($9, eight hours).

Buses to Macas ($5, four hours) leave every hour and go as far as Río Pastaza, where you have to transfer (see p262). There are two early morning departures to Coca ($10, nine hours).

Centinela del Oriente, located at the bus terminal, runs ancient buses to various small villages in the surrounding jungle.

Getting Around

A taxi ride from downtown to the bus terminal costs $1. Small local buses go to Shell ($0.30) about every 30 minutes or so from south of the market along 27 de Febrero.

THE SOUTHERN ORIENTE

So what if former head hunters now wear Polo shirts? The southern Oriente is still the backwater of the Ecuadorian Amazon, with reams of roadless land, far-flung indigenous settlements and nary a jungle lodge in sight (OK, there's one). Tourism in the region is nascent. The best opportunities for visitors are with cultural tours; unpolished excursions which afford a very real glimpse of local life.

The central highway runs north–south, coming in from Puyo and connecting Macas with smaller towns all the way to Zamora. Beautiful highland roads swoop down from Cuenca and Loja to join with the central highway (both described in the Cuenca & the Southern Highlands chap-

ter). With broken buses, unpaved roads and rainy-season landslides the norm, travelers need patience and fortitude. June to August are the rainiest months.

MACAS
☎ 07 / pop 13,600

Mission roots burrow back to 1563, but they are just a layer in the complex scaffolding of this old trading post at the tip of Shuar and Achuar territories. The provincial capital of Morona-Santiago, Macas is essentially a burgeoning modern town whose identity ebbs between colonial and indigenous. Its slow and steady pace and approachable locals make it a welcoming stop for the visitor and an excellent launch pad for adventures further afield.

Information

Banco del Austro (cnr 24 de Mayo & 10 de Agosto) May change traveler's checks; offers ATM and cash advances on Visa.

Banco del Pinchincha (cnr 10 de Agosto & Soasti) Has an ATM.

Cámara de Turismo (☎ 270 1606, 270 0300; Comin; 🕐 8am-1pm Mon-Sat) Useful information kiosk

Centro de Interpretación (cnr Juan de la Cruz & 29 de Mayo) Small exhibit and information about Parque Nacional Sangay.

Cyber Vision (☎ 270 1212; Soasti; per hr $1.50; 🕐 9am-1pm & 1:30-10pm Mon-Fri, 10am-3pm Sat & Sun)

Orientravel (☎ 270 0371; ortravel@cue.satnet.net; cnr 10 de Agosto & Soasti) To book national and international airline tickets.

Pacifictel (24 de Mayo; 🕐 8am-10pm) Long-distance call center.

Post office (9 de Octubre)

Sights & Activities

The main activity centers on Soasti but a few blocks past it you'll find Our Lady of Macas, a **cathedral** whose Technicolor virgin looms over the manicured plaza. Miracles are attributed to the painting of the Virgin of Macas (c 1592) on the altar. Inside, you can gawp at the deco-style altar and the lace-curtain confessionals. Each August 4, a 23km procession in honor of the Virgin arrives from Sucúa.

The **casa de la cultura** (free admission; 🕐 8am-noon, 1:30-5pm Mon-Fri) offers a glimpse of Shuar artifacts, including pottery, hunting bows and basketry.

The perfect snow-covered cone of **Volcán Sangay** (5230m), some 40km to the northwest,

THE ORIENTE

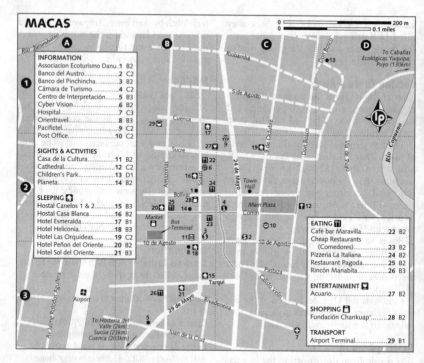

MACAS

INFORMATION
Asociacion Ecoturismo Danu..1 B2
Banco del Austro.....................2 C2
Banco del Pinchincha..............3 B2
Cámara de Turismo..................4 C2
Centro de Interpretación.........5 B3
Cyber Vision............................6 B2
Hospital..................................7 C3
Orientravel..............................8 B3
Pacifictel.................................9 C2
Post Office...........................10 C2

SIGHTS & ACTIVITIES
Casa de la Cultura.................11 B2
Cathedral..............................12 C2
Children's Park......................13 D1
Planeta.................................14 B2

SLEEPING
Hostal Canelos 1 & 2............15 B3
Hostal Casa Blanca...............16 B2
Hotel Esmeralda...................17 B1
Hotel Heliconia....................18 B3
Hotel Las Orquideas.............19 C2
Hotel Peñon del Oriente......20 B2
Hotel Sol del Oriente...........21 B3

EATING
Café bar Maravilla................22 B2
Cheap Restaurants
   (Comedores)....................23 B2
Pizzeria La Italiana...............24 B2
Restaurant Pagoda...............25 B2
Rincón Manabita..................26 B3

ENTERTAINMENT
Acuario................................27 B2

SHOPPING
Fundación Chankuap'...........28 B2

TRANSPORT
Airport Terminal..................29 B1

can be glimpsed on a clear day. It is Ecuador's seventh-highest mountain and one of the world's most active volcanoes; early missionaries construed it as hell. It may be climbed, but only from its highland side.

A few blocks northeast of the center, is a small **children's park** (Don Bosco & Zabala).

Approaching the last week of May is the **Chonta Festival**, the most important Shuar celebration of the year. If you speak with a Shuar guide, it is possible to garner an invitation to this grand event, where participants dance for four consecutive hours to help ferment the *chicha* (a corn drink; see p262).

Tours

There are many wonderful and fascinating trips to be had in the southern Oriente and Macas is the place to book them. It has the best infrastructure of guides and tours to Cuevas de los Tayos and other attractions much further south.

That said, tourism is still fledgling and its services are not as comprehensive as those in the northern Oriente. Adventure – sure, there's plenty, but don't expect many creature comforts. Be aware that the Shuar do not want unguided visitors in their villages and certain villages refuse visitors. Given the negative impact of outside encounters in the past, this stance is certainly understandable.

Asociación Ecoturismo Danu (☎ 270 1300; 2nd fl, Soasti & Bolivar) Runs trips near and into Parque Nacional Sangay. A three-day tour for two people costs $45 per day. Park entry fee is $10 extra.

Planeta Tours (☎ 270 1328; Comin at Soasti; ☼ 8am-10pm Mon-Fri, 8am-noon Sat & Sun) Offers cultural tours in Shuar territory, waterfall hikes, fishing and some whitewater canoeing. Some English is spoken.

Yacu Amu Rafting (Quito ☎ 02-223 6844; www.yacu amu.com) offers eight-day trips through Río Upano's wild Namangosa Gorge, whose magnificent scenery comes from high waterfalls spilling over the lip of the gorge. The Class III to IV white water is also suitable for kayakers. See p89.

Independent guides who can take you into remote Shuar communities and caves include: **Tsunki Marcelo Cajecal** (tourshuar@hotmail.com), a licensed guide with basic English; **Bolivar Caita** (☎ 270 1690; bolicaita@hotmail.com), a knowledgeable longtime guide; and **Nanki Wampankit** (nanki_82@hotmail.com). All are Shuar.

Sleeping

Hotel Heliconia (☎ 270 1956; h_heilconia_macas@ hotmail.com; Soasti & 10 de Agosto; s/d $13/22) Posh by Macas standards, this high-rise is decked out in parquet floors and glass-walled panoramic views. Bedrooms feature cable TV and phones as well as thick comforters, finer furnishings and marble bathrooms. The staff is eager to help and restaurant service is available on request.

Hotel Sol del Oriente (☎ 270 2911; Tarqui & Soasti; r per person $8) Another new high-rise with large, bright tiled rooms and city views.

Hotel Las Orquideas (☎ 270 0970; 9 de Octubre; r per person with shared/private bathroom $7/8) Excellent value, with prim pink rooms away from the noise. The hard beds and singles-only contribute to the conventlike ambience of this large, old-fashioned *pensión* (inexpensive boarding house.

Hostal Casa Blanca (☎ 270 0195; Soasti; r per person incl breakfast $11) A modern white multistory whose most coveted rooms line the garden out back. Interior rooms are dim and airless, but clean. Has a restaurant attached.

Hotel Esmeralda (☎ 270 0130; Cuenca 612; r per person $8) Beds sag and rooms are on the small side but the friendly owner makes travelers welcome.

Hostal Los Canelos (☎ 270 0113, 270 2942; Soasti & Tarqui; r per person $7-8) Offers two locations on the same block; the corner lot is glossier with bright tiles and immaculate beds. Try to get a room with a balcony.

Hotel Milenium (☎ 270 0805; Amazonas & Tarqui; r per person with shared/private bathroom $6/8) Locate the plant-lined balcony outside and step inside to spotless, unadorned rooms.

Hotel Peñon del Oriente (☎ 270 0124; Amazonas & Conin; r per person $6-8) Make sure you have a sense of humor for the Barbie bedspreads and Bible sayings, but with rooms this worn, you might consider venturing further from the bus station.

Hostería del Valle (☎ 270 0226, 270 1143; Vía Macas-Sucua (km2); r per person $10) Rustic bungalows offer private hot bathroom, TV and breakfast.

Cabañas Ecológicas Yuquipa (☎ 270 0071; r per person $35) These rudimentary huts offer a rural experience near Río Yuquipa, a small tributary of Río Upano. Your guide will show you plants and take you through San Vicente, a Shuar outpost. Rates include meals and Spanish-speaking guides.

Eating

Café bar Maravilla (☎ 270 0158; Soasti near Sucre; mains $4-6; ☺ 4pm-1am Mon-Sat) This blue casita is all ambience, from the twinkling porch lights to the stuffed red leather armchairs. It is a great place to chill, with *tablas* (cutting boards) of meat and cheese and yuca fries. The drink menu gets creative, with herbal aphrodisiacs and *hueso de chuchuguazo* (a root mixed with rum).

La Italiana (☎ 270 2893; Bolívar & Soasti; mains $1.50-4; ☺ 11am-midnight Tue-Sun) Wedged into a side street, this is a pleasant spot to hang out and eat crisp pizza with a smattering of sausage and mushrooms; there's burritos and pasta too.

Restaurant Pagoda (☎ 270 0280; cnr Amazonas & Comín; mains $4-6; ☺ 9:30am-10:30pm) The best *chifa* (Chinese restaurant) in Macas is this red-lacquered diner serving steamy beef and noodles, and fried rice.

Rincón Manabita (Amazonas; mains $1.50-3; ☺ 7am-10pm Mon-Fri, 7am-3pm Sat & Sun) A no-fuss, rambling outfit offering ceviche and fish plates, located down a slim passage, behind the swinging doors.

The *comedores* (cheap restaurants) situated on Comín near Soasti sell tasty *ayampacos*, a jungle speciality of meat, chicken or fish grilled in *bijao* leaves.

Entertainment

Bust up your mellow weekend with a trip to **Café bar Maravilla** (see above) for live Andean music or jaunt to **Acuario** (☎ 270 1601; Sucre; ☺ 9pm-1am Thu-Sat), a small, popular disco.

Shopping

Fundación Chankuap' (☎ 270 1176; www.chankuap .com; cnr Bolívar & Soasti; ☺ 9am-noon & 2-6pm Mon-Fri, 8am-1pm Sun) Aids the Shuar, Achuar and area colonists produce and sell crafts, herbal remedies and beauty products. Its cool products can also be seen online at www .camari.org/chankuap/ES.

Getting There & Away

AIR

Monday through Friday **TAME** (☎ /fax 270 1162, 270 1978; airport) flies from Quito to Macas ($43) at 2pm and returns at 3pm. If flying from Macas to Quito, the left-hand side of the plane offers the best mountain views, including Sangay and Cotopaxi if the weather is clear.

THE ORIENTE

CHICHA – THE BREAKFAST OF CHAMPIONS?

Before you could get even a Coke and a smile in the Amazon Basin, there was *chicha*, not the boiled highland version, but a highly portable nutritional drink taken 'to go' as a paste wrapped in leaves that – presto! – becomes a liquid lunch when you arrive at the next river and mix up a batch.

The recipe is simple – *chicha* is yuca or chonta palm masticated by women (yes, just women). It's an important staple of the jungle, where people eat very little and drink up to 6L a day. For millenia *chicha* has been a prime source of nutrition and vitamins for remote communities, far superior to plain old water. When fresh it's mild and yogurtlike. As time passes, *chicha* becomes more alcoholic as bacteria from the saliva breaks carbohydrates down into simple sugars. The older it is, the stronger the vintage, so to speak. Its taste depends on who made your *chicha*; with different bacterias seeding each fermentation, the *chicha* of each woman has a distinctive taste. Really terrible *chicha* is considered a portent that something bad will happen.

Will something bad happen to you, the visitor, if you try it? It might. But contrary to what you might assume, most problems come not from the *chicha* itself but the unfiltered river water it might be mixed with. As it's considered very bad form to refuse *chicha*, in one way or another, you'll be taking your chances.

Small aircraft can sometimes be chartered to various jungle villages, but are expensive; ask a local tour agency or guide.

BUS

In late 2006 all departures will be from the bus terminal but while it is remodeled, the various bus companies line Guamote and 10 de Agosto. Centinela del Oriente goes to Quito ($10, 10 hours) in the morning and evening. Buses Macas offers several departures a day for Cuenca ($8.50, eight hours) and Coop Sucua goes to Gualaquiza ($8, nine hours), passing Limon and Mendez. Buses to Sucúa ($1, 45 minutes) run every 30 minutes from 6am to 7pm.

Buses north to Puyo ($4, four hours) leave several times a day; some continue to Tena. About halfway to Puyo at Chuitayo, passengers tumble out and walk across a suspension bridge over Río Pastaza to a designated second bus. Cars can cross a small bridge. The thatched hut, Aqui me Quedo, provides humor, drinks and snacks.

The old mule trail joining Macas with the highland town of Guamote (near Riobamba) is now a paved road. At the close of this edition, there was a weekend bus service but passengers were required to walk a short unfinished section and catch a second bus on the other side. Also see p177.

Transportes Macas runs small buses and pickup trucks to various remote parts of the province, including 9 de Octubre (for Parque Nacional Sangay) and Morona.

PARQUE NACIONAL SANGAY

This **national park** (admission $10) is more fully described on p176. Most access to the park is from the north and west; access from the south and east is very difficult. If starting from Macas, make your goal the alpine lakes or surrounding wilderness, since the volcano itself proves rather inaccessible from here.

Buses from Macas go to 9 de Octubre and San Vicente, where you'll find a small German-run **hospedaje** (boarding house; ☎ 09-420 8127; correo.martinriester59@hotmail.com; r per person with breakfast $15) whose owner also guides tours into the park for $60 per day.

The small settlement of Purshi is the official entrance to Parque Nacional Sangay. Ask a ranger or locals for trail advice. It's best to go with a guide. Trails are faint and advancing will often require acute navigation and machete skills in this steep and broken terrain: this is not a trip for the uninitiated outdoorsperson.

Road service between Macas and Riobamba has been initiated via this pass. At the time of writing, the road was only open on weekends and bus passengers were required to walk an unfinished stint and change buses on the other side. Inquire about further developments with the helpful Macas tourism office (see p259). Also see p177.

KAPAWAI ECOLODGE & RESERVE

Located in the heart of Achuar wilderness in one of most remote parts of the Ecuadorian Amazon, **Kapawi** (Map pp228–9; www.kapawi.com)

garners international fame and rightly so. With ecologically sound practices, it has shown an alternative to petroleum exploitation through cultural preservation and tourism. Many outfits make the same claim, but few practice it.

Tour operator Canodros built the lodge but rents the land and has trained Achuar participants in guiding, tourism and hospitality. They make up over half the staff, to eventually take over in 2011. Low-impact technology such as solar power, trash management and recycling, and biodegradable soaps are used in daily operations. The lodge has 20 thatched cabins built around a lagoon, each with private bathroom and a balcony with lake views.

Tourism as you know it is put on its head. Instead of photographing the Achuar, guests are invited to their homes, offered manioc beer and asked questions about their lives to begin the cultural exchange. Small groups are accompanied by an Achuar guide and a bilingual naturalist, who work in tandem to explain the intricacies of the rain forest, both from an ecological and a cultural point of view.

Kapawi received Conservation International's 'Ecotourism Excellence Award' and the British Airways 'Tourism for Tomorrow' award.

The lodge is just off Río Pastaza, on an oxbow lake on Río Capahuari. Visitors must reach it via light aircraft, followed by a boat ride. Make reservations at the main **Canodros office** (Guayaquil ☎ 04-228 0880; www.cano

dros.com; packages per person 4 days/5 nights $870), or at the **branch office** (Guayaquil ☎ 04-228 5711, Urbanizacion Santa Leonor, Manzana 5, Solar 10) or at most major travel agencies. Transportation from Quito costs $224 round trip. Package rates are based on double occupancy and include all meals and guided tours. For a student discount, present a valid ISIC student ID. Visitors pay a tax of $10 per person levied by the Achuar community.

THE JUNGLE FROM MACAS

Many Ecuadorian maps show tracks or trails leading from Macas into the interior. These often lead to Shuar indigenous villages and missions further into the Oriente. Going into these areas on your own is not recommended, as tourists may be unwelcome and some communities that do welcome guests insist they be accompanied by a guide.

Frequent buses from Macas go to the mission (church and school) of **Sevilla** (Don Bosco), about an hour's walk away on the other side of Río Upano. This is a good place to buy Shuar crafts from local artisans. From here a broad track leads to the village of **San Luís**, about a four-hour walk. Brothers Lino and Marcelino Juanga have a basic guest **cabaña** (☎ 09-178 0685; r per person & meals $30); in addition to sharing cultural dances and typical food, Lino sings in Shuar in a techno-*cumbia* band – surely something you haven't seen before. If going in on your own, be sure to ask permission from the locals upon entering; they may, in fact, require that a 'guide' accompany you.

OILBIRDS

When palm fruits ripen, thousands of oilbirds come to roost in remote caves filling southeast Ecuador. Small, reddish and whiskered, the oilbird is related to the nightjar but is so unusual that it is classified in its own family, the *Steatornithidae*. Known for their exceptionally acute vision and fine sense of smell which sniffs out fruity fragrances, the world's only nocturnal fruit-eating birds have been prized for centuries for their oil.

The Shuar use oil extracted from plump young birds as a medicine for parasites; a spoonful cleans out the kidneys and liver. It is also considered to be effective against rheumatism and used for cooking and lighting. Over the centuries its remarkable usefulness, in a culture without ready access to a pharmacy, has contributed to the decline in oilbirds.

These days to see a roosting cave, a visitor must journey at least several hours on foot into this secluded area. Cuevas de los Tayos is actually a body of more than 30 caves; Churitayo being one of the more accessible. Coangos cave, of greater interest to scientists, requires a multiday underground expedition which starts with a 70m rappel – not for claustrophobes. Underground, sounds of screaming calls and clicks (a form of echolocation also used by bats) fill the blackness. With larger colonies the din is deafening. Welcome to the world of the oilbird.

THE ORIENTE

Trails leading into remote jungle communities are an unmarked tangle, with some paths overgrown. This is one more reason to hire a guide. A charter *expreso* light aircraft can take you by air to some of the better-known centers, such as **Taisha**, 70km due east of Macas. Salesian mission aircraft fly here, but locals are given preference and flights are often full. Hiring your own aircraft costs about $60 per person per hour for a five-seater, usually with at least a $200 minimum fee. Expect delays when there's inclement weather.

To satisfy your craving for **caving** or to sight the rare oilbird (The Cave of the Oilbirds – see the boxed text, p263), grab a guide and head to **Las Cueva de los Tayos** between Méndez and Morona. A five-hour trail leads to the extensive Coangos cave system, where you can spend a week exploring these underground caverns laced with stalactites and stalagmites. This visit requires technical equipment, as the journey starts with a 70m drop into the caves. Sound too serious? The Curitayo cave, a two-hour hike, can be visited without any technical equipment. However, you will need gloves to protect your hands, rubber boots to slog through deep puddles and a flashlight when you lose your guide!

A river trip down Río Santiago toward Peru (not an authorized crossing) will get you way off the beaten path and into very remote jungle. Trips of this nature can be arranged with the more experienced guides in Macas.

SUCÚA
☎ 07 / pop 6310

Limp and languid in the hot tropical sun, this dusty town 23km south of Macas has little to offer but peace. There is a small plaza with ficus trees and chirping cicadas. From the plaza, it's a short walk down the main street to the **Federación Shuar** (☎ 274 0108; Domingo Comín 17-38). It's of little interest to casual visitors, but useful to people working with the Shuar. Market day is Sunday.

If you decide to stay, **Hotel Athenas** (☎ 274 0216; Comín & Solís; s/d $8/12) is posh for the price, with sparkling parquet floors and rattan bed covers. Nearby **Bar-Restaurant Esmeralda** (☎ 274 0140; Comín & Bernal; mains $3; ☽ 8am-10pm) caters to local tastes, but these coastal transplants can fry up a damn good *camarones*

apanados (butterfly shrimp) or *encocado* (fish or seafood cooked in spicy coconut sauce) on request.

Frequent buses or pickups leave for Macas ($1, one hour) from dawn until dusk at the corner of the main plaza.

FROM MÉNDEZ TO LIMÓN
☎ 07

The road south passes banana plantations and papaya groves surrounded by shaggy tropical forest. A little surprise is **Méndez**, at the bend in the Río Paute, its rows of bright colonials with sagging balconies squeezed into the hills. At noon a storekeeper plays solitaire on the countertop. It's more than quaint; this picturesque oblivion seems made to order for Witness Protection Program participants. Immune to its charms, Méndez has no tourist industry whatsoever. It's the crossroads for travel west to Cuenca (five hours), east toward the Peruvian border via Santiago (a rough and bumpy road), north to Macas (three hours) and south to Gualaquiza.

The best place to stay is **Los Ceibos** (☎ 276 0133; Cuenca near Comín; r per person $6), a spick-and-span hotel with peach and terra-cotta tiles. Eat at **Saboy** (Cuenca near Comín; menu $3) across the street, a typical lunch of meat and *menestra* (beans) with rice and fried bananas on the side.

The scenery on offer between Méndez and Gualaquiza is simply stunning. The road winds south along the Río Upano, courting views of buttressed walls and conical hills. **Limón**, also known as General Leonidas Plaza Gutiérrez, is a small, unprepossessing jungle town 35km after Méndez. It has one main street with a Pacifictel office, a few hotels, simple restaurants and bus offices. **Hotel Dream House** (☎ 277 0166; r per person $12) offers adequate rooms with shared bathrooms and a restaurant.

An hour south of Limón the road passes through the missions of San Juan Bosco and Indanza (also known as Plan de Milagro), and then continues through the countryside until it reaches Gualaquiza, four hours from Limón.

GUALAQUIZA
☎ 07 / approximate pop 6340 / elevation 950m

A colonial gem tucked into the tropical hills, Gualaquiza has happily forgotten the world. In this tranquil town, newspapers (if they arrive) don't hit the streets until late afternoon, women stroll with parasols to block the dazzling sun and a child skips home from Sunday market with grandma's cherries clutched in her fist. Visitors be forewarned: if you come here it is to flout the march of time and enjoy a little wandering.

Information isn't easy to rustle up in Gualaquiza but the locals are friendly and patient with inquiries. A **tourist booth** (☎ 278 0109; García Moreno near Pesantez; ⊗ 9am-5pm Mon-Fri) has information about nearby Inca sites and attractions. There's supposedly excellent **caving** 15km west of town near the village of Nueva Tarquí (spare flashlights and batteries are essential). A visit to **Ciclos** (☎ 278 0579; Orellana 4-35 near the market) bike shop run by Angel and Erwin Barros may yield useful advice on outings. An excellent **ride** swoops through the hills to La Florida (2½ hours by bike) and options abound for countryside jaunts. It is best to have your own bike, but they may be willing to rent.

Accommodations are limited, but your best bet is **Hotel Internacional** (☎ 278 0781; r per person $7.50), a modern multistory with narrow, well-kept rooms and varnished plywood floors. A half-block off the plaza you'll find **Residencial Guadalupe** (☎ 278 0113; Calle Gonzalo Pezantez; r per person with shared/private bathroom $3.50/6) a friendly old bunkhouse with sagging beds and faded rooms. Nonetheless, it's clean. For a slow bite, head to **Restaurant Copacabana** (☎ 278 0353; 2nd fl, Gualaquiza & 12 de Febrero; mains $3; ⊗ 7:30am-10pm). Their scrambled eggs with tomatoes are divine, and you'll have fine views of town in this spacious, open-air restaurant.

The **bus terminal** is downhill from the center. Ten buses a day go to Loja ($6, six hours) via Zamora ($4, four hours). There are two routes to Cuenca: the Sígsíg route ($7, six hours) saves two hours. Buses north go to Limón ($4, four hours), and after that Sucúa and Macas ($7.50, nine hours). Rancheras outside the terminal go to the villages in the pretty hillsides, which could make for an interesting outing.

Finally, before you leave, stop by the **market** next to the terminal, where you'll find sweet, creamy mangoes to dribble all over your bus seat on the way out.

FROM GUALAQUIZA TO ZAMORA
☎ 07
Several kilometers south of Gualaquiza, a turnoff to the right leads to Bomboiza, where a **Salesian mission** educates Shuar and colonist children.

Soon thereafter, the road crosses the provincial line into Zamora-Chinchipe province and then rises before passing through the village of **El Panguí**. Ask locals here for directions to *la cascada*, a beautiful waterfall two hours east on foot. South of El Panguí the road descends from tableland hills into a gaping, lush valley where the paved road turns to dirt.

The road continues through the village of **Los Encuentros** and, about 3½ hours from Gualaquiza, reaches **Yantzaza**, the only sizable village before Zamora, 1½ hours further south. In Yantzaza there are restaurants and some basic hotels (likely to be full of gold miners) near the main plaza.

Río Zamora zigzags the emerald valley floor parallel to the road. These rich-soil floodplains are populated with colonists from Loja and native Shuar. Indigenous hamlets and *fincas* (farms) grow tropical produce such as coffee, sugarcane and citrus fruit.

Just before Zamora you'll hit **Nambija**. A 1980s gold rush created a wild-west atmosphere of prostitution and crime against the backdrop of frenzied mining action. A landslide in the late 1980s killed many, and the town has calmed down in recent years. Rather than stay in a basic hotel here, it's preferable to move on.

About five hours from Gualaquiza, you finally reach the southern belle of **Zamora**, which is an excellent base from which to explore Parque Nacional Podocarpus. Although Zamora is geographically part of the Oriente, it is best accessed from the highland city of Loja (only two hours west by bus) – for more information see p218.

North Coast & Lowlands

In San Lorenzo you arrive to fissured streets and wobbly shacks propped up on the mudflats. You take your doubt to a concrete café where in 10 minutes you're sharing a beer with the next table. In 20 minutes your fish arrives, stewed in peppery coconut. An hour later, emboldened by the trumpets pounding on the boom box, your new friends kick away the chairs for an impromptu salsa lesson. Even if you have two left feet, there's something to be learned here.

The northern coast and lowlands usually take low priority on visitors' long lists of where to go and what to see. But those who want to sidestep the gringo circuit will find a friendly reception, some unique landscapes and magnificent, mouth-watering seafood.

Lush tangles of mangroves may be losing ground but they're the main attraction at Reserva Ecológica de Manglares Cayapas Mataje in northern Esmeraldas. If you're looking for adventure, turn back the hands of time with a canoe journey upriver out of Borbón, where you can glimpse remote river life in the tropics and hike in the tracks of big cats.

Moving from the exuberant vegetation and Afro-Ecuadorian flavor of the north, you find Atacames, the most developed coastal resort, next to the quiet charmers of Same and Súa. Surf-seekers shouldn't miss Canoa and Mompiche, whose killer waves have been known to trap surfers into setting up hostels and staying.

Almost as good is the trip you take to get there: choose from a handful of highland routes that swoop into the lowlands, making giddy turns through lovely panoramas.

HIGHLIGHTS

- Follow the tracks of big jungle cats in the **Playa de Oro Reserva de Tigrillos** (p276)
- Play in the waves in **Canoa's** (p287) surf paradise
- Soak in the tropical grooves of **Atacame's** (p280) thatched beach bars and discos
- Attend **Kasama** (p269) – the Tsáchila's New Year celebration of their indigenous roots
- Explore the tangled mangroves and seascapes of the **Reserva Biológica Bilsa** (p271)

- AVERAGE TEMPERATURE IN ESMERALDAS: 26°C (79°F)
- RAINIEST MONTH IN ESMERALDAS: MARCH

NORTH COAST & LOWLANDS

Climate

The northern coast has two seasons: rainy and dry. The rainy season lasts from December to May, and the dry season the rest of the year. Rainy season is marked by sporadic downpours but also by the hot, bright sun. The dry season is often overcast, grey and cool. Ecuadorians jam the beaches during the rainy season, for July and August school vacations and from January to Easter when the water is warmest. The coast is relatively abandoned from September to November.

Malaria can be a problem in the northern region, mostly during the rainy season. It's less prevalent south of Esmeraldas province.

National Parks

Mangroves, estuaries and beaches comprise the **Reserva Ecológica de Manglares Cayapas Mataje**, which is best accessed by boat from either San Lorenzo or La Tola. Also found within the diverse Chocó bioregion is the remote **Reserva Ecológica Cotacachi-Cayapas**. This 204,000-hectare forest is filled with such plant species as mahogany, ferns and orchids and is reached via canoe from Borbón. Further south of here you will find the **Reserva Ecológica Mache Chindul**, which is a 70,000-hectare humid tropical forest filled with waterfalls and swimming holes. It borders the private **Reserva Biológica Bilsa** and also the areas of Atacames and Muisne.

Dangers & Annoyances

Solo female travelers get stares, dares and offers from some local males, who are far less reserved than their highland counterparts. While the problem is mostly endemic to beaches, it pervades buses as well. If you have any opportunity to choose your seat partner, do so with this in mind.

Getting There & Around

A direct bus from Quito can zip you to the coast in just a day. If you're coming from another area you can get a connection in Santo Domingo, the transportation hub between the Andes and the coast. From Quito two roads reach Santo Domingo de los Colorados. The new road takes three hours, and the old road via Mindo takes about five hours, but also distracts with some fabulous diversions (for information on this route, see p139).

San Lorenzo can be reached by paved road from Ibarra (in the northern highlands) in only four hours. From Latacunga in the central highlands, a spectacular five-hour bus ride will take you to Quevedo in the western lowlands, from where it's about four hours to Portoviejo.

It used to be more convenient to travel the northern coast by boat, but with the paving of the coastal highway it is cheaper and more efficient to now go by road.

WESTERN LOWLANDS

The flat farmland still cultivates remnants of the old-time banana-republic of Ecuador that predated oil discovery. Witness its forgotten country houses and the starchy formality of its provincial gentlemen, contrasted with the bustle and grime of its fast growing lowland cities. Now that the small farmer has been replaced with international heavy hitters, you'll see enormous name-brand plantations spanning the smooth green horizon for miles.

This area is sandwiched between the coastal hills and the Andes. Former forest land was burned in the last century and replaced with crops of cacao, African palm oil and banana plantations. Botanists estimate that about half the plant species that once grew on the western Andean slopes and lowlands were found nowhere else. The last forested pockets of this unique ecosystem, vastly distinct from the Amazonian rain forest, merit a good look before they disappear from the globe.

QUITO TO SANTO DOMINGO DE LOS COLORADOS
☎ 02

Steep pitches plunge you toward the cottony void, past misty views of humpback hills. It is best to travel this stretch in the morning, when skies are more likely to be clear. This route attracts the most aggressive drivers, undeterred by the white crosses which dot the way

For visitors headed to the coast, the road from Quito through Santo Domingo is the most direct route. From there you can head south through Quevedo and Babahoyo, in the lowland province of Los Ríos, and on to Guayaquil, on the south coast; or you can go northwest toward Esmeraldas, on the north coast.

Outside of Quito the road climbs into the high *páramo* (Andean grasslands), with views of the extinct **Volcanes Atacazo** (4463m) and **Corazón** (4788m) to the north and south, respectively. The tortuous descent leads into the Río Toachi valley where the air thickens and tropical plants begin sprouting up. The trans-Ecuadorian oil pipeline parallels the road for the last third of the distance. If your bus is continuing beyond Santo Domingo it may bypass the city altogether.

About 16km outside of Santo Domingo, **Tinalandia** (Map p270; Quito ☎ 02-244 9028; www .tinalandia.com; s/d $65/85) was built for golfing but receives much greater acclaim for its top-notch bird-watching. This rustic resort sits at 600m in a wet premontane forest. Guests stay in weathered bungalows with private bathrooms and hot showers. The driest months (May and June) are particularly popular with bird-watchers, who can come for day visits (day pass $10). Delicious meals with fresh veggies from the hydroponics farm cost extra. Reservations may be necessary. Make them on your own or through major travel agencies in Ecuador.

Tinalandia is about 86km after the turnoff from the Panamericana in Alóag. Ask your driver to drop you off at Tinalandia, or don't miss the small stone sign on the right side of the road as you drive from Quito. The hotel is 500m away on the left.

LOS TSÁCHILAS

In a yard of thatched huts surrounded by sugarcane, a river that no longer has fish and tattered forest remnants that no longer bear wild game, stands grandfather Oeido Aguabil. Dressed in traditional Tsáchila finery, he sweeps a look at his surroundings and family and wonders aloud, 'Do you think this is worth it?'

The family, part of the small community of 70 families in El Poste, 12km outside of Santo Domingo, is part of a group interested in reviving customs and dress and sharing its culture with the public in hopes of keeping what's left of it intact. The many alterations to their environment and the often abrasive contact with the outside world makes the challenge justifiably daunting.

The Tsáchila, dubbed the Colorados by colonists, have well-known *curanderos* (medicine men) and the women craft beautiful wovens in shocks of rainbow colors on the backstrap loom. The group's signature dress is easy to recognize: they paint their faces with black stripes and men dye their bowl-shaped haircuts red. Aguabil says that the natural dye from the achiote plant was long ago used as a protection from Yellow Fever. Ritual painting, such as the black stripes, is also considered a form of shield or protection.

Nowadays it is much more probable to see Westernized Tsáchila. With bus drivers protesting that the hair dye stains the backs of their seats, curio shops selling their postcard images, and gawkers in the city calling them 'painted tigers' it's no wonder that these customs have been closeted.

The community's most important celebration was shelved for 30 years and began again only in 1998. Kasama, the New Year, is a time for the Tsáchila to reaffirm their roots. Coinciding with the Catholic Holy Saturday (day before Easter Sunday), it unites all of the villages to wish prosperity for one another and revisit their millenary traditions. Cane sugar *chicha* (a fermented drink) is served and the festive atmosphere ignites with music, dance and theater. With the return of this celebration springs the small hope that other important features of the landscape – such as the guatusa and the armadillo, will eventually return as well.

While most communities are reticent to welcome visitors (much less have their photograph taken), visitors are welcome in Chihuilpe and El Poste, both south of Santo Domingo on the road to Quevedo. Apart from going to the **tourist center** in Chihuilpe, you can also visit one of the *curanderos* who sell curative herbs or offer treatments. **El Poste** welcomes visitors for the annual Kasama festival (see above).

SANTO DOMINGO DE LOS COLORADOS

☎ 02 / pop 199,850 / elevation 500m

At noon the thoroughfare of 29 de Mayo reaches boiling point. Sidewalks brim with crowds, piles of coconuts, bicycle cages stuffed with clucking hens and there's a derelict sprawled flat on the sidewalk. Even if the sight grabs your attention, the busy surroundings remain unfazed. Welcome to Santo Domingo de los Colorados (usually shortened to Santo Domingo). As this tropical town becomes an important commercial center, unchecked growth also expands its seedier side. Visitors should be somewhat wary and avoid the market area and 3 de Julio after dark.

Information

Andinatel (Av Quito near Río Toachi)

Bancos del Pichincha (Iturralde, Main Plaza) There's also a branch on Avenida Quinindé. Both branches have ATMs.

Hard Soft Net (Av Quito 127 near Los Tsáchilas; per hr $0.80; ☯ 8am-8pm) A friendly, modern Internet center with a quiet 2nd-floor location.

Post office (Av Tsáchilas near Río Baba) Just north of downtown.

Sights & Activities

Downtown's concrete structures plastered with signage are not conducive to admiration, but the **street markets** are lively; selling, among other things, clothing and electronics. The Sunday market gets crowded, so watch your belongings carefully.

The most interesting excursion is going to see the **Tsáchila**. Contact **José Aguabil** (☎ 09-770 8703), leader of the community El Poste, to arrange a visit. This group, eager to revive cultural traditions that are quickly being left behind (above), offers a community tour that includes a demonstration of plants used for medicinal purposes, an explanation of

SANTO DOMINGO DE LOS COLORADOS

INFORMATION	
Andinatel................................1 D2	
Banco del Pichincha..............2 A2	
Banco del Pichincha..............3 C2	
Hard Soft Net.........................4 D3	
Post Office............................5 C1	
SLEEPING	
Gran Hotel Santo Domingo....6 D3	
Hostal Jennefer......................7 C2	

Hotel Diana Real....................8 A2	
Hotel El Colorado..................9 A2	
EATING	
Chifa Happy........................10 C2	
La Tonga.........................(see 6)	
Restaurante Timoneiro.........11 D3	
TRANSPORT	
Local Bus Plaza...................12 A2	

customs and traditions, and even dancing. They produce lovely hand-woven goods in their signature wild rainbow colors as well as jewelry. While they speak only Tsa'fiki and Spanish, an English-speaking volunteer is currently on-site. Another contact for tours and directions on how to arrive solo is **Annabell Acurio** (☎ 370 1039; annabellrocio@yahoo .com; tour $10).

Festivals & Events

Santo Domingo is the capital of its canton and celebrates its **cantonization day** on July 3, when the town packs with visitors attending the fairs and agricultural festivals. Rooms are harder to come by during this week.

Sleeping

Most of the cheapest hotels are downtown, near the market area, which is not very safe at night.

Hotel Diana Real (☎ 275 1380; cnr 29 de Mayo & Loja; s/d $13/17) Soothing, quiet rooms in cream and tan, with fan, cable TV, hot shower and telephone. The staff is friendly, and homey, bland fare is available in the restaurant.

Hotel Sheraton (☎ 276 7901; Av Calazacón 111; s/ d $7/10) Not to be confused with the chain hotel, this cheery and cheap option is outside the bus terminal. Plain rooms are jazzed up with scrubbed tiles and silk flowers, and there's cable TV and fans.

Gran Hotel Santo Domingo (☎ 276 7950; www .granhotelsd.com; Río Toachi & Galapagos; s/d with aircon $42/62; ❷ ❷) Bowtied bellhops, plump couches and plush grounds showcase the city's swankiest hotel. It's nothing out of this world, but its location in Santo Domingo makes it seem so. Rooms have snug fittings, cable TV, minibar and air-conditioning. The restaurant on-site is reputable and there's a baguette bakery next door.

Hotel El Colorado (☎ 275 4299; 29 de Mayo 110; r per person $7) Kind hospitality and cleanliness will distract you from the appalling Indian statuettes, and sketchy neighborhood. Basic rooms have phones but no hot water.

Hostal Jennefer (☎ 275 0577; 29 de Mayo near Ibarra; s/d $7/10) A serviceable option with somewhat cranky attention. Rooms here are large, but most beds sag and smoky odors linger.

Eating

Restaurante Timoneiro (Av Quito 115; mains $2-4; ☺ 8am-4pm) Sunken and softly lit, this traditional restaurant has hearty fare, full dinners and chicken soup with all the bones.

El Hornero Pizzeria (☎ 1-800 500 500; Av Quito km2 & Madrid; pizzas $3-5; ☺ 7am-10:30pm) The delicious cheesy pizzas are worth the taxi ride out here.

La Tonga (☎ 276 7950; Río Toachi & Galapagos; mains $4-5; ☺ 7am-10:30pm) A crisp and formal setting with a varied menu of well-prepared international dishes, vegetarian options and criollo (of Spanish influence) specialities. Located in the Gran Hotel Santo Domingo.

Chifa Happy (☎ 275 0121; Tulcán 117; mains $2-4; ☺ noon-10pm) Chinese food right on the plaza but the steamed veggies and lo mein are on the salty side.

Drinking & Entertainment

Lined on the far end of Avenida Quito are a number of small atmospheric joints geared mostly to the younger crowd. For salsa dancing, hail a taxi to **Salsoteca the Jungle** (☺ 9pm-late), east on Avenida Quito.

Getting There & Away

Santo Domingo is an important transportation hub, with connections all over Ecuador. The bus terminal is almost 2km north of downtown and has frequent buses to many major towns, as well as Internet and an ATM. Quito ($3, three hours) and Guayaquil ($5, five hours) are the most frequent destinations, with several buses going every hour. Those headed to Guayaquil pass Quevedo. To get to Mindo ($4, 3½ hours) try **Transportes Kennedy** (☎ 275 8740).

Costal-bound buses include **Transportes Occidentales** (☎ 275 8741), with several departures a day to Machala ($5 to $6, seven hours) and Reina de Camino, which goes to Puerto Lopez every day at 11am ($7, eight hours). Every hour buses depart to the north-coast town of Esmeraldas ($4, 3½ hours), stopping at La Concordia and Quinindé. After going through Esmeraldas, some may continue to Atacames or Muisne. Buses also go to Bahía de Caráquez ($6, six hours) and Manta ($6, six hours).

Highland-bound buses go to Ambato ($4, four hours), Baños ($5, five hours), Ríobamba ($5, five hours) and Loja ($13, 12 hours). Several companies have a daily trip to Lago Agrio ($10, 12 hours) and Coca ($12, 14 hours).

The local bus plaza at the west end of 3 de Julio serves nearby villages.

Getting Around

Look for the city bus marked 'Centro.' It loops past the bus terminal, through downtown and out along Avenida Quito. The return bus, signed 'Terminal Terrestre,' heads west along 29 de Mayo, picking up passengers for the terminal.

NORTH OF SANTO DOMINGO DE LOS COLORADOS

☎ 02

The road rumbles northwest of Santo Domingo to Esmeraldas, almost 200km away. Amid African oil palm and banana groves you'll find **Bosque Protectora La Perla** (☎ 272 5344; admission $5), a 250-hectare reserve ideal for bird-watching and guided walks. You can even stake a tent on the grounds. Obtain exact directions when making a reservation.

Shortly after the village of **La Concordia** (about 50km northwest of Santo Domingo) a paved road leads eastward toward Mindo via Puerto Quito and Pedro Vicente Maldonado (see p143), eventually spitting out at Mitad del Mundo.

On the way to Esmeraldas, the small town of **Quinindé** (also known as Rosa Zárate; the area code is ☎ 06), 86km from Santo Domingo, has a couple of basic hotels.

Rugged adventurers should head to **Reserva Biológica Bilsa**, 30km west of Quinindé. Crashing waterfalls and spectacular wildlife adorn this biological station. This 30-sq-km reserve in the Montañas de Mache (a small range of mountains) is administered by **Fundación Jatun Sacha** (☎ 243 2240/6, 243 2173; www.jatunsacha .org; Pasaje Eugenio de Santillán N34-248 & Maurián, Urbanización Rumipamba, PO Box 17-12-867). Biodiversity is exceptionally high in these last vestiges of premontane tropical wet forest. Visitors may see howler monkeys and endangered birds such as birders' coveted long wattled umbrella bird. Jaguar and puma are also afoot. This trip is not for the feeble or frail: rainy season access (January to June) requires hiking or mule riding a mud-splattered 25km trail. Contact Jatun Sacha (above) for reservations and volunteer or research information (rooms per person with three meals $34; discounts for groups and students).

SOUTH OF SANTO DOMINGO DE LOS COLORADOS

The road from Santo Domingo descends 100m to Quevedo through banana plantations, African palm and papaya groves. Villages off the main road are part of the shrinking territory of the Tsáchila indigenous (known also as the Colorados) whose *curanderos* (medicine men) have great acclaim.

About 46km south of Santo Domingo, you'll see a sign for the **Reserva Río Palenque** (day-use $5), a 110-hectare reserve run by Fundación Wong. It has one of the few remaining stands of western lowlands forest left in the area. There are facilities for researchers, 3km of trails and excellent bird-watching. Past counts noted 1200 plants and 360 bird species but with development infringing, some species have become scarce. The proposal of a government-sponsored dam on Río Palenque threatens to flood part of this important biodiversity pocket.

Still, an overnight stop here is a relaxing countryside alternative. Visitors can sleep in the **field station** (Guayaquil ☎ 04-220 8670, ext 1470; 09-751 9465; fundacion@grupowong.com; r per person $30, dm $12.50) where rooms are quite comfortable and meals are $3. Advance reservations are necessary. Any bus between Santo Domingo and Quevedo can drop you off or pick you up at the entrance road to the field station.

QUEVEDO

☎ 05 / pop 120,380

Hot and sticky, Quevedo is a busy hub of motorbikes, street vendors and Chinese immigrants. For most people, the main attraction is striving to the coast via the gorgeous drive linking Latacunga to Quevedo.

If you need a place to stay try **Hotel Casablanca** (☎ 275 4144; Décima 416 near 7 de Octubre; s/d with fan $10/14, with air-con $20/24), whose echoey tile rooms beg a homey touch. On the south end of town the high-end **Hotel Olímpico** (☎ 275 0455; Calle 19na 107 & Av Jaime Roldós; s/d $40/50; 🏊) falls short of high expectations but it's coveted by lap swimmers. Meals here are $7 to $10.

Quevedo claims to have the best Chinese food in the country. At **Café Fenix** (☎ 276 1460; 12 de Octubre; mains $3-5; 🕑 9:30am-9pm) you'll note the blending of cultures in dishes such as *mondongo* (tripe stew) curry.

The new terminal is located off of Avenida Walter Andrades on the edge of town.

The following bus companies are all found within the terminal:

Transportes Macuchi has regular direct buses to Quito ($5, four hours). Transportes Sucre has buses to Santo Domingo (one hour), from where there are frequent buses to Quito. Transportes Sucre and TIA go frequently to Guayaquil ($3, 2½ hours) both via Daule or Babahoyo. Transportes Cotopaxi has hourly departures from 3am to 5pm to Latacunga ($5, 5½ hours), as well as an 8am and a 1pm bus to Portoviejo ($5, four hours).

QUEVEDO TO GUAYAQUIL

Overtaking is a competitive sport on these roads. If you're easily rattled, sit in the back of the bus and fix your concentration on the in-house kung fu movie to avoid witnessing trucks passing double. If your southbound bus crosses Río Quevedo, then you are going to Babahoyo; if it doesn't, then you are heading to Daule. Both roads lead to Guayaquil. On the three-hour drive you'll see the banana plantations give way to rice paddies and husking-and-drying factories called *piladoras* along the road.

BABAHOYO

☎ 05 / pop 76,870

The provincial capital of Los Ríos, Babahoyo translates as 'slime pit.' Stationed on flooding lowlands, the city is surrounded by rice paddies and banana plantations. Although tourists are rare here, it's an OK spot to get a bed or a bite midjourney.

You can grab a few winks at **Hotel Cachari** (☎ 273 4443; Bolívar 111; s/d with bathroom $14/15, with air-con $18/26; 🗙) or the dated but trustworthy **Hotel Emperador** (☎ 273 0535; Barona near 27 de Mayo; s/d with fan $12/15, with air-con $17/24; 🗙). Outdoor café breakfasts are available from **Restaurant Munich** (10 de Agosto & Eloy Alfaro; mains $3; 🕑 7.30am-10pm) near the plaza, where you can also find filling ceviche with *mote* (maize) and *patacones* (fried plantain slices).

Babahoyo has no proper bus terminal. Most buses depart from a couple of blocks southwest of the plaza. There are frequent services to Guayaquil ($1, 1½ hours). Buses to the highlands climb steeply to the skirts of Volcán Chimborazo and Ambato ($5, five hours) and to Ríobamba ($4.50, 4½ hours).

THE NORTH COAST

Paradise with a jagged edge, the north coast features verdant jungle toppling onto beaches, dank backwaters and lush forests, as well as lively (and sometimes dodgy) towns. Good sense and a taste for adventure are essential tools for travelers to this region, some of whom may be turned off by its rawness and lack of upkeep.

SAN LORENZO

☎ 06 / pop 14,600

Encircled by verdant jungle, at the edge of a dank, still river, San Lorenzo is a decrepit, lively hodge-podge of blaring heat, tropical beats and crumbling storefronts. Hollow marimba notes and salsa flavor this mostly African-Ecuadorian outpost, which goes all out in August with an annual music festival.

With road access only completed in the mid-1990s, the area still has the air of a forgotten outpost. It is extremely poor, tourism is barely developed and getting around isn't easy. Its treasure is its people, the most spirited you'll encounter, and the real reason to come all this way. With little in common with the Ecuador that most visitors know, San Lorenzo makes an intimidating but nonetheless fascinating visit.

Orientation

Coming into San Lorenzo, you'll pass the old train station and follow Calle Imbabura, the main street, for several blocks. The better hotels are to the left. The road narrows and ends at the small plaza of Parque Central near the Río San Antonio. The main pier is to the left, a few blocks beyond the park.

The town itself is extremely poor with cracked, flooded streets and falling-down buildings all around. Locals are the first to warn visitors to stay safe in San Lorenzo, not to wander off the main road and plaza area, and not to stay out long after dark.

Information

The **police station** (☎ 278 0672) faces the Parque Central, and the **capitanía** (port captain) is at the main pier; if you're traveling into or out of Colombia (which is not recommended), take care of passport formalities at one of these places.

San Lorenzo's Catholic hospital, a short taxi ride from downtown, is reputedly the best in the area north of Esmeraldas.

Andinatel (Calle Imbabura) Opposite Gran Hotel San Carlos.

Ministerio del Ambiente (☎ 278 0184; main plaza; usually ⏰ 9am-12:30pm & 2-7pm Mon-Fri) On the far side of the park; with information on Reserva Ecológica de Manglares Cayapas Mataje.

Papeleria Gamel (Calle Imbabura at Tácito Ortíz; ⏰ 8am-8pm) Slow Internet for $2 per hour.

Sleeping

Pickings are slim, but consider mosquito nets and fans as essentials, especially in rainy season. The following places all have mosquito nets.

Hotel Pampa de Oro (☎ 278 0214; Calle Tácito Ortíz; r per person $6; 🕸) The most circumspect hotel in appearance; its spacious pastel rooms have thick mattresses and old-fashioned ceiling fans. Located on a side-street off Imbabura.

Hotel Continental (☎ 278 0125; Imbabura; r per person with fan/air-con $7/10; 🕸) Fishing murals and creaky floorboards adorn this antiquated building. The rooms are sizable and clean, with TV and warm showers.

Hotel Carondelet (☎ 278 0202; Parque Central; r per person with shared/private bathroom $3.50/4.50) Shoehorn your way into one of these diminutive rooms with tin-roof views, but make sure the sheets are clean. The shower is bracing.

Gran Hotel San Carlos (☎ /fax 278 0284; cnr Imbabura & José Garcés; r per person with shared/private bathroom $4/6) A worn-down bunkhouse with a tropical theme and rainbow stripes running down the hallway. The rooms are passable, with satellite TV and phones.

Eating

La Red (☎ 278 0710; Isidro Ayora near Imbabura; mains $3-10; ⏰ 7am-10pm) The ambience isn't much at this cement-block café, but the food is lip-smackingly good. Try the spicy *encocado* (fish in chili and coconut sauce) while chatting with the locals above the grainy tunes.

Ballet Azul (Imbabura; mains $2-6; ⏰ 8:30am-10pm Mon-Sat) Shrimp is the specialty at this matchbox-sized dive. *Ceviche de camarón* (shrimp ceviche) and *camarones al ajillo* (garlic shrimp) mate perfectly with a bottle of beer.

The $2 *almuerzo* (set-lunch menu) is popular at **El Condorito** (Eloy Alfaro; mains $2) or try the **Hotel Carondelet** (☎ 278 0202; Parque Central) restaurant with whimsical hours (see above).

Getting There & Away

BOAT

Ecuador Pacífico (☎ 278 0181, 278 1603; andrescar vache@yahoo.es) departs to Limones ($3, 1½ hours) and continues to La Tola ($6, 45 minutes) at 8:30am and 11:30am. With the early departure to La Tola, you can connect with a bus to Esmeraldas. Trips to nearby beaches leave at 7am and 2pm and cost $3. Andres Carvache guides these and other trips. He can be found on the pier in a stilted storefront to the right.

To cross the Colombian border there are departures at 7:30am and 2pm ($15), which also requires bus connections to Tumaco in Colombia. Given nearby guerilla activity which occasionally sends refugees spilling over, it is not recommended to cross the border here.

Touring the mangroves isn't really possible via public transportation. To arrange a trip contract **Cooperativa de Servicios Turisticos** (☎ 278 0181, 278 1603), an authorized service offering private tours in boats with capacity for four to 70 passengers. The outfit is also run by Sr Carvache. Tours cost between $20 and $50 and chartered service is $20 per person per hour to go to nearby reserves.

BUS

La Costeñita and Transportes del Pacífico alternate departures for Borbón ($1.20, one hour) and Esmeraldas ($5, five hours). They leave the Parque Central hourly from 5am to 4pm. The road is mostly paved except for a few monstrous potholes and jackhammer-rough patches.

Aerotaxi buses leave at 1pm and 3pm to Ibarra ($4, four hours) from the corner of Imbabura and Tácito Ortíz. Both buses continue on to Quito ($5, five to six hours).

TRAIN

The scenic highland-to-coast train from Ibarra was washed out in 1998's El Niño storms. Locals yen for its return, but as of yet there are no projects in the works to rebuild.

RESERVA ECOLÓGICA DE MANGLARES CAYAPAS MATAJE

Millions of migratory birds pass through this coastal reserve in June to July, creating a cacophonous and memorable spectacle. This 51,300-hectare reserve supports five species of mangroves, including the tallest mangrove forest in the world, Manglares de Majagual, near the villages of La Tola and Olmedo. The town of San Lorenzo lies in the middle of the reserve and makes a good base. Most of the reserve is at sea level and none of it is above 35m. A highlight of the reserve is the pristine 11km island beach of **San Pedro** near the Colombian border but visitors should inquire about safety before venturing into this area.

There are basic, community-run cabañas nearby at the settlement of **Palmareal**. If you stay, bring a mosquito net and water (or purification tablets). The reserve is accessible almost solely by boat.

LIMONES

☎ 06

This island lumber town scratches out a living at the deltas of Río Santiago and Río Cayapas. You'll find wilting wooden homes perched above the water, a humble plaza flanking the foot of the pier, and all the bananas you can peel. Most of the timber logged in the area is floated downriver to Limones' sawmill. Rough-and-tumble, the place has few amenities, but it's interesting nonetheless. Sometimes indigenous Chachis (formerly known as the Cayapas) come to trade. Get your 40 winks at **Hotel Mauricio Real** (☎ 278 9219; r per person $12), a tolerable spot at the end of the pier.

See left for details about boat travel.

LA TOLA

☎ 06

This small fishing village is usually bypassed now that road travel is the norm. The main attraction is the Tolita archaeological site on the nearby island of **Manta de Oro**, but since the gold ornaments found here are now in museums, there is not much left to see.

You can still hop a ferry from San Lorenzo via Limones, arrive at La Tola and continue by bus to Esmeraldas, or by foot to nearby Olmedo. La Costeñita and Transportes del Pacífico run buses to and from Esmeraldas ($3, three hours) and boats to and from Limones ($3, one hour); see left. If you take a morning bus from Esmeraldas, you can connect here with a boat to San Lorenzo and vice versa.

If you need to stay in La Tola, ask around for Señora Olin at Hostal Doña F for reasonable lodgings. She can also guide you to the mangroves.

OLMEDO
☎ 06

Hoof it for 20 minutes from La Tola's pier to Olmedo, a spit of land in the estuary, engulfed in mangroves, shrimp farms and the sea. This mostly Afro-Ecuadorian fishing village offers boat and fishing tours. You can stay at **Cabañas de los Manglares de Olmedo** (San Lorenzo ☎ 278 0357, La Tola 278 6133, Olmedo ☎ 278 6126; r per person $5), a welcoming but basic community-run *hostal* (small hotel) right on the estuary – at high tide the water laps the deck. The shared bathrooms have cold showers, and meals are $4 each. At low tide roll up your pant legs and grab a pail to go clamming on the wide, silty beach.

The nearby **Manglares de Majagual** boasts the tallest mangrove forest in the world (64m). Visit the forest on your own or hire a guide in Olmedo or La Tola.

BORBÓN
☎ 06

Borbón is a muddy and ramshackle lumber port, its main strip lined with *comedores* (cheap restaurants) where men play dominoes and drink beer at any given hour. The attraction here is to make boat connections upriver to the remote settlements of Afro-Ecuadorians and indigenous Chachi. Boats up Río Cayapas continue up Río San Miguel to the Reserva Ecológica Cotacachi-Cayapas. Boats also depart sporadically for Río Santiago.

If you need assistance, ask locals to direct you to the US-run mission. **La Tolita Pampa de Oro** (r per person with shared/private bathroom $3/5) offers basic lodging in a rambling blue boarding house. You'll find it on a street parallel to the river, left of the boat dock.

Getting There & Away

La Costeñita and Transportes del Pacífico run buses to Esmeraldas ($3, four hours) or San Lorenzo ($1.20, one hour) about every hour from 7am to 6pm. Most of the roads are paved, although some sections have murderous potholes.

A daily passenger boat leaves at 11am for San Miguel ($8, five hours). This boat can drop you at any location on Río Cayapas or at San Miguel. Various boats run irregularly

to other destinations – ask around at the docks. *Fletes* (private boats) can usually be hired if you have the money, but these are not cheap – expect to pay at least $100 per day per group.

ALONG RÍO CAYAPAS
Borbón to San Miguel

Borbón's daily passenger boat to San Miguel (below) is a fascinating trip into the little-explored interior, described by one visitor as 'the other heart of darkness.'

The boat to San Miguel stops at a number of communities and missions. Passengers here range from nuns to indigenous Chachi embarking or disembarking in the various ports, which are usually no more than a few planks at the water's edge.

The first mission is the Catholic **Santa María** where there is a clean dormitory for six guests, a basic *pensión* (boarding house) and camping. The next mission, Protestant **Zapallo Grande**, also offers basic accommodations. There are a number of other villages, such as Pichiyacu, Playa Grande, Atahualpa and Telembi, where Afro-Ecuadorians or Chachi indigenous live, some with crafts for sale.

San Miguel

San Miguel is a modest and friendly Afro-Ecuadorian community of stilted thatched huts set in the forest. Chachi homes are scattered nearby along the shores of the river. The village is the main base from which to visit the lowland sections of the Reserva Ecológica Cotacachi-Cayapas.

The **San Miguel Eco-project** (Quito ☎ 02-252 8769; www.ecosanmiguel.org; accommodations & tour package per day $30) is a community-run program offering two- and three-day trips into the rain forest. Visitors can fish and kick around a soccer ball with locals. Accommodations are in a basic lodge with mosquito nets, or camping. Trips start in Borbón. The contact in Quito is Carlos Donoso at **Books & Coffee** (Quito ☎ 02-252 8769; Juan Leon Mera 12-27 & Calama, Quito).

The **ranger station** (per person $5) perched on a small hill with spectacular views of the rain forest and river, has basic accommodations. Ask the *guardaparque* (park ranger) for permission to stay here. If you camp, load up on insect repellent because the grass is loaded with chiggers. The station has a cold-water shower, a toilet and kitchen facilities. A shop in the village sells basic provisions or sympathetic locals can cook up simple meals of soup, rice and plantains for about $5.

The driver of the daily passenger canoe from Borbón spends the night about 15 minutes downriver from San Miguel. He will not return to San Miguel unless passengers have made previous arrangements, so advise ahead. The canoe leaves San Miguel around 4am.

PLAYA DE ORO

The other river leading inland from Borbón is Río Santiago. The furthest community up the river is the remote settlement of **Playa de Oro** (below), near the border of Reserva Ecológica Cotacachi-Cayapas. Playa de Oro means 'Beach of Gold.'

Half an hour upstream from Playa de Oro is the **Playa de Oro Reserva de Tigrillos**, a 10,000-hectare reserve owned and operated by the community of Playa de Oro. The reserve, which borders Cotacachi-Cayapas, protects native jungle cats, which are more plentiful here than elsewhere, but nonethe-

less elusive. The best way to experience it is by staying at the community operated riverside **jungle lodge** (www.touchthejungle.org; accommodations & tour package per day $50). Prices include three meals, laundry service and local guides.

Playa de Oro's charm is its authenticity. Locals do what they and their ancestors have always done, whether that be roaming the forest, riding the river current, panning for gold, making drums or encouraging their children in traditional dances. When visitors find that interesting, locals are quietly proud.

The village of Playa de Oro is about five hours upstream from Borbón, but there are no regular boats. You have to take the 7:30am bus from Borbón to Selva Alegre ($3, two hours). From Selva Alegre, if you made a reservation, a boat from Playa de Oro will motor you up to the village or the reserve. The two-hour river trip (2½ hours if you're going to the reserve) from Selva Alegre costs $50, split among the number in your group. Reservations must be made at least a month in advance with **Rosa Jordan** (rosaj@look.ca) who speaks English.

ONE MAN'S GOLD

Playa de Oro's end-of-the-earth location is the defining point of its existence. The huffing of margays can be heard at night outside a cabin window. The village is populated with the Afro-Ecuadorian descendants of slaves brought here to pan for gold 500 years ago. Located hours inland from the coast in a remote, roadless wilderness, Playa de Oro's near-inaccessibility has kept it a natural paradise.

To ensure that it would stay that way, the community designated 10,000 of its hectares as **Playa de Oro Tigrillos Reserve**, a wildlife area protecting all species of indigenous wildcats – jaguars, cougars, ocelots, margays, oncillas and jaguarundi. They passed on registering the reserve with the national government, given its history of cozying up to industry keen on entering its national parks, and decided to manage it as a community.

Designating a protected area and protecting it turn out to be two distinct pursuits. Tree thefts along the reserve's borders and the encroachment of slash-and-burn squatters created the need for a conservation patrol. In the background the threat of commercial logging remains. There's additional concern that economic need will outstrip the community's good intentions. In an area so poor that it has no doctor, no electricity and no secondary school, what happens when a big multinational offers it $10,000 a month for as many months as it takes to clearcut their near-virgin forest?

In Playa de Oro, every villager over the age of 14 has a vote on important issues. The farsighted among them have long argued that ecotourism is the sensible, nondestructive way to go. But their insistence on maintaining control of their own ecotourism, and not allowing it to fall into the hands of large tour agencies who take a big cut, forces them to rely on independent travelers and small groups. The question remains whether the income that trickles in from these sources will sustain their paradise for the years to come.

For more information on Playa de Oro, see above.

RESERVA ECOLÓGICA COTACACHI-CAYAPAS

This 204,420-hectare **reserve** (admission $5) is by far the largest protected area of Ecuador's western Andean habitats. Altitude ranges from about 200m above sea level around San Miguel to 4939m above sea level at the summit of Cotacachi. Habitats change quickly from lowland, tropical, wet forest to premontane and montane cloud forest to *páramo*, with many intermediate habitat types. This rapid change of habitat produces the so-called 'edge effect' that gives rise to an incredible diversity of flora and fauna.

These hills are the haunts of such rarely seen mammals as giant anteaters, Baird's tapirs, jaguars and, in the upper reaches of the reserve, spectacled bears. The chances of seeing these animals are remote, however. You may see monkeys, squirrels, sloths, nine-banded armadillos, bats and a huge variety of bird species.

To visit the reserve you can approach from the highlands (as described on p127), or San Miguel, as described earlier in this chapter (p275). Hiking between the two regions may well be impossible; the steep and thickly vegetated western Andean slopes are almost impenetrable. This is good news for the species existing there – they will probably be left alone for a little while longer.

The lower reaches of the reserve and rivers are the home of the indigenous Chachi. About 5000 remain, mostly fishermen and subsistence farmers, living in open-sided, thatched river houses built on stilts. The Chachi are famous for their basketwork; try buying their crafts directly from the river folk, although many speak only Chachi. Over the last few decades, the Chachi have been swept by an epidemic of river blindness carried by black flies, which are particularly prevalent in April and May. Some 80% have the disease to some extent. To protect yourself while traveling use insect repellent and take malaria pills.

When to Go

River levels are high during rainy season (December to May), making for swifter travel. At this time mosquitoes, black flies and other insects are at their highest concentrations; definitely cover up at dawn and dusk when they come out in full force. Even during the rainy months, mornings are often clear. Up to 5000mm of rain has been reported in some of the more inland areas, although San Miguel is somewhat drier. The drier months of September to the start of December are usually less buggy, and there is a better chance of seeing wildlife, although river navigation may be limited.

Getting There & Around

Entrance into the reserve is payable at the ranger station in San Miguel (p275). The rangers can serve as guides, and charge about $10 per day, plus food. Two guides are needed for trips – one for each end of the dugout canoe. These canoes are paddled and poled, engines are scarce out here. Alternatively, you can visit on a guided tour with one of the lodges. The lodge in Playa de Oro (opposite) is also an access point for the reserve.

It is about two or three hours by canoe from San Miguel to the park boundaries. Another one or two hours brings the visitor to a gorgeous little waterfall in the jungle. A guide is essential as the few trails are poorly marked. There are places to camp if you have tents and the necessary gear.

THE ROAD TO ESMERALDAS

☎ 06

The bus journey to Esmeraldas from San Lorenzo via Borbón is dusty in the dry season, muddy in the wet season and bumpy year-round. It starts along the Ibarra road and turns inland through the forest. Beyond Borbón, there are a number of villages, most with a basic *residencial* (cheap hotel) if you get stuck. One of these villages is **Lagarto**, where Río Lagarto is crossed.

Soon after crossing Río Lagarto, the routes from Borbón and La Tola unite. Then the road passes on to the coastal village of **Rocafuerte**, which has very basic *residenciales* and simple restaurants selling tasty fresh seafood to weekenders from the city out for a stroll in the countryside.

A few kilometers further, the road passes through the two coastal villages of Río Verde: **Palestina de Río Verde**, just beyond the river, and then **Río Verde**, a few kilometers further. Río Verde was the setting of Moritz Thomsen's fine memoir *Living Poor*. At the river crossing, look for a large frigatebird colony visible in the trees along the banks. Palestina de Río Verde has a few simple hotels.

Between the two coastal villages **Hostería y Restaurante Pura Vida** (☎ 274 4203; r per person $10, cabañas $15) is the best place to stay between San Lorenzo and Esmeraldas. This lovely remote *hostal* arranges rental bikes, fishing, excursions and volunteering in local schools. Some rooms have private bathrooms, and there's a pool and very good restaurant (meals $3 to $5). The phone lines are sometimes out, so try emailing or just show up.

Almost 20km beyond Río Verde is the village of **Camarones**, which, as its name implies, sells fresh shrimp concoctions in its simple beachfront restaurants open weekends and vacations. Ask around about cabins for rent if you want to stay by the beach; Cabañas Fragatas is one such place.

A few kilometers beyond Camarones, the road passes the Esmeraldas airport on the east side of Río Esmeraldas. The city is on the west side, but there is no bridge until San Mateo, about 10km upriver. It is a half-hour drive from the airport to Esmeraldas.

ESMERALDAS

☎ 06 / pop 95,124

The Spanish conquistadors made their first Ecuadorian landfall on this broad, sandy bank flanked by a sparkling river and surrounded by low green hills. Esmeraldas has been an influential port town throughout history but its modern incarnation is not pretty. Many of its cement structures are either half-finished or half-fallen, the frenzied streets harbor drugs and petty crime and the forests have surrendered to scrub brush.

These days fishing and shipping take a backseat to the oil refinery processing the contents of the trans-Ecuadorian oil pipeline, which adds its share of noise and pollution. This, combined with the fact that Esmeraldas is considered one of Ecuador's most dangerous major cities, makes it an improbable destination.

Still, visitors should know that *esmeraldeños* (residents of Esmeraldas) are seriously preoccupied about their reputation and some will go out of their way to prove how amenable they are. If you can negotiate the mean streets, you'll find a fun and gregarious culture under hard times. Most tourists just spend the night (if they have to) and continue southwest to the towns of Atacames, Súa and Mompiche, where the best beaches are found.

Information

Andinatel (cnr Malecón Maldonado & Montalvo)

Banco del Pichincha (Olmedo & Mejía; Bolívar & 9 de Octubre) Changes traveler's checks and has an ATM.

Banco Popular (cnr Piedrahita & Bolívar) Changes traveler's checks and has an ATM.

Hospital (☎ 271 0012; Av Libertad) Between Esmeraldas and Las Palmas, at the north end of town.

Immigration office (☎ 271 0156, 272 4624) At the Policía Civil Nacional, 3km out of town (take a taxi). Have your passport stamped here for entry or exit via the rarely used coastal route to Colombia.

Planeta.net (☎ 09-959 3441; cnr Olmedo & Cañizares; per hr $1; ⏰ 9am-9:30pm) Internet access.

Police station (cnr Bolívar & Cañizares) Two blocks south of the plaza.

Post office (Colón near 10 de Agosto) Two blocks east of the main plaza.

Tourist office (☎ 271 1370; www.viveecuador.com; Cañizales, 2nd fl; ⏰ 9am-12:30pm, 2:30-6pm) Helpful and arranges student-guided city tours. Located between Bolívar and Sucre.

Dangers & Annoyances

Esmeraldas is striving to beat its notorious rap. In the meantime, avoid arriving after dark or take a taxi if you do. Busy Olmedo is the safest street to walk at night. Be careful in the market areas (especially the south end of the Malecón Maldonado) and away from the main streets. Single women get hit on and hooted at more often than elsewhere. Many reactions are tempting, but just ignore them. Incidences of malaria increase during the wet months.

Sights & Activities

A great new addition to the city is **Centro Cultural Esmeraldas** (☎ 272 2078; Bolívar 427; admission $1; ⏰ Tue-Fri 9am-5pm, Sat & Sun 10am-4pm), a museum, library and bookstore. Material ranges from recent local history to fine ceramics and gold work from the ancient Tolita culture. Some exhibit signs and documentary videos are in English and the staff is very obliging.

Sleeping

Hotels are plentiful here, but the cheapest ones tend toward intolerable. During the wet months you should have a fan or a mosquito net in your room.

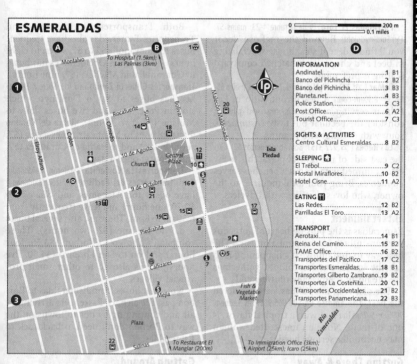

ESMERALDAS

| 0 | 200 m |
| 0 | 0.1 miles |

INFORMATION
Andinatel.................................1 B1
Banco del Pichincha..................2 B2
Banco del Pichincha..................3 B3
Planeta.net...............................4 B3
Police Station...........................5 C3
Post Office...............................6 A2
Tourist Office...........................7 C3

SIGHTS & ACTIVITIES
Centro Cultural Esmeraldas.......8 B2

SLEEPING
El Trébol..................................9 C2
Hostal Miraflores....................10 B2
Hotel Cisne.............................11 A2

EATING
Las Redes...............................12 B2
Parrilladas El Toro....................13 A2

TRANSPORT
Aerotaxi.................................14 B1
Reina del Camino....................15 B2
TAME Office...........................16 B2
Transportes del Pacífico...........17 C2
Transportes Esmeraldas...........18 B1
Transportes Gilberto Zambrano.19 B2
Transportes La Costeñita.........20 C1
Transportes Occidentales.........21 B2
Transportes Panamericana.......22 B3

El Trébol (☎ 272 8031; Cañizares 1-18; r per person $13.50; ✷) Immaculate fern-lined modern hotel offering oversized rooms with a crisp finish and cable TV, but no hot water.

Hotel Cisne (☎ 272 1588; 10 de Agosto; s/d $10/16; ✷) Off the street and quieter, these Spartan rooms are sparkling and there's laundry service and a restaurant.

Hostal Miraflores (☎ 272 3077; 2nd fl, Bolivar 6-04 on plaza; r per person $4) The best bet for backpackers. Granny is your decorator at this old wooden *hostal* adorned with bubblegum colors and plastic bouquets. Pocket-sized rooms have high ceilings and mosquito nets, and the shared bathrooms are clean.

The resort-suburb of Las Palmas, situated 3km north of downtown, offers considerably better accommodations and nightlife. Most of the hotels and restaurants are on Avenida Kennedy, which is the main street parallel to the beach. Reach it by heading north on Libertad.

Hotel Cayapas (☎ 722 1318; Av Kennedy 401; s/d $24/51; ✷) Decorated with festive paintings by local artists, rooms are comfortable and bright, with cushiony mattresses, phone, TV

and hot water. There's also room service and the restaurant has delicious seafood dishes.

Hostal Kennedy (☎ 272 1141; Av Kennedy 7-03; r per person $20; ✷) Snug and spacious rooms in an adorable house with a gated patio out front. Cable TV included and it's family-run.

Hotel Costa Verde (☎ 272 8714; calmar@andinanet .net; Luis Tello 809; r/ste ind breakfast $41/$50; ✷) This flamingo-pink high-rise by the beach has comfy, modern rooms and is on a tranquil side-street location. It caters partly to the business crowd and has a good restaurant.

Eating

The food in the many cheap sidewalk cafés and *comedores* is often good – try along Olmedo between Mejía and Piedrahita.

Restaurant El Manglar (☎ 272 7112; Quito 3-03; mains $5-12; ☽ 11:30am-4pm, 6-11pm) Considered the best dining downtown, this earthy stucco restaurant is split between two chefs and as many menus. Grab pizza or pasta for lunch and come back at the dinner hour for grilled lobster or roasted conch in herbs and lemon. Food is flavorful and you will love the air-conditioning here.

Parrilladas El Toro (9 de Octubre 4-23; mains $7; 5pm-midnight) Beyond the mafioso decor you'll find a decent steakhouse specializing in beef and chops. The thatched courtyard seating is preferable.

O' Mar (272 0688; Malecón de las Palmas; mains $5-11; 8:30am-6pm) A beachfront patio in Las Palmas serving monstrous seafood plates; consider the peculiar but tasty *ensumacao*, soup with coconut and peanuts.

Las Redes (272 3151; Bolívar; almuerzos $2) On the east side of the central plaza, this teeny café crammed with wooden benches serves *almuerzos*. Bring your local inquiries to the owner, who loves chatting with travelers.

Entertainment

Esmeraldas is the pulsing heart of gorgeous African-influenced marimba music. The best way to find out what's happening is to ask the locals, but impromptu gatherings are the norm – especially on weekends.

The discos in Las Palmas are considered the best, the **Empire** (09-966 9817; Av Kennedy 909; 9-2pm Thu-Sun), with a tropical flavor, is one of them. Note: an unescorted woman may encounter serious hassles.

Getting There & Away

AIR

The **TAME office** (272 6863; Bolívar near 9 de Octubre; 8:30am-12:30pm & 3-6pm Mon-Fri) is just off the central plaza. TAME flies from Quito to Esmeraldas and back on Tuesday, Thursday, Friday and Sunday afternoons. The one-way fare is $33. The 30-minute flight leaves Quito at 4pm and Esmeraldas at 5pm. You can also purchase a plane ticket at the **airport office** (272 7058) if the flight isn't full; arrive early and make sure you get a seat assignment. **Icaro** (www.icaro.com.ec) flies to Quito and back daily. Check the website for flight times.

BUS

There is no central bus terminal. **Aerotaxi** (Sucre), between Rocafuerte and 10 de Agosto, rockets to Quito ($6, five hours). **Transportes Occidentales** (9 de Octubre) and **Transportes Esmeraldas** (10 de Agosto at Plaza Central) both near the central plaza, are slower and a little cheaper. **Transportes Panamericana** (Colón & Salinas), behind the playground, has the most luxurious buses to Quito, but the fare is a few dollars more, and the trip takes seven to eight hours.

Both Transportes Occidentales and Transportes Esmeraldas also have frequent buses to Guayaquil ($5 to $7, seven to eight hours). Transportes Occidentales has buses to Guayaquil and Machala ($7, nine hours). **Transportes Gilberto Zambrano** (cnr Sucre & Piedrahita) has buses to Santo Domingo which stop in Pedernales and five buses daily to Muisne ($2, two hours). **Reina del Camino** (Piedrahita) goes to Manta six times a day ($7, seven hours) and to Bahía de Caráquez ($7, eight hours) once a day.

Transportes La Costeñita (Malecón Maldonado) and **Transportes del Pacífico** (Malecón Maldonado) have buses for Atacames and Súa (both $0.70, one hour) and leave frequently from 6:30am to 8pm. There are also several buses a day to Muisne ($2, two hours). These companies also go to Borbón ($3.50, four hours) and on to San Lorenzo ($4.50, five hours). Buses also go to other small provincial villages.

Note that buses from Esmeraldas to Borbón pass the airport. Passengers arriving by air and continuing by bus to towns on the way to Borbón don't need to backtrack to Esmeraldas.

Getting Around

The airport is 25km from town, across the Río Esmeraldas. Passengers and taxi drivers gather in front of the TAME office in town a couple of hours before the flight, and four or five passengers cram a taxi for $3 per person (15 minutes). Incoming passengers get together to do the same thing at the airport. At the airport, a taxi charges about $25 to go directly to Atacames, thus avoiding Esmeraldas completely.

A taxi to the beach costs $1, or otherwise take a Selectivo bus signed 'Las Palmas No 1' northbound along Bolívar.

Taxis charge a $1 minimum, which doubles after 11pm.

To avoid the area of the bus terminals you can catch buses to Atacames on Calle Olmedo after Calle Quito.

ATACAMES

06 / pop 9785

Atacames' rolling cobalt waves set the stage for Ecuador's most popular beach, crowded with thatched bars and sarong shops. If you enjoy the accoutrements of urban beaches, this place is for you. The strip is the lively haunt of all-night revelers with blaring music and coconuts waiting to be split, spiked with rum and served up with a Chinese umbrella. Revelry thrives during high season (July to mid-September, Christmas through New Year, Carnaval and Easter) when *serranos* (highlanders) pour into town to party. In low season it drops dead and becomes a cloudy, brooding refuge.

For those who want a quiet getaway, the nearby villages of Súa (p283) and Same (p283) offer open, empty expanses of sun and sea.

Orientation

The main road from Esmeraldas goes through the center of town and continues south past Súa and Same. Ask the bus driver to leave you at *taxis ecológicos*, the tricycle rickshaw stand. The beach is on a peninsula on the opposite bank of the Río Atacames. Take Prado west a couple blocks to the small footbridge over the river to the beach and hotel area. Hotels and restaurants line the east–west Malecón. The street parallel to the Malecón is the Calle Principal.

The beach itself is a pretty strip extending 4km to its southern terminus at 'suicide rock.' Buses do not reach the beach area. To skip the walk, hail a tricycle 'ecotaxi' to take you (via the other bridge) to your hotel for $1. The actual center of town is inland from the highway but there is little reason to go there other than to go to the bank.

Information

Andinatel (Malecón)

Banco del Pichincha (Roberto Luis Cervantes s/n; 8am-2pm Mon-Fri) Changes traveler's checks and has an ATM.

Café Net (Malecón; per hr $2.40) A 2nd-floor Internet café facing the beach.

Dangers & Annoyances

The beach has a powerful undertow and lifeguards work only midweek to weekends. People drown here every year, so stay within your limits.

The beach is considered unsafe at night when assaults and rapes have been reported. Visitors should stay near the well-lit areas in front of the hotels. Stay away from the

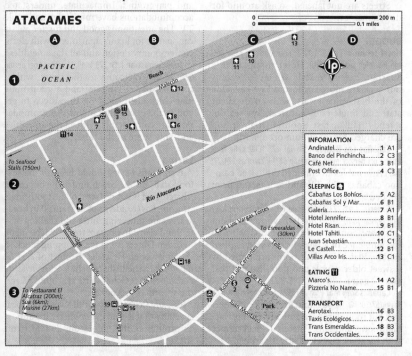

ATACAMES

0 ——— 200 m
0 ——— 0.1 miles

PACIFIC OCEAN

Beach

Malecón

Río Atacames

To Seafood Stalls (150m)

To Restaurant El Alcatraz (200m); Súa (6km); Muisne (27km)

INFORMATION	
Andinatel	1 A1
Banco del Pichincha	2 C3
Café Net	3 B1
Post Office	4 C3

SLEEPING	
Cabañas Los Bohíos	5 A2
Cabañas Sol y Mar	6 B1
Galería	7 A1
Hotel Jennifer	8 B1
Hotel Risan	9 B1
Hotel Tahiti	10 C1
Juan Sebastián	11 C1
Le Castell	12 B1
Villas Arco Iris	13 C1

EATING	
Marco's	14 A2
Pizzeria No Name	15 B1

TRANSPORT	
Aerotaxi	16 B3
Taxis Ecológicos	17 C3
Trans Esmeraldas	18 B3
Trans Occidentales	19 B3

isolated stretch between Atacames and Súa, as knifepoint robberies have been reported. Needless to say, the beach is not a place to bring your valuables. It should be fine during daylight hours but if you're a woman alone you may find you attract more attention than you'd like. Little can be done, but if there are other beachgoers set up near a family for less hassle. Camping here would be ludicrous.

Sleeping

Atacames has over 12,000 beds to choose from, yet it is surprisingly hard to find a decent one on weekends, and especially over the vacation periods, when prices opportunistically skyrocket. During high-season weekends you must pay for the number of beds in the room (upward of four or six) regardless of the number in your party. Rates are best from Sunday to Wednesday, when you can try bargaining, especially if you plan on staying a few days. Single travelers usually pay the double rate. Most hotels have only cold water (which they will call 'natural,' meaning unheated), due to the plumbing in this part of town.

Streets are not labeled, so ask around for directions.

BUDGET

Hotel Jennifer (☎ 273 1055; near Malecón; r per person low/high season $8/10) Hotel rooms have a Spartan, executive style while the cabins out back are more rustic and low-key. One of the best-value locals, with an excellent staff and single rates midweek/low season, it tends to fill up fast. Rooms in high-season are charged for maximum occupancy.

Cabañas Los Bohios (☎ /fax 273 1089; Calle Principal; r per person low/high season $8/14; cabañas $24/27; ☒) Amenable but cramped doll-sized bamboo cabañas with TV and fans, set in prim clipped gardens.

Galería (☎ 273 1149; Malecón; r per person low/high season $6/8; ☒) Guests have raved about this bare-bones beachfront motel with all the ambience of a pile of driftwood washed ashore. Plain, boarded rooms are rented by a sweet older couple and pool-use will cost you $2 extra.

Cabañas Sol y Mar (☎ 273 1524; r per person low/high season $7/10; ☒) You'll find the service indifferent, but rooms are tiled and airy with private bathrooms and fans. There's a small terrace with hammocks and off-street parking.

MIDRANGE

Villas Arco Iris (☎ 273 1069; www.villasarcoiris.com; Malecón; r per person low season $20, high season $22; ☒ ☒) Atacames' coziest retreat, these beachside villas are reached along a shady palm-lined path. Cabañas are snuggly, with bright rooms, firm beds and hammock decks. The larger ones have kitchenettes. The service is friendly, and the atmosphere is relaxing, whether you putter about the pool or grab seafood in the restaurant. Cash prices are about 20% lower.

Hotel Risan (☎ 273 1609; Las Tavas; r per person low/high season $10/20; ☒) Chipper, tiled rooms are sparkling clean with fans, cable TV and a pint-sized on-site pool. Find the building with the giant smiley painted on it.

Hotel Tahiti (☎ 273 1078; Malecón; r per person low/high season $13/20; cabañas $8/12; ☒) Beachfront digs with cheap cabins or hotel rooms, which leave options for everyone. While cabins are on the dark and shaggy side, the hotel rooms offer hot water, fans and cable TV.

Le Castell (☎ 273 1476/08; Malecón; d low/high season incl breakfast $45/90; ☒ ☒) Smart, flower-filled grounds include a swimming pool and playground. Immaculate, understated accommodations have minifridge and cable TV. The attention is good and fussier guests can splurge for luxury apartments with clean, contemporary design and all the amenities.

Juan Sebastian (☎ 273 1049; Malecón; r per person $29; ☒ ☒) Welcome to the show, with a thatched bar at the pool and a giant nude hair-chick airbrushed on the stucco to get you in the good-time mood. Accommodations are comfortable, with all the amenities and only some of the taste.

Eating

Adventurous eaters should head to the seafood stalls on the beach under the big *choza* (thatch-roof building) west of the footbridge. *Atacameñas* (residents of Atacames) in headscarves are squeezing limes and shelling oysters and clams to prepare fresh ceviche made to order. Diners eat at the chopping block in the noisy open air stalls. A bowl of *ceviche de concha* (shellfish ceviche) or *ceviche de pescado* (fish ceviche) starts at around $3 and the shrimp is precooked.

Cocada (a chewy coconut sweet) is a local specialty that is sold everywhere. It's almost as prolific as the ubiquitous *batido* (fruit shake).

Thatched parasols on the beach serve sunbathers *batidos* and the catch of the day. A whole fish dinner will start at around $4 or $5. Most of these spots double as bars in the evenings.

Pizzería No Name (Malecón; pizzas $5-8; ⏰ 6:30pm-1am) A 2nd-floor bamboo café with views to the sea. Try the pizza fresca, with tomatoes and fresh basil. Shrimp and garlic topping options impart a seaside flavor.

Restaurant El Alcatraz (☎ 273 1453; Rd to Súa; mains $5-15) This fashionable eatery serves great Esmeraldan cuisine, with fresh seafood. A full plate of *mariscos* (seafood) features various clams and shellfish, simmered in spices.

Marco's (Malecón; mains $5; ⏰ 11am-11pm) A little eatery offering appetizing steaks and seafood. The food is good, if a little bland.

Drinking & Entertainment

On high-season weekends the Malecón packs with revelers well into the night. Merry-makers pour into the loud competing beachside bars and swill fruity rum cocktails. The only discos in town are on the Malecón so they're easy to stumble into after you've barhopped. Try **Sambayé** or **Scala**; both get going after midnight. During the low season and midweek, things are mellow, if not dead.

Getting There & Away

All buses stop by the *taxis ecologicas* on the main road to/from Esmeraldas; there is no bus terminal. Buses for Esmeraldas ($0.80, one hour) normally begin from Súa, and there are plenty of seats. Most buses from Esmeraldas to Atacames continue on to Súa (10 minutes), Same and Tonchigüe for about $0.50. There are regular buses to Muisne ($1.50, 1½ hours).

Daily service to Quito (seven hours) can be found with **Transportes Occidentales** (☎ 09-981 9743; Barrio El Prado) for $7, **Trans Esmeraldas** (☎ 273 1550; Calle Luis Vargas Torres & Juan Montalvo) for $8 and **Aerotaxi** (☎ 273 1112; Calle Cuarta) for $9. If you're returning to Quito on a Sunday in the high season be sure to buy your ticket in advance.

SÚA
☎ 06

Fishing boats bob in the bay, encircled by frigates, pelicans and other seabirds. This village boasts tranquil waters ideal for a dip

and a slow-churning pace, although early morning finds the bay busy with trawlers. Súa is family-oriented, quieter and less popular than Atacames, with more reasonable weekend prices. Humpback whales can be seen off the coast from June to September. There is an Andinatel office.

Hostal Las Buganvillas (☎ 273 1008; Malecón; r per person $8; ☒) is a family-run hotel with clean, high-ceiling rooms with fans and balconies with views out to sea. A large pool is perfect for laps.

Hotel Chagra Ramos (☎ 273 1006; Malecón; r per person $7) is a wind-battered, salt-stained classic snuggled against the beach. Rooms are adequate but on the shaggy side, with antiquated bathrooms, TV, fans, and nice views. There's no hot water.

Cold concrete-block ambience is on offer at **Hotel El Peñón de Súa** (☎ 273 1013; near plaza; r per person $8), about 300m off the beach. Rooms are adequate and you'll find a convenient pool and on-site restaurant.

For a bamboo beachfront eatery, try **Kikes** (Malecón; ⏰ 9am-evening mains $4). It serves up mouth-watering *encocada de camarón* (shrimp and coconut stew).

Buses to and from Esmeraldas run about every 45 minutes. It takes 10 minutes to get to Atacames ($0.30) and about an hour to get to Esmeraldas ($1). If you want to go further along the coast to Muisne, you have to wait out of town along the main road for a bus headed south from Esmeraldas.

SAME & TONCHIGÜE
☎ 06

Exclusive hotels hug the palm-fringed coast of Same (pronounced sah-may), a resort village 6km southwest of Súa. A notch tamer than even Súa, its gray-sand beaches shun the flash and bustle of Atacames. Expect to pay more here.

Tonchigüe is a tiny fishing village about 3km west of Same, along the same stretch of beach.

Sleeping & Eating

El Acantilado (☎ 273 3466, Quito ☎ 02-245 3606; www.hosteriaelacantilado.com; high-season cabañas $52, s/d/tr low season $16/29/40) You'll love the smashing views of the surf and the private beach. Rustic suites and cabañas have blue tiles, wood furnishings and hot water. Larger accommodations fit up to eight occupants.

Each room has a garden hammock and sea view and there's a little pool and glassed-in restaurant with views. Run by a hospitable young family who speaks English. Located 1km south of Same.

Azuca (☎ 273 3343; Entrada Las Canoas, Carretera; r per person incl breakfast low/high season $5/10) Guests feel welcome in this Colombian-owned home pleasantly disheveled with oil paintings and interesting memorabilia. Three simple guest rooms sit over the restaurant. Meals are quite good. It is nowhere near the beach, but at the corner of the highway and the entrance road into town.

La Terraza (☎ 273 3320; Same; r for 2-4 persons $45, cabañas $35) Offers spacious, stark rooms with terraces, two of which face the beach. The cabañas are cement with wooden decks and floors. La Terraza's restaurant and bar is popular; the pizza is excellent.

Hotel Club Casablanca (Quito ☎ 02-225 2077; www.ccasablanca.com; Same; d incl breakfast $61-80; 🖳) With Dockers and a polo shirt you'll fit right into this first-class beach resort, resembling a Greek villa. Rooms are sprite and cushiony, each with its own deck or balcony. The extensive property includes a golf course, two kinds of tennis courts, a sprawling pool deck with wait staff and games facilities. An airport shuttle from Esmeraldas is offered.

Buffalo (☎ 09-539 7471; r per person form $10) A new hotel in a crisp Santa Fe adobe style. The rooms are snug but spare, and a restaurant and a bar are going on-site.

Playa Escondida (☎ 273 3122, 09-973 3368; www .playaescondida.com.ec; campsites per person $5, r per person $8-12) A set of rustic cabins with composting toilets, located 3km west of Tonchigüe and 10km down the road to Punta Galeras. It's an out-of-the-way and precious stretch, backed by rumpled woods, and run by a Canadian named Judy.

Seaflower (☎ 273 3369; Same; mains $9-22; 🕙 10am-4pm & 6-10pm) This former hotel is now an upscale restaurant, with delicious homemade pastas, steaks and lobster. The house's countryside ambience is warm and eclectic, with bright, candlelit tables both indoors and out. It's a shell's throw from the beach.

Rincón del Sabor (Calle Principal, Same; mains $3-5) Slip into this thimble space for delicious seafood, especially the spicy *encocado*.

Buses heading east to Esmeraldas and south to Muisne pick up and drop passengers at both Same and Tonchigüe. Rancheras (open-sided buses) head to Tonchigüe from Esmeraldas.

MUISNE & AROUND
☎ 05

Muisne is a tumble-down, working-class island surrounded by river and sea, off the end of the road from Esmeraldas. Its little ramshackle port bustles with a minor banana-shipping industry. Relatively remote, Muisne attracts far fewer visitors than the more popular beaches, but it makes an interesting foray off the beaten track. The long and lonely palm-lined beach at its back is its best feature.

The few remaining mangroves in the area are protected and worth a visit (see the boxed text, opposite).

Orientation
Buses from Esmeraldas get as far as the cement launch of El Relleno. From here take a motorized canoe across the mottled blue Río Muisne to the island ($0.20). Muisne's main road leads directly away from the pier, crossing the center to the beach. It's 2km end to end. Ecotaxis vie for passengers at the pier. It's worth the $1 for the wild ride at top rickshaw speed through muddy potholes and over sharp, rolling rubble. The beautiful beach is fronted by worn wooden boarding houses.

Information
There's no bank in Musine and the post office, near the telephone office, is open sporadically. An Andinatel office is just off the main plaza.

Dangers & Annoyances
Some beach cabins have had thefts so check the security of the room you choose before you head out. Single travelers, women especially, should stick to the area of hotels and restaurants on the beach.

Tours
Community and mangrove tours are organized by **Fundecol** (☎ 248 0519; www.fundecol.org; 🕙 8:30am-noon & 2:30-5:30pm Mon-Fri), the Foundation for Ecological Defense. Costs range from $25 to $50 per person per day (depending on the tour and the group size) and include boat trips up Río Muisne to see the remaining mangroves and the impact

MALTREATED MANGROVES

Ecuador's coastal mangroves are an important habitat. In addition to helping to control the erosion of the coast, they provide homes, protection and nutrients for numerous species of fish, birds, mollusks and crustaceans. Unfortunately, mangroves have been in no-man's land, and it has been difficult to say who owns these coastal tropical forests that are semipermanently inundated. Squatters took over areas of mangroves as their own, but this was not a problem in itself, because they were able to use the mangroves sustainably. The mangroves also supported cottage industries, such as fishing, shrimping and crabbing, as well as some sport fishing. Thousands of families along the coast were gainfully employed in these industries without impacting the mangroves.

This all changed in the 1980s with the arrival of shrimp farms, which produced shrimp in artificial conditions in numbers many times greater than could be caught by traditional shrimping methods. To build the farms, it was necessary to cut down the mangroves. The prospective owner of a shrimp farm simply took over an area of mangrove forest, paid off anyone who was living there, cut down the mangroves, and began the shrimp-farming process. The net profits of the shrimp farms were very high, and the idea soon caught on and spread rapidly along the coast, resulting in the complete destruction of 80% to 90% of Ecuador's mangroves during the 1980s and early 1990s.

Although there are now laws controlling this destruction, it has continued because the laws are difficult to enforce in the remote coastal areas. There have been many negative short- and long-term effects of the shrimp farms. Previously, many families could find a sustainable livelihood in the mangroves, whereas shrimp farms employ only a handful of seasonal workers. Where before there were mangroves protecting a large diversity of species, now there's just commercial shrimp. Coastal erosion and pollution from the wastes of the shrimp farms have become serious problems. It is yet another case of a handful of entrepreneurs getting very rich at the expense of thousands of families' livelihoods and the environment.

In 1999, the shrimp industry suffered dramatically when diseases such as *mancha blanca* (whitespot) wiped out entire shrimp farms in a matter of days. Many farms now lie abandoned. Meanwhile, desperate efforts are being made in Muisne, Bahía de Caráquez and a few other coastal towns to start replanting mangroves.

of commercial shrimping (see the boxed text, above).

Only 2km from Muisne is the **Congal Biostation**, a 250-hectare marine reserve working with mangrove conservation and organic aquaculture. Volunteers are needed, but visitors are welcome as well. There are great opportunities for snorkeling and scuba diving and comfortable private cabins with seafood on the menu. Contact **Fundación Jatun Sacha** (☎ 02-243 2240; www.jatunsacha.org; Pasaje Eugenio de Santillán N34-248 & Maurián, Urbanización Rumipamba, PO Box 17-12-867; r per person with 3 meals $34, discounts for groups & students).

Sleeping & Eating

There are only budget options in Muisne. Avoid the bleak hotels across the river and head to the island where you'll find beachfront cabañas. During the rainy months, mosquitoes can be bad, so get a room with a net. All hotels have cold water.

Hotel Playa Paraíso (☎ 248 0192; r per person $5, cabañas $8) Your best bet is this rambling pink house on the beach run by a friendly English-speaking couple. Small rooms with shared bathroom are no-frills. The cabañas with hammocks in the back are better and reasonably priced. Both have mosquito nets. Palms shade the immense garden where there's a billiard table and barbecue area. The restaurant serves good food (including veggie options) with advance requests.

El Oasis (☎ 248 0186; Manabí; r per person $8) This British-owned house is a block off the beach behind an enormous cement wall. You'll find the lawn is perfect and the miniature cabins are prodigiously clean. Bargaining the room price is frowned upon. Located 200m from the beach.

Spondylus (☎ 248 0279; r per person with shared/ private bathroom $7/9) Just down the beach, this place is friendly and has small rooms spruced up with a splashy paint job and candy-colored mosquito nets. Front rooms have ocean views.

A couple of other cheap hostels and inexpensive restaurants and bars line the beach. Everything is within a five-minute walk; look around for what looks best for you.

Getting There & Away

Several companies have buses departing from El Relleno across the river about every 30 minutes to Esmeraldas ($2, 2½ hours) passing Same, Súa and Atacames en route. There are five buses a day to Santo Domingo de los Colorados ($5, five hours) where connections to Quito or Guayaquil are made. **Transportes Occidentales** (Calle Principal at El Relleno) has a nightly bus at 10:30pm to Quito ($8, 8½ hours); it runs a night bus from Quito at 10:45pm which arrives in Muisne at 7am. Buses or pickups (depending on road conditions) go south to Daule about every hour, from where boats go on to Cojimíes. It's easier, however, to take an Esmeraldas bus for 30 minutes ($0.50) to El Salto (a road junction with a basic *comedor*) and wait there for southbound traffic heading to Daule. To get further south, get a bus to El Salto ($0.50, 30 minutes) and then a bus to Pedernales ($3, three hours), from where there are buses heading in all directions. Between El Salto and Pedernales, you often have to change buses in San José de Chamanga (you'll know you're in Chamanga by the floating piles of garbage and stilted houses). Ask your driver.

MOMPICHE

☎ 05

Besides a fabulous stretch of palm-fringed sands, Mompiche has little else. That's the beauty. Its claim to fame is its world-class wave – a left point-break that you'll find during big swells. Fanatics can click onto the latest **surf reports** (www.surf-forecast.com/breaks /Mompiche.shtml).

You can get your 40 winks at **Gabeal** (☎ 09-969 6543; east beach; r per person low/high season $10/15, camping $3), a set of basic bamboo cabins with cold-water bathrooms. The amenable owner can arrange horseback riding and surf lessons. You'll find it two blocks to the right of the bus stop.

Iruña (☎ 09-754 725; r per person), with its pale Easter-egg cabins, offers isolated tranquility. Talk to Marco to arrange a visit; you'll need to arrive by boat or truck at low tide.

Rancheras go to and from Esmeraldas every day ($3.50, 3½ hours), passing Atacames on the way.

COJIMÍES

☎ 05

The diminutive port of **Cojimíes** teeters on a headland getting gobbled up by the ocean. The village has to keep moving inland, which means that the cemetery is gaining beachfront vistas. There is a Pacifictel office here and a few very basic wash-in-a-bucket-type places to stay at. Ask around for small *comedores* in people's houses – the meals are cheaper and often better than the overpriced restaurants.

Hotel Coco Solo (☎ 09-921 5078, Pedernales ☎ 05-268 1156; cabins per person $8) is a coconut grove hideaway 14km south of Cojimíes. Some visitors have commented that it is becoming run down, but it still offers horses to gallop the deserted beaches and seaside cabins. The restaurant offers just a limited menu and there's a pool table for entertainment. The hotel is notoriously difficult to reach by phone. Visitors can also reserve through Guacamayo Bahíatours; see p290.

The Costa del Norte bus office on the main street can give transportation information. Trucks run along the beach at low tide, racing the tide at breakneck speeds, to Pedernales (from $10, 40 minutes). Buses take the 'road' ($1.50, 1½ hours); the last one leaves at around 3pm. To head north, you have to take a boat across to Daule, from where there are buses to the junction of El Salto where you can change direction to Muisne or Esmeraldas (those to Esmeraldas pass through other coastal towns).

PEDERNALES

☎ 05

Chevys with tinted windows thump down the strip where street-side grills soak up the action. The beach here attracts *serranos* but there are better options around. This unattractive yet important hub and shrimping center 40km south of Cojimíes may be a necessary juncture for connections south to Canoa or north to Esmeraldas.

Hotel Arenas (☎ 268 1170; Av Plaza Acosta & Robles; r per person with fan/air-con $8/10;) is the best value, with spacious, airy rooms and cable TV. It's located a few blocks from the beach. The modernish **Hotel América** (☎ 268

1174; García Moreno; r per person $8; ⌨) is well-kept but the walls are paper thin.

Buses leave the terminal for destinations south along the coast including Canoa ($4, three to 3½ hours) and San Vicente ($3, four hours). Regular buses go to Santo Domingo ($4, three hours), Quito ($6, six hours) and Guayaquil ($9, seven hours). The road via Chamango to El Salto leaves you near Muisne to make connections there or further north. Full-speed trucks take the beach north to Cojimíes ($1.45) during low tide.

CANOA

☎ 05 / pop 6086

Surf addicts, artisan fishermen and increasing numbers of sun-seekers all share this gorgeous, fat strip of beach. In the meantime the village continues to grow and spruce up. International surf competitions come in high season when waves reach up to 2m and accommodations become downright scarce (unless you want to camp on the beach). Obviously, the swimming is better after surf season. At low tide you can reach caves at the north end of the beach, which house hundreds of roosting bats.

There are no banks, but there is a public phone, and Internet access is available at La Posada de Daniel. Hotel Bambu and La Posada de Daniel both rent surfboards. Buses between Pedernales and San Vicente come through Canoa about every hour.

Tours

San Tour (☎ 261 6536; ⌚ 7am-6pm high season) Next to and affiliated with Pais Libre, this agency offers snorkeling, sport fishing, horseback riding ($2 per hour) as well as surfboard ($3 per hour) and bike rentals ($2 per hour).

Hostal Posada de Daniel (right) Also rents bikes, has a good in-house tour agency to arrange local hikes and outings to the Río Muchacho farm, and also offers surfing 101 ($15 per two hours). The owner is a former junior surf champ.

Sleeping & Eating

All of the following accommodations offer mosquito nets in rooms.

Hotel Bambu (☎ 261 6370; www.ecuadorexplorer .com/bambu; campsites $2, s with shared/private bathroom $7/12) A beachfront surfer resort able to sustain your urges for fruit shakes, hammock naps, big meals and bigger waves. Reserve early because this is the one place that fills up even in off-season. Firm beds fill these

smallish thatched rooms, kept cool with a bamboo-plaster construction. Shared bathrooms are spotless and all have hot water. You can rent surfboards, body boards and a beach sailer, or hang out in the communal lounge with games. English and Dutch are spoken.

Hotel Pais Libre (☎ 261 6536; r per person with shared/private bathroom $6/10; ⌨) A thatched multistory worthy of Noah, with bamboo-crafted rooms accented with brick and wood. The effect is eclectic but inviting. It has its own disco and swimming pool, and hammocks on the upper decks. The squat but cozy rooms come equipped with fans as well as hot water.

Hostal Shelmar (☎ 09-864 4892; shelmar66@hot mail.com; Av Javier Santos 304; r per person $6) Piping hot showers and friendly service make Shelmar a great deal. Rooms are nicely finished and there are mosquito nets and fans too. Sandwiched in the middle of the main strip, it's a few blocks from the beach.

La Posada de Daniel (☎ 261 6373; posadadedani el183@hotmail.com; r per person $8, camping $4; ⌨) A hipster hangout with Internet café ($2 per hour) and thatched-bar social scene. The campsites are decked out with tents and thick air mattresses good to go. Doubles and bunk rooms are borderline shabby but a whole new section is being built. You'll find this place next to the plaza a few blocks inland. They also arrange tours.

Take your pick from the lot of casual beachfront restaurants cooking up seafood fresh off the boat. A number of bars and cafés line the main strip, their waiters eager to lure in customers with any old line.

Arenabar (☎ 269 2542; Malecón; pizzas $2-3) A serene and happy ambience pervades this surfer-run restaurant, whose gooey pizza pies and healthy salads will perk you up on your board. Saturday nights are dance nights.

AROUND CANOA

The **Río Muchacho Organic Farm** is a tropical organic farm where guests and locals get their hands dirty engaging in and learning about sustainable farming practices. The farm is proactive in the community and built a primary school that teaches children about reforestation and waste management, in addition to their ABCs.

The farm lies along the river of the same name and is reached by a rough 8km track branching inland from the road north of Canoa. Transportation to the farm is normally on horseback, which is how the local *montubios* (coastal farmers) get around. After touring the farm, inspecting the crops and learning about permaculture and organic farming, visitors are free to choose from a variety of activities. They can help with farm chores, fish for river shrimp or make ornaments from tagua nuts. Those who want unadulterated nature can take guided hikes, go horseback riding or bird-watching.

Cabins are Thoreau-approved rustic, with shared showers and composting toilets. The coveted spot is a treehouse bunk. Guest groups are kept small, and reservations are a must.

Volunteers are welcome to stay longer and work in the school or on the farm, and are charged $250 a month for food and lodging. Spanish courses are offered and the farm now hosts a month-long apprenticeship in organic agriculture (billed as a course).

For more information contact **Guacamayo Bahíatours** (☎ 269 1107, 269 1412; www.riomuchacho .com; packages per person 1/2 nights $64/90) in Bahía de Caráquez (see p290). Guacamayo earmarks 10% of tour fees to support the school and other conservation work.

SAN VICENTE
☎ 05

Travelers usually beeline to Bahía, the shiny white city across the bay. If you have time to look around, check out the brisk market and the colorful murals and stained glass in the church on the beach. Buses to various destinations can be found here.

On the way to Canoa, there are several hotels, such as **Hotel Monte Mar** (☎ 267 4778; r $15-30), which has the best views of Bahía de Caráquez, as well as a pool, a restaurant, and the option of air-conditioning.

Hostal San Vicente (☎ 267 4182; r per person with shared/private bathroom $2/4), located near the center, is the best of the basic places. For air-conditioned rooms go to **Hotel Vacaciones** (☎ 267 4116; r per person with fan/air-con $8/10; 🏊) on the Malecón in front of the gas station. It also has a pool and a decent restaurant.

Buses leave hourly from near the market (by the passenger-ferry dock) to Pedernales ($3, three hours). Reina del Camino has several buses a day to Chone ($1.50, 1½ hours), Santo Domingo and Guayaquil ($7,

six hours), as well as morning and evening buses to Quito ($8, eight hours). Buses head regularly to Canoa ($0.35, 30 minutes).

Passenger ferries cross Río Chone several times an hour between 6am and 10pm ($0.35). It takes 10 minutes to reach Bahía de Caráquez. A car ferry leaves about every half-hour – foot passengers can cross at no charge.

BAHÍA DE CARÁQUEZ
☎ 05 / pop 19,700

Chalk-colored high-rises and red-tile roofs fill this tiny peninsula, whose manicured yards and swept sidewalks give a tidy impression. In the first half of the 20th century, the city was Ecuador's principal port, but eroding sandbanks let the honor drift to Guayaquil and Manta, and Bahía (as the locals call it) was left to its housekeeping.

Calamities seem to collect here. When the 1998 El Niño hit Bahía particularly badly it was cut off by landslides, and streets turned into rivers of mud. In the same year an earthquake measuring 7.2 on the Richter scale toppled or severely damaged some buildings. Only one person was killed in the quake, but at least 20 died in the horrendous mudslides that followed, literally wiping out the poorer neighborhoods on the edge of town.

However dismal things get, Bahía's buoyant nature is to reinvent itself after each knock. When President Sixto Durán (1992–96) got a holiday home here, many upper-class Ecuadorians followed suit. Most recently, in 1999, the city declared itself an 'ecocity,' creating a community culture of recycling and sustainable living that has attracted worldwide attention.

Bahíans get an ecocity pamphlet with environmental tips for everyone – from children to taxi drivers. The market recycles and organic farms are within a stone's throw of town. Reforestation projects target hillsides damaged after 1998's El Niño and mangroves desiccated by shrimp farming. Various other agroecological and recycling ventures are promoted by a handful of visionary locals.

Information
Banco de Guayaquil (☎ 269 2205; cnr Bolívar & Riofrío) Cashes traveler's checks and has an ATM.
Clínica Bahía (☎ 269 0957; Hidalgo near Intriago) Recommended by locals.

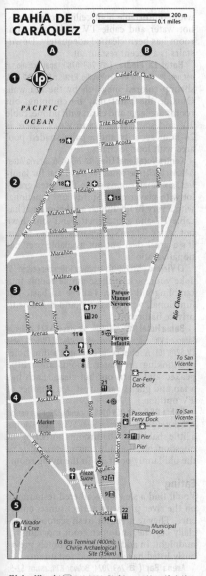

BAHÍA DE CARÁQUEZ

0   200 m
0   0.1 miles

INFORMATION

Banco de Guayaquil	1 A4
Clínica Bahía	2 A2
Clínica Viteri	3 A4
Genesis Net	4 B4
Pacifictel	5 B3
Post Office	6 A5
Tourist Office	7 A3

SIGHTS & ACTIVITIES

Bahía Dolphin Tours	8 A4
Casa de Cultura	9 B5
Church of La Merced	10 A5
Guacamayo Bahíatours	11 A3
Museo Bahía de Caráquez	12 B5

SLEEPING

Bahía B&B	13 A4
Bahía Hotel	14 B5
Centro Vocacional Life	15 B2
Hotel El Viajero	16 A4
Hotel Italia	17 A3
Hotel La Herradura	18 A2
Hotel La Piedra	19 A2

EATING

Arena Bar	20 A3
Picantería La Patineta	21 B4
Puerto Amistad	22 B5
Riverside Restaurants	23 B4

TRANSPORT

Repsol Gas Station	24 B4

Sights & Activities

Take a peek at **Casa de Cultura**, a century-old building, in front of the **Museo Bahía de Caráquez** (☎ 269 2285; cnr Malecón Santos & Peña; admission $1; ☼ 10am-5pm Tue-Sat, 11am-3pm Sun). The museum has a small collection of pre-Columbian pottery, a library, cheap Internet and local crafts for sale. The **Mirador La Cruz** (lookout) at the south end of town gives good views of the area and can be reached on foot or by a short taxi ride.

Chirije archaeological site, 15km south of Bahía and 3km north of San Clemente, is an earthen hill riddled with artifacts – such as ceramics, burials, cooking areas, garbage dumps and jewelry – dating mainly from the Bahía culture (500 BC–AD 500). The site is owned by Bahía Dolphin Tours (p290), and to visit you must arrange a guided trip through the agency. The sheer number of remains leads archaeologists to think this was once an important ancient port. Only small sections of the site have been professionally excavated, and some pieces are exhibited in the tiny on-site museum, but visitors will find shards of pottery all over the place.

Chirije is cut off by high tides, so visits have to be planned with this in mind (Bahía

Clínica Viteri (☎ 269 0429; Riofrío near Montúfar) Also recommended by locals.
Genesis Net (☎ 269 2400; Malecón Santos 1302; per hr $1.60; ☼ 7am-10pm Mon-Fri, 8am-8pm Sat & Sun) Internet.
Pacifictel (cnr Intriago & Arenas)
Post office (Aguilera 108)
Tourist office (☎ 269 1124; mturlitoral@ec-gov.net; Bolívar; ☼ 8:30am-5pm Mon-Fri)

Dolphin Tours will have this info). Visitors can spend the night and take advantage of trails into the coastal, tropical dry forest. Five large solar cabins sleep up to eight (a squeeze) and have a porch, private bathroom and kitchen. Rates are $50 to $80 per cabin and meals are available on request.

Tours

The following agencies are useful local resources. In addition to describing tours and attractions, they can provide information on volunteering in local schools and other excellent opportunities for community work.

Guacamayo Bahíatours (☎ 269 1412; www.gua camayotours.com; Bolívar at Arenas; ♥ 7:30am-7pm Mon-Fri, 9am-5pm Sat, 10am-2pm Sun) is owned by an Ecuadorian/New Zealand couple. The company arranges tours to Río Muchacho Organic Farm (p287), daytrips to other agroecological projects, such as an organic shrimp farm, in addition to organizing a number of active tours.

Canoe tours through mangrove forests with abundant birdlife are paddled by a local fisherman. Trips to local islands with seabird colonies (including one of the coast's largest frigatebird colonies) also educate about the problems facing the mangrove habitat and visit a private zoo. Whale-watching runs from late September to early October.

Bahía Dolphin Tours (☎ 269 2097/86; Bolívar 1004) owns the Chirije archaeological site, and day visits or overnight tours to the site can be arranged. The staff can arrange packages with overnight stays at Chirije and in Bahía, combined with visits to panama-hat workshops, an organic shrimp farm, frigatebird islands and other local points of interest. Guides speak English, French and German.

Sleeping

Some of the cheap places have water-supply problems.

La Herradura (☎ 269 0446; Bolívar 202; s/d with fan & cold water $8/20, with air-con & hot water $16/25; ❄) An old Spanish home with antiques and artwork brimming from its nooks. The cheaper rooms are smaller with funky old chenille spreads; you'll find better options upstairs where the ambience is more airy and contemporary. Look for the upper-level balconies and the two rooms with ocean views.

Hotel Italia (☎ 269 1137; cnr Bolívar & Checa; r per person $10) An old-fashioned four-story hotel

with comfortable high-ceiling rooms, fans, hot water and cable TV. Make sure your room has been cleaned adequately. Downstairs is a decent restaurant.

Hotel La Piedra (☎ 269 0780; apartec@uio.sat net.net; Av Circunvalación Virgilio Ratti; r $49; ❄) A shrimp-colored megalith by the sea wall. Outside the paint may be chipping, but rooms are large and clean with phone, cable TV and spectacular ocean views. There is 24-hour security and a palm-shaded pool area with lounge chairs.

Centro Vocational Life (☎ 269 0496; Octavio Vitteri & Muñoz Dávila; r per person $10; ❄) Ideal for families, six small cabins sit on this gated grassy lot with playground. Sturdy and functional with a very Brady Bunch aesthetic. Each has cable TV and a kitchenette, and some have hot water. There's a separate games room. It's a great deal but not available over national vacations.

El Viajero (☎ 269 0792; Bolívar 910; r per person $8) Take your pick of these ample rooms in a rambling old house. They're all basic but functional, with fans, TV and a few with private bathroom.

Bahía Hotel (☎ 269 0509, ☎ /fax 693 833; Malecón Santos at Vinueza; r per person without/with TV/with cable TV $7/8/10) A cheery green and white hotel overlooking the water. Rooms are a little peaked and worn-out but clean. Each has a fan and guests can invest in a number of TV options.

Bahía B&B (☎ 269 0146; Ascázubi 322; r per person with shared/private bathroom $6/8) With the rooms a little shabby, and bathrooms bordering on questionable, the only charm left may be in the old family portraits in the living room.

Eating

You'll find a slew of weathered restaurants on the river pier with perfect sunset ambience. They're great for fresh seafood, especially ceviche, and open from morning till midnight. In addition, several hotels previously listed have very good restaurants.

Arena Bar (☎ 269 2024; Bolívar 811; mains $2-5; ♥ 5pm-midnight) Chow down to international rhythms and casual surf decor. Pizza is the staple but the salads, spruced up with olives and cheese, make a nice change from the norm, as do the homey grilled cheese sandwiches.

La Herradura (☎ 269 0446; Bolívar 202; mains $5) The high ceilings and wrought-iron chandeliers lend a formality to this affordable restaurant. The original menu offers delicious green plantain bread and tart ceviches sprinkled with cilantro. For the more conservative diners, there's always the Spanish omelet.

Puerto Amistad (Malecón Santos; mains $4-9) An upscale restaurant with a lovely deck over the river. Grilled meat and quesadillas are favorites on the menu. Across from the Bahía Hotel.

Picantería la Patineta (Ascázubi; soups $1; 8:30am-12:30pm) Serves *encebollado,* an Ecuadorian breakfast favorite soup made of seafood, yucca and onion soup garnished with *chifles* (crispy banana slices).

Getting There & Away

The new bus terminal is at the far southern end of the Malecón. From there **Coactur** (269 0014) has buses to Portoviejo ($1.50, 1½ hours) hourly from 4am to 8pm; some continue to Manta ($2.90, two hours) and Guayaquil ($4.50, six hours). **Reina del Camino** (269 0636) offers two classes of service – regular and *ejecutivo* (1st class) – to Quito

($9, eight hours) and Guayaquil ($7, seven hours). The company also serves Ambato ($9, nine hours) and Santo Domingo ($4, four hours). Buses to local towns such as Chone are often rancheras and they leave from various places in town.

To Canoa and points north, cross the river to San Vicente – see p288 for boat information. The passenger and car-ferry docks are on the eastern side of town, off Malecón Santos.

PORTOVIEJO

05 / pop 171,850

Government workers, business people, everyone in this city rushes around its bleak and stuffy streets. Despite an industrious appearance, Portoviejo remains uninspiring to visitors. Founded in 1535, Portoviejo is the capital of Manabí province and vital for coffee, cattle and fishing. Much of its commercial success is based on the agricultural-processing industry. If it doesn't float your boat, at least it has scores of bus connections and is a reasonable overnight stop from Quito en route to the coast.

Information

Banco de Guayaquil (Parque Central, Bolívar & Ricaurte) Changes traveler's checks and has an ATM.

Banco del Pacífico (☎ 263 9300; cnr 10 de Agosto & Chile) Changes traveler's checks and has an ATM.

Clínica Metropolitana (☎ 263 4207; cnr 9 de Octubre & Rocafuerte)

Cybercafé Mr Chat (Sucre 715; per hr $1; ⌚ Mon-Sat)

Metropolitan Touring (☎ 265 1070, 263 1761; Olmedo 706; ⌚ 8:30am-1pm & 3-7pm Mon-Fri) For standard tours and airline tickets.

Miky Cyber Café (Chile 621; per hr $1.20) Internet access.

Pacifictel (cnr 10 de Agosto & Pacheco)

Post office (Ricaurte; ⌚ 8am-6:30pm Mon-Fri, 8am-12:30pm Sat) Between Sucre and Bolívar.

Tourist office (☎ 263 0877; Gual 234; ⌚ 8:30am-5pm Mon-Fri)

Sights

Despite the town's colonial history, there's little to see. Wander down to the pleasant **Parque Eloy Alfaro**, which has what may well be the starkest, barest modern **cathedral** in Ecuador. Next to the cathedral is a **statue of Francisco Pacheco**, who is the founder of Portoviejo.

The **street market** (Chile), between Duarte and Gual, makes for an interesting stroll; it's impassable to cars during the day. If you want to browse around a mall, **Paseo Portoviejo** by the Parque Central has some shops.

Sleeping

Hostal Colón (☎ 263 4004; Colón & Olmedo; r per person $8; 🖥) As long as large rooms with metal beds don't give you nurse nightmares, this is a great option. Bathrooms are spit-shine clean, owners are chilled and you get TV and your choice of fan or air-conditioning.

Hotel Ejecutivo (☎ 263 2105; fax 263 0876; 18 de Octubre near 10 de Agosto; s/d $17/22) Polished and elegant rooms are tasteful and snug. Considered the best hotel in town, with an attitude to match. The fully equipped, carpeted rooms are often booked. The hotel provides car rental and has a very good, but not cheap, restaurant.

Hotel New York (☎ 263 2395; Olmedo & F de Moreira; s/d $18/25, with window $20/28; 🖥) A plain hotel gussied up with air fresheners and tacky homages to the red-white-and-blue. Rooms are clean and the beds are comfortable. There's hot water and cable TV.

Hotel Paris (☎ 265 7272; Sucre 513; r per person $4) Lest you wax romantic over the name, this is, truly, a $4 hotel. However, the old building does have remnant charms, such as the pressed-tin ceiling and the long shuttered windows that gaze out over the plaza.

Hotel Conquistador (☎ 263 1678; 18 de Octubre & Gual; s/d with fan $10/16, with air-con $16/20) With worn floor boards, cold water and sagging beds, you will hopefully find refuge in the cable TV provided.

Eating

La Carreta (☎ 265 2108; Olmedo; mains $2-5; ⌚ 7am-10pm Mon-Fri, 7am-3pm Sat) Tie-clad waiters serve up delicious Ecuadorian fare in this slick and starched eatery by the cathedral.

Soda Bar Caramel (Colón; ⌚ 8am-10pm) Slip onto a bench and satisfy your yen for grilled cheese sandwiches in the popular minimarket atmosphere.

Fruta Prohibida (☎ 263 7167; Chile 607; ⌚ 9:45am-11pm) Creamy *batidos*, fresh juices, fruit salads and hamburgers can be chowed at outdoor tables observing the street action.

Chicken roasters and other cheap eateries can be found on Gual between 18 de Octubre and Pacheco, as well as on the block of Morales south of Gual.

Getting There & Away

At the time of writing, flights in and out of Portoviejo were being served out of Manta. Look for changes on the Tame website (www.tameairlines.com).

Most travelers arrive at the bus terminal 1km southwest of downtown. Take a taxi ($1) to/from the terminal for security reasons.

Buses depart every half-hour or so to Manta ($0.75, 40 minutes) and every 45 minutes to Jipijapa ($1.20, 40 minutes). Carlos Aray buses to Jipijapa continue on to Puerto López ($2, two hours). There are frequent departures to Guayaquil ($4, four hours) and Salinas ($5.50, five hours), and daily departures to Esmeraldas ($7, seven hours). Several companies offer a service to Quito ($9, eight hours); **Reina del Camino** (Gual & Rocafuerte) has *ejecutivo* (first class) buses to Quito if you want a little more comfort.

Other small nearby villages are frequently served by small bus companies.

DASHBOARD INVENTORY – THE COASTAL BUS

Bored on the bus? See how many dashboard items you can inventory while you hurtle past African palm plantations at warp speed.

- Two photographs of driver with his bus: right angle, left angle
- One CD player, four hairy speakers thumping 'psycho cumbia' (accelerated version)
- One floral scarf tied over dash, secured by a pink banana clip
- Stickers: one rainbow Jesus; two regular Jesuses (miniature); two Virgin Marys; one saint (unknown); four football logos; two 'chick idol' Bart Simpsons; one crowned Virgin Mary holding scepter in left hand, baby Jesus in right
- One magazine cutout of nude female backside wrapped in white bow (in privileged location) next to rearview mirror; one XL Playboy logo; one 18-inch blonde in bikini
- Approximately two dozen Tweety and Pooh stickers on red fur trimmed rear-view mirrors
- Three old air-fresheners
- One wooden keychain carved with palm tree and TERESA
- Marbleized steering wheel, red
- One window inscription: '*Me sigieras viendo toda la vida*' (You'll keep seeing me all your life)…

INLAND FROM PORTOVIEJO
☎ 05

These marketplaces of coffee, cattle, corn, cotton and bananas are the very essence of lowland Ecuador. Folks are old-fashioned and amiable and coming here provides a glimpse of provincial life off the beaten track.

Approximately 20km north of Portoviejo, **Rocafuerte** is known for its sticky coconut and caramel confections. **Calceta**, 43km northeast of Portoviejo, produces *sisal*, the strong fiber gathered from the spiny-leaved agave plant. It's used for ropes and sandals; you'll even see them on the locals in the Otavalo market.

A good road continues about 25km northeast to the sizable town of **Chone**, known for cowboy machos who supposedly keep the local beauties under wraps. Keep this in mind when seeking a dance partner.

From Chone, a paved road continues northeast, linking the coastal lowlands with Santo Domingo. This road climbs to over 600m above sea level as it crosses the coastal mountains, then drops over the eastern side to the canton capitals and market towns of **Flavio Alfaro** and **El Carmen** before reaching Santo Domingo. From El Carmen buses loop back to the coast via Pedernales.

CRUCITA AREA
☎ 05

North of Manta, you'll find small villages popular with national tourists. The fishing town of **Crucita** has superlative winds for paragliding and kite-surfing. If you're interested in taking the leap, call Raúl or Luis Tobar at the friendly and family-oriented **Hostal Los Voladores** (☎ 234 0200; hvoladores@hotmail .com; r per person with shared/private bathroom $6/8; 🖳). **Hostería Zucasa** (☎ 234 0133; r per person with cold/ hot water $14/17; 🖳) offers comfortable cabins around a shady pool area.

Sandwiched between **San Jacinto** (13km beyond Crucita) and **San Clemente** (3km further) there's a few nice beaches with nearby lodging and restaurant options. Beyond San Clemente, a road continues northeast along the coast to Bahía de Caráquez, about 20km away.

MANTA
☎ 05 / pop 183,100

Come daylight, little boats of Manteño fishing crews haul in their lines and Tarqui beach churns to life with prattling housewives and restaurant owners haggling for the best of the catch. This is the daily ritual of an old seafaring society which has transformed into a frenetic, major port. While Manta depends on fishing, the artisan fisherman battles daily against the massive industrialized fishing industry. A large US military base whose mission is Plan Colombia fills the backdrop.

With the economy somewhat depressed, a large portion of the population openly daydreams of slipping away to New York or Spain. Still, the city's friendly populous, wide beaches and happening nightlife make it a popular destination for national tourists. While not the place for empty, paradisiacal surf and sun, Manta has an interesting atmosphere to soak up.

Orientation

The town is divided into two by Río Manta. Manta is joined by the more easterly Tarqui by road bridges. Manta has the main offices, shopping areas, first-class hotels and bus terminal. Tarqui has a number of hotels aimed at budget travelers. They are generally older and run down, and the area is more prone to theft and security problems, particularly at night. The main residential areas are to the southwest of the Manta business district, while the cleanest beaches are to the northwest of Manta. Addresses are rarely used.

Information

Banco del Pacífico (☎ 262 3212; cnr Av 2 & Calle 13; ☯ 8:30am-5pm Mon-Fri) Changes traveler's checks; has an ATM.

Banco del Pacífico ATM (cnr Av 107 & Calle 103) In Tarqui.

Banco del Pichincha (☎ 262 6844; Av 2 at Calle 11) Changes traveler's checks; has an ATM.

Cámara de Turismo (☎ 262 0192; Malecón de Manta & Circunvalación, Tramo 1; ☯ 9am-6pm) Provides tourist information.

Clínica Manta (☎ 292 1566) Has doctors of various specialties.

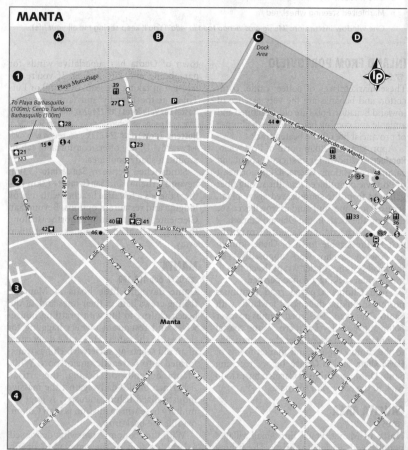

Cyber Café (Av 1 near Calle 14; per hr $0.70) Internet
Metropolitan Touring (☎ 262 3090, 613 366; Av 4 at Calle 12) Reliable full-service travel agency.
Municipal tourist office (☎ 261 1471; Calle 9, Municipio; ☽ 8am-5pm Mon-Fri) Well-staffed and friendly; located in the town hall.
Pacifictel (Malecón de Manta) On the Manta waterfront.
Police station (☎ 292 0900; 4 de Noviembre) Tourist embarkation card extensions can be done in the immigration office – this street is a continuation of Malecón de Manta.
Post office (Calle 8) At the town hall.
Publicomp (☎ 261 0306; Av 3 1245; per hr $0.70; ☽ 6:30am-9:30pm Mon-Sat) Internet.

Sights & Activities

The **Museo del Banco Central** (Malecón de Manta; admission $1 Mon-Sat, free Sun; ☽ 9am-5pm Mon-Sat, 11am-3pm Sun) has valuable artifacts from pre-Columbian Manta culture, as well as quirky fishing memorabilia.

You know you're in Tarqui when you stumble upon the enormous **Manabí fisherman statue**. Beyond it is **Tarqui beach**, whose east end is a hive of activity early in the mornings. Vendors' carts tail the morning crowd, selling rows upon rows of shark, tuna, swordfish, dorado and others (whose size decrease with each passing year). Nearby is Manta's **boatyard**, where giant wooden fishing boats are built by hand on the edge of the sand. The whole scene merits an early wake-up call. The **fishing-boat harbor**, between Manta and Tarqui, is busy and picturesque at high tide and dead in the mud at low tide.

| 0 | 400 m |
| 0 | 0.2 miles |

INFORMATION		
Banco del Pacífico	1	D2
Banco del Pacífico ATM	2	G4
Banco del Pichincha	3	D2
Cámara de Turismo	4	A2
Cyber Café	5	D2
Metropolitan Touring	6	D2
Municipal Tourist Office	(see 10)	
Pacifictel	7	E2
Post Office	8	E3
Publicomp	9	D2
Town Hall	10	E3

SIGHTS & ACTIVITIES		
Church	11	H4
Manabí Fisherman Statue	12	F4
Museo del Banco Central	13	E3

| Playground | 14 | E2 |
| Supermaxi | 15 | A2 |

SLEEPING 🏠		
Boulevard Hotel	16	G4
Boulevard Hotel Annex	17	H4
Hostal Astoria 2	18	H4
Hostal del Mar	19	G4
Hostal Las Velas	20	G4
Hostal Manta Aeropuerto	21	H4
Hostal Miami	22	H4
Hotel Cabañas Balandra	23	B2
Hotel El Inca	24	C4
Hotel Las Gaviotas	25	H4
Hotel Lun Fun	26	F4
Hotel Manta Imperial	27	B1
Hotel Oro Verde	28	A1

Hotel Pacífico Inn	29	G4
Hotel Panorama Inn	30	G4
Hotel Panorma Inn (Annex)	31	G4
Leo Hotel	32	E3

EATING 🍴		
Bufalo Grill	33	D2
Cheap Comedores	34	H3
Comedor Malibu	35	H3
Fruta del Tiempo	36	D2
Picantería El Marino	37	H3
Pizzería Topi	38	D2
Playa Murciélago Cafés	39	B1
Rincon Criollo	40	B2

ENTERTAINMENT 🎭 🎵		
Krug	41	B2
Madera Fina	42	A2
Tantra	43	B2

TRANSPORT		
Budget	44	C1
Bus Terminal	45	E3
Icaro	(see 28)	
Localiza	46	A2
Panamericana Terminal	47	D3
TAME Office	48	D2

Open-Air Theater & Plaza

Plaza 4 de Noviembre

Breakwater

Plaza
Civic Plaza

PACIFIC OCEAN

Fishing-Boat Harbor

Breakwater

Tarqui Beach

Av Jaime Chavez Gutierrez (Malecón de Manta)

24 de Mayo

Av 9

Malecón de Tarqui

Río Manta

Av 107

Tarqui

Av 11

Av 12

Av 24 de Mayo

To Police Station (100m); Clínica Manta (500m); Montecristi (11km); Portoviejo (39km)

Market

To Airport (3km)

In Manta, **Playa Murciélago** is a less protected beach and has bigger waves (although they're not very big, there's a powerful undertow). It is a couple of kilometers northwest of downtown and is the town's most popular beach, backed by snack bars and restaurants and umbrella rental spots. Shopping can be done at the new **Supermaxi**, located diagonally across from Hotel Oro Verde. Further northwest, **Playa Barbasquillo** is a more tranquil resort area.

Sleeping

Prices rise during vacation weekends and during the high seasons (December to March, and June to August), when single rooms can be hard to find. At other times of the year you can bargain for cheaper rates. While most of the better bars and discos are in Manta proper, the cheaper hotels are in Tarqui. If you stay here definitely take a taxi if you're out after dark.

TARQUI

Unless noted all of the following hotels have cold-water showers.

Hotel Panorama Inn (☎ 261 1552; Calle 103 near Av 105; r per person $6, annexe $20; ✷) The budget version of this hotel is worn out, but welcoming. Large tiled rooms have teeny balconies and (some have) views of the water. The staff is attentive. Its newer incarnation across the road has air-conditioning and a courtyard pool.

Hostal Astoria 2 (☎ 262 8045; Av 105 at Calle 106; r per person $5) Fresh paint and new furnishings make this well-kept cheapie great value.

Hotel El Inca (☎ 262 0440; Calle 105 & Malecón de Tarqui; r per person $10) An old-world-style *pensión*, with small, neat rooms and large wall murals. Despite worn edges, it has appeal. There are discounts for groups and there's a TV in the rooms.

Boulevard Hotel (☎ 262 5333; Calle 103; r per person $6, annexe $12) Dumpy but friendly, instead try the annex further down the block. It's much better value, with hot water, cable TV and an indoor pool, although the rooms can be musty.

Hostal Miami (☎ 262 2055; cnr Av 102 & Calle 107; r per person $5) Spacious but Spartan rooms in seafoam-green offer ocean views from the balconies. The bathroom is antiquated and there are fans in each room.

Hostal Las Velas (☎ 262 4409; Av 106 at Calle 101; s/d with fan $12/16, with air-con $16/22; ✷) Electric-blue rooms with firm mattresses and TV as well as modern bathrooms. Ask for hot water, only a few rooms have it.

Hotel Las Gaviotas (☎ 262 0140; hotelgav@interactive.net.ec; Malecón de Tarqui 1109; s/d with fan $10/18, with air-con $15/25; ✷) Popular with weekending families who crowd the pool, the hotel is squeaky clean but generic in its cement and tile construction. It features 24-hour security, hot water and phones. You can smash balls around on the tennis court and socialize in the affable restaurant and bar. Ocean-view rooms cost extra.

Other cheap but basic places in Tarqui include the **Hostal del Mar** (Calle 104; r per person $4) and nearby **Hotel Pacífico Inn** (☎ 262 3584; Av 106 near Calle 102; r per person $10).

MANTA

Hotel Cabañas Balandra (☎ 262 0316, 262 0915; www.hotelbalandramanta.com; Calle 20; s/d/tr $80/88/95; ✷ ✷) The urban hideaway of these upscale hillside cabañas has large appeal. Two-bedroom cabins have small, snug rooms in ocean tones with balconies looking out to sea. Amenities include minifridge, TV and telephone. Outside you'll find sculpted shrubbery, a tiled dining deck and a pleasing pool area. Located north of downtown Manta, two blocks from Playa Murciélago.

Hotel Lun Fun (☎ 262 2966, 261 2400; lunfunhotel@yahoo.com, Calle 2; s/d $39/50; ✷ ▢) Slick, Asian-influenced decor sets the mood for this upscale hotel. Plush and modern, the rooms have modern bathrooms, hot water, air-conditioning, minifridge, TV and telephone. You'll also find a business center and wi-fi Internet. Unfortunately, the location is only convenient to the bus terminal. The attached Chinese restaurant is the best in town (opposite).

Hotel Oro Verde (☎ 262 9200/9; www.oroverdehotels.com; Playa Murciélago at Calle 23; s/d $95/100, ste $120-150; ✷ ▢ ✷) Recline into the lap of luxury in this high-rise full-service resort. Impeccable rooms are decked out in cream tones and have wi-fi access and smashing sea views. Relaxation massages are $20, or you can head to the private beach and pool area for catered drink service. A casino, tennis court, gym and sauna round out the offerings.

Hostal Manta Aeropuerto (☎ 262 8040; Barrio Playa Murciélago, Av M3 & Calle 24; r per person $20; ✷) This B&B offers a quiet urban getaway still in walking distance to most of the nightlife.

Hotel Manta Imperial (☎ 262 2016; Malecón at Calle 20; s/d with fan $27/34, with air-con $32/40; ✷ ✧) This 1960s concrete palace has seen better days. Guests will find the rooms battered but clean. There's a casino and disco and it's next to the popular Playa Murciélago.

Centro Turístico Barbasquillo (☎ 262 0718; fax 622 456; r per person from $30; ✷ ✧) A comfortable beach resort located on the next beach (Barbasquillo) northwest of Murciélago. There is private beach access and a beach bar, pool, sauna, gym, disco, playground and a restaurant. Rates for air-conditioned rooms with TV and telephone include breakfast.

Leo Hotel (☎ 262 3159; 24 de Mayo; s with fan/air-con $12/15; ✷) Across from the bus station, this hotel's ample tiled rooms are far more tolerable than its next door neighbor's. Very convenient if you're just passing through.

Eating

Lun Fun (☎ 262 2966; mains $7) Chinese with a Latin twist. Try the beef in sweet tomato sauce or a noodle dish. The black-lacquered dining room is sophisticated and fun.

Bufalo Grill (☎ 272 3853; Av Seis; lunch $2; ✧ 11:30am-3pm) Freddy cooks up tasty lunch specials in this local hole-in-the-wall favorite located between Calles 13 and 14.

Rincon Criollo (☎ 226 4668; Av Flavio Reyes & Calle 20; lunch $3.50; ✧ lunch only) This hopping local haunt serves up *almuerzos* such as traditional peanut soup, chicken and rice.

Picantería El Marino (Malecón de Tarqui & Calle 110; mains $4-6; ✧ 8am-5pm) This whitewashed café is more upscale than its Tarqui neighbors, with blue checkered tablecloths and whopping seafood plates. Enjoy the water views and the icy air-conditioning.

Comedor Malibu (Malecón de Tarqui; mains $4-6) One of many thatched huts with irregular hours serving heaping plates of fish (fried or steamed), but this one is particularly friendly.

Fruta del Tiempo (☎ 262 5920; cnr Av 1 & Calle 12; mains $1-3; ✧ 7:30am-2am Mon-Sat, 4-10pm Sun) Slip into a bamboo chair on the plaza for great juices, breakfasts, filling lunches and ice-cream sundaes.

Pizzería Topi (☎ 262 1180; Malecón de Manta; mains $3-6; ✧ noon-1am) Serves spicy Italian sausage pizzas till the wee hours.

If you're in the mood to stroll for your supper, consider the following options. In Tarqui, seafood *comedores* line the east end of the beach along Malecón de Tarqui. Behind them are several restaurants. Playa Murciélago has numerous cafés, front and center to enjoy beach action from beach-volleyball to beauty contests. The Hotel Oro Verde complex includes an American-style delicatessen and sushi restaurant.

Drinking & Entertainment

At night, downtown is deserted for the more fashionable karaoke, bar and *discoteca* neighborhood further south. Take a taxi to the intersection of Flavio Reyes and Calle 20, uphill from Playa Murciélago, and check out the options. Since many fashionable discos open and close in a drum beat, ask around for the latest hot spots. Don't bother going early in the week or before 11pm.

Tantra (☎ 261 3727; Av Flavio Reyes & Calle 20) Packs on the weekend with stilettoed salsa dancers and merengue mavens.

Madera Fina (☎ 262 6573; Av Flavio Reyes) Another long-time favorite featuring salsa, reggae and tropical rhythms.

Krug (Av Flavio Reyes; ✧ 4pm-late) An amenable bar with both a relaxed and welcoming atmosphere.

Getting There & Away

AIR

Located on the Manta waterfront, past the open-air theater, is the **TAME office** (☎ 262 2006; Malecón de Manta). TAME has daily 30-minute flights to/from Quito ($45 one way). Monday through Saturday flights leave Quito at 7am and return at 8am from Manta, Friday and Sunday flights leave Quito at 7:15pm and return at 8:15pm from Manta. **Icaro** (☎ 262 7327; www.icaro.com.ec; Hotel Oro Verde tower) has a couple flights per day to Quito. You can buy tickets at the airport on the morning of the flight, but the planes are full on weekends and vacations.

The **airport** (☎ 262 1580) is some 3km east of Tarqui, and a taxi costs about $1.

BUS

Most buses depart from the central bus terminal in front of the fishing-boat harbor in Manta. Buses to nearby Manabí towns and villages such as Montecristi ($0.30, 15 minutes) also leave from the terminal.

Trans Crucita goes hourly to Crucita ($1.50, 1½ hours). Reales Tamarindo has frequent departures to Portoviejo ($0.75, 40

1500 YEARS OF SEAFARING

Is it possible that something as simple and worthless as a shell moved an entire culture toward trade and exploration? The desire for shells, pottery and gold drove the Manteño to become world-renowned navigators and seamen. They set out in rudimentary vessels made of balsa trunks and, guided by the Southern Cross, arrived as far as the modern day Chile and Mexico. In those ancient times the settlement where Manta now sits was called Jocay, which, long before the Spanish 'founded' it in 1535, was a regional capital of sea exploration, trade and fishing.

Locals can pick out a fisherman in a crowd. Crow's feet ring his eyes, his back is thick as a hull, and his hands are split and swollen. Numbering around 2000, the modern-day incarnation of the Manta fisherman straddles modernity and tradition. He goes to sea in three-day stints, in three-man boats supplied with only canned goods, water and the occasional orange. He uses fiberglass boats with an outboard motor or traditional wooden *bongos*. But before embarking he visits the church altar and asks his family's ancestral patron saint to provide him with safe passage. He knows the sea like a shopper does a grocery store and has memorized the aisles for shark, swordfish, octopus, crab, whitefish, sea bass, dorado and squid among others.

In spite of fishing's new expediency, the Manteño remembers his traditions. On the feast days of Saint Peter and Paul, nautical processions with the saints' images are launched to sea. According to local historian José Elías Sánchez, this is a time for the fisherman to give thanks and ask, not for safety or prosperity, but simply for peace. A raging fiesta, presided over by a queen, breaks out only after a formal visit to church. These shindigs are not cheap – they set a fisherman back between $10,000 and $15,000 dollars, but each is obligated to host at least one in his career to retain his respect in the community.

The artisan fisherman, hard pressed to compete with commercial fishing fleets, survives day by day, with neither social security nor a sure-fire catch. 'There is progress,' Sánchez points out, 'the son of the fisherman finished high school and today his grandson is a doctor. AND, you better believe, a damn good fisherman.'

minutes), Jipijapa ($1, one hour), Montañita ($5, 3½ hours), La Libertad ($6, five hours) and Quevedo ($5, four hours). Coactur goes to Pedernales ($4.60, seven hours) and Canoa ($4, 3½ to four hours). Transportes Manglaralto goes hourly to Puerto López ($2.50, 2½ hours) and Manglaralto ($6, 4½ hours).

Reina del Camino and Flota Imbabura have hourly departures to Guayaquil ($5, four hours) and Quito ($8.50, eight hours) as well as several departures for Esmeraldas ($10, 10 hours) and Ambato ($7, 10 hours).

If you want to avoid the terminal altogether, **Panamericana** (☎ 262 5898; Av Cuatro & Calle 12) has *ejecutivo* buses to Quito at 9pm and 9:45pm.

CAR

You can rent cars through **Localiza** (☎ 262 2434; cnr Flavio Reyes & Av 21) and **Budget** (☎ 262 9919; Malecón de Manta & Calle 16).

MONTECRISTI
☎ 05

Montecristi produces the finest straw hat on the planet, even if it is mistakenly la-

beled as the panama hat; see the boxed text, p206. Ask for yours as a *sombrero de paja toquilla* (hats made of *paja toquilla*, a fine, fibrous straw endemic to this region). Hat stores line the road leading into town and the plaza, but most of their wares are cheap and loosely woven. Proper *super-fino* (the finest, tightest weave of all) is available at the shop and home of **José Chávez Franco** (☎ 260 6343; stelios@manta.telconet.net; Rocafuerte 386), between Eloy Alfaro and 10 de Agosto, behind the church. Here you can snatch up high-quality hats for under $100, but check them closely. None are blocked or banded but they're cheaper than just about anywhere else in the world. If you shop around you'll find other good shops which carry local wickerwork and basketry as well.

Montecristi was founded around 1628 when Manteños fled inland to avoid the frequent plundering by pirates. The town's many unrestored colonial houses give the village a rather tumbledown and ghostly atmosphere. The main plaza has a beautiful church dating back to the early part of the last century. It contains a statue of the

Virgin (to which miracles have been attributed) and is worth a visit. In the plaza is a statue of Eloy Alfaro, who was born in Montecristi and was president of Ecuador at the beginning of the 20th century. His tomb is in the town hall by the plaza.

Montecristi can be reached during the day by frequent buses ($0.20, 15 minutes) from the bus terminal in Manta.

JIPIJAPA
☎ 05

This hill city is surrounded by burned fields, set among the gnarled, spooky ceibas. Pronounced 'Hipihapa,' it is an important agricultural center, especially busy on Sun-

days when market stands hawk fish and vegetables. You can buy *paja toquilla* hats here. Signs outside many stores read 'Compro Café' (Coffee Bought Here) but you'd be hard pressed to find a decent cup because it's bought, not sold. The bus terminal on the outskirts facilitates fast onward travel. A few basic hotels are available.

From the terminal, buses to Portoviejo, Manta and Puerto López leave frequently; fares are about $1. Buses to Guayaquil and Quito ($9, 10 hours) leave several times a day. Vendors board the buses with baskets of sticky *pan almodón*, delicious gooey buns baked with yuca root. It's worth buying a hot handful for the journey.

The South Coast

THE SOUTH COAST

While some would sum up the south coast in two words – sun and surf – this region can't be so easily pigeonholed. Stretching all the way from Puerto López in the north to the Peruvian border in the south, it undoubtedly does include a long, sandy coastline. This draws and sucks in a motley crew of international travelers, who head mostly to mellow hangouts like Montañita and around the Parque Nacional Machalilla, while the resorts further south on the Santa Elena peninsula serve more as weekend and holiday spots for wealthy *Guayacos*. During the off season, some of the coastal resorts feel like ghost towns – with the only thing missing a piece of scrub brush blowing in the wind.

But the south coast also includes Guayaquil: Ecuador's largest city, its commercial and business capital and, more importantly for travelers, an emerging city that is just beginning to come into its own. The rejuvenated waterfront, a far cry from the old Malecón of concrete and shady characters, is more like Disneyworld these days, filled with children and families and couples succumbing to the universal romance of a bench, a river and piped-in salsa music.

South of Guayaquil is mostly banana country, with miles and miles of the green fruit – or 'oro verde' as it's referred to down here. Machala, the regional capital, while not especially appealing in its own right, has a good choice of accommodation and makes a convenient stopover for those heading to Peru or for exploring the nearby mountain towns of Zaruma and Piñas.

HIGHLIGHTS

- Witness the flipping and singing of the cirque de humpback whales off **Isla de las Plata** (p303)
- Lay low on the quiet sands of the beach towns of **Ruta del Sol** (p302)
- Tune out and take in the surfer scene at **Montañita** (p309)
- Wander along Guayaquil's riverfront public playground, the **Malecón** (p323)
- Cool off in the mountains in chilled little **Zaruma** (p343)

Isla de la Plata
★

★ Ruta del Sol
★ Montañita

the Malecón, Guayaquil
★

Zaruma
★

■ AVERAGE TEMPERATURE IN GUAYAQUIL: 26°C (79°F)   ■ RAINIEST MONTH IN GUAYAQUIL: MARCH

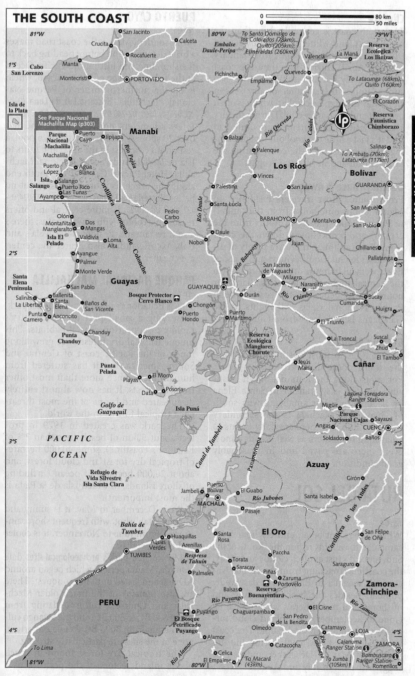

THE SOUTH COAST

THE SOUTH COAST

Climate

The south coast is generally drier than the north coast, and winter or the rainy season (this gets confusing) lasts only from January through April. During this time the coast is oppressively hot and humid, but it's also sunny, unlike the summer or dry season from May through December, which is often overcast and pleasantly cool. During the dry season, visitors are often disappointed to find it's just a little too cool out for sunbathing. Ecuadorians visit the coast during the rainy season and in July and August.

Getting There & Away

From Quito, most travelers head first to Manta (about nine hours from the capital) or Puerto López (nearly 11 hours from the capital) and work slowly down the coast from there (although there are plenty of direct buses to Guayaquil). Guayaquil is about five spectacular hours from Guaranda (in the central highlands) and less than four hours from Cuenca via the road through Parque Nacional Cajas. All flights to the Galápagos Islands leave from Guayaquil.

Getting Around

You can get to most destinations around the south coast direct from Guayaquil. For spots along the Ruta del Sol, it's usually only one easy transfer in Santa Elena or La Libertad. For smaller towns south of Guayaquil, Machala is the secondary transport hub and there are daily flights to Guayaquil from there as well. Roads almost everywhere are paved and in reasonably good condition.

RUTA DEL SOL

☎ 04
While it may not be an entirely honest PR campaign to call this region the 'Route of the Sun,' since it's just as often cloudy and misty, the coastline stretching from the Parque Nacional Machalilla to Ballenita is deservedly popular. Besides the beaches, surfing and offshore coral reefs, there's whale-watching (June to September) and inland cloud forests with unique flora and fauna. The coast is often overcast and cool during the dry months of May to December and can be soggy with mist in July and August.

PUERTO CAYO
☎ 05
From south of Manta, the coast road makes a brief detour inland before heading back to the shoreline and hitting the Pacific Ocean at the fishing village of Puerto Cayo, which is on the northern border of Parque Nacional Machalilla. **Hostería Luz de Luna** (Quito ☎ 02-240 0563, 02-240 0562; r per person $25; 🏊) is a few kilometers north of town, and has over 20 spotless cabins with baths, a pool, a restaurant (the best in the area) and tours to Isla de la Plata and Parque Nacional Machalilla. Hotel Puerto Cayo, at the south end along the beach, is more expensive but no better. **Hostería Los Frailes** (Jipijapa ☎ 261 6014, 09-127 2012; s/d $16/25) is more central and offers reasonable rooms with private baths; there's also a restaurant. Residencial Zavala's and Cabañas Alejandra, also nearer the center, are cheaper.

PARQUE NACIONAL MACHALILLA
☎ 05
This is Ecuador's only coastal national park, preserving a small part of the country's rapidly disappearing coastal habitats. This unique tropical dry forest once grew along much of the Pacific coast of Central and South America, but it has suffered from human interference more than most other tropical forests. It has now almost entirely disappeared and is one of the most threatened tropical forests in the world.

The park was created in 1979 to protect about 50km of beach (less than 2% of Ecuador's coastline), some 40,000 hectares of tropical dry forest and cloud forest, and about 20,000 hectares of ocean (including offshore islands, of which Isla de la Plata is the most important).

From December to May, it is sunny and uncomfortably hot, with frequent short rainstorms. From June to November, it is cooler and often overcast.

Most of the park's **archaeological sites** date from the Manta period, which began around AD 500 and lasted until the conquest. There are also remains of the much older Machalilla and Chorrera cultures, dating from about 800 BC to 500 BC, and the Salango culture dating from 3000 BC. While important, none of the sites are particularly striking.

The tropical dry forest found in much of the inland sectors of the park forms a strange and wonderful landscape of characteristically bottle-shaped trees with small crowns and heavy spines – a protection against herbivores. In the upper reaches of the park, humid cloud forest is encountered. Some of the most common species include the *leguminous algarrobo*, which has green bark and is able to photosynthesize even when it loses its leaves. The kapok (or ceiba) tree has fruits that yield a fiber that floats and doesn't get waterlogged. Before the advent of modern synthetics it was used in life jackets. Fig, laurel and palo santo trees are also commonly seen. Tall, spindly candelabra cacti are abundant on the hillsides, as is prickly pear.

Within this strange-looking forest, a variety of bird and animal life is found. Well over 200 species of birds have been recorded, including a range of coastal parrots, parrotlets and parakeets, as well seabirds such as frigatebirds, pelicans and boobies – some of which nest in the offshore islands. Other animals include deer, squirrels, howler monkeys, anteaters and a variety of lizards, snakes and iguanas.

Information

The **park headquarters** (☎ 260 4170; ☒ 8am-5pm Mon-Fri) and the small **museum** (admission free; ☒ 8am-5pm) share a building in Puerto López. The park-entrance fee is $20 and covers any or all sectors of the park (including the islands) and is valid for five days. If you plan to visit *only* Isla de la Plata, the fee is $15; the mainland-only fee is $12. The fee is charged in all sectors of the park, so carry your ticket.

Sights & Activities
ISLA DE LA PLATA

If Sir Francis Drake buried treasure here, only the blue-footed boobies and frigates would know it. Of course, their abundant shiny glops of guano also may have inspired the name 'Silver Island.' The island has many nesting colonies of seabirds – red-footed boobies and pelicans have also been frequently recorded, as well as a variety of gulls, terns and petrels. Albatrosses can be seen from April to October, dolphins pass by and there's year-round snorkeling in the coral reefs around the island.

THE SOUTH COAST

PARQUE NACIONAL MACHALILLA

The attraction of the island itself is dwarfed by the awesome sight of mating **humpback whales**, which abound in these waters between mid-June and early October (especially July and August). Tour boats approach to observe the spectacle, which biologists fear will negatively affect mating patterns. Etiquette of boats has been hotly debated and today there are strict guidelines in place for observance.

The island has a steep climb from the boat landing to two loop hikes: the 3.5km **Sendero Machete** and the 5km **Sendero Punta Escaleras**. Either way, the trail is rough, and good footwear is advised. There's absolutely no shade so come prepared.

The only way to enjoy this 'poor person's Galápagos' is by taking a guided boat tour from Puerto López (see opposite).

LOS FRAILES BEACH

About 10km north of Puerto López, this gorgeous virgin beach is an excellent spot for a dip (although watch the undertow). Just before the town of Machalilla, a ranger station admits you to a dirt road going 3km to the coast. Hikers can take a 4km trail through the coastal forest, but leave your camera and valuables behind as there have been thefts. There are two lookouts – keep your eye out for blue-footed boobies.

AGUA BLANCA

Agua Blanca is the territory of an indigenous community and there is a $3 charge simply to use the roads, but this fee also covers the museum and museum guiding. You'll find the park entrance about 5.5km north of Puerto López on the right side of the road. A dirt road leads through tropical dry forest to the village of Agua Blanca, 6km from the entrance. The village has an **archaeological museum** (admission free with community pass; ⏲ 8am-6pm) with funeral urns, artifacts and snakes. The Manta site is about a half-hour walk away and visitors must go guided. Only the bases of the buildings can be seen, but there are plans to restore some of the approximately 400 buildings excavated at the site, which is thought to have been an important political capital of the Manta people.

You can finish your visit with a soak in the nearby **sulphur pool**. The water is hot and you can slather the therapeutic mud on your skin and bake in the sun. This area gets merciless sun, so bring hats and sunscreen.

SAN SEBASTIÁN & JULCUY

This excellent four-hour hike or horseback ride lies to the southeast of Agua Blanca. The trail ascends a transition zone to humid

---

HUMPBACK HIGHLIGHTS AND HARDSHIPS

The humpback whale has one of the most arduous yet predictable travel itineraries around. Each year a group of these mammals undertakes one of the longest migrations on earth. The swim from summer feeding grounds in Antarctica to breeding and birthing grounds at the equator takes about five weeks. Once they arrive it's all play – with a purpose, that is. In the quest to breed, males the size of semi trucks romance their sweethearts with blows, acrobatics and songs that amount to one of nature's most phenomenal spectacles.

Visitors to Parque Nacional Machalilla get a front row seat at this mammalian peep show. Puerto López is considered the epicenter of whale breeding grounds, with an annual population of around 400, though whales can be seen from Súa to Salinas from June to September. The humpback preference for coastal waters means their antics are that much easier to follow. So much so that it has created a sticky issue.

In the glee of the chase, etiquette has sometimes been brushed aside. Boats jockeying to get the best views have encircled and crowded whales: harassing behavior that scientists think may scare them off in the long run. Education is altering this practice. New strict rules for observation mandate that observers keep a distance of 100m, no more than four or five boats should approach one whale, and all must remain off to one side, giving the whale an exit.

A much bigger threat is whaling, which, believe it or not, is coming back. A Japanese government proposal to dramatically increase the practice would endanger this population of humpbacks. In spite of a worldwide ban, several countries still participate in whaling. Those interested in humpbacks can visit the Pacific Whale Foundation website (www.pacificwhale.org) or Hostería Mandala in Puerto López (p306), where a whale museum is in the works.

remnant cloud forest at San Sebastián, about 600m above sea level. Horses ($5 per person) can be hired if you don't want to hike the 20km round-trip, and guides ($20) are mandatory. Contract one in Agua Blanca for either the archaeological site or San Sebastián. It's best to stay overnight, but camping or staying with local people are the only accommodations.

Another option is to continue through Agua Blanca up the Río Julcuy valley to the northeast. From Agua Blanca, it is a six- to seven-hour hike through the park, coming out at the village of Julcuy, just beyond the park boundary. From Julcuy, it's about another three hours to the main Jipijapa–Guayaquil road. Four-wheel drives may be able to pass this road in good weather, but it is mainly a horse trail.

Sleeping

There's camping in the park, but check with park authorities about the availability of water – particularly during the May-to-December dry season. Inquire about homestays in the communities of San Sebastián and Agua Blanca. Local tour agencies may also be able to make arrangements.

Getting There & Away

At least every hour, buses run up and down the coast between Puerto López and Jipijapa. You should have no difficulty, therefore, in getting a bus to drop you off at the park entrance or in finding one to pick you up when you are ready to leave.

Trucks occasionally go from the main road to Agua Blanca and back. However, you'll probably have to walk or hire a taxi in Puerto López to get to Agua Blanca.

You can arrange boat trips to Isla de la Plata through the tour agencies in Puerto López (see right).

PUERTO LÓPEZ
☎ 05 / pop 7720

This pretty seaside village, with its dusty streets and chipped blue boats bobbing in the bay, is fast becoming a hub for travelers hot to explore Parque Nacional Machalilla, whale-watch, swim and sunbathe. With cheap and cheerful hotels, a smattering of expats, slow smiles, happy cafés and safe streets, it is just about an obligatory stop on any coastal pilgrimage.

Of course, the 'other' Puerto López is the fishing village, which is best witnessed and understood in the wee morning hours when fishermen gut their catch on the beach and the air teems with wheeling frigatebirds and vultures diving at the scraps.

Information

The post office and police station are on the same block as Pacifictel telephone center, and there's a small medical clinic north of town.

Banco de Pichincha (cnr Machalilla & General Córdova) Changes travelers checks and has an ATM.
Muyuyo Internet (General Córdova; per hr $2; ☯ 8am-11pm)
Pacifictel (cnr Machalilla & Eloy Alfaro) Near the market.

Tours

Numerous agencies offer tours to Isla de la Plata and/or the mainland part of the park. Some are licensed, some aren't.

From June through September, whale-watching tours combined with visits to Isla de la Plata are popular. During both July and August, good whale-sightings are pretty much guaranteed, and in June and September sightings may be brief, distant or just of single animals. On Isla de La Plata groups have lunch, a guided hike and a brief opportunity to snorkel. The trip to the island takes well over an hour going flat out, and can be rough, so take motion-sickness medication if necessary, and bring a rain jacket for the wind and spray.

Licensed companies charge a standard price ($35) plus the park-entry fee ($15 to $20). They all have boats with two outboard engines (both are used for speed, but the boat can return on one if the other breaks down), and are equipped with life jackets, radios and basic toilet facilities. These agencies are found along General Córdova and Malecón Julio Izurieta. They offer similar services and take turns, so just ask in any agency.

On the Malecón, you'll be approached by folks offering much cheaper whale-watching expeditions on fishing boats. It skips the park fee by not visiting the island. Be wary of these trips. These slower, smaller boats are an invitation to seasickness. Worse, they may lack a radio, spare engine, bathroom or sufficient life jackets. Lastly, if you book on the street and things go awry, there will be no one to complain to.

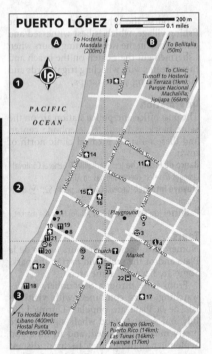

INFORMATION
Banco del Pichincha...(see 23)
Machalilla Tours...**1** A2
Muyuyo Internet...**2** A3
Pacifictel...**3** B2
Parque Nacional Machalilla Headquarters &
    Museum...**4** B3
Police Station...**5** B2
Post Office...**6** A3

SIGHTS & ACTIVITIES
Exploramar..**7** A2
Mantaraya...**8** A2

SLEEPING
Hostal Flipper..**9** A3
Hostal Isla Los Islotes.......................................**10** A2
Hostal Maxima..**11** A3
Hostal Turismar...**12** A3
Hostería Itapoá..**13** B1
Hotel & Cabañas Pacífico.................................**14** A2
Residencial Paola..**15** A2
Sol Inn...**16** A2
Villa Colombia...**17** B3

EATING
Café Ballena/The Whale Café..........................**18** A3
Mayflower...(see 21)
Patacón Pisa'o..**19** A2
Picantería Rey Hojas...**20** A3
Restaurant Carmita...**21** A2

TRANSPORT
Reina del Camino..**22** B3
Taxis..(see 23)
Transportes Carlos A Aray & Other Buses............**23** B3

Outside of the whale-watching season, similar tours to the island are offered to see birds and sea lions, and dolphins may well be spotted. Most of the operators will also arrange a variety of other local trips, such as camping and/or horse riding in the Agua Blanca/San Sebastián areas and visits to local beaches. It is usually cheaper to make your own way to Agua Blanca. The $3 entry to the area includes museum guide and visit.

Exploramar (Malecón), **Machalilla Tours** (☎ 230 0206; Malecón) and **Mantaraya** (☎ 230 0233; General Córdova at Juan Montalvo) offer scuba-diving trips to people with certification; both have received good reports, and all equipment is provided. Exploramar also offers PADI (Professional Association of Diving Instructors) dive courses.

Sleeping

Accommodations in Puerto López are practically guaranteed to have a hammock but not hot water. Still, there's a great selection of budget hotels and even the simplest ones are usually spanking clean. Reserve ahead

during the busy whale-watching season, and during the coastal high-season from January to April.

Hostería Mandala (☎ /fax 230 0181, 09-950 0880; s/d/tr cabin $15/24/36) A feat of the imagination, this beautiful beachfront hostel has a handful of ecologically minded cabins in its labyrinthine gardens. Fragrant hibiscus, orchids and poinsettias are tucked behind the enormous entry gates. The lodge has a bar, game room, a quirky instrument collection and multilingual library. The restaurant serves delectable breakfasts with homemade bread, as well as excellent Italian and local seafood. It's a 10-minute walk north on the beach, or ask your bus driver for the roadside entrance. Owners are a friendly Italian/Swiss couple passionately dedicated to whale conservation. Look for the 'Extinction is Forever' whale museum they are building next door.

Sol Inn (☎ 230 0248; hostal_solinn@hotmail.com; Juan Montalvo near Eloy Alfaro; r per person with shared/private bathroom $5/6) Rooms are funky and colorful in this mellow *hostal* owned by outgoing ex-backpackers. The two-story bamboo house has an outdoor kitchen and living area, hammocks strewn about and a book exchange. English and French are spoken.

Hostería Itapoá (☎ 09-984 3042, in Quito 02-255 1569; Abdón Calderón; cabañas per person $7.50) An affordable retreat of whitewashed cabañas set around a blooming garden bordered by hammocks, this hospitable Brazilian/Ecuadorian place offers screened, clean rooms and a small path leading directly to the beach. Breakfast is included but other meals are available on request. The owners also run a small farm-*hostal* in Puerto Quito.

Hostal Flipper (☎ 230 0221; General Córdova at Rocafuerte; r per person $6) An immaculate new *hostal*, it has terracotta walls and airy rooms, plus an attached restaurant.

Hostería La Terraza (☎ 260 4235; s/d $14/22) Perched on an arid hill overlooking the town and the broad Pacific, this whole place has a 'do not disturb' feel. Cabins are quaint and tidy, each with a piping-hot shower, and a porch with a hammock. Peter, the German owner (who speaks English too) might even loan out a beat-up Panama hat for hiking. Proper breakfasts on the tiled patio are available and dinners can be arranged. Call to be picked up or hike the 1km from town.

Hostal Monte Libano (☎ 230 0231; Malecón; r per person $5-6) Rooms are not for claustrophobes, but the place is nonetheless clean and friendly. The beachfront property and 2nd-floor terrace edge up the desirability of this quiet spot on the southern end of the Malecón.

Villa Colombia (☎ 230 0105; hostalvillacolombia@ hotmail.com; off General Córdova; r per person $6) Families and budget travelers find this out-of-the fray *hostal* quiet and relaxing. It's several blocks from the beach and offers simple rooms with hot water, kitchen and laundry facilities.

Hostal Isla Los Islotes (☎ 260 4108; hostallos islotes@hotmail.com; Malecón at General Córdova; r per person $10) A good choice. Comfortable, un-adorned modern rooms all have hot water and fan. If you want a discount you'll have to forgo the ocean views. Breakfast on the terrace is included.

Hotel & Cabañas Pacífico (☎ 230 0147; hpacific@ manta.ecua.net.ec; Lascano at Malecón; s/d with fan $15/20, with air-con $30/40; 🏊) Quality and pricing varies with rooms, which are attractive but not

extraordinary. The centerpiece is the lovely backyard pool. In high season this can be a noisy spot.

Hostal Punta Piedrero (☎ 230 0013; puntapiedre ro@hispavista.com; Malecón; r per person $8) Quiet solace and sea access are the pluses of this last spot on the beach, south of town. The new tiled rooms have bunks and singles with gnarled wood bed frames and stark white walls. Has hot water.

Hostal Maxima (☎ 09-953 4282; www.hotelmaxima .net; Gonzáles Suarez at Machalilla; r per person with shared/ private bathroom $5/6) A colorful three-story tower will guide you across town to this clean no-frills hostel run by a guy from Jersey.

If you want nothing more than a cheap place to crash the night, try the very basic beachfront **Hostal Turismar** (☎ 260 4114; General Córdova; r per person $5) or **Residencial Paola** (☎ 260 4162; Juan Montalvo; r per person with shared/private bath $2/3).

Eating
Patacon Pisa'o (☎ 09-127 4206; General Córdova; mains $3) Forget seafood – this tiny Colombian joint serves fantastic *arepas* (maize pancakes) with shredded beef, chicken or beans as well as its whopping namesake. That and a steaming cup of java make this friendly little café the best new addition to the town.

Bellitalia (🕑 from 6pm; Juan Montalvo s/n) This candle-lit little number offers authentic Italian food. The spaghetti *di mare* is divine, the wine delicious and the tiramisu tops it all off nicely. You'll love the garden ambience. This place has received rave reviews from local cognoscentie.

Café Ballena/The Whale Café (Malecón; mains $2-6; 🕑 8am-9pm, low-season hr variable) Walk down toward the fishing fleets to find this laid-back American café. High season means you might have to wait for your morning latte and banana pancakes. The dinner menu includes a tasty stir-fry choc full of veggies, as well as pastas and pizza. Don't skip dessert – homemade apple pie and rich chocolate cake await.

Along the Malecón you will find traditional seafood restaurants with patio dining. **Restaurant Carmita** (☎ 260 4149; mains $2-3; 🕑 8am-11pm) is the best known of the bunch, but others, including Picantería Rey Hojas and Mayflower, serve up comparable fresh fare.

Getting There & Away

In recent years armed robberies have been a problem on long-distance buses. **Reina de Camino** (☎ 230 0207; General Córdova) has the fastest, most secure service to Quito with a new *ejecutivo* (first class) bus at 8:15am and 8pm ($12, 11 hours). Passengers can get off at Santo Domingo de los Colorados, but cannot get on the bus, so it's a faster service. It doesn't stop for dinner either. Show up 20 minutes early for security checks.

Transportes Carlos A Aray (☎ 230 0178; cnr General Córdova & Machalilla) has direct buses to Quito ($10, 11 hours) at 5am, 9am and 7pm. Alternatively, you can catch the bus to Portoviejo or Manta to make connections.

Several other companies between Jipijapa and La Libertad stop at the corner of General Córdova and Machalilla at least every hour during daylight hours. These buses will drop you off at any point you want along the coast, including the surfing town of Montañita ($2.50, one hour). There are also buses to and from Santa Elena (on the south coast) about every hour.

Getting Around

The whole town is walkable and secure, but if you're feeling sluggish, Ecotaxi tricycles can be found on the Malecón or near the buses. The **Associacion de Camioneros** (☎ 230 0127) has cars and pickups in front of the church. The 24-hour service goes to Agua Blanca for $10 roundtrip and to Los Frailes and Agua Blanca for $15. Another reliable driver is **Tito Hidalgo** (☎ 09-951 4182).

SALANGO
☎ 04

This little fishing town 6km south of Puerto López is a lazy place to wander. You can hire fishing boats to buzz the 2km out to **Isla Salango**, a haven for bird life and scuba diving. In the town itself take a peek in the small archaeological **Museo Salango** (☎ /fax 290 1195, 290 1208; admission $1.50; ☽ 9am-5pm Wed-Sun). Many signs are in English, and the gift shop offers crafts by local artisans.

One of the best seafood restaurants around is **El Delfín Mágico** (☎ 278 0291; Parque Central; mains $3-8; ☽ 10am-7pm). Order your favorite seafood in their divine peanut or garlic sauces. *Spondylus* (a spiny, red oyster) is a local specialty but also endangered. One more on a plate is one less in the sea.

You can avoid the eternal wait for your order by visiting the museum. **El Pelicano** (☎ 278 3752; ☽ 8am-8pm), near the church, is another sure bet.

A fun spot 2km south of Salango is the **Hostería Piqueros Patas Azules** (☎ 278 0279; s/d from $25/35) where the cabins perched on a lip of land over the sea are decent, if a bit garish. With the surf rippin', landlubbers can opt for volleyball or soccer on the beach. Although the small archaeological museum is in the throes of disrepair, there's a good restaurant and medicinal mudbaths to wallow in. The hotel also offers reputable whale-watching tours.

PUERTO RICO
☎ 04

About 8km south of Salango, the road passes through the village of Puerto Rico, whose claim to fame is the **Hostería Alandaluz** (☎ 278 0690, Quito ☎ 02-254 3042; www.andaluzhosteria.com; camping $4, r per person $14-33), one of Ecuador's very first self-sustaining, low-impact resorts. Located south of the village, this hotel has inviting and innovative interiors of wood, bamboo and stone set off with a zing of lusty color. Local, fast-growing, easily replenishable materials are used in construction. The lavatories are self-composting, and everything that can be recycled is. A variety of designs and locations (seaside or across the highway) result in prices and tastes for all. When hunger strikes, the dining room serves excellent food bent toward seafood and vegetarian options and there's a bar as well. Swimmers should proceed with caution as there are strong currents here.

LAS TUNAS
☎ 04

This is another wide sweep of sand just begging for you and your beach blanket. You'll know you've arrived when you spot **La Barquita** (☎ 278 0051, 278 0683; www.labarquita-ec.com; dm/d/tr $10/28/36), a beautiful wooden boat-shaped hotel. If you can't stay, at least have a drink in the cool bar with fine views of surf off stern. Rustic ambience pervades the surrounding thatched wooden cabins.

The best new find is **Hosteria La Perla** (☎ 278 0701; www.proyectospondylus.org; r per person in low/high season incl breakfast $15/20), a romantic beach house weathered by sun and sand. Rooms are dark wood with bright-blue doors. The common area is cozied up with burgundy antiques and views of the tumbling surf. Sauna and massage are available. The owner, Mónica Fabara, is a marine biologist and highly regarded local guide.

The nearby **Tsafiki Hosteria** (☎ 278 0556; s/d cabañas $25/45) has a stable of *Paso Peruano* show horses and others available for riding, while surfboards and body boards can be rented. Just a few immaculate thatched cabins decorated in sea stars, this place is made for peace and quiet.

AYAMPE

☎ 04

'Unwind' is the name of the game on this wide flap of sand 17km south of Puerto López. The Río Ayampe, a fine source of freshwater shrimp, weaves down from deliciously green hills into the ocean, irrigating patches of watermelon, melon and papaya groves. Putter the beach and make sandcastles or hit the wooded hills – you'll find everything from horseback riding to surfing to better napping in this welcoming and incorrigibly relaxed atmosphere.

The somewhat earthy and abandoned feel of **Finca Punta Ayampe** (☎ 278 0616; www.fincapuntaayampe.com; r/cabaña per person $8/12) isn't for everyone, but some will love this wooded hideout. The high-ceilinged, two-bedroom cabañas built of *caña de guadúa* (a local bamboo species) peer out to sea. The main lodge has basic rooms and a comfy, lived-in common area. Surfing, scuba-diving, birdwatching and other tours can be arranged. Prices rise during the high season.

Almare (☎ 278 0611/12; www.hotelalmare.net; r per person low/high season $10/15; mains $5-7), a lovely house by the sea, flaunts a big cedar deck, central chimney and patio dining room. Screened-in rooms have modern touches of ambient lighting, large tubs and hot water. A sandy path to the beach tops off this great-value place.

Ideal for families, **Cabañas La Tortuga** (☎ 278 0613, 09-995 6015; s/d/tr $15/24/30) is a beachfront retreat that offers plenty of diversions, from movies, table tennis and billiards to kayaking and walks on the beach. Five can bunk in the tidy thatched brick cabins with firm beds, mosquito nets and hot showers. There's also a restaurant, bar and satellite TV.

Cabañas de la Iguana (☎ 278 0605; www.ayampeiguana.com; r per person with shared/private bathroom

SAVING PRIVATE CHOCOLATE

Ecuador was once one of the world's largest producers of high-quality cocoa. In the early part of the last century at the industry's high point there were 80 million cocoa trees growing in the country's coastal region. Prized because of the hint of bananas and other tropical fruit that grew alongside it, Ecuador's cocoa farms were once everywhere along the coast where the rain forests provided shade. A combination of more aggressive industries in other countries, plant diseases and higher-yield hybrids shrank the industry in Ecuador to a bon-bon of its former Mars Bar self. Since 1997 the Conservacion y Desarollo, an Ecuadorian non-profit organization, has worked to help rescue the country's cocoa industry by reviving varieties on the edge of extinction or by introducing new hardier and tastier ones. Small producers have been organized into cooperatives, pooled their resources, equipment and expertise, and are beginning to again satisfy sweet tooths everywhere.

$7/8) is a modest spread of four bright rooms with snug, well-dressed beds and hot water. The hosts are a friendly husband-and-wife team with a back-to-nature vibe. Home-cooked meals including organic salads, Spanish lessons ($5 per hour) and day hikes ($5 per person) are available. Prices surge on holidays.

MONTAÑITA

☎ 04

From the baggy shorts to the friendly, sleepy demeanor, surfer-dude culture is universal. The good surf at the beach here insures a steady stream of travelers, some you'll see settling up their bills after weeks and months, or taking up trades like hair braiding and wristband weaving. The accompanying Rasta vibe and laid-back ethos means the end of the road for some. Most of the buildings lining one of the several dirt streets in town house a restaurant on the ground floor and either residences or rooms for rent above.

The beach break is rideable most of the year – though it's best from December to May – but beginners should keep in mind that waves can get big and riptides are

THE SOUTH COAST

common. Real surfers ride the wave at the north end of the beach at *la punta* (the point), a right that can reach 2m to 3m on good swells. An international surf competition is usually held around Carnaval.

A few kilometers further north from Montañita is the coastal village of **Olón**, which has a long though not especially attractive beach and a couple of inexpensive hotels. Seven kilometers north of Olón, the province of Guayas ends and Manabí begins.

Information

Banco de Guayaquil has an ATM in front of the Hotel Montañita. There are two cyber-cafés in town, **Montañita Express** (⊗ 8am-midnight) and the **Cyber Hostal Mona Loa** (⊗ 8am-midnight). **Fuzzy Laundry** (Papaya Hostal) charges $1.30 per kilogram.

Activities

Most *hostals* can arrange surfboard rentals ($4 per hour) and lessons ($12 for two hours), as does **Balsa Custom Surfboards** (☎ 757 2450; www.balsanova.uk.com). Wetsuits and body boards are also available.

Sleeping

Noise is an issue and earplugs are recommended at many of the hotels in town during the high season. The partying is more subdued at other times of the year, but if you're interested in peace and quiet it makes sense to check out the places just outside of town.

Unless specified, the prices quoted here are for the high season (mid-December through April). Almost all hotels cut their rates significantly for the rest of the year and discounts are available for extended stays.

The Calle Principal is the main drag down to the beach. Most hotels in town are on the streets leading away from the Calle Principal. Most have mosquito nets, hot water and sea breezes for ventilation.

IN TOWN

Cabañas Pakaloro (☎ 290 1366; pakaloro69@hotmail .com; s/d $6/11) This beautifully crafted place stands out from the others, especially because of the attention to detail and loving care that its immaculate rooms and polished wood floors obviously receive. Each room has a small modern bathroom and a terrace with a hammock, with the only downside being that privacy is in short supply since there isn't much separating you from your neighbors.

Charo Hostal (☎ 290 1344; charo117@msn.com; r from $8) Though the faux brick and wood building lacks both charm and the rustic laid-back vibe of others in town, Charo is recommended for its beachfront location and clean, well-kept rooms. The top floor loft-like room with wood floors and modern bathroom has its own large balcony and you can fall asleep to the sounds of waves rather than reggae. During the high season it's potentially noisy since there is a bar on the premises.

Tiki Limbo Backpackers Hostel (☎ 254 0607; tikilimbo@hotmail.com; r from per person $5) As with any of the places on this road, noise can be an enemy of sleep, but the Tiki Limbo outdoes the others in terms of bright colors and large bamboo beds, which are nicer than its competitors. The fantastic 2nd-floor lounge area has stylish bamboo bar stools and comfy couches for hanging out (but no hammocks). There's a good vegetarian restaurant attached.

Papaya Hostel (☎ 09-911 6889; hostalpapaya@ yahoo.com; r from per person $5) Next door to the Tiki Limbo, the Papaya's rooms aren't quite as charming but each simple room does have its own hammock on the balcony, which is where you'll probably spend most of your time anyway.

El Centro del Mundo (☎ 278 2831; r per person with shared/private bathroom $5/6) A large three-story behemoth close to the beach, El Centro del Mundo wears its rustic simplicity proudly. The no-frills rooms are all wood, and the common toilet and showers are rather makeshift, but the small communal balconies face the ocean and there's a pool table. The dorm area is a loft with room for almost 20 mattresses. Hiking and horseback riding trips can be arranged here.

El Velero (☎ 290 1364; r $5) One of the first places you come to on the Calle Principal, this tall, narrow family run guesthouse has two rustic, all-timber rooms that sleep up to four. Each has a kitchenette and balcony.

OUT OF TOWN

All of these places are only a short walk from town, and all bar the Nativa Bambu Eco Lodge are located near or on the beach just to the north.

Nativa Bambu Eco Lodge (☎ 290 1293, 713 1478; www.nativabambu.com; cabañas $30) Perched on a hill overlooking the town on the other side of the highway from the beach, this lodge is a good choice if you're after privacy and quiet. Each of the charming wood, stone, bamboo and thatched-roof cottages has a porch with hammock providing bird's-eye views of the surf. The toilet and shower are strangely separated from the bedroom only by low stone partitions. It's owned by a friendly Ecuadorian couple who can arrange surfing, horseback riding, mountain biking and whale-watching tours.

La Casa del Sol (☎ 290 1302; www.casasol.com; r per person $4-10) Like a deceptively well-designed pair of Billabong shorts (comfortable and just the right fit), La Casa del Sol knows what surfers or wannabes want in accommodations – comfortable but not too luxurious; laid-back but welcoming to party types. The rooms are charming, done in stone and stucco, and the bar and restaurant are great spots to talk about the big one that got away. To find it, walk towards the point on the beach.

Paradise South (☎ 290 1185; www.paradisesouthec .com; r $10-20) Another good choice for those seeking silence, Paradise South is just north of the river on the way to the point. Set in a well-kept grassy lawn are several stone and thatched-roof cottages with spotless adobe-walled rooms with ceramic tiled floors and modern bathrooms. More expensive rooms have air-con and all have hammocks. There's a large grassy area with a volleyball court and pool table.

Hotel Baja Montañita (☎ 232 8498; s/d $25/35; ✂ ◆) At the far north end of the beach, the Baja is a large (though not particularly attractive) compound whose whitewashed buildings are topped with Mediterranean-style red-tile roofs. Rooms themselves are surprisingly basic and it can feel either lonely or secluded during the low season. It has a swimming pool, Jacuzzi and a restaurant (only open in the high season).

Eating

Almost every street side space has been converted into an informal restaurant. Spanish and English menus cater to foreigners' taste buds, serving everything from pizzas to empanadas and bubbling *cazuelas* (seafood stew). Those serving Ecuadorians are more likely to offer economical *almuerzos* (set lunches) and *meriendas* (set dinners). Many double as game rooms during the day and bars at night.

Cevicheria Lojanita (mains $3-7) A place frequented by locals as much by foreign tourists, Lojanita serves up every manner of seafood from ceviches (uncooked marinated seafood) to *cazuelas,* breaded fish and lobster omelettes.

Viejamar (mains $4) A mellow place on the main road – especially at night when the tables are lit by candles – Viejamar probably does the best empanadas in Montañita, with shrimp, chicken, cheese or vegetable fillings.

Café Hola Ola (mains $4) One of the more popular restaurants, Hola Ola has a cheap and filling breakfast ($2.50) and a large menu of grilled meats and seafood, plus a few Israeli-inspired dishes. There's two-for-one drinks in the early evening.

Karukera (mains $3) This small, charmingly decorated café across from the Papaya Hostal is good for people-watching. Excellent choices include the chicken crepes ($3) and shrimp with garlic ($5), while ice cream, cake and coffee drinks are served as well.

Tiburón Restaurant (mains $4) Another small spot as good for drinks as for the menu of pancakes, omelettes, empanadas, salads and ceviches. Also has tourist info about Puerto López and whale-watching.

Getting There & Away

CLP buses pass by Montañita on their way south to Guayaquil at 5am, 1pm and 5pm ($5, 3½ to four hours). These are more comfortable than other buses that stop past on their way to Santa Elena ($1.50, 1¼ hours), La Libertad or north to Puerto López ($1.50, one hour). These depart every 15 minutes or so.

DOS MANGAS

☎ 04

Most often visited as a side trip from Montañita a few kilometers away, the inland village of Dos Mangas is a starting point for walks or horseback rides further into the Cordillera Chongón de Colonche – coastal hills reaching an elevation of 834m and covered by tropical, humid forest. Tagua carvings and *paja toquilla* (toquilla straw) crafts can be purchased in the village.

Guides and horses can be hired at the Centro de Información Sendero Las Cascadas, a small kiosk in the village. The friendly guides speak Spanish only and will take you on a four- to five-hour hike through the forest to an elevation of 60m and to the 80m **waterfalls** (these dry up in the dry season). They charge $10 for up to three people and an extra $3 per person for horses, and lunch can be arranged in local homes. The park entrance fee is $1.

Trucks to Dos Mangas ($0.25, 15 minutes) leave the highway from Manglaralto every hour or so.

MANGLARALTO
☎ 04

If the surf was steady and strong, no doubt Manglaralto would look more like Montañita 5km to the north rather than a typical Ecuadorian coastal village. Several paved streets emanate from a town plaza and it's a nice walk along the beach to Montañita at low tide.

Hoping to attract the non-surf-oriented travelers from its neighbor, Manglaralto has developed some ecotourism ventures, community projects and volunteer opportunities. **Fundación Pro-Pueblo** (☎ 278 0231; www .propueblo.com) offers travelers the chance to visit remote coastal villages and stay overnight with local families for a nominal fee that also includes meals, guides and mules. The villages are usually an easy day's walk or horse ride from Manglaralto and each other. Overnight tours can be arranged for bird-watching and visiting remote waterfalls and other natural attractions.

Kamala Hostería (☎ 242 3754; www.kamalahos teria.com; dm per person $3, cabañas $25-$45) On the beach just north of town, friendly Kamala is a hodge-podge of jerry-rigged cabañas with mismatched parts owned by four backpackers. Nevertheless, it's popular with travelers seeking a low-key alternative to Montañita – except for its monthly full moon parties that draw in the crowds. They offer diving and PADI certification, kayak rental ($5 per hour), horseback riding ($15 per hour) and other trips. A restaurant/café/bar is on the grounds.

Sunset Hostel (☎ 244 0797; manglaralto_beach@ yahoo.com; s/d $8/15) Though it lacks charm or a beachfront location, the Sunset Hostel, located on a semi-paved street in the center of town, has several immaculate rooms with tile floors and modern bathrooms. There's a hammock in front of each room, though the view is decidedly uninspiring.

VALDIVIA TO BALLENITA

Most visitors pass through this coastal area dotted with fishing villages and high- and low-rise condo developments, vacation homes for the Guayaquil upper-class, on their way from Puerto López or Montañita to Guayaquil. The beaches en route are often immaculate stretches of sand, though the landscape inland is an uninspiring mix of dry scrub and cactus.

Valdivia, a village 7km south of Manglaralto, has a small **museum** (☎ 202 8035; adult/child $1/0.50; ⏲ 9am-5pm) displaying artifacts from the Valdivia period (around 3000 BC). About 3km south of Valdivia, you pass the fishing village of **Ayangue** and another 6km south the village of **Palmar**. The area can get crowded with day-trip visitors to the beaches during high-season weekends, but only Ayangue has a couple of small budget hotels.

On the outskirts of Ballenita, just north of Santa Elena, is **Farallón Dillon** (☎ 278 6643; ddillon@gu.pro.ec; s/d $24/38; 🏊), a whitewashed complex perched on a cliff with rooms, a nautical museum and a lookout point from which migrating whales can be seen from June to September.

SANTA ELENA PENINSULA
☎ 04

Combining industrial sprawl and the popular beachside resort of Salinas, the Santa Elena Peninsula is usually bypassed by foreign travelers on their way between Guayaquil and the Ruta del Sol. *Guayaquileños* pack the hotels and condominiums from mid-December through April and sport fishermen and international yachties stop here as well.

Getting There & Away

La Libertad is the center of bus services on the peninsula, but if you're bypassing Salinas it's easier to simply be let off in Santa Elena and make the transfer to another bus heading either north along the Ruta del Sol or east to Guayaquil.

To get to Guayaquil ($2, 2½ hours) you can take buses with either **Cooperativa Libertad Peninsular** (CLP; cnr 9 de Octubre & Guerro Barreiro) or **Cooperativa Intercantonal Costa Azul** (CICA; 9 de Octubre & Diagonal 2) opposite the Residencial Turis Palm in La Libertad. Buses from Guayaquil continue to Salinas and then return to Guayaquil via La Libertad.

Also in La Libertad, Transportes San Agustín is in a bus terminal near the market and has buses to Chanduy (see p315). Several coastal villages to the north (including Ballenita, Valdivia, Ayangue and Palmar) are also served by transportation from the market area. Cooperativa Manglaralto and CITM have several daily buses to Manglaralto and Montañita (both just under an hour from La Libertad), Puerto López ($2.80, three hours) and on to Jipijapa ($3.50, five hours). Note that buses may be booked out in advance during weekends in the high season.

To get to Santa Elena from La Libertad, flag down one of the minibuses that run frequently along 9 de Octubre. Frequent buses to Salinas run all day from Calle 8 and Avenida 2.

For information about getting to/from Salinas see p315.

La Libertad & Santa Elena

The area around La Libertad and Santa Elena toward the end of the peninsula is a dusty urban zone with few open spaces. The road forks at Santa Elena, where you can head west to La Libertad (largest town on the peninsula and a noisy, dusty place with a mainly rubble beach) and to Salinas, east to Guayaquil or north along the coast. If you're en route to/from the northern beach towns, it's easier to change buses at the fork – just ask the driver – than going into La Libertad.

Besides an oil refinery and the peninsula's radio station, Santa Elena is home to the archaeological museum **Los Amantes de Sumpa** (☎ 278 6149; admission $1; ⏰ 9am-1:30pm & 2:30-5pm Mon-Tue & Thu-Fri). It has an interesting display of 8000-year-old skeletons shown in the positions that they were found, including two embracing as *amantes* (lovers). The museum is a couple of blocks from the main road on the west side of town.

There's no reason to stay in either place since better accommodation is available in nearby Salinas.

Punta Carnero

This is a point of land in the middle of a wild and largely deserted beach some 15km

in length. The ocean in front of the hotels is considered too rough for swimming, but the beach is good for walks. Sports fishing is a popular activity and boats and equipment can be chartered from Salinas. The area has also been recommended for bird-watching. Whales may be observed from July to September.

Out on the point, the resort-hotel **Punta Carnero Inn** (☎ 277 5450, 294 8477; www.puntacarnero .com; r $70; 🅿 🏊) overlooks the ocean from a cliff top and has comfortable rooms with balconies, plus a restaurant and swimming pool. Nearby, **Hostería Vista del Mar** (☎ 277 5370; www.hosteriadelmar.com; d $20-50; 🅿 🏊) has better-value rooms and cabins, a restaurant, swimming pool and tennis court. Fan rooms are a good deal.

Buses from La Libertad go to Punta Carnero, but most visitors come with their own vehicle.

Salinas

From afar, Salinas looks like Miami beach, a row of tall white condominiums fronting a white sandy expanse filled with sun worshippers and yachts docked nearby. Up close it's not so glamorous, especially since only a block behind the beach the streets look more down-and-out than a playground for wealthy Ecuadorians. Nevertheless, Salinas is the biggest resort town on the south coast and the most westerly town on the Ecuadorian mainland.

Upon entering Salinas, before reaching the beach, you pass through blocks and blocks of blighted semi-industrial landscape. The resort itself stretches for several kilometers along the beachfront, the more visited and popular part and where most of the hotels are located are fronted by a Malecón with restaurants and bars. On one side it ends at the large Barcelo Colón hotel and on the other side is the town plaza and church. West of here is an equally nice sandy stretch though the apartment buildings are directly on the beach. At the time of research a water park was being built right behind the Malecón. The streets are poorly signed, so most locals go by landmarks rather than street names. Salinas is overpriced yet crowded during the high season (mid-December through April) when international yachts dock at the Yacht Club on the west end of the waterfront. The water is warmest for swimming from January to March. In July and August, Salinas is overcast and dreary and, although the sunbathing is lousy during this time, whale- and bird-watching is fairly good. During Carnaval (in February), the place is completely full.

INFORMATION

There are banks with ATMs along Malecón.

Camara de Turismo (☎ 277 1690; captursalinas@hotmail.com; Malecón) Open during high season.

Capitaña (Malecón) Where to go if arriving by private boat or looking to sign on with one as a crew member.

Cybermar (Calle Fidon Tohala Reyes; per hr $1; ⏱ 9.30am-9.30pm) Internet access.

Lavenderia de Tostito (Calle Ruminahui) Around the corner from Hostal Francisco II.

SIGHTS & ACTIVITIES

Beginning about 13km offshore from Salinas, the continental shelf drops from 400m to over 3000m (about 40km offshore), so a short, one-hour sail can take you into really deep water for excellent **sportsfishing**. Swordfish, sailfish, tuna, dorado and Black marlin call these waters home. **Pesca Tours** (☎ 277 2391, in Guayaquil 244 3365; www.pescatours .com.ec; Malecón) charters boats for about $350 a day (6am to 4:30pm). Boats take up to six anglers and include a captain, two crew members and all fishing gear, but you have to provide your own lunch and drinks. The best season (for marlin, dorado and wahoo) is September to December.

Bird-watchers need to seek out the **Oystercatcher Bar** (☎ 277 8329; bhaase@ecua.net.ec; Av 2), between Calle 47 and Calle 50. The owner, Ben Haase, knows more about coastal birds than anyone in the area and is permitted to lead tours (group of eight $30) to the private Ecuasal lakes by the Salinas salt factory, where 109 species of birds have been recorded. The bar, which has a small whale museum and a 10m humpback whale skeleton out the back, is an equally good place to set up **whale-watching** trips (June through October only).

SLEEPING

There is no very cheap accommodation and hotels may close down in the off season. Prices quoted here are for the high season – they often drop 20% to 30% from May to mid-December. Prices will be higher than those quoted here during Easter week, Christmas, New Year and Carnaval.

Hotel Francisco I (☎ 277 4106; Enríquez near Rumiñahui; s/d $25/35; 🟦 🟦) Maybe the most pleasant hotel located within only a block of the beach, Francisco I has very clean, tile-floored rooms tucked back in a concrete building. A small pool occupies the courtyard and there's a nice little restaurant/café attached. The entrance faces the street behind the Malecón across from the Mi Comiserato supermarket.

Hotel Yulee (☎ 277 2028; r $15-30; 🟦) The Yulee is a compound surrounded by high yellow walls near the main plaza just off the beach. From the outside the elegant facade and grilled ironwork suggest colonial elegance, but the rooms are simply basic. They do have cable TV and large bathrooms, though the hot water is erratic. There's a nice courtyard and restaurant attached.

Hotel Francisco II (☎ 277 3471; hotel_francisco_2@ yahoo.com; s/d $25/35; 🟦) On the Malecón between Calle 17 and 19, Francisco II is a four-story yellow building with around-the-clock security and clean, well-kept rooms, hot water and cable TV. A restaurant is attached.

El Carruaje (☎ 277 4282; r from $30; 🟦) Some of the rooms at this friendly hotel on the Malecón are weirdly designed and have a couch in the gargantuan bathroom. Balconies and sea views cost more.

Barceló Colón Miramar (☎ 277 1610; www.barcelo .com; Malecón; s/d from $125/160; 🟦 🖥 🟦) This is the most luxurious hotel in Salinas though the big bucks are more warranted for the facilities like the pool, Jacuzzi, gym, spa and tennis courts than the rooms. It also has three restaurants, several bars and lounges. Deep-sea fishing trips, windsurfing and all manner of tours can be arranged through the hotel. During the low season you can often get all-inclusive deals at substantial discounts.

EATING

Most of the restaurants are located either on the Malecón or a block or two away. Many, however, may be closed or have limited hours during the low season. Cevichelandia, the nickname for a series of cheap seafood stalls at Calle 17 and Enríquez, are mainly open for lunch.

La Bella Italia (☎ 277 1361; mains $4) The best pizza on the Malecón is cooked in a large wood-burning oven in La Bella Italia's dining room. There's street-side seating and, as you'd expect from a place decorated with aquariums, there's lots of seafood available.

Cafeteria del Sol (⏰ 7am-2am; mains $5) This trellis-covered restaurant isn't cheap, but it's open late and it has a large menu with all manner of seafood and meat dishes and large breakfasts. It's between the Banco del Pichincha and Calypso Hotel on the Malecón.

Amazon Restaurant (☎ 277 3671; Malecón & 24 de Mayo; mains $5) This restaurant which looks like a Mexican villa from the outside is one of the nicer restaurants in Salinas. The menu is eclectic, serving everything from pizzas to *parrilladas* to seafood. It's next to the Banco de Guayaquil.

La Ostra Nostra Cevicheria (☎ 277 4028; mains $4) You can't miss this restaurant's large sign off the town plaza and near the church. Ceviches, *cazuelas*, soups and other seafood dishes are served up quick. Another good cevicheria is next door.

Vrouw Maria (mains $5) in front of Hotel Carruaje and the boat-shaped **Mar Y Tierra** (mains $5) are two recommended seafood restaurants on the Malecón.

ENTERTAINMENT

The bars and discos on the Malecón come alive during high-season weekends. Also check the **Oystercatcher Bar** (☎ 277 8329; bhaase@ ecua.net.ec; Av 2). Salinas is almost comatose during the low season.

GETTING THERE & AWAY

Buses enter town along the Malecón and continue to the naval base, where they turn around and head back along Enríquez to La Libertad ($0.25, 20 minutes) and Guayaquil ($3, 2½ hours). There's a **CLP bus office** (Calle 7 near Avenida 5). There are direct buses to Guayaquil 163km away, though they stop again in La Libertad to fill up with passengers, so it may be easier to wait for the bus there. To continue further north to destinations along the Ruta del Sol like Montañita ($1.50, two hours), catch a CITUP bus in La Libertad. See p312 for details of services out of La Libertad.

A taxi from Salinas to La Libertad costs about $2.

SANTA ELENA PENINSULA TO GUAYAQUIL

☎ 04
East of Santa Elena Peninsula, the landscape seems fit for a cowboy. It becomes increasingly dry and scrubby and the ceiba trees give way to 5m-high candelabra cacti. Few people and animals are seen, although herds of tough, half-wild goats seem to thrive. Some of the few inhabitants scratch a living from burning the scrub to make charcoal.

To the south along the coast, the resorts draw *guayaquileños* but few foreigners, since the beachfronts – primarily Salinas and to a lesser extent Playas – are backed by concrete and buildings, and outside of the water itself, the towns hold little appeal.

CHANDUY

☎ 04
Just over halfway between Santa Elena and Progreso, a signed road to the right indicates the archaeology museum in the coastal village of **Chanduy**, 12km to the south. Archaeological excavations nearby led to the opening of the small **Museo Real Alto** (☎ 230 6683; admission $1; ⏰ 9am-4pm Mon, 9am-5pm Tue-Sun), on the outskirts of the village, which has displays on the 6000-year-old archaeology of the area.

Chanduy is reached by bus or taxi from La Libertad.

PLAYAS

☎ 04
A long, broad expanse of beach backed by crumbling buildings, Playas (called General Villamil on some maps) is the closest beach resort to Guayaquil. The sand and the surf aside, it's not a pleasant place and at night the streets and beachfront feel slightly dodgy. Besides serving as a weekend retreat for guayacos, Playas is also an important fishing village. A generation ago, many of the fishing craft were small balsa rafts with one sail, similar to the boats that were used before the Spanish conquest. Now more modern crafts are mainly used, but a few of the old balsa rafts can be seen unloading

THE SOUTH COAST

their catch at the west end of the beach. Playa is busy from December to April but quiet at other times. It can be depressing on an overcast midweek day in the low season.

Information

There's a **Camara de Turismo** (☺ high season) on the beachfront road. Banco de Guayaquil and Banco de Boliviano are on the central plaza, and have ATMs. There are several Internet cafés in town, including **Cybe Alev@Net** (☎ 9am-9pm; $1 per hour), also on the central plaza, and telephone center on Jaime Roldos Aguilera, **Cyber Claudia.com** (☺ 8am-9pm) and **Cyber Playas** (☺ 9am-1am).

Activities

There's some good **surfing** around Playas and the best place for information is the local surf club, **Playas Club Surf** (☎ 09-272 9056; cnr Paquisha & Av 7), based at Restaurant Jalisco (opposite).

Sleeping

Rates here are for the high season but are around 10% to 20% more for holiday week-

ends and the same percentage less during the low season. Couch potatoes be warned: there's no cable TV in Playas hotels yet.

Several cheap hotels are scattered around the central plaza, where earplugs are de rigueur on noisy holiday weekends.

Hotel Arena Caliente (☎ 228 4097; www.hotel arenacaliente.com; Av Paquisha; s/d $28/35; ☒ ☒) Easily the best of the lot, the four-story Arena Caliente has spotless tiled rooms with large baths and TV; many have small balconies as well. Look for the green awning out front above the hotel's modern and good restaurant. There's a nice swimming pool and lounge area in the inner courtyard.

Hotel Nevada (☎ 276 0759; Av Paquisha; r from $25; ☒ ☒) The Nevada, a good second choice, is like a miniaturized version of the Arena Caliente across the street. Rooms here are slightly smaller but modern and clean. The best feature is a little rooftop pool with hammock, chairs and good views of the city.

En route to Data, southeast of the center, are several quiet places near the beach that tend to fill up and overcharge on high-season weekends. They're usually quiet midweek.

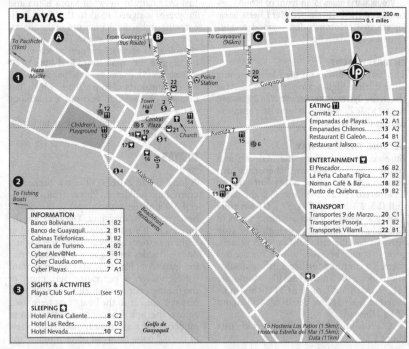

PLAYAS

0 — 200 m
0 — 0.1 miles

INFORMATION
Banco Boliviana.................1 B2
Banco de Guayaquil..............2 B1
Cabinas Telefonicas............3 B2
Camara de Turismo..............4 B2
Cyber Alev@Net.................5 B1
Cyber Claudia.com..............6 C2
Cyber Playas...................7 A1

SIGHTS & ACTIVITIES
Playas Club Surf...............(see 15)

SLEEPING
Hotel Arena Caliente...........8 C2
Hotel Las Redes................9 D3
Hotel Nevada..................10 C2

EATING
Carmita 2.....................11 C2
Empanadas de Playas...........12 A1
Empanades Chilenos............13 A2
Restaurant El Galeón..........14 B1
Restaurant Jalisco............15 C2

ENTERTAINMENT
El Pescador...................16 B2
La Peña Cabaña Típica.........17 B2
Norman Café & Bar.............18 B2
Punto de Quiebra..............19 B2

TRANSPORT
Transportes 9 de Marzo........20 C1
Transportes Posorja...........21 B2
Transportes Villamil..........22 B1

To Pacifictel (1km)

Plaza Madre

From Guayaquil (Bus Route)

To Guayaquil (96km)

Av Paquisha

Police Station

Guayaquil

Town Hall

Central Plaza

Church

Avenida 7

Children's Playground

Malecón

To Fishing Boats

Beachfront Restaurant

Av Jaime Roldos Aguilera

Golfo de Guayaquil

To Hosteria Los Patios (1.5km); Hosteria Estrella del Mar (1.5km); Data (11km)

Hotel Las Redes (☎ 276 0222; r with fan/air-con from $15/22; ❄) The first place you come to south of town on Avenida Jaime Roldos Aguilera, the Las Redes probably has the nicest rooms of the bunch of hotels outside of town. Each has tile floors, TV and hot water and, a bunch of hammocks hang in the central courtyard. There is a restaurant attached.

Hosteria Los Patios (☎ 276 1115; s/d $10/25; ❄ ❄) The best place on (or rather just off) the beach, Los Patios even has a small pool and hammocks in the lounge area in the back. Rooms here have old furniture but are kept clean, and there is a nice modern restaurant as well.

Hosteria Estrella del Mar (☎ 276 0430; r from $12) Next door to Los Patios, down the same dirt road off the highway, is the family-run Estrella del Mar. Rooms in this two-story white building are clean and each has one old lounge chair seemingly as an afterthought. Several hammocks are on a 2nd-floor porch-like area.

Eating

It's *comedore* central around the intersection of Jaime Roldos Aguilera and Paquisha. These cheap restaurants have piles of oysters and crabs on display and serve up the seafood in a myriad of ways. There are several *comedores* along the beach, where staff compete for your patronage by waving menus and shouting specials upon your approach.

Carmita 2 (cnr Paquisha & Av Jaime Roldos Aguilera; mains $3.50) One of a number of cevicherias grouped at this corner and does an especially good and thick shrimp *cazuela* served sizzling in a clay pot.

Empanadas de Playas (Av Jaime Roldos Aguilera) and **Empanades Chilenos** (Av Jaime Roldos Aguilera) No-frills restaurants with plastic tables serving cheap chicken and meat empanadas (each $0.60).

Restaurant Jalisco (cnr Av Paquisha & Av 7; mains $3; ⏰ 8am-5pm) Does good, cheap *almuerzos* and seafood plates. It's a simple place but the food's good enough that it's been in business for some 40 years.

Restaurant El Galeón (cnr Guayaquil & Asisclo G Garay; ⏰ 8am-8pm Sun-Thu, 8am-midnight Fri & Sat) Below Residencial El Galeón, this place is friendly and serves good, cheap, standard Ecuadorian fare.

Entertainment

During high season, *discotecas* are open every night, but only on weekends during low season. Most of them are near the central plaza. The dancing and/or karaoke don't really kick in till late.

Punto de Quiebra and Norman Café & Bar are both on the west side of the plaza. La Peña Cabaña Tipica and El Pescador are two more nearby drinking spots.

Getting There & Away

Transportes Villamil (☎ 276 0190; Avenida Pedro Mendez Gilbert) and **Transportes Posorja** (☎ 214 0284) have buses to Guayaquil 97km away ($2.50, 1¾ hours) though Villamil is a much better choice since they go direct rather than pass through Posorja. Buses leave every 15 minutes with either company from 4am until 8pm. **Transportes 9 de Marzo** (Guayaquil at Av Paquisha) has frequent buses to Posorja ($0.50, 30 minutes) during the day.

To get to Santa Elena and then further north along the Ruta del Sol, go to Progreso ($0.50, 25 minutes) on any Guayaquil-bound bus and change buses there. However, the buses that you may catch in Progreso for Santa Elena are often full upon leaving Guayaquil during the holidays.

On Sunday afternoons in the high season (December to April), everybody is returning to Guayaquil. The road becomes a one-way bus-fest and few (if any) vehicles can travel south into Playas.

AROUND PLAYAS

There are two roads south of Playas – one follows the coast and the other heads inland. The coastal road goes through the villages of Data de Villamil and Data de Posorja, which are often collectively called **Data**. These places are known for boat building. The inland road passes through the old village of **El Morro**, which has a huge old wooden church with dilapidated bamboo walls and three white wooden towers.

Both the inland and coastal roads lead to **Posorja**, a fishing village 20km southeast of Playas with many working boats and hundreds of seabirds wheeling overhead a dirty beach. Buses frequently go there from Playas with Transportes 9 de Marzo.

Stretching northwest from Playas, **Punta Pelada** is a long and fairly deserted beach backed by salt flats, cliffs and cacti. There is some good surfing here. The dirt road along the beach is a popular drive for those with their own vehicles – there is no public transportation here.

PUERTO HONDO

A little west of Cerro Blanco is the small community of Puerto Hondo, at Km 17 on the south side of the Guayaquil–Salinas highway. It can be reached the same way as Cerro Blanco.

There are basic stores and supplies. **Club Ecológico Puerto Hondo** (☺ 9am-4pm) will take visitors on canoe rides ($9) into the mangroves in the area, which can be arranged through **Fundación Pro-Bosque** (☎ 241 6975; Eloy Alfaro & Cuenca, Edificio Promocentro, Office 16) in Guayaquil. This has to be arranged in advance, as tours can only take place at high tide.

BOSQUE PROTECTOR CERRO BLANCO

About 15km west of Guayaquil, this is one of the few areas of tropical dry forests left in the country, and counts jaguars, pumas, monkeys, deer and raccoons among its wildlife. Over 200 bird species, including the rare Great Green Macaw (the reserve's symbol), call Cerro Blanco home. There are stands of dry forest with huge ceiba (kapok) trees and over 100 other tree species, as well as views of coastal mangrove forests in the distance and several trails that take you into this area of rolling coastal hills.

From January to May there's plenty of water and the plants are green, but there are lots of mosquitoes so bring repellent. From June to December (the dry season) the trees flower and it's easier to see wildlife since the animals concentrate in the remaining wet areas. Early morning and late afternoon are, as always, the best times to see wildlife.

This is a private **reserve** (admission $4; ☺ 8am-4pm Sat & Sun, weekdays by reservation) owned by the Cemento Nacional factory and administered by Fundación Pro-Bosque. There's also a wildlife **rescue center** (admission $2), where endangered species are cared for. Many of the center's animals have been recovered from illegal poaching.

Information

Cerro Blanco has a visitors center and a **camping ground** (3-person tent rental $8), with the charge for camping included in the admission price. The ground features barbecues, bathrooms

and running water (even showers), while one cabin with shower and bathroom is also available. The visitors center sells a bird list and booklets, and dispenses information and trail maps. Back-country camping may be permitted and early entry to the reserve can be arranged in advance. Reservations are requested for weekday visits (two days' advance warning), but on weekends you can just show up.

Spanish-speaking guides are available for $7 to $12 per group (up to eight) though it's always best to arrange in advance in Guayaquil through **Fundación Pro-Bosque** (☎ 241 6975; Eloy Alfaro & Cuenca, Edificio Promocentro, Office 16) or otherwise directly through the director, **Eric Horstman** (☎ 287 4946; vonhorst@ecua.net.ec), who speaks English.

Getting There & Away

Cooperativa de Transportes Chongón buses leave Guayaquil's bus terminal heading west and will drop you at the park entrance at Km 16. Get off before the cement factory; you'll see a sign. Chongón buses also leave from Moncayo at Sucre in downtown Guayaquil, allowing you to avoid the trip out to the terminal if you're already downtown. A taxi will cost about $7 to $10.

From the reserve entrance, it is about a 10-minute walk to the information center and camping area.

GUAYAQUIL

☎ 04 / pop 2,117,553

Certainly the image of a butterfly emerging from its cocoon is too poetic for a city that is the economic engine of the country. However, get caught up in the streams of *guayacos* wandering the Malecón (the city's riverfront town square-cum-eatery-cum-cultural center) and there's a feeling of a new and proud identity in the air. If Quito's geography and identity is determined by the mountains, then Guayaquil's is influenced by the river. Besides the amusement park–like development along the Río Guayas, there's the historic *barrio* of Las Peñas, which perches over the riverfront – looking like a cross between a Mexican and Greek fishing village – and now boasts several happening restaurants and bars. Running away from the river is 9 de Octubre, the principal downtown thoroughfare, pedestrian walkway and shopping district.

Of course the massive urban renewal projects, and there are more in the works, also highlight the differences between the new Guayaquil and the old neighborhoods that recall what most of the city was like only a decade ago. Walking the downtown streets is like traversing a glacier: full of uneven surfaces and crevices. But even here among the revitalized squares and parks you can tell it's a city in the midst of change.

Guayaquil is the commercial center of the country, with more than half the companies in Ecuador based here, but the city is also beginning to challenge the cultural hegemony of Quito. Apart from shrimp exporting, petroleum refining, food processing and manufacturing, you'll find a theater, film and art scene growing alongside an already lively club and bar scene that's fuelled in part by several large universities.

Note that all flights to the Galápagos Islands either stop or originate in Guayaquil, so the city is the next best place after Quito to set up a trip.

HISTORY

Popular legend has it that Guayaquil's name comes from Guayas (the great Puna Indian chief who fought bravely against the Incas and then later against the Spanish), and Quill, the wife of Guayas, whom he is said to have killed before drowning himself, rather than allowing her to be captured by the conquistadors. However, several historians claim the city's name comes from the words 'Hua' or land, and 'Illa' meaning beautiful prairie and 'Quilca,' one of the Guyas River's tributaries where the Quilca tribe lived until being wiped out in the 17th century. Thus Guayaquil is literally 'the land like a beautiful prairie on the land of the Quilcas.'

Whatever the origin of the name, a settlement was first established in the area around 1534 until moving permanently to the Santa Ana Hill in 1547. The city was an important port and ship-building center for the Spanish, but it was plagued by pirate attacks and several devastating fires, including one in 1896 – known as the 'Great Fire' – in which huge parts of the city were simply burnt to the ground. Guayaquil achieved its independence from the Spaniards on October 9th, 1820 and was an independent province until Simón Bolívar annexed it as part of Gran Columbia in 1822. When Bolivar's experiment and dream failed in 1830, Guayaquil became part of the newly formed republic of Ecuador.

ORIENTATION

Most travelers stay in the center of town, which is organized in a grid-like fashion on the west bank of Río Guayas. The main east–west street is 9 de Octubre, which runs from the Estero Salado (a brackish estuary bordering the west side of the center) to La Rotonda (the famous statue of liberators Simón Bolívar and José de San Martín) on the Río Guayas. La Rotonda marks the halfway point of the Malecón 2000, which stretches along the bank of the Río Guayas, from the Mercado Sur (near the diagonal Blvd Olmedo) at its southern tip to Las Peñas and the hill of Cerro Santa Ana to the north.

The airport is about 5km north of the center and the bus terminal is about 2km north of the airport entrance. The suburb of Urdesa, which is frequently visited for its restaurants and nightlife, is about 4km northwest and 1.5km west of the airport. The city sprawls in other directions including across the river, but most of these areas are residential or industrial and of little interest to the traveler.

INFORMATION
Bookshops
International Bookshop (Map pp320-1; Luque near Pichincha)

Librería Científica (Map pp320-1; Luque 225 at Carbo)

Mr Books (Map p327; Mall del Sol) Large, modern store in the mall.

Cultural Centers
Alliance Française (Map pp320-1; ☎ 253 2009; Hurtado 436 & José Mascote) French cultural center located near the American embassy holds exhibitions, concerts and various courses and lectures.

Casa de Cultura (Map pp320-1; ☎ 230 0500; cnr 9 de Octubre & Moncayo; ☯ 10am-6pm Tue-Fri, 9am-3pm Sat) Holds art exhibitions, lectures, poetry readings and has a small gold collection. Also a bookstore, small café and cinema (see p331) that shows foreign and art house films.

Internet Access
Most of the top-end hotels and a few of the midrange ones offer wi-fi Internet in their lobbies, rooms and/or their own Internet

GUAYAQUIL – CITY CENTER

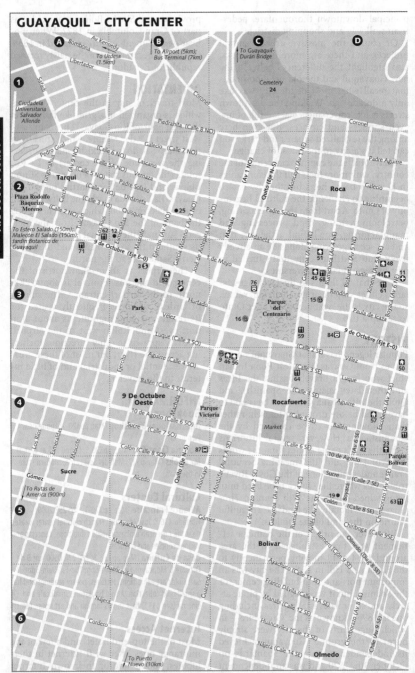

THE SOUTH COAST

THE SOUTH COAST

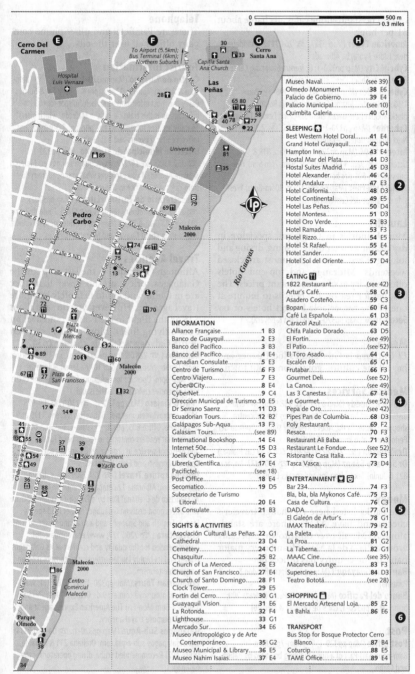

0 500 m
0 0.3 miles

Museo Naval....................(see 39)
Olmedo Monument................38 E6
Palacio de Gobierno..............39 E4
Palacio Municipal...............(see 10)
Quimbita Galería.................40 G1

SLEEPING
Best Western Hotel Doral.....41 E4
Grand Hotel Guayaquil........42 D4
Hampton Inn.....................43 E4
Hostal Mar del Plata...........44 D3
Hostal Suites Madrid...........45 D3
Hotel Alexander.................46 C4
Hotel Andaluz....................47 E3
Hotel California.................48 D3
Hotel Continental...............49 E5
Hotel Las Peñas.................50 D4
Hotel Montesa...................51 D3
Hotel Oro Verde.................52 B3
Hotel Ramada....................53 F3
Hotel Rizzo.......................54 E5
Hotel St Rafael..................55 E4
Hotel Sander.....................56 C4
Hotel Sol del Oriente...........57 D4

EATING
1822 Restaurant................(see 42)
Artur's Café......................58 G1
Asadero Costeño.................59 C3
Bopan.............................60 F4
Café La Española................61 D3
Caracol Azul.....................62 A2
Chifa Palacio Dorado...........63 D5
El Fortín..........................(see 49)
El Patio..........................(see 52)
El Toro Asado....................64 C4
Escalón 69.......................65 G1
Frutabar..........................66 F3
Gourmet Deli....................(see 52)
La Canoa.........................(see 49)
Las 3 Canestas..................67 E4
Le Gourmet......................(see 52)
Pepa de Oro.....................(see 42)
Pipes Pan de Columbia........68 D3
Poly Restaurant..................69 E2
Resaca............................70 F3
Restaurant Ali Baba.............71 A3
Restaurant Le Fondue..........(see 52)
Ristorante Casa Italia..........72 E3
Tasca Vasca......................73 D4

ENTERTAINMENT
Bar 234...........................74 F3
Bla, bla, bla Mykonos Café.....75 F3
Casa de Cultura.................76 G1
DADA.............................77 G1
El Galeón de Artur's.............(see 58)
IMAX Theater....................79 F2
La Paleta.........................80 G1
La Proa...........................81 G2
La Taberna.......................82 G1
MAAC Cine.......................(see 35)
Macarena Lounge................83 F3
Supercines.......................84 D3
Teatro Bototá....................(see 28)

SHOPPING
El Mercado Artesanal Loja.....85 E2
La Bahía..........................86 E6

TRANSPORT
Bus Stop for Bosque Protector Cerro
Blanco..........................87 B4
Coturcip..........................88 E5
TAME Office......................89 E4

INFORMATION
Alliance Française.................1 B3
Banco de Guayaquil...............2 E3
Banco del Pacífico.................3 B3
Banco del Pacífico.................4 E4
Canadian Consulate...............5 E3
Centro de Turismo.................6 F3
Centro Viajero.....................7 E3
Cyber@City........................8 E4
CyberNet..........................9 C4
Dirección Municipal de Turismo.10 E5
Dr Serrano Saenz.................11 D3
Ecuadorian Tours.................12 B2
Galápagos Sub-Aqua.............13 F3
Galasam Tours....................(see 89)
International Bookshop...........14 E4
Internet 50¢......................15 D3
Joelik Cybernet...................16 C3
Librería Científica.................17 E4
Pacifictel.........................(see 18)
Post Office........................18 E4
Secomatico.......................19 D5
Subsecretario de Turismo
Litoral.........................20 E4
US Consulate.....................21 B3

SIGHTS & ACTIVITIES
Asociación Cultural Las Peñas..22 G1
Cathedral.........................23 D4
Cemetery.........................24 C1
Chasquitur........................25 B2
Church of La Merced.............26 E3
Church of San Francisco.........27 E4
Church of Santo Domingo.......28 F1
Clock Tower......................29 E5
Fortín del Cerro..................30 G1
Guayaquil Vision.................31 E6
La Rotonda.......................32 F4
Lighthouse........................33 G1
Mercado Sur.....................34 E6
Museo Antropológico y de Arte
Contemporáneo...............35 G2
Museo Municipal & Library......36 E4
Museo Nahim Isaias.............37 E4

cafés. The stand-alone cafés all charge about $1 per hour.

American Cyber (Map p327; ☎ 264 7112; Oxandaberro near Isidro Ayora, La Alborada)

Cyber@City (Map pp320-1; Unicentro Shopping Center, Ballén near Chile; ✆ 9.30am-8pm)

Cyberin@Net (Map p327; ☎ 224 1196; ✆ 8am-1:30am) Located just off Guillermo Pareja Rolando, a few blocks south of the Garzocentro Shopping Center, La Garzota.

CyberNet (Map pp320-1; Luque 1115; ✆ 7.30am-10pm) Next door to Hotel Alexander.

Internet 50¢ (Map pp320-1; Rumichaca 818 & 9 de Octubre; ✆ 9am-11pm Mon-Sat, 9am-7pm Sun) You guessed it – 50¢ per hour.

Joelik Cybernet (Map pp320-1; ✆ 10am-8pm) West side of Parque del Centenario.

Laundry

Most laundries in Guayaquil specialize in dry cleaning rather than washing, drying and folding. Keep in mind that most are closed weekends. Midrange and top-end hotels offer laundry at often exorbitant prices. The best bet for reasonable rates is to inquire at one of the respectable budget hotels or try **Secomatico** (Map pp320-1; cnr Colón & Boyaca).

Media

El Universo is Guayaquil's local paper and has all the cultural goings-on about town.

Medical Services

Clínica Kennedy (Map p327; ☎ 238 9666; Av Periodista) The best hospital in Guayaquil, by the Policentro shopping center in the Nueva Kennedy suburb. Avenida del Periodista is also known as San Jorge.

Dr Peterson (☎ 288 8717; Acacias 608 & Av Las Monjas)

Dr Serrano Sáenz (Map pp320-1; ☎ 230 1373; Boyaca 821 & Junín) Takes drop-ins and speaks English.

Money

The banks listed here all change traveler's checks and have ATMs. There are stand-alone ATMs all over downtown, especially around Plaza de la Merced, and every major bank in the country has offices here.

Banco de Guayaquil (Map pp320-1; cnr Rendón & Panamá)

Banco del Pacífico (Map pp320-1; Paula de Icaza 200; branch Map pp320-1; cnr 9 de Octubre & Ejército)

Post

Post office (Map pp320-1; ✆ 8am-7pm Mon-Fri, 8am-noon Sat) Part of a huge building bounded by Ballén and Carbo.

Telephone

There are Pacifictel and other phone company offices all over the city.

Tourist Information

Centro de Turismo (Map pp320-1; Malecón; ✆ 10am-1pm & 2-7pm Mon-Fri, 11am-1pm & 2-6pm Sat & Sun) Easily the most informative and helpful spot for tourist information is this train car on the Malecón, which offers 15 minutes' free Internet access, plus good city maps and info on cultural events and happenings.

Dirección Municipal de Turismo (Map pp320-1; ☎ 252 4100, ext 3477/9; www.guayaquil.gov.ec; Malecón & 10 de Agosto) If you can't get what you need from the train car, try this office in the town hall.

Subsecretario de Turismo Litoral (Map pp320-1; ☎ 256 8764; infotour@telconet.net; 5th fl, Paula de Icaza 203; ✆ 8.30am-4.30pm Mon-Fri) Provides general tourist information about Guayas and Manabí Provinces.

Travel Agencies

Although Guayaquil is the last stop for the Galápagos, prices are no lower than they are in Quito, and Quito definitely has more travel agencies. However, you do save about $45 on the flight to the islands (and over an hour's flying time). More details are given in the Galápagos Islands chapter (p347).

Canodros (☎ 228 0880; www.canodros.com; Urbanización Santa Leonor, Manzana 5, Solar 10, Vía Terminal Terrestre; ✆ 9am-6pm) Operator for *Galápagos Explorer II* – one of the most expensive cruise ships in the islands.

Centro Viajero (Map pp320-1; ☎ 230 1283, 09-975 2433; centrovi@telconet.net; Baquerizo Moreno 1119 at 9 de Octubre, Office 805, 8th fl; ✆ 9am-7:30pm) A travel agency that readers continue to recommend for its honest and personal service in organizing Galápagos packages. Spanish, English and French spoken.

Dreamkapture Travel (☎ 224 2909; www.dreamkapture.com; Alborada 12a etapa, Av Benjamín Carrión at Av Francisco de Orellana) Run by a French-Canadian woman who offers good deals on Galápagos cruises (and speaks French, English and Spanish) and also arranges surfing trips.

Ecoventura (☎ 220 7177; www.ecoventura.com) Recommended for the quality and comfort of its Galápagos cruises and its highly lauded attention to conservation and sustainable tourism.

Ecuadorian Tours (Map pp320-1; ☎ 228 7111; www.ecuadoriantoursgye.com.ec; 9 de Octubre 1900; ✆ 9am-1pm & 2-6pm Mon-Fri) The American Express agent and good all-purpose travel agency.

Galápagos Sub-Aqua (Map pp320-1; ☎ 04-230 5514; www.galapagos-sub-aqua.com; Orellana 211 & Panamá, Office 402) Recommended scuba-diving operator for the Galápagos.

Galasam Tours (Map pp320-1; ☎ 230 4488; www
.galapagos-islands.com; 9 de Octubre 424, Office 9A;
⏲ 9am-6:30pm Mon-Fri, 10am-1pm Sat) Known for
economical Galápagos cruises. Some people have negotiated good deals, but Lonely Planet has also received many
complaints from readers of bad service and trips gone
wrong. Go in with your eyes open.
Metropolitan Touring (Map p327; ☎ 233 0300; www
.metropolitantouring.com; Hilton Colón Hotel, Av Francisco
de Orellana) Can arrange luxury trips to the Galápagos and
also book tours throughout the country.

DANGERS & ANNOYANCES

Guayaquil has its fair share of poverty and
urban woes, though statistically and anecdo-
tally it is certainly no more dangerous than
Quito and doesn't deserve the bleak tag that
is bandied about by foreigners who spend
only a few hours in the city. There is a persistent problem with post–ATM withdrawal
robberies, so it's worth being extra aware
for at least a few blocks after leaving the
bank. However, the main tourist areas of 9
de Octubre, the Malecón and Las Peñas are
perfectly safe – not simply because there is a
visible police presence but also because these
are lively, vibrant areas clogged with couples
and families, and not the predatory gangs
that some would have you believe. The area
directly north and south of the Parque del
Centenario can feel dodgy at night, but simply use common sense and take the normal
precautions when visiting any large city.

SIGHTS & ACTIVITIES

The city has its fair share of sights, most
within walking distance of one another. If
your time is limited be sure to walk the
Malecón 2000 (also called Malecón Simón
Bolívar or simply El Malecón) and visit
the northern neighborhood of Las Peñas –
an especially pleasant destination at night
when cool breezes blow off the Río Guayas and the bright lights of the city sparkle
below. Sunday is a good day to foot it because traffic is limited.

Malecón 2000

The riverfront promenade is Guayaquil's
own Central Park – minus grass but plus
a river – and it's where the city comes to
shop, eat, stroll and just plain congregate.
Malecón 2000 (Map pp320-1; ⏲ 7am-midnight),
one of the most extensive urban renewal
projects in South America, is made up of

ponds, playgrounds, sculptures, gardens
and river views. From its southernmost
point at the Mercado Sur to Cerro Santa
Ana and Las Peñas in the north, the Malecón stretches 2.5km along the bank of
the wide Río Guayas. It's a gated, policed
public space with restaurants, a museum,
performance space, IMAX movie theater
and a shopping mall.

At the southern end of the Malecón
stands the handsome, steel **Mercado Sur** (Map
pp320-1), sometimes called the Crystal Palace, a Belgium-designed covered market built
in 1907 – at the time the biggest marketplace
in Guayaquil. It has now been restored, with
giant glass walls, and is periodically filled
with art and commercial exhibitions.

Just north of the Mercado Sur is the **Olmedo monument** (Map pp320-1) honoring
José Joaquín de Olmedo (1780–1847), who
was an Ecuadorian poet and the president of
the first Ecuadorian territory independent of
Spanish rule. Just to the north, outside the
Malecón's blue fence, is the sprawling street
market known as La Bahía (p332) where you
can pick up everything from underwear to
DVDs of the Latin Grammy awards.

Where 10 de Agosto hits the Malecón
you'll see the famous Moorish-style **clock
tower** (Map pp320-1; ⏲ 9am-6pm Mon-Fri), which
originally dates from 1770 but has been replaced several times. The 23m-high tower is
open to visitors to climb the narrow spiral
staircase inside.

Across the street from the clock tower is
the **Palacio Municipal** (Map pp320-1), an ornate, gray building that is separated from
the simple and solid **Palacio de Gobierno** by
a small but pleasant pedestrian mall. Both
buildings date from the 1920s. The Palacio
de Gobierno replaced the original wooden
structure, which was destroyed in the great
fire of 1917. The little-visited **Museo Naval**
(Map pp320-1; ☎ 232 4249; Government Bldg, Malecón &
Ballén; admission free; ⏲ 8.15am-noon & 1-4pm Mon-Fri),
entered through the door on the Malecón
side, has four large galleries with maps, documents, models and other curio of the seafaring history of the country.

A few blocks away in the Plaza de Admin-
istración building is the new **Museo Nahim Isaias**
(Map pp320-1; Pichincha & Ballén; adults/children $1.50/0.50;
⏲ 10am-6pm Tue-Sat, 11am-4pm Sun), which exhibits
a collection of sculptures, paintings and artifacts of the colonial period.

THE SOUTH COAST

THE SOUTH COAST

Continuing north along the Malecón, you will soon come to the famous statue of **La Rotonda** (Map pp320–1), one of Guayaquil's more impressive monuments, particularly when illuminated at night. Flanked by small fountains, it depicts the historic but enigmatic meeting between Bolívar and San Martín that took place here in 1822. Few people realize that the curved wall behind the statue acts as an acoustic reflector. If two people stand at either end of it, the whisper of one into the wall will be carried around to the other person.

From La Rotonda, there are good views north, along the riverfront, of the colonial district of Las Peñas and Cerro Santa Ana and, far beyond, the impressive Guayaquil–Durán bridge – the biggest in the country. To the east of La Rotonda, **9 de Octubre** (Map pp320–1), downtown Guayaquil's main commercial street stretches off toward Parque del Centenario.

At the far northern end of the Malecón is the modern **Museo Antropológico y de Arte Contemporáneo** (Map pp320–1; MAAC; ☎ 230 9400; Malecón & Loja; admission $3 Wed-Sat, $1.50 Tue & Sun; ☽ 10am-6pm Tue-Sat, 10am-4pm Sun), a museum of anthropology, archaeology and (most importantly for the average visitor) a superb and well-curated collection of contemporary Ecuadorian art. MAAC also has a modern 400-seat theater for plays, concerts and film. Behind the museum is an open-air stage, where musical and theatrical performances are occasionally given. Beside the museum is a modern food court.

Las Peñas & Cerro Santa Ana

These two historic neighborhoods (Map pp320–1) have been refurbished into an idealized version of a quaint South American hillside village, all brightly painted homes and cobblestone alleyways. If you peek inside an open door or window, however, you realize it's a bit of a Potemkin village that's not entirely sanitized as residents still live their everyday lives as they would elsewhere in the city. Everyone strolling the Malecón ends up here, especially at night when the views from the top are spectacular. There are several stylish and attractive bars, and it's completely safe – though one of the friendly security officers may stop you for walking up or down the wrong side of the steep stairway so as

not to impede the heavy foot traffic. There are future plans to create a Disneyfied port area below Las Peñas.

The historic street of **Numa Pompillo Llona**, named after the *guayaquileño* (1832–1907) who wrote the national anthem, begins at the northern end of the Malecón, to the right of the stairs that head up the hill called Cerro Santa Ana. The narrow, winding street has several unobtrusive plaques set into the walls of some of its houses, indicating the simple residences of past presidents. The colonial wooden architecture has been allowed to age elegantly, albeit with a gloss of paint. Several artists live in the area, and there are a few good galleries, including the eponymous **Quimbita Galeria** (Map pp320–1; ☎ 231 0785; www.quimbita.com; Cerro Santa Ana; ☽ 2pm-11pm Tue-Thu & Sun, 2pm-2am Fri & Sat), which doubles as a bar and showpiece for the large canvasses of this highly regarded artist. The **Asociación Cultural Las Peñas** (Map pp320–1; ☎ 235 1891; Numa Pompillo Llona 173; ☽ 10am-4pm) is in a lovely old house over the river and sells paintings by local artists.

Numa Pompillo Llona is a dead-end street, so retrace your footsteps and instead of continuing back along the Malecón, hang a sharp right and head up the steps of **Cerro Santa Ana** (Map pp320–1). The stairs lead past dozens of refurbished, brightly painted homes, cafés, bars and souvenir shops, and up to the hilltop fort **Fortín del Cerro** ('Fort of the Hill'; Map pp320–1). Cannons, which were once used to protect Guayaquil from pirates, aim over the parapet toward the river and are still fired today during celebrations. You can climb the **lighthouse** (Map pp320–1; admission free; ☽ 10am-10pm) for spectacular 360-degree views of the city and its rivers.

Back at the bottom of the hill, if you walk inland from the stairway, you'll see the open-air theater **Teatro Bogotá** (Map pp320–1). Behind the theater is the oldest church in Guayaquil, the **Church of Santo Domingo** (Map pp320–1). The church, which is worth a look, was founded in 1548 and restored in 1938.

Downtown Area

There are several ordinary colonial-era buildings in the streets immediately south of Las Peñas, but soon all the architecture turns mostly modern and dull. The **Church of La Merced** (Map pp320–1; Rendón at Rocafuerte) dates from 1938 and has a richly decorated golden altar, but the original wooden church built in 1787, like most of Guayaquil's colonial buildings, was destroyed by fire.

The **Church of San Francisco** (Map pp320-1; 9 de Octubre near Chile) was originally built in the early 18th century, destroyed by the devastating fire in 1896 that destroyed huge swathes of the city, reconstructed in 1902 and beautifully restored in the late 90s. The plaza in front contains Guayaquil's first public monument, unveiled on New Year's Day in 1880. It is a statue of Vicente Rocafuerte, Ecuador's first native president who held office 1835–39. (Ecuador's first president, Juan Flores, was a Venezuelan.)

The main thoroughfare, **9 de Octubre** (Map pp320-1), is definitely worth a stroll, even if you're not shopping, if only to experience the commercial vibrancy of the city.

Parque Bolívar Area

Guayaquil may be the only city in the world that has land iguanas, some over a meter in length, living downtown. These prehistoric-looking animals, a different species from those found in the Galápagos, are a startling sight in one of Guayaquil's most famous plazas, **Parque Bolívar** (Map pp320-1) which is also known as Parque Seminario. Around its small ornamental gardens are many of Guayaquil's first-class hotels.

On the west side of Parque Bolívar is the **cathedral** (Map pp320-1). The original building on this site dates from 1547, but – as is common with most of Guayaquil's original wooden buildings – it burnt down. The present structure was completed in 1948 and renovated in 1978. The front entrance is extremely ornate, but inside it is simple, high-vaulted and modern.

A block south of Parque Bolívar, you find the **Museo Municipal** (Map pp320-1; ☎ 252 4100; Sucre; admission free; ☒ 8:30am-4:30pm Tue-Fri, 10am-2pm Sat & Sun) and the municipal **library**. The archaeology room on the ground floor has mainly Inca and pre-Inca ceramics, and several figurines from the oldest culture in Ecuador, the Valdivia (c 3200 BC). Also on the ground floor is a colonial room with mainly religious paintings and a few period household items. Upstairs, there is a jumble of modern art and ethnography rooms with regional costumes, handicrafts and several shrunken heads.

Parque del Centenario

This plaza, found along 9 de Octubre (Map pp320-1), is the largest in Guayaquil and marks the midway point between the Río Guayas and the Estero Salado. It's four square city blocks of manicured gardens, benches and monuments, the most important of which is the central Liberty column surrounded by the founding fathers of the country.

Parque Histórico Guayaquil

Historic Williamsburg meets the zoo at this large **park** (Map p327; ☎ 283 3807; www.parquehistorico.com; adult/child Tue-Sat $3/1.50, Sun $4.50/3; ☒ 9am-4:30pm Tue-Sun) across the Guayaquil–Durán bridge, on the east side of Río Daule. The park is divided into three 'zones:' the Endangered Wildlife Zone, which has 45 species of birds, animals and reptiles in a seminatural habitat; the Urban Architecture Zone, which has a restaurant and showcases the development of early 20th-century architecture in Guayaquil; and the Traditions Zone, which focuses on local traditions, with an emphasis on rural customs, crafts and agriculture.

A taxi from the city costs between $3 and $4 or take the red-and-white Duran number 4/30 bus. It's easier to catch the bus back to the city from in front of the large mall on the main road about a 200m walk from the park.

Malecón El Salado

Like its more famous sister development on the Río Guayas to the east, the Malecón El Salado is an attempt to reclaim the city's waterfront for the everyday use of its residents. There are several eateries and cafés in a streamlined modern mall-like building along the estuary and a walkway above. Previously known as the Guayaquil Park, the large square just south of the Malecón, now called the **Rodolfo Baquerizo Moreno Plaza**, is dominated by a large modernist structure, and expositions and events are held here periodically. A series of gardens, playgrounds and manicured public walkways, collectively called Parque Lineal, is being constructed on the other side of the waterway just to the north.

City Cemetery

Incorporated into the city landscape a short ride from the center is this **cemetery** (Map pp320-1; Coronel & Moncayo) containing hundreds of above-ground tombs stacked atop one another so that it resembles a mini apartment complex rather than a final resting place. A walkway leads to several monuments and huge mausoleums, including the impressive grave of President Vicente Rocafuerte.

Jardín Botánico de Guayaquil

About a half-hour drive north of town near Cerro Colorado, this **botanical garden** (☎ 256 0519; jbotanic@interactive.net.ec; Av Francisco de Orellana; adults/children & students $3/1.50; ☽ 9am-4pm) has over 80 orchid varieties and nearly 700 plant species. Paths and trails lead you past the plant exhibits and tropical birds flutter overhead. There is a gift shop, café, butterfly garden and an auditorium.

Insect repellent is recommended in the rainy months. With a few days' advance notice, a guided tour can be arranged.

The most efficient way of getting there is to take a taxi and ask for Urbanización de Los Orquídeas. Chasquitur (below) offers tours and has information.

TOURS

Chasquitur (Map pp320-1; ☎ 228 1084/85; chasquit@gye.satnet.net; Urdaneta 1418; ☽ 10am-6pm Mon-Fri) Good for local day tours, city tours and ecotourism.

Ecuandino (☎ 232 6375; ecuandin@telconet.net) A panama-hat exporter and an organizer of local tours, especially to see how *toquilla* (fine, fibrous straw) is split, boiled, bleached and dried in preparation for weaving. Ask for Alejandro Lecaro who speaks English. See the boxed text 'It's not a Panama, it's a Montecristi!' on p206.

Ecuatrails (☎ 239 3944; ecuatrails@ecutel.net) Can arrange visits to banana or cocoa plantations in the region.

Guayaquil Vision (☎ 230 6444; www.guayaquilvision.com; adults/children $5/3) Double decker bus tours of the city (1½ hours). Starts from the Plaza Olmedo on the Malecón.

Nancy Hilgert (☎ 210 3416; nancyperegrinus@yahoo.com) Expert bird-watching guide. Works with professional and academic tour groups as well as individuals.

Sans Souci Tours (☎ 288 7494; www.sanssouci.com.ec) Another operator offering half-day tours of banana and cocoa plantations.

FESTIVALS & EVENTS

Simón Bolívar's birthday & Founding of Guayaquil Falling on July 24 and 25 respectively, the city goes wild with parades, art shows, beauty pageants, fireworks and plenty of drinking and dancing. Hotels are booked well

in advance. The festivities often begin July 23 or even July 22, depending on which day of the week the holiday falls. Banking and other services are usually disrupted.

Independence Day & Día de la Raza These two combine to create another long holiday full of cultural events, parades and bigger than usual crowds on the Malecón. Independence Day is October 9 (1820) and Día de la Raza is October 12.

New Year's Eve Celebrated with bonfires and life-sized puppets called *viejos* (the old ones), which are made by stuffing old clothes – they represent the old year. The *viejos* are displayed on the main streets of the city, especially the Malecón, and then burned at midnight in bonfires.

Carnaval Movable feast held on the days immediately preceding Ash Wednesday and Lent, which, in addition to the traditional throwing of water, is 'celebrated' by dousing passersbys with all manner of unpleasant liquids.

SLEEPING

Some people choose to stay in the northern suburbs, but it's really no more convenient to the airport or bus terminal than staying downtown and you'll be forced to take taxis wherever you go. It's also no safer than downtown, so if you do choose to stay here, decide on the merits of the accommodation alone.

Each hotel is officially required to post its approved prices near the entrance. You may be charged up to 22% tax on their listed price, but most of the cheaper hotels don't bother. The better hotels often have a two-tiered pricing system in which foreigners are charged about twice as much as residents.

During holiday periods, finding a room can be problematic, especially in the better hotels, and prices are usually higher than the listed price. Outside the holiday season, single travelers can often get a double room for the price of a single.

The heat and humidity in Guayaquil are especially oppressive from January to April, when air-conditioning is highly desirable.

Downtown
BUDGET

Cheap hotels in Guayaquil aren't built with foreigners on a tight budget in mind and there are none of the backpacker havens that you find elsewhere in the country. Most of the budget accommodation is found within several blocks of the Parque del Centenario and street noise can be an annoyance so earplugs are advised.

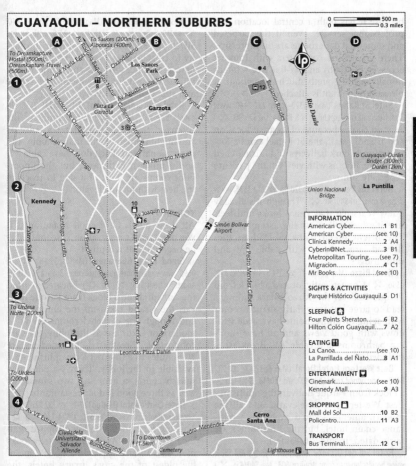

GUAYAQUIL – NORTHERN SUBURBS

INFORMATION
American Cyber..............1 B1
American Cyber..........(see 10)
Clínica Kennedy...........2 A4
Cyberin@Net.................3 B1
Metropolitan Touring......(see 7)
Migracion.....................4 C1
Mr Books...................(see 10)

SIGHTS & ACTIVITIES
Parque Histórico Guayaquil..5 D1

SLEEPING
Four Points Sheraton.........6 B2
Hilton Colón Guayaquil....7 A2

EATING
La Canoa...................(see 10)
La Parrillada del Ñato.......8 A1

ENTERTAINMENT
Cinemark.....................(see 10)
Kennedy Mall................9 A3

SHOPPING
Mall del Sol...................10 B2
Policentro....................11 A3

TRANSPORT
Bus Terminal..................12 C1

Hostal Suites Madrid (Map pp320-1; ☎ 230 7804; Quisquis 305; r with fan/air-con $12/15;) The large, modern rooms here are kept spotless and bright. And unlike much of the accommodation in this range (though not listed here), it won't make you feel down and out. It's only a block north of the Parque del Centenario, but the entrance is not so easy to spot. The manager at the time was especially friendly and helpful.

Hotel Montesa (Map pp320-1; ☎ 231 2526; Urdaneta 817 & Rumichaca; r with fan/air-con $12/15;) Another good budget choice only a block north of Suites Madrid, this new hotel has a gleaming marble and tile lobby to match the small but gleaming rooms. Hot water is hit and miss, but the staff are friendly and professional.

Hotel Sander (Map pp320-1; ☎ 232 0030; Luque 1101; r per person with fan/air-con $9/11;) What makes the large bunker-like Sander one of the better cheapies is the 24-hour security, friendly front desk and elevator to take you to the top floors. Otherwise the almost bare (except for a piece of old wooden furniture), tiled-floor rooms aren't much to get excited about.

MIDRANGE
The hotels in this category are more secure and have modern amenities like cable TV, telephones and air-conditioning.

Hotel Alexander (Map pp320-1; ☎ 253 2000; hotel alexander@hotmail.com; Luque 1107; s/d $25/30;) The Alexander is one of the best-value places because it has both a central location and professional service, even if the carpeted and somewhat dark rooms are unimpressive. There are several computers with Internet access in the lobby and wi-fi is free – intentionally or not – pretty much throughout. A pleasant restaurant is attached.

Hotel St Rafael (Map pp320-1; ☎ 232 7140; www .hotelstrafaplz.com.ec; Chile 414 & Ballén; s/d $25/30; 🔀) A good choice because of its great location and friendly staff, the St Rafael can be forgiven for its dark hallways and mismatched furniture. Rooms with views of the park are especially sunny.

Hotel Las Penas (Map pp320-1; ☎ 232 3355; www .hlpgye.com; s/d $40/50; 🔀) Though it's already a few years old, Las Penas looks and feels like it's just rolled off the assembly line. The bright green hallways lead to tile-floored large rooms with cable TV and mini fridges.

Hotel Rizzo (Map pp320-1; ☎ 232 5210; Ballén 319; r $36; 🔀) Conveniently located a block from Parque Bolívar, the Rizzo's dark hallways lead to large but irregularly shaped rooms with aging furniture. Some have wide windows with good views and all have modern bathrooms and cable TV. Breakfast is included.

Best Western Hotel Doral (Map pp320-1; ☎ 232 8490; www.hdoral.com; Chile 402; s/d $40/48; 🔀) Only a block from Parque Bolívar, the multistory Best Western has an elevator and all the modern amenities you'd expect of a midrange chain hotel, but the furnishings are fairly dated. Includes breakfast.

Hotel Sol del Oriente (Map pp320-1; ☎ 232 5500; www.hotelsoloriente.com; Aguirre 603; s/d $40/45; 🔀) This high-rise is popular with groups, less for its large carpeted, geometrically challenged rooms than for the fact that it has three restaurants and a small gym and sauna ($5 to $10). Ask for a top-floor room with a view. Rooms sleeping four at only $54 are excellent value.

Hotel Andaluz (Map pp320-1; ☎ 231 1057; hotel _andaluz@yahoo.com; Junín 852; s/d $18/36; 🔀) The attractive facade of the Andaluz suggests an elegant colonial-era building, while the tiny lobby with the cashier locked behind a security grate leaves an unfortunate impression. Through a maze of hallways and a little garden, the rooms themselves are clean and comfortable. Each has a separate shower and toilet, as well as TV (sans cable).

Hostal Mar del Plata (Map pp320-1; ☎ 230 7610; Junín 718 & Boyacá; s/d with fan $12/20, with air-con $18/23; 🔀) Rooms here are similar in quality to Hostal Suites Madrid except the TVs here are noticeably old and some of the toilets are seat-free. It's clean and secure and still a good choice.

Hotel California (Map pp320-1; ☎ 230 2538; Urdaneta 529; s/d $20/24; 🔀) Unfortunately the rooms at the California aren't as nice as you might think from the marble lobby and professional staff. Each does have cable TV and a modern bathroom, but the upper-floor rooms are a bit of a slog to reach in the heat without an elevator.

TOP END
All these hotels have good restaurants. If you don't have a reservation, discounts may be negotiated at reception.

Grand Hotel Guayaquil (Map pp320-1; ☎ 232 9690; www.grandhotelguayaquil.com; Boyacá & 10 de Agosto; r from $85; 🔀 🏊 💻) Located behind the cathedral and a block from Parque Bolívar, the Grand takes up the entire block and though the carpeted rooms aren't as modern or luxurious as the lobby, they are comfortable. Breakfast is included, as are 30 minutes free Internet a day, plus wi-fi is available in the lobby. There's a pool, two squash courts, a gym and two saunas, as well as three good indoor restaurants.

Hotel Continental (Map pp320-1; ☎ 232 9270; www .hotelcontinental.com.ec; Chile 510; r $74-140; 🔀 💻) This big fortress-like building topped with the flags of South American countries looks more like an embassy than a hotel. One of the oldest of the city's luxury hotels, the Continental's carpeted rooms are comfortable though not especially large. It's right across from Parque Bolívar and has several good restaurants.

Hampton Inn (Map pp320-1; ☎ 256 6700; www .hampton.com.ec; 9 de Octubre 432 & Baquerizo Moreno; r $85-350; 🔀 💻) In the heart of the action, the high-rise Hampton Inn is your standard comfortable chain hotel. It has a deli, sushi bar and restaurant, and includes a spa, gym, business center and free buffet breakfast for guests, plus wi-fi Internet in the lobby.

Hotel Oro Verde (Map pp320-1; ☎ 232 7999; www.ororverdehotels.com; 9 de Octubre & García Moreno; r $152-317; 🔀 💻 🏊) The Oro Verde is considered the classiest of the bunch. About four blocks east of Parque del Centenario, t has over 250 rooms and suites, although he rooms aren't really much superior to ts competitors. You pay extra for the service and the facilities, which include a pool, gym, sauna, casino, shops and several excellent restaurants. Low walk-in rates are sometimes available.

Hotel Ramada (Map pp320-1; ☎ 256 5555; Malecón 606; s/d $65/75; ✖ 🖳 ☎) Easily the best feature of this aging hotel is its location on the Malecón. Rooms here cry out for a decorator to do away with the strangely mismatched furniture, plastic lawn-chairs and large, marble bathrooms. There's a small indoor pool covered by a greenhouse and surrounded by artificial turf. A restaurant, bar and casino are attached. Some rooms have direct river views, others angled and some have no view at all.

Northern Suburbs

Parts of the northern suburbs are technically closer to the airport and bus terminal than downtown, but because of traffic and roundabout routes it's really no more convenient to stay here. It is slightly quieter and closer to the large Mall del Sol, the bars of Kennedy and the restaurants of Urdesa. Buses connect the suburbs with downtown and a cab ride to the Malecón costs about $4.

Dreamkapture Hostal (☎ 224 2909; www.dreamkap ture.com; Alborada 12a etapa, Manzana 2, Villa 21, Juan Sixto Bernal; s/d with shared bath $12/20, with private bath $18/28; ✖ ☎) A small, friendly Canadian/Ecuadorian-owned hostal with a garden courtyard and tiny pool for cooling off on a side street in the suburb of Alborada. There are several rooms including one good for groups of four or five and breakfast is included. One of the owners operates a travel agency (p322) and can arrange economic tours of the Galápagos. Even with the address the hostal is hard to find – it's on Juan Sixto Bernal near the intersection of Avenida Benjamín Carrión and Avenida Francisco de Orellana. There's no sign, so look for the fantasy paintings on the compound walls.

Hilton Colón Guayaquil (Map p327; ☎ 268 9000; www.hiltoncolon.com; Av Francisco de Orellana; r from $185; ✖ 🖳 ☎) This massive complex occupies several blocks almost equidistant to the airport, Mall del Sol shopping center and the restaurants of Urdesa. It's probably the most luxurious choice and the suites have balconies with spectacular views. Two

restaurants, a 24-hour café, two bars and a deli all serve good meals. Also has a pool, shops, casino, gym and sauna.

Four Points Sheraton (Map p327; ☎ 269 1888; www.fourpoints.com; Av Joaquin Orrantia G; r from $140; ✖ 🖳 ☎) The Four Points is much more of a standard international business hotel, though travelers with just a night before catching an onward flight to the Galápagos find it convenient for its proximity to the airport and the Mall del Sol. It also has a large outdoor pool, small gym, sauna, restaurant and café. Substantial discounts are available on weekends.

EATING

In terms of eating, downtown Guayaquil hasn't kept pace with other changes in the city. There are bunches of little, inexpensive eateries catering to working folk though there are few standout restaurants. Informal parillas are everywhere, with a particular cluster around the Parque del Centenario, and there are several concentrations of bright, clean fast-food restaurants along the Malecón 2000, the Malecón Estero Salado. There's also a large food court in the Mall del Sol north of downtown, while 9 de Octubre has several fast-food joints.

Guayacos love their *encebollado*, a tasty soup made with seafood, yucca and onion and garnished with popcorn and *chifles* (crispy fried bananas). The best *encebollados* are sold in cheap mom-and-pop restaurants. They usually sell out by lunchtime. *Cangrejo* (crab) is another local favorite.

The best dining experiences are in hotels downtown or in the northwestern suburb of Urdesa.

Downtown
RESTAURANTS

Escalón 69 (Map pp320-1; ☎ 230 9828; Cerro Santa Ana; mains $4-8; ✖ Tue-Sun noon-2am) On the steps of Las Peñas, this is a charming mix of romantic elegance and casual local spot, with a menu of creative interpretations of typical Ecuadorian dishes: yucca patties served with honey lemon sauce ($5), squid stuffed with Spanish sausage ($5) and rock bass ceviche ($4.50). It's decorated with flowing yellow drapes, hammocks and handwoven tablecloths.

Tasca Vasca (Map pp320-1; ☎ 253 4599; Ballén 422 & Chimborazo; mains $8-14; ✖ noon-11pm Mon-Sat) From the waiters' uniforms to the chalkboard menus, from the exposed brick to the smoky cellar-like atmosphere, Tasca Vasca is more Spanish than a restaurant in Madrid. Choose from plates such as grilled octopus, *zarzuela de mariscos* (seafood stew) and baby eels, tapas and paella ($8).

Caracol Azul (Map pp320-1; ☎ 228 0461; 9 de Octubre 1918 & Los Ríos; mains $10-20; ☕ noon-3:30pm & 7pm-midnight Mon-Sat) One the city's few gourmet restaurants, Caracol Azul serves French-Peruvian haute cuisine in an elegant dining room for very haute French prices. Try the *corvina a lo macho* (sea bass smothered in a rich shellfish sauce; $13).

Bopan (Map pp320-1; ☎ 231 0094; Malecón & Paula de Icaza; mains $3-7; ☕ Mon-Sat 9am-9pm) A good place to break up a walk along the Malecón, Bopan has an extensive menu of crepes, tortillas, sandwiches and pastas.

Restaurant Ali Baba (Map pp320-1; 9 de Octubre; mains $2) For a little variety, head to Ali Baba for Middle Eastern staples like hummus and falafel. It's a small but charming place with several tables open to the street.

Asadero Costeño (Map pp320-1; Garaycoa 929; almuerzos $1.50) This is a large, bare-bones eatery serving grilled chicken, rice and beans on the east side of the Parque del Centenario. Order and pay at the caged cashier before sitting. Next door is the curiously named Parrallidas Beefs & Salads, another busy local eatery.

Ristorante Casa Italia (Map pp320-1; ☎ 230 2490; Rendon 438; mains $3) One of the few stand-alone Italian restaurants downtown, Casa Italia is a casual, informal place with cheap *almuerzos* ($2) with your choice of pastas.

Resaca (Map pp320-1; ☎ 242 3390; Malecón at Roca; mains $5-9) This restaurant on the Malecón feels a little like TGI Fridays, what with the red checkered tablecloths, salads, chicken wings, pasta dishes and friendly waiters. It's also a popular bar open late on weekend nights.

Poly Restaurant (Map pp320-1; ☎ 230 4754; Malecón 303; almuerzos $1.50) One of the few authentic local-style eateries left around the area of the Malecón and Las Peñas.

Chifa Palacio Dorado (Map pp320-1; ☎ 232 8070; Chile 712 & Sucre; mains $3) One of several Chinese restaurants within a few blocks' radius, Palacio Dorado has a large dining room and good-sized portions.

CAFES & QUICK EATS

Frutabar (Map pp320-1; ☎ 282 0609; Malecón; drinks from $1.50; ☕ 8am-midnight) From the surfboards,

tropical-themed murals and artwork, everything about this little café shouts Hawaii. Besides the 20-plus types of *batidos* (fruit shakes) and dozens of fruit juices, there are sandwiches, snacks and light meals. There's another branch in Urdesa.

Artur's Café (Map pp320-1; ☎ 231 2230; Numa pillo Llona 127, Las Peñas; mains $3-7; ☕ 6pm-3am, closed Sun) Unlike most of the refurbished facades in the neighborhood, Artur's looks like it's been around for a while – this is a good thing. It feels like a local's secret hideaway, perched over the Río Guayas in Las Peñas, and the slightly chintzy decor only adds to its charm. There's drinks, Ecuadorian food and live music on many weekends.

Las 3 Canastas (Map pp320-1; cnr Velez & Chile) A downtown spot for fruit shakes, fruit juices and ice cream. Sidle up to the bar stools or hang out at one of the street-side tables.

Café La Española (Map pp320-1; ☎ 230 2710; Junín 705 & Boyacá; sandwiches $2) The super-clean and air-conditioned dining area more than makes up for this chain outlet's lack of charm. Good deli sandwiches and meal deals, baked sweets and breads are the specialty here.

El Toro Asado (Map pp320-1; cnr Garaycoa & Luque, mains $1.50-4; ☕ noon-1:30am) Serves good, reasonably priced grilled meats in a casual and busy atmosphere. *Almuerzos* only cost $1.50. *Asado y menestra* (grilled beef with lentils or beans) is the specialty.

Pipes Pan de Columbia (Map pp320-1; cnr Junín & Rumichaca) Piping hot baked goods served up late just northeast of the Parque del Centenario.

HOTEL RESTAURANTS

La Canoa (Map pp320-1; ☎ 232 9270; Chile 510; mains $3-7; ☕ 24hr) In the Hotel Continental, this is a bustling popular diner, Ecuadorian-style, which means instead of hamburgers, the quick dish of choice is a ceviche or fried rice with crab. There's also a branch in the Mall del Sol (Map pp320–1). Also in the hotel is the expensive El Fortín (Map pp320–1), which has won international gastronomic awards.

1822 Restaurant (Map pp320-1; ☎ 232 9690; Boyacá & 10 de Agosto; mains $10-23) Grand Hotel Guayaquil's restaurant serves excellent international food in a Mexican/Spanish villa setting, replete with stucco and tile and Simón Bolívar portraits. Up in Pepa de Oro, the coffee is excellent and refills are free.

Le Gourmet (Map pp320-1; ☒ 232 7999; de Octubre & García Moreno; ☒ 7pm-1am) One of several excellent restaurants in Hotel Oro Verde, Le Gourmet is a top-flight French place. If you're in the mood for a splurge, start off with the warm smoked duck breast salad with caramelized apple and emulsion of raspberry ($14) and then the crab claws flambéed with Armagnac and pastis ($25). Elsewhere in the hotel, El Patio (Map pp320-1) serves delicious Ecuadorian dishes at upscale prices; it's open for breakfast, lunch and dinner. Easier on the pocket book is the hotel's Restaurant Le Fondue (Map pp320-1), which serves Swiss food and stays open late; the specialty, of course, is fondue. The Gourmet Deli (Map pp320-1) serves cakes and pastries throughout the day.

Northern Suburbs
Avenida Estrada, the main drag in the suburb of Urdesa 4km northwest of downtown, is one big American-style strip mall of fast food joints and restaurants – some slick and upscale. Other good eateries are scattered throughout the suburbs of Alborada, La Garzota and Los Sauces.

La Parrillada del Ñato (Map p327; ☒ 238 7098; Estrada 1219 at Laureles; mains $6-10) Still Guayaquil's most famous grill and one of the city's institutions, del Ñato does barbecue in a big way, a reference both to the size of the dining room and the large portions. There's also a branch in Alborada at the corner of Demetrio Aguilera Malta and Avenida Rodolfo Baquirizo Nazur.

Lo Nuestro (☒ 238 6398; Estrada 903; mains $6-15) Housed in a century-old mansion complete with wooden shutters and period furniture, Lo Nuestro is one of the most atmospheric places in Guayaquil to eat seafood dishes typical of the region. Musicians play on Friday and Saturday evenings when reservations are recommended and the place fills at lunch time with local bigwigs.

Trattoria da Enrico (☒ 238 7079; Bálsamos 504, Central Urdesa; mains $9-30) One of the more expensive but also more romantic places to eat in Guayaquil, da Enrico makes its intentions loud and clear by the dim mood-lighting, low cellar-like ceiling and, well, the prices on the menu. Serves conventional Italian fare and has an extensive wine selection.

Tsuji (☒ 288 1183; Estrada 816, Urdesa; mains $12) A stylish, upscale Japanese restaurant that wouldn't be out of place in New York City, or Tokyo for that matter. Sushi, sashimi, noodle and tempura dishes are all on the menu.

Siam Thai Cuisine (☒ 223 9404; Calama; mains $10) On the corner of Juan León Mera, this is one of the few Thai restaurants in town and, like other restaurants in the neighborhood, is as much focused on its cool and hip design scheme as it is on its menu – though the usual standards are done well.

Grand Banquete Buffet (☒ 238 5768; Estrada 618; buffet lunch $6) This unassuming, large Chinese restaurant in Urdesa is a good choice if you're hungry – the buffet packs a wallop. Besides a selection of seafood, it has salads and meat and veggie dishes; chicken and pork are grilled to order.

ENTERTAINMENT
The *farra* (nightlife or party) in Guayaquil is spread around town, but some of the most interesting, welcoming and stylish bars are conveniently found in the neighborhood of Las Peñas. There are also several downtown near the Malecón 2000. Alborada, Kennedy Norte and Urdesa also have their fair share of clubs and bars. The local newspapers *El Telégrafo* and *El Universo* have up-to-date entertainment listings. The city's luxury hotels all have casinos and sedate bars.

Bars
La Paleta (Map pp320-1; ☒ 231 2329; Numa Pompillo Llona; ☒ Wed-Sat 6pm to late) Probably the most bohemian and coolest bar in the city. La Paleta is found along the cobblestone streets of Las Peñas and is all cave-like nooks, comfy benches and dark wood. There are bars on the 1st- and 2nd-floors, plus $8 martinis.

DADA (Map pp320-1; ☒ 230 2828; Numa Pompillo Llona 177; ☒ Tue-Sat 6pm-3am) A beautiful new bar just past the Galería Angel Zalmada on Calle Numa Pomilio in Las Peñas, DADA is both hip and stylish and warm and welcoming because of its all-wood interior and picture windows with views of the river.

Escalón 69 (Map pp320-1; ☒ 230 9828; Cerro Santa Ana; ☒ Tue-Sun noon-2am) Above the restaurant of the same name, there's a welcoming bar with karaoke and live music on weekends.

El Galeón de Artur's (Map pp320-1; ☒ 230 3574; Cerro Santa Ana; ☒ 6pm-1:30am) Near the bottom of the stairs in Las Peñas and next to Escalon 69, El Galeón is a casual place for a drink if you don't mind the loud music.

La Proa (Map pp320-1; ☎ 277 2511; Malecón at Vernaza y Carbo; $10 cover; ⌚ 6.30pm-late Wed-Sat) A beautiful and hip bar next to the MAAC cinema – you'd think you were in downtown Manhattan. La Proa has unobstructed river views and happy hour is Wednesday and Thursday from 7pm to 10pm.

La Taberna (Map pp320-1; Cerro Santa Ana) Just to the left at the bottom of the steps in Las Peñas, La Taberna is a drinking bar with Latin rock and pop in the background. The walls are a hodgepodge of soccer jerseys, newspaper clippings, cigarette cartons and photographs.

Piranha Bar (☎ 224 8250; Av Augustin Freire; ⌚ from 4pm Mon-Sat; Garzota, north of the airport) An informal laid-back bar done in wood and bamboo with an eclectic variety of live music Thursday, Friday and Saturday when there's also a small cover charge.

Bar de los Ochenta (Centro Comercial Albán Borja, Av Carlos Julio Arosemena, Km 2.7) In Urdesa, where La Crème used to be, this club plays all 80s music all the time.

Nightclubs
DOWNTOWN
Macarena Lounge (Map pp320-1; Malecón 602 & Imbabura; ⌚ 7pm-4am Mon-Fri), **Bar 234** (Map pp320-1; Imbabura 234; Tue-Sat 6pm-3am) and **Bla, bla, bla Mykonos Café** (Map pp320-1; Imbabura 229 & Rocafuerte) turn into raucous discotheques most weekend nights.

NORTHERN SUBURBS
Barhopping is easy at **Kennedy Mall** (Map p327; Av Francisco de Orellana), which is not a shopping mall but rather a concentration of bars and discos in Kennedy Norte. Have a cabbie drop you off and pick what looks right since they're generally all situated next to each other. Most have a cover charge, but also an open bar, meaning you drink for free after paying admission. The main drag in Urdesa, Estrada, still has a number of happening clubs despite the neighborhood's upper-class residents' desire to keep things low key. Names, locations and hotspots change with frequency.

Mumba (☎ 209 7766; Centro Comercial Bocca, Vía Samborondón; ⌚ 8pm-late) An upscale club with a DJ spinning music on weekend nights.

El Jardín de Salsa (☎ 239 6083; Américas) All salsa all the time. The dance floor here is one of the biggest in Ecuador, but wallflow-

ers can enjoy themselves equally well since there's plenty of space simply for drinking and admiring. It's near the airport.

Fizz (Map p327; Av Francisco de Orellana)

Cinemas
El Telégrafo and *El Universo* publish show times for all cinemas in the city. English-language movies with Spanish subtitles are usually shown, although downtown there are a few B-rated movie houses screening porno flicks and schlock. For Hollywood fare downtown, check out the six-screen **Supercines** (Map pp320-1; ☎ 252 2054; 9 de Octubre 823 & Avilés; $2) or the **Imax theater** (Map pp320-1; ☎ 256 3078; $4) cinema on the Malecón connected to the MAAC; the latter also has the **MAAC Cine** (Map pp320-1; ☎ 230 9400), a nice art-house cinema. The **Casa de Cultura** (Map pp320-1; cnr 9 de Octubre & Moncayo) shows good foreign films and art flicks. The multiscreen **Cinemark** (Map p327; ☎ 269 2014; www.cinemark.com.ec) in the Mall del Sol in the northern suburbs is the largest in the city.

Theater
In addition to a building boom, Guayaquil is also going through somewhat of a cultural renaissance, especially in terms of live theater. Besides performances at the MAAC, several other venues to check out include **Centro Cultural Sarao** (☎ 229 5118; Oeste 313 & Av del Periodista, Kennedy), **Teatro del Ángel** (☎ 238 0585; Bálsamos 620 & Las Monjas, Urdesa), and **Teatro Centro de Arte** (☎ 235 1367; Av del Bombero, Km 4.5).

SHOPPING
El Mercado Artesanal Loja (Map pp320-1; Baquerizo Moreno; ⌚ 9am-7pm Mon-Sat, 10am-5pm Sun) This is a large artisans' market in a building taking up an entire block downtown. It has a huge variety of crafts from all over Ecuador including Otavalo-style sweaters, Panama hats, nicely carved chess boards, mass-produced paintings and just about every knick-knack imaginable. Bargaining is expected.

La Bahía (Map pp320-1; Carbo & Villamil) *Guayacos* like to shop at this sprawling street market between Olmedo and Colón. It's crowded, busy and colorful, and you'll find everything from knock-off name-brand watches to brassieres and bootleg CDs.

(Continued on page 337)

La Virgen de Quito (p77), Quito

Equator line monument, la Mitad del Mundo (p108)

Plaza Grande (p73), Quito

ALFREDO MAIQUEZ

Guagua Pichincha (p111)

Street scene, Cuenca (p195)

DAVID PEEVERS

Volcán El Altar (p177), Candeleria

BRENT WINEBRENNER

ALFREDO MAIQUEZ

Reserva Producción Fanustíca Cuyabeno (p236), northern Oriente

GRANT DIXON

Native plants, Volcán El
Reventador (p232)

Bataburo Lodge (p241), Huaorani territory

KRISTIN PILJAY

PAUL KENNEDY

Seaside cattle-drive, Mompiche (p286)

Isla Rábida (p375)

DONALD C. & PRISCILLA ALEXANDER EASTMAN

PAUL KENNEDY

Church of Santo Domingo (p324), Guayaquil

Las Peñas (p324), Guayaquil

RICHARD I'A

(Continued from page 332)

If you prefer a more sedate shopping atmosphere, try one of the indoor shopping malls along the Malecón or the department stores along 9 de Octubre. The biggest mall in Guayaquil, similar to any you find in the US, is **Mall del Sol** (Map p327; Av Juan Tanca Maarengo) near the airport. **Policentro** (Map p327; Av del Periodista) in the Kennedy suburb has many modern stores, restaurants and a movie theater. Also in Urdesa is **Centro Comercial Albán Borja** (Av Carlos J Arosemena).

GETTING THERE & AWAY
Air
Guayaquil's **Simón Bolívar Airport** (Map p327) is one of Ecuador's two major international airports and is about as busy as Quito's. It's currently located on the east side of Avenida de las Américas, about 5km north of downtown; the international and national terminals are side by side but a brand new terminal next door was under construction at the time of research. Anyone flying to the Galápagos Islands either leaves from here or stops here on their way from Quito; those flying from Quito rarely have to change planes.

There is a *casa de cambio* (currency-exchange bureau) at the airport, which pays about as much as the downtown rate and is open for most incoming international flights. There are also the usual cafeterias, car-rental agencies, gift shops, ATMs and international telephone facilities.

About 1km south of the main airport is the Terminal de Avionetas (small-aircraft terminal).

There are many internal flights to all parts of the country, but times, days and fares change constantly, so check the following information. The most frequent flights are to Quito with TAME, which charges about $58 one way. For the best views, sit on the right side when flying to Quito.

TAME also flies to Cuenca ($48) and Loja ($48) daily, Machala ($48) on weekday mornings and Lago Agrio ($55, via Quito). There are usually flights to Tulcán and Esmeraldas as well.

TAME and AeroGal fly to Baltra and San Cristóbal in the Galápagos. There are two morning flights every day, costing $344 per round-trip ($300 in the low season – mid-January to mid-June and September

to November). Ecuadorian residents pay $80 all year.

Icaro flies to Quito ($57) four times a day Monday to Friday and twice daily on weekends. It flies twice daily (except weekends) to Cuenca ($45) and Monday, Wednesday and Friday to San Cristóbal in the Galápagos.

Austro Aéreo, at the airport, has two flights Monday to Friday to Cuenca ($50).

All the aforementioned flights leave from the main national terminal. Several small airlines have flights leaving from the Terminal de Avionetas. These airlines use small aircraft to service various coastal towns, such as Portoviejo and Esmeraldas. Flights are subject to demand. Baggage is limited to a 10kg bag and passenger weight is limited to 100kg.

The following is a list of domestic airline offices in Guayaquil.

AECA (☎ 228 8110; Terminal de Avionetas)
AeroGal (☎ 228 4218; www.aerogal.com.ec; main airport)
Aerolitoral (☎ 228 0864; Terminal de Avionetas)
Austro Aéreo (☎ 229 6685/87, 228 4084; main airport)
Icaro (☎ 229 4265; www.icaro.com.ec; main airport)
TAME Gran Pasaje (Map pp320-1; ☎ 256 0778, 256 0920; www.tame.com.ec; Paula de Icaza 424, Gran Pasaje); main airport (☎ 228 2062, 228 7155; main airport) Enter the Gran Pasaje office from 9 de Octubre.

See left for information about international flights in and out of Guayaquil.

Boat
Cruise lines occasionally call at Guayaquil, and passengers may make brief forays ashore. A few cargo boats will take passengers to and from North America or Europe (for more information see p404).

Bus & Vans
The **bus terminal** (Map p327) is just north of the airport, though a new one was under construction across the street at the time of research. It has a few simple restaurants, a bank, an Internet café, hairdresser etc. There are scores of bus company offices with their destinations clearly marked and you can get just about anywhere. Keep some loose change handy since it's $0.10 to pass through the turnstiles to get to the buses.

NATIONAL
For the Santa Elena Peninsula, you can take Transportes Villamil or Transportes Posorja, which have buses every 10 minutes to Playas

($2.50, 1¾ hours) and Posorja ($2.10, 2¼ hours). Costa Azul, Co-op Libertad Peninsular (which have air-conditioned buses) and CICA have buses to Salinas ($3, 2½ hours) every 15 minutes. To get to Bosque Protector Cerro Blanco (p318), you can take a bus marked 'Chongón' from the stop at Moncayo and Sucre. All the drivers know where to stop for the entrance to the reserve.

The best services to Quito are with the companies **Transportes Ecuador** (☎ 214 0592), **Flota Imbabura** (☎ 214 0649) and **Panamericana** (☎ 214 0638). They all cost around $9 and do the trip in eight hours.

Several companies run buses to Cuenca, but if you want to get there fast, try the vans run by **Supertaxis Cuenca** (☎ 229 7026); they charge $7. The fastest route (3½ hours) is via Parque Nacional Cajas. **Coturcip** (Map pp320-1; ☎ 251 8895; Sucre 202 & Pichincha) has comfortable air-conditioned vans to Machala ($8).

Most bus companies sell tickets in advance, which will guarantee you a seat. Otherwise, just show up at the terminal and you'll often find a bus to your destination leaving soon. Friday nights and holidays can get booked up. The following table should give you an idea of fares and travel times.

Destination	Cost ($)	Duration (hr)
Ambato	6	6
Atacames	8	8
Babahoyo	2	1
Bahía de Caráquez	4.50	5½
Cuenca	7	3½ to 4½
Esmeraldas	7	7
Huaquillas	4.50	4
Ibarra	10	10
Lago Agrio	10	16
Loja	6	9
Macará	9	11
Machala	4.50	3
Manta	4.50	3½
Muisne	9	9
Piñas	4.50	5
Portoviejo	4.50	4
Puyo	9	7
Quito	9	7 to 10
Riobamba	5	4½
San Lorenzo	10	10
Santo Domingo	4	5
San Vicente	5	6
Tulcán	13	13
Zaruma	7	5

INTERNATIONAL

Ecuadorian bus companies such as CIFA, Transportes Rutas Orenses and Ecuatoriana Pullman go to Machala and Huaquillas on the Peruvian border. Transportes Loja has one bus in the evening to the border at Macará.

The easiest way to Peru, however, is with one of the international lines. **Rutas de America** (☎ 229 7383; www.rutasdeamerica.com; Los Rios 3012 at Letamendi), whose office and terminal is south of downtown, has direct buses to Lima ($50, 24 hours) every day at 6am. **Expresso Internacional Ormeno** (Map p327; ☎ 229 7362; Centro de Negocios El Terminal, Bahia Norte, Office 34, Bloque C) goes daily to Lima ($55) at 2pm, stopping in Tumbes ($20, five hours). Their office and terminal is on Americas, just north of the main bus terminal. These services are very convenient because you do not have to get off the bus to take care of border formalities.

GETTING AROUND

Walking is the easiest and most convenient way of getting around downtown. An above ground metro rail route was under construction at the time of research that will cross the city north to south on Avenida Rocafuerte.

To/From the Airport

The **airport** (Américas) is about 5km north of downtown. A taxi from the airport to the center should cost no more than $4; in the other direction $3. Taxi drivers will likely try to charge much more from the airport – be sure to bargain. Taxis are cheaper if you hail one from the street outside the terminal.

If you cross the street in front of the airport, you can take a bus downtown. From the center, the best bus to take to the airport is the No 2 Especial, which only costs $0.25 and takes under an hour. It runs along the Malecón but is sometimes full, so you should leave yourself plenty of time.

To/From the Bus Terminal

From the airport, the bus terminal is about 2km away. You can walk the distance if you want – turn right out of the airport and head for the obvious huge terminal. Or you can take a bus or taxi (about $1.50).

Buses from the center to the bus terminal leave from Parque Victoria, near 10 de Agosto and Moncayo.

Several buses leave from the terminal for downtown including the No 71. A taxi to or from downtown is about $3.

Bus
City buses are cheap (about $0.20) but the routes are complicated and are not much use for getting around downtown. What with waiting and traffic, you're better off walking.

Car
There are several car-rental agencies at the airport including **Hertz** (☎ 229 3011; www.hertz .com) and **Localiza** (☎ 228 1463; www.localiza .ec), although both are expensive; make sure insurance, tax and mileage are included in your rate. See p407 for more details.

Taxi
Always agree on the fare before you get into the cab, otherwise you will surely be overcharged. You should be able to get between any two points downtown for about $1.50 and to the airport, the bus terminal or Urdesa for between $3 to $4.

There are air-conditioned minicabs called 'Taxi Amigos' that respond quickly once called and charge even slightly less than yellow cabs. **VIPCAR** (☎ 239 3000) is one.

SOUTH OF GUAYAQUIL

Though primarily seen by travelers simply as a place to pass through on their way south to Peru, this agriculturally important part of the country boasts two national reserves and several charming mountain towns.

RESERVA ECOLÓGICA MANGLARES CHURUTE
☎ 04
This 50,000-hectare **national reserve** (admission $10) protects an area of mangroves southeast of Guayaquil. Much of the coast used to be mangrove forest – an important and unique habitat (see p44). This is one of Ecuador's few remaining mangrove coastlands – the rest have been destroyed by the shrimp industry. Inland is some tropical dry forest on hills reaching 700m above sea level.

Studies of the area within the reserve indicate that the changing habitat from coastal mangroves to hilly forest supports a wide biodiversity with a high degree of endemism. Dolphins have frequently been reported along the coast and many other animal and bird species are seen by wildlife-watchers, who are the main visitors.

The reserve entrance is on the left side of the main Guayaquil–Machala highway, about 46km south of Guayaquil. At the entrance is an **information center** (☎ 09-276 3653) where you pay the entrance fee. The park rangers can arrange boats for you to visit the mangroves (about $60 for the whole day for four or five people). There are also several kilometers of hiking trails. The best season for boats is January to May, when water levels are high (but there are more insects then). There is room at the information center for a few people to sleep.

Bordering the reserve is another area protected by Fundación Andrade. Nancy Hilgert (p326) is the contact and she can guide you. Chasquitur (p326) also does tours to Manglares Churute.

Contact Dreamkapture Hostal (p329) in Guayaquil about cabañas in the reserve.

Any bus between Guayaquil and Naranjal or Machala can drop you off at the information center. When you are ready to leave, you can flag buses down. There is a sign on the road and drivers know it.

MACHALA
☎ 07 / pop 216,900
Surrounded by banana plantations – the *oro verde* (green gold), which is the province's moniker – Machala is the commercial and administrative capital of El Oro Province. The city is a convenient stop south from Guayaquil on the way to the Peruvian border or as a place to base yourself for journeys further into the mountains directly to the east. Puerto Bolívar (p342), only 7km away, is the local international port and seafood central.

Information
Banco del Pacífico (cnr Junín & Rocafuerte) ATM.
Banco del Pichincha (cnr Guayas & Rocafuerte) Changes traveler's checks and has an ATM.
CLIC Internet (9 de Octubre; ☽ 8am-10pm) Internet access.
Copy@Comp (Sucre; ☽ 8am-8pm)
Easy Net Café (9 de Octubre; ☽ 8am-10pm) Good speed, flat screens.
Hospital (☎ cnr Colón & Boyacácnr)

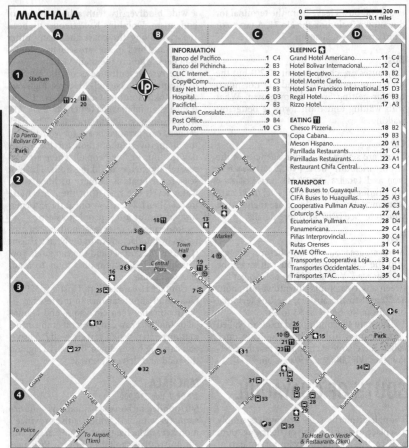

MACHALA

0 _____ 200 m
0 _____ 0.1 miles

INFORMATION
Banco del Pacífico.........................1 C4
Banco del Pichincha......................2 B3
CLIC Internet................................3 B2
Copy@Comp.................................4 C3
Easy Net Internet Café..................5 B3
Hospital......................................6 D3
Pacifictel....................................7 B3
Peruvian Consulate.......................8 C4
Post Office..................................9 B4
Punto.com.................................10 C3

SLEEPING
Grand Hotel Americano.................11 C4
Hotel Bolivar Internacional............12 C4
Hotel Ejecutivo...........................13 B2
Hotel Monte Carlo.......................14 C2
Hotel San Francisco International.....15 D3
Regal Hotel................................16 B3
Rizzo Hotel................................17 A3

EATING
Chesco Pizzeria...........................18 B2
Copa Cabana..............................19 B3
Meson Hispano............................20 A1
Parrillada Restaurants...................21 C4
Parrilladas Restaurants.................22 A1
Restaurant Chifa Central...............23 C4

TRANSPORT
CIFA Buses to Guayaquil................24 C4
CIFA Buses to Huaquillas...............25 A3
Cooperativa Pullman Azuay............26 C3
Coturcip SA................................27 A4
Ecuatoriana Pullman.....................28 D4
Panamericana.............................29 C4
Piñas Interprovincial.....................30 C4
Rutas Orenses 31 C4
TAME Office................................32 B4
Transportes Cooperativa Loja.........33 C4
Transportes Occidentales..............34 D4
Transportes TAC..........................35 C4

Stadium

To Puerto
Bolívar (7km)
Park

Las Palmeras

Vela

Santa Rosa

Ayacucho

Sucre

Guayas

Boyacá

Pasaje

Olmedo

9 de Mayo

Market

Church

Town
Hall

Central
Plaza

9 de Octubre

Montalvo

Páez

Rocafuerte

Bolívar

Junín

Olmedo

Park

Pichincha

Junín

Tarqui

Sucre

Colón

Buenavista

Guayas

9 de Mayo

Arizaga

Montalvo

Tarqui

To Police
To Airport
(1km)

To Hotel Oro Verde
& Restaurants (2km)

Pacifictel (cnr Montalvo near 9 de Octubre)
Post office (cnr Montalvo & Bolívar)
Provincial Government Office (Map p340; ☎ 293 5871; Ayacucho btwn Pasaje & Sucre) Has some tourism information, including info on Bosque Petrificado Puyango.
Punto.com (Sucre; ☺ 8am-8pm)

Festivals & Events
Machala celebrates the **Feria Mundial del Banano** during the third week in September, when an international contest is held to elect La Reina del Banano ('The Banana Queen').

Sleeping
Machala has a number of good-value hotels and it makes sense to spend the night here rather than Huaquillas if heading to or from Peru. Prices may rise for September's Banana Festival and national holidays.

Grand Hotel Americano (☎ 296 6400; www.hotel smachala.com; Tarqui & 9 de Octubre; r from $20; ☒) The best choice in terms of overall value, the Grand Hotel Americano has clean, modern rooms, professional staff and a central location. The one downside is potentially annoying street noise. All rooms have air-conditioning and cable TV, and breakfast is included in the attached restaurant.

Regal Hotel (☎ 296 0000; www.regalhotel.com.ec; Bolívar near Guayas; s/d $42/55; ☒) A big step up in terms of price though not a huge one in terms of comfort, the Regal nevertheless is the classiest hotel in downtown Machala.

There are hints of Spanish villa in the floor tiles and the wall murals. The popular Cafeteria Las Rocas is attached. Look for the tall glass-fronted building only a block from the main plaza.

Hotel Monte Carlo (☎ 293 3462; montecarlo@asap -tel.net; Guayas near Olmedo; s/d $23/35; 🔀) Another good central choice, the Monte Carlo has nothing of its namesake's luxury (except maybe a fake marble floor) but the rooms are large and sunny and have cable TV. A nice restaurant is attached.

Rizzo Hotel (☎ 293 3651; Guayas 2123; s/d $25/42; 🔀 🏊) The architecture of the Rizzo screams 70s and the furniture probably hasn't been replaced since then, but there is a pool and patio area. Rooms at the Rizzo are clean and have cable TV though they are a little dark. Breakfast is included.

Hotel Bolivar Internacional (☎ 293 0727; cnr Bolívar & Colón; r $16) A short walk from the busy center, the Hotel Bolivar is a small sparkling new hotel. Some of the tiled rooms are actually too large with too many beds.

Hotel Ejecutivo (☎ 292 3162; Sucre & 9 de Mayo; s/d $18/25; 🔀) Rooms in the Ejecutivo have great views of the busy downtown streets and the hallways are bright and sunny which helps offset the old TV and slightly mismatched furniture.

Hotel San Francisco International (☎ 293 0445, 293 0457; Tarqui near Sucre; s/d with fan $12/18, with aircon $17/23; 🔀) The fan rooms at this centrally located hotel are small and have old furniture and chipped paint. Although the rooms in the newer wing are much nicer and better kept, they aren't nearly as good value as those in the Grand Hotel Americano only a block away.

Eating

There are several cheap *parrillada* restaurants serving inexpensive grilled chicken and steaks on Sucre near Tarqui and on Las Palmeras in front of the stadium. All the hotels listed earlier have restaurants and most are air-conditioned. Consider heading over to Puerto Bolívar (p342) for a fresh seafood lunch.

Meson Hispano (☎ 293 6769; Av Las Palmeras & Sucre; mains $5-12; ⏱ 11am-midnight Mon-Thu, 11-1am Fri & Sat) This restaurant is where the elite of Machala go to eat. Meson Hispano is modern, has uniformed waiters and accepts credit cards. The chef does the grilling in the dining room

and the menu includes everything from *ceviche de concho* ($5) to paella for two ($12) to chateaubriand ($7).

Chesco Pizzeria (☎ 293 6418; Guayas 1050 & 9 de Octubre; mains $4) Easily one of the best restaurants in town, Chesco serves up piping-hot deep-dish pizzas plus pasta and hamburgers in a modern dining room.

Copa Cabana (☎ 292 3491; 9 de Octubre 111; mains $3) An American diner wannabe complete with booth seating and banana splits ($3.50), Copa Cabana's menu has chicken sandwiches, hamburgers, fries and more.

Restaurant Chifa Central (Tarqui near Sucre; mains $2-5; ⏱ 11am-10pm) This Chinese restaurant across from the Grand Hotel Americano has large portions and a modern dining room with family-style seating.

There are several restaurants in the **Hotel Oro Verde** (☎ 293 3140; www.oroverdehotels.com; Circunvalación Norte & Calle Vehicular V7), Machala's only luxury hotel a few kilometers south of town.

Getting There & Away

AIR

Weekday morning flights to Guayaquil ($30), continuing to Quito ($55), are available with **TAME** (☎ 293 0139; www.tame.com.ec; Montalvo near Pichincha). The airport is barely 1km from downtown and a taxi ride there will cost about $1. If you're on foot, walk southwest along Montalvo.

BUS

Machala has no central bus terminal. There are **CIFA** (☎ 293 1164; Guayas & Bolivar) buses that go to the Peruvian border at Huaquillas ($1.50, 1½ hours) every 20 minutes during daylight from the corner of Bolívar and Guayas. These buses go via the towns of Santa Rosa and Arenillas.

CIFA buses also go to Guayaquil ($4.50, three hours) from its depot on 9 de Octubre near Tarqui. **Rutas Orenses** (☎ 293 7661; Rocafuerte near Tarqui) and **Ecuatoriana Pullman** (☎ 293 1164; 9 de Octubre near Colón) have more comfortable air-conditioned buses and frequent services to Guayaquil as well.

Piñas Interprovincial (☎ 229 3689; Colón & Rocafuerte) and **Transportes TAC** (Colón) both leave regularly from early morning to around 7pm for Piñas ($2, two hours) and Zaruma ($3, three hours).

Panamericana (☎ 293 0141; Colón & Rocafuerte) has regular daily buses to Quito ($7, 11

THE SOUTH COAST

hours). It also has buses to Santo Domingo ($6, eight hours) and an evening bus to Tulcán. **Transportes Occidentales** (Buenavista & Olmedo) has regular buses to Quito and a night bus to Esmeraldas ($7, nine hours).

Cooperative Pullman Azuay (☎ 293 0539; Sucre at Tarqui) has many buses daily to Cuenca ($3.60, four hours). A few direct buses take three hours.

Transportes Cooperativa Loja (☎ 293 2030; Tarqui & Bolivar) goes to Loja ($4.50) several times a day; the ride takes six to seven hours on the old (but very scenic) dirt road via Piñas and four to five hours on the newer paved road.

VAN

For both a more comfortable and faster option, **Coturcip SA** (☎ 296 0849, in Guayaquil 251 8895; Guayas 2223) has several departures leaving daily in air-conditioned mini vans to Guayaquil ($7).

Getting Around

The No 1 bus, which is usually crowded, goes northwest from the central plaza along 9 de Octubre to Puerto Bolívar ($0.20, 15 minutes). It returns along Pichincha and goes southeast as far as the statue of El Bananero, almost 2km from the center. A taxi to Puerto Bolívar costs no more than $2.

At the airport, **Localiza** (☎ 293 5455) rents out cars. Hotel Oro Verde (p328) also arranges car rental.

PUERTO BOLÍVAR & JAMBELÍ

☎ 07

The port of Puerto Bolívar, only 7km from Machala, is of interest to seafood connoisseurs and those who want to glimpse the final stop for the southern coast's bananas and shrimp before it's shipped overseas. Protected from the ocean by islands and a diminishing supply of mangroves, the port itself is really nothing more than a concrete Malecón with over a dozen cevicherias and a slightly dodgy feel at night. The **Waikiki Restaurant** (☎ 292 9810; mains $4.50) is a more upscale and modern version of these and a secure destination if you decide to visit after dark.

Motorized dugouts can be hired for cruising the mangroves, for **bird-watching** or to visit the nearby island beach at **Jambelí** (mosquito-ridden during the wet months). While it's understandably popular for Machala residents seeking a quick escape from the city, it's not an especially attractive destination in and of itself. Jambelí can be busy on weekends and completely overcrowded during **Carnaval** and **Semana Santa**.

Maria Sol (☎ 293 7461; r per person $5) is a small place with fan rooms on the beach. Numerous beach-side shacks serve seafood on weekends, but many are closed midweek.

Take the No 1 bus from Machala's central plaza; a taxi should cost about $2. To Jambelí you can either charter a boat from Puerto Bolívar or take one of the passenger

---

THE FRUIT OF LABOR

Much like big oil, 'big banana' is controlled by a handful of powerful companies. The biggest of the big in Ecuador (which is now the world's largest banana exporter) is Exportadora Bananero Noboa, owned by Alvaro Noboa, who lost to Lucio Gutiérrez in the 2002 presidential election and is one of the country's wealthiest people. Followed closely by a consortium called La Favorita, and then the US companies Chiquita (formerly United Fruit), Dole and Del Monte, together these companies control the world market in bananas. Ecuador has trumped its South American competitors like Columbia, Panama, Guatemala and Costa Rica at least in part because the cost of labor is lower here than elsewhere.

Only 1% of the 150,000 people working in the banana industry in Ecuador are unionized. As a point of comparison, in Columbia around 90% of the banana workers belong to a union. To help offset the low wages of their parents – around $6 a day – an estimated 6000 children work on the plantations in often unsafe and dangerous working conditions and the big banana companies use only short-term contracts to avoid labor protections. There have been calls for reform both within Ecuador and from labor groups abroad, but the companies have responded with sometimes violent intimidation and the claim that they are forced to lower their wages because big wholesale and retail chains in the US like Costco and Walmart demand lower and lower prices.

shuttle boats that head to Jambelí (round-trip $2.40, 20 minutes) every half hour from 7.30am to 6pm. The boats drop you off on a canal on the mainland side of the island and you have to walk the few hundred meters to the beach.

ZARUMA
☎ 07 / elevation 1150m

Climbing the road to Zaruma in the mountains southeast of Machala, the country and the views open up, providing a refreshing change of perspective and feel from that of the lowlands. Once you reach the narrow, hilly streets of this old gold-mining town – which is lined with quaint timber buildings and where everyone knows everyone else's name – you'll feel like you're in a different country.

While the mines are mostly exhausted, you can arrange a visit at the friendly and helpful **tourism office** (☎ 297 3101; turismo zaruma07@yahoo.com; ○8am-5pm Mon-Sat, 9am-4pm Sat, 9am-1pm Sun) just off the Plaza de Independencia. In town there's a Banco de Guayaquil and a Banco de Machala, both with ATMs, and one or two Internet cafés.

None of the hotels have air-conditioning because night-time temperatures here are comfortable.

Roland Hotel (☎ 297 2800; s/d $12-18/24-30; 🛋) is the best place to stay in Zaruma. The carpeted modern rooms have TVs, hot showers and fantastic views of the surrounding mountains and valley. There are more expensive small chalets around the pool in the courtyard. It is a short hike uphill to the plaza; look for it on the main road before you reach the town proper.

A close second is **Hotel Blacio** (☎ 297 2045; www.hotelblacio.com; Calle El Sexmo; s/d $10/20), a friendly new hotel on the main street a block or so above the bus stop. Rooms here are very comfortable and have cable TV, hot water and some even have small balconies. Tourist information is readily available here.

Yet another good choice is **Romeria Hostal** (☎ 297 2173; romeriahostal@hotmail.com; s/d $7/15), a well-run, 12-room place right on the Plaza Independencia. The carpeted rooms are bright and also have TV and hot water, but it's the wood floors and public balcony that give the place character. A café is attached.

There are several casual eateries within a few blocks of Plaza Independencia. Tango-

bar Restaurant has charming wood floors and good and cheap *almuerzos*.

Piñas (☎ 297 6167) has departures every hour on the half hour and TAC leaves every hour on the hour for Piñas (1$, one hour) and Machala ($3, three hours).

PIÑAS
☎ 07 / elevation 1014

Architecturally more modern and less charming, Piñas is probably best visited as a side trip while based in Zaruma. In 1980, a new bird species – the El Oro parakeet – was discovered near here. The best place to see the bird is Fundación Jocotoco's **Reserva Buenaventura**, a 1500-hectare cloud-forest reserve about 9km from Piñas.

About five blocks from the bus stop is the **Orquideario** (Sucre & Olmedo), a small orchid garden with bromeliads, heleconias and a talapia-fish breeding pond. You can walk or take a taxi to a cross on a nearby hilltop for good views of the surrounding hills.

Though the choice of accommodation is far superior in Zaruma, if you're stuck for the night, check out the **Residencial Dumari** (☎ 297 6118; Av 8 de Noviembre & Loja; r without/with private bathroom $6/9). There's no fan or air-conditioning and the furniture is old and mismatched, but the wooden floors are attractive and some rooms have good views of town.

The Calypso Heladeria & Café is across the street from the Piñas bus stop and ticket office, a block from the TAC stop. It is a clean little place with ice cream and snacks, and a good place to wait for the bus. There are several simple eateries in town including Magic Pizzeria and Naomi's Café & Bar.

Piñas and TAC run frequent buses to/from Machala ($2, two hours). Buses to/from Zaruma ($1, one hour) all pass through here.

EL BOSQUE PETRIFICADO PUYANGO
☎ 07

This is the largest petrified forest (2659 hectares) in Ecuador and probably the whole continent. Fossilized Araucaria tree trunks – many of them millions of years old and up to 11m long and 1.6m in diameter – have been found and the reserve is also home to over 130 bird species.

Puyango is in a valley at about 360m above sea level, some 55km inland from the coast. The valley is separated from the ocean by the Cordillera Larga, which reaches over 900m above sea level. Despite the separation, the area experiences a coastal weather pattern, with warm temperatures and most of the annual 1000mm of rainfall occurring from January to May.

Camping is allowed for a small fee; ask at the information center. A lookout point and trails have been constructed.

In the small nearby village of **Puyango** there is no hotel as such, although the villagers will find you a bed or floor space. Locals know the reserve and some will act as guides. The nearest village with basic *hostals* is **Alamor**, just south of Puyango.

For more information, call the **Provincial Government Office** (Map p340; ☎ 293 5871; Ayacucho btwn Pasaje & Sucre).

Transportes Cooperativa Loja buses from Machala and Loja will drop you in Puyango. Alternatively, take a CIFA bus to the town of Arenillas, where you can catch an infrequent local bus to Puyango. Since Puyango is close to the border there may be passport checks.

TO/FROM THE PERUVIAN BORDER

It's about 80km from Machala to the border town of Huaquillas, the route taken by most overland travelers to Peru. The bus passes through banana and palm plantations, as well as through the dusty market towns of **Santa Rosa** and **Arenillas**. The border itself is at **Río Zarumilla** (☼ 24hr), which is crossed by an international bridge linking Huaquillas to **Augas Verdes** in Peru. Many travelers report that crossing at night is much easier – it allows you to avoid the crowds, touts and overzealous immigration officials (as opposed to the sleepy immigration officials who, in the middle of the night, simply want you on your way).

The **Ecuadorian Immigrations office** (☼ 24hr) is inconveniently located about 3km north of the bridge; all entrance and exit formalities are carried out here. The Peruvian immigration office is about 2km south of the border.

If you are leaving Peru and entering Ecuador, first obtain an exit stamp in your passport from the Peruvian authorities. After walking across the international bridge, you'll find yourself on the main road, which is crowded with market stalls and stretches

out through Huaquillas. Take a taxi (about $1.50) or a Machala-bound bus to the Ecuadorian immigration office.

If you are leaving Ecuador, stop at the Ecuadorian *migraciones* office, 3km before the border. If you're traveling by bus from Machala, the driver usually does not wait for you. You must save your ticket and board the next Machala–Huaquillas bus (they pass every 20 minutes or so) or continue on to the border by taxi.

As you cross the international bridge, you may be asked to show the exit stamp in your passport to the Ecuadorian and Peruvian (Aguas Verdes) bridge guards, or you may not be bothered until full entrance formalities are carried out in the immigration building about 2km from the border. Taxis are available for about $0.50 per person.

Although an exit ticket out of Peru is officially required, travelers are rarely asked for this unless they look thoroughly disreputable. Other Latin American travelers are often asked for an exit ticket, however. If necessary, there is a bus office in Aguas Verdes that sells (nonrefundable) bus tickets out of Peru. The immigration official will tell you where it is.

From the immigration building in Peru, *colectivos* (shared taxis; about $1.50 per person) go to Tumbes – beware of overcharging. Tumbes has plenty of hotels, as well as transportation to take you further into Peru. See Lonely Planet's *Peru* for more information.

Huaquillas
☎ 07 / pop 30,000
If you don't look up and miss the huge 'Welcome to Ecuador' or 'Welcome to Peru' signs you'd never know you crossed over into another country. The police uniforms are different colors and the Ecuadorian side is more hectic and crowded, but other than that both sides of the frontier hold little appeal except as places that have to be passed through on the way to somewhere else. The Río Zarumilla, which separates the two, is a dry riverbed for much of the year. There is a busy street market by the border and the place is full of Peruvians shopping on day passes.

There are several Internet cafés in town including **Rifynet** (6 de Agosto) across from Hotel Rody.

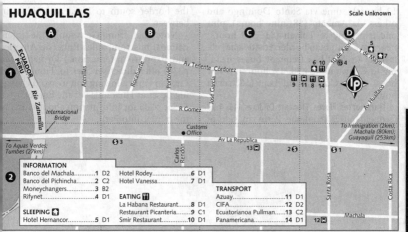

MONEY

It's best to avoid the informal moneychangers – the guys with the briefcases sitting on plastic chairs – on the Ecuadorian side of the border. A number of travelers report being passed fake currency. In order to get your business, moneychangers will tell patent lies like 'banks are closed,' 'the machines don't work' or 'there's a strike.' Banks in Huaquillas or Aguas Verdes do not normally do exchange transactions, but it's worth trying and there are a number of ATMs on the Ecuadorian side including a **Banco de Pichincha** (La Republica) and a **Banco de Machala** (La Republica).

If leaving Peru, it's best to get rid of as much Peruvian currency as possible before arriving in Ecuador and preferably before arriving at the border since there are reports that moneychangers on the Peruvian side are equally likely to cheat on transactions. If leaving Ecuador, your US currency is easily exchanged in Peru, but again it's best to wait to do the bulk of your transactions further south in Tumbes. Traveler's checks can also be exchanged, but with some difficulty and at lower rates than cash.

SLEEPING & EATING

Most travelers leaving Ecuador sleep in Machala and go straight through to Tumbes (or vice versa); both places have plenty of hotels. However, if you're stuck for the night there are a few adequate options.

Hotel Hernancor (☎ 299 5467; 1 de Mayo; s/d $13/16; ❄) High ceilings and a black-and-white tile floor pass for charm in Huaquillas, which makes the Hernancor the best bet. Plus the rooms are large and the front desk is friendly and can help with transport questions.

Hotel Rody (☎ 299 5581; Av Teriente Córdorez & 10 de Agosto; s/d from $5/10) The Rody looks quite nice from the outside, but rooms are small and the paint is peeling. More expensive rooms have air-conditioning.

Hotel Vanessa (☎ 299 6263; 1 de Mayo & Av Hualtaco; r $10) A not entirely lovely choice because of the old furniture, broken TVs and chipped paint, the Vanessa does have hot water and some rooms have air-conditioning.

Smir Restaurant (cnr 10 de Agosto & Teriente Córdorez) serves ceviches, tortillas and other fare in an air-conditioned modern dining room. **La Habana Restaurant** (Teriente Córdorez) and **Restaurant Picanteria** (Teriente Córdorez) are both across the street; the former does good *parrilladas* and the latter has cheap *almuerzos*. There are several other small hole-in-the-wall eateries around town.

GETTING THERE & AWAY

Huaquillas does not have a main bus terminal, but you will see buses on the main street a few blocks from the border. **CIFA** buses run frequently to Machala ($4.50, 1½ hours). Taxi drivers at the border will tell you there are no buses or *colectivios* running to Tumbes when in fact there are.

Panamericana (cnr Teriente Córdorez & 10 de Agosto) has six buses a day heading to Quito ($10,

12 hours), some via Santo Domingo and others via Ambato ($8, nine hours), plus one trip daily to Tulcan ($15, 18 hours) near the Columbian border. **Ecuatoriana Pullman** (La Republica) has frequent buses heading to Guayaquil ($4.50, 4½ hours). A few buses go to Cuenca and Loja ($8, seven hours).

Transportes Flores (Teniente Cordoves 116) has frequent buses from the Peruvian side of the border south to Lima and points in between.

Note that from Guayaquil, the international bus companies Rutas de America and Expresso Internacional Ormeno (see p338) offer direct services to Tumbes and Lima in Peru, allowing you to avoid changing buses at Huaquillas or the border.

See p403 for information about crossing the border into Peru.

The Galápagos Islands

Much like the revolutionary scientific idea it's become synonymous with, the Galápagos Islands may inspire you to think differently about the world. Nowhere else can you engage in a staring contest with wild animals and lose. You can't help thinking you've stumbled upon an alternate universe, some strange utopian colony organized by sea lions – the golden retrievers of the Galápagos – and arranged on principles of mutual cooperation. Don't come expecting to see bizarre wildlife – there are no half-penguin, half-turtle 'penurtles,' no large mammals with shark fins. What's truly special is that the creatures that call the islands home act as if humans are nothing more than slightly annoying paparazzi.

This is not the Bahamas – though some of the boats that cruise these islands will remind you of a Caribbean luxury resort – and these aren't Pacific paradises; in fact, most of the islands are devoid of vegetation and look more like the moon than Hawaii. There are more humans living here than most people assume, more than 30,000 and the population is growing; and for such isolated specks of land over 1000km from mainland Ecuador, there's a surprising level of development – of course most of it is geared toward sustaining a thriving tourism industry.

The islands have taken on a mythological status. Their relationship with Charles Darwin, the islands' most famous visitor who undoubtedly violated several park rules in riding and eating the Galápagos turtles, has become distorted and romanticized. Yet you don't have to be an evolutionary biologist or an ornithologist to appreciate one of the few places left on the planet where the footprint of the human presence is kept to a minimum.

THE GALÁPAGOS ISLANDS

HIGHLIGHTS

- Swim after frisky penguins off **Isla Bartolomé** (p375)
- Meet iguanas face-to-scary-face on **Isla Fernandina** (p378)
- Tip-toe up to seabirds along the dramatic cliffs at **Punta Suárez** on Isla Española (p379)
- Sunbathe at **Playa Tortuga** or dive in **Academy Bay** near Puerto Ayora (p362)
- Catch some rip-roaring surf off **Isla San Cristóbal** (p371)

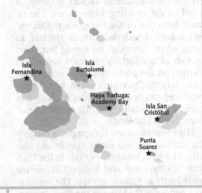

■ AVERAGE TEMPERATURE IN PUERTO BAQUERIZO MORENO: 23°C (73°F)

■ RAINIEST MONTH IN PUERTO BAQUERIZO MORENO: FEBRUARY

Orientation

There are around 12 main islands and 12 minor islands. Five of the islands are inhabited. About half the residents live in Puerto Ayora, on Isla Santa Cruz in the middle of the archipelago, which is also the most important island from the traveler's point of view. North of Santa Cruz, separated by a narrow strait, is Isla Baltra, which is home to one of the islands' major airports. A public bus and a ferry connect the Isla Baltra airport with Puerto Ayora (see p368).

Puerto Baquerizo Moreno on Isla San Cristóbal, the easternmost island, continues to grow and develop and is becoming more important with regards to tourism. Its airport is receiving an increasing number of flights from the mainland and while more tours start from Isla Santa Cruz, Puerto Baquerizo Moreno is another option.

The other inhabited islands are Isla Isabela, with the small port of Puerto Villamil; and Isla Santa María (Floreana), with Puerto Velasco Ibarra – both have places to stay and eat. Regular public ferries or private boats provide interisland transportation (see p359).

The remaining islands are not inhabited by people but are visited on tours. See p14 for information on planning your trip and for recommended books about the islands. See p49 for a brief introduction to the wildlife of the islands.

When to Visit

There really isn't a bad time to visit, however there are several factors to keep in mind in determining when to go. The islands have two distinct seasons: the warm/wet season which lasts from January to June, when there can be strong but short periods of rain but it's generally sunny and warm; and the cool/dry season which lasts from July to December when water temperatures can become decidedly chilly and a misty precipitation known as the 'garúa' impacts the highlands.

High season in the Galápagos is roughly the same as the warm/wet season and also coincides with vacation periods in the USA such as Christmas and Easter. This means more boats and more groups. The low season, generally the same as the cool/dry season means fewer visitors which is a plus, but while the air temperature is extremely

WHAT TO PACK

- Ear plugs – in case your cabin is too close to the engine
- Motion sickness pills – nighttime crossings can feel like a roller coaster ride during certain times of the year
- Wet suit – all the higher-end boats provide these but they might not always fit so snug
- Snorkeling gear – again, all the higher-end boats provide this and it's of generally good quality; however lower-end boats may not provide gear or, if they do, it may be of poor quality

pleasant, the water is colder (wet suits are definitely needed) and the seas can be rough during the overnight passages between islands. Sea sickness is not uncommon and some people have difficulty sleeping.

History

The Galápagos Archipelago was discovered by accident in 1535, when Tomás de Berlanga, the first Bishop of Panama, drifted off course while sailing from Panama to Peru. The bishop reported his discovery to King Charles V of Spain and included in his report a description of the giant Galápagos tortoises from which the islands received their name, and an amusing note about the islands' birds that any visitor today can appreciate, '…so silly that they didn't know how to flee and many were caught by hand.'

It is possible that the indigenous inhabitants of South America were aware of the islands' existence before 1535, but there are no definite records of this and the islands don't appear on a world map until 1570 when they are identified as the 'island of the tortoises.' In 1953, Norwegian explorer Thor Heyerdahl discovered what he thought to be pre-Columbian pottery shards on the islands, but the evidence seems inconclusive.

For more than three centuries after their discovery, the Galápagos were used as a base by a succession of buccaneers, sealers and whalers. The islands provided sheltered anchorage, firewood, water and an abundance of fresh food in the form of the giant Galápagos tortoises, which were caught by the thousands and stacked, alive, in the ships' holds. More than 100,000 are estimated to have been taken between 1811 and 1844. The tortoises could survive for a year or more and thus provided fresh meat for the sailors long after they had left the islands.

The first rough charts of the archipelago were made by buccaneers in the late 17th century, and scientific exploration began in the late 18th century. The Galápagos' most famous visitor was Charles Darwin, who arrived in 1835 aboard the British naval vessel the *Beagle*. Darwin stayed for five weeks, 19 days of which were spent on four of the larger islands, making notes and collecting specimens that provided important evidence for his theory of evolution, which he would later formulate and publish, but not for decades after. He spent the most time on Isla San Salvador observing and, for that matter, eating tortoises. The truth is that Darwin devoted as much of his attention to geology and botany as he did to the animals and marine life of the Galápagos.

The first resident of the islands was Patrick Watkins, an Irishman who was marooned on Isla Santa Maria in 1807 and spent two years living there, growing vegetables and trading his produce for rum from passing boats. The story goes that he managed to remain drunk for most of his stay, then stole a ship's boat and set out for Guayaquil accompanied by five slaves. No one knows what happened to the slaves – only Watkins reached the mainland.

Ecuador officially claimed the Galápagos Archipelago in 1832. For roughly one century thereafter, the islands were inhabited by only a few settlers and were used as penal colonies, the last of which were closed in 1959.

Some islands were declared wildlife sanctuaries in 1934, and 97% of the archipelago officially became a national park in 1959. Organized tourism began in the late 1960s and now, an estimated 80,000 foreign visitors visit the islands each year. Another 20,000 or so are businesspeople or Ecuadorians visiting family and friends and don't enter the protected reserve.

Geography

The Galápagos are an isolated group of volcanic islands that lie in the Pacific Ocean on the equator about 90 degrees west of Greenwich. The nearest mainland is Ecua-dor, some 1000km to the east, and Costa Rica, almost 1100km to the northeast. The land mass of the archipelago covers 7882 sq km, of which well over half consists of Isla Isabela, the largest island within the archipelago and the 12th-largest in the South Pacific. There are 13 major islands (ranging in area from 14 sq km to 4588 sq km), six small islands (1 sq km to 5 sq km) and scores of islets, of which only some are named. The islands are spread over roughly 50,000 sq km of ocean. The highest point in the Galápagos is Volcán Wolf (1646m), on Isla Isabela.

Most of the islands have two – sometimes three – names. The earliest charts gave the islands both Spanish and English names (many of these refer to pirates or English noblemen assigned by Ambrose Cowley who drew up the first navigational charts of the islands), and the Ecuadorian government assigned official names in 1892. An island can thus have a Spanish name, an English name and an official name. The official names are used here in most cases.

Geology

The oldest of the islands visible today were formed roughly four to five million years ago by underwater volcanoes erupting and rising above the ocean's surface (the islands were never connected to the mainland). The Galápagos region is volcanically very active – more than 50 eruptions have been recorded since their discovery in 1535. The most recent eruption occurred in October, 2005 when Volcán Sierra Negra on Isabela spewed ash and lava for several days. Thus, the formation of the islands is an ongoing process; the archipelago is relatively young compared with the age of the earth (which is about 1000 times older).

Geologists generally agree that two relatively new geological theories explain the islands' formation. The theory of plate tectonics holds that the earth's crust consists of several rigid plates that, over geological time, move relative to one another over the surface of the earth. The Galápagos lie on the northern edge of the Nazca Plate, close to its junction with the Cocos Plate. These two plates are spreading apart at a rate of about 1km every 14,000 years, pretty fast by plate-tectonic standards.

The hotspot theory states that deep within the earth (below the moving tectonic plates)

GALÁPAGOS ISLANDS

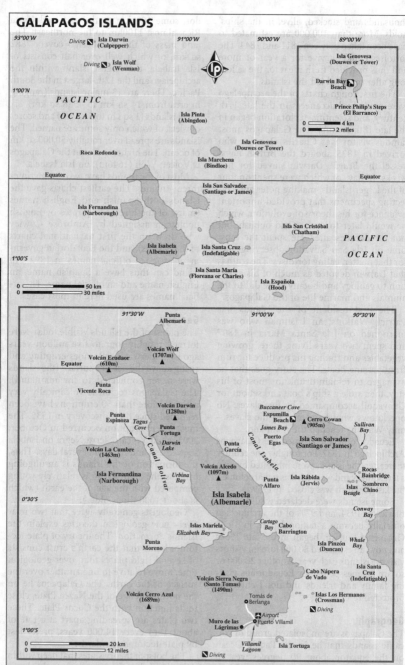

THE GALÁPAGOS ISLANDS

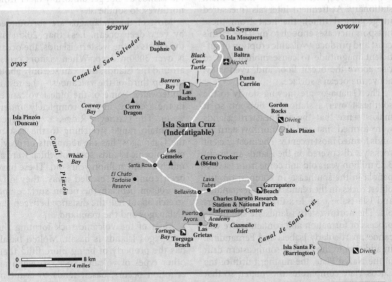

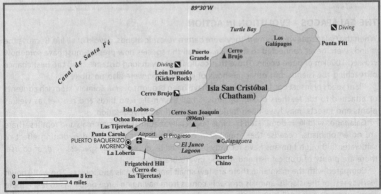

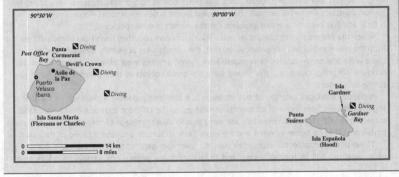

THE GALÁPAGOS ISLANDS

are certain superheated areas that remain stationary. At frequent intervals (measured in geological time), the heat from these hotspots increases enough to melt the earth's crust and produce a volcanic eruption of sufficient magnitude to cause molten lava to rise above the ocean floor and, eventually, above the ocean's surface.

The Galápagos are moving slowly to the southeast over a stationary hotspot, so it makes sense that the southeastern islands were formed first and the northwestern islands formed most recently. The most ancient rocks yet discovered on the islands are about 3.25 million years old and come from Isla Española in the southeast. In comparison, the oldest rocks on the islands of Isla Fernandina and Isla Isabela are less than 750,000 years old. The northwestern islands are still in the process of formation and contain active volcanoes, particularly Isabela and Fernandina. In addition to the gradual southeastern drift of the Nazca Plate, the northern drift of the Cocos Plate complicates the matter, so that the islands do not get uniformly older from northwest to southeast.

Most of the Galápagos are surrounded by very deep ocean. Less than 20km off the coasts of the western islands, the ocean is over 3000m deep. When visitors cruise around the islands, they can see only about the top third of the volcanoes – the rest is underwater. Some of the oldest volcanoes in the area are, in fact, completely underwater. The Carnegie Ridge, a submerged mountain range stretching to the east of the Galápagos, has the remnants of previous volcanic islands, some of which were as much as nine million years old. These have been completely eroded away; they now lie 2000m beneath the ocean surface and stretch about half the distance between the Galápagos and the mainland.

Most of the volcanic rock forming the Galápagos Islands is basalt. Molten basalt has the property of being more fluid than other types of volcanic rock, so when an eruption occurs, basalt tends to erupt in

THE GALÁPAGOS – EVOLUTION IN ACTION

When the Galápagos were formed, they were barren volcanic islands, devoid of all life. Because the islands were never connected to the mainland, all the species now present must have somehow crossed 1000km of open ocean. Those that could fly or swim long distances had the best chance of reaching the islands, but other methods of colonization were also possible.

Plant seeds or insect eggs and larvae may have been brought over in animals' stomach contents or attached to the feathers or feet of birds. Small mammals, land birds and reptiles, as well as plants and insects, may have been ferried across on floating vegetation.

Galápagos wildlife is dominated by birds (especially seabirds), sea mammals and reptiles. There are no amphibians, because their moist skin is unable to withstand the dehydrating effect of salt water (although humans have recently introduced a couple of frog species). And, of course, there are plenty of tropical fish and marine invertebrates.

Compared with the mainland, there are few small land mammals and insects. The well-known fearlessness of the islands' animals probably comes from having no large predators to fear – there simply weren't any until pigs, goats, cats and other domesticated animals were introduced by human colonists. Domestic animals that escaped found little competition – now, their offspring is feral and has become a major problem for the islands' native species.

When the first migrating species arrived millions of years ago, they found the islands different from the mainland in two important ways: first, the islands were physically different, and second, there were few other species to compete with. Some animals were able to survive, breed and produce offspring. Obviously, the young were the same species as their parents, but some had subtle differences.

A classic Galápagos example of this situation is a bird that produces a chick with a bill that is slightly different from those of its parents or siblings. In the different environment of the islands, some chicks with slightly different bills are more able to take advantage of the surroundings. These birds are said to be better adapted and are more likely to survive and raise a brood of their own.

These better-adapted survivors may pass on favorable genetic traits (in this case, a slightly better-adapted bill) to their offspring, and thus, over many generations, certain favorable traits the form of lava flows rather than in the form of explosions. Hence the Galápagos Islands have gently rounded shield volcanoes rather than the cone-shaped variety most people associate with the formations.

Ecology & Environment

Every plant and animal species arrived in the Galápagos from somewhere else after journeys of several hundred to thousands of kilometers on fortuitous wind, air and sea currents, mostly from South America and the Caribbean. Of course some flora and fauna arrived later more unnaturally, brought by settlers and others visiting the islands. There are no large terrestrial mammals.

As early as 1934, the Ecuadorian government set aside some of the islands as wildlife sanctuaries, but it was not until 1959 that the Galápagos were officially declared a national park. The construction of the Charles Darwin Research Station on Isla Santa Cruz began soon after, and the station began operating in 1964 as an international non-governmental organization (NGO). (The Galápagos National Park Service began operating in 1968 and is the key institution of the Ecuadorian government responsible for the park. Both entities work together to manage the islands.) In 1986, the Ecuadorian government granted more protection to the islands by creating the Galápagos Marine Resources Reserve.

For more on the fascinating wildlife of the Galápagos, see the Galápagos Wildlife chapter (p49).

The national park covers approximately 97% of the total land mass – the rest is taken up by urban areas and farms that existed prior to the creation of the park. The Galápagos Marine Resources Reserve covers the 133,000 sq km of ocean and seabed within which the islands are located, plus a 20,000-sq-km buffer zone. A law that was passed in 1998 enables the park and reserve to protect and conserve the islands and surrounding ocean; it also encourages educational and scientific research while

are selected for and other less favorable traits are selected against. Eventually, the difference between the original colonizers and their distant descendants is so great that the descendants can be considered a different species altogether. This is the essence of Darwin's theory of evolution by natural selection.

The earliest colonizers had little competition and a variety habitats to choose from, and so adaptive changes could occur in to take advantage of different habitats or islands. Thus it wasn't only that a longer, broader or smaller bill would be better adapted – it could be that various types of bills could confer adaptive advantages to birds in different ecological niches. One ancestral species could therefore give rise to several modern species in this evolutionary process, which is called adaptive radiation. This explains the presence in the Galápagos of 13 similar, endemic species of finches – called 'Darwin's finches' in honor of the founder of evolutionary theory.

Charles Darwin, during his visit in 1835, noted the differences in bills in these 13 species of finches; he also noted similar differences in other groups of animals. These observations, combined with many others, led to the 1859 publication of Darwin's the *Origin of Species,* which is one of the most influential books ever published and remains the mainstay of modern biological thought.

It's generally assumed that these evolutionary processes take thousands or millions of generations – new species don't normally appear over a single generation – making evolution in action impossible to observe. That evolutionary science was based on inferences made from the geological or skeletal records was assumed until the last several decades when teams of researchers around the world have made attempts to document evolution in the same way scientists document climatic change. One of the more influential studies has taken place in the Galápagos themselves, headed by a husband-wife team from Princeton University.

For many years, evolutionary biologists were puzzled over how so many unique species could have evolved in the Galápagos over the relatively short period of about four million years (the age of the oldest islands). The answer has recently been provided by the geologists and oceanographers who found nine-million-year-old remnants of islands under the ocean to the east of the existing islands. Presumably, the ancestors of the present wildlife once lived on these lost islands, and therefore had at least nine million years to evolve – a figure that evolutionary biologists find acceptable.

allowing sustainable development of the islands as an Ecuadorian province.

TOURISM

Few tourists had visited the islands before the station opened, but by the mid-1960s, organized tourism began, with a little over 1000 visitors a year. This figure soon increased dramatically. By 1971, there were six small boats and one large cruise ship operating in the islands. In less than two decades, the number of visitors had increased tenfold; in the early 1990s, an estimated 60,000 visited annually. The most current figures indicate that 108,000 people visited the islands in 2004; this includes Ecuadorian residents as well as foreign visitors.

To cope with the increased demands of tourism, a second airport with regular flights to the mainland opened in the mid-1980s. The number of hotels in Puerto Ayora and Puerto Baquerizo Moreno doubled from 15 in 1981 to about 30 a decade later. New hotel growth is now restricted. There are more than 80 boats (with sleeping accommodations) carrying four to 96 passengers; the majority carry fewer than 20. The resident population of the islands is growing at about 10% annually to provide labor for the booming tourism industry.

While this is good for the economy of Ecuador, inevitable problems have resulted. Fortunately, the Ecuadorian government has seen the sense of preventing the building of luxurious high-rise hotels and introducing as many cruise ships as demand calls for. However, some see the coming of the *MV Discovery*, a 500-passenger cruise ship owned and operated by Discovery World Cruises, as the writing on the wall as far as mass tourism is concerned. Starting in 2006, this luxury yacht will stop in the islands for a few days, part of a much longer cruise, and be allowed to dock only in Puerto Baquerizo Moreno on San Cristóbal. People have begun to ask whether this is the final step in the evolution or devolution to unhindered Caribbean-style tourism and if so, can the direction be reversed for the benefit of the flora, fauna and people of the Galápagos.

OVERFISHING

Overfishing has been a major problem. Although sea-cucumber fishing became illegal back in December, 1994, the Charles Dar-win Foundation reports that more than one and a half million sea-cucumbers per month continued to be exported in 2005, chiefly for their purported aphrodisiac properties. Other illegal fishing activities include taking shark fins for shark-fin soup, killing sea lions for bait, and overfishing lobster to feed tourists and locals.

There have been periodic protests by fishermen unhappy with the restrictions on various fisheries. The most serious incidents occurred in 1995 when armed fishermen occupied the Charles Darwin Research Station and threatened to kill tortoises, beat up station personnel and burn portions of the park. More recently, in April, 2004 a group of fishermen occupied the research station, demanding the right to use longer lines and bigger nets. The stand-off was temporarily settled, but the conflict is far from resolved.

Sport fishing for tourists was encouraged for a short time and in 2005 a tournament was held, however several boats remained and continued to fish illegally once it was over. It has since been banned until strict controls are in place.

OTHER ISSUES

The introduction of domestic animals onto the islands is only one of various difficulties that the archipelago faces. Feral goats and pigs and introduced rats decimate (or cause the extinction of) native species in just a few years – the goats themselves are thought to be responsible for the extinction of four to five species. It took more than 127 years to eliminate the feral pig population on the island of Santiago. A newly introduced wasp species is feared to be the cause of a declining number of caterpillar larvae, an important food for finches.

Some islanders see the national park as a barrier to making a living in agriculture and argue that the more food cultivated locally, the less that has to be exported and the cheaper the cost of living for residents.

One of the more serious incidents within the reserve occurred in January, 2001, when a Ecuadorian oil tanker ran aground near Puerto Baquerizo Moreno on San Cristóbal. Fortunately much of the oil was carried away from the islands by favorable winds and ocean currents and the effects were widespread but minimal.

CONSERVATION EFFORTS

There are various solutions to the problems facing the Galápagos Islands. One extreme view is to prohibit all colonization and tourism – an option that appeals to few. Many colonists act responsibly and actively oppose the disruptive and dangerous tactics of the protesting fishermen. The tourist industry is important for Ecuador's economy, and the best solution is a combination of environmental education for both residents and visitors and a program of responsible tourism.

By law, tour boats must be accompanied by certified naturalist guides that have been trained by the National Park Service. In reality however, guides on less expensive boats may lack any kind of certification and there are very few Naturalist III Guides – the most qualified, usually multilingual, university-educated biologists with very real interests in preserving and explaining wildlife – left working in the islands. This is mostly due to the fact that the qualifying exams have not been given for years, after mostly local guides – who tended to not do as well on the tests – came together to change the laws in order to keep foreigners out of the guide game. Some local Naturalist II guides were also bumped up to level III without having to meet the demanding criteria. In 2000 a level one course and exam, open only to Galápagos residents, was given.

On the cheapest boats, guides may speak little English and may know less about the wildlife. Some of the interested parties, including several tour boat companies are pushing to reinstate the exams, open them to mainlanders and foreigners, and in general to reinvigorate the quality and number of guides working in the islands.

Visitors to the islands are restricted to the official visitor sites. Important park rules protect wildlife and the environment; these are mostly a matter of courtesy and common sense: don't feed or handle the animals; don't litter; don't remove any natural object (living or not); do not bring pets; and do not buy objects made of sea lion teeth, black coral, tortoise or turtle shells, or other artifacts made from plants or animals. You are not allowed to enter the visitor sites after dark or without a qualified guide, and a guide will accompany every boat. On all shore trips, the guide will be there to answer your questions and show you the best sites – and also to ensure that you follow park rules.

Tours

There are basically three kinds of tours in the Galápagos: the most common and most recommended are boat-based trips with nights spent aboard; there are also daytrips returning to the same hotel each night; and hotel-based trips staying on different islands. Once you decide on what kind of tour you want, you can either fly to the islands and find a tour there, or make reservations in advance on the mainland or through a travel agency in your home country. There is public transportation only between Isla Santa Cruz, Isla San Cristóbal and Isla Isabela, and the crossings can be rough.

BOAT TOURS

Most visitors tour the Galápagos on boat tours, sleeping aboard the boat. Tours can last from three days to three weeks, although tours lasting from four to eight days are the most common. It's difficult to do the Galápagos justice on a tour lasting less than a week, but five days is just acceptable. If you want to visit the outlying islands of Isabela and Fernandina, a cruise of eight days or more is recommended. On the first day of a tour, you arrive from the mainland by air before lunchtime, so this is really only half a day in the Galápagos, and on the last day, you have to be at the airport in the morning. Thus, a five-day tour gives only three full days in the islands. Shorter tours are advertised, but with the travel time at either end, they are not recommended.

You can find boats to go to almost any island, although it takes more time to reach the outlying ones and cramming as many ports of call as possible into your cruise means you probably won't have time to do justice to any. Boats have fixed itineraries, so you need to think ahead if you want a tour that visits a specific island. Make sure the tour doesn't include more than one night in Puerto Ayora since you can always tack on a few days (or weeks for that matter) at the beginning or end on your own.

Boats used for tours range from small yachts to large cruise ships. By far the most common type of boat is the motorsailer (a medium-sized motor boat), which carries eight to 20 passengers.

SHOPPING FOR A SMOOTH SAIL

There are five boats (*Galápagos Explorer, Expedition, Galápagos Legend, Santa Cruz* and *Polaris*) that carry up to 98 passengers and three boats (*Isabela II, Eclipse* and *Islander*) that carry up to 48 passengers; all these boats are considered luxury or first-class ships. The majority of the boats or yachts, close to 75 to choose from, carry up to 20 people or less. There are several catamarans as well.

The $100 park fee, airfare and bottled drinks are not included in any fare quote. Boats are divided roughly into the following categories (prices are per week):

- Luxury ships: $2500 to $3500
- First-class ships: $1900 to $2500
- Deluxe yachts: $2500 to $3000
- Superior first-class yachts: $1900 to $2400
- First-class yachts: $1500 to $1900
- Superior tourist-class yachts: $1200 to $1500
- Tourist-class yachts: $900 to $1100
- Economic-class yachts: $700 to $900
- Dedicated Dive Liveboards: per week $2900

For practical reasons it's obviously impossible to provide reviews for all or most of the boats servicing the islands. It's also quite common for boats and companies to receive favorable reviews from some and unfavorable from others. Expectations and standards differ and sometimes things go wrong on one trip but smoothly on another. The chemistry between you and your fellow passengers is another important factor and so the smaller the boat the more important it is that you get along.

These caveats aside, there are a few boats and companies that are worth checking out:

Archipell A new and recommended catamaran.

Ecoventura (Quito ☎ 02-290 7396, Guayaquil ☎ 04-220 7177; www.ecoventura.com) Recommended for the quality and comfort of its cruises and its highly lauded attention to conservation and sustainable tourism.

Ecuador Travel (www.ecuador-travel.net/Galapagos.htm) Owner Erich Lehenbauer comes across as an honest businessman in a field of slick salesmen.

Floreana Considered a superior tourist-class yacht. Positive reviews.

Free Enterprise Booked through various agencies online. Relatively inexpensive first-class boat. Sleeps 20, hot water with private bathroom, comfortable cabins, and good basic food.

Galacruises Expeditions (www.galacruisesexpeditions.com) Cheaper than others, great service.

Safari Tours (admin@safari.com.ec) A database of tours and can often get you on a boat quickly at a reasonable price.

Sangay Touring (www.sangay.com) Has a good range of choices at fair prices.

Conditions on the cheapest boats can be cramped and primitive. Ask about washing facilities – they can vary from deck hoses on the cheapest boats to communal showers on the better boats and private showers in more expensive boats. Also inquire about water – on the cheaper boats, you may need to bring your own large containers of water. Bottled drinks are carried but cost extra – agree on the price before you leave, and make sure that enough beer and soda is loaded aboard. There's nothing to stop you from bringing your own supply.

If you're going to spend such a large chunk of change to get to the islands, then seeing the Galápagos is probably important to you, so it might be worthwhile to consider spending an extra few hundred dollars to go on a more comfortable, reliable boat and getting a decent guide (although more expensive boats have their problems too). For about $800 to $1600 for eight days, you can take a more comfortable tourist-class tour – the usual extra costs (airfare, fees and tips) apply. Many companies in Quito offer tours at about this price.

It is customary to tip the crew at the end of a trip. A tip may be anywhere between $20 and $200 per passenger per week, depending on the quality and cost of the tour. On exceptionally good and higher-end boats, a tip amount is usually suggested and you aren't responsible for dividing the amount up among the crew members as you might on the cheaper boats where the guide generally gets the most, then the cook and captain, and then the other crew members.

Arranged Locally

Most people arrive in the islands with a pre-arranged tour, although it's generally cheaper to arrange a tour in Puerto Ayora or Baquerizo Moreno. Generally, only the cheaper boats are available in the Galápagos; the better boats are almost always booked. Don't fly to the Galápagos hoping to get on a really good boat for less money. Arranging a tour from the Galápagos is not uncommon, but neither is it as straightforward as it sounds. It can take several days – sometimes a week or more – and is therefore not an option for people with a limited amount of time.

The best place to organize a tour is from Puerto Ayora. It is also possible to arrange it in Baquerizo Moreno, but there are fewer boats available. If you are alone or with a friend, you'll need to find more people, as even the smallest boats take no fewer than four passengers. There are usually people looking for boats, and agencies can help in putting travelers and boats together.

Finding boats both in August and around Christmas and Easter is especially difficult. The less busy months have fewer travelers on the islands, but boats are often being repaired or overhauled at this time, particularly in October. Despite the caveats, travelers who arrive in Puerto Ayora looking for a boat can almost always find one within a week (often in just a few days) if they work at it. This method isn't always cost effective since by the time you pay for hotels and meals in Puerto Ayora, you may not save anything.

The most important thing to find is a good captain and an enthusiastic naturalist guide. You should be able to meet both and inspect the boat before booking.

Prearranged

Most visitors arrange tours before arriving at the islands. You can do this in your home country (expensive but efficient), or you can arrange something in Quito or Guayaquil (cheaper, but you sometimes have to wait several days or weeks during the high season). See p89 and p322 for more information on agencies that book Galápagos tours.

Dangers & Annoyances

Judging by a fair number of letters Lonely Planet has received, there are some common pitfalls and hassles to Galápagos boat tours. It's difficult to make blanket statements concerning specific boats or companies, however it does seem safe to say that the cheaper the trip the more likely you are to experience problems. That's not to say costly boats are glitch free, only that because the crew and company expect you to have higher expectations, they are more attentive and quick to respond to any complaints.

Five tourist-class boats – *Darwin Explorer, Antartida, Golondrina, Pulsar* and *Fragata* – have sunk in the past two years.

Some of the recurring complaints involve last-minute changes of boat (which the contractual small print allows), poor crew, lack of bottled drinks, changes in the itinerary, mechanical breakdowns, bad smells, bug infestations and overbooking. Passengers share cabins and are not guaranteed that their cabin mates will be of the same gender; if you are uncomfortable, get a guarantee in writing that you won't have to do this. If at all possible ask to see a photograph or layout of the boat including those of the cabins before booking.

When things go wrong, a refund is difficult to obtain. If you have a problem, report it at the *capitanía* (port captain) in Puerto Ayora. If you are unable to do so while in the islands, reports can be mailed to **El Capitán del Puerto** (La Capitanía, Puerto Ayora, Galápagos, Ecuador). Reports are taken seriously, and repeat offenders get their comeuppance. You should also report problems (in person or by email) to the **Cámara de Turismo** (tourist information office; infocptg@capturgal.org.ec) in Puerto Ayora, which keeps a database of complaints to share with agencies and tourists.

There have also been reports of crew members of tourist boats and more commonly small fishing boats, illegally fishing and killing wildlife. Complaints of this kind should be reported to the Natural Reserve office, a green building just to the left of the information booth at the entrance to the Charles Darwin Research Station in Puerto Ayora.

Though not usually publicly disclosed, there have been a handful of shark attacks over the years. One reader reports that a member of his group was bitten by a Galápagos shark while swimming in a channel near the Plaza Islands in 2004. Odds are slim to nil this will happen but worth mentioning in the interests of full disclosure.

With all the boats cruising the islands it's easy to forget that these are remote, inhospitable and dangerous places to be marooned. Seventeen people have disappeared since 1990, most were found alive though a few have died after straying from the designated paths.

DAY TOURS

Daytrips are based in either Puerto Ayora or Baquerizo Moreno. Several hours are spent sailing to and from the day's visitor site(s) so only a few central islands are feasible destinations. Some trips may involve visiting sites on other parts of Isla Santa Cruz or Isla San Cristóbal.

One of the downsides of this kind of tour is that there is no chance of visiting the islands early or late in the day. The cheapest boats may be slow and overcrowded; their visits may be too brief; the guides may be poorly informed; and the crew may be lacking an adequate conservationist attitude. Nevertheless, daytrips are useful for severe seasickness sufferers and if your time and budget is extremely limited.

Operators in Puerto Ayora and Baquerizo Moreno typically charge from $40 to $120 per person per day, depending on the destination on offer and the quality of the boat and guides.

HOTEL-BASED TOURS

These tours go from island to island, and you sleep in hotels on three or four different islands (Santa Cruz, San Cristóbal, Santa Maria, Isabela). Tours typically last a week and cost $800 to over $1000 per person, plus airfare and park fee. However, there aren't too many companies offering this kind of tour. One company that does is **Surtrek** (☎ 02-223 1534, 250 0530; www.surtrek.com, www.galapagosyachts.com; Av Amazonas 897), based in Quito (p90). Also check with other agencies in Quito or Puerto Ayora, and possibly Baquerizo Moreno.

GALÁPAGOS ON A SHOESTRING

Regardless of the corners you cut, a trip to the Galápagos takes a significant chunk of change. Travelers touring the continent usually take a pass since a week in the islands may cost as much as a month or two backpacking. There are however some strategies to reducing costs, though they also may reduce the pleasure involved in a trip.

Talk to the ship-owners directly to avoid having to pay commission to an agency. Ecuadorian agencies are generally at least 30% cheaper than agencies booking trips in the USA and Europe. You may find that you can get a substantial discount by checking various agencies and seeing if they have any spaces to fill on departures leaving in the next day or two. This applies both to the cheaper tours and to some of the pricier ones. Particularly out of the high season, agencies may well let you travel cheaply at the last minute rather than leave berths unfilled.

Individuals and couples have a better chance of grabbing a last-minute discounted spot than do large groups. All cabins are not the same size. Book the smaller ones to save money.

For boats in this price range, owners, captains, guides and cooks all change frequently; in addition, many boats make changes and improvements from year to year. Generally speaking, a boat is only as good as its crew. You can deal with a crew member or boat representative during your search, but don't hand over any money until you have an agreed itinerary in writing to avoid disagreements with other passengers and the crew during the cruise.

Getting There & Away

AIR

Flights from the mainland arrive at two airports: Isla Baltra just north of Santa Cruz and Isla San Cristóbal. There are almost an equal number of flights to Baltra and San Cristóbal. Every two or three years the Baltra airport undergoes repairs and all flights are diverted to San Cristóbal for up to several months.

Two major airlines flying to the Galápagos Islands are TAME (p367) and Aerogal (p367). TAME operates two morning flights daily from Quito via Guayaquil to both the Isla Baltra airport, just over an hour away from Puerto Ayora by public transportation (see p368) and the San Cristóbal airport. AeroGal has three flights daily from Quito to Isla Baltra and San Cristóbal via Guayaquil. All return flights are in the early afternoons of the same days. Icaro (Guayaquil ☎ 04-229 4265; www.icaro.com.ec) also flies to San Cristóbal three times a week.

Flights from Guayaquil cost high season/low season $344/300 round-trip and take 1½ hours. From Quito, flights cost $390/344 round-trip and take 3¼ hours, due to the layover in Guayaquil (you do not have to get off the plane). It's also possible to fly from Quito and return to Guayaquil or vice versa. There is a limit of 20kg of checked luggage (per person) on the flight to the Galápagos.

Ecuadorian nationals can fly from Guayaquil for half the price foreigners pay, and Galápagos residents pay half that again. Some foreign residents of Ecuador or workers in the islands are also eligible, so if you have a residence visa you should make inquiries.

There is a Hercules military plane that flies to the islands every other Wednesday that occasionally has room for foreign passengers. Make inquiries at Avenida de la Prensa 3570, a few hundred meters from the Quito airport (ask for Departamento de Operaciones, Fuerza Aerea del Ecuador). Flights go from Quito via Guayaquil and stop at both San Cristóbal and Baltra. Foreigners pay about $300 round-trip for either destination.

Flights to the Galápagos are sometimes booked solid well in advance, but you'll often find that there are many no-shows. Travel agencies book blocks of seats for their all-inclusive Galápagos Islands tours. They will release the seats on the day of the flight when there is no longer any hope of selling their tour.

Getting Around
Most people get around the islands by organized boat tours, but it's entirely possible to visit some of the islands independently. Santa Cruz, San Cristóbal, Santa María (Floreana) and Isabela all have accommodations and are reachable by interisland boat rides or flights (which are pricey). Keep in mind however that you'll only scratch the surface of the archipelago's natural wonders traveling independently.

AIR
The small airline, EMETEBE (Puerto Ayora ☎ 05-252 6177, San Cristóbal ☎ 05-252 0036, Puerto Villamil ☎ 05-252 9155, Guayaquil ☎ 04-229 2492), flies a five-passenger aircraft between the islands. It offers two to three flights a week between Baltra and Puerto Villamil (Isla Isabela), between Baltra and San Cristóbal, and between San Cristóbal and Puerto Villamil. Fares are about $120 one way, and there is a 13kg baggage limit per person (although this is flexible if the plane isn't full).

BOAT
Ingala (Puerto Ayora ☎ 05-252 6151), a government-run company, operates passenger ferry services aboard the Ingala II. It goes from Santa Cruz to San Cristóbal Monday, Wednesday and Friday and from Santa Cruz to Isabela about twice monthly (usually on a Friday) and once a month from Isabela to Floreana. The office in Puerto Ayora can give you up-to-date details, as can the Camará de Turismo (tourist information office) in Puerto Ayora (p362). The departure times change periodically.

Fares are $50 for foreigners (sometimes cheaper in low season) on any passage and are purchased either on the day before or the day of departure. Ask around in Puerto Ayora and Puerto Baquerizo Moreno for private companies that ply the same routes daily or weekly; these are cheaper and faster but also tend to be smaller and more sensitive to rough seas.

Fees & Taxes
The $100 Galápagos national park fee must be paid in cash at one of the airports after you arrive or can be paid in advance through a prebooked tour. You will not be allowed to leave the airport until you pay. Make sure you have your passport available when you pay your fees and hang onto your ticket until you leave.

ISLA SANTA CRUZ (INDEFATIGABLE)
The island of Santa Cruz has the largest and most developed town in the Galápagos; almost every visitor to the islands spends at least some time here even if it's simply commuting from the airport on nearby Isla Baltra to a cruise ship in the harbor of Puerto Ayora. However to anyone who stays for longer, the island of Santa Cruz is more

than just a way station or place to feel connected to the modern, man-made world; it's a destination in itself, full of visitor sites, easily accessible beaches, remote highlands in the interior and a base for adventurous activities far from the tourism trail.

Visitor Sites

CHARLES DARWIN RESEARCH STATION

About a 20-minute walk by road northeast of Puerto Ayora, the **Charles Darwin Research Station** (www.galapagos.org; ☉ 7:30am-5pm) can also be reached by dry landing from Academy Bay. It contains a national-park information center; an informative museum in the Van Straelen Exhibition Center (where a video in English or Spanish is presented several times a day); a baby-tortoise house with incubators, where you can see hatchlings and young tortoises; and a walk-in adult tortoise enclosure, where you can meet the Galápagos giants face to face. The tiny tortoises in the baby-tortoise house are repatriated to their home islands when they weigh about 1.5kg (or are about four years old) – some 2000 have been repatriated so far.

Several of the 11 remaining subspecies of tortoise can be seen here. **Lonesome George**, the only surviving member of the Isla Pinta subspecies, is also here. George's chances to shack up with a comely female become more remote as he crawls slowly into his ninth decade.

Other attractions include paths through arid-zone vegetation, such as salt bush, mangroves and prickly pear and other cacti. A variety of land birds, including Darwin's finches, can be seen.

TURTLE BAY

A 3km paved trail southwest from Puerto Ayora takes you to Turtle Bay, a beautiful white-sand beach good for swimming, surfing or just sunbathing. A spit of land provides protection for swimmers (there are strong currents on the exposed side of the spit) and you can see sharks, marine iguanas, pelicans and the occasional flamingo. There's no drinking water or other facilities. It's about a half-hour walk from the start of the path – often used by local runners – where you must sign in (between 6am and 6pm).

HIGHLANDS

Several sites of interest in the highlands of Santa Cruz can be reached from the trans-island road and are part of the itineraries of many cruises. Access to some sites is through colonized areas, so respect private property. From the village of Bellavista, 7km north of Puerto Ayora by road, one can turn either west on the main road continuing to Isla Baltra or east on a road leading about 2km to the **lava tubes** (admission $3). These underground tunnels are more than a

---

CHARLES DARWIN FOUNDATION

Most tourists have the opportunity to visit the Charles Darwin Research Station, founded in 1959, the same year the national park was established. More than 200 scientists and volunteers are involved with research and conservation efforts, the most well known of which involves a captive breeding program for giant tortoises. The 14 surviving tortoises on Española in 1965 produced nearly 1000 offspring which were reintroduced to the wild thanks in part to the mating skills of Diego, a frisky lothario returned to the islands from the San Diego Zoo. Visitors are encouraged to make donations to the organization, which carries out research and advises government and tourist agencies on minimizing the impact of tourism on the islands. (None of the $100 park fee goes toward the research station.)

Outside of the islands, the research station is supported by contributions to the Charles Darwin Foundation. Donors contributing $25 or more each year receive the English-language bulletin *Galápagos News* and the English-language scientific journal *Noticias de Galápagos*. These journals are great for keeping up with the latest happenings on the islands, including information about conservation issues, as well as interesting recent research and unusual wildlife observations.

Donations are tax deductible for citizens of the USA and several European countries. Addresses for donations are easily obtained in the research station and at most boats or hotels in the Galápagos. United States citizens may contact the **Charles Darwin Foundation** (☎ 703-538-6833; www.darwinfoundation.org; 407 N Washington St, Suite 105, Falls Church, VA 22046, USA).

kilometer in length and were formed by the solidifying of the outside skin of a molten-lava flow. When the lava flow ceased, the molten lava inside the flow kept going, emptying out of the solidified skin and thus leaving tunnels. Because they are on private property, the tunnels can be visited without an official guide. The owners of the land provide information, guides and flashlights (included in the entrance fee). Tours to the lava tubes are offered in Puerto Ayora.

North of Bellavista is the national park land known as the highlands. A path from Bellavista leads toward **Cerro Crocker** (864m) and other hills and extinct volcanoes. This is a good chance to see the vegetation of the Scalesia, Miconia and fern-sedge zones (see p44) and to look for birds such as the vermilion flycatcher or the elusive Galápagos rail, and paint-billed crake. It is around 5km from Bellavista to the crescent-shaped hill of Media Luna and 3km further to the base of Cerro Crocker. This is national park, so a guide is required.

Part of the highlands that can be visited from the road are the twin craters called **Los Gemelos**. These are actually sinkholes, not volcanic craters, and they are surrounded by Scalesia forest. Vermilion flycatchers are often seen here, as well as short-eared owls on occasion. Los Gemelos are reached by taking the road to the village of Santa Rosa, about 12km west of Bellavista, and continuing about 2km beyond Santa Rosa on the trans-island road. Although the craters lie only 25m and 125m on either side of the road, they are hidden by vegetation, so ask your driver to stop at the short trailhead.

EL CHATO TORTOISE RESERVE & RANCHO PERMISO

Near Santa Rosa, is El Chato Tortoise Reserve, where you can observe giant tortoises in the wild. The reserve is also a good place to look for short-eared owls, Darwin's finches, yellow warblers, Galápagos rails and paint-billed crakes (these last two are difficult to see in the long grass).

A trail from Santa Rosa leads through private property to parkland about 3km away. The trail is downhill and often muddy. Horses can be hired in Santa Rosa – ask at the store/bar on the main road for directions to the outfitter's house. The trail forks at the park boundary, with the right fork going

up to the small hill of Cerro Chato (3km further) and the left fork going to **La Caseta** (2km). The trails can be hard to follow, and you should carry water. The reserve is part of the national park, and a guide is required.

Next to the reserve is **Rancho Permiso** (admission $4), a private ranch owned by the Devine family. This place often has dozens of giant tortoises, and you can wander around at will and take photos for a fee. The entrance is beyond Santa Rosa, off the main road – ask locals for directions. Stay on the main tracks to avoid getting lost. Remember to close any gates that you go through. There is a café selling cold drinks and hot tea, which is welcome if the highland mist has soaked you.

OTHER SITES

There are several attractive spots in or around Puerto Ayora. The small white-sand **beach** in front of the Finch Bay Hotel (p366) is a good place to while away a few hours. The water here is pristine and sharks have been known to pass through the cove. For nice swimming and snorkeling, head to **Las Grietas**, a water-filled crevice in the rocks. Take a water taxi (per person $0.50) to the dock for the Angermeyer Point restaurant (p366), then walk past the Finch Bay Hotel, then through an interesting salt mine and finally hike down to the water. Good shoes are needed for the walk which takes about 30 minutes. Just behind the Casa de Lago and Hotel Fiesta is the **Laguna Las Ninfas**, an emerald-green watering hole popular with cannon-balling children.

A beautiful 40-minute taxi ride from Puerto Ayora (per person $5) through the highlands brings you to **Garrapatero beach** which has tidal pools good for exploring, a lagoon with flamingos and nice snorkeling on calm days.

The remaining Santa Cruz visitor sites are reached by boat and with guides. On the west coast are **Whale Bay** and **Conway Bay**, and on the north coast are **Black Turtle Cove** (Caleta Tortuga Negra) and **Las Bachas**. Between these two areas is the relatively new visitor site of **Cerro Dragón**. Conway Bay has a 1.5km trail passing a lagoon with flamingos; Whale Bay isn't visited very often. North of Conway Bay, Cerro Dragón has two small lagoons that may have flamingos and a 1.75km trail that leads through a forest of *palo santo* (holy wood) trees and opuntia cacti to a small hill with good views. There are some large repatriated land iguanas here.

There is no landing site in Black Turtle Cove, which is normally visited by *panga* (small boats). The cove has many little inlets and is surrounded by mangroves, where you can see lava herons and pelicans. The main attraction is in the water: marine turtles are sometimes seen mating, schools of golden mustard rays are often present, and white-tipped sharks may be seen basking in the shallows. This site is occasionally visited by day boats from Puerto Ayora. The nearby Las Bachas beach, although popular for sunbathing and swimming, is often deserted.

Puerto Ayora
☎ 05 / pop 12,000
This town, the largest in terms of population and size in the Galápagos, is a surprise to most visitors, who don't expect to find anything but plants and animals in the islands. Puerto Ayora looks and feels like a fairly prosperous mainland Ecuadorian coastal town, that is if it weren't for the sea lion, iguana and albatross or two that lounge around the waterfront. Most of the hotels, restaurants and tourist facilities line Avenida Charles Darwin and the airport is on Isla Baltra, around an hour away to the north (see p368).

INFORMATION
Cultural Center
Casa de Lago Cultural Centre (☎ 271 4647; www .galapagoscultural.com) Occasionally has readings, performances, live music, film screenings (on weekends) and photo exhibitions, all with a Galápagos, Ecuador or South American focus. Also a highly recommended place to stay (see p365).

Internet Access
Some of the midrange and top-end hotels offer Internet access. The stand-alone cafés all charge around $2 per hour.
Chosen Internet (Av Padre Julio Herrera; ⏰ 7am-11pm)
Cyber Café (Av Bolívar Naveda; ⏰ 9am-10pm)
Galápagos Online (Av Charles Darwin; ⏰ 8am-8pm)
Limón y Café (Av Charles Darwin) You can drink a beer while you type; it's also a popular bar.
Pelikan.net (Av Charles Darwin; ⏰ 7:30am-11pm) Has a call center as well.

Laundry
Laundry Lava Flash (Av Bolívar Naveda; per kg $1; ⏰ 8am-1pm & 2-7pm) Drop off or do-it-yourself machines.
Lavenderia La Peregrina (Av Indefatigable)

Left Luggage
Passengers of the commuter interisland boats to Isla San Cristóbal or Isla Isabela can leave their luggage for a few hours at the little office near the passenger wharf.

Medical Services
Protesub (☎ 252 6911; 18 de Febrero) Has a state-of-the-art recompression chamber for divers with the bends and offers 24-hour emergency medical service. Several languages are spoken.

Money
Banco del Pacífico (Av Charles Darwin; ⏰ 8am-3:30pm Mon-Fri, 9:30am-12:30pm Sat) Maybe the only bank in the world where pelicans and iguanas queue for the ATM. Does not accept Plus cards. Cash advances on credit cards – up to US$2000 – but each transaction costs $10 (not revealed until you receive credit card bill). Changes traveler's checks.

Post
There's a post office near the harbor.

Telephone
There are several Paciftel and other booths along Avenida Charles Darwin.

Tourist Information
Cámara de Turismo (tourist information office; ☎ 252 6153; www.galapagostour.org; Av Charles Darwin; ⏰ 7:30am-noon & 2-5:30pm Mon-Fri) Hotel information, maps and schedules for local boat transportation available. Some of the staff speak English. Report any complaints here about boats, tours, guides or crew – it's kept on file to provide ratings to other tourists and agencies.
i-Tur (Water taxi pier) A sometimes staffed booth with flyers and basic hotel and travel agency info.
Ministry of Tourism (Av Charles Darwin) Less suited for general queries and not much English spoken.

ACTIVITIES
Diving
Not surprisingly for a place whose underwater habitat resembles a well-stocked aquarium, scuba diving in the Galápagos is world class. The conditions aren't suitable for beginners because of strong currents, sometimes murky visibility and cold temperatures. When the water is warm there's

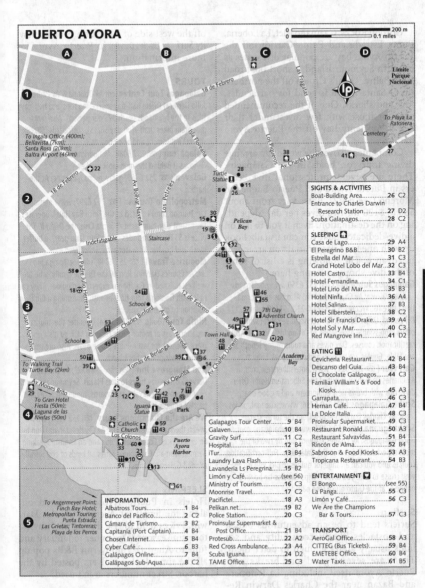

PUERTO AYORA

0   200 m
0   0.1 miles

Limite
Parque
Nacional

To Ingala Office (400m);
Bellavista (7km);
Santa Rosa (20km);
Baltra Airport (46km)

18 de Febrero

18 de Febrero

Isla Floreana

Los Piqueros

Las Fragatas

To Playa La
Ratonera

Cemetery

Av Charles Darwin

Av Bolívar Naveda

Los Petreles

Turtle
Statue

Pelican
Bay

Indefatigable

Staircase

Av Padre Julio Herrera (Av Baltra)

Juan Montalvo

School

12 de Febrero

Av Bolívar Naveda

Charles Binford

School

Town Hall

7th Day
Adventist Church

Tomás de Berlanga

Av Opuntia

Av Charles Darwin

Academy
Bay

To Walking Trail
to Turtle Bay (2km)

Av Moises Brito

To Gran Hotel
Fiesta (50m);
Laguna de las
Ninfas (50m)

Iguana
Statue

Park

Catholic
Church

Los Colonos

Puerto
Ayora
Harbor

To Angermeyer Point;
Finch Bay Hotel;
Metropolitan Touring;
Punta Estrada;
Las Grietas; Tintoreras;
Playa de los Perros

SIGHTS & ACTIVITIES
Boat-Building Area	26 C2
Entrance to Charles Darwin Research Station	27 D2
Scuba Galapagos	28 C2

SLEEPING
Casa de Lago	29 A4
El Peregrino B&B	30 B2
Estrella del Mar	31 C3
Grand Hotel Lobo del Mar	32 C3
Hotel Castro	33 B3
Hotel Fernandina	34 C1
Hotel Lirio del Mar	35 B3
Hotel Ninfa	36 A4
Hotel Salinas	37 B3
Hotel Silberstein	38 C2
Hotel Sir Francis Drake	39 A4
Hotel Sol y Mar	40 C3
Red Mangrove Inn	41 D2

EATING
Cevicheria Restaurant	42 B4
Descanso del Guia	43 B4
El Chocolate Galápagos	44 C3
Familiar William's & Food Kiosks	45 A3
Garrapata	46 B4
Hernan Café	47 B4
La Dolce Italia	48 B4
Proinsular Supermarket	49 C3
Restaurant Ronald	50 A3
Restaurant Salvadias	51 B4
Rincón de Alma	52 B4
Sabroson & Food Kiosks	53 A3
Tropicana Restaurant	54 B3

ENTERTAINMENT
El Bongo	(see 55)
La Panga	55 C3
Limón y Café	56 C3
We Are the Champions Bar & Tours	57 C3

TRANSPORT
AeroGal Office	58 A3
CITTEG (Bus Tickets)	59 B4
EMETEBE Office	60 B4
Water Taxis	61 B5

Galapagos Tour Center	9	B4
Galaven	10	B4
Gravity Surf	11	C2
Hospital	12	B4
iTur	13	B4
Laundry Lava Flash	14	B4
Lavanderia Ls Peregrina	15	B2
Limón y Café	(see 56)	
Ministry of Tourism	16	C3
Moonrise Travel	17	C2
Pacifictel	18	A3
Pelikan.net	19	B2
Police Station	20	C3
Proinsular Supermarket & Post Office	21	B4
Protesub	22	A2
Red Cross Ambulance	23	A4
Scuba Iguana	24	D2
TAME Office	25	C3

INFORMATION
Albatross Tours	1	B4
Banco del Pacífico	2	C2
Cámara de Turismo	3	B2
Capitanía (Port Captain)	4	B4
Chosen Internet	5	B4
Cyber Café	6	B3
Galápagos Online	7	B4
Galápagos Sub-Aqua	8	C2

THE GALÁPAGOS ISLANDS

not much of a current so it's also a little murky (January to March); there is better visibility but colder water temperatures from July to October.

Besides an array of tropical fish there are plenty of whale sharks, hammerheads, manta rays and even sea horses to be seen. The average cost of one week on a live-aboard is from \$2500 to \$3000 and includes up to four or five dives a day plus stops at some visitor sites on land. Most live-aboard boats go to Wolf and Darwin, northwest of the major islands where there's a large number of different species of sharks. The best month to dive with whale sharks is July but they're around from May to October.

Gordon Rocks, Caamaño islet, La Lobería, Punta Estrada and Punta Carrión off the Puerto Ayora bay are popular dives sites as is North Seymour island, a short boat road from Baltra. Devil's Crown off the northern tip of Santa Maria is good for barracudas, rays and sharks. One of the recommended sites for those with few dives under their belt is Academy Bay off the Puerto Ayora harbor.

Companies all over the world can arrange diving tours on boats in the Galápagos. There are several professional dive centers in Puerto Ayora and Puerto Baquerizo Moreno (see p372). Rates vary from about $80 to $120 for two dives per day, depending on the destination. Even if you're not on a dive-dedicated boat you can usually hook up with one for a day or so if you arrange it in advance. The following is a list of some of the dive shops operating here:

Galápagos Sub-Aqua (☎ 252 6350; www.galapagos -sub-aqua.com; Av Charles Darwin) Also has an information office (Guayaquil ☎ /fax 04-230 5514; Orellana 211 & Panamá, Office 402). A full-service dive center which offers Professional Association of Diving Instructors (PADI) certification courses. Day dives and tours of any length are available. Guides are friendly and most speak English.

Galextur (☎ 252 6277; www.hotelsilberstein.com; Av Charles Darwin) Run out of the Silberstein Hotel. Offers dive trips with brand new equipment and a good boat.

Scuba Galápagos (☎ 250 5756; www.scubagalapagos .com; Av Charles Darwin) Across from the turtle statue.

Scuba Iguana (☎ 252 6497; www.scubaiguana.com; Hotel Galápagos; Av Charles Darwin) Run by two of the most experienced divers in the Galápagos. Full-certification courses and you can arrange for guides to pick you up on your cruise to take you diving. Trips can also be booked online or at the Quito office (see p89).

Surfing

Surfers tend to be an adventurous bunch and obstacles like inaccessibility and sea lions usually aren't enough to deter them. There are several good surf breaks near Puerto Ayora itself including La Ratonera and Bazán near the Charles Darwin Research Station beach. If hauling your board a few kilometers is no problem Tortuga Bay has several breaks.

An hour or so by boat takes you to Punta Blanca and further north to Cerro Gallina, Las Palmas Chica and Las Palmas Grande, considered to be three of the best breaks in the Galápagos. There are also several breaks off the west side of Isla Baltra. Stop by **Gravity Surf** (Av Charles Darwin) in Puerto Ayora for more information.

TOURS

Galápagos Tour Center (cnr Av Opuntia & Av Padre Julio Herrera) Offers half-day snorkeling trips and half-day trips to the highlands (each $25 per person). Also rents mountain bikes (half-/full day $8/15), surfboards ($8/18), snorkel equipment and body boards.

Galapatour (☎ 252 6088; Av Rodriguez Lara & Genovesa) Behind the municipal market.

Galaven (☎ 252 6359; galaven@pa.ga.pro.ec) At the harbor.

Metropolitan Touring (☎ 252 6297; www.metropoli tan-touring.com) Located at the Finch Bay Hotel, operates the fastest day-tour yacht at Santa Cruz, the *Delfín II*. The price is $115, and includes snorkeling (and gear), a buffet lunch and guides. All water activities offered.

Moonrise Travel (☎ 252 6348; sdevine@pa.ga.pro .ec; Av Charles Darwin) Run by the Devine family, who are well established as Galápagos experts and guides. They can help with finding a tour boat or with confirming a flight, in addition to other things.

Ninfa Tour (Quito ☎ 222 3124) Operates the 'tourist-superior' class of motor yacht *Lobo del Mar*, so it's a good place to check for last minute cruise deals. Also organizes various daytrips to other islands.

Red Mangrove Inn (☎ /fax 252 6277; Av Charles Darwin) Offers day tours to Islas Plazas, Seymour and Santa Fé. Also rents sea kayaks, surfboards, mountain bikes and snorkel equipment.

We Are the Champions Tours (☎ 252 6951; www .wearethechampionstours.com; Av Charles Darwin) Run by an experienced Ecuadorian guide and an English-speaking German woman, Champions offers all kinds of ecologically minded Galápagos trips.

SLEEPING

Hotels in Puerto Ayora are spread out along the length of Avenida Charles Darwin. Prices tend to rise during the heaviest tourism seasons (December to January and June to August). Family-run B&Bs pop up all the time; look for flyers posted by the harbor. Street numbers aren't used.

Budget

Hotel Salinas (☎ 252 6107; fax 252 6072; Av Bolívar Naveda; s/d from $10/15) Some of the 2nd-floor rooms at Salinas have high ceilings and are much nicer than the dark and small ground-floor rooms. All have hot water, TV and tile floors. Look for the white building with blue trim.

AUTHOR'S CHOICE

Casa de Lago (☎ 271 4647; www.galapagoscultural.com; Moisés Brito & Juan Montalvo; r from $35; ☒ ▢) By far the best place to feel at home in the islands. There are only two large suites – a third was under construction at the time of research – made from recycled materials and filled with attractive tiles and textiles. Both also have large kitchens with stove and refrigerator. The Casa de Lago is only about 350m from the harbor and a short walk to the Laguna las Ninfas; the perfect place to base yourself for a long-term stay. Owned and operated by a friendly, culturally- and environmentally-conscious couple who regularly host photographic exhibitions and music and theater performances in the charming, wooden main building. They also serve good vegetarian food, coffee, bagels and exotic flavors of homemade ice cream. Can help arrange trips around the island and there's an inflatable kayak available for rent. Free Internet is available for guests.

El Peregrino B&B (☎ 252 6323; Av Charles Darwin; r per person incl breakfast $13) This small place, only four simple rooms in total, is popular because of its central location and warm, family-like atmosphere.

Hotel Sir Francis Drake (☎ 252 6221; Av Padre Julio Herrera; s/d $8/15) Just up the street from the harbor, this grandiosely named hotel won't disappoint if you only expect bare bones simplicity. While the dull grey colors and concrete won't delight the eye, the tile rooms are well maintained.

Hotel Lirio del Mar (☎ 252 6212; Av Bolívar Naveda; r per person $8) Across the street from Hotel Salinas, the Lirio del Mar is a slight step down in quality though the basic concrete rooms here are kept clean. A terrace on the 2nd floor catches a bit of a breeze.

Midrange
Gran Hotel Fiesta (☎ 252 6348; s/d incl breakfast $33/56; ☒ ▢) The Fiesta is both quiet and almost directly in front of the Laguna Las Ninfas, perfect for a quick dip. Rooms in this orange and yellow concrete building are well kept and have hot water. There's a pool table and modern restaurant on the grounds.

Hotel Castro (☎ 252 6173; Av Padre Julio Herrera; s/d $20/30) The most affordable option in this category, the Castro has clean, well-maintained rooms with tile floors and hot water; air-conditioning is available if needed and it's only a block from the harbor.

Hotel Ninfa (☎ 252 6127; galaven@pa.ga.pro.ec; Moisés Brito; s/d from $50/65; ☒ ▢) While the rooms at the Ninfa aren't twice as nice as the Castro across the street, this hotel does boast a sunny courtyard and nice restaurant. Rooms here do have cable TV and little decorative touches.

Estrella del Mar (☎ 252 6427; estrellademar@ayora .ecua.net.ec; s/d from $28/40) Though the rooms at this friendly, family-run hotel are basic and the furniture is old, those with windows and ocean views make up for the shortcomings; others are less expensive. It's on the waterfront behind the school playground and near the police station.

Hotel Fernandina (☎ 252 6499; cnr 18 de Febrero & Los Piqueros; s/d $50/80; ☒ ▢) Only a short walk from Avenida Charles Darwin, this friendly, family-run hotel nevertheless feels pleasantly secluded. Rooms are surrounded by a nicely landscaped garden, and there's a pool and Jacuzzi on the premises.

Grand Hotel Lobo del Mar (☎ 252 6188; 12 de Febrero; s/d from incl breakfast $50/65; ☒ ▢) From the outside this hotel does look somewhat grand, however inside it's fairly spare and the spacious rooms are basic. The central courtyard has a little pool. It also has a bar, restaurant and a 4th-floor terrace.

Hotel Sol y Mar (☎ 252 6281; Av Charles Darwin; r $30-60) The Sol y Mar's saving grace is its waterfront location where you can share the patio with sea lions and iguanas. The rooms are decidedly unattractive, the furniture old and mismatched and the tile floor reminiscent of a school cafeteria.

Top End
Red Mangrove Inn (☎ 252 7011; www.redmangrove .com; Av Charles Darwin; s/d $115/145; ☒ ▢) This charmingly decorated inn at the northern end of Avenida Charles Darwin has the most character of any top-end hotel in Puerto Ayora. Each of the rooms are bright and sunny with white adobe walls and colorful tiled bathrooms. There are good views of the water from the attached Japanese restaurant and the common areas are outfitted with

hammocks and a Jacuzzi. Sea-kayaking, windsurfing, horseback riding, mountain biking, fishing and camping trips can be arranged.

Finch Bay Hotel (☎ 252 6297; www.finchbayhotel.com; r from $200; ✗ ☐ ✈) This boutiquelike hotel across the bay from Puerto Ayora would not look out of place in Santa Fe, New Mexico, that is if it weren't situated on an exceptionally pretty little beach (open to the public). The rooms themselves, a mix of tasteful wood and modern appliances, aren't especially large or luxurious but the grounds which include a pool, Jacuzzi and barbecue area, justify the splurge. Water taxis ($0.50) can zip you back and forth to the harbor. Metropolitan Touring (see p89) based in the hotel, can arrange kayaking, snorkeling, scuba diving, boat trips and any outdoor activity imaginable in the Galápagos.

Hotel Silberstein (☎ 252 6277; www.hotelsilberstein.com; Av Charles Darwin; s/d $79/105; ✗ ☐ ✈) Previously known as the Hotel Angermeyer, the Silberstein looks like a whitewashed Mexican villa from the outside, however once through the opening archway, an attractive pool and garden area reveals itself. While the surrounding rooms are simple, modern and clean, but not exceptional, the hotel is near the Charles Darwin Research Station at the quieter end of town. An in-house agency offers island tours with overnights here.

EATING

Often it's only higher prices that distinguish the restaurants that cater to locals from those that cater to tourists; although all the latter are congregated along Avenida Charles Darwin from the harbor to the Charles Darwin Research Station. Most of the hotels have restaurants as well. Proinsular is the cheapest and best-stocked market by the harbor.

Restaurants

Angermeyer Point (☎ 252 7007; mains from $11) It's only a two-minute water taxi ride ($0.50) from the harbor to this picturesque spot perched over the water. The restaurant, in the former home of painter Carl Angermeyer, serves up mostly seafood and Western mains and is often booked by large groups. Breakfast and lunch by reservation. Set menus change monthly and there are

specials every night. Saturday's happy hour means two-for-one drinks.

La Dolce Italia (☎ 284 8666; Av Charles Darwin; mains $9; ⏰ 11am-3pm & 6-10pm) The Sicilian owner of this upscale Italian bistro is a boisterous and welcoming booster who may accost you on the street and draw you in. The interior is nautically inspired and excellent pizzas and pastas are served up on white tablecloths. Does Dominoes one better and delivers to boats.

Garrapata (☎ 252 6264; Av Charles Darwin; mains $4-9; ⏰ 7-10pm Mon-Sat) This popular outdoor restaurant serves basic sandwiches ($4) to more substantial fare such as chicken in pineapple sauce ($9) and shrimp in garlic sauce ($9). Next to the La Panga disco, it catches a nice offshore breeze.

Hernan Café (Av Padre Julio Herrera; mains $3-9; ⏰ 7am-9pm) With the same owner as La Dolce Italia and much of the same menu, Hernan Café is an excellent more affordable and casual choice. Near the central park and iguana statues, Hernan serves sandwiches ($2), hamburgers ($3), pizzas ($5) and slightly pricier ceviches, fish and Western dishes in an outdoor setting.

Rincón de Alma (☎ 252 6196; Av Charles Darwin; mains $6-9; ⏰ 7am-9pm) A streetside casual restaurant that serves ceviches and other seafood dishes such as a lobster omelet ($16). Inexpensive ($3) *almuerzos* (set lunches) are also available.

Restaurant Salvavidas (☎ 252 6418; mains $6-16; ⏰ 9am-8pm Mon-Sat) Frequented as much because of it's convenient dockside location as because of its standard seafood and snack menu, Salvavidas has been the daytime harbor hangout of choice for years.

Cevicheria Restaurant (Av Padre Julio Herrera; ceviches $4; ⏰ 9am-8pm) This *cevichería* (ceviche restaurant) is nothing more than a few outdoor tables next to Rincó de Alma. Specializes in, you guessed it, ceviches.

Descanso Del Guia (Av Charles Darwin; ⏰ 9am-8pm) Like the name suggests, this is a favorite with boat crews and guides.

Cafés & Quick Eats

The cheapest places to eat are found along Avenida Padre Julio Herrera. East from this street, along Charles Binford, are some very popular kiosks selling cheap and well-prepared meals – mainly fish and meat dishes.

El Chocolate Galápagos (Av Charles Darwin; mains $3-6; ⏰7:30am-10pm Mon-Sat) This café across from the bank is an excellent place for people watching. Besides coffee, fruit drinks and chocolate cake, there's an extensive menu with everything from sandwiches ($3) and burgers ($3) to ceviches ($7) and salads ($4).

Familiar William's (Charles Binford; encocados $4-7; ⏰6-10pm Tue-Sun) One of the many eateries lining both sides of this street, William's stands out because of its delicious *encocados* (fish, shrimp or lobster smothered in a savory coconut sauce).

Restaurant Ronald (Av Padre Julio Herrera; almuerzos $2) A hole in the wall frequented by locals. Serves up filling and cheap *almuerzos*.

Tropicana Restaurant (Av Bolívar Naveda; mains $2) Another inexpensive local option, Tropicana does *almuerzos* and standard seafood dishes.

Casa de Lago Café (☎271 4647; cnr Moisés Brito & Juan Montalvo) A great place to while away a few hours, the café serves excellent homemade ice cream, coffee, fruit drinks and bagels with cream cheese. There's a small bar and 2nd-floor balcony (see p365).

DRINKING & ENTERTAINMENT

La Panga (Av Charles Darwin) The most popular disco in town, next to Garrapata.

El Bongo (Av Charles Darwin) This popular bar downstairs from La Panga is where most people start out the night.

Limón y Café (Av Charles Darwin) An outdoor bar with a gravel floor heavy on the maritime and surf decor. Always busy on weekends.

Champions Bar (Av Charles Darwin) This bar is a cool, laid-back hang out serving up good *capahrinas* (a sugarcane-based drink), *cuba libres* (a rum-based cocktail) and other drinks.

La Taberna del Duende (Barrio Miraflores) Live music Thursday through Saturday nights. A taxi ride there should cost $0.80 – cab drivers know the place.

SHOPPING

Every imaginable item has been covered with a Galápagos logo and is on sale in Puerto Ayora. Cute and kitschy T-shirts are available everywhere. The profits from gifts and clothes sold at the Charles Darwin Research Station go to support the institution, and the national park boutique is the only place to get things emblazoned with its logo. Avoid buying objects made from black coral, turtle and tortoise shell. These threatened species are protected, and it is illegal to use these animal products for the manufacture of novelties.

Stock up on sunblock, insect repellent, toiletries, film and medications on the mainland. These are available in Puerto Ayora, but selection is slimmer and more expensive.

GETTING THERE & AWAY

Air

For more information on flights to and from Santa Cruz see p358. Reconfirming your flight departures at either the **Aerogal** (☎252 6798; www.aerogal.com.ec; Av Padre Julio Herrera) or **TAME office** (☎252 6165; www.tame.com.ec; Av Charles Darwin; ⏰8am-noon & 2-10pm Mon-Fri, 4-6pm Sat) is essential. Flights are often full, and there is sometimes difficulty in changing your reservation or buying a ticket. **EMETEBE** (☎252 6177; Av Charles Darwin) has small aircraft that fly between Baltra and San Cristóbal and Isabela. You must reserve your ticket at least a few days in advance. Departure times vary.

Boat

The *capitanía* has information about (infrequent) boats to the mainland and has details of every boat sailing from Puerto Ayora.

The passenger ferry *Ingala II* sails Monday, Wednesday and Friday to San Cristóbal and two Fridays each month to Isabela. Both trips are about four hours and cost $50. Tickets are sold the day of departure below the EMETEBE office near the harbor. You can pick up schedules at the Cámara de Turismo, at the *capitanía* and at the main **Ingala office** (☎252 6151), north of the harbor off Avenida Padre Julio Herrera.

Ask at Restaurant Salvavidas about smaller boats that usually head daily to Isabela (one trip at 2pm) and San Cristóbal (up to eight trips in the morning). They reach the islands in less than three hours and charge about $30. There are no toilets on these little boats and the ride can be rough and even terrifying to some.

One recommended company that plies the Santa Cruz–San Cristóbal route in a larger, more trustworthy and comfortable boat than most is *Blue Attractions* (p372).

GETTING AROUND

Most hotels and some cafés rent bicycles (per hour $1), a good way to get around town and the highlands for the aerobically ambitious.

To/From Airport

The airport is on Isla Baltra, a small island practically touching the far northern edge of Isla Santa Cruz. If you are booked on a prearranged tour you will be met by a boat representative upon arrival and ushered onto a bus for the 10-minute drive to the channel – separating Baltra from Santa Cruz – and the boat dock.

If you are traveling independently, don't take these buses. Instead, take the public bus that's signed 'Muelle' to the dock (a 10-minute ride, free) for the ferry to Isla Santa Cruz. A 10-minute ferry ride ($0.80) will take you across to Santa Cruz, where you will be met by a CITTEG bus to take you to Puerto Ayora, about 45 minutes away ($1.80). This drive (on a paved road) provides a good look at the interior and the highlands of Santa Cruz. There isn't much waiting involved and you should be in Puerto Ayora about an hour after leaving the airport.

You can buy your ticket on the bus or at one of the ticket booths near the airport exit. The ride is always crowded.

Buses from Puerto Ayora to Baltra (via the ferry) leave early every morning to meet the first flight from Baltra, and again later timed to meet any other incoming flights. Tickets are sold at the CITTEG bus station around 2km north of the harbor at the corner of Padre Julio Herrera and Charles Binford.

Taxis are also available on the Santa Cruz side of the channel to take you to Puerto Ayora ($15, 30 minutes).

Buses & Taxis

Taxis from anywhere in town to the CITTEG bus station cost $1. Buses from Puerto Ayora to Santa Rosa (about $1) leave from the bus station four or five times a day Monday to Saturday and less often on Sunday. Charters can be arranged for groups.

The most convenient way of seeing the interior and ensuring that you don't get stuck is to hire a bus or truck for the day with a group of other travelers.

All taxis are pickups which means you can toss your bike in the back if you want to return to Puerto Ayora by pedal power. To Bellavista by taxi is around $2 and to Santa Rosa is around $15 – both one way.

AROUND ISLA SANTA CRUZ

The one sizable island in the central part of the archipelago that has no visitor sites is **Isla Pinzón** (Duncan). It is a cliff-bound island, which makes landing difficult, and a permit is required to visit it (permits are usually reserved for scientists and researchers).

Isla Baltra

Most visitors' first experience of the Galápagos is from the archipelago's main airport at Isla Baltra. Baltra is a small island (27 sq km) off the north coast of Santa Cruz. Nearly all tours begin here or in the town of Puerto Ayora, about one hour away (by a bus-boat-bus combination) on Isla Santa Cruz. There are no visitor sites or accommodations. Those on a prearranged tour are often met at the airport and taken to their boats – a host of pelicans and noddies will greet you as you arrive at the harbor, and you can begin your wildlife-watching within minutes of leaving the airport. Public transportation for here is described under Puerto Ayora (see left).

Islas Seymour & Mosquera

Separated from Isla Baltra by a channel, Isla Seymour is a 1.9-sq-km uplifted island with a dry landing. There is a rocky, circular trail (about 2.5km) leading through some of the largest and most active seabird-breeding colonies in the islands. Magnificent frigatebirds and blue-footed boobies are the main attractions. Whatever time of year you come, there is always some kind of courtship, mating, nesting or chick rearing to observe. You can get close to the nests, as there is always at least one pair of silly boobies that chooses the middle of the trail as the best place to build their nest. Swallow-tailed gulls also nest here, and other birds are often seen as well. Sea lions, and land and marine iguanas are common, while occasional fur sea lions, lava lizards and Galápagos snakes are seen too. It's well worth visiting for the wildlife.

Isla Mosquera is a tiny sandy island (about 120m by 600m) that lies in the channel between Islas Baltra and Seymour. There's no trail, but visitors land on the sandy beach to see or swim with the sea lion colony.

Islas Plazas

These two small islands are just off the east coast of Santa Cruz and can be visited on a daytrip from Puerto Ayora.

The two islands were formed by uplift due to faulting. Boats anchor between them, and visitors can land on **South Plaza** (the larger of the islands), which is only about 13 hectares in area. A dry landing on a jetty brings you to an opuntia cactus forest, where there are many land iguanas. A 1km trail circuit leads visitors through sea lion colonies and along a clifftop walk where swallow-tailed gulls and other species nest. The 25m-high cliffs offer a superb vantage point to watch various seabirds, such as red-billed tropic-birds, frigatebirds, pelicans and Audubon's shearwaters. Snorkeling with the sea lions is a possibility.

Islas Daphne

These two islands of obviously volcanic origin are roughly 10km west of Seymour. **Daphne Minor** is the one that is very eroded, while **Daphne Major** retains most of its typically volcanic shape (called a tuff cone). A short but steep trail leads to the 120m-high summit of this tiny island.

There are two small craters at the top of the cone, and they contain hundreds of blue-footed booby nests. Nazca boobies nest on the crater rims, and a few red-billed trop-icbirds nest in rocky crevices in the steep sides of the islands.

The island is difficult to visit because of the acrobatic landing – visitors have to jump from a moving *panga* on to a vertical cliff and scramble their way up the rocks. The steep slopes are fragile and susceptible to erosion, which has led the national park authorities to limit visits to the island. You must arrange special permission in advance (groups no larger than 12).

Isla Santa Fé (Barrington)

This 24-sq-km island, about 20km southeast of Santa Cruz, is a popular destination for daytrips. There is a good anchorage in an attractive bay on the northeast coast, and a wet landing gives the visitor a choice of two trails. A 300m trail takes you to one of the

tallest stands of opuntia cactus in the islands. Some of the cacti here are over 10m high. A somewhat more strenuous 1.5km rough trail goes into the highlands, where the Santa Fé land iguana (found nowhere else in the world) may be seen if you are lucky. Other attractions include a sea lion colony, excellent snorkeling, marine iguanas and, of course, birds.

ISLA SAN CRISTÓBAL (CHATHAM)

Some local boosters say that San Cristóbal is the capital of paradise, which it technically is since the port town of Baquerizo Moreno on the southwest point is the political seat of the Galápagos. It's the only island with fresh water, the only island with an airport in town, and has several easily accessible visitor sites, all of which means that its tourism profile is second only to Santa Cruz. San Cristóbal is the fifth-largest island in the archipelago and has the second-largest population. The Chatham mockingbird, common throughout the island, is found nowhere else.

Though first settled in 1880, it was the establishment of a sugar factory by Manuel J Cobos in 1891 that signaled the start of any significant human presence on the island. Cobos recruited jailed mainlanders to work in his factory at El Progreso, imported train cars and minted his own money called the cobo. The experimental utopian project lasted for 25 years until the workers revolted and killed him in 1904. His son took over but was not very successful; it's now a small village and you can see the factory ruins and the site where Cobos is buried.

Visitor Sites

EL JUNCO LAGOON

A road leads from the capital to the village of **El Progreso**, about 8km to the east and at the base of the 896m-high Cerro San Joaquín, the highest point on San Cristóbal (buses go here several times a day from Puerto Baquerizo Moreno or you can hire a taxi to take you for about $20 round trip). Rent a jeep or walk east along a dirt road about 10km further to El Junco Lagoon – a freshwater lake at about 700m above sea level. It's one of the few permanent freshwater bodies in the Galápagos. Here you can see frigatebirds shower in the freshwater (to remove the salt from their feathers), white-cheeked pintails and common gallinules and observe the typical highland Miconia vegetation and endemic tree ferns. The weather is often misty or rainy.

The road to El Junco continues across the island to the isolated beach of **Puerto Chino**.

PUERTO GRANDE

Smaller than its name suggests, Puerto Grande is a well-protected little cove on San Cristóbal's northwestern coast. There is a good, sandy beach suitable for swimming and various seabirds can be seen.

ISLA LOBOS

About an hour northeast of Puerto Baquerizo Moreno by boat is the tiny, rocky Isla Lobos, the main sea lion and blue-footed booby colony for visitors to San Cristóbal. There is a 300m-long trail where lava lizards are often seen. Both the boat crossing and the trail tend to be rough, and there are better wildlife colonies elsewhere.

LEÓN DORMIDO (KICKER ROCK)

About a half-hour boat ride northeast of Puerto Baquerizo Moreno is little rocky island that, because of a resemblance to a sleeping lion, is named León Dormido. However, it's more commonly referred as Kicker Rock. The island is a sheer-walled tuff cone that has been eroded in half; smaller boats can sail between the two rocks. Because there's no place to land, this site is usually only seen from a passing boat, often to dramatic effect when the sun is setting.

LOS GALÁPAGOS

At the northern end of the island is Los Galápagos, where you can often see giant Galápagos tortoises in the wild, although it takes some effort to get to the highland area where they live. One way is to land in a bay at the north end of the island and hike up – it takes about two hours to reach the tortoise area by the trail. Some visitors report seeing many tortoises, others see none. It's also possible to get to Los Galápagos by taking the road from Puerto Baquerizo Moreno through El Progreso and on to El Junco Lagoon from where you can hike in.

OTHER SITES

The northeasternmost point of the island is **Punta Pitt**, where volcanic tuff formations

are of interest to geologists (and attractive in their own right), but the unique feature of the site is that it's the only one where you can see all three Galápagos booby species nesting. The walk is a little strenuous but rewarding.

Maybe one of the nicest beaches in the Galápagos is **Cerro Brujo**, a huge white sandy expanse at the northeast end of the island that feels like sifted powdered sugar. A colony of sea lions and blue-footed boobies call Cerro Brujo home and behind the beach is a lagoon where you find great egrets and great blue herons. There's good snorkeling in the turquoise waters. Also nearby is **Turtle Bay** where you can see flamingos, turtles and other wildlife; both Turtle Bay and Cerro Brujo can be visited as part of a trip to Punta Pitt and Los Galápagos.

On the northwest side is **Ochoa Beach**, a horseshoe-shaped cove with a white sandy beach and shallow water good for snorkeling. Sea lions, frigate birds, pelicans, blue-footed boobies can all be found frolicking here however it's only accessible by boat and usually with a guide.

Part of the national park on the southeastern part of San Cristóbal is **Galapaguera**, a corral of giant tortoises living in seminatural conditions. A taxi can take you there and back for around $30.

Puerto Baquerizo Moreno

☎ 05 / pop 7000

In an attempt to come out from under the shadow of Puerto Ayora, its larger and more high profile sister city in the Galápagos, Puerto Baquerizo Moreno is experiencing something of a mini boom. Not that it's in danger of losing its sleepy, time-stands-still fishing village feel, but there are more hotels, restaurants and gift shops going up than in years past. More flights are arriving daily and some boat companies begin their island tours from here. Locals affectionately call it 'Cristóbal' (even though that's the name of the island). The surfing is world-class, and you can explore many places on the island from here on your own.

INFORMATION
Internet Access

Cyber Jean Carlos (Calle Española; per hr $2; ⏰ 8am-10pm Mon-Fri, 8am-5pm Sat, 8am-3pm Sun)
Miconia (Av Charles Darwin) A row of computers in the hotel of the same name.

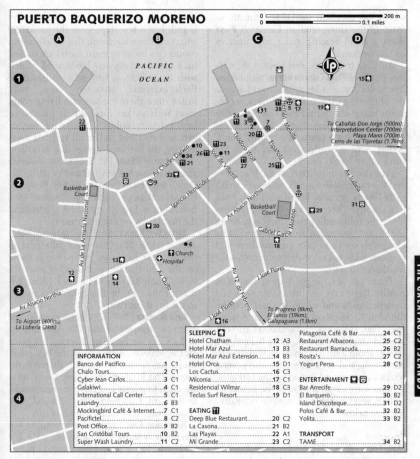

PUERTO BAQUERIZO MORENO

PACIFIC
OCEAN

To Cabañas Don Jorge (500m);
Interpretation Center (700m);
Playa Mann (700m);
Cerro de las Tijeretas (1.7km)

Basketball
Court

Av de la Armada Nacional

Av Charles Darwin

José de Villamil

Teodoro Wolf

Herman Melville

Española

Ignacio Hernández

Av Alsacio Northia

Basketball
Court

Gabriel García Moreno

Av Isabela

Church
Hospital

Av Quito

Av 12 de Febrero

I José Flores

I José Flores

Av Alsacio Northia

To Airport (400m);
La Lobería (2km)

To Progreso (8km);
El Junco (19km);
Galapaguera (13km)

THE GALÁPAGOS ISLANDS

INFORMATION	
Banco del Pacifico	1 C1
Chalo Tours	2 C1
Cyber Jean Carlos	3 C1
Galakiwi	4 C1
International Call Center	5 C1
Laundry	6 B3
Mockingbird Café & Internet	7 C1
Pacifictel	8 C2
Post Office	9 B2
San Cristóbal Tours	10 B2
Super Wash Laundry	11 C2

SLEEPING	
Hotel Chatham	12 A3
Hotel Mar Azul	13 B3
Hotel Mar Azul Extension	14 B3
Hotel Orca	15 D1
Los Cactus	16 C3
Miconia	17 C1
Residencial Wilmar	18 C3
Teclas Surf Resort	19 D1

EATING	
Deep Blue Restaurant	20 C2
La Casona	21 B2
Las Playas	22 A1
Mi Grande	23 C2

Patagonia Café & Bar	24 C1
Restaurant Albacora	25 C2
Restaurant Barracuda	26 B2
Rosita's	27 C2
Yogurt Persa	28 C1

ENTERTAINMENT	
Bar Arrecife	29 D2
El Barquero	30 B2
Island Discoteque	31 D2
Polos Café & Bar	32 B2
Yolita	33 B2

TRANSPORT	
TAME	34 B2

Mockingbird Café/Internet (Española) Good place for coffee and snacks.

Laundry
Laundry (Av Alsacio Northia; per kg $1; ⏰ 8am-1pm & 2-8pm Mon-Sat, 8am-1pm Sun) Next to the church. Machine-washed and dried clothes in an hour and a half.
Superwash Laundry (J Villamil; per kg $1)

Money
Banco de Pacifico (Av Charles Darwin; ⏰ 8am-3:30pm Mon-Fri, 10am-noon Sat) Changes traveler's checks and has an ATM.

Telephone
There's an international call center at the corner of Avenida Charles Darwin and Ave-

nida Herman Melville, only a block from the pier.

SIGHTS & ACTIVITIES
The modern and easy to digest **Interpretation Center** (☎ 252 0358, ext 102) on the north side of the bay explains the history and significance of the Galápagos better than anywhere else in the islands or the country. Exhibits deal with the biology, geology and human history of the islands; definitely deserves a visit even if you've already been inundated with facts from boat guides. From the center there are various well-marked trails that wind around the cactus- and scrub-covered **Cerro de las Tijeretas** (Frigatebird Hill). One trail leads over the hill to the small Las Tijeretas bay,

which has excellent **snorkeling**. Directly in front of the Interpretation Center is **Playa Mann**, a small beach popular with townies on the weekends.

Another trail leads west toward the narrow beach of **Playa Cabo de Horno**, nicknamed 'Playa del Amor' (Beach of Love) because the sheltering little mangrove trees are favorite make-out spots. From this beach you can often see surfers ripping up the waves peeling off **Punta Carola**, the nearby point. **Surfing** here is world-class and there are three other breaks nearby.

From beside the airport a road leads several kilometers (about half-an-hour's walk) to **La Lobería**, a rocky beach with a lazy sea lion colony. There are lots of land iguanas along the trail leading past the beach. Bring water and protection from the sun. Taxis charge about $3 to take you out here and you can walk back (or pay an extra $4 for the driver to wait).

There are several good spots for **diving** nearby. Eagle rays, sea turtles, sea lions and hammerheads and white-tip sharks can be found at Kicker Rock. Big schools of jacks, eagle rays, stingrays, and seahorses are seen around Stephanie's Rock. Roca Ballena is a cave at about 23m to 24m down with corals, parrotfish, and rays. There are also several wreck dives around including the *Caragua*, a 100m-long cargo ship near the *Jessica* oil spill. Several companies in town offer diving (see below).

Tours

Chalo Tours (☎ 252 0953; chalotours@hotmail.com; Espanola) Offers day and overnight scuba trips, daytrips on San Cristóbal and more expensive daytrips to nearby islands; also rents snorkel, kayaking and biking equipment.

Galakiwi (☎ 252 0873; www.southernexposuretours.co .nz; Av Charles Darwin) Run by a New Zealand-Galápagean couple. Land tours and snorkeling around San Cristóbal per person $30; full-day tours to Espanola Island ($85); five-day boat tours with overnights on islands from per person $300; rents snorkeling gear; daily dive tours (two dives $100).

San Cristóbal Tours (☎ 252 0124, 09-970 4415; Av Charles Darwin) Daily and live-aboard diving cruises. PADI-run courses. Also operates the *Blue Attractions* boat service to Santa Cruz and Isabela. Run by Harry Jiménez, a friendly, enthusiastic and knowledgeable guide.

SLEEPING

Miconia (☎ 252 0608; www.miconia.tk; Av Charles Darwin; s/d incl breakfast $40/60; 🍴 🖥 🏊) The Mico-

nia is easily the nicest place to stay on the island. Just a few steps from the passenger wharf on the waterfront, this hotel's seven rooms (it's building eight more) are tucked back quietly in a nicely landscaped garden with hammocks, a tiny pool and Jacuzzi. Each extremely attractive room, really suites since there are separate living room areas with wicker furniture, is painted in bright cheerful colors. There's a full-service gym and excellent restaurant and café overlooking the harbor. Internet café as well.

Residencial Wilmar (☎ 252 0706; rafriv@ecuaenlace .com; Gabriel García Moreno; s/d incl breakfast $25/50; 🍴) Only a few blocks from the harbor, this place has several large, comfortable rooms in a family home. Everything is kept spotless and the mattresses are especially good.

Teclas Surf Resort (☎ 252 0632; teclagenoa@yahoo .com; s/d $30/60; 🍴) This white villa next to the Miconia has large, basic rooms; those on the 2nd floor have balconies with sea views. There's a pool in the back (though it may or may not be filled) and hammocks in the front courtyard.

Casa Nuestra (☎ 252 0258; berenicenorris@hotmail .com; r per person incl breakfast $22) Also known as La Casa de Berenice Norris, this place on the Malecón across from the basketball courts has several rooms with shared bathroom. The kitchen and living room areas are open to guests and there are hammocks in the yard. Can help with tours and refer you to other homestays on the island.

Hotel Mar Azul (☎ 252 0139; hotelmarazul_ex@ hotmail.com; Av Alsacio Northia at Av Quito; s $12-20, d $20-25; 🍴) Friendly and has pleasant patios and rooms with private hot shower, TV and fan. The Mar Azul Extension is a modern building across the street. Rooms here are a little more expensive.

Los Cactus (☎ 252 0078; hostal_cactus@hotmail .com; J Jose Flores near Av Quito; s/d/tr incl breakfast $15/24/33) A friendly family-run place, the Los Cactus however isn't much to look at since everything is concrete. The fan-cooled rooms have TV. A terrace with good views of town was in the works at the time of research.

Hotel Chatham (☎ 252 0137; Av Alsacio Northia; r $15-25) The Chatham has a concrete patio with hammocks, but it's an old building and the rooms are basic.

Cabañas Don Jorge (☎ 252 0208; Av Alsacio Northia; r per person $8-15) Don Jorge consists of several old cabañas, probably not much changed since Darwin's day, set amid unkempt grounds directly across from Playa Mann on the way to the Interpretation Center. Each room is a rustic hodgepodge of furniture and has a separate ancient kitchen.

Hotel Orca (☎ /fax 252 0233, Quito ☎ 02-256 4565; s/d about $45/55) This is the largest hotel on the island, although besides its convenience for big groups there's not much to recommend about the Orca. It's near the beach and the 20 basic rooms have hot water and fans.

Casa del Ceibo (☎ 252 0248; r per person $4) Known to locals in the highlands of Progreso as Tarzan's House because of its address – a large ceibo tree – there are two basic rooms available. There's kitchen access and a restaurant is open on weekends.

EATING

For better or worse there aren't many restaurants catering to tourists in Baquerizo Moreno. Most are informal spots with a few tables on the street and close early on Sundays. Women sell *chuzos* (thinly sliced steak grilled on a stick) along Alsacio Northia, near the school in the evenings.

Miconia (☎ 252 0035; Av Charles Darwin; mains $6-12; ⏱ 7am-8pm) Part of the hotel of the same name, this is the most modern and comfortable restaurant in town. The 2nd-floor dining room has great views of the harbor and serves pizza ($8), pasta ($7) and seafood ($8). Cheap *almuerzos* are also available.

Las Playas (☎ 252 0577; Av de la Armada Nacional; mains $6) This restaurant in an attractive yellow building along the waterfront to the west of town has outdoor seating and, more importantly, large portions. The shrimp cooked in coconut milk ($7) is especially good as is the conch ceviche ($6) and the personal pizzas ($7).

Yogurt Persa (Av Charles Darwin; burgers $2) A good spot to watch new arrivals and old hands come and go on the pier just opposite. It's fast food all the way, from the bright lights to the chicken meals.

La Casona (☎ 252 0292; Av Charles Darwin) Look for the yellow and blue facade at the southern end of the Malecón for good sandwiches, shakes and coffee.

Mi Grande (Jose de Villamil; drinks $0.90-1.50) Famous for its array of *batidos* (fruit shakes).

Rosita's (Ignacio Hernandez & Wolf) and **Restaurant Albacora** (Alsacio Northia & Española) both serve tasty fresh-caught fish ($4) and cheap *almuerzos* ($3).

Patagonia Café & Bar (Av Charles Darwin), **Deep Blue Restaurant** (Av Española) and **Restaurant Barracuda** are similar places on or just off the Malecón serving inexpensive *almuerzos* and snacks throughout the day and evening.

DRINKING & ENTERTAINMENT

Bar Arrecife is the place for karaoke filled evenings and the rustic **Polos Cafe & Bar** (Av 12 de Febrero) is sometimes turned into a discotheque but always does good *capahrinas*.

The **Island Discoteque** (Av Isabela) is perched on a hill in town. Side by side, **Neptuno** (Av Charles Darwin) and **Yolita** (Av Charles Darwin) are the local discos; both are on the Malecón near the *capitanía*.

El Barquero is a good hang-out with outdoor tables, though usually only open on weekends.

GETTING THERE & AWAY
Air

The airport is half a kilometer from town – a five-minute walk or a $1 taxi ride (taxis are white pickup cabs). For information on flights to Guayaquil and Quito see p358. A Hercules plane seconded from the air force, flies tourists from Guayaquil to San Cristóbal, Baltra and Isabela every 15 days and costs half of other fares (see p358). Regardless of the airline you should try to check your luggage at least two hours in advance; you can always easily return to town to spend your final hours in the islands more comfortably.

AeroGal (☎ 252 1117; www.aerogal.com.ec) Office at the airport.

EMETEBE (☎ 252 0036) Office at the airport. Flies within the islands.

TAME (☎ 252 1089; www.tame.com.ec; Av Charles Darwin) Office in town and at the airport.

Boat

Ingala II sails two to three times per week to Puerto Ayora, Santa Cruz ($50, about four hours). Small boats head to Santa Cruz and occasionally to Floreana and Isabela; ask about the *Blue Attractions* boat at San Cristóbal Tours (see opposite). Rates are $20 to $30 (two to 2½ hours).

GETTING AROUND

To get to the farming center of El Progreso 8km into the highlands, hire a taxi $2 (one

THE GALÁPAGOS ISLANDS

THE MAN BEHIND THE MYTH

The life and work of Charles Darwin is so closely connected in the general public's mind with the Galápagos Islands that most people assume he spent a significant amount of time here and that the inspiration for ideas he sketches out in the *Origin of Species* came to him in a eureka moment while touring the islands. Neither assumption is in fact true.

Darwin spent only five weeks in the Galápagos and his later observations of pigeons and the methods of dog breeders in England were both much more influential to Darwin than the finches that have become the poster children of evolutionary theory.

Darwin lived in London for five years after he returned from the Galápagos and then retreated to an estate in the countryside. From then on he hardly traveled and was confined to a sedentary lifestyle in part because of chronic health concerns.

From an early age he was inspired more by free-thinking religious figures than secular atheists and was never motivated to disprove the role of a divine figure. After he spent 22 years trying to prove his theory, he renounced Christianity in his middle ages and described himself an agnostic.

Originally sent to Cambridge to be a clergyman, Darwin instead became inspired by the botany lessons of his mentor JS Henslow. He collected beetles as a hobby and formed a club organized around the eating of animals unknown to the European kitchen. It was only after his uncle Josiah Wedgwood intervened that Darwin's father allowed him to go on a voyage at the age of 22. Darwin slept on a hammock on the *Beagle*, rode on top of Galápagos turtles, and in what is surely a violation of park rules today, he dined on their meat.

From 1831 to 1836 the *Beagle* was tasked to survey the South American coastline and chart harbors for the British navy; the boat stopped in Brazil, the Falklands, Argentina and Chile before the Galápagos. Darwin returned with more than 1500 specimens, though for many of those found in the Galápagos he neglected to label where each was found.

By the time the boat reached Bahía, Brazil in 1836 Darwin was ready to return, writing in his journal, 'I loathe, I abhor the sea and all ships which sail on it.' In 1859 the *Origin of the Species* sold out on its first day in print. Only 1% of the book refers to the Galápagos.

way). In El Progreso, you can hire a vehicle ($20), walk or hitchhike, for the final 10km ride to the visitor site of El Junco Lagoon. Some taxi drivers are licensed to give tours of the lagoon.

In Puerto Baquerizo Moreno, taxis hang out along the Malecón and have fixed rates to island destinations, but don't always stick to them. They'll take you to La Lobería, El Progreso, El Junco Lagoon, La Galapaguera and Puerto Chino.

ISLA SAN SALVADOR (SANTIAGO OR JAMES)

Once a hideout for British buccaneers and one of the stops on Darwin's itinerary, Isla Santiago, whose little used official name is San Salvador, is the fourth-largest of the islands. It's a frequent stop on boat tours because there are several interesting visitor sites and its terrain of rough lava fields is an example of the island's challenging beauty.

One of the most popular sites in all the islands is **Puerto Egas**, on James Bay, on the west side of Santiago. Here, there is a long, flat, black lava shoreline where eroded shapes form lava pools, caves and inlets that house a great variety of wildlife. This is a great place to see colonies of marine iguanas basking in the sun. The tide pools contain hundreds of red Sally Lightfoot crabs, which attract hunting herons of all the commonly found species.

Named after Dario Egas, the owner of a salt mine on the island that was once, as a result of presidential patronage, the only producer of salt in all the country.

The inlets are favorite haunts of the Galápagos fur sea lion, and this is a great opportunity to snorkel with the surprisingly agile animals as well as many species of tropical fish, moray eels, sharks and octopuses.

Behind the black lava shoreline is Sugarloaf Volcano, which can be reached via a 2km path. Lava lizards, Darwin's finches and Galápagos doves are often seen on this path. It peters out near the top of the 395m summit, but from here, the views are stupendous. There is an extinct crater in which feral goats are often seen (wild goats are a major problem on Santiago), and Galápagos hawks often hover a few meters above the top of the volcano. North of the volcano is a crater where the salt mine used to be; its remains can be visited by walking along a 3km trail from the coast.

At the north end of James Bay, about 5km from Puerto Egas, is the brown-sand **Espumilla Beach**, which can be reached with a wet landing. The swimming is good here, and by the small lagoon behind the beach you can see various wading birds – including, at times, flamingos. A 2km trail leads inland through transitional vegetation where there are various finches and the Galápagos flycatcher.

At the northwestern end of Santiago, another site that is normally visited by boat is **Buccaneer Cove**, so called because it was a popular place for 17th- and 18th-century buccaneers to careen their vessels. The cliffs and pinnacles, which are used as nesting areas by several species of seabirds, are the main attraction these days. This is best appreciated from the sea, but it is possible to land in the cove, where there are beaches.

Sullivan Bay is on Santiago's east coast. Here, a huge, black, century-old lava flow has solidified into a sheet that reaches to the edge of the sea. A dry landing enables visitors to step onto the flow and follow a trail of white posts in a 2km circuit on the lava. You can see uneroded volcanic formations, such as *pahoehoe* lava, lava bubbles and tree-trunk molds in the surface. This site is of particular interest to those interested in volcanology or geology.

AROUND ISLA SAN SALVADOR
Isla Bartolomé
Panoramic views and frisky penguins make this tiny island just off Sullivan Bay a common stop for boat tours. A path from a jetty (dry landing) leads up to the wind-whipped 114m summit of the island where the dramatic views make it a de rigeur spot for group photos. This trail leads through a wild and unearthly looking lava landscape; a wooden boardwalk and stairs have been built, both to aid visitors and to protect the trail from erosion.

The other visitor site is a small, sandy beach in a cove (wet landing) from where

you can don your snorkel gear and swim after the speedy Galápagos penguins that frequent this cove. Marine turtles and a gaudy variety of tropical fish are also frequently seen.

The best way to photograph the penguins is by taking a *panga* ride close to the rocks on either side of the cove – particularly around the aptly named Pinnacle Rock, to the right of the cove from the seaward side. You can often get within a few meters of these fascinating birds – the closest point to Puerto Ayora where you can do so. Other penguin colonies are on the western side of Isabela.

From the beach, a 100m trail leads across the narrowest part of Bartolomé to another sandy beach on the opposite side of the island. Marine turtles may nest here between January and March.

Sombrero Chino
This tiny island, a fairly recent volcanic cone, just off the southeastern tip of Santiago is less than a quarter of 1 sq km in size. Its accuracy of its descriptive name, translated as 'Chinese Hat,' is best appreciated from the north. There is a small sea lion cove on the north shore, where you can anchor and land at the visitor site. Opposite Sombrero Chino, on the rocky shoreline of nearby Santiago, penguins are often seen.

A 400m trail goes around the cove, where there's snorkeling and swimming opportunities, and through a sea lion colony – marine iguanas scurry everywhere.

Isla Rábida
This approximately 5-sq-km island, also known as Jervis, lies 5km south of Santiago. There is a wet landing onto a comparatively dark red beach where sea lions haul out and pelicans nest. This is one of the best places to see these birds nesting.

Behind the beach, there is a saltwater lagoon where flamingos and white-cheeked pintails are sometimes seen. This lagoon is also the site of a sea lion colony where the *solteros* (lone males), deposed by the dominant bull, while away their days in bachelor ignominy.

There is a 750m trail with good views of the island's 367m volcanic peak, which is covered with *palo santo* trees. At the end of the trail, there is a great snorkeling spot.

ISLA ISABELA (ALBEMARLE)

Despite its size – Isabela is the largest island in the archipelago at 4588-sq-km – and imposing skyline of volcanoes, most still active, it's the delicate sights like frigates flying as high as the clouds or penguins making their way tentatively along the cliffs that reward visitors to Isabela.

It's a relatively recent island and consists of a chain of five fairly young and intermittently active volcanoes, including Volcán Sierra Negra which erupted in late 2005 sending up a 20km-high smoke column. Puerto Villamil, 22km to the south, and nearby wildlife were not in danger. One of the island's volcanoes, Volcán Wolf, is the highest point in the Galápagos at 1707m (some sources claim 1646m). There is also one small older volcano, Volcán Ecuador (610m).

Volcán Alcedo (1097m) has the largest tortoise population in the Galápagos, however more than 50,000 feral goats also call the volcano home, threatening to out-compete the tortoises for the limited food stuffs available. The campaign to preserve the tortoise population on Alcedo is a joint venture between the Charles Darwin Research Station and the Galápagos National Park Service.

Although Isabela's volcanoes dominate the westward view during passages to the western part of Santa Cruz, the island itself is not frequently visited by smaller boats because most of the best visitor sites are on the west side of the island which is reached only after a long passage (over 200km) from Santa Cruz.

Visitor Sites

As you'd expect from an island that occupies over 58% of the entire land mass of the Galápagos, there are many visitor sites on Isabela. One of these is the summit of **Volcán Alcedo** (1097m), which is famous for its 7km-wide caldera and steaming fumaroles, where hundreds of giant tortoises can be seen, especially from June to December. The view is fantastic. Permits are required to hike this long, steep and waterless trail and camp near the summit (two days required).

A few kilometers north of the landing for Alcedo is **Punta García**, which consists mainly of very rough *aa* lava, a sharp, jagged lava; there are no proper trails, but you can land. This is one of the few places where you can see the endemic flightless cormorant without having to take the long passage around to the west side (sightings are not guaranteed).

At the northern tip of Isabela is **Punta Albemarle**, which used to be a US radar base during WWII. There are no trails, and the site is known for the flightless cormorants, which normally are not found further to the east. Further west are several points where flightless cormorants, Galápagos penguins and other seabirds can be seen, but there are no visitor sites. You must view the birds from your boat.

At the west end of the northern arm of Isabela is the small, old Volcán Ecuador (610m), which comes down almost to the sea. **Punta Vicente Roca**, at the volcano's base, is a rocky point with a good snorkeling and diving area, but there is no official landing site.

The first official visitor-landing site on the western side of Isabela is **Punta Tortuga**, a mangrove-surrounded beach at the base of Volcán Darwin (1280m). Although there is no trail, you can land on the beach and explore the mangroves for the mangrove finch, which is present here but not always easy to see. This finch is found only on Islas Isabela and Fernandina.

Just south of the point is **Tagus Cove**, where early sailors frequently anchored and scratched the names of their vessels into the cliffs around the cove. It's a strange sight to behold graffiti, the oldest from 1836, in an otherwise pristine environment next to where sea lions roam.

A dry landing deposits you at the beginning of a 2km-long trail that brings you past a postcard-perfect saltwater lagoon, twice the salinity of the ocean, called **Darwin Lake**; it's a tuff cone, like a chimney from the main volcano. Here the trail leads to the lower lava slopes of Volcán Darwin, where various volcanic formations and stunning views of surrounding slopes can be observed. There are some steep sections on this trail. A *panga* ride along the cliffs will enable you to see the historical graffiti and various seabirds, usually including Galápagos penguins and flightless cormorants. There are snorkeling opportunities in the cove.

Urbina Bay lies around the middle of the western shore of Isabela and is a flat area formed by an uplift from the sea in 1954. Evidence of the uplift includes a coral reef on the land. Flightless cormorants, pelicans, giant tortoises and land and marine iguanas can be observed on land, and rays and turtles can be seen in the bay. A wet landing onto a beach brings you to a 1km trail that leads to the corals. There is a good view of Volcán Alcedo.

Near where the western shoreline of Isabela bends sharply toward the lower arm of the island, there is a visitor site that's known for its marine life. **Elizabeth Bay** is best visited by a *panga* ride, as there are no landing sites. Marine turtles and rays can usually be seen in the water, and various seabirds and shorebirds are often present. Islas Mariela are at the entrance of the bay and are frequented by penguins.

West of Elizabeth Bay is **Punta Moreno**. You can make a dry landing on to a lava flow, where there are some brackish pools. Flamingos, white-cheeked pintails and common gallinules are sometimes seen, and various pioneer plants and insects are found in the area.

On the southeastern corner of Isabela, there is the small village of Puerto Villamil. Behind and to the west of the village is the **Villamil Lagoon**. This visitor site is known for its migrant birds – especially waders, more than 20 species have been reported here. The surrounding vegetation is dense and without trails, but the road to the highlands and the open beach do give reasonable access to the lagoons. Also west of Puerto Villamil is a visitor site, **Muro de las Lágrimas** (Wall of Tears), which was built by convicts.

To the northwest near the tiny settlement of Santo Tomás lies the massive **Volcán Sierra Negra** (1490m), which erupted in late 2005. Trucks or jeeps can be hired for the 18km ride from Puerto Villamil ($40 round-trip). From Santo Tomás, it is 9km further up a steep trail to the rim of the volcano – horses can be rented in the village ($10, one hour).

The caldera is roughly 10km in diameter and is a spectacular sight with magnificent views. An 8km trail leads around the east side of the volcano to some active fumaroles. It is possible to walk all the way around the caldera, but the trail peters out. You should carry all your food and water or rent horses. Galápagos hawks, short-eared owls, finches and flycatchers are among the birds commonly seen on this trip. The summit is often foggy (especially during the June-to-

December *garúa* season) and it is easy to get lost. Nearby is Volcán Chico, a subcrater where you can see more fumaroles. These volcanoes are very infrequently visited.

Puerto Villamil

☎ 05 / pop 1500

This quaint palm-fringed village fronted by a beautiful white-sand beach and backed by a lagoon is not a bad place to call home. Undoubtedly when General Jose Villamil moved here in 1832 with hopes of organizing a model community made up mostly of whalers he found the location as beguiling as today's visitors do. Unfortunately, the draftees peaceful inclinations proved to be more utopian than real and ended up destroying the colony. Villamil later introduced cows, horses and donkeys which quickly reproduced and threatened the island's delicate ecosystem.

You can change traveler's checks at Gram Money; bring US cash. There is a Pacifictel office. Access the Internet at Easy Cyber Café on Avenida Escalesias.

SLEEPING & EATING

La Casa Marita (☎ 252 9238; www.galapagosisabela .com; s/d/tr/q incl breakfast $35/50/65/80; 🞩 🖳) Close to the beach with sea views, each uniquely decorated room at the Marita has its own color scheme as well as hot showers and kitchenettes. There's a Jacuzzi, bar, library and hammocks in the garden.

Hostería Isabela del Mar (☎ 252 9030; www.hos teriaisabela.com.ec; r per person $20) Really two hotels in one, the Isabela del Mar also includes rooms in another building called Hotel Ballena Azul, which serves good food. Some rooms have shared and some have private bathrooms; ask for an ocean view.

Cormorant Beach House (☎ 252 9200; www.gala pagoss.com; Av Antonio Gill & Malecón; r from $20) has two large cabañas by the beach and **Hotel Las Gardenia** (☎ 252 9115; r $10) is one of the cheapest options in town.

Ballena Azul (☎ 252 9030) Has good food with many choices but very slow service so order ahead of time.

There are several restaurants located on Av Antonio Gill near the central square including charming Pepas's which serves delicious seafood and European dishes and El Toque del Sabor which has set breakfasts, *almuerzos* and pizzas.

THE GALÁPAGOS ISLANDS

GETTING THERE & AWAY
Air
Two times a week, **EMETEBE** (☎ 252 9155) flies from Baltra to San Cristóbal to Isabela to Baltra. Each leg is around $100. Its office is at the airport. See p359 for more information. The Isabela stop may be canceled if there aren't enough passengers.

Hercules military flights also fly periodically from San Cristóbal and Baltra.

Boat
There are daily boats to Santa Cruz ($30, two hours, 8am) from Puerto Villamil. From Santa Cruz boats leave at 2pm. Tickets can be purchased at the dock near the restaurant Salvavidas in Puerto Ayora.

Otherwise you can charter a boat from Puerto Ayora ($400, up to 16 people) or Puerto Baquerizo Moreno ($700, up to 16 people).

GETTING AROUND
Buses to/from Villamil to Santo Tomás and further into the highlands leave at 7am and noon, returning two hours later. Trucks can be rented at other times.

ISLA FERNANDINA (NARBOROUGH)
Even by Galápagos standards, Fernandina is especially unique. It's home to thousands of lethargic marine iguanas and for the volcanically minded it's the island you'll most likely witness an eruption; the most recent occurred in May 2005. At 642 sq km, Fernandina is the third-largest island and the westernmost and youngest of the main islands. Unlike other parts of the Galápagos, no introduced species have taken root here.

The one visitor site at **Punta Espinoza**, just across from Tagus Cove on Isabela is a memorable one. Marine iguanas, too many to count, can be seen sunning themselves on the black lava formations, a dramatic sight that looks like a museum diorama on dinosaurs come to life. Flightless cormorants nest nearby and Galápagos penguins, turtles and sea lions sometimes frolic in an admirable display of multispecies tolerance in the lagoon near the landing.

A dry landing brings you to two trails: a 250m trail to the point and a 750m trail to recently formed lava fields. Here you can see various pioneering plants, such as the *Brachycereus* cactus, as well as *pahoehoe* and *aa* lava formations. Several movies, most famously *Master and Commander*, filmed scenes here in front of a now iconic white mangrove tree.

SOUTHERN ISLANDS
Isla Santa María (Floreana, Charles)
This, the sixth-largest of the islands, is known as much for the tragic history of its first residents, as for its intensely pink flamingos and snorkeling sites. After the departure of Patrick Watkins, the first known resident in all the archipelago, Floreana was turned into an Ecuadorian penal colony. Then in the 1930s, three groups of German settlers arrived and strange stories have been told about them ever since.

The most colorful of the settlers was a baroness who arrived with three lovers. Antoher settler, Dr Friedrich Ritter, an eccentric who had all of his teeth removed before arriving to avoid having dental problems, was accompanied by his mistress. The third group was a young couple from Cologne, the Wittmers.

Despite their common nationality, there was a great deal of friction among the groups, and one by one the settlers died under mysterious circumstances. The baroness and one of her lovers simply disappeared, while another lover died in a boating accident. The vegetarian Dr Ritter died of food poisoning after eating chicken. The only ones to survive were the Wittmers; the last, Margaret Wittmer, died in 2000 at the age of 95.

Her children and grandchildren run a small hotel and restaurant in Puerto Velasco Ibarra. Although several books and articles have been written about the strange happenings on Floreana (including one by Wittmer herself), no one is really sure of the truth.

VISITOR SITES
From the village of Puerto Velasco Ibarra, a road runs inland for a few kilometers to an area where you can see the endemic medium tree finch (this finch exists only on Floreana). Early settlers once lived in the nearby caves. This area, called **Asilo de la Paz**, is an official visitor site. It is an all-day hike there and back – you can hire a guide. There are no taxis.

There are three visitor sites on the north coast of Floreana. **Post Office Bay** used to have a barrel where whalers left mail. The site continues to be used, but obviously the barrel has been changed many times. About 300m behind the barrel is a lava cave that can be descended with the aid of a short rope. Nearby is a pleasant swimming beach and the remains of a canning factory; a wet landing is necessary.

Also reached with a wet landing is **Punta Cormorant**, a greenish beach (green because it contains crystals of the mineral olivine) where sea lions play and the swimming and snorkeling are good. A 400m trail leads across an isthmus to a white-sand beach where turtles sometimes lay their eggs. The beach is also good for swimming, but beware of stingrays.

Between the two beaches is a lagoon where several dozen flamingos are normally seen. This is also a good place to see other wading birds, such as the black-necked stilts, oystercatchers, willets and whimbrels. White-cheeked pintail ducks are often seen in the lagoon, and Galápagos hawks wheel overhead.

Another Floreana visitor site is the remains of a half-submerged volcanic cone poking up out of the ocean a few hundred meters from Punta Cormorant. Aptly named the **Devil's Crown**, this ragged semicircle of rocks is one of the most outstanding marine sites in the Galápagos.

A *panga* ride around the cone will give views of red-billed tropicbirds, pelicans, herons and lava gulls nesting on the rocks, but the greater attraction is the snorkeling in and around the crater. There are thousands of bright tropical fish, a small coral formation, sea lions and the occasional shark.

PUERTO VELASCO IBARRA

Only several dozen people call this tiny port home, and it's the only settlement on Isla Santa María (Floreana). However, it wouldn't be the Galápagos without animals as neighbors – there's a sea lion colony on a nearby black-sand beach and a flamingo lagoon within walking distance. The highlands are accessed by a road, though it sees little traffic other than that of the foot variety.

The descendants of the Wittmers run the small **Floreana Hotel & Restaurant** (☎ 05-252 0250; s/d/tr $30/50/70) which also doubles as the island post office, best eatery and information and guide center. Beachfront rooms have hot water and fans, and meals can be provided though they are not inexpensive. If it's full, which is rare, they can point you in the direction of a homestay.

Once a month, the passenger ferry *Ingala II* goes from Isabela to Floreana to Santa Cruz. Other boats can be arranged, especially between Floreana and Santa Cruz.

Isla Española (Hood)

Certainly one of the more dramatically beautiful of all the islands in the Galápagos, Española is also the most southerly in the archipelago. Because it's somewhat outlying (about 90km southeast of Santa Cruz), captains of some of the smaller boats may be reluctant to go this far. The 61–sq-km Española is especially well-worth visiting from late March to December, because it has the only colony of the waved albatross, one of the Galápagos' most spectacular seabirds.

A wet landing at **Punta Suárez**, on the western end of the island, leads to a rocky 2km-long trail that takes visitors through masked and blue-footed booby colonies, a beach full of marine iguanas and the waved albatross colony when these spectacular birds call Española home (late March to early December). But equally breathtaking are the views from the wave-battered cliffs; blow holes in the rocky shore below shoot water high into the air and seabirds perform their aerial acrobatics and their more clumsy take offs and landings.

Other birds to look out for are the Hood mockingbird (found nowhere else), swallow-tailed gulls, red-billed tropicbirds and oystercatchers. There are three species of finches: large cactus, small ground, and warbler – all part of the Darwin's finch family that may hop along after you hoping to get at some of your fresh water. The large cactus finch is found on few other islands.

Reached with a wet landing at the east end of Isla Española is **Gardner Bay**, a beautiful white-sand beach with good swimming and a large sea lion colony. It's a little like walking through a mine field, albeit one that moves occasionally, and it's a good idea to give the large male bulls a wide berth lest they interpret your curiosity as a challenge to their dominance. An island a short distance offshore provides good but sometimes rough snorkeling and scuba diving – there's one rock that often has white-tipped reef sharks basking under it, and hammerheads, sea stars and red-lip bat fish are often seen.

NORTHERN ISLANDS
Isla Genovesa (Tower)

Whatever you call it, Isla Genovesa or Tower Island or even Booby Island, lovers of the sometimes goofy- and cuddly-looking boobie won't want to miss this, the northeasternmost of the Galápagos Islands. Watch your feet since it's quite easy to miss a fluffy little baby booby or a camouflaged iguana while scanning the horizon for sperm whale passing in the distance or the hard-to-sight Galápagos owl. Tower Island covers only 14 sq km and is the only regularly visited island that lies entirely north of the equator (the northernmost part of Isabela pokes above the line) and so is often an opportunity for a little shipboard humorous advice to 'hold tight as we pass over the bump.'

As it is an outlying island, Tower is infrequently included on shorter itineraries. It is the best place to see a red-footed booby colony, and it provides visitors with the opportunity to visit colonies of great frigatebirds, red-billed tropicbirds, swallow-tailed gulls, Nazca boobies and many thousands of storm petrels. Other bird attractions include Galápagos doves and short-eared owls. Both sea lions and fur sea lions are present, and there's the chance to snorkel with groups of hammerhead sharks.

The island is fairly flat and round, with a large, almost landlocked, cove named Darwin Bay on the south side. There are two visitor sites, both on Darwin Bay. **Prince Philip's Steps** (also called El Barranco) is on the eastern arm of the bay and can be reached with a dry landing. A steep and rocky path leads to the top of 25m-high cliffs, and nesting seabirds are sometimes found right on the narrow path.

At the top of the cliffs, the 1km-long trail leads inland, past dry-forest vegetation and various seabird colonies, to a cracked expanse of lava, where thousands of storm petrels make their nests and wheel overhead. Short-eared owls are sometimes seen here.

The second visitor site, **Darwin Bay Beach**, is a coral beach reached by a wet landing. There is a 750m trail along the beach that passes through more seabird colonies.

You can take a pleasant *panga* ride along the cliffs, often followed by playful sea lions. This recommended excursion gives a good view of the cliffs and of the birds nesting on them.

Islas Marchena (Bindloe) & Pinta (Abington)

Isla Marchena, at 130 sq km is the seventh-largest island in the archipelago and the largest one to have no official visitor sites. There are some good scuba-diving sites, however, so you may get to see the island up close if on a dive trip. The 343m-high volcano in the middle of the island was very active during 1991 – ask your guide about its current degree of activity.

Isla Pinta is the original home of Lonesome George, the tortoise described earlier (p360). Pinta is the ninth-largest of the Galápagos Islands and is further north than any of the bigger islands. There are landing sites, but the island has no visitor sites, and researchers require a permit to visit.

Isla Wolf (Wenman) & Isla Darwin (Culpepper)

The northernmost islands are the twin islands of **Isla Wolf** and **Isla Darwin**. They are about 100km northwest of the rest of the archipelago and are very seldom visited, except on scuba-diving trips. Both have nearly vertical cliffs that make landing difficult; Isla Darwin was first visited in 1964, when a helicopter expedition landed on the summit.

Directory

CONTENTS

Accommodations 381
Activities 383
Business Hours 386
Children 386
Climate Charts 386
Courses 387
Customs 387
Dangers & Annoyances 387
Disabled Travelers 388
Discount Cards 389
Embassies & Consulates 389
Festivals & Events 390
Food 390
Gay & Lesbian Travelers 390
Holidays 391
Insurance 391
Internet Access 391
Legal Matters 391
Maps 392
Money 392
Photography 393
Post 394
Shopping 394
Solo Travelers 396
Telephone 396
Time 397
Toilets 397
Tourist Information 397
Visas 397
Women Travelers 398
Work 398

PRACTICALITIES

- Ecuador uses 110V AC, 60Hz (the same as in North America). Plugs have two flat prongs, as in North America.

- Ecuador uses the metric system for weights and measures.

- In Ecuadorian addresses, the term 's/n' refers to 'sin numero' (without number), meaning the address has no street number.

- Quito's two biggest newspapers are **El Comercio** (www.elcomercio.com) and the more liberal **Hoy** (www.hoy.com.ec). Guayaquil's papers are **El Telégrafo** (www.telegrafo.com.ec) and **El Universo** (www.eluniverso.com). Ecuador's best-known news magazine is **Vistazo** (www.vistazo.com). International newspapers, including a locally published edition of the *Miami Herald*, can be found in Quito (p70).

- Ecuador uses VHS NTSC video format (the same as North America).

ACCOMMODATIONS

The range of accommodations in Ecuador spans from wooden shacks in the mangroves of Esmeraldas province, to luxurious haciendas on the flanks of Andean volcanoes. How you sleep really comes down to how you *want* to sleep, though you'll be limiting yourself to certain experiences if you only want posh.

Nearly every town of any size has a hotel, but unless you stick to the most touristy destinations, you'll have to tolerate the occasional saggy bed, lousy shower or noisy neighbor. But that's all in the spirit of travel on the equator. Most hotels are respectable, well-run places – they can just be a little…unsophisticated sometimes.

Most hotel rooms have private bathrooms, and reviews throughout this book assume so unless shared bathrooms are specified. Hot water is hardest to come by along the coast and in the Oriente, where most locals might call you crazy for wanting it in the first place. In the highlands, assume water is hot unless noted in a review.

It is virtually unheard of to arrive in a town and be unable to find somewhere to sleep, but during major fiestas or on the night before market day, accommodations can be extremely tight.

Prices

Throughout this book, accommodations are often grouped by the following categories when a town offers numerous choices: budget (up to $16 per double), midrange ($17 to $60 per double) and top end (over $60 per

---

BOOK ACCOMMODATIONS ONLINE

For more reviews of accommodations and recommendations by Lonely Planet authors, check out the online booking service at www.lonelyplanet.com. You'll find the true, insider lowdown on the best places to stay. Reviews are thorough and independent. Best of all, you can book online.

---

double). Within these budget categories, hotels are listed in order of preference.

Room rates are highest throughout Ecuador around Christmas and New Year's Eve, around Semana Santa (Easter week) and during July and August. They also peak during local fiestas. Hotels are required to charge 12% sales tax (called IVA), though it's often already included in the hotel's quoted rate. Better hotels often tack on an additional 10% service charge (bringing the grand total to 22% more than the advertised price!), so be sure to check. To the best of our knowledge, rates throughout this book include tax and service.

Accommodations are most expensive in Quito, Cuenca and Guayaquil, but there are still scores of cheap, traveler-friendly places to choose from. The main exception is the Galápagos, where there are few rock-bottom hotels.

Most hotels charge per person, which is great for the single traveler.

Reservations

Most hotels accept reservations without you having to cough up your credit card number. If you haven't prepaid, however, always confirm your reservation if you're arriving late in the day to avoid it being given to someone else. Pricier hotels may want a prepayment either by credit card or by means of a deposit to the hotel's bank account.

Reservations definitely ease the mind, but walking in off the street can sometimes get you a better rate. This is especially true for luxury hotels in the big cities, which often offer cut-rate prices on weekends (at times up to 50%), when their usual business clientele is at home.

B&Bs

Bed and breakfasts are a tried and true concept in Ecuador and especially popular in tourist destinations such as Quito, Baños, Cuenca and Otavalo. Once you're out in the countryside, there's a fine line between B&Bs and *hosterías* (inns), which are described later.

Camping

Camping is allowed on the grounds of a few rural hotels, in the countryside and most national parks. There are no campgrounds in towns. The constant availability of cheap hotels makes them superfluous. There are climbers' *refugios* (refuges) on some of the major mountains, in some national parks, but you need to bring a sleeping bag.

Remember, if you're bringing a camp stove, be sure the fuel bottle is unused; otherwise the airline may not allow it on the plane. Camping supplies are available in Quito, but they're pricey and pickings are usually limited.

Haciendas & Hosterías

The Ecuadorian highlands have some fabulous haciendas, historic family ranches that have been refurbished to accept tourists. They usually fall into the top-end price bracket, but the price almost always includes outstanding home-cooked meals as well as activities such as horseback riding or fishing. The best known haciendas are in the northern and central highlands.

Hosterías are similar but often smaller. They're usually intimate, unique and comfortable places to stay in country settings. *Hosterías* regularly have rates that include full board and/or activities and can be great places to stay. They're usually cheaper than haciendas, though the line between the two can be hazy.

Homestays

Homestays are normally organized by Spanish schools to enable travelers to practice Spanish in a home environment and eat meals with the family. You may want to 'try out' your family for a week before you commit to a longer period. Occasionally (though not often), families are in it only for the money, giving a less than warm experience. Homestays are mostly available in Quito and Cuenca and are difficult to find elsewhere.

In the most rural communities, where there are no hotels, you can sometimes ask around and be offered a place to sleep in a local family's home. This happens only in the most off-the-beaten-track places, and you should always offer payment (though it may not be accepted).

Hostels

Ecuador has a limited hostel system, primarily because there are so many cheap hotels. Hostelling International cards get you a 10% discount at member facilities, but it's hardly worth getting one for the trip. The cheapest hostels start at around $5 per person in dorms. Most are clean and well run, but usually have the requisite saggy beds and that lived-in smell. Most hostels have more expensive private rooms as well. One of the best things about hostels are their communal kitchens, which allow you to save money on food.

Hotels

Budget hotels are the cheapest, but not necessarily the worst options for accommodations. Although rooms are usually basic, with just a bed and four walls, they can nevertheless be well looked after, very clean and excellent value. They can also be good places to meet other travelers. Prices in this category range from about $4 to $16 per person. Every town has hotels in this price range, and in smaller towns, that's often all there is. The cheapest hotels have communal bathrooms, but you can often find rooms with a private bathroom for as little as $6 per person. Generally, you'll pay about $8 per person for something decent.

Midrange hotels, on the whole, are Ecuador's best bargains. They're often cool little places, usually with cable TV, and the hot water is often infallible.

Top-end hotels are found in only the larger cities. They're generally luxurious and may have a two-tiered pricing system in which foreigners pay more. This system stinks, but is legal, and there's not much you can do about it other than avoid staying in luxury hotels.

Make sure to never rent a room without looking at it first. In most hotels – even the cheapest – the staff will happily let you see the room first. Check out the bathroom and make sure that the water runs if you want a wash. This little screening process sometimes gives the staff time to contemplate dropping the price a bit.

Lodges

Ecolodges and jungle lodges are one of the most wonderful ways to experience Ecuador. They're almost exclusively the haunt of foreigners, but often offer the chance to experience traditional culture up close, albeit in a staged but still intimately educational way. Lodges are most popular in the Oriente and in the cloud forests of the western Andean slopes, and are often the only way to really experience these unique ecosystems. The lodges in the Oriente are generally only available as part of a three- to five-day package, but this usually includes all your meals and activities. The lodge will arrange any river or jungle transportation, but you generally have to get to the nearest departure town on your own.

ACTIVITIES

Where to begin? There are so many exciting activities in Ecuador that any list of suggestions will certainly miss something. The following are Ecuador's most popular outdoor activities.

Bird-Watching

Ecuador boasts some of the world's best bird-watching. Where you watch depends entirely upon what interests you. The cloud forests around both Mindo and Tandayapa (p139) will send the average birder out of their mind: during the Audubon Society's 2004/2005 Christmas Bird Count, a total of 420 species were spotted and logged here in a single day. The count was topped only by the lower Río Napo region of the Amazon (p241), where 471 bird species were logged. The Galápagos Islands have 28 endemic bird species. A Guayaquil ornithologist claims that within 50km of that city, you can find more than 50 Ecuadorian mainland endemic species. Let's just say that, for bird-lovers, a visit to Ecuador is more akin to a pilgrimage than a vacation.

Hiking & Trekking

The opportunities for hiking and trekking are practically limitless. Most of the best independent hiking is in the national parks: Parques Nacionales Cotopaxi (p150), Las Cajas (p209) and Podocarpus (p216) in the highlands, and Parque Nacional Machalilla (p303) on the coast, all offer excellent hiking without the need of a guide. The Lagunas de Mojanda (p123) area near Otavalo and, for shorter walks, the countryside around Vilcabamba (p219) and Baños (p167) are all beautiful. There's great hiking in the cloud forests around Mindo (p141) and elsewhere along the western Andean slopes. The Inca trail to the archaeological site of Ingapirca (p194) is a popular three-day trek.

Topographical maps are available from the Instituto Geográfico Militar (p70), located in Quito. Also pick up a copy of Lonely Planet's *Trekking in the Central Andes*.

Horseback Riding

Ecuador has some great horseback-riding opportunities, especially in the highlands. Unfortunately, the standards of care for horses used for tourism is low, and several travelers have written to say that their horses were old, overworked and underfed. There are, however, some agencies that do look after their animals, but they charge more for tours. Those travelers looking for the cheapest rates are going to get a hack and contribute to its misery. Haciendas throughout the highlands generally use good horses and offer some of the best opportunities for horseback riding. Vilcabamba (p219), Baños (p167) and Otavalo (p116) are some of the best places to set up horseback rides if you're not staying at a hacienda.

An expensive but fully reputable company is **RideAndes** (www.rideandes.com). It offers day tours, multiday tours and custom-made tours for both experienced and inexperienced riders. Horses and guides are top notch.

Mountaineering

Pull your boots on – Ecuador is a climbers' paradise. The country boast 10 peaks over 5000m, eight of which are in the central highlands (p145). This is where you'll find Ecuador's two highest peaks: Chimborazo (6310m) and Cotopaxi (5897m). Both can be climbed in one long day from their respective climbers' refuges, but sane people allow for two days. Climbers must acclimatize for several days before attempting an ascent. Lodges in and around Cotopaxi (p150) and the Ilinizas (p148) are great for acclimatization.

The Ilinizas also offer excellent climbing; Iliniza Sur (5248m) is Ecuador's sixth-highest peak and one of the country's most difficult climbs. Iliniza Norte (5126m) is a rough scramble and can be climbed by acclimatized, experienced hikers. In Parque Nacional Sangay (p177), El Altar (5319m) is widely considered the most beautiful and most technical of Ecuador's mountains.

Mountaineers will require standard snow and ice gear: a rope, crampons, ice axe, high-altitude sun protection and cold-weather clothing as a minimum. Unless you are very experienced, hiring a guide from Quito or Riobamba is recommended. The weather can turn bad quickly in the Andes, and even experienced climbers have been killed. Several agencies offer both rental gear and guides: very roughly expect to pay $60 to $80 per person per day to climb a major peak. The best guides have a card accrediting them to the Ecuadorian Mountain Guides Association (ASEGUIM).

You can climb year-round, but the best months are considered to be June to August and December to February.

Mountain Biking

Mountain biking has grown increasingly popular, especially the adrenaline-charged downhills on the flanks of Cotopaxi and Chimborazo. The best mountain-biking operators (with the best bikes, guides and equipment) can be found in Quito (p86) and Riobamba (p183). Baños (p170) is also awash in midrange mountain bikes, thanks to the popular and excellent downhill ride (by road) to Puyo.

If you're doing any serious cycling on your own, bring all your own gear and replacement parts as speciality parts are only available in Quito or, if you're lucky, from one of the operators in Riobamba or Baños. Also remember the very real threat of dehydration; in Ecuador you're either riding at altitude or in the extreme heat of the lowlands, so always carry plenty of water.

Rafting & Kayaking

Both in terms of white water and scenery, Ecuador boasts world-class river-rafting and kayaking year-round. Its importance as a white-water destination was solidified in 2005 when the IRF World Rafting Championship was held on the Río Quijos, a spectacular Class IV to V river on the eastern slopes of the Andes, not far from the town of Baeza (p231).

In the Oriente, the town of Tena (p247) has become Ecuador's de facto white-water capital. Near it, the upper Río Napo (Class III) and the feisty Río Misahuallí (Class IV) are the country's best known rivers, after the Quijos. The Misahuallí is best during the dry months of October through March. There are several other Class IV and V runs around Tena as well, making the town a great base for kayakers.

Further south, the Río Upano (Class IV to IV+), near Macas (see p260), is excellent for multiday trips and outrageous jungle scenery, including the spectacular stretch along the Namangosa Gorge, where more than a dozen waterfalls plummet into the river. The Upano is best from about September to February.

On the western slopes of the Andes, about 2½ hours west of Quito, the Río Blanco (Class III to IV), is a year-round possibility and a favorite daytrip from the capital, with wildest conditions from February to about June. There are several Class II to III runs suitable for complete beginners near Quito as well. See p89 for rafting operators in the capital.

The Río Pastaza and Río Patate, are two of the country's most popular rivers thanks to their proximity to the tourist mecca of Baños (see p167), but the Patate is very polluted.

Kayakers regularly bring their own boats to Ecuador, while rafters usually sign on with a local operator. Even beginners can enjoy the activity, as rafts are captained by seasoned and qualified experts. Ecuador's river-guide association is called Asociación de Guías de Aguas Rapidas del Ecuador (AGAR; Ecuadorian White-Water Guides Association). Only reputable companies are listed in this book.

Rafting Ecuador (www.raftingecuador.org) is an informative online resource.

Scuba Diving & Snorkeling

The Galápagos Islands are one of the world's great dive destinations, offering opportunities to see dramatic underwater wildlife: hammerhead and other sharks, a variety of rays (occasionally a manta ray will appear), turtles, penguins, sea lions, moray eels, huge numbers of fish of many kinds and, if you're very lucky, dolphins or even whales. The conditions here, however, are difficult for beginners. There are four dive operators based in Puerto Ayora (p362).

Diving has also become popular out of the coastal town of Puerto López (p305).

When it comes to snorkeling, again, think Galápagos. If you're off to the islands, snorkeling will expose you to a completely new world. Baby sea lions swim up and stare at you through your mask, various species of rays slowly undulate by, and penguins dart past you in a stream of bubbles. The hundreds of species of fish are spectacularly colorful, and you can watch the round, flapping shapes of sea turtles as they circle you.

You may be able to buy a mask and snorkel in sporting goods stores in Quito or Guayaquil, and they can sometimes be borrowed or rented in the Galápagos, but you're better off bringing a mask from home to ensure a good fit. The water temperature is around 22°C (72°F) from January to April and about 18°C (64°F) during the rest of the year, so consider bringing a spring-suit (shorty) with you, too.

Surfing

Ecuador isn't a huge surf destination, but it has some excellent breaks if you know where to go. Surf season is generally November through April with peak months in January and February. Localism is generally minimal, with Ecuadorians and foreigners mixing it up pretty peacefully.

The classic mainland break is Montañita (p309), a fast, powerful reef-break that can cough up some of the mainland's best barrels. It also has some tolerable beach-breaks nearby. Near Muisne, in Esmeraldas province, Mompiche (p286) is a world-class left point-break offering rides up to 500m on top days. Canoa (p287) is a fun spot for beach-breaks, if only because the town here is a great little hangout and the beach is beautiful.

There are dozens of other good breaks – including left and right beach-, reef- and point-breaks – along the mainland coast that are beyond the scope of this book. The great majority of them are south of Manta and most are hidden and require tapping local resources. For information's sake, the best place to start is Montañita.

In the Galápagos, Isla San Cristóbal is home to three world-class reef-breaks, all near the town of Puerto Baquerizo Moreno. They're extremely fast however, and manageable only for experienced surfers. The high price of getting there keeps the crowds down.

Two excellent online resources are **Wannasurf** (www.wannasurf.com) and **Wavehunters** (www.wavehunters.com); both provide comprehensive sections on Ecuador.

BUSINESS HOURS

Reviews found throughout this book provide opening hours when they differ from the following standard hours.

Banks open at 8am and close sometime between 2pm and 4pm Monday to Friday (though money-changing services usually stops around 2pm). Andinatel, Pacifictel and Etapa telephone call centers are almost invariably open 8am to 10pm daily. Post offices are generally open 8am to 6pm Monday through Friday and 8am to 1pm Saturday. In smaller towns they'll close for lunch.

In Quito and Guayaquil, most stores and businesses of interest to tourists stay open from 9am to 7pm Monday through Saturday, usually with an hour off for lunch (around 1pm). Government offices and businesses such as Amex are open from about 9am to 5:30pm Monday to Friday, also with an hour off for lunch around 1pm. In smaller towns, especially in the hotter lowlands, lunch breaks of two hours are not uncommon. On Saturday, many stores and some businesses are open 9am to noon. Stores in major shopping malls are open between 8am and 10pm daily.

Restaurant hours vary widely, so complete hours are given in the reviews throughout this book. Restaurants often close on Sunday. Bars usually open between 5pm and 7pm and close between midnight and 2am.

CHILDREN

Foreigners traveling with children are still a curiosity in Ecuador (especially if they are gringos), and a crying or laughing child at your side can quickly break down barriers between you and locals. Parents will likely be met with extra, and extra-friendly, attention. As throughout most of the world, people love children. Lonely Planet's *Travel with Children* is an excellent resource.

Practicalities

Children pay full fare on buses if they occupy a seat, but they often ride for free if they sit on a parent's lap. The fare for children under

12 is halved for domestic flights (and they get a seat), while infants under two cost 10% of the fare (but they don't get a seat). In hotels, the general rule is simply to bargain. The charge for children should never be as much as that for an adult, but whether they stay for half price or free is open to discussion.

While kids' meals are not normally offered in restaurants, it is perfectly acceptable to order a meal to split between two children or an adult and a child.

Changing facilities are rarities in all but the best restaurants. Breast feeding is acceptable in public. Formula foods can be difficult to come by outside the large big-city supermarkets, but disposable diapers are sold at most markets throughout the country.

Safety seats are generally hard to come by in rental cars (be sure to arrange one ahead of time), and in taxis they're unheard of. This is, after all, a country where a family of four can get across town on a motorcycle.

Sights & Activities

Ecuador is not a country that's big on funparks, children's rides and first world–type spectacles for kids. Yours will definitely have to appreciate the outdoors if you want to keep the peace. But rare is the kid – X-Box addicts aside – that's uninterested in tramping through the rain forest, canoeing down a river or watching whales from a boat.

Whale-watching is a must while in Puerto López (p305). Older children will likely go berserk snorkeling and animal-watching in the Galápagos (p347). Quito (p88) has a healthy number of activities that the young ones will enjoy, including a reptile zoo, a theme park and several good museums.

CLIMATE CHARTS

The following climate charts are handy for planning, but for specifics on the best time to visit Ecuador, see p14.

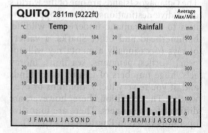

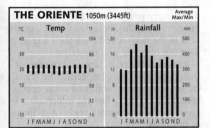

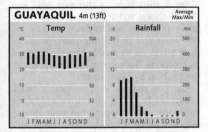

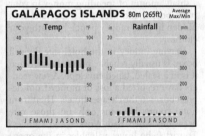

COURSES

Ecuador is one of the best places to study Spanish in South America. Ecuadorian Spanish is clear and precise, and similar to Mexican and Central American Spanish, and rates are cheap. Quito (p88) and Cuenca (p200) are the best places to study, and both have a plethora of language schools. Expect to pay between $5 and $10 per hour for private lessons. Accommodations with local families can be arranged. There are also schools in Baños (p171) and Otavalo (p118) if you want a more small-town experience.

Dance schools in Quito (see p88) offer private lessons in salsa and other Latin dances at prices unheard of in North America and Europe.

CUSTOMS

Each traveler is able to import 1L of spirits, 300 cigarettes and an unspecified 'reasonable' amount of perfume – all items are duty free. There is no problem bringing in the usual personal belongings, but if you plan on bringing in something that might not be considered a 'usual personal belonging,' you should check with an Ecuadorian consulate.

Pre-Columbian artifacts and endangered-animal products (including mounted butterflies and beetles) are not allowed to be taken out of Ecuador or imported into most other countries.

DANGERS & ANNOYANCES

The purpose of this section is not to scare you. Just remember: *most crimes and accidents can be avoided by using common sense.* Ecuador is a safe and wonderful country for travel. No matter where you travel, it's wise to get some travel insurance; see p391 for more information.

Drowning & Shipwreck

Nasty stuff. Much of the coast suffers from riptides, especially during the highest tides and biggest waves. In one weekend alone in February 2003, 11 people drowned along the coast. Some beaches use flags – red indicates dangerous conditions, while yellow indicates that it's OK to swim. Many beaches don't have flags, however, so be aware of riptides.

Most boats in the Galápagos are shipshape, but captains don't always make the best decisions. In 2005 a tourist cruiser was hit by a freak wave in bad weather and immediately sunk, sending the boat and everyone's belongings to the bottom. Out of sheer luck, no one was injured, but few were fully compensated for what they lost. Consider planning your Galápagos visit outside the foul-weather season (see p348).

Drugs

Imbibing illegal drugs such as marijuana and cocaine can either land you in jail, land your money in the hands of a thief, or worse. Unless you are willing to take these risks, avoid illegal drugs.

Lonely Planet has received a couple of letters from travelers who were unwittingly drugged and robbed after accepting food from a stranger. You can see the mistake that was made here.

Robbery

Every year or so, you hear of long-distance, nighttime bus robberies. Night buses are simply held up at a road block and robbed by a group of armed men. It happens to one bus in many thousands, so don't get too paranoid if your schedule demands a night bus. However day buses are best.

If you are driving a car in Ecuador, never park it unattended. Never leave any valuables in sight in the car – even attended cars will have their windows smashed by hit-and-run merchants.

Make sure to never leave your gear unattended in a mountain hut while you are out hiking. Some huts, such as those on Cotopaxi or Chimborazo, have guardians and a place to lock up your gear when you climb, and these are relatively safe.

Rucu Pichincha (p87), near Quito, and Lagunas de Mojanda (p123), near Otavalo, were once plagued by armed robbers, but they've gotten much safer over the last few years. South American Explorers in Quito (p397) is the best place for up-to-date information on issues such as this is.

On the off chance you are robbed, you should file a police report as soon as possible. This is a requirement for any insurance claim, although it is unlikely that the police will be able to recover the property. Normally, only the main police station in a town will deal with this.

Scams

Be wary of false or crooked police. Plainclothes 'policemen' may produce official-looking documents, but always treat these with suspicion, or simply walk away with a smile and a shrug. On the other hand, a uniformed official who asks to see your passport in broad daylight in the middle of a busy street is probably just doing a job.

Theft

If travelers had to confess their top five stresses, one would surely be Backpack Separation Anxiety (BSA). It's most commonly experienced when travelers are required to place their backpacks in a bus's luggage compartment or overhead rack. Aside from craning your neck at every stop until it snaps, there's little you can do to prevent it being stolen. But rest assured – for the most part, the bag-checker is on your side and knows whose bags are whose. Definitely keep your eye on it (or carry a pack small enough to bring on the bus), but

don't worry yourself silly. Bag theft occurs, but not very often. Some people buy a grain sack in the market and pack their bag in it so it will blend in with the cargo.

Armed robbery is rare in Ecuador, although parts of Quito (especially the Mariscal Sucre neighborhood) and some coastal areas are dangerous. Specific information is given in the appropriate regional chapters of this book.

Sneak theft is more common, and you should always watch your back (and back pockets) in busy bus stations, on crowded city buses and in bustling markets. All of these places are worked by bag-slashers and pick pockets. But you can avoid playing victim to them by being smart.

Carrying your wallet or passport in a back pocket is advertising. But also avoid lifting your shirt and whipping out your money pouch in public. Instead carry a wallet with a small amount of spending money in your front pocket and keep the important stuff hidden in your money pouch beneath your clothes.

Leaving money in the hotel safe deposit boxes is usually reliable, but make sure that it is in a sealed, taped envelope. A few readers have reported a loss of money from deposit boxes in the cheaper hotels. Theft from hotel rooms happens only on those rare occasions when Bad Worker and Careless Tourist (who leaves valuables in the open) cross paths.

Trouble Spots

Due to the armed conflict in neighboring Colombia, areas along the Colombian border (particularly in the northern Oriente) can be dangerous. Tours into the Oriente are almost invariably safe, but there have been a few isolated incidents of armed robbery in which no one was hurt. Lago Agrio (p232) is dodgy once you leave the main drag.

DISABLED TRAVELERS

Unfortunately, Ecuador's infrastructure for disabled travelers is virtually nonexistent. Wheelchair ramps are few and far between, and sidewalks are often badly potholed and cracked. Bathrooms and toilets are often too small for wheelchairs. Signs in Braille or telephones for the hearing impaired are practically unheard of.

Nevertheless, disabled Ecuadorians get around, mainly through the help of others. It's not particularly unusual to see disabled travelers being carried onto a bus, for example. Buses are (legally) supposed to carry disabled travelers for free. Local city buses, which are already overcrowded, won't do that, but long-distance city buses sometimes do. Disabled travelers are also eligible for 50% discounts on domestic airfares.

When it comes to hotels, the only truly accessible rooms are found at the international chain hotels in Quito and Guayaquil.

DISCOUNT CARDS

Generally, student cards are less useful in Ecuador than in European countries. Aside from reduced museum entrance fees (which can add up), the only substantial discount is 15% off high-season flights to the Galápagos. The **International Student Identity Card** (ISIC; www.isic.org) is generally accepted only when issued from the traveler's home country and presented in combination with a valid student ID card.

EMBASSIES & CONSULATES

It's important to realize what your own embassy can and can't do to help you if you get into trouble. Generally speaking, it won't be much help in emergencies if the trouble you're in is remotely your own fault. Remember that you are bound by the laws of the country you are in. Your embassy will not be sympathetic if you end up in jail after committing a crime locally, even if such actions are legal in your own country.

In genuine emergencies, you might get some assistance from your embassy, but only if other channels have been exhausted. If you need to get home urgently, a free ticket home is exceedingly unlikely – the embassy would expect you to have insurance. If all your money and documents are stolen, it might assist you with getting a new passport, but a loan for onward travel would be out of the question.

Ecuadorian Embassies & Consulates

Ecuador has diplomatic representation in Latin America, North America, Western Europe and Australia.

Australia & New Zealand (☎ 02-6286 4021, 6286 1231; www.embassyecuadoraustralia.org.au; 6 Pindari Crescent, O'Malley, ACT 2606)

Canada (☎ 613-563 8206; www.ncf.ca/ecuador; 50 O'Connor St, Suite 316, Ottawa, Ontario K1P 6L2)
France (☎ 01-45-61-10-21; www.ambassade-equateur .fr; 34 Av de Messine 75008 Paris)
Germany (☎ 030-238 6217; www.embajada-ecuador .org; Kaiser-Friedrich Strasse 90, 1 0G,10585 Berlin)
Netherlands (70-346 3753, 346 9563; www.embajada ecuador.nl; Koninginnegracht 84, 2514 AJ Den Haag)
Peru (☎ 01-212 4171, 212 5481; www.mecuadorperu .org.pe; Las Palmeras 356, San Isidro, Lima 27)
UK (☎ 020-7584 2648, 7584 1367; www.ecuador.embas syhomepage.com/; Flat 3, 3 Hans Crescent, Knightsbridge, London SW1X 0LS)
USA (☎ 202-234 7200; www.ecuador.org/esp/principal .htm; 2535 15th St NW, Washington, DC 20009)

Embassies & Consulates in Ecuador

Many countries have embassies in Quito and consulates in Quito or Guayaquil and in other provincial capitals or border towns. Hours are short and change regularly, so it's a good idea to call ahead. Australia and New Zealand do not have embassies or consulates in Ecuador.

Canada Quito (Map pp80-1; ☎ 02-256 3580, 223 2114, 250 6162; www.dfait-maeci.gc.ca/Ecuador; Av 6 de Diciembre 2816 & P Rivet, 4th fl; ◷ 9am-noon Mon-Fri); Guayaquil (☎ 04-256 3580, 256 6747; consulc1@gye.sat net.net; Córdova 810, 4th fl)
Colombia Quito (☎ 02-245 8012; www.embajadadeco lombiaenecuador.org; Atahualpa 955 & Av de la República, 3rd fl; ◷ 8:30am-1:30pm Mon-Fri); Guayaquil (☎ 04-263 0674/5; Francisco de Orellana, World Trade Center, Tower B, 11th fl; ◷ 9am-1:30pm Mon-Fri); Tulcán (☎ 06-298 0559; Av Manabí 58-087; ◷ 8:30am-1pm, 2:30-3:30pm Mon-Fri); Lago Agrio (☎ 06-283 0084; Av Quito 1-52; ◷ 8am-2pm & 3-5pm Mon-Fri)
France Quito (Map pp80-1; ☎ 02-254 3101, 254 3110; franciac@andinanet.net; Diego de Almagro 1550 & Pradera; ◷ 8:30am-1pm & 3-5:30pm Mon-Fri); Guayaquil (☎ 04-232 8442; José Mascote 909 & Hurtado)
Germany Quito (Map p78; ☎ 02-297 0820; www.emba jada-quito.de; Naciones Unidas E10-44 at República de El Salvador, Edificio Citiplaza, 12th fl; ◷ 9am-noon & 2-4pm Mon-Thu, 9am-noon Fri); Guayaquil (☎ 04-220 6867/8; Av Las Monjas & Av CJ Arosemena, Km 2.5, Edificio Berlin)
Ireland (☎ 245 1577; Antonio de Ulloa 2651 & Rumi-pamba, Quito)
Netherlands Quito (Map pp80-1; ☎ 02-222 9230, 222 9229; www.embajadadeholanda.com; 12 de Octubre 1942 & Cordero, World Trade Center, Tower 1, 1st fl; ◷ 8:30am-1pm Mon-Fri); Guayaquil (☎ 04-256 6789, 256 2777, 256 3857; Córdova 1004 & P de Icaza)

Panama (☎ 02-256 6449; www.embajadapanamaecua
dor.com; Alpallana 581 & Whymper, Edificio Pradera 2, 5th
fl, Quito; ☾ 9am-2pm Mon-Fri)
Peru Quito (☎ 02-246 8410, 246 8389; embpeecu@uio
.satnet.net; Republica de El Salvador 495 & Irlanda;
☾ 9am-1pm & 3-6pm Mon-Fri); Guayaquil (☎ 04-228
114; conperu@gye.satnet.net; Av Francisco de Orellana
501); Loja (Map p213; ☎ 07-257 9068; Sucre 10-56;
☾ 8:30am-1:30pm & 3-5pm Mon-Fri); Machala (☎ 07-
930 680; cnr Bolívar & Colón; ☾ 9am-6pm Mon-Fri)
UK Quito (Map p78; ☎ 02-297 0800/1; www.britemb
quito.org.ec; Naciones Unidas & República de El Salvador,
Edificio Citiplaza, 14th fl; ☾ 8:30am-12:30pm & 1:30-
5pm Mon-Thu, 8:30am-1:30pm Fri); Guayaquil (☎ 04-256
0400, 256 3850; Córdova 623 & Padre; ☾ 9am-noon &
2:30-4pm Mon-Fri)
USA Quito (Map pp80-1; ☎ 02-256 2890; www.usem
bassy.org.ec; Av Patria & Av 12 de Octubre; ☾ 8am-
12:30pm & 1:30-5pm Mon-Fri); Guayaquil (☎ 04-232 3570;
9 de Octubre & García Moreno; ☾ 7:30am-5pm Mon-Fri)

FESTIVALS & EVENTS

Every city, town and village in Ecuador has
its local festivals, which are invariably celebrated with great vigor and a generous dose
of fireworks, alcohol, music, dancing and, in
some cases, an infectious disregard for public safety. They're worth planning around,
especially the more important ones. Many
that seem outwardly Catholic are actually
indigenous fiestas at their core.

The following are the country's biggest festivals and events. Local festivals are covered
in town sections throughout this book. For a
list of national public holidays, see opposite.

February/March
Carnaval Held the last few days before Lent, Carnaval
is celebrated with water fights throughout the country.
Guaranda (p178) is famous for its Carnaval celebrations.
Ambato (p162) has a lovely fruit and flowers festival,
which also coincides with Carnaval.

March/April
Semana Santa (Holy Week) Beginning the week before
Easter Sunday, Semana Santa is celebrated with religious
processions throughout Ecuador. The Good Friday procession in Quito is especially colorful and definitely worth
seeing.

June
Corpus Christi This religious feast day, falling on the
ninth Thursday after Easter, combines with a traditional
harvest fiesta in many highland towns and features processions and street dancing.

Inti Raymi This millennia-old indigenous celebration of
the summer equinox and harvest (June 21–29) is celebrated throughout the northern highlands and especially
in the Otavalo area (p116) where it is combined with
celebrations of St John the Baptist (June 24) and Sts Peter
& Paul (June 29).

July
Founding of Guayaquil Make your way to Guayaquil
(p318) for this wild celebration of the city's founding (July
25). Combined with the national holiday of July 24, the city
closes down and parties hard.

September
Fiesta del Yamor Imbabura province's biggest festival
celebrates the fall equinox and Colla Raimi (festival of
the moon) with bullfights, dancing, cock fights, partying,
feasts and lots of yamor (a nonalcoholic corn drink made
with seven types of corn). Held September 1–15.
Fiesta de la Mamá Negra One of the highland's most
famous, fascinating and colorful celebrations is held in
Latacunga in honor of the La Virgen de las Mercedes
(September 23–24). Its central character is a man dressed
as a black woman, La Mamá Negra, in honor of the 19th-
century liberation of African slaves.

December
Founding of Quito Quito whoops it up with bullfights,
parades and street dances throughout the first week of
December.
End-of-year celebrations Parades and dances starting
on December 28 culminate in the burning of life-size effi-
gies in the streets on New Year's Eve. Biggest in Guayaquil
and Quito.

FOOD

For a mouth-watering idea of all the food
you can eat while traveling in Ecuador, see
p61. In the Eating sections throughout this
book, restaurants are listed in order of preference and grouped either by cuisine type
or neighborhood.

GAY & LESBIAN TRAVELERS

Same-sex couples traveling in Ecuador should
be wary of showing affection when in public. Gay rights in a political or legal con-
text are a nonissue for most Ecuadorians.
Homosexuality was technically illegal until
1998, and antigay bias still exists. As in most
Latin American countries, sexuality is more
stereotyped than it is in Europe or North
America, with the man playing a dominant
macho role and the woman tagging along
with that. This attitude spills over into the

perception of homosexuality. A straight-acting macho man will seldom be considered gay, even if he is, while an effeminate man, regardless of his sexual orientation, may be called a *maricón*, a mildly derogatory term for a homosexual man.

Several fiestas in Ecuador have parades with men cross-dressing as women. This is all meant in fun, rather than as an open acceptance of sexual alternatives, but it does provide the public at large (both gay and straight) a popular cultural situation in which to enjoy themselves in an accepting environment. On New Year's Eve, puppets representing the old year are burned at midnight. Meanwhile, men dressed as women (posing as the puppets' widows) walk the streets, asking passers-by for spare change that will later be used for the year-end party. More entertaining still, Latacunga's incredible Mamá Negra festival, in late September, features cross-dressing men brandishing whips!

The best website about gay Quito is the incredibly detailed **Gay Guide to Quito** (http://gayquitoec.tripod.com). Also check out **Gay Ecuador** (www.gayecuador.com). There is a community center for lesbian, gay, bisexual and transsexual people, as well as an AIDS-activist organization called **FEDAEPS** (☎ 02-222 3298; www.fedaeps.org; Baquerizo Moreno 166 & Tamayo, Quito). It's open to the public on Thursday at 3pm; gay and lesbian literature is available, and there are often discussions held at 6:30pm.

Zenith Travel (☎ 02-252 9993; www.galapagosgay.com; Juan Leon Mera 453 & Roca, Edificio Chiriboga No 202, Quito) specializes in gay and lesbian tours.

HOLIDAYS

On major holidays, banks, offices and other services close. Transportation a gets very crowded, so buy bus tickets in advance. Major holidays are sometimes celebrated for several days around the actual date. If an official public holiday falls on a weekend, offices may be closed on the nearest Friday or Monday. If an official holiday falls midweek, it may be moved to the nearest Friday or Monday to create a long weekend.

New Year's Day January 1.
Epiphany January 6.
Semana Santa (Easter Week) March/April.
Labor Day May 1.
Battle of Pichincha May 24. This honors the decisive battle of independence from Spain in 1822.

Simón Bolívar's Birthday July 24.
Quito Independence Day August 10.
Guayaquil Independence Day October 9. This combines with the October 12 national holiday and is an important festival in Guayaquil.
Columbus Day/Día de la Raza October 12.
All Saints' Day November 1.
Day of the Dead (All Souls' Day) November 2. Celebrated by flower-laying ceremonies in cemeteries, it's especially colorful in rural areas, where entire Indian families show up at cemeteries to eat, drink and leave offerings in memory of the departed.
Cuenca Independence Day November 3. Combines with the national holidays of November 1 and 2 to give Cuenca its most important fiesta of the year.
Christmas Eve December 24.
Christmas Day December 25.

INSURANCE

In addition to health insurance (see p412) and car insurance (see p409), a policy that protects baggage and valuables, like cameras and camcorders, is a good idea. Keep your insurance records separate from other possessions in case you have to make a claim.

Worldwide cover for travelers from more than 44 countries is available online at www.lonelyplanet.com/travel_services.

INTERNET ACCESS

You'll be hard pressed to find a town without its cybercafé. They're *everywhere,* and computers are generally of good quality, with USB connections and CD players and burners. Rates average about $1 an hour.

If you're carrying a laptop, some hotels (usually the pricier ones) allow you to connect to their telephone lines; Ecuador uses RJ-11 plug types, the same as those used in North America. One of the best online resources is Steve Kropla's comprehensive website at www.kropla.com.

For Internet resources, see p16.

LEGAL MATTERS

If you get into legal trouble and are jailed, your embassy can offer only limited assistance. This may include an occasional visit from an embassy staff member to make sure that your human rights haven't been violated, letting your family know where you are and putting you in contact with an Ecuadorian lawyer (whom you must pay yourself). Embassy officials will not bail you out, and you are subject to the laws

DIRECTORY

of Ecuador, not to the laws of your home country.

Drug penalties in Ecuador for possession of even small amounts of illegal drugs are much stricter than in the USA or Europe. Defendants often spend many months in jail before they are brought to trial, and if convicted (as is usually the case), they can expect several years in jail.

Businesspeople should be aware that a legal dispute that may be of a civil nature in their home country may be handled as a criminal proceeding in Ecuador. This may mean that you are not allowed to leave Ecuador while your dispute is being settled, and that it could possibly lead to your arrest and jailing until the case is settled.

Drivers should carry their passport, as well as their driver's license. In the event of an accident, unless extremely minor, the vehicles should stay where they are until the police arrive and make a report. This is essential for all insurance claims. If the accident results in injury and you are unhurt, you should take the victim to obtain medical help, particularly in the case of a pedestrian accident. You are legally responsible for the pedestrian's injuries and will be jailed unless you pay, even if the accident was not your fault. Drive defensively.

MAPS

Anyone planning serious treks or backcountry walking should visit the Instituto Geográfico Militar (IGM) in Quito (see p70 for more details). It publishes excellent topographical maps of the entire country, ranging from a 1:1,000,000 single-sheet map of Ecuador to 1:50,000 regional sheets. Best part – they cost only $2 each. Few city maps are published anywhere and (not to toot anyone's horn) you'll often find the ones in this book the most useful.

The blue-cover Nelson Gómez Guía Vial del Ecuador is a pocketbook size, countrywide road map available at most bookstores in Quito, Cuenca and Guayaquil. Another good country map available internationally is the 1:1,000,000 single sheet published by International Travel Maps & Books (ITMB; www.itmb.com).

MONEY

Ecuador's official currency is the US dollar (see the boxed text, p31). If you're not traveling from the USA, consider bringing a small supply of US dollars with you on your trip in case you have trouble exchanging currency from your home country. Western Unions are in most big cities.

For exchange rates, see this book's inside front cover. For an idea of what things cost, see p14.

ATMs

ATMs are the easiest way of getting cash, period. They're found in most cities and even in smaller towns, though they are occasionally out of order. Make sure you have a four-digit PIN; many Ecuadorian ATMs don't recognize longer ones. Bancos del Pacífico and Bancos del Pichincha have MasterCard/Cirrus ATMs. Bancos de Guayaquil and Bancos La Provisora have Visa/Plus ATMs.

Black Market

Quito and many border towns have black markets, which are generally best avoided unless you have no alternative. If you plan to change cash from a moneychanger on the street, look up the current exchange rate before you do it. The **Yahoo! Currency Converter** (http://finance.yahoo.com/currency) is as good as any. Folks entering the country along infrequently used border crossings (such as Macará or Zumba from Peru) will find the black market the only alternative. Change only as much as you need to get you to a major town, where you can change the rest.

Cash

Again, US dollar bills are the official currency. They are identical to those issued in the USA. Coins of one, five, 10, 25 and 50 cents are identical in shape, size and color as their US equivalents, but bear images of famous Ecuadorians rather than US presidents. Both US and Ecuadorian coins are used in Ecuador. There are no plans to print Ecuadorian versions of US dollar bills. The US$1 'Sacajawea' coin is widely used.

The biggest problem when it comes to cash is finding change. It can be hard to cash a $20 bill even in big cities. No one ever has sueltos (literally 'loose ones,' meaning 'change'), so change your bills when you can. Forget about changing a $50 or $100 bill outside a bank.

Credit Cards

Credit cards are great as backup. Visa, MasterCard and Diners Club are the most widely accepted cards. First-class restaurants, hotels, gift shops and travel agencies almost always accept MasterCard or Visa. Small hotels, restaurants and stores don't. Even if an establishment has a credit-card sticker in the window, don't assume that credit cards are accepted. In Ecuador, merchants accepting credit cards will often add between 4% and 10% to the bill. Paying cash is often better value.

Moneychangers

It is best to change money in the major cities of Quito, Guayaquil and Cuenca, where rates are best. Because banks have limited hours (see p386), *casas de cambio* (currency-exchange bureaus) are sometimes the only option for changing money. They are usually open 9am to 6pm Monday to Friday and until at least noon on Saturday. They're entirely credible places, though the exchange rate might be a percentage point or so lower than that given by banks.

If you're in a pinch, *cambios* (as they're abbreviated) at the airports and major hotels in Quito and Guayaquil stay open past the usual hours.

Euros, Peruvian *pesos* and Colombian *nuevos soles* are the easiest currencies to exchange in Ecuador.

Tipping

Better restaurants add a 12% tax and a 10% service charge to the bill. If the service has been satisfactory, you can add another 5% for the waiter. Cheaper restaurants don't include a tax or service charge. If you want to tip your server, do so directly – don't just leave the money on the table.

Tip porters at the airport about $0.25 per bag and bellboys at a first-class hotel about $1 per bag. Hairdressers receive $0.50 or more for special services. Taxi drivers are not normally tipped, but you can leave them the small change from a metered ride.

Guides are usually paid low-wages, and tips are greatly appreciated. If you go on a guided tour, a tip is expected. If you are in a group, tip a top-notch guide about $5 per person per day. Tip the driver about half that. If you hire a private guide, tip about $10 per day.

If you are going on a long tour that involves guides, cooks and crew (eg the Galápagos Islands), tip about $25 to $50 per client per week, and distribute among all the personnel.

Traveler's Checks

Commission for changing traveler's checks ranges from 1% to 4%, with the highest rates charged in small towns. Traveler's checks are safer than cash because they are refunded if they are lost or stolen. Don't bring all of your money in traveler's checks, however. It's always useful to have a supply of US cash and an ATM card.

PHOTOGRAPHY

Bring everything you think you'll need as camera gear is expensive in Ecuador. Standard films are available in most towns, but Quito, Cuenca and Guayaquil are the only places you'll find speeds other than ASA 200 or 400. E6 (slide) films are available in Quito and Guayaquil. Standard print processing is easy to find, but E6 processing is available only in Quito, Cuenca and Guayaquil. Check the expiration date when you buy film.

The bright equatorial sun washes out photos and exaggerates shadows. Try to shoot using a polarizing lens, and shoot in the morning and afternoon. Bring fast films (ASA 800 is usually fine) for the rain forest, where light is low. People rarely prepare themselves for the amount of pictures they take of animals in the Galápagos – bring extra film and batteries.

For digital photographers, most cybercafés have at least one computer with USB ports and a CD burner. Your best bet (if you can afford it) is to buy a portable hard drive.

Lonely Planet's *Travel Photography* book is packed with useful tips.

Photographing People

The Ecuadorian people make wonderful subjects for photos. From an indigenous child to the handsomely uniformed presidential guard, the possibilities of 'people pictures' are endless. However, most people resent having a camera thrust in their faces, and people in markets will often proudly turn their backs on pushy photographers. Ask for permission with a smile or a joke, and if this is refused, don't become offended. Some people believe that bad luck

DIRECTORY

can be brought upon them by the eye of the camera. Others are just fed up with seeing their pictures used in books, magazines and postcards; somebody is making money at their expense. Sometimes a 'tip' is asked. Be aware and sensitive of people's feelings.

POST

Ecuador's postal service is reliable. Allow one to two weeks for a letter or package to reach its destination. A postcard or letter up to 20g costs $1.25 to North America, $2 to Europe and $2.25 to the rest of the world. To the same destinations, a letter weighing between 20g and 100g costs $2.15, $3 and $3.75. Sending any letter certified costs $1 more. Packages weighing 1kg/2kg cost $15.40/26.40 to the US, $24/43.30 to Europe and $28/50 to the rest of the world.

Packages usually have no problem arriving their destinations (so go ahead and ship that panama hat!), but always bring your box to the post office unsealed. Postal officials may be required to inspect what you're sending. If you're sending packages, do so from a major city.

Courier services including FedEx, DHL and UPS are readily available in sizable towns, but the service is extremely costly. For example, a legal document envelope costs $35 to the USA. A 2kg box costs $95.

You can receive mail in Ecuador using the post office's *lista de correos* (general delivery). Mail sent to the post office is filed alphabetically. Instruct your correspondents to address letters clearly (capitalizing your last name) and in the following manner:

Johanna SMITH (surname capitalized)
Lista de Correos
Correo Central
Quito (or town and province of your choice)
Ecuador

Receiving small packages is usually no problem. If the package weighs more than 2kg, however, you will have to go to customs to retrieve it and perhaps pay duty tax.

SHOPPING

Souvenirs in Ecuador are good, varied and also cheap. Although going to village markets is a blast, don't worry about getting ripped off too badly if you only have time to shop

in Quito. Items for sale in the main cities are often not that much more expensive, so if you're limited on time, you can shop in Quito. If you only have the time or inclination to go on one big shopping expedition, the Saturday market at Otavalo (p116) is one of the largest in South America and the best one for most types of crafts. Many other markets are colorful events for locals rather than tourists.

Some of the best stores are quite expensive; on the other hand, the quality of their products is often superior. Shopping in markets is more traditional and fun.

Bags

Apart from bags made from two small weavings stitched together, you can buy *shigras*, or shoulder bags made from agave fiber, that are strong, colorful and eminently practical. They come in a variety of sizes and are expandable. The best places to look for them are the markets in Latacunga and Riobamba. Agave fiber is also used to make macramé bags.

Bargaining

In markets and smaller stores, bargaining is acceptable, indeed expected, and you can sometimes lower the original price by 20% to 40%. Other times (and tourists find this happens in Otavalo) a vender won't budge an inch. In 'tourist stores' in Quito, prices are usually fixed.

Clothing

Woolen goods, particularly sweaters, are popular and are often made of a pleasantly coarse homespun wool. Otavalo is great for sweaters, scarves, hats, gloves and vests. In the central Highlands, Salinas (p180) is a great place to pick up a wool sweater. In both Otavalo and Salinas, the price of a thick sweater will begin around $15, depending on size and quality; fashionable boutique sweaters, like those sold at Galería Latina in Quito (p104) can fetch $50. Wool is also spun into a much finer and tighter textile for making ponchos: indigenous ponchos from Otavalo and the Riobamba area are among the best.

Hand-embroidered clothes are also attractive, but it's worth getting them from a reputable shop; otherwise they may shrink or run. Cotton blouses, shirts, skirts, dresses and shawls are available.

NOT SO STANDARD SOUVENIRS

Sure, you can dazzle your friends back home with the classic Ecuadorian wool sweater (like they've never seen *that* before), or a panama hat (you'll never wear it) or a goofy set of coasters (getting better). But why not bring home something a wee bit...different. With the following, you can't go wrong:

- Banana press – This wooden hand press used to make *patacones* (flattened fried plantain slices) is available at most supermarkets.
- Virgin Mary gear shift handle – A bright green plastic shifter knob, complete with a floating Virgin Mary inside. Who's gonna call you a bad driver with that screwed onto your stick? Check small auto parts stores and highland markets.
- San Pedro cactus-seed crucifix – Definitely a weird one: a crucifix made with the pearly seeds of the San Pedro cactus (sorry, only the cactus itself is psychoactive). Often sold in stores outside churches; try the ones in front of Basílica del Voto Nacional (p75).
- F**king figurines – Keep your eyes peeled for the replicas of pre-Hispanic ceramic figurines engaged in various versions of 'mating rituals.'
- Espíritu del Ecuador – It might look like a tacky miniature of the equator monument, but it's full of Ecuador's sweet liqueur. Delicious over ice cream. Available in liquor stores.
- Shrunken head – OK, so it's not a real shrunken head, but it stinks like one. Made from sheepskin, these are morbid enough to freak your friends out. Find them at crafts stores in Quito.
- Pilsener T-shirt – You can't go home without supporting Ecuador's national beer. Available at Café Kallari (p101) in Quito.
- Fire water – A bottle of Zhumir or Cristal will put the zing in your friends back home (and make them believe your stories). Available at liquor stores.
- Polaroid picture – Even in this age of digital, nothing replaces the Polaroid picture, snapped for $2 a pop by the old photographers on Plaza Grande, Quito (p73).

Panama hats are one of the best buys you can make. The finest hats are found in Quito, Cuenca, Sigsig (near Cuenca) and Montecristi (on the Pacific coast). Also see the boxed text on p206.

Jewelry
Ecuador isn't famous for its gemstones, but it does have some good silverwork. Chordeleg (p210), near Cuenca, has beautifully filigreed silver items. The Amazon area produces necklaces made from nuts, seeds and other rain forest products.

Leather
Cotacachi (p126), located north of Otavalo, and Quisapincha (p165), situated near Ambato, are both famous centers for leatherwork. Items range from jackets and luggage to wide-brimmed hats to coin purses. Prices are extremely cheap (especially in Quisapincha, where you can pick up a jacket for about $35), but quality varies, so examine items carefully.

Other Items
Baskets made of straw, reeds or agave fibers are common everywhere. Onyx (a pale, translucent quartz with parallel layers of different colors) is carved into chess sets and other objects. Miniature blowpipes modeled after those used by indigenous groups from the Amazon are also popular, and you'll find plenty of other choices as well.

Tree Products
Ecuador's most important woodworking center is San Antonio de Ibarra (p129), where you'll find everything from utilitarian bowls, salad utensils, chess sets and candlesticks to ornately decorative crucifixes, statues and wall plaques. Again, the prices are low, but quality varies. Colorful balsa-wood birds carved into all sizes are extremely popular. They're made in the Oriente and sold throughout Quito. Carvings from the tagua nut (which resembles ivory) are common souvenirs.

DIRECTORY

Weavings

Woolen weavings are beautiful and range from square-foot pieces that can be sewn together to make throw cushions or shoulder bags, to weavings large enough to be used as floor rugs or wall hangings. Otavalo has a huge selection of mediocre-quality but very colorful weavings. The village of Salasaca (p166) is famous for its weavings. You'll see plenty of the same patterns at stores throughout Ecuador, but for something really unique, drop by the store Folklore Olga Fisch (p104) in Quito. It's pricey, but worth it.

SOLO TRAVELERS

Traveling alone can be one of the most rewarding experiences in life. You're far more likely to meet locals and fellow travelers – which is really what travel's all about, isn't it? – without the shell of companionship. Mind you, it can get lonely at times, and it's certainly nice to have a mate to watch your bags or go to the bar with you, but the benefits of solo travel can outweigh companionship in numerous ways.

If you do get lonely, Ecuador has an abundance of traveler-oriented hotels that make hooking up with other travelers easy. On the financial side, midrange and budget hotels often charge per person, which means you won't spend *that* much more than you would while traveling with others.

Women traveling anywhere are inherently at a greater risk than are men traveling alone. But countless women travel alone safely in Ecuador every day. For more information for women travelers, see p398.

TELEPHONE

For important nationwide numbers see the inside front cover of this book. Telephone service is readily available throughout Ecuador and is operated, depending on where you are, by one of three regional companies: Andinatel (mainly in the highlands and Oriente), Pacifictel (mainly in the coastal lowlands) and Etapa (in Cuenca). These companies operate *centros de llamadas* (telephone call centers) in nearly every town in the country, and they are the best places to make calls. Most call centers are open 8am to 10pm daily. Other private companies, including Alegro, Movistar and Porta, have call centers that operate on cellular networks.

Public street phones are also common. Some use phone cards, which are sold in convenient places such as corner stores. Others accept only coins. For local calls within a city, you can often borrow a phone in a store or use a private phone offered by entrepreneurs on the street. You'll be charged a small amount for the service, of course. All but the most basic hotels will allow you to make local city calls.

International calls from an Andinatel, Pacifictel or Etapa office are as cheap as $0.35 per minute to the USA and $0.45 to the UK and Australia. Rates are 20% cheaper on Sunday and after 7pm on all other days. Internet cafés provide even cheaper 'Net-to-phone' services.

Hotels that provide international phone connections very often surcharge extremely heavily. Collect (reverse-charge) calls are possible to a few countries that have reciprocal agreements with Ecuador; these agreements vary from year to year, so ask at the nearest telephone office.

All telephone numbers in Ecuador have seven digits, and the first digit – except for cellular phone numbers – is always a '2'. If someone gives you a six-digit number (which happens often), simply put a '2' in front of it.

Cell Phones

Cellular telephone numbers in Ecuador are always preceded with the prefix ☎ 09. As far as bringing your own phone, only GSM cell phones operating at 850 Mhz (GSM 850) function in Ecuador, and rates are extremely high. A tri-band GSM cellular will not currently work in Ecuador. Neither are prepaid SIM cards currently available without purchasing a local phone. This is a rapidly changing field and you can stay up to date by checking www.kropla.com and www.gsmworld.com.

Phone Codes

Two-digit area codes beginning with '0' are used throughout Ecuador; these are provided beneath each destination heading in this book. Area codes are not dialed if calling from within that area code, unless dialing from a cellular phone.

Ecuador's country code is ☎ 593. To call a number in Ecuador from abroad, call your international access code, Ecuador's country code, the area code *without* the 0, and the seven-digit local telephone number.

Phonecards

International calling cards from your country don't work well in Ecuador, because the local telephone companies don't make any money from them and are reluctant to use them. Buy local cards instead; some have instructions in English.

TIME

The Ecuadorian mainland is five hours behind Greenwich Mean Time, and the Galápagos are six hours behind. Mainland time here is equivalent to Eastern Standard Time in North America. When it's noon in Quito, it's noon in New York, 5pm in London and 4am (daylight saving time) in Melbourne. Because of Ecuador's location on the equator, days and nights are of equal length year-round, and there is no daylight-saving time.

For world time zones, see pp438–9.

TOILETS

As throughout South America, Ecuadorian plumbing has very low pressure, and putting toilet paper into the bowl is a serious no-no anywhere except in the fanciest hotels. Always put your used toilet paper in the basket (it's better than a clogged and overflowing toilet!). A well-run cheap hotel will ensure that the receptacle is emptied and the toilet cleaned daily.

Public toilets are limited mainly to bus terminals, airports and restaurants. Lavatories are called *servicios higiénicos* and are usually marked 'SS.HH.' You can simply ask to use the *baño* (bathroom) in a restaurant. Toilet paper is rarely available, so the experienced traveler always carries a personal supply. Remember 'M' on the door means *mujeres* (women) not 'men.' Men's toilets are signed with an 'H' for *hombres* (men) or a 'C' for *caballeros* (gentlemen).

TOURIST INFORMATION

Ecuador's system of government-run tourist offices is hit or miss, but is getting better. Tourist information in Quito and Cuenca is excellent.

The government run **Ministerio de Turismo** (www.vivecuador.com) is responsible for tourist information at the national level. It is slowly opening tourist information offices –

known as iTur offices – in important towns throughout Ecuador. Even if there's not an iTur office in a town, there's usually a municipal or provincial tourist office. The quality of information you'll get depends entirely on the enthusiasm of the person behind the desk. Most of the time, the staff is good at answering the majority of questions.

An excellent resource, especially once you've arrived in Ecuador, is **South American Explorers** (SAE; ☎ 02-222 5228; www.saexplorers.org; Jorge Washington 311 & Leonidas Plaza Gutiérrez, Quito; ⏰ 9:30am-5pm Mon-Fri, 9:30am-6pm Thu, 9am-noon Sat), a member-supported nonprofit organization with clubhouses in Quito; Lima, Peru; Cuzco, Peru; and a head office in Ithaca, New York. The clubhouses function as information centers for travelers, adventurers, researchers etc, and provide a wealth of advice about traveling in Latin America.

Annual SAE membership is $50/80 per individual/couple or $30 per person with a group of four or more. Membership includes the use of all three clubhouses, plus four quarterly issues of the informative *South American Explorer* magazine (members from countries outside the USA must add $10 for postage). The Quito clubhouse has the following services: a lending library; maps; an outstanding compilation of trip reports left by other travelers; storage of luggage; storage of mail addressed to you at the club; relaxing reading and TV rooms; current advice about travel conditions; volunteer information; a book exchange; a notice board; extra activities, such as Thursday-night talks and comedy nights; and many other services.

Services for nonmembers are limited to the purchase of useful information sheets. Paid-up members can stay all day.

VISAS

Most travelers entering Ecuador as tourists, including citizens of Australia, New Zealand, Japan, the EU, Canada and the USA, do not require visas. Upon entry, they will be issued a T-3 embarkation card valid for 90 days. Sixty-day stamps are rarely given, but double check if you're going to be in the country for a while. Residents of most Central American and some Asian countries require visas.

All travelers entering as diplomats, students, laborers, religious workers, businesspeople, volunteers and cultural-exchange visitors require nonimmigrant visas. Various immigrant visas are also available.

Obtaining a visa is time consuming, so commence the process as far ahead of your visit as possible. Visas enable holders to apply for a *censo* (temporary-residence card) and pay resident prices in national parks, as well as on trains and planes. Visas must be obtained from an Ecuadorian embassy and cannot be arranged within Ecuador. See p389 for a partial list of Ecuadorian embassies.

All (nontourist) visa holders must register at the **Dirección General de Extranjería** (☎ 02-223 1022/3; 10 de Agosto & General Murgeón, Edificio Autorepuestos, 4th fl; ☽ 8am-1pm Mon-Fri) in Quito within 30 days of arrival in Ecuador. If visa holders wish to leave the country and return, they need a *salida* (exit) form from the Jefatura Provincial de Migración (described in the following section), which can be used for multiple exits and re-entries. Visa holders who apply for residency need to get an exit permit from the immigration authorities in Quito before they leave the country.

Stay Extensions
Embarkation card extensions can be obtained from the **Jefatura Provincial de Migración** (Map p78; ☎ 02-224 7510; Isla Seymour 1152 near Río Coca, Quito; ☽ 8:30am-noon & 3-5pm Mon-Fri). On top of the original 90 days, you can obtain a maximum of 30 additional days, a process that can be performed three times, for a maximum of 180 days (six months) per year. You cannot get an extension until the day your embarkation card expires.

WOMEN TRAVELERS
Generally, women travelers will find Ecuador safe and pleasant, despite the fact that machismo is alive and well. Ecuadorian men often make flirtatious comments and whistle at single women, both Ecuadorian and foreigners. Really, it's just sport – a sort of hormonal babbling among groups of guys – and the best strategy is to brush them off. Women who firmly ignore unwanted verbal advances are often treated with respect.

Women who speak Spanish find that it is easier to deal with persistent questions from men, which generally follow the classic: 'Where are you from?' 'How old are you?' 'Are you married?'. If you're not interested in conversation, consider beginning your response with 'My husband…' even if it's fiction. Sometimes this is all it takes. If the come-ons get really bad, a firm '¡No, me molestes!' ('Don't bother me!') should do the trick. In general, don't let comments on how pretty you are get under your skin, unless they're rude. Either say 'Thank you,' or ignore them (and remember them back home when no one comments on your eyes unless they're red!).

On the coast, come-ons are more predatory, and solo female travelers should take precautions such as staying away from bars and discos where they'll obviously get hit on, opting for taxis over walking etc. Racy conversation with a guy, while it may be ironic or humorous, is not common here, and a man will probably assume you're after one thing.

There have been stories about foreign women who have been put into a compromising position with a guide or boss at a volunteer organization. In the rare chance this happens to you, report the person to the organization and any parent organization. The SAE in Quito (p72) will take reports and maintains a list of problem organizations or tour groups. Most of the licensed guides in Ecuador, however, have a high level of professionalism. Women-only travel groups or guides are available in a few situations.

Finally, very occasional reports have been received of women being harassed by hotel owners or peaked at through bathroom windows that won't close, but this seems a rarity. Try to rent a room with a secure lock and throw a towel over the bathroom window in the rare event it won't close.

WORK
Ecuador has 11% unemployment and 47% underemployment, so finding work here isn't easy. Officially, you need a worker's visa to be allowed to work in Ecuador. Aside from the occasional job opening at a tourist lodge or B&B, there is little opportunity for paid work. The one exception is teaching English.

Most paid English-teaching job openings are in Quito and Guayaquil. Schools sometimes advertise for teachers on the bulletin boards of hotels and restaurants. Pay is just enough to live on unless you've acquired a full-time position from home.

If you have a bona-fide teaching credential, so much the better. Schools such as the

American School in Quito will often hire teachers of mathematics, biology and other subjects, and may help you get a work visa if you want to stay on. They also pay much better than the language schools. Check ads in local hotels and newspapers.

One of the best online ESL resources, complete with job boards, is **Dave's ESL Café** (www.eslcafé.com).

Volunteer Work

Numerous organizations look for the services of volunteers, however the vast majority require at least a minimal grasp of Spanish, a minimum commitment of several weeks or months, as well as fees (anywhere from $10 per day to $300 per month) to cover the costs of room and board. Volunteers can work in conservation programs, help street kids, teach, build nature trails, construct websites, do medical or agricultural work – the possibilities are endless. If you're wanting to keep your volunteer costs down, your best bet is to look when you get to Ecuador. Plenty of places need volunteers who only have their hard work to offer.

SAE (see p397) in Quito has a volunteer desk where current offerings are posted. The clubhouse itself often needs volunteers. The classifieds section on **Ecuador Explorer** (www.ecuadorexplorer.com) has a lengthy list of organizations of all types that are seeking volunteers.

Organizations in Ecuador that often need volunteers:

Bosque Nublado Santa Lucía (www.santa-lucia.org, www.santaluciaecuador.com) Community-based ecotourism project in the cloud forests of northwest Ecuador. It regularly contracts volunteers to work in reforestation, trail maintenance, construction, teaching English and more.

FEVI (www.fevi.org) This Ecuadorian nonprofit places volunteers in communities throughout Ecuador. FEVI works with children, the elderly, women's groups and indigenous communities, so it's good for those seeking a cultural-exchange type experience.

Fundación Natura (www.fnatura.org) Important Ecuadorian nongovernment organization (NGO) that regularly hires Spanish-speaking volunteers to work in research, reforestation and more.

Jatun Sacha Foundation (www.jatunsacha.org) Offers volunteer positions in plant conservation, reserve maintenance, environmental education, community service, agroforestry and other fields at one of 10 biological stations in Ecuador.

Junto con los Niños (www.juconi.org.ec) Excellent organization that works with street kids in the slum areas of Guayaquil. One-month minimum preferred.

New Era Galápagos Foundation (www.neweragalapagos.org) Unique nonprofit offering volunteerships focused on community empowerment and sustainable tourism in the Galápagos. Volunteers live and work on Isla San Cristóbal.

Rainforest Concern (www.rainforestconcern.org) British nonprofit offering paid but very affordable volunteer positions in forest environments in Ecuador.

Reserva Biológica Los Cedros (www.reservaloscedros.org) This biological reserve in the cloud forests of the western Andean slopes often needs volunteers. One month minimum. Also see p129.

Río Muchacho Organic Farm (www.riomuchacho.com) Coastal ecotourism project offering one-month apprenticeships in organic agriculture with volunteer opportunities. Also see p287.

Transportation

CONTENTS

Getting There & Away	**400**
Entering the Country	400
Air	400
Land	403
River	404
Sea	404
Getting Around	**404**
Air	404
Bicycle	405
Boat	406
Bus	406
Car & Motorcycle	407
Hitchhiking	409
Local Transportation	409
Tours	410
Train	411
Trucks	411

THINGS CHANGE...

The information in this chapter is particularly vulnerable to change. Check directly with the airline or a travel agent to make sure you understand how a fare (and ticket you may buy) works and be aware of the security requirements for international travel. Shop carefully. The details given in this chapter should be regarded as pointers and are no substitute for careful, up-to-date research.

GETTING THERE & AWAY

ENTERING THE COUNTRY

Entering the country is straightforward, and border officials, especially at the airports, mince few words whisking you through. At land borders, officers may take a little more time examining your passport, if only to kill a little time. Officially, you need proof of onward travel and evidence of sufficient funds for your stay, but this is rarely – if ever – asked for. Proof of $20 per day or a credit card is usually evidence of sufficient funds. However, international airlines flying to Quito may require a round-trip or onward ticket or a residence visa before they let you on the plane; you should be prepared for this possibility, though it's unlikely. Though not law, you may be required to show proof of vaccination against yellow fever if you are entering Ecuador from an infected area.

Flights, tours and rail tickets can all be booked online at www.lonelyplanet.com/travel_services.

Passport

All nationals entering as tourists need a passport that is valid for at least six months after arrival. You are legally required to have your passport on you at all times. Many people carry only a copy when they're hanging around a town, though this is not an officially acceptable form of ID. Never take buses, boats, drives or otherwise travel without your passport. For visa requirements, see p397.

AIR

Airports & Airlines

Two major international airports serve Ecuador: Quito's **Aeropuerto Mariscal Sucre** (UIO; ☎ 02-294 4900; www.quitoairport.com; Av Amazonas at Av de la Prensa) and Guayaquil's **Aeropuerto Simón Bolívar** (GYE; ☎ 04-228 2100, 228 9616; Av de las Américas s/n).

TAME (www.tame.com.ec) is Ecuador's main airline, but aside from its short border-hopper flight from Tulcán to Cali, Colombia, it offers no international flights.

The following international airlines serve Ecuador. Unless otherwise noted, the telephone numbers given are for the airlines' Quito offices.

Aeropostal Alas de Venezuela (airline code VH; ☎ 02-226 4392/6; www.aeropostal.com; hub Caracas, Venezuela)
Air Europa (airline code UX; ☎ 02-2567646/7; www.aireuropa.com; hub Madrid, Spain)
Air France (airline code AF; ☎ 02-222 4818, 222 1605; www.airfrance.com; hub Paris, France)
Air Madrid (airline code NM; ☎ 02-227 4919; www.airmadrid.com; hub Madrid, Spain)

American Airlines (airline code AA; ☎ 02-226 0900; www.aa.com; hubs Dallas, TX & Chicago, IL, USA)

Avianca (airline code AV; ☎ 02-223 2015/16/20; www .avianca.com; hub Bogotá, Colombia)

Continental Airlines (airline code CO; ☎ 02-255 7170/64/65/66; www.continental.com; hub Houston, TX, USA)

Copa (airline code CM; ☎ 02-230 3227/39/11; www .copaair.com; hub Panama City, Panama)

Grupo TACA (airline code TA; ☎ 02-292 3170/69/68/67; www.grupotaca.com; hub San Salvador, El Salvador)

Iberia (airline code IB; ☎ 02-256 6009; www.iberia.com; hub Madrid, Spain)

KLM (airline code KL; ☎ 02-298 6828; www.klm.com; hub Amsterdam, Holland)

LAN Airlines (airline code LA; ☎ 02-250 8396; 250 8400; www.lanchile.com, www.lan.com; hub Santiago, Chile)

Lufthansa (airline code LH; ☎ 02-254 1300, 250 8396; www.lufthansa.com; hub Cologne, Germany)

Santa Bárbara Airlines (airline code S3; ☎ 02-225 3972; www.santabaraairlines.com; hub Caracas, Venezuela)

Tickets

Airfares to South America are fairly costly from just about anywhere outside the continent. Ticket prices are highest during the tourist high seasons of mid-June through early September, and then December through mid-January. Working with a travel agent that deals specifically in Latin American travel is always an advantage.

COURIER FLIGHTS

Courier flights are rarely offered to Ecuador, but you might find something to another South American capital with **International Association of Air Travel Couriers** (www .courier.org) or **Air Courier Association** (www.aircourier .org). You'll have to be flexible with your dates and can only bring carry-on luggage.

INTERCONTINENTAL (RTW) TICKETS

Some of the best deals for travelers visiting many countries on different continents are Round-the-World (RTW) tickets. Itineraries from the USA, Europe or Australia can include five or more layovers (including Quito). Similar 'Circle Pacific' fares allow excursions between Australasia and South America. Another option is putting together your own ticket with two or three stops and a round trip from another country. If you work with a travel agent, it might work out cheaper than a RTW ticket.

> ### DEPARTURE TAX
>
> A $25 departure tax is levied on all international flights from Quito or Guayaquil. This tax is not included in ticket prices and must be paid in cash at the airport. Short cross-border hops, such as Tulcán–Cali (Colombia), are not taxed.

Fares for RTW and Circle Pacific tickets can vary widely, but to get an idea, shop around at the following websites:

Airbrokers (www.airbrokers.com) US based.

Airtreks (www.airtreks.com) US based.

Oneworld (www.oneworld.com) Alliance between nine airlines that offer circle and RTW tickets. Quito is on the list of destination cities for its 'Visit South America' ticket.

Roundtheworldflights.com (www.roundtheworld flights.com) UK based.

Star Alliance (www.staralliance.com) Airline alliance that allows you to build your own RTW ticket.

Australia

There is no real choice of routes between Australia and South America, and there are certainly no bargain fares available. The two most straightforward options are: fly Qantas or Air New Zealand to Los Angeles (USA) and fly from there (most easily via Houston or Miami) to Quito; or fly Aerolíneas Argentinas to Buenos Aires, from where there are direct flights to Quito. Another alternative is flying Qantas to Santiago, Chile and connecting with a LanChile flight north to Ecuador.

Some of the cheapest tickets are available through **STA Travel** (☎ 1300 733 035; www.statravel .com.au) and **Flight Centre** (☎ 133 133; www.flight centre.com.au), both of which have dozens of offices in the country. For online bookings, try www.travel.com.au.

Canada

Air Canada, American Airlines and United fly from Toronto or Montreal via New York or Miami to Guayaquil or Quito. The most direct flights (one stop only) are with Air Canada via Miami or with Continental via Houston, Texas. Flights from Montreal via New York also stop in Miami before continuing to Quito.

Travel Cuts (☎ 800-667-2887; www.travelcuts.com) is Canada's national student travel agency. For online bookings try www.expedia.ca and www.travelocity.ca.

TRANSPORTATION

TRANSPORTATION

Continental Europe

There are few direct flights from Europe to Ecuador; most involve a change of plane and airline in Miami or Houston, or in a South American capital other than Quito. Iberia, Air Europa, Air Madrid and LAN Airlines (LanChile/LanEcuador) all fly non-stop to Quito or Guayaquil from Madrid. There are no other nonstop flights from Continental Europe.

The following travel agencies are good possibilities for bargain fares from Continental Europe.

FRANCE
Anyway (☎ 08 92 89 38 92; www.anyway.fr)
Lastminute (☎ 08 92 70 50 00; www.lastminute.fr)
Nouvelles Frontiéres (☎ 08 25 00 07 47; www.nouvelles-frontieres.fr)
OTU Voyages (www.otu.fr) This agency specializes in student and youth travelers.
Voyageurs du Monde (☎ 01 40 15 11 15; www.vdm.com)

GERMANY
Expedia (www.expedia.de)
Just Travel (☎ 089 747 3330; www.justtravel.de)
Lastminute (☎ 01805 284 366; www.lastminute.de)
STA Travel (☎ 01805 456 422; www.statravel.de) For travelers under the age of 26.

ITALY
One recommended agency is **CTS Viaggi** (☎ 06 462 0431; www.cts.it), which specializes in student and youth travel.

NETHERLANDS
Try **Airfair** (☎ 020 620 5121; www.airfair.nl).

Latin America

There are loads of flights from Quito or Guayaquil to South American countries, including Colombia (Bogotá, Cali and Cartagena); Argentina (Buenos Aires); Venezuela (Caracas); Bolivia (La Paz); Peru (Lima); Chile (Santiago); and Brazil (Sao Paulo and Río de Janeiro). There are also direct flights to Mexico City, Panama City and Havana, Cuba.

New Zealand

As with Australia, there are no direct routes to Ecuador from New Zealand. Your best bets are flying Air New Zealand to Los Angeles (USA) or Aerolíneas Argentinas to

Buenos Aires and connecting from either of these cities to Quito. Qantas also flies from Auckland to Santiago, Chile, where you can connect with a LanChile flight to Ecuador.

Both **Flight Centre** (☎ 0800 243 544; www.flightcentre.co.nz) and **STA Travel** (☎ 0508 782 872; www.statravel.co.nz) have branches throughout the country. For online bookings try www.travel.co.nz.

UK & Ireland

There are no direct flights from the UK or Ireland to Ecuador. Fares from London are often cheaper than those from other European cities, even though your flight route may take you from London through a European city.

Discount air travel is big business in London. Advertisements for many travel agencies can be found in the travel pages of the weekend broadsheet newspapers, in *Time Out*, the *Evening Standard* and in the free online magazine *TNT* (www.tntmagazine.com).

Recommended travel agencies in the UK include the following:
Bridge the World (☎ 0870 444 7474; www.b-t-w.co.uk)
Flightbookers (☎ 0870 814 4001; www.ebookers.com)
Flight Centre (☎ 0870 890 8099; www.flightcentre.co.uk)
North-South Travel (☎ 01245 608 291; www.northsouthtravel.co.uk) North-South Travel donate part of their profit to projects in the developing world.
Quest Travel (☎ 0870 442 3542; www.questtravel.com)
STA Travel (☎ 0870 160 0599; www.statravel.co.uk) For travelers under the age of 26.
Trailfinders (www.trailfinders.co.uk)
Travel Bag (☎ 0870 890 1456; www.travelbag.co.uk)

USA

From the USA, you can get a direct flight nonstop to Quito or Guayaquil from the gateways of New York, Houston and Miami. American Airlines and Continental are the main US carriers, and some Latin American airlines, especially LanChile/LanEcuador and Grupo TACA fly to Ecuador; in the case of the latter, via Central America. Flights from other cities or with any of the other airlines require an aircraft change in the US gateways listed earlier, or in another Latin American capital.

Latin American travel specialist **eXito Travel** (☎ 800-655-4053; www.exitotravel.com) offers some of the cheapest fares around as well as personal service (such as flight changes from abroad, travel recommendations and more) from an impressively well-informed staff.

Discount travel agents in the USA are known as consolidators (although you won't see a sign on the door saying 'Consolidator'). San Francisco is the nation's consolidator capital, although some good deals can be found in Los Angeles, New York and other big cities.

The following agencies are recommended for online bookings:

Cheap Tickets (www.cheaptickets.com)
Expedia (www.expedia.com)
Lowestfare.com (www.lowestfare.com)
Orbitz (www.orbitz.com)
STA Travel (www.sta.com) Best for travelers under the age of 26.
Travelocity (www.travelocity.com)

LAND

If you live in the Americas, it is possible to travel overland by bus. However, if you want to start from North or Central America, the Panamericana (Pan–American Highway) stops in Panama and begins again in Colombia, leaving a 200km roadless section of jungle known as the Darien Gap. The Darien Gap has become increasingly dangerous because of banditry and drug-related problems, especially on the Colombian side, so you are advised *not* to try to cross it. Most overland travelers fly over the Darien Gap or hire on as a crew member on a private yacht that will sail from Panama to Colombia.

Once in South America, it is relatively straightforward to travel by public bus from the neighboring Andean countries. See the Lonely Planet guidebooks to those countries for full details.

Bicycle

There is no extra charge for entering Ecuador by land with a bicycle; it's as straightforward as entering by foot. For additional cycling information see p384.

Border Crossings

Peru and Colombia are the only two countries sharing borders with Ecuador. If you are entering or leaving Ecuador, border formalities are straightforward if your documents are in order. No taxes are levied on tourists when entering or exiting overland.

If you're leaving the country and have lost your embarkation card (see p397), you should be able to get a free replacement at the border, assuming that the stamp in your passport has not expired. If your documents aren't in order, several things might happen. If you've overstayed the allowed time by a few days, you'll likely be required to pay a fine, usually about $10. (This really is a fine, not a bribe.) If you've overstayed by several months, you may have to pay a hefty fine or you will be sent back to Quito. If you don't have an *entrada* (entrance) stamp, you will also be sent back.

PERU

There are three important border posts connecting Ecuador and Peru. All are safe. The Huaquillas crossing (p344), south of Machala, gets almost 100% of the international traffic between the two countries. A second crossing, at Macará, has recently become popular because it's more relaxed than the Huaquillas crossing, and the journey from Loja (p212) in the southern highlands is beautiful. Direct buses run between Loja and Piura, Peru (eight hours) via Macará and wait for you at the border while you take care of formalities. It's easy. The least used crossing is the La Balsa crossing at Zumba (p223), south of Vilcabamba (p219). This is a remote and interesting crossing that gets little traffic. People often hang out in Vilcabamba for a few days before heading to Zumba and Peru.

A fourth crossing is by river via the outpost of Nuevo Rocafuerte (p245) on the Río Napo in the Oriente. This is a long journey that is rarely undertaken by foreigners – but it's possible.

COLOMBIA

The main border crossing to Colombia is via Tulcán (p138) in the northern highlands. It's currently the only safe place to cross into Colombia. The border crossing north of Lago Agrio (p235) in the Oriente is unsafe due to smuggling and conflict in Colombia.

Bus

Bussing into Ecuador from Colombia or Peru is straightforward and usually requires walking across one of the earlier mentioned international borders and catching another bus once you're across. Some international bus companies offer direct, long-haul services from major cities such as Lima or Bogotá.

Car & Motorcycle

Driving a private vehicle into Ecuador can be a huge hassle, depending largely upon the mood of the official who stops you at the border. To bring your car into Ecuador, you are officially required to have a Carnet de Passage en Douane (CPD), an internationally recognized customs document that allows you to temporarily 'import' a vehicle into Ecuador without paying an import tax. The document is issued through an automobile club in the country where the car is registered, and you are strongly advised to obtain one well in advance. Motorcycles seem to present fewer hassles at the border.

RIVER

Since the 1998 peace treaty was signed with Peru, it has been possible to travel down the Río Napo from Ecuador to Peru, joining the Amazon near Iquitos. The border facilities are minimal, and the boats doing the journey are infrequent, but it is possible to do the trip – see p245. It is also geographically possible to travel down Río Putumayo into Colombia and Peru, but this is a dangerous region because of drug smuggling and terrorism, and is not recommended.

SEA

Very few cruise ships use Guayaquil as a port of call as they head down the Pacific coast of South America. Occasionally you can find a ship going to Guayaquil, Ecuador's main port, although this is a very unusual way to arrive in Ecuador. It's certainly cheaper and more convenient to fly.

A few cargo lines will carry passengers, though it usually costs more than flying. If you're determined to get here by freighter, you can start your research online at www .travel-library.com/rtw/html/rtwfreighters .html and at the **Internet Guide to Freighter Travel** (www.geocities.com/freighterman.geo/mainmenu .html).

It is possible to arrive in Ecuador on your own sailing boat or, if you don't happen to have one, as a crew member. In Ecuador, Salinas is the port most frequented by international yachts. For further information, read the *World Cruising Handbook* by Jimmy Cornell.

GETTING AROUND

Ecuador has an efficient transportation system, and because of its small size, you can usually get anywhere and everywhere quickly, easily and enjoyably.

AIR
Airlines in Ecuador

Ecuador's most important domestic airline is TAME, followed by Icaro and al. Except for TAME's flight from Tulcán to Cali, Colombia, none fly internationally. All three enjoy safety records on par with most world airlines, although some of the planes look a little old.

With the exception of flying to the Galápagos Islands, internal flights are generally fairly cheap, rarely exceeding $70 for a one-way ticket. All mainland flights are under an hour and often provide you with incredible views over the Andes. There is a two-tier pricing system on flights to and from the Oriente and to/from the Galápagos, on which foreigners pay more than Ecuadorians.

If you can't get a ticket, go to the airport early and get on a waiting list – passengers often don't show up. If you do have a reservation, reconfirm your flight 72 hours in advance.

Flights to most destinations originate in Quito or Guayaquil only. Detailed flight information is given under the appropriate cities throughout this book. The following are Ecuador's three passenger airlines with their reservation numbers in Quito:

AeroGal (02-292 0510-4; www.aerogal.com.ec) Serves Quito, Guayaquil, Cuenca, Isla Baltra (Galápagos) and Isla San Cristóbal (Galápagos).

Icaro (☎ 02-245 0928; www.icaro.com.ec) Serves Quito, Guayaquil, Cuenca, Manta, Coca, Lago Agrio and Esmeraldas.

TAME (☎ 02-290 9900-9; www.tame.com.ec) Serves Coca, Cuenca, Esmeraldas, Isla Baltra (Galápagos), Isla San Cristóbal (Galápagos), Guayaquil, Lago Agrio, Loja, Macas, Manta, Portoviejo, Quito, Tulcán and Cali (Colombia).

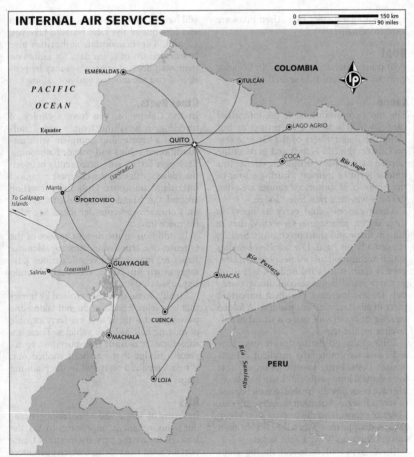

INTERNAL AIR SERVICES

BICYCLE

Each year a handful of cyclists attempt to ride from Alaska to Argentina, or any number of shorter long-distance rides, and manage to get through Ecuador just fine, despite the fact that road rules are few, bike lanes are nonexistent and roads are poor. Cycling in the Andes is strenuous, not only because of hill climbs but because of the altitudes. Mountain bikes are recommended, as road bikes don't stand up to the poor road quality.

Bike shops are scarce outside of Quito, and those that do exist usually have a very limited selection of parts. Bring all important spare parts and tools from home. For mountain-biking destinations in Ecuador,

see p384. The country's best mountain bike tour operators are in Quito (p86) and Riobamba (p183).

Hire

Renting bikes has only recently become an option in Ecuador, and is mainly for short tours, mostly from Quito, Riobamba and Cuenca. The main exception is the Andean town of Baños (p167) which has a wonderful paved ride nearby and is therefore full of mountain bike rentals.

Purchase

Bicycles are extremely expensive in Ecuador, and outside of Quito or Guayaquil it is very difficult to find anything even approaching a quality bike. Used bikes are hard to come by.

BOAT

Boat transportation is common in Ecuador and can be divided into several types.

Canoe

The most common boat is the motorized canoe, which acts as a water taxi or bus along the major rivers of the Oriente (especially on the Río Napo) and parts of the northern coast. Most people experience this unique form of transport during a tour in the Amazon, as motorized canoes are often the only way to a rain forest lodge.

These canoes often carry as many as three dozen passengers. Generally, they're long in shape and short on comfort. Seating is normally on hard, low wooden benches which accommodate two people each. Luggage is stashed forward under a tarpaulin, so carry hand baggage containing essentials for the journey. The most important piece of advice: *bring seat padding*. A folded sweater or towel will make a world of difference on the trip.

Pelting rain and glaring sun are major hazards, and an umbrella is excellent defense against both. Bring suntan lotion or wear long sleeves, long pants and a sun hat – people have been literally unable to walk because of second-degree burns on their legs after six hours of exposure to the tropical sun. When the sun disappears or when the rain begins, it can get chilly, so bring a light jacket.

Insect repellent is useful during stops along the river. Bottled water and something to snack on will complete your hand baggage.

Once you're off the main branch of a river, you may have to navigate smaller tributaries in a paddled (or motorized) dugout canoe. The paddled dugout canoe is one of the most divine modes of transportation because it moves along stealthily and silently. Tours from a jungle lodge usually involve paddled dugout canoes.

Private Yacht

The idea of sailing your own yacht around the Galápagos might sound splendid, but to do so, you need a license, and licenses are all limited to Galápagos boats. If you arrive at the islands in your own boat, you will have to moor the boat in Puerto Ayora and hire one of the local boats to take you around. The Ecuadorian authorities give transit permits of seven days for sailors on their own boats. Longer stays may be possible if you are moored and not sailing.

Other Boats

In the Galápagos, you have a choice of traveling in anything from a small sailboat to a cruise ship complete with air-conditioned cabins and private bathrooms. Passenger ferries run infrequently between the islands, offering the cheapest means of interisland transport. Only folks traveling around the islands independently (ie not on a cruise) need consider these. See p359 for more info.

In addition to the dugout canoes of the Oriente, one cruise ship, *Amazon Manatee Explorer,* makes relatively luxurious passages down Río Napo; see Nuevo Mundo Expeditions, p90.

Finally, some rivers are crossed by ferries that vary from a paddled dugout taking one passenger at a time, to a car ferry capable of moving half-a-dozen vehicles. These are sometimes makeshift transportation to replace a bridge that has been washed out, is being repaired or is still in the planning stages.

BUS

In terms of scope and affordability, Ecuador's bus system is impressive, to say the least. Buses are the primary means of transport for most Ecuadorians, which guarantees buses to just about anywhere. They can be exciting, cramped, comfy, smelly, fun, scary, sociable and grueling, depending on your state of mind, where you're going and who's driving.

In terms of safety, sure, you're safer at home. To avoid mincing words, the majority of Ecuadorian bus drivers are maniacs. They pass on blind turns, they ride the airbrakes till they smoke, they hit the gas going downhill and they race other buses for fun. But, to their credit, most are amazingly skillful drivers. If they get too crazy, people on the bus start to complain, which can either settle the driver down or piss him off and make him drive faster. Overall, buses are a wonderful experience, and, more often than not, you're in good hands.

Every major city and nearly every siz-able town has a main *terminal terrestre* (bus terminal) for most arriving and departing buses. Almost all are walking distance or a short cab ride from the town's center. Smaller towns are occasionally served by passing buses, in which case you have to walk from the highway into town. It's usu-ally only a short walk, since only the small-est towns lack terminals.

If you're traveling lightly, take your lug-gage inside the bus with you. If your luggage has to go on top or in a luggage compart-ment, pack your gear in garbage bags in case of rain. The luggage compartment is sometimes filthy or leaky, so using a protec-tive sack is a good idea (though not crucial if rain is out of the question). Many locals use grain sacks as luggage; you can buy them for a few cents in general stores or markets and toss your bag inside it. For information on luggage theft, see p388.

On average, bus journeys cost about $1 per hour of travel. Remember to always have your passport handy when you're going anywhere by bus, as they are frequently stopped for checks. This is especially true in the Oriente.

Classes

There are rarely classes to choose from – whatever's available is the class you ride. Most *autobuses* (buses) are nondescript pas-senger (as opposed to school-type) buses, and they rarely have a bathroom on board unless they're traveling over about four hours. Some of the long-haul rides between large cities have air-conditioned buses with on-board toilets, though are few and far be-tween. When a bus does have a bathroom, you usually have to ask the driver's assistant for the key. If a bus doesn't have a toilet, and you're not going to make it to the next stop without your bowels exploding, simply put a panicked look on your face and tell the driver, *'necesito orinar'* ('I need to urinate'). and he'll know to stop and let you out. It's not a big deal.

Long-Distance Buses

Long-distance buses usually stop for a 20-minute meal break at the appropriate times. The food in terminal restaurants may be somewhat basic, so if you're a picky eater you should bring food with you.

On remote routes, full buses allow pas-sengers to travel on the roof. This can be fun, with great views but minimal comfort!

Reservations & Schedules

Most companies have scheduled departures, but they change often and may not always be adhered to. If a bus is full, it might leave early. Conversely – and this one will surely drive you bonkers – an almost empty bus may spend half an hour *dando vueltas* (driv-ing around), with the driver's assistant yell-ing out of the door in the hope of attracting more passengers. The upside is, you'll carry these songlike hollers (¡*Saquisilí, Saquisilí, venga venga Saquisilí!*) home like souvenirs and hear them for years to come. The larger terminals often have traveler information booths that can advise you about routes, fares and times.

For rides over four hours, you can usu-ally purchase a ticket up to eight days in ad-vance. Tickets must be purchased in person at the bus terminal. Except on weekends and during vacations, you'll rarely have trouble getting a ticket, but it never hurts to buy one a day in advance or arrive an hour or two early. Doing so also allows you to score a better seat. The suspension at the back of a bus is usually far worse than anywhere else, so try to avoid the back rows altogether. Anyone over 180cm (6ft) should buy tickets in advance and ask for a seat with *mucho espacio* (lots of space), usually toward the front.

Bus companies with frequent departures (twice an hour or more) usually only sell tickets for the next departure.

CAR & MOTORCYCLE

Driving a car or motorcycle in Ecuador defi-nitely has its challenges. The main north–south artery, the one you'll surely drive if you do any driving at all, is the Panameri-cana. This international highway, one of the world's most famous roads, passes through Ecuador and is fairly well surfaced but not without its potholes, blind turns, and in-sanely fast bus and truck drivers. It's quite an experience, to say the least.

Automobile Associations

Ecuador's automobile association is **Aneta** (Quito ☎ 02-250 4961, 222 9020; www.aneta.org.ec), which offers a few member services to members of foreign automobile clubs, including Canadian and US AAA members. It provides 24-hour roadside assistance to Aneta members.

Bring Your Own Vehicle

Unless your visit to Ecuador is part of a longer multicountry or continent-wide road trip, it's hardly worth shipping your own vehicle to Ecuador. The cost is high and, unless you choose to container your vehicle, theft of items from inside the car is a serious problem. Containerless Ro-Ro (roll on, roll off) shipping is not recommended.

Driver's License

An international driver's license is not officially required to drive in Ecuador, but it can be beneficial as a familiar document to the officer who has never seen, say, a Nebraska state driver's license. You are required to have a driver's license from your home country and a passport whenever you're driving. The international driver's license can also come in handy when renting a car.

Fuel & Spare Parts

There are two octane ratings for gasoline in Ecuador: 'Extra' (82-octane) and 'Super' (92-octane). Gasoline is sold by the gallon and costs about $1.50 per gallon for Extra and about $2 per gallon for Super. Super is not always available in rural areas. Dirty diesel is available throughout the country. Depending on your vehicle, spare parts can be difficult to come by outside the main urban areas.

Hire

Few people rent cars in Ecuador, mainly because public transport makes getting around so easy. To get to really out-of-the-way places, however, a rental car can come in handy. Most of the international car rental companies, including **Avis** (www .avis.com), **Budget** (www.budget.com), **Hertz** (www .hertz.com) and **Localiza** (www.localiza.com.ec), have outlets in Ecuador, but it is difficult to find any agency outside of Guayaquil, Quito and Cuenca.

To rent a car you must be 25 years old and have a credit card, a valid driver's li-

DRIVING DISTANCES (KM)

	Ambato	Bahía de Caráquez	Baños	Cuenca	Esmeraldas	Guayaquil	Huaquillas	Ibarra	Loja	Macará	Macas	Manta.	Otavalo	Quito	Riobamba	Tena
Bahía de Caráquez	406															
Baños	40	446														
Cuenca	306	530	309													
Esmeraldas	390	392	430	667												
Guayaquil	288	280	288	235	472											
Huaquillas	440	533	445	242	670	253										
Ibarra	251	455	291	557	433	535	693									
Loja	511	695	514	205	832	415	233	762								
Macará	701	682	704	395	819	402	195	952	190							
Macas	230	642	190	231	620	432	473	479	436	626						
Manta	404	120	444	446	442	196	449	505	611	598	628					
Otavalo	231	435	271	537	413	515	673	20	742	932	459	485				
Quito	136	340	176	442	318	420	578	115	647	837	366	390	95			
Riobamba	52	464	55	254	442	233	390	303	459	649	245	456	283	188		
Tena	180	586	140	449	497	428	585	271	598	788	208	584	251	186	195	
Tulcán	376	580	416	682	558	660	818	125	887	1077	604	630	145	240	428	396

cense and a passport. Occasionally a company will rent to someone between 21 and 25 years old, though it may require a higher deposit. Typical rates start at around $40 per day for a compact car, but can go over $100 for a 4WD vehicle (high clearance can be a life saver during ventures off the beaten track). It's well worth shopping around for the best price. As you do, be sure to ask if the quoted rate includes *seguro* (insurance), *kilometraje libre* (unlimited kilometres) and IVA (tax); most likely it won't.

As with renting a car anywhere, make sure existing damage to the vehicle is noted on the rental form. Be absolutely certain there's a spare tire (with air!) and a jack. Rental cars are targets for thieves, so don't leave your car parked with bags or other valuables in sight. When leaving your car for any period, especially overnight, park it in a guarded lot.

Motorcycle rental is hard to find in Ecuador. One of the only options is Baños (p167) where 250cc Enduro-type motorcycles are available for about $10 per hour or $40 per day. Riders with their own machines will find an endless amount of information at www.horizonsunlimited.com.

Some international rental agencies will make reservations for you from your home country.

Insurance

Car rental companies offer insurance policies on their vehicles but they can carry a hefty deductible – anywhere between $1000 and $3500, depending on the company – so be sure you read the fine print. Even if an accident is not your fault, you will likely be responsible for the deductible in the event of a collision.

Road Hazards

Hazards in Ecuador include potholes, blind turns and, most obvious of all, bus and truck drivers who pass other buses and trucks at seemingly impossible moments. Always be alert for stopped vehicles, sudden road blocks and occasional livestock on the road. Signage in Ecuador is poor.

Road Rules

Ecuadorians drive on the right side of the road. Lanes, however, especially on the Panamericana, are a loose interpretation

of the driver. In essence, the Panamericana has three lanes: one goes one direction, a second goes the opposite direction, and a hazily defined no-man's land between the two serves as a de facto passing lane. As you can imagine, this middle lane offers plenty of nerve-racking games of chicken and chance, and you should be extremely cautious when overtaking other vehicles.

Road signs and traffic lights should always be obeyed even though they only seem symbolic to Ecuadorian drivers. To that end, even if a light is green, look both directions before entering an junction.

Military checkpoints are common along the Panamericana, so be certain to have all your papers in order to avoid hassle.

HITCHHIKING

Hitchhiking is never entirely safe in any country in the world, and we don't recommend it. Travelers who decide to hitchhike should understand that they are taking a small but potentially serious risk. People who do choose to hitchhike will be safer if they travel in pairs and let someone know where they are planning to go.

Hitching is not very practical in Ecuador for three reasons: there are few private cars, public transportation is relatively cheap and trucks are used as public transportation in remote areas, so trying to hitch a free ride on one is the same as trying to hitch a free ride on a bus. Many drivers of *any* vehicle will pick you up but will also expect payment, which is usually minimal.

LOCAL TRANSPORTATION

Bus

Local buses are usually slow and crowded, but they are also very cheap. You can get around most towns for $0.20 to $0.25. Local buses often travel to nearby villages, and riding along is a good, inexpensive way to see the area.

Outside of Quito, the concept of a fixed bus stop is pretty much nonexistent. Buses stop (or at least come to a slow roll) when people flag them down. When you want to get off a local bus, yell '¡Baja!,' which means 'Down!' (as in 'the passenger is getting down'). Another favorite way of getting the driver to stop is by yelling '¡Gracias!' ('Thank you!') which is unmistakably polite.

Taxi

Ecuadorian taxis come in a variety of shapes and sizes, but they are all yellow. Most taxis have a lit 'taxi' sign on top or a 'taxi' sticker in the windshield. Taxis often belong to cooperatives; the name and telephone number of the cooperative is usually printed on the door.

Always ask the fare beforehand, or you'll be overcharged more often than not. Meters are rarely seen, except in Quito, where they are obligatory. For variations on the use of the taxi meter in Quito, see p107. A long ride in a large city such as Quito or Guayaquil shouldn't go over $4. The minimum fare nearly everywhere is $1, and will be required to pay $1 in Quito even if the meter only says $0.80. Fares from international airports (Quito and Guayaquil) can be exorbitantly high if you're not careful. See those towns for tips on how to avoid getting burned. On weekends and at night, fares are always about 25% to 50% higher. Taxis can be hard to flag down during rush hours.

You can hire a taxi for a day for about $40 to $60. Hiring a taxi for a few days is comparable to renting a car, except that you don't have to drive. But you will have to pay for the driver's food and room. Some tour companies in Quito rent 4WD vehicles with experienced drivers.

Tricycle Taxi

The closest thing to a bicycle when it comes to local public transportation is a tricycle with a covered seat on the back. These tricycle taxis are pedaled by local entrepreneurs in a few coastal towns, most notably Muisne (p284). Keenly exploiting the complexes of foreigners, tricycle owners refer to their vehicles as 'ecotaxis,' and they're certainly correct.

Trucks

In certain towns, especially in rural areas where there are many dirt roads, pickup trucks act as taxis. If you need to get to a national park, a climbers' refuge or a trailhead from a town, often the best way to do so is hiring a pickup, which is usually as easy as asking around.

TOURS

Whether you can stomach the idea or not, there are a great many places in Ecuador that are accessible only by taking an organized tour. This is not necessarily a bad thing – in fact, you end up learning a lot from a good guide. You don't always have to put up with strangers either; some tour operators, particularly those offering climbing, horseback-riding or trekking tours, will send out a guide for as few as two people. Usually, however, the more people you can get to go with you, the cheaper the per-person rates will be.

If you're short on time, the best place to organize a tour is Quito. A plethora of operators in the capital offer trips including Galápagos cruises, climbing and trekking tours, horseback riding, jungle tours, mountain-biking tours, hacienda tours, tours to major cities – you name it. There's something on offer for every budget and every taste.

It was once cheapest to book a tour close to where you will be touring, and this is occasionally still true. For example, some travelers try to arrange a tour in the Galápagos from Puerto Ayora or Puerto Baquerizo Moreno or to the Oriente from Misahuallí or Coca. You may get lucky, but you may also face several problems. During the Galápagos' high seasons, many boats are full and it may be difficult to find one available. During the low seasons (and at anytime in the Oriente), it may take several days to get a group of people together who are interested in doing the same thing. In the Oriente, the great majority of local guides now work for companies operating out of Quito, which means they're hard to find. But again, it's possible. You just have to allow yourself plenty of time to hang around to make it work. Towns throughout Ecuador have tour operators, and they usually cost about the same as trips sold in Quito.

The upside of going to a town in the Oriente and setting something up there is that you get a more local experience and you get to spend some time (for better or worse) in the jungle towns themselves, rather than just rushing through.

Tour costs vary tremendously depending on what your requirements are. The cheapest camping jungle tour can be as low as $40 per person, per day, while the most expensive lodges can be $200 per person per night, including all meals and tours. Climbs of the volcanoes average about $160 per person for a two-day climb. Galápagos boat cruises range from $700 to over $3000 per week, excluding air fare, taxes and entrance fees. Day tours out of Quito range from $25 to $80 per person per day.

See p355 and p227 for more general information on tours in those areas. For a list of operators in Quito, see p89.

TRAIN

Ecuador's rail system is now extremely limited and consists primarily of two tourist trains. The most famous is the dramatic descent from Alausí along La Nariz del Diablo (The Devil's Nose; see the boxed text, p186), a spectacular section of train track that was one of the world's greatest feats of railroad engineering. The second is the weekend train excursion between Quito and the Area de Recreación El Boliche, near Cotopaxi (see p106 and p150). Passengers are allowed to ride on the roof of some cars, and these are very popular trips.

Reservations are generally not necessary for the El Boliche run. For the Devil's Nose ride, you can buy your tickets a day in advance from the train station in Riobamba. There's one class – roof class. Well, you can ride inside if you really want.

TRUCKS

In remote areas, trucks often double as buses. Sometimes these are large, flatbed trucks with a tin roof, open wooden sides and uncomfortable wooden-plank seats. These curious-looking 'buses' are called rancheras or *chivas,* and are seen on the coast and in the Oriente. If you get an outside seat, they're actually a blast, provided you're not going *too* far.

In the remote parts of the highlands, *camionetas* (ordinary trucks or pickups) are used to carry passengers; you just climb in the back. If the weather is good, you get fabulous views and the refreshing sensation of Andean wind in your face. If the weather is bad, you hunker down beneath a tarpaulin with the other passengers. These rides are certainly far from comfortable, but are some of the most interesting (not to mention fun) experiences you'll have in Ecuador.

Payment for these rides is usually determined by the driver and is a standard fare depending on the distance. You can ask other passengers how much they are paying; usually you'll find that the trucks double as buses and charge almost as much.

TRANSPORTATION

Health David Goldberg, MD

CONTENTS

Before You Go 412
Insurance 412
Recommended Vaccinations 413
Medical Checklist 413
Internet Resources 413
In Transit 413
Deep Vein Thrombosis (DVT) 413
Jet Lag & Motion Sickness 413
In Ecuador 414
Availability & Cost of Health Care 414
Infectious Diseases 414
Traveler's Diarrhea 416
Environmental Hazards 416
Traveling with Children 417
Women's Health 417

Your health depends on your predeparture preparations, your daily health care while traveling and how you handle any medical

problem that does develop. While the potential dangers can seem quite frightening, in reality, few travelers experience anything more than an upset stomach.

BEFORE YOU GO

Make sure you're healthy before traveling. If going on a long trip, make sure your teeth are OK. If you wear glasses, take a spare pair and your prescription.

If you require a particular medication, take an adequate supply, as it may not be available locally. Know the generic name, as well as the brand, to make getting replacements easier. To avoid problems, have a legible prescription or letter from your doctor to show that you legally use the medication.

INSURANCE

Make sure that you have adequate health insurance. See p391.

IMMUNIZATIONS

Although no vaccines are legally mandated, a number are strongly recommended:

Vaccine	Recommended for	Dosage	Side effects
chickenpox	travelers who've never had chickenpox	2 doses 1 month apart	fever; mild case of chickenpox
hepatitis A	all travelers	1 dose before trip; booster 6-12 months later	soreness at injection site; headaches; body aches
hepatitis B	long-term travelers in close contact with the local population	3 doses over a 6-month period	soreness at injection site; low-grade fever
measles	travelers born after 1956 who've had only 1 measles vaccination	1 dose	fever; rash; joint pains; allergic reactions
rabies	travelers who may have contact with animals & may not have access to medical care	3 doses over 3-4 weeks	soreness at injection site; . headaches; body aches
tetanus-diphtheria	all travelers who haven't had booster within 10 years	1 dose lasts 10 years	soreness at injection site
typhoid	all travelers	4 capsules by mouth, 1 taken every other day	abdominal pain; nausea; rash
yellow fever	all travelers	1 dose lasts 10 years	headaches; body aches; severe reactions are rare

RECOMMENDED VACCINATIONS

Plan ahead for getting your vaccinations: some require several injections, and some vaccinations should not be given together or should be avoided during pregnancy and by people with allergies – discuss this with your doctor at least six weeks before travel. Be aware that there is often a greater risk of disease for children and pregnant women.

MEDICAL CHECKLIST

Give some thought to a medical kit for your trip, particularly if you're going far off the beaten track.

It's not necessary to take every remedy for every illness you might contract during your trip. Ecuadorian pharmacies stock all kinds of drugs, and medication can be cheaper than in other counties. Almost everything is sold over the counter. Be sure to check expiry dates.

- antibiotics
- antidiarrheal drugs (eg loperamide)
- acetaminophen (Tylenol) or aspirin
- anti-inflammatory drugs (eg ibuprofen)
- antihistamines (for hay fever and allergic reactions)
- antibacterial ointment (eg Bactroban; for cuts and abrasions)
- steroid cream or cortisone (for poison ivy and other allergic rashes)
- bandages, gauze
- adhesive or paper tape
- scissors, safety pins, tweezers
- thermometer
- pocketknife
- DEET-containing insect repellent for the skin
- permethrin-containing insect spray for clothing, tents and bed nets
- sun block
- oral rehydration salts
- iodine tablets (for water purification)
- syringes and sterile needles
- acetazolamide (Diamox; to help with altitude sickness)

INTERNET RESOURCES

There are some excellent travel-health sites that can be found on the Internet. From the Lonely Planet home page, there are links at www.lonelyplanet.com/weblinks/wlheal. htm to both the World Health Organization and the US Center for Disease Control and Prevention.

> **THE MAN SAYS...**
>
> It's usually a good idea to consult your government's travel health website before departure (if one is available):
>
> ■ **Australia** (www.dfat.gov.au/travel/)
> ■ **Canada** (www.travelhealth.gc.ca)
> ■ **UK** (www.doh.gov.uk/traveladvice/)
> ■ **USA** (www.cdc.gov/travel/)

IN TRANSIT

DEEP VEIN THROMBOSIS (DVT)

Blood clots may form in the legs (deep vein thrombosis) during long plane flights, chiefly because of prolonged immobility. Though most blood clots are reabsorbed uneventfully, some may break off and travel through the blood vessels to the lungs, where they could cause life-threatening complications.

The chief symptom of DVT is swelling or pain of the foot, ankle or calf, usually but not always on just one side. When a blood clot travels to the lungs, it may cause chest pain and some difficulties in breathing.

To prevent the development of DVT on long flights you should walk about the cabin, perform isometric compressions of the leg muscles (ie contract the leg muscles while sitting), drink plenty of fluids and avoid alcohol.

JET LAG & MOTION SICKNESS

Jet lag is common when crossing more than five time zones and usually results in insomnia, fatigue, malaise or nausea. To avoid jet lag make sure to drink plenty of fluids (nonalcoholic) and by eating light meals. Upon arrival, be sure to get exposure to natural sunlight and readjust your schedule (as for meals, sleep etc) as soon as possible.

Antihistamines such as dimenhydrinate (Dramamine) and meclizine (Antivert, Bonine) are usually the first choice for treating motion sickness. Their main side-effect is drowsiness. Ginger is a good herbal alternative, which works like a charm for some people.

HEALTH

FOLK REMEDIES

Problem	Treatment
altitude sickness	gingko
jet lag	melatonin
motion sickness	ginger
mosquito bite prevention	oil of eucalyptus

IN ECUADOR

AVAILABILITY & COST OF HEALTH CARE

Medical care is available in major cities, but may be difficult to find in rural areas. Most doctors and hospitals will expect payment in cash, regardless of whether you have travel health insurance. If you develop a life-threatening medical problem, you'll want to be evacuated to a country with state-of-the-art medical care. Since this may cost tens of thousands of dollars, be sure you have insurance to cover this before you depart. Pharmacies in Ecuador are known as *farmacias*.

INFECTIOUS DISEASES

Cholera

This is the worst of the watery diarrheas, and medical help should be sought. Outbreaks of cholera are generally widely reported, so you can avoid such problem areas. Fluid replacement is the most vital treatment – the risk of dehydration is severe, as you may lose up to 20L a day. If there is a delay in getting to a hospital, then begin taking tetracycline. The adult dose is 250mg four times daily. Tetracycline is not recommended for children under the age of nine or for pregnant women. Tetracycline may help shorten the illness, but adequate fluids are required to save lives.

Dengue

This viral disease is transmitted by mosquitoes and is fast becoming one of the top public-health problems in the tropical world. Unlike the malaria mosquito, the *Aedes aegypti* mosquito, which transmits the dengue virus, is most active during the day and is found mainly in urban areas, in and around human dwellings.

Signs and symptoms of dengue fever include a sudden onset of high fever, headache, joint and muscle pains (hence its old name, 'breakbone fever'), and nausea and vomiting. A rash of small red spots sometimes appears three to four days after the onset of fever. In the early phase of illness, dengue fever may be mistaken for other infectious diseases, including malaria and influenza. You should seek medical attention as soon as possible if you think you may be infected.

Hepatitis A

Hepatitis A is the second most common travel-related infection (after traveler's diarrhea). It's a viral infection of the liver that's usually acquired by ingestion of contaminated water, food or ice, as well as through direct contact with infected persons. The illness occurs throughout the world, but the incidence is higher in developing nations. Symptoms may include fever, malaise, jaundice, nausea, vomiting and abdominal pain. Most cases resolve without complications, though hepatitis A occasionally causes severe liver damage. There is no treatment.

The vaccine for hepatitis A is safe and highly effective. If you get a booster six to 12 months later, it lasts for at least 10 years. Because the safety of hepatitis A vaccine has not been established for pregnant women or children under age two, they should instead be given a gamma globulin injection.

Hepatitis B

Like hepatitis A, hepatitis B is a liver infection that occurs worldwide but is more common in developing nations. Unlike hepatitis A, the disease is usually acquired by sexual contact or by exposure to infected blood, generally through blood transfusions or contaminated needles. The vaccine is recommended only for long-term travelers (on the road more than six months) who expect to live in rural areas or have close physical contact with the local population.

Hepatitis B vaccine is safe and highly effective. However, a total of three injections are necessary to establish full immunity. Several countries added hepatitis B vaccine to the list of routine childhood immunizations in the 1980s, so many young adults are already protected.

HIV & AIDS

Infection with the human immunodeficiency virus (HIV) may lead to acquired immune deficiency syndrome (AIDS), which is a fatal disease. Any exposure to contaminated blood, blood products or body fluids may put the individual at risk. The disease is often transmitted through sexual contact or dirty needles – vaccinations, acupuncture, tattooing and body piercing can be potentially as dangerous as intravenous drug use. HIV/AIDS can also be spread through infected blood transfusions; Ecuador's best clinics screen their blood supply. If you do need an injection, ask to see the syringe unwrapped in front of you, or take a needle and syringe pack with you.

Leishmaniasis

This is a group of parasitic diseases transmitted by sandflies. Cutaneous leishmaniasis affects the skin tissue, causing ulceration and disfigurement, and visceral leishmaniasis affects the internal organs. Seek medical advice, as laboratory testing is required for diagnosis and correct treatment. Avoiding sandfly bites is the best precaution. Bites are usually painless but itchy. Cover up and use insect repellant.

Malaria

Malaria is transmitted by mosquito bites, usually between dusk and dawn. The main symptom is high spiking fevers, often accompanied by chills, sweats, headache, body aches, weakness, vomiting or diarrhea. Severe cases may involve the central nervous system and lead to seizures, confusion, coma and death.

Taking malaria pills is recommended for all rural areas below 1500m. Risk is highest along the northernmost coast and in the northern Oriente. There is no malaria risk in the highlands.

There is a choice of three malaria pills, all of which work about equally well. Mefloquine (Lariam) is taken once weekly, starting one to two weeks before arrival and continuing through the trip and for four weeks after return. The problem is that a certain percentage of people develop neuropsychiatric side effects, which may range from mild to severe. Atovaquone/proguanil (Malarone) is a newly approved combination pill taken once daily with food starting two days before arrival and continuing through the trip and for seven days after departure. Side effects are typically mild.

Doxycycline is a third alternative, but may cause an exaggerated sunburn reaction.

In general, Malarone seems to cause fewer side-effects than mefloquine and is becoming more popular. The chief disadvantage is that it has to be taken daily.

Protecting yourself against mosquito bites is just as important as taking malaria pills, since none of the pills are 100% effective.

If you do not have access to medical care while traveling, you should bring along additional pills for emergency self-treatment, which you should take if you can't reach a doctor and you develop symptoms that suggest malaria, such as high spiking fevers. One option is to take four tablets of Malarone once daily for three days. However, Malarone should not be used for treatment if you're already taking it for prevention.

If you develop a fever after returning home, see a physician, as malaria symptoms may not occur for months.

Rabies

This viral infection is fatal. Many animals can be infected (dogs, cats, bats and monkeys etc), and it is their saliva that is infectious. Any bite, scratch or even lick from an animal should be cleaned immediately and thoroughly. Scrub with soap and running water, and then apply alcohol or iodine solution. Medical help should be sought promptly to receive a course of injections to prevent the onset of symptoms and/or death.

Sexually Transmitted Diseases

Sexual contact with an infected partner can result in you contracting a number of diseases. While abstinence is the only 100% effective prevention, the use of condoms lessens the risk of infection considerably.

The most common sexually transmitted diseases are gonorrhoea and syphilis, which in men first appear as sores, blisters or rashes around the genitals and a discharge or pain when urinating. Symptoms may be less marked or not present at all in women. Syphilis symptoms eventually disappear, but the disease continues and may cause severe problems in later years. Gonorrhoea and syphilis are treatable with antibiotics.

Tetanus

This disease is caused by a germ that lives in soil and in the feces of horses and other animals. It enters the body via breaks in the skin. The first symptom may be discomfort in swallowing, or a stiffening of the jaw and neck; this is followed by painful convulsions of the jaw and whole body. The disease can be fatal. It can be prevented by vaccination.

Typhoid

A dangerous gut infection, typhoid fever is caused by contaminated water and food. Medical help must be sought.

In its early stages, sufferers may feel they have a bad cold or flu on the way, as initial symptoms are a headache, body aches and a fever that rises a little each day until it is around 40°C (104°F) or more. The victim's pulse is often slow relative to the degree of fever present – unlike a normal fever, during which the pulse increases. There may also be vomiting, abdominal pain, diarrhea or constipation.

In the second week, the high fever and slow pulse continue, and a few pink spots may appear on the body; trembling, delirium, weakness, weight loss and dehydration may occur. Complications such as pneumonia or perforated bowel may occur.

Typhus

This is spread by ticks, mites and lice. It begins as a severe cold followed by a fever, chills, headaches, muscle pains and a body rash. There is often a large and painful sore at the site of the bite, and nearby lymph nodes become swollen and painful.

Yellow Fever

This viral disease is endemic in South America and is transmitted by mosquitoes. The initial symptoms are fever, headache, abdominal pain and vomiting. Seek medical care urgently and drink lots of fluids.

TRAVELER'S DIARRHEA

To prevent diarrhea, avoid tap water unless it has been boiled, filtered or chemically disinfected (iodine tablets); only eat fresh fruits or vegetables if cooked or peeled; be wary of dairy products that might contain unpasteurized milk; and be highly selective when eating food from street vendors.

If you develop diarrhea, be sure to drink plenty of fluids, preferably an oral rehydration solution containing lots of salt and sugar. A few loose stools don't require treatment but, if you have more than four or five stools a day, you should start taking an antibiotic (usually a quinolone drug) and an antidiarrheal agent (such as loperamide). If diarrhea is bloody or persists for more than 72 hours or is accompanied by fever, shaking chills or severe abdominal pain you should seek medical attention.

ENVIRONMENTAL HAZARDS
Altitude Sickness

Altitude sickness may develop in travelers who ascend rapidly to altitudes greater than 2500m, including those flying directly to Quito. Being physically fit does not in any way lessen your risk of altitude sickness. Symptoms may include headaches, nausea, vomiting, dizziness, malaise, insomnia and loss of appetite. Severe cases may be complicated by fluid in the lungs (high-altitude pulmonary edema) or swelling of the brain (high-altitude cerebral edema). Most deaths are caused by high-altitude pulmonary edema.

The standard medication to prevent altitude sickness is a mild diuretic called acetazolamide (Diamox), which should be started 24 hours before ascent and continued for 48 hours after arrival at altitude. Possible side effects include increased urination, numbness, tingling, nausea, drowsiness, nearsightedness and temporary impotence. For those who cannot tolerate acetazolamide, most physicians prescribe dexamethasone, which is a type of steroid. A natural alternative is gingko, which some people find quite helpful. The usual dosage is 100mg twice daily.

To lessen the chance of getting altitude sickness, you should also be sure to ascend gradually or by increments to higher altitudes, avoid overexertion, eat light meals and avoid alcohol.

If you or any of your companions show any symptoms of altitude sickness, you should be sure not to ascend to a higher altitude until the symptoms have cleared. If the symptoms become worse, immediately descend to a lower altitude. Acetazolamide and dexamethasone may be used to treat altitude sickness as well as prevent it.

Hypothermia

If you are trekking at high altitudes, be prepared. Symptoms of hypothermia are exhaustion, numb skin (particularly in the toes and fingers), shivering, slurred speech, irrational or violent behavior, lethargy, stumbling, dizzy spells, muscle cramps and violent bursts of energy. To treat mild hypothermia, first get the victims out of the wind and/or rain, remove their clothing if it is wet and replace it with dry, warm clothing. Give them hot liquids – not alcohol – and some high-energy, easily digestible food. Do not rub victims; instead, allow them to slowly warm themselves.

Parasites

Intestinal worms are most common in rural, tropical areas. Some worms, such as tapeworms, may be ingested by eating food such as undercooked meat, and some, such as hookworms, enter through your skin. Infestations may not show up for some time, and although they are generally not serious, if left untreated, some can cause severe health problems later. Consider having a stool test when you return home to check for these.

You should always check all over your body if you have been walking through a potentially tick-infested area, as ticks can cause skin infections and other, more serious, diseases.

Snakes

To minimize your chances of being bitten, always wear boots, socks and long trousers when walking through undergrowth where snakes may be present. Don't put your hands into holes and crevices, and be careful when collecting firewood.

Snakebites do not cause instantaneous death, and antivenins are usually available. Immediately wrap the bitten limb tightly, as you would for a sprained ankle, and then attach a splint to immobilize it. Keep the victim still and seek medical help, bringing the dead snake, if possible, for identification. Don't attempt to catch the snake if there is a possibility of being bitten again. Tourniquets and sucking out the poison are now comprehensively discredited.

Water & Sun

The number one rule is *be careful drinking the water*. If you don't know for certain that the water is safe, assume the worst. Take care with fruit juice, particularly if water may have been added. Tea or coffee should also be OK, since the water should have been boiled. At altitudes greater than 2000m (6500ft), boil water for three minutes. Another option is to disinfect water with iodine pills.

In the tropics or at high altitudes you can get sunburned surprisingly quickly, even through cloud cover. Use sunscreen, a hat and a barrier cream for your nose and lips. Calamine lotion or a commercial after-sun preparation are good for mild sunburn. Protect your eyes with good-quality sunglasses, particularly if you will be near water, sand or snow.

TRAVELING WITH CHILDREN

Travel with Children, by Cathy Lanigan, includes advice on travel health for younger children.

WOMEN'S HEALTH

Antibiotic use, synthetic underwear, sweating and contraceptive pills can lead to fungal vaginal infections when traveling in hot climates. Maintaining good personal hygiene, and loose-fitting clothes and cotton underwear will help to prevent these.

Women who are pregnant need to take special care on the road. Most miscarriages occur during the first three months of pregnancy, so this is the most risky time to travel. The last three months should also be spent within reasonable reach of good medical care because serious problems can develop at this stage. Pregnant women should avoid all unnecessary medication, but vaccinations and malarial prophylactics should still be taken when possible.

Birth control pills are readily available at pharmacies throughout Ecuador.

Tampons are harder to come by than pads (which are readily available), so bring your preferred brand from home if you use the former.

Language

CONTENTS

Phrasebooks & Dictionaries	418
Ecuadorian Spanish	419
Pronunciation	419
Gender & Plurals	419
Accommodations	419
Conversation & Essentials	420
Directions	420
Emergencies	421
Health	421
Language Difficulties	421
Numbers	421
Shopping & Services	422
Time & Dates	422
Transport	423
Travel with Children	424

Spanish is the official language of Ecuador, however, travelers to the region will encounter a mix of other European tongues, indigenous languages and colorful dialects.

Most Indigenous groups are bilingual, with Quichua (known as Quechua in Peru) being their mother tongue and Spanish their second language. There are also several small lowland groups that speak their own languages. The Quichua spoken in Ecuador is quite different from that spoken in Peru and Bolivia, so it can be difficult for highland natives from these countries to communicate easily. It's rare to encounter indigenous people who understand no Spanish at all, although they certainly exist in the more remote communities.

The basic elements of Spanish are easy to pick up, and a month-long language course taken before departure can go a long way toward facilitating communication and comfort on the road. Travelers who make the effort to learn a few basic phrases and pleasantries are met with enthusiasm and appreciation.

PHRASEBOOKS & DICTIONARIES

Lonely Planet's compact *Latin American Spanish Phrasebook* is an excellent addition

---

QUICHUA

The following list of words and phrases is obviously minimal, but it could be useful in areas where Ecuadorian Quichua is spoken. Pronounce them as you would a Spanish word. An apostrophe represents a glottal stop, which is the 'non-sound' that occurs in the middle of 'uh-oh.'

Hello.	Napaykullayki.
Please.	Allichu.
Thank you.	Yusulipayki.
Yes/No.	Ari/Mana.
How do you say ...?	Imainata nincha chaita ...?
It is called ...	Chaipa'g sutin'ha ...
Please repeat.	Ua'manta niway.
How much?	Maik'ata'g?
father	tayta
food	mikiuy
mother	mama
river	mayu
snowy peak	riti-orko
water	yacu

1	u'
2	iskai
3	quinsa
4	tahua
5	phiska
6	so'gta
7	khanchis
8	pusa'g
9	iskon
10	chunca

---

to your backpack. Another very useful resource is the University of Chicago *Spanish-English, English-Spanish Dictionary* – with its small size, light weight and thorough entries, it's ideal for use when traveling. Upon your departure it can also make a welcome gift for any newfound friends.

Lonely Planet's *Quechua Phrasebook* is based on the Cuzco variety of the language (southern Quichua), but can still be useful in getting your basic message across, and any attempts to speak Quichua in Ecuador will be greatly appreciated. See the Quichua box above for a few Quichua basics.

ECUADORIAN SPANISH

The Spanish of Ecuador sounds different from the Spanish of Spain and it includes regional vocabulary, much of which is derived from indigenous languages. Throughout Latin America, the Spanish language is referred to as *castellano* more often than *español*. Unlike in Spain, the plural of the familiar 'you' *(tú)* is *ustedes* rather than *vosotros*; the latter term will sound quaint and archaic in the Americas. In addition, the letters **c** and **z** are never lisped in Latin America; attempts to do so could well provoke amusement or even contempt.

PRONUNCIATION

Pronunciation of Spanish is not difficult. Many Spanish sounds are similar to their English counterparts, and the relationship between pronunciation and spelling is clear and consistent. Unless otherwise indicated, the English examples used below take standard American pronunciation.

Vowels & Diphthongs

a	as in 'father'
e	as in 'met'
i	as the 'i' in 'police'
o	as in British English 'hot'
u	as the 'u' in 'rude'
ai	as in 'aisle'
au	as the 'ow' in 'how'
ei	as in 'vein'
ia	as the 'ya' in 'yard'
ie	as the 'ye' in 'yes'
oi	as in 'coin'
ua	as the 'wa' in 'wash'
ue	as the 'we' in 'well'

Consonants

Spanish consonants are generally the same as in English, with the exception of those listed below.

The consonants **ch**, **ll** and **ñ** are generally considered distinct letters, but in dictionaries **ch** and **ll** are now often listed alphabetically under **c** and **l** respectively. The letter **ñ** still has a separate entry after **n** in alphabetical listings.

b	similar to English 'b,' but softer; referred to as 'b larga'
c	as in 'celery' before **e** and **i**; elsewhere as the 'k' in 'king'
ch	as in 'choose'
d	as in 'dog'; between vowels and after **l** or **n**, it's closer to the 'th' in 'this'
g	as the 'ch' in the Scottish *loch* before **e** and **i** ('kh' in our pronunciation guides); elsewhere, as in 'go'
h	invariably silent
j	as the 'ch' in the Scottish *loch* ('kh' in our pronunciation guides)
ll	as the 'y' in 'yellow'
ñ	as the 'ni' in 'onion'
r	as in 'run,' but strongly rolled
rr	very strongly rolled
v	similar to English 'b,' but softer; referred to as 'b corta'
x	usually pronounced as **j** above; as in 'taxi' in other instances
z	as the 's' in 'sun'

Word Stress

In general, words ending in vowels or the letters **n** or **s** are stressed on the second-last syllable, while those with other endings have stress on the last syllable. Thus *vaca* (cow) and *caballos* (horses) are both stressed on the next-to-last syllable, while *ciudad* (city) and *infeliz* (unhappy) are stressed on the last syllable.

Written accents generally indicate words that don't follow the rules above, eg *sótano* (basement), *América* and *porción* (portion).

GENDER & PLURALS

Spanish nouns are either masculine or feminine, and there are ways to help determine gender (there are of course some exceptions). Feminine nouns generally end with **-a** or with the groups **-ción**, **-sión** or **-dad**. Other endings typically signify a masculine noun. Endings for adjectives also change to agree with the gender of the noun they modify (masculine/feminine singular **-o/-a**). Where both masculine and feminine forms are included in this language guide, they are separated by a slash, with the masculine form first, eg *perdido/a* (lost).

If a noun or adjective ends in a vowel, the plural is formed by adding **s** to the end. If it ends in a consonant, the plural is formed by adding **es** to the end.

ACCOMMODATIONS

Are there any rooms available?

¿Hay habitaciones libres?	ay a·bee·ta·*syon*·es *lee*·bres

I'm looking for ...
Estoy buscando ... e-stoy boos-kan-do ...
Where is ...?
¿Dónde hay ...? don-de ai ...
  a hotel
  un hotel oon o-tel
  a boarding house
  una pensión oo-na pen-syon
  a youth hostel
  un albergue juvenil oon al-ber-gekhoo-ve-neel

MAKING A RESERVATION

(for phone or written requests)

To ...	A ...
From ...	De ...
Date	Fecha
I'd like to book ...	Quisiera reservar ...
	(see the list under
	'Accommodations' for bed
	and room options)
in the name of ...	en nombre de ...
for the nights of ...	para las noches del ...
credit card ...	tarjeta de crédito ...
number	número
expiry date	fecha de vencimiento
Please confirm ...	Puede confirmar ...
availability	la disponibilidad
price	el precio

I'd like a ... *Quisiera una* kee-sye-ra oo-na
room. *habitación ...* a-bee-ta-syon ...
  double *doble* do-ble
  single *individual* een-dee-bee-dwal
  twin *con dos camas* kon dos ka-mas

How much is it *¿Cuánto cuesta* kwan-to kwes-ta
per ...? *por ...?* por ...
  night *noche* no-che
  person *persona* per-so-na
  week *semana* se-ma-na

private/shared *baño privado/* ba-nyo pree-va-do/
  bathroom *compartido* kom-par-tee-do
full board *pensión* pen-syon
  completa kom-ple-ta
too expensive *demasiado caro* de-ma-sya-do ka-ro
cheaper *más económico* mas e-ko-no-mee-ko
discount *descuento* des-kwen-to

May I see the *¿Puedo ver la* pwe-do ver la
  room? *habitación?* a-bee-ta-syon

Does it include breakfast?
¿Incluye el desayuno? een-kloo-ye el de-sa-yoo-no
I don't like it.
No me gusta. no me goos-ta
It's fine. I'll take it.
OK. La alquilo. o-kay la al-kee-lo
I'm leaving now.
Me voy ahora. me voy a-o-ra

CONVERSATION & ESSENTIALS

Hello. *Hola.* o-la
Good morning. *Buenos días.* bwe-nos dee-as
Good afternoon. *Buenas tardes.* bwe-nas tar-des
Good evening/ *Buenas noches.* bwe-nas no-ches
night.
Bye/See you soon. *Hasta luego.* as-ta lwe-go
Yes. *Sí.* see
No. *No.* no
Please. *Por favor.* por fa-vor
Thank you. *Gracias.* gra-syas
Many thanks. *Muchas gracias.* moo-chas gra-syas
You're welcome. *De nada.* de na-da
Pardon me. *Perdón.* per-don
Excuse me. *Permiso.* per-mee-so
  (used when asking permission)
Forgive me. *Disculpe.* dees-kool-pe
  (used when apologizing)

How are things?
¿Qué tal? ke tal
What's your name?
¿Cómo se llama? (pol) ko-mo se ya-ma
¿Cómo te llamas? (inf) ko-mo te ya-mas
My name is ...
Me llamo ... me ya-mo ...
It's a pleasure to meet you.
Mucho gusto. moo-cho goos-to
The pleasure is mine.
El gusto es mío. el goos-to es mee-o
Where are you from?
¿De dónde es? (pol) de don-de es
¿De dónde eres? (inf) de don-de er-es
I'm from ...
Soy de ... soy de ...
Where are you staying?
¿Dónde está alojado/a? (pol) don-de es-ta a-lo-kha-do/a
¿Dónde estás alojado/a? (inf) don-de es-tas a-lo-kha-do/a
May I take a photo?
¿Puedo sacar una foto? pwe-do sa-kar oo-na fo-to

DIRECTIONS

How do I get to ...?
¿Cómo puedo llegar a ...? ko-mo pwe-do ye-gar a ...
Is it far?
¿Está lejos? es-ta le-khos

EMERGENCIES

Help!	¡Socorro!	so·ko·ro
Fire!	¡Fuego!	fwe·go
Go away!	¡Déjeme!	de·khe·me
Get lost!	¡Váyase!	va·ya·se

Call ...!	¡Llame a ...!	ya·me a
an ambulance	una ambulancia	oo·na am·boo·lan·sya
a doctor	un médico	oon me·dee·ko
the police	la policía	la po·lee·see·a

It's an emergency.
Es una emergencia. es oo·na e·mer·khen·sya
Could you help me, please?
¿Me puede ayudar, me pwe·de a·yoo·dar
por favor? por fa·vor
I'm lost.
Estoy perdido/a. (m/f) es·toy per·dee·do/a
Where are the toilets?
¿Dónde están los baños? don·de es·tan los ba·nyos

Go straight ahead.
Siga derecho. see·ga de·re·cho
Turn left.
Voltée a la izquierda. vol·te·e a la ees·kyer·da
Turn right.
Voltée a la derecha. vol·te·e a la de·re·cha
Can you show me (on the map)?
¿Me lo podría indicar me lo po·dree·a een·dee·kar
(en el mapa)? (en el ma·pa)

north	norte	nor·te
south	sur	soor
east	este	es·te
west	oeste	o·es·te
here	aquí	a·kee
there	allí	a·yee
avenue	avenida	a·ve·nee·da
block	cuadra	kwa·dra
street	calle	ka·ye

HEALTH

I'm sick.
Estoy enfermo/a. es·toy en·fer·mo/a
I need a doctor.
Necesito un médico. ne·se·see·to oon me·dee·ko
Where's the hospital?
¿Dónde está el hospital? don·de es·ta el os·pee·tal
I'm pregnant.
Estoy embarazada. es·toy em·ba·ra·sa·da
I've been vaccinated.
Estoy vacunado/a. es·toy va·koo·na·do/a

I'm ...	Soy ...	soy ...
asthmatic	asmático/a	as·ma·tee·ko/a
diabetic	diabético/a	dee·ya·be·tee·ko/a
epileptic	epiléptico/a	e·pee·lep·tee·ko/a

I'm allergic	Soy alérgico/a	soy a·ler·khee·ko/a
to ...	a ...	a ...
antibiotics	los antibióticos	los an·tee·byo·tee·kos
nuts	las fruta secas	las froo·tas se·kas
penicillin	la penicilina	la pe·nee·see·lee·na

I have ...	Tengo ...	ten·go ...
a cough	tos	tos
diarrhea	diarrea	dya·re·a
a headache	un dolor de	oon do·lor de
	cabeza	ka·be·sa
nausea	náusea	now·se·a

LANGUAGE DIFFICULTIES

Do you speak (English)?
¿Habla/Hablas (inglés)? a·bla/a·blas (een·gles) (pol/inf)
Does anyone here speak English?
¿Hay alguien que hable ai al·gyen ke a·ble
inglés? een·gles
I (don't) understand.
(No) Entiendo. (no) en·tyen·do
How do you say ...?
¿Cómo se dice ...? ko·mo se dee·se ...
What does ... mean?
¿Qué quiere decir ...? ke kye·re de·seer ...

Could you	¿Puede ..., por	pwe·de ... por
please ...?	favor?	fa·vor
repeat that	repetirlo	re·pe·teer·lo
speak more	hablar más	a·blar mas
slowly	despacio	des·pa·syo
write it down	escribirlo	es·kree·beer·lo

NUMBERS

0	cero	ce·ro
1	uno/a	oo·no/a
2	dos	dos

3	tres	tres
4	cuatro	kwa·tro
5	cinco	seen·ko
6	seis	seys
7	siete	sye·te
8	ocho	o·cho
9	nueve	nwe·ve
10	diez	dyes
11	once	on·se
12	doce	do·se
13	trece	tre·se
14	catorce	ka·tor·se
15	quince	keen·se
16	dieciséis	dye·see·seys
17	diecisiete	dye·see·sye·te
18	dieciocho	dye·see·o·cho
19	diecinueve	dye·see·nwe·ve
20	veinte	vayn·te
21	veintiuno	vayn·tee·oo·no
30	treinta	trayn·ta
31	treinta y uno	trayn·tai oo·no
40	cuarenta	kwa·ren·ta
50	cincuenta	seen·kwen·ta
60	sesenta	se·sen·ta
70	setenta	se·ten·ta
80	ochenta	o·chen·ta
90	noventa	no·ven·ta
100	cien	syen
101	ciento uno	syen·to oo·no
200	doscientos	do·syen·tos
1000	mil	meel

SHOPPING & SERVICES

I'm looking for (the) ...   Estoy buscando ...   es·toy boos·kan·do

ATM	el cajero automático	el ka·khe·ro ow·to·ma·tee·ko
bank	el banco	el ban·ko
bookstore	la librería	la lee·bre·ree·a
embassy	la embajada	la em·ba·kha·da
exchange office	la casa de cambio	la ka·sa de kam·byo
general store	la tienda	la tyen·da
laundry	la lavandería	la la·van·de·ree·a
market	el mercado	el mer·ka·do
pharmacy	la farmacia/ la droguería	la far·ma·sya/ la dro·ge·ree·a
post office	los correos	los ko·re·os
supermarket	el supermercado	el soo·per·mer·ka·do
tourist office	la oficina de turismo	la o·fee·see·na de too·rees·mo

I'd like to buy ...
  Quisiera comprar ...   kee·sye·ra kom·prar ...

I'm just looking.
  Sólo estoy mirando.   so·lo es·toy mee·ran·do

May I look at it?
  ¿Puedo mirarlo?   pwe·do mee·rar·lo

How much is it?
  ¿Cuánto cuesta?   kwan·to kwes·ta

I don't like it.
  No me gusta.   no me goos·ta

That's too expensive for me.
  Es demasiado caro   es de·ma·sya·do ka·ro
    para mí.   pa·ra mee

Could you lower the price?
  ¿Podría bajar un poco   po·dree·a ba·khar oon po·ko
    el precio?   el pre·syo

I'll take it.
  Lo llevo.   lo ye·vo

less	menos	me·nos
more	más	mas
large	grande	gran·de
small	pequeño	pe·ke·nyo

Do you accept ...?	¿Aceptan ...?	a·sep·tan ...
credit cards	tarjetas de crédito	tar·khe·tas de kre·dee·to
traveler's checks	cheques de viajero	che·kes de vya·khe·ro

What time does it open/close?
  ¿A qué hora abre/cierra?   a ke o·ra a·bre/sye·ra

I want to change some money/traveler's checks.
  Quiero cambiar dinero/   kye·ro kam·byar dee·ne·ro/
  cheques de viajero.   che·kes de vya·khe·ro

What's the exchange rate?
  ¿Cuál es el tipo de   kwal es el tee·po de
    cambio?   kam·byo

I want to call ...
  Quiero llamar a ...   kye·ro ya·mar a ...

airmail	correo aéreo	ko·re·o a·e·re·o
letter	carta	kar·ta
registered mail	certificado	ser·tee·fee·ka·do
stamps	estampillas	es·tam·pee·yas

TIME & DATES

What time is it?	¿Qué hora es?	ke o·ra es
It's (one) o'clock.	Es la (una).	es la (oo·na)
It's (seven) o'clock.	Son las (siete).	son las (sye·te)
midnight	medianoche	me·dya·no·che
noon	mediodía	me·dyo·dee·a
half past two	dos y media	dos ee me·dya

now	ahora	a·o·ra
today	hoy	oy
tonight	esta noche	es·ta no·che
tomorrow	mañana	ma·nya·na
yesterday	ayer	a·yer
Monday	lunes	loo·nes
Tuesday	martes	mar·tes
Wednesday	miércoles	myer·ko·les
Thursday	jueves	khwe·ves
Friday	viernes	vyer·nes
Saturday	sábado	sa·ba·do
Sunday	domingo	do·meen·go
January	enero	e·ne·ro
February	febrero	fe·bre·ro
March	marzo	mar·so
April	abril	a·breel
May	mayo	ma·yo
June	junio	khoo·nyo
July	julio	khoo·lyo
August	agosto	a·gos·to
September	septiembre	sep·tyem·bre
October	octubre	ok·too·bre
November	noviembre	no·vyem·bre
December	diciembre	dee·syem·bre

TRANSPORT
Public Transport

What time does	¿A qué hora ...	a ke o·ra ...
... leave/arrive?	sale/llega?	sa·le/ye·ga
the bus	el autobus	el ow·to·boos
the plane	el avión	el a·vyon
the ship	el barco	el bar·ko
airport	el aeropuerto	el a·e·ro·pwer·to
bus station	la estación de	la es·ta·syon de
	autobuses	ow·to·boo·ses
bus stop	la parada de	la pa·ra·da de
	autobuses	ow·to·boo·ses
luggage check	guardería/	gwar·de·ree·a/
room	equipaje	e·kee·pa·khe
ticket office	la boletería	la bo·le·te·ree·a

I'd like a ticket to ...
Quiero un boleto a ... kye·ro oon bo·le·to a ...
What's the fare to ...?
¿Cuánto cuesta hasta ...? kwan·to kwes·ta a·sta ...

student's (fare)	de estudiante	de es·too·dyan·te
1st class	primera clase	pree·me·ra kla·se
2nd class	segunda clase	se·goon·da kla·se
one-way	ida	ee·da
return	ida y vuelta	ee·da ee vwel·ta
taxi	taxi	tak·see

ROAD SIGNS

Acceso	Entrance
Aparcamiento	Parking
Ceda el Paso	Give Way
Despacio	Slow
Dirección Única	One-Way
Mantenga Su Derecha	Keep to the Right
No Adelantar/	No Passing
No Rebase	
Peaje	Toll
Peligro	Danger
Prohibido Aparcar/	No Parking
No Estacionar	
Prohibido el Paso	No Entry
Pare	Stop
Salida de Autopista	Exit Freeway

Private Transport

pickup (truck)	camioneta	ka·myo·ne·ta
truck	camión	ka·myon
hitchhike	hacer dedo	a·ser de·do
I'd like to hire	Quisiera	kee·sye·ra
a/an ...	alquilar ...	al·kee·lar ...
bicycle	una bicicleta	oo·na bee·see·kle·ta
car	un auto/	oon ow·to/
	un coche	oon ko·che
4WD	un todo terreno	oon to·do te·re·no
motorbike	una moto	oo·na mo·to

Is this the road to ...?
¿Se va a ... por se va a ... por
esta carretera? es·ta ka·re·te·ra
Where's a gas/petrol station?
¿Dónde hay una don·de ai oo·na
gasolinera? ga·so·lee·ne·ra
Please fill it up.
Lleno, por favor. ye·no por fa·vor
I'd like (10) gallons.
Quiero (diez) galones. kye·ro (dyes) ga·lo·nes

diesel	diesel	dee·sel
leaded (regular)	gasolina con	ga·so·lee·na kon
	plomo	plo·mo
gas/petrol	gasolina	ga·so·lee·na
unleaded	gasolina sin	ga·so·lee·na seen
	plomo	plo·mo

(How long) Can I park here?
¿(Por cuánto tiempo) (por kwan·to tyem·po)
Puedo aparcar aquí? pwe·do a·par·kar a·kee

Where do I pay?
¿Dónde se paga?   don·de se pa·ga
I need a mechanic.
Necesito un mecánico.   ne·se·see·to oon me·ka·nee·ko
The car has broken down in ...
El carro se ha averiado el ka·ro se a a·ve·rya·do
en ...   en ...
The motorbike won't start.
No arranca la moto.   no a·ran·ka la mo·to
I have a flat tire.
Tengo un pinchazo.   ten·go oon peen·cha·so
I've run out of gas/petrol.
Me quedé sin gasolina. me ke·de seen ga·so·lee·na
I've had an accident.
Tuve un accidente.   too·ve oon ak·see·den·te

TRAVEL WITH CHILDREN

I need ...   *Necesito ...*   ne·se·see·to ...
Do you have ...?   *¿Hay ...?*   ai ...
  a car baby seat
  un asiento de seguridad para bebés
  oon a·syen·to de se·goo·ree·da pa·ra be·bes
  a child-minding service
  un servicio de cuidado de niños
  oon ser·vee·syo de kwee·da·do de nee·nyos
  a children's menu
  una carta infantil
  oo·na kar·ta een·fan·teel

  a creche
  una guardería
  oo·na gwar·de·ree·a
  (disposable) diapers/nappies
  pañales (de usar y tirar)
  pa·nya·les de oo·sar ee tee·rar
  an (English-speaking) babysitter
  una niñera (que habla inglesa)
  oo·na nee·nye·ra (ke a·bla een·gle·sa)
  infant formula (milk)
  leche en polvo para bebés
  le·che en pol·vo pa·ra be·bes
  a highchair
  una trona
  oo·na tro·na
  a potty (toddler's portable toilet)
  una pelela
  oo·na pe·le·la
  a stroller
  un cochecito
  oon ko·che·see·to

Do you mind if I breast-feed here?
¿Le molesta que dé   le mo·les·ta ke de
de pecho aquí?   de pe·cho a·kee
Are children allowed?
¿Se admiten niños?   se ad·mee·ten nee·nyos

Also available from Lonely Planet:
Latin American Spanish Phrasebook

Glossary

For help translating eating- and drinking-related words and phrases, see p61.

abrazo – backslapping hug exchanged between men
AGAR – Asociación de Guías de Aguas Rapidas del Ecuador (Ecuadorian White-Water Guides Association)
aguardiente – sugarcane alcohol
apartado – post office box (also called *apdo*)
ASEC – Asociación Ecuatoriana de Ecoturismo (Ecuadorian Ecotourism Association)
ASEGUIM – Asociación Ecuatoriana de Guías de Montaña (Ecuadorian Mountain Guides Association)
autobus – large intercity bus; also called *bus grande*

balneario – literally 'spa', but any place where you can swim or soak
baño – bathroom or toilet
buseta – small intercity bus which usually has about 22 seats

cabañas – cabins found both on the coast and in the *Oriente*
camioneta – pickup or light truck
campesino – peasant
capitanía – port captain
casas de cambio – currency-exchange bureaus
casilla – post-office box
censo – temporary-residence cards
centros comerciales – often abbreviated to 'CC'; shopping centers
chiva – open-sided bus, or truck mounted with uncomfortably narrow bench seats; also called *ranchera*
colectivos – shared taxis
comedores – cheap restaurants
Conaie – Confederation of Indigenous Nationalities of Ecuador
cuartel – army barracks
curanderos – medicine men

endemic – species which breed only in one place – in the Galápagos Islands, for instance
entrada – entrance

FARC – Revolutionary Armed Forces of Colombia

guardaparque – park ranger

hostal – small and reasonably priced hotel; not a youth hostel
hostería – small hotel, which tends to be a midpriced country inn; often, but not always, found in rural areas

IGM – Instituto Geográfico Militar, the Ecuadorian government agency which produces topographic and other maps
indígena – indigenous person

kushma – knee-length smock worn by Cofan men

malecón – waterfront
mestizo – person of mixed indigenous and Spanish descent
migraciones – immigration offices
música folklórica – traditional Andean folk music
nevado – permanently glaciated or snow-capped mountain peak

pachamama – earth mother
Panamericana – Pan-American Highway, which is the main route joining Latin American countries with one another; it is called the Interamericana in some countries
panga – small boat used to ferry passengers, especially in the Galápagos Islands, but also on the rivers and lakes of the *Oriente* and along the coast
páramo – high-altitude Andean grasslands of Ecuador, which continue north into Colombia with relics in the highest parts of Costa Rica
parque nacional – national park
peña – bar or club featuring live folkloric music
pensión – boarding house or family-run lodging
playa – beach
pucarás – pre-Inca hill fortresses
puente – bridge

quinta – fine house or villa found in the countryside

ranchera – see *chiva*
refugios – mountain refuges
residencial – cheap hotel

salsoteca – (also salsateca) nightclub where dancing to salsa music is the main attraction
serranos – people from the highlands
shigra – small string bag
soroche – altitude sickness
SS.HH. – *servicios higiénicos*, or public toilets

tagua nut – from a palm tree grown in local forest; the 'nuts' are actually hard seeds that are carved into a variety of ornaments
terminal terrestre – central bus terminal for many different companies

Behind the Scenes

THIS BOOK

This 7th edition of *Ecuador & the Galápagos Islands* was written by Danny Palmerlee, Michael Grosberg and Carolyn McCarthy. Danny Palmerlee served as coordinating author, writing all the front and back chapters as well as the Quito, Central Highlands and Southern Highlands chapters. Michael Grosberg covered the South Coast and the Galápagos Islands chapters. Carolyn McCarthy researched and wrote the Northern Highlands, the Oriente and North Coast & Lowlands chapters. David Andrew contributed the Galápagos Wildlife chapter and Dr David Goldberg MD wrote the Health chapter. The 6th edition was written by Danny Palmerlee and Rob Rachowiecki. The first five editions were written by Rob Rachowiecki.

Commissioning Editor Kathleen Munnelly
Coordinating Editor Trent Holden
Coordinating Cartographer Emma McNicol
Coordinating Layout Designer Wibowo Rusli
Managing Cartographer Alison Lyall, Andrew Smith
Managing Editors Suzannah Shwer, Carolyn Boicos
Assisting Editors Pete Cruttenden
Assisting Cartographer Joshua Geoghegan
Proofreader Kate Evans
Cover Designer Jim Hsu
Colour Designer Jacqui Saunders
Project Manager Eoin Dunlevy
Language Content Coordinator Quentin Frayne

Thanks to Jessa Boanas-Dewes, Melanie Dankel, Sally Darmody, Jennye Garibaldi, Kate McDonald, Jessica Van-Dam, Celia Wood

THANKS
DANNY PALMERLEE

First and foremost I thank Aimee Sabri, my eternal partner in crime, who accompanied me on this trip (and down the road of write-up madness) and made the book possible in every way. You rock! As always, a huge thanks goes out to the folks at all the Ecuadorian tourist offices who fielded my barrage of seemingly mundane questions. Cristina Guerrero de Miranda at Quito's Corporación Metropolitana de Turismo went above and beyond anything I could have imagined, supplying me with loads of information and wonderful insights on *quiteño* culture. In Mindo, a big hug and many thanks to Mariela Tenorio and Tom Quesenberry for their help (keep up the great work, guys!). In Quito, thanks to Eran Hayoun of Hostería Papagayo and Mogge and Ely at Moggely climbing for lending friendly, helpful hands. Christine and the entire staff at SAE were extremely helpful and welcoming. Thanks to Michele and Andy in Chugchilán for their warm assistance. On the LP front, a round of beers and cheers (if we ever end up in the same country) to my co-authors Michael and Carolyn, to cartographer Alison Lyall and to our rockin' and always-available commissioning editor, Kathleen Munnelly.

MICHAEL GROSBERG

Gracias goes out to Harry Jiménez and Juan Carlos for sharing their knowledge of the Galápagos Islands and injecting humor into the tour; to Annie, Susan and April, three fellow boat passengers, for their efforts at restoring my frayed wardrobe; to

THE LONELY PLANET STORY

The story begins with a classic travel adventure: Tony and Maureen Wheeler's 1972 journey across Europe and Asia to Australia. There was no useful information about the overland trail then, so Tony and Maureen published the first Lonely Planet guidebook to meet a growing need.

From a kitchen table, Lonely Planet has grown to become the largest independent travel publisher in the world, with offices in Melbourne (Australia), Oakland (USA) and London (UK). Today Lonely Planet guidebooks cover the globe. There is an ever-growing list of books and information in a variety of media. Some things haven't changed. The main aim is still to make it possible for adventurous travelers to get out there – to explore and better understand the world.

At Lonely Planet we believe travelers can make a positive contribution to the countries they visit – if they respect their host communities and spend their money wisely. Every year 5% of company profit is donated to charities around the world.

Wail, Kate and Baheya MacNeil, three other boat companions, for their advice on Santa Cruz; to Doris J Welsh and Simon Heyes for sharing their knowledge and experience about travel in the Galápagos; to Francisco Gutierrez who provided transport and local knowledge about the area between Machala and the Peruvian border; to Bennett Zamoff for sharing his enthusiasm about Ecuador and to my niece Sashi.

CAROLYN MCCARTHY

They say the first time's a doozy. I couldn't have done the research without great people on the ground. *Muchos agradecimientos y saludos van a* Lupe De Heredia, Christine at South American Explorers, my Napo co-expeditioner Col. Luis Hernandez, Rodrigo Mora, Laura Barniak, Kevin, Raul and Patricia in Puerto López; Chris Canady in Puyo; Tom and Mariela in Mindo; Dorothy and the 'machine,' Carlos Cano and his family; José Elías Sánchez in Manta; David and Maryellen in Intag; Penti Baihua, Jarol Fernandez Vaca, Kirin the brujo, Tsunki Marcel Cajecai and Douglas McMeekin in the Oriente; Oeido and José Aguabil, Trent Blare; as well as Rosa Jordan, Oswaldo Muñoz, Dominic Hamilton, Jean Brown, Olmedo Moncayo, Alex García and the strangers I may never bump into again. My co-conspirators Danny Palmerlee, Michael Grosberg and Kathleen Munnelly guided me out of heaps of pickles. Thanks for your patience and advice. I am also indebted to the production team at Lonely Planet. Finally, my family and friends Judianne and Cathy Bérard deserve tremendous gratitude for everything.

OUR READERS
Many thanks to the travellers who used the last edition and wrote to us with helpful hints, useful advice and interesting anecdotes:

A Annika Achberger, Paul Adderley, Evelyn Aguilar, Sheela Ahluwalia, Sharifah Albukhary, Paolo Alessio, Henrik Almblad, Maria Alvarez Sanz, Veronika Ambertson, Julie Andersen, Frida Andrae, Margara Anhalzer, Julie Archer, Sharon Ashcroft, Chris Askew, Kate Attard, Mary & Fred Attick, Isabelle Auclair, Eric Avery **B** Hank Baca, Prisca Baeni, Veronica Bakker, Matt Bannister, David Barmettler, Vincent Barnes, Eileen Barnett, Denise Baron, Sam Barr, Katy Battrick, Helen Baumgartner, Tal Bechar, Charo Bellas, Virginia Berg, Janine Berger, Caryl Bergeron, Clark Bernard, Sarit & Alex Bernstein, David Berry, Lucas Binnenkade, Clint & Carly Blackbourn, David Bloch, Bert Bloemsma, Ken Blum, Arthur Blume, Christel Bockting, Ben Bogaerts, Hendrick Bohne, Philippa Boland, Karin Boon, Adi Borovich, Brenda Bosch, Jenny Bourquin, Carl Boyer, Nathalie Bridey, David Brierley, Chris Briggs, Sandy Brown, Victoria Buksbazen, Adam Burdick, Peter Burkett, Stefan

Burmeister, Mike Burrell, Bill Bushnell, Jane Bussmann, Sarah & Ernest Butler, Neil Buyers **C** Eduardo Caballero, Cristina Caprari, Louise & Kevin Carling, Danielle Carpenter, Gill Castle, Dan Cauley, Simon Cernuta, John Chadwin, Matthew Chell, Alexandra Chevrolet, Raffaele Chiacchia, Adam Clanton, Jeff Clewell, Diane Clifton, Michael Cohan, Philippa Collier, Ed Comber, Steve Cooper, Matthew Courtney, Samantha Cowen, Barry Cowperthwaite, Sebastian Crespo, Natasha Cridler **D** Whitney Dafoe, Jennifer Dahnke, Ana Dassum, Sian Davies, Anna Davison, Andrew de Courtenay, Richard de Laat, Marleen de Smet, Luca de Vincentis, Patrick Debouck, Rosemarijn & Joost Dekker, Franz Dellacasa, Marco Dello Sbarba, George Demosthenes, Liesbeth den Hartigh, Ingrid den Uijl, Ali Deneira, Kelly Dortmans, Tawnya Dozier, Dana Drake, Koen Dreijerink, Chris & Sally Drysdale, James Dunan, Bettina Dworschak **E** Henrik Ebne, Guy Edwards, Robert Ehlert, Michael Eiche, Anne Eller, Kathryn Elmer, Janet Elphick, Nina Elter, Rob Elze, Judit Emodi, Bethany Ericson, Sherry Essnaashari, Galo Estrada, Barbara Etter **F** Tarla Fallgatter, Jasper Feiner, Ross Ferguson, Joshua Feyen, Antoinette Figliola-Kaderli, Sharon Finch, Kathy Fisher, Lindsey Fitch, Michael Fleishman, Isabelle Fragniere, Karyne Framand, Nancy Frank, Gerald Frankl, Steve Franklin, Jam Fritz, Liese Fritze, Geert Froyen, Brian R Fryer, Joanna Furnell **G** Susanne Galla, Jim Galloway, Cristina Garcia, Robert Garnsworthy, Gaby Gebus, Ziegler Georg, Jean Pierre & Fernande Gigoux, Lee Gimpel, Luke Gingerich, Elizabeth Gledhill, Kristin Godfrey, Daniel Goergen, Jeff Gold, Cristina Gomezjurado, Alexander Gordon, Ross Gordon, Guy Goyvaerts, Lisa Grabenwöger, Melvern Graham, Terry Grant, Marilyn Grayson, Joris Gresnigt, Annabelle Groenendijk, Erik Groeneveld, Jose Groothuis **H** Joerg Haas, Miira Hackenberger, Frank Hall, Suzanne Halliwell, Arne Hannibal, Florian Hanslik, Christopher Hardyment, Jesse Harris, Tim Harrison, Edwina Hart, Claudia Hauser, Christian Hausladen, Anna Healy, Peter & Izabella Hearn, Staley & Meg Heatly, Sol Heber, Kim Hendrikx, René Henke, Roger Hennekens, Martha Henson, Jenny Hill, Mark Hillick, Gerald Hinxman, Tom Hiskey, Mary Holozubiec, Mary & Peter Tucci Holozubiec, James Holzgraf, Monica Homma, Isabelle Honnore, Jurgen Hoogland, Jamie Horejs, Tim Howard, Irene Huber **I** Blanche Iberg, Philipp Irniger, Kristine Iverson, Susan Iwanicki **J** Amy Jackson, Dean Jacobs, Neha Jain, Lian Janse, Gerbert Jansen, Sven Janssen, Annie Jespersen, Anthony Joffe, Catherine Johnson, Lynn Johnson, Peter Johnson, Thea Johnson, Mark Jones, Caroline Joyner **K** William Kaderli, Grant Kapteyn, Karen Kawasaki, Matthew Keilty, Minhee Kim, Jean King, Jay Kloss, Richard Knapp, Ilkka Koskinen, Ben Kosleck, Mike Kozel, Paulina Kramarz, Marloes Krol, Wolfgang Krueger, Gerald Kuhl, Elizabeth Kupchick **L** Connie Lam, Daniel Lang, Mirjam Lang, Jane Langille, Morgan Barlow, Ryszard Laskowski, Rex Last, Pascal le Colletter, Stieve Lederer, Tania Ledergerber, Katherine Legione, Gerard Leitner, Anders Lennartsson, Alejandra Leonard, Michel Leseigneur, Mariah Levinson, Andreas Lomborg, Katherine Love, Markus Low, Martin Lundgren, Timothy Lynch, Chris Lyons **M** Campbell Macdonald, Markus Maerkl, Nicholas Magness, Patricia Maier, Joe Mailhot, Neil Makin, Tina Manley, Christian Marchel, Elizabeth Marron, Dom Martin, Tanya Martz, Susanne Mascow, Mardi Mastain, Susan Matt, Chantal Matthee,

Tobias Mauche, Ulrike May, Laurie Mayer, Michael McClure, Ralph McCuen, Diana McCulloch, Paul Mccutchen, Carole McKeown, Stephanie Mcmahon, Kevin Mcnamee, Ricki Mehnert, Frank Meriwether, Colleen Meyer, William Midmer, Bryan Miles, Mollie Milesi, Horacio Miller, Julie Miller, Simona Miller, Erika Millstein, Thomas Ming, Paulina Miranda, Maxim Mironov, Ian Mitchell, Brigitte Monfils, Francisco Montesdeoca, Ed Moore, Jessica Moore, Stephen Moore, Tom Moore, Ted Morrison, Christian Mueller, Harald Mueller, Nicole Mueller, Susanne Mueller, Benjy Munro, Adam Musbach, Wim Muys **N** Menkin Nelson, Simon Nettleton, Christopher Newton, Roel Nieuwenkamp, Dave Nix, Caroline Norman, John Nunes **O** Lisa O Connell, Rita Odenheimer, Melanie Olding, Barak Orbach, Lindsey Oswald, Jolanda Oudeman, Remco Oudhoff **P** Amy Parker, Caroline Parrott, Matthew Paterson, Cristina Paz, Jorge Paz, Carlos Pazmiño, Lisa Peake, Kerry Pennings, Betty Petheram, Barbara Phillips, Tanner Pinney, Rebecca Plofker, Nicole Pointecker, Dennis Poland, Sally Pope, Alex Prince, Anna Przybysz **Q** Renate Quell **R** Wolfgang Rainer, Sandhya Rao, Jane Reason, Armin Rechberger, Brian Reilly, Georg & Julia Renöckl, Deborah Rhodes, Margarita Ricaurte, Maggie Richards, Greta Richter, Niall Riddell, Patrick Riedijk, Reidun Riisehagen, Ross Rivas, Giovanna Robbiani, Sara Roberts, Scott Roberts, Caroline Rodgers, Piet Romein, Alison Rowe, Martina & Brian Rowe, Matthew Royston, Gabrielle Rozing, Steven Rubenstein, Fernando Schettini, Jenny Russell, Jakob Rutqvist, Paul Rutter **S** Tomasz Sajovic, Tomasz & Anna Sajovic, Steve Samis, Sten Sannerholt, Morard Sanny, Thomas Sarosy, Celia Schatzky, Catherine Schloegel, Linette Schlup, Katharina Schneider, Stephan Schneider, Nancy Schneider-Deacon, Laima & Bradley Schnell, Rene Schnyder, Claudia Schreiner, Ingo Schultz, Tara Schulz, Ivana & Nicolas Schwab, Emma Scragg, Sybille Seliner, Peter Sels, Carol Severino, Devi & Hunter Sharp, Eugene Shepard, Brett Sheperson, Darren Shepherd, Allan Shlossberg, Amanda Sierra, Kip Sikora, Evan Siljander, Gioconda Simmonds, Diane Simpo, Michael Slatnik, Martin Smetacek, Joan Smith, Richard Smith, Stacey Smith, Thomas Sondergaard, Nicky Spencer-Jones, Meghan St John, Joe Stemig, Rolf Stengl, Bart Sterenborg, Hesther Sterk, Benjamin Sternthal, Barbara Stewart, Cheryl Stewart, Gary Stocker, Hans Stragier, Helena Striwing, Joe Sullivan, Meghan Sullivan, Sarah Swannet, Michelle Swanson, Katie Symons, Rebecca Szper **T** Jude Talbot, Ron Tamari, Rasmus Tangen, Joe Taschetta, Ilka Theis, Enrico Thiel, Laura Thielges, Diana Thompson, Lizzie Thompson, Elizabeth Thomsic, Erica Tieman, Henk Timmer, Robert Tinker, Colin Tinto, Dan Tintor, Barbara Tomasella, Amanda Ton, Kate Tornblom, Andrew Townsend, Jan-Peter Trautwein, Peter Turk, Dana Turner **U** Mark Unger, Jon Unoson **V** Rouzita Vahhabaghai,

SEND US YOUR FEEDBACK

We love to hear from travelers – your comments keep us on our toes and help make our books better. Our well-traveled team reads every word on what you loved or loathed about this book. Although we cannot reply individually to postal submissions, we always guarantee that your feedback goes straight to the appropriate authors, in time for the next edition. Each person who sends us information is thanked in the next edition – and the most useful submissions are rewarded with a free book.

To send us your updates – and find out about Lonely Planet events, newsletters and travel news – visit our award-winning website: **www.lonelyplanet.com/feedback**.

Note: We may edit, reproduce and incorporate your comments in Lonely Planet products such as guidebooks, websites and digital products, so let us know if you don't want your comments reproduced or your name acknowledged. For a copy of our privacy policy visit www.lonelyplanet.com/privacy.

Erik van Arend, Maarten van Beek, Louis van den Berg, Peggy van den Bogaart, Renske van den Broek, Odette & Paul van Galen, Anouk van Limpt, Oliver van Straaten, Carl Vannetelbosch, Linda Veldmeijer, Clem Vetters, Andre Villasenor, Christopher Vinegra, Yvonne & Michael Vintiner, Jessica Vivar, Maria Belen Vizcaino Borrego, Scott Vomvolakis, Antonius von Gagern, Joel von Trapp, Christoph von Uthmann, Kristien Vrancken, Nander Vrees **W** Weston Wagner, Rashida & Dieter Wahl, Jürgen Walravens, John Walters, Toni Walters, Monika Wanek, Peter Ward, Lynda Watson, Karyn Wesselingh, Clodagh Whelan, Siobhan Whooley, Siw Wikstrom, CeCe Wilkens, Jeb Wittgenstein, Oswald Wolf, Mike Woodworth, Megan Wroster, Fiona Wuerthner, Rene Wuest, Miriam Wunderwald **Y** Tai-shung Yeung, Ani Youatt, Susan Young **Z** Tara Zadeh, Sarah Zipkin, Romain Zivy, Jan Zoells, Udi Zohar

ACKNOWLEDGEMENTS

Many thanks to the following for the use of their content: Mountain High Maps® ©1993 Digital Wisdom, Inc.

Index

A

accommodations 381-3
activities 383-6, *see also individual activities*
Agato 122, 126
Agua Blanca 304
Aguilera, Jaime Roldos 30
Ahuano 254
air travel 400-3
  airfares 401
  airline offices 400-1
  airports 400
  domestic airlines 404
  to/from Ecuador 401-3
  within Ecuador 404
Alamor 344
Alao 177
Alarcón, Fabián 31
Alausí 189-90
albatross 50, 59
alcohol 64
Alfaro, Eloy 28
Aloasí 147
altitude sickness 72, 416
Amazon 44, 45, 46, 47, 167, 175
AmaZOOnico 254-5
Ambato 162-5, **163**
Ambuquí 134
amphibians 42
animals 40-3, *see also individual species*
Apuela 128
Arajuno Jungle Lodge 255
archaeological sites
  Agua Blanca 304
  Chirije 289
  Cochasquí 114-15
  Ingapirca 194-5
  Manta de Oro 274
  Parque Nacional Machalilla 302
  Rumicucho 109
Archidona 246-7
architecture 37-8
Arco de la Reina 76
Area Nacional de Recreación El Boliche 150
Arenillas 344

Arteaga, Rosalía 31
arts 37-9
Asilo de la Paz 378
Atacames 280-3, **281**
Atahualpa 25-6, 165
Atillo 177
ATMs 392
Avenue of the Volcanoes, the 40, 145
ayahuasca 251
Ayampe 309
Ayangue 312
Azogues 195

B

Babahoyo 272
Baeza 231-2
Bahía de Caráquez 288-91, **289**
Ballén, Sixto Durán 30
Ballenita 312
bananas 342
Baños 167-75, **168**, 7
  accommodations 172-3
  entertainment 174-5
  festivals 171, 7
  food 173-4
  shopping 175
  travel to/from 175
  travel within 175
Baños (Cuenca) 208
Basílica del Voto Nacional 75
Basílica de Nuestra Señora de Agua Santa 170
bathrooms 397
beaches, *see also individual beaches*
  Atacames 280-1
  Ayampe 309
  Canoa 287
  Cerro Brujo 370
  Gardner Bay 379, 5
  Las Tunas 308-9
  Los Frailes 304
  Manglaralto 312
  Mompiche 286, 336
  Montañita 309-10
  Ochoa Beach 370
  Playas 315-16
  Punta Carnero 313
  Punta Cormorant 379
  Salinas 313-14
  Tarqui 295

beer 64
begging 33, 194
Benalcázar, Sebastián de 26
Biblián 195
bicycle travel, *see* cycling, mountain-biking
birds 41, 49-53, 217, 57, 58, 59
bird-watching 41, 49, 383
  Bosque de los Arreyanes 134
  Bosque Protector Cerro Blanco 318
  Intag Valley 128
  Isla Genovesa 380
  Isla San Cristóbal 370
  Isla Santa Cruz 361, 368, 369
  Isla Santa María 379
  Isla Isabela 376, 377
  Mindo 141-2
  Parque Nacional Cajas 208
  Parque Nacional Machalilla 303
  Puerto Bolívar 342
  Reserva Biológica Bilsa 271
  Reserva Biológica Los Cedros 129
  Reserva Río Palenque 272
  Tinalandia 268
black market 392
Black Turtle Cove 361-2
boat travel, *see also* kayaking, river-rafting
  to/from Ecuador 404
  within Ecuador 406
Bolívar 134
Bolívar, Simón 28, 82, 125, 319, 326
boobies 49-50, 57
books 16, 39
  bird-watching 41
  cooking 61
  environment 47
  fiction 39
  food 66
  history 27
  indigenous peoples 30, 37, 38, 39, 116
  nature 44
  politics 31
  travel 16
  wildlife 40-2, 49
Borbón 275-6
border crossings 403
  to/from Colombia 138-9, 235-6, 403
  to/from Peru 223, 245, 344-6, 403

000 Map pages
000 Photograph pages

Borja, Rodrigo 30
Bosque Protector Cerro Blanco 318
Bosque Protector Mindo-Nambillo 141
Bosque Protectora La Perla 271
Bucaram, Abdala 29, 30, 31, 32
Buccaneer Cove 375
bullfighting 36
bus travel
   to/from Ecuador 403-4
   within Ecuador 406-7, 409
business hours 386
butterflies 42

C

caiman 42
Cajabamba 187
Calceta 293
Calderón 110
Camarones 278
camping 382
Cañar 195
Cañari people 25, 35, 194
Candelaria 177
Canoa 287
Capac, Huayna 25
car travel 404, 407-9
   driver's license 408
   insurance 409
   organizations 407-8
   rental 408-9
   road distance travel 408
   road rules 409
Caras 115
Cariamanga 224
Casa de Sucre 76
Casa Museo María Augusta Urrutía 76
Catacocha 224
Catamayo 223-4
Catedral de la Inmaculada Concepción
   196, 8
cathedral (Quito) 73-5
catholicism 36
caving 249, 264, 265
Cayambe 115-16
central highlands 145-90, **146**
Centro Cultural Metropolitano 75
Cerro Brujo 370
Cerro de las Tijeretas 371
Cerro Dragón 361
Cerro Santa Ana 324
Chachi people 35, 277
Chanduy 315
Charles Darwin Foundation 48, 360
Charles Darwin Research Station 353,
   360, 367

chicha 262
Chihuilpe 269
children, travel with 88-9, 386, 417
Chirije archaeological site 289
cholera 414
Chone 293
Chordeleg 209-10
Chugchilán 159
churches
   Basílica del Voto Nacional 75
   Basílica de Nuestra Señora de Agua
      Santa 170
   Church of El Carmen de la
      Asunción 197
   Church of El Sagrario 76
   Church of Santo Domingo (Cuenca)
      197
   Church of Santo Domingo
      (Guayaquil) 324, **336**
   Church of Santo Domingo (Quito) 77
   Church of San Francisco (Cuenca)
      197
   Church of San Sebastián (Loja) 213
   La Compañía de Jesús 76
   La Merced 75
   Monastery of San Agustín 75
   Monastery of San Diego 79
   Monastery of San Francisco 77
   Monastery of Santa Catalina 76
   Santuario de la Virgen del Rocío 195
cinema, see film
climate 14, 386
climbing 86, 148, 150, 171, 187-8,
   384
clothing 394
cloud forest 43, 139, 141
Coca 238-41, **239**
Cochasquí archaeological site 114-15
cockfighting 36, 121-22
cocoa 309
Cofan people 35, 236
Cojimíes 286
Colombia border crossings 138-9,
   235-6, 403
Colonial Era
   architecture 38
   history 26-8
Congal Biostation 285
conservation 47
consulates 389-90
Conway Bay 361
Cordero, León Febres 30
cormorant 50
costs 14, see also money
Cotacachi 126-7

courses 88, 387
   dancing 387
   language 88, 118-19, 131, 171,
      200, 387
crafts 39
credit cards 393
Crucita 293
Cuenca 195-208, **198-9**, 7, 8, **334**
   accommodations 201-3
   entertainment 205
   festivals 201
   food 203-5
   Internet access 196
   markets 200
   medical services 196
   shopping 205-7
   tourist information 196
   tours 200-1
   travel to/from 207
   travel within 207-8
cultural centers
   Guayaquil 319
   Puerto Ayora 362
   Quito 70
culture 33-9
customs regulations 387
cycling 86-7, 403, 405-6, see also
   mountain-biking

D

Dahik, Alberto 30
dance 88
Daphne Major 369
Daphne Minor 369
Darwin Bay Beach 380
Darwin, Charles 49, 52, 347, 349,
   353, 374
Darwin Lake 376
Darwin's finches 52
Data 317
deep vein thrombosis (DVT) 413
deforestation 46
dengue fever 414
departure tax 401
Devil's Crown 379
diarrhea 416
disabled travelers 388-9
diving 385
   Congal Biostation 285
   Puerto Ayora 362-4
   Puerto Baquerizo Moreno 372
   Puerto López 306
   Salango 308
dollarization 31, 33
dolphins 42, 55, 339, **60**

Dos Mangas 311-12
drinks 63-4
driving, see car travel
drugs, illegal 387
dry forests 44
Dureno 236

E
economy 23, 33
ecotourism 48
  Black Sheep Inn 159
  Bosque Nublado Santa Lucía 140
  Cerro Golondrinas Project 135
  Mamá Kinua Cultural Center 201
  Manglaralto 312
  Napo Wildlife Center 242-3
  Proyecto El Cóndor 188-9
  Reserva Producción Fanustíca
    Cuyabeno 236, **335**
  volunteer work 399
Egas, Camilo 39
El Altar 256-7
El Ángel 135
El Bosque Petrificado Puyango 343-4
El Carmen 293
El Chato Tortoise Reserve 361
El Chaupi 148
El Cisne 224
El Junco Lagoon 369-70
El Lecehro 118
El Morro 317
El Panecillo 77-9
El Panguí 265
El Progreso 369
El Quinche 111
electricity 381
Elizabeth Bay 377
embassies 389-90
environmental issues 46-8
  deforestation 46
  Galápagos Islands 353-5
  oil exploration 235, 245-6
equator 108, 109, **333**
Esmeraldas 278-80, **279**
exchange rates, see inside front cover
Espumilla Beach 375

F
festivals 15, 390
  drinks 64-5
  food 64-5

film 39
fish 43, 56
fishing 313, 314
flamingos 51, **57**
Flavio Alfaro 293
food 61-7, 390
  customs 66
  festivals 64-5
  vegetarian 65-6
football 23, 35, 39
frigatebirds 50, **59**
frogs 42, 151
Fundación Golondrinas 135
Fundación Jatun Sacha 253, 271, 285
Funedesin 255
Fuya Fuya 123

G
Galápagos Islands 45-6, 347-80,
  350-1, see also specific islands
  books 49
  environment issues 353-5
  geography 349
  geology 349, 352
  history 348-9
  plants 44
  tours 355-8, 364
  travel to/from 358-9
  travel within 359
Galápagos Marine Resources Reserve
  353-4
Galápagos tortoises 53-4, 370, **60**
Galápagos Wildlife Guide 49-56
Gardner Bay 379, **5**
Garrapatero beach 361
gay travelers 390-1
geography 40
geology 40
giant tortoises 53-4, **60**
Girón 210
Gonzanamá 224
Gordon Rocks 56, 364
Gualaceo 209-10
Gualaquiza 264-5
Guamote 189
Guano 186-7
Guápulo 86
Guaranda 178-80, **178**
Guayaquil 318-39, **320-1**, **327**, **336**
  accommodations 326-9
  drinking 331-2
  entertainment 331-2
  festivals 326
  food 329-31
  history 319

Internet access 319-22
  medical services 322
  shopping 332, 337
  tourist information 322
  tours 326
  travel to/from 337-8
  travel within 338-9
Guayasamín, Oswaldo 39
Guayllabamba 110
Gutiérrez, Lucio 23, 29, 31-2, 34

H
haciendas 382
health 412-17
  child travelers 417
  infectious diseases 414-16
  insurance 412
  Internet resources 413
  vaccinations 412-13
  women travelers 417
Hepatitis A 414
hiking 383-4
  Baños 170
  Bosque Nublado Santa Lucía 140
  Dos Mangas 311-12
  Intag Valley 128
  Los Frailes beach 304
  Parque Nacional Cajas 208-9
  Parque Nacional Cotopaxi 150
  Quilotoa Loop 156, 158
  Quito 87
  Vilcabamba 220
  Volcán Carihuairazo 188
  Zumbahua 157
history 24-32
  colonial era 26-8
  early cultures 24
  Inca Empire 25
  independence 28
  politics 28-32
  Spanish conquest 26
hitching 409
HIV/AIDS 414-15
holidays 14, 391
homestays 382
horse riding 171, 201, 220, 384
hostels 383
hosterías 382
hot springs 115, see also thermal
  baths
hotels 383
Huamaní 246
Huaorani people 35, 238, 241, 257
Huaquillas 344-6, **345**
Huáscar 25

Humboldt, Alexander von 40, 145, 151
hypothermia 416-17

I

Ibarra 129-34, **130**
   accommodations 131-2
   drinking 133
   entertainment 133
   food 132-3
   travel to/from 133-4
   travel within 134
Ibarra, José María Velasco 29
iguanas 42, 54, **58**
Ilinizas 147-9
Ilumán 122, 126
immigration 33-4
Incas 25-6, 194, 200
independence 28
indigenous peoples 35, *see also*
   individual ethnic groups
   books 116
   environmental issues 45, 47, 237
   Internet resources 35, 45
   markets 160
   museums 83, 118, 197, 257
   Oriente, the 226, 236, 265
   Parque Nacional Yasuní 245-6
   Tsáchila people 269
   weaving 125
Ingapirca 194-5
insects 42
insurance 391
   car 409
   health 412
Intag Cloud Forest Reserve 128
Intag Valley 127-9
Internet access 391
Internet resources 16-17, 35, 40
   ecotourism 48
   environment 47
   health 413
   indigenous peoples 35, 45
   Quito 70
   volcanoes 167
Isinliví 159
Isla Baltra 368
Isla Bartolomé 375
Isla Darwin 380
Isla de la Plata 303-4
Isla Española 379, 5
Isla Fernandina 378
Isla Genovesa 380
Isla Isabela 376-8
Isla Lobos 370
Isla Marchena 380

Isla Mosquera 368-9
Isla Pinta 380
Isla Pinzón 368
Isla Rábida 375
Isla San Cristóbal 369-74
Isla San Salvador 374-5
Isla Santa Cruz 359-68
Isla Santa Fé 369
Isla Santa María 378
Isla Seymour 368-9
Isla Wolf 380
Islas Daphne 369
Islas Plazas 369
Ítapoa Reserve 144
itineraries 18-22
   Andean mountain high 19
   author's favourite trip 12
   best of Ecuador 18
   marimbas & mangroves 20
   peak experience 22
   southern Ecuador 21
   surf & sun 22

J

Jambelí 342-3
Jardín Botánico de Guayaquil 326
Jardín Botánico las Orquídeas 257
Jardín Botánico (Quito) 83
jet lag 413
jewelry 395
Jima 210
Jipijapa 299
Julcuy 304-5
Juncal 134
jungle lodges 227, 241-5, 253-6, 276
jungle tours 230
Junín 129

K

Kapawai Ecolodge & Reserve 262-3
kayaking 90, 171, 247-9, 384-5
Kingman, Eduardo 39

L

La Balsa 223, 403
La Cima de la Libertad 79
La Compañía de Jesús 76
La Concordia 271
La Esperanza 134-5
La Joya de las Sachas 238
La Libertad 313
La Merced 75
La Mitad del Mundo 108-9, 333
La Paz 134, 136
La Piscina de La Virgen 169

La Selva Jungle Lodge 243
La Tola 274-5
La Virgen de Quito 77, 333
La Virgen del Cisne 224
Lagarto 277
Lago Agrio 232-6, **233**
Laguna de Colta 187
Laguna de Cuicocha 127
Laguna de San Pablo 124
Laguna Las Ninfas 361
Laguna Limpiopungo 151
Laguna Puruhanta 134
Laguna Quilotoa 157-9
Laguna Yaguarcocha 131
Lagunas de Atillo 177
Lagunas de Mojanda 123-4
language 418-24
   courses 88, 118-9, 131, 171,
      200, 387
   food vocabulary 66-7
   glossary 425
Larrea, Osvaldo Hurtado 30
Las Bachas 361-2
Las Cascadas de Paluz 134
Las Cueva de los Tayos 264
Las Peñas 324, **336**
Las Tunas 308-9
Latacunga 152-6, **153**
lava tubes 360-1
leather 395
legal matters 391
legislative palace 82
leishmaniasis 415
León Dormido (Kicker Rock) 370
lesbian travelers 390-1
Liana Lodge 254-5
Licto 177
Limón 264
Limonal 135
Limoncocha 241
Limones 274
literature 39, *see also* books
lizards 54-5, **58**, 60
llamas 42
Loja 212-16, **213**
Los Amantes de Sumpa 313
Los Encuentros 265
Los Frailes Beach 304
Los Galápagos 370
Los Gemelos 361

M

Macará 225
Macas 259-62, **260**
Machachi 147

Machala 339-42, **340**
Machay 176
magazines 381
Mahuad, Jamil 29, 31
malaria 415
Malecón 2000 323-4
Manatee riverboat 241
Manglaralto 312
Manglares de Majagual 275
mangroves 44, 285
Manta de Oro 274
Manta people 298
Manta (town) 293-8, **294-5**
Manto de La Novia waterfalls 175
maps 392
Mariscal Sucre 69, 72, 82, 83, **84**
markets 15, 394
    Ambato 162
    Cajabamba 187
    Chordeleg 209-10
    Cuenca 200
    Gualaceo 209-10
    Guamote 189
    Guaranda 178
    Guayaquil 323
    Latacunga 153-4
    Machachi 147
    Otavalo 118, 125, 6
    Riobamba 181
    Sangolqui 111
    Santo Domingo de los Colorados 269
    Saquisilí 160-1, 6
    Saraguro 211
    Sigsig 209-10
    Zumbahua 157
measures & weights 381, *see also inside front cover*
medical services 414
Méndez 264
Mera 176
mestizos 28, 35
metric conversions, *see inside front cover*
Mindo 141-3
Misahuallí 251-3
Mompiche 286, **336**
Monasterio de Carmen Alto 76-7
Monastery of Santa Catalina 76
Monastery of San Agustín 75
Monastery of San Diego 79
Monastery of San Francisco 77

money 14, 392-3, *see also inside front cover*
    dollarization 31
moneychangers 393
monkeys 41
Montañita 309-11
Montecristi 298-9
Montúfar, Juan Pío 28
Moreno, Gabriel García 28
motion sickness 413
motorcycle travel 404, 407-9
mountain biking 86-7, 170, 183, 384, 405
Muisne 284-6
Muro de las Lágrimas 377
museums
    Capilla del Hombre 83, 85, 86
    Casa de la Cultura (Latacunga) 154
    Casa de la Cultura (Macas) 259
    Casa Museo María Augusta Urrutía 76
    Centro Cultural Esmeraldas 278
    Centro Interamericano de Artes Populares 197
    Instituto Otavaleño de Antropología 118
    La Cima de la Libertad 79
    Los Amantes de Sumpa 313
    Museo Alberto Mena Caamaño 75
    Museo Amazónico 83
    Museo Antropológico y de Arte Contemporáneo 324
    Museo Bahía de Caráquez 289
    Museo Camilo Egas 75
    Museo de Arte Colonial 75
    Museo de Arte Moderno 197
    Museo de Arte Religioso 181
    Museo de Ciencias Naturales (Ambato) 163
    Museo de Ciencias Naturales (Quito) 83
    Museo de Jacinto Jijón y Caamaño 83
    Museo de la Ciudad 76, 181
    Museo de las Conceptas 200
    Museo de las Culturas 126
    Museo de las Culturas Aborígenes 197-8
    Museo de San Agustín 76
    Museo del Banco Central (Loja) 212
    Museo del Banco Central (Manta) 295
    Museo del Banco Central 'Pumapungo' 200
    Museo del Banco Central (Quito) 39, 82

Museo del Quito en Miniatura 108
Museo Etnoarqueológico 257
Museo Etnográfico Huaorani 257
Museo Etnográfico de Artesanía de Ecuador 83
Museo Franciscano 77
Museo Guayasamín 83
Museo Herman Bastidas Vaca 136
Museo Manuel Agustín Landivar 200
Museo Municipal 325
Museo Nahim Isaias 323
Museo Naval 323
Museo Real Alto 315
Museo Remigio Crespo Toral 197
Museo Salango 308
Museo Solar Inti Ñan 108-9
music 37, 5

N
Nambija 265
Nanegal 140
Nanegalito 139
Napo Wildlife Center 242
Nariz del Diablo 150, 180, 186, 190, 411
national parks & reserves 15, 45-6, **46**
    Bosque Protector Cerro Blanco 318
    Bosque Protector Mindo-Nambillo 141
    Bosque Protectora La Perla 271
    El Bosque Petrificado Puyango 343-4
    Galápagos Marine Resources Reserve 353-4
    Kapawai Ecolodge & Reserve 262-3
    Parque Nacional Cajas 193, 208-9
    Parque Nacional Cotopaxi 147, 149-52
    Parque Nacional Llanganates 147, 165
    Parque Nacional Machalilla 302-5
    Parque Nacional Podocarpus 193, 216-18
    Parque Nacional Sangay 147, 176-7, 227, 262
    Parque Nacional Sumaco-Galeras 227, 246
    Parque Nacional Yasuní 227, 245-6
    Playa de Oro Reserva de Tigrillos 276
    Refugio de Vida Silvestre Pasochoa 111
    Reserva Bellavista 140-1
    Reserva Biológica Bilsa 267, 271
    Reserva Biológica Guandera 135-6

000 Map pages
000 Photograph pages

INDEX

Reserva Biológica Jatun Sacha 253-4
Reserva Biológica Limoncocha 241
Reserva Biológica Los Cedros 129
Reserva Biológica Maquipucuna 140
Reserva Buenaventura 343
Reserva de Producción Faunística
    Chimborazo 147
Reserva Ecológica Cayambe-Coca
    114
Reserva Ecológica Cotacachi-
    Cayapas 114, 127, 267, 277
Reserva Ecológica de Manglares
    Cayapas Mataje 267, 274
Reserva Ecológica El Ángel 114,
    135
Reserva Ecológica Mache Chindul
    267
Reserva Ecológica Manglares
    Churute 339
Reserva Geobotánica Pululahua
    109-10
Reserva Producción Fanustíca
    Cuyabeno 236-7, **335**
Reserva Río Palenque 272
Nebot, Jaime 30
newspapers 381
Noboa, Alvaro 31
Noboa, Gustavo 31-2
north coast & lowlands 266-99, **267**
northern highlands 113-44, **114**
Nuevo Rocafuerte 244-5

O
Ochoa Beach 370
oil industry
    books 30, 47
    environmental issues 46, 235,
        237, 245-6
    Internet resources 45
Olmedo 275
Olón 310
Orellana, Francisco de 26
Oriente 226-65, **228-9**
    northern 229-259, **335**
    southern 259-265
Otavaleños people 35, 116
Otavalo 116-22, **117**
    accommodations 119-21
    entertainment 121-2
    festivals 119
    food 121
    markets 118, 125, **6**
    tours 119
    travel to/from 122
Oyacachi 115-16

P
Pailón del Diablo waterfalls 175
painting 38-9
Palacio, Alfredo 23, 32
Palacio Arzobispal 75, **8**
Palacio de Gobierno (Guayaquil) 323
Palacio del Gobierno (Quito) 73
Palacio Municipal 323
Palestina de Río Verde 277
Palmar 312
Palmareal 274
Pañacocha 244
panama hats 205-6, **4**, **7**
panamericana 403, 407, 409
Papallacta 229-31
páramo 43
parasites 417
Parque Amazónico 247
Parque Bolívar 325
Parque Calderón 196
Parque Condor 118
Parque del Centenario 325
Parque El Ejido 82
Parque Histórico Guayaquil 325
Parque Itchimbia 79
Parque Juan Montalvo 163
Parque La Alameda 79-82
Parque La Carolina 83
Parque La Merced 131
Parque Nacional Cajas 45-6, 193,
    208-9, **208**
Parque Nacional Cotopaxi 45-6, 147,
    149-52, **149**
Parque Nacional Llanganates 45-6,
    147, 165
Parque Nacional Machalilla 45-6,
    302-5, **303**
Parque Nacional Podocarpus 45-6,
    193, 216-18
Parque Nacional Sangay 45-6, 147,
    176-7, 227, 262
Parque Nacional Sumaco-Galeras
    45-6, 227, 246
Parque Nacional Yasuní 45-6, 227, 245-6
Parque Omaere 257
Parque Pedro Moncayo 131
Parque Santo Domingo 131
Parque Vicente León 153
Pasaje 211
passports 400
Patate 166
Pedernales 286-7
Pedro Vicente Maldonado 143
Peguche 122, 125-6
Pelileo 165, 166

penguins 50, 375, **58**
Peru
    border crossings to/from 29, 223,
        245, 344-6, 403
    relations with 27-8
photography 393-4
Pifo 111
Píllaro 165
Pimampiro 134
Piñas 343
Pizarro, Francisco 25-6
planetarium 108
planning 14-17, *see also* itineraries
plants 43-4
Playas 315-17, **316**
Playa de Oro 276
Playa de Oro Reserva de Tigrillos 276
Plaza de San Francisco (Cuenca)
    197, 200
Plaza del Teatro 76
Plaza Grande 73-5, **333**
Plaza San Francisco (Quito) 77
politics 23, 28-32
Pompeya 241
population 23, 35
Portoviejo 291-2, **291**
Posorja 317
Post Office Bay 378-9
postal services 394
Prince Philip's Steps 380
provinces **27**
Puerto Ayora 362-8, **363**, **5**
    accommodations 364-66
    activities 362-4
    food 366-7
    entertainment 367
    Internet access 362
    medical services 362
    tourist information 362
    tours 364
    travel to/from 367
    travel within 368
Puerto Baquerizo Moreno 370-5, **371**
Puerto Bolívar 342-3
Puerto Cayo 302
Puerto Chino 370
Puerto Egas 374-5
Puerto Grande 370
Puerto Hondo 318
Puerto López 305-8, **306**
Puerto Quito 144
Puerto Rico 308
Puerto Velasco Ibarra 379
Puerto Villamil 377-8
Pujilí 156-7

Pungalá 177
Punta Albemarle 376
Punta Carnero 313
Punta Cormorant 379
Punta García 376
Punta Moreno 377
Punta Pelada 317-18
Punta Pitt 370
Punta Suárez 379
Punta Tortuga 376
Punta Vicente Roca 376
Puyango 344
Puyo 256-9, **257**

Q

Quevedo 272
Quichua people 35
Quilotoa Loop 156-61, **156**
Quinindé 271
Quisapincha 165
Quito 68-112, **78**, **7**, **8**, **333**
    accommodations 90-6
    activities 86-7
    clubbing 103
    drinking 102-3
    entertainment 102-4
    festivals 90, **7**
    food 96-102
    Guápulo 86
    history 69
    Internet access 70
    itineraries 69
    Mariscal Sucre 83-6, **84**
    medical services 71
    music 103
    new town 79-86, **80-1**
    old town 73-9, **74**, **8**
    shopping 104-5
    sights 73-85
    tourist information 72
    tours 89-90
    travel to/from 105-7
    travel within 107
    walking tour 87-8, **87**
Quito Observatory 82
Quito School of Art 28, 38
Quito Zoo 89, 110

R

rabies 415
rafting, see river-rafting

000 Map pages
000 Photograph pages

rain forests 44
Rancho Permiso 361
Refugio de Vida Silvestre Pasochoa
    111
religion 36
reptiles 42-3, 53-5
Reserva Bellavista 140-1
Reserva Biológica Bilsa 267, 271
Reserva Biológica Guandera 135-6
Reserva Biológica Jatun Sacha 253-4
Reserva Biológica Limoncocha 241
Reserva Biológica Los Cedros 129
Reserva Biológica Maquipucuna 140
Reserva Buenaventura 343
Reserva de Producción Faunística
    Chimborazo 147
Reserva Ecológica Cayambe-Coca 114
Reserva Ecológica Cotacachi-Cayapas
    114, 127, 267, 277
Reserva Ecológica de Manglares
    Cayapas Mataje 267, 274
Reserva Ecológica El Ángel 114, 135
Reserva Ecológica Mache Chindul 267
Reserva Ecológica Manglares Churute
    339
Reserva Geobotánica Pululahua 109-10
Reserva Producción Fanustíca
    Cuyabeno 236, **335**
Reserva Río Palenque 272
restaurants 65, 390
Río Aguarico 236
Río Blanco Area 135
Río Cayapas 275-6
Río Chota valley 134
Río Muchacho Organic Farm 287-8
Río Napo 241-5, 253-6
Río Negro 176
Río Pastaza 166, 227
Río Tomebamba 197
Río Verde 176, 277
Riobamba 180-6, **182**
    accommodations 183-4
    entertainment 185
    festivals 183
    food 184-5
    shopping 185
    tours 183
    travel to/from 185
    travel within 186
river-rafting 384-5
    Baeza 231
    Baños 171
    Macas 260
    Tena 247-9
    tours 90

Rocafuerte 277, 293
Romerillos 218
Rumicucho 109
Rumiñahui 26, 165

S

Sacha Lodge 242
SAE (South American Explorers) 397
safe travel 387-8
    drowning 387
    road hazards 409
    road rules 409
    robbery 387-8
Salango 308
Salasaca 166
Salasaca people 35
Salinas 180, 313
Sally Lightfoot crab 56
Same 283-4
San Antonio de Ibarra 129
San Bartolomé 210
San Clemente 293
San Francisco 176
San Gabriel 134
San Jacinto 293
San Lorenzo 266, 273-4
San Luís 263
San Miguel 275-6
San Miguel de Salcedo 161-2
San Pablo del Lago 122
San Pedro 274
San Pedro de la Bendita 224
San Rafael Falls 232
San Sebastián 304-5
San Vicente 177, 288
Sanctuary of El Guápulo 86
Sangolquí 111
Sani Lodge 243
Santa Elena 313
Santa Elena Peninsula 312-15
Santa Isabel 210
Santa Lucía 140
Santa Rosa 344
Santa Teresita 187
Santo Domingo de los Colorados
    269-71, **270**
Santuario de la Virgen del Rocío 195
Saquisilí 160-1, **6**
Saraguro 211-12
Saraguro people 35
scams 388
scuba diving, see diving
sculpture 38-9
sea lions 55, **58**
Selva Viva Lodge 254-5

Sevilla 263
sexually transmitted diseases 415
sharks 56
Shell 176
shopping 394-6, *see also* markets
Shuar people 35, 259, 260, 263
Shushufindi 241
Shyris 25, 69
Sigchos 159
Sigsig 209-10
Siona-Secoya people 35
sloths 41
snakes 42-3, 417
snorkeling 348, 385
    Congal Biostation 285
    Garrapatero beach 361
    Isla de la Plata 303
    Isla Rábida 375, 336
    Isla Santa Fé 369
    Islas Plazas 369
soccer 23, 35, 39
Solorzano, Carlos 31
Sombrero Chino 375
South American Explorers (SAE) 397
south coast, the 300-46, **301**
southern highlands 191-225, **192-3**
South Plaza 369
Sozoranga 224
Spanish conquest 26
special events 390
sportfishing, *see* fishing
sports 35-6
Súa 283
Sucre, Antonio José de 28, 79
Sucúa 264
Sullivan Bay 375
surfing 286, 287, 309-10, 364, 372, 385

T
Tagaeri people 245-6
tagua nut 395
Tagus Cove 376
Taisha 264
Tandayapa 139
tapir
Taromenani people 245-6
Tarqui 294-5
taxis 410
Teatro Sucre 76
telefériQo 79
telephone services 396-7
Tena 247-51, **248**
Termas de Papallacta 231

tetanus 415-16
theft 388
theme park 89
thermal baths 128, 136, 169-70, 208, 304
Tigua 157
Tiguino 241
time 397
Tinalandia 268
tipping 393
Toaquiza, Alfredo 39
toilets 397
Tonchigüe 283-4
tortoises 42, 53, 60
tourist information 397
tours 410-11
train travel 411
traveler's checks 393
trekking, *see* hiking
tricycle taxi 410
truck travel 410, 411
Tsáchila 35, 269
tubing 141, 144
Tulcán 136-9, **137**
Tumbaco 111
Turtle Bay 360, 370
turtles 53
typhoid 416
typhus 416

U
Urbina Bay 376-7

V
vaccinations 412-13
Valdivia 312
Vargas, Antonio 31
vegetarian travelers 65-6
Vía Auca 241
video systems 381
Vilcabamba 219-23, **221**
Villamil 377
visas 397-8
Vivarium 83
Volcán Alcedo 376
Volcán Antisana 231
Volcán Atacazo 268
Volcán Carihuairazo 187-9
Volcán Cayambe 116
Volcán Chimborazo 39, 40, 187-88
Volcán Corazón 147, 268
Volcán Cotacachi 124
Volcán Cotopaxi 149, 5
Volcán El Altar 177, 334

Volcán El Reventador 232, 335
Volcán Imbabura 124, 134
Volcán Pichincha 111-12, 334
Volcán Rumiñahui 149
Volcán Sangay 177, 259-60
Volcán Sierra Negra 377
Volcán Sumaco 246
Volcán Tungurahua 167, 170, 176-7
volunteer work 127-8, 129, 288, 399

W
walking, *see* hiking
Wall of Tears 377
Watkins, Patrick 349, 378
water 417
weavings 125, 126, 396
websites, *see* Internet resources
weights & measures 381, *see also inside front cover*
Whale Bay 361
whales 55-6, 304
whale-watching 304, 305, 312, 313, 314
white-water rafting, *see* river-rafting
wildlife 40-4, 149, 352, *see also individual animals*
    books 40-2
    conservation 127-8
    Galápagos 49-56
Wittmer, Margaret 16, 378
women in Ecuador 36-7
women travelers 268, 396, 398, 417
work 398
world heritage sites 48
    Cuenca 195-208
    Galápagos Islands 347-80
    Quito (old town) 73-9
    Parque Nacional Sangay 176-7

Y
Yachana Lodge 255-6
yachts 356
Yantzaza 265
Yarina Lodge 241-2
yellow fever 416
Yupanqui, Tupac 25
Yuturi Lodge 244

Z
Zábalo 236
Zamora 218-19, 265, **218**
Zaruma 343
Zumba 223
Zumbahua 157

INDEX

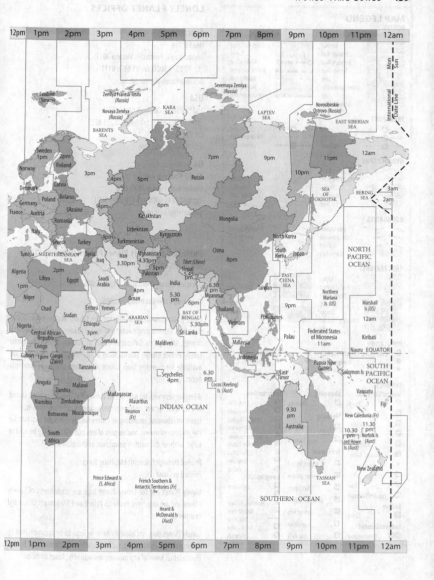

MAP LEGEND

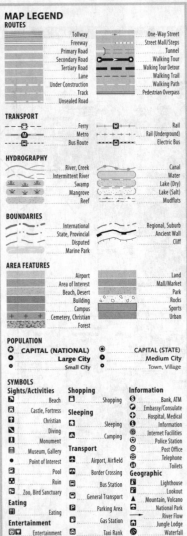

ROUTES

Tollway	One-Way Street
Freeway	Street Mall/Steps
Primary Road	Tunnel
Secondary Road	Walking Tour
Tertiary Road	Walking Tour Detour
Lane	Walking Trail
Under Construction	Walking Path
Track	Pedestrian Overpass
Unsealed Road	

TRANSPORT

Ferry	Rail
Metro	Rail (Underground)
Bus Route	Electric Bus

HYDROGRAPHY

River, Creek	Canal
Intermittent River	Water
Swamp	Lake (Dry)
Mangrove	Lake (Salt)
Reef	Mudflats

BOUNDARIES

International	Regional, Suburb
State, Provincial	Ancient Wall
Disputed	Cliff
Marine Park	

AREA FEATURES

Airport	Land
Area of Interest	Mall/Market
Beach, Desert	Park
Building	Rocks
Campus	Sports
Cemetery, Christian	Urban
Forest	

POPULATION

CAPITAL (NATIONAL)	CAPITAL (STATE)
Large City	Medium City
Small City	Town, Village

SYMBOLS

Sights/Activities
- Beach
- Castle, Fortress
- Christian
- Diving
- Monument
- Museum, Gallery
- Point of Interest
- Pool
- Ruin
- Zoo, Bird Sanctuary

Eating
- Eating

Entertainment
- Entertainment

Shopping
- Shopping

Sleeping
- Sleeping
- Camping

Transport
- Airport, Airfield
- Border Crossing
- Bus Station
- General Transport
- Parking Area
- Gas Station
- Taxi Rank

Information
- Bank, ATM
- Embassy/Consulate
- Hospital, Medical
- Information
- Internet Facilities
- Police Station
- Post Office
- Telephone
- Toilets

Geographic
- Lighthouse
- Lookout
- Mountain, Volcano
- National Park
- River Flow
- Jungle Lodge
- Waterfall

LONELY PLANET OFFICES

Australia
Head Office
Locked Bag 1, Footscray, Victoria 3011
☎ 03 8379 8000, fax 03 8379 8111
talk2us@lonelyplanet.com.au

USA
150 Linden St, Oakland, CA 94607
☎ 510 893 8555, toll free 800 275 8555
fax 510 893 8572
info@lonelyplanet.com

UK
72–82 Rosebery Ave,
Clerkenwell, London EC1R 4RW
☎ 020 7841 9000, fax 020 7841 9001
go@lonelyplanet.co.uk

Published by Lonely Planet Publications Pty Ltd
ABN 36 005 607 983

© Lonely Planet Publications Pty Ltd 2006

© photographers as indicated 2006

Cover photographs: Shuar tribesperson taking shelter under a banana leaf, Oriente jungle area near Tena, Ecuador, Yadid Levy/Alamy (front); Sea lion on Galapagos beach at sunset, Ernest Manewal/Lonely Planet Images (back). Many of the images in this guide are available for licensing from Lonely Planet Images: www.lonelyplanetimages.com.

Printed through Colorcraft Ltd, Hong Kong.
Printed in China